# Women and International Human Rights in Modern Times

# Women and International Human Rights in Modern Times

A Contemporary Casebook

Rosa Celorio

*Burnett Family Associate Dean and Professorial Lecturer for International and Comparative Legal Studies, George Washington University Law School, USA*

 Edward Elgar
PUBLISHING

Cheltenham, UK • Northampton, MA, USA

Published by
Edward Elgar Publishing Limited
The Lypiatts
15 Lansdown Road
Cheltenham
Glos GL50 2JA
UK

Edward Elgar Publishing, Inc.
William Pratt House
9 Dewey Court
Northampton
Massachusetts 01060
USA

Paperback edition 2022

A catalogue record for this book
is available from the British Library

Library of Congress Control Number: 2021952861

This book is available electronically in the **Elgar**online
Law subject collection
http://dx.doi.org/10.4337/9781800889392

Printed on elemental chlorine free (ECF)
recycled paper containing 30% Post-Consumer Waste

ISBN 978 1 80088 938 5 (cased)
ISBN 978 1 80088 939 2 (eBook)
ISBN 978 1 0353 0030 3 (paperback)

Printed and bound in the USA

# Contents

# Preface

This casebook is intended for students of issues concerning women, gender equality, human rights, and international law. It provides an overview of the main international and regional legal standards related to the human rights of women, and explores their development and practical application in light of contemporary times, challenges, and advances. This book navigates the nuances of the ongoing problems of discrimination and gender-based violence, and discusses them in the context of modern challenges, such as the COVID-19 pandemic, the *MeToo* movement, the growth of non-state actors, environment and climate change, sexual orientation and gender identity, and the digital world, among others.

The human rights of women today find expression in many legal instruments. They are reflected at the national level in many countries in constitutions, legislation, and national policies. They are addressed in case judgments by supreme, constitutional, and lower courts. There is also an international law framework designed to govern the human rights of women with direct and comprehensive obligations for states. The efforts of this universal system are greatly complemented by active regional human rights protection systems in Europe, the Americas, and Africa, and emerging regional approaches in Asia and the Middle East. There are also many bodies created at the international and national levels with the objective of advancing the protection of the rights of women.

Despite these advances, however, women still experience daily violations of their civil, political, economic, social, and cultural rights. The Beijing Declaration and Platform of Action adopted in 1995 reaffirmed women's equality as a basic human right and the paramount nature of their rights to live free from discrimination and gender-based violence. Twenty-five years later, women still face formidable challenges to see their human rights fully respected, protected, and fulfilled. One hundred years have passed since the adoption of the Nineteenth Amendment of the United States Constitution, granting women the right to vote, but the struggle continues to see their full citizenship rights respected, and for women to fully and effectively participate in public and political life.

Women and girls still constitute the vast majority of gender-based violence victims, suffering widespread domestic violence, sexual violence, psychological, and economic harm. They also experience forms of discrimination, inequality, and exclusion. Women still carry most of the burden of unpaid work at home, caring for children, the elderly, and the sick. Women are also affected by poverty, and constitute a large component of workers in the informal economy, lacking many social and employment protections. Women are still largely absent from decision-making positions in the political, civil, social, and economic affairs of their countries. Women and girls moreover face significant restrictions to accessing the information necessary to make autonomous decisions concerning their sexual and reproductive lives, and daunting barriers to accessing health services they only need due to their biological differences. Female human rights defenders still lose their lives and suffer forms of harassment and violence for voicing concerns and defying social expectations. We live in societies where equality for women and a full protection of their human rights is still a distant dream. A full and multidisciplinary gender perspective is still lacking from most decision-making.

The study of the rights of women is made more intricate in the present by the fact that many new social developments greatly impact the way women exercise their human rights. These include the digital age, the COVID-19 pandemic and its aftermath, environmental degradation and climate change, unregulated business practices, and gender ideology. Women in different circumstances still face structural discrimination, racially motivated bias and violence, hate speech, xenophobia, and violence in the internet and technology realms. The study of women's rights today involves contemplating the modern scenarios in which these rights are limited, but also exercised.

This casebook combines and reconciles the history of the human rights of women with its modern scenarios and manifestations, encouraging readers to adapt the current legal framework to the contemporary challenges that women face to see their human rights fully protected. This book discusses the history of the rights of women, including an overview of the main universal and regional instruments and institutions, and national progress. It analyzes this history and connects it with modern issues faced by women in 13 chapters. Chapter 1 analyzes the development of the prohibition of discrimination against women as a foundational international human rights law principle through the adoption of the Convention on the Elimination of All Forms of Discrimination against Women (CEDAW). Chapter 2 reviews the widespread nature of the problem of gender-based violence as a form of discrimination and international human rights problem, and the regional treaties specialized on this issue. Chapter 3 analyzes the intricacies of the problems of intersectionality and multiple forms of discrimination, discussing the concrete case of indigenous women. Chapter 4 looks closely at the development of an international legal framework of protection for persons discriminated against on the basis of their sexual orientation and gender identity, and problems such as violence, discrimination, prejudice, and stigma.

Chapter 5 analyzes the rights of women in times of emergency, analyzing as an example the impact of the 2020–2021 coronavirus pandemic – better known as COVID-19 – on the exercise of the rights of women. The pandemic represents a major and unforeseeable event which produced a global crisis of magnitude with dire consequences for women. In the author's view, it represents a pivotal moment in which all of the human rights of women were put to the test and challenged in some way. The COVID-19 pandemic may also constitute a major turning point for the exercise of and full respect for the rights of women.

Chapter 6 addresses the due diligence obligation of states to prevent and respond to the problem of gender-based violence. As examples, the chapter explores the impact of the *MeToo* movement, the evolving role of non-state actors in women's rights issues, and social protest campaigns demanding change and accountability. Chapter 7 delves into the many forms of discrimination that women still face, and the conceptualization of vulnerabilities, stereotypes, strict scrutiny, and temporary special measures, and their connection with an intersectional discrimination lens. Chapter 7 also discusses the problems of hate speech and gender ideology as forms of backlash to progress in the protection of the human rights of women. Chapter 8 looks at the various barriers that women still face to fully exercise their sexual and reproductive rights in the areas of availability and quality of services and information, maternal health, the regulation of abortion, and assisted reproductive technologies. Chapter 9 explores different areas related to the economic, social, and cultural rights of women, including their economic autonomy and dignified life; decent and quality employment; and food and water resources.

Chapter 10 examines environmental law issues with a gender and human rights lens, discussing the right to a safe and healthy environment, natural disasters and their impact on women, and the effects of climate change. Chapter 11 navigates the world of regional human rights protection systems in the Americas, Europe, Africa, Asia, and the Middle East, and their statements advancing the human rights of women.

Chapter 12 discusses the complex nature and potential conflicts between culture, religion, and the rights of women. Chapter 13 examines developments concerning the human rights of women in the digital world, including the problems of online violence, barriers to access and use technology, and the right to privacy.

In each chapter, students are encouraged to reflect and answer questions alluding to the intricacies, challenges, and advances in the protection and exercise of women's rights in modern times. Some of the chapters also include practical exercises designed to delve in more detail into important issues concerning the rights of women. Many primary sources in the form of universal and regional human rights treaties and instruments are discussed throughout this book. The chapters also include many case judgments, decisions, views, and general recommendations adopted by international and regional bodies and courts advancing the development of women's human rights issues. This analysis is complemented by key scholarship, reports, and statements produced in the area of the human rights of women and its different features. This volume also reviews emblematic decisions from national courts and their cross-cutting nature with existing international legal standards concerning women.

This book is not intended to provide a comprehensive survey of each subject, but navigates and provides snapshots of priority issues and themes in the field of the human rights of women. An important learning goal of this book is to provide students with knowledge and understanding of the main universal and regional standards related to the human rights of women, their development, and application to contemporary issues and in diverse contexts. This book also aims to provide students with exposure to a range of crucial issues affecting the protection, practice, and exercise of the rights of women today.

Many of the issues discussed in this book will be reviewed in light of the text, language, and obligations contained in the Convention on the Elimination of all Forms of Discrimination against Women (hereinafter "CEDAW"), adopted in 1979, which is still the leading treaty in the world on women. CEDAW prohibits all direct and indirect discrimination against women, and enumerates a comprehensive set of state obligations to advance their human rights. It is the second most ratified of the universal human rights treaties, including 189 state parties. It has also been complemented by 38 General Recommendations adopted by the CEDAW Committee, providing salient interpretive content to treaty dispositions. This book explores the promise of CEDAW, and how its provisions are still relevant today based on ongoing developments concerning the rights of women and the challenges that women and girls still face in their daily lives.

The author also refers to the web of universal human rights treaties outlining a vast range of human rights applicable and pertinent to the situation of women. In this sense, the author discusses extensively the work of the regional human rights protection systems – particularly those of Europe and the Americas – as these have extensive jurisprudence and statements setting important legal standards for women's rights. A noticeable body of regional human rights treaties has been adopted, shedding light on important state obligations concerning the protection of and respect for the civil, political, economic, social, and cultural rights of women.

This book offers the term "women" a broad definition including those of all ages – including girls under 18 years old and women over 60 – and those with diverse and non-conforming sexual orientations and gender identities. The chapters will allude in several parts to issues which specifically affect girls under 18 years old, and women who self-identify or are perceived to be lesbian, bisexual, transgender, and intersex.

I hope this book offers students a framework understanding of the international human rights law governing the rights of women and its contemporary application. I also want to encourage students to appreciate the complexities and intricacies of issues affecting women. My foremost hope is that this book inspires students to work to advance the protection, respect, and fulfillment of the rights of women, in any careers they pursue in the future.

Lastly, it is also my wish that this book awakens a passion in its readers to advance human dignity, and to contribute to societies guided by equality, inclusion, diversity, and justice.

# Acknowledgements

I would like to dedicate these pages to Eric and Sebastian, who are the loves of my life, and were incredibly patient and supportive throughout this project. I am also grateful to my parents, Lydia and Raul, who continue to inspire me and taught me to lead life with empathy, care, kindness, and the pursuit of human dignity and equality.

I am also grateful to my research assistants, Janina Heller, Sabrina Rodriguez, and Johana Vargas, for their support with this project. Thank you also to Traci Emerson Spackey, our expert librarian at GW Law School on international law, for her guidance and support. I also salute all of my students over the years with gratitude and the hope that they use the knowledge imparted to help many people in their life paths.

I express my deep appreciation to all of the organizations and entities which granted permission to reproduce materials in this casebook. I am also deeply grateful to Edward Elgar Publishing and to all of those involved in the editing and publishing of this book.

Lastly, I want to express my gratitude to all the women, girls, and organizations, working tirelessly to advance human rights, that I have met globally. Thank you for sharing your work, stories, and wisdom with me. I am in awe of your dedication, grit, determination, courage, and resilience.

# 1. Discrimination against women: doctrine, practice, and the path forward

## I INTRODUCTION: DISCRIMINATION AGAINST WOMEN THROUGH THE LENS OF INTERNATIONAL HUMAN RIGHTS LAW

The international human rights law regime, as we understand it today, was established post World War II. This global conflict resulted in the loss of millions of lives and the total destruction of entire countries and cities. Foremost, the Holocaust took place at the hands of Nazi Germany and their collaborators, leading to the execution of about six million Jews.[1] International human rights law was adopted after World War II to restore and build new societies based on human dignity, rule of law, and peace. After World War II, the United Nations was created in 1945, through the adoption of the United Nations Charter,[2] to advance international peace and security and to promote economic and social progress for all peoples.

A key instrument in the development of international human rights law was the Universal Declaration of Human Rights, adopted in 1948.[3] The Universal Declaration of Human Rights, now considered a source of customary international law, recognized for the first time many of the civil, political, economic, social, and cultural rights that permeate most international treaties today. The Universal Declaration includes paramount rights to life, to be free from slavery and torture, to an effective remedy, to work, and to an education, among others. Acknowledging the need for binding documents, the international community adopted the International Covenants on Civil and Political Rights (hereinafter "ICCPR")[4] and Economic, Social and Cultural Rights (hereinafter "ICESCR")[5] in 1966 codifying for the first time the rights contained in the Universal Declaration.

---

[1] For more reading, *see* United States Holocaust Memorial Museum, *Introduction to the Holocaust*, https://encyclopedia.ushmm.org/content/en/article/introduction-to-the-holocaust (last visited on May 19, 2021).

[2] *See generally* U.N. Charter, June 26, 1945, 59 Stat. 1031, T.S. 993, 3 Bevans 1153, entered into force Oct. 24, 1945.

[3] *See generally* Universal Declaration of Human Rights, G.A. Res. 217A (III), U.N. Doc. A/810 at 71 (1948).

[4] *See generally* International Covenant on Civil and Political Rights, G.A. Res. 2200A (XXI), 21 U.N. GAOR Supp. (No. 16) at 52, U.N. Doc. A/6316 (1966), 999 U.N.T.S. 171, entered into force Mar. 23, 1976.

[5] *See generally* International Covenant on Economic, Social and Cultural Rights, G.A. Res. 2200A (XXI), 21 U.N. GAOR Supp. (No. 16) at 49, U.N. Doc. A/6316 (1966), 993 U.N.T.S. 3, entered into force Jan. 3, 1976.

The human rights system was created to restrain the activity and power of states towards the individual. It was the result of wars driven by totalitarian states in which many abuses against people had been committed. The system first greatly emphasized civil and political rights as a key to safeguarding the human person, peace, and security. The Soviet Bloc in particular highlighted the equal importance of economic, social, and cultural rights and the need to subject compliance of these rights to the availability of state resources.

References to the rights of women appear early in international human rights law instruments. The United Nations Charter refers in its Preamble to the equal rights of men and women. The Universal Declaration of Human Rights recognizes in Articles 1 and 7 the principle of equality, and in Article 2 it prohibits distinctions on the basis of sex. Both the ICCPR and the ICESCR prohibit discrimination on the basis of sex in Article 2 and advance the equality of men and women in Article 3.[6]

These instruments, however, proved insufficient to improve the situation of women and to advance the respect and protection of their human rights. In parallel with the development of the international human rights law system, the work of the women's rights movement and the Commission on the Status of Women were key to bring visibility to the need for a specialized treaty that exclusively addressed the realities faced by women. The Commission on the Status of Women was established in 1946 as part of the United Nations to adopt strategies and recommendations which could advance the equality of women. The Commission actively propelled the adoption of a number of treaties and instruments by the United Nations General Assembly, including the Convention on the Political Rights of Women (1953), the Convention on the Nationality of Married Women (1957), the Convention on Consent to Marriage, Minimum Age for Marriage, and Registration of Marriages (1962), and the Declaration on the Elimination of Discrimination against Women (1967). These were all precursor instruments to the eventual adoption of the Convention on the Elimination of all Forms of Discrimination against Women, covering different dimensions of the human rights of women.

All these efforts raised the awareness of the international community of the need to adopt a more multifaceted and comprehensive instrument related to the rights of women. This led to the drafting of the Convention on the Elimination of all Forms of Discrimination against Women (hereinafter "CEDAW")[7] by the Commission on the Status of Women and its eventual adoption in 1979. The adoption of CEDAW was joined by the establishment of its monitoring committee as disposed in Article 17. Civil society organizations were crucial in the growing visibility of women's rights issues among decision-makers in the international community and the eventual text of the treaty. CEDAW – which will be discussed in detail in this section – is centered on the issue of discrimination against women and its many layers and intricacies. CEDAW is a watershed moment in the history of the human rights of women, recognizing

---

6   The ICCPR also provides in Article 26 that
    All persons are equal before the law and are entitled without any discrimination to the equal
    protection of the law. In this respect, the law shall prohibit any discrimination and guarantee to all
    persons equal and effective protection against discrimination on any ground such as race, colour,
    sex, language, religion, political or other opinion, national or social origin, property, birth or other
    status.
7   *See generally* Convention on the Elimination of All Forms of Discrimination against Women,
G.A. Res. 34/180, 34 U.N. GAOR Supp. (No. 46) at 193, U.N. Doc. A/34/46, entered into force Sept. 3,
1981.

state responsibility to prevent and respond to discrimination against women, both in the family and in all spheres of public life.

The right of women to be free from all forms of discrimination is still a pillar of their human rights and a basic principle and state obligation. The CEDAW, and its goals to advance women's equality and non-discrimination, were cross-cutting themes in the adoption of the Beijing Declaration and Platform of Action.[8] The Beijing Declaration and Platform of Action was the product of the Fourth World Conference on Women held in September of 1995, including approximately 17,000 participants and 30,000 activists.[9] The resulting document is historic in calling for the empowerment and equal participation of women in all social dimensions.[10] The document also underscored women's human rights as human rights.[11]

Most of the international law treaties today advancing human rights contain a prohibition of all forms of discrimination on the basis of sex. There has also been a growing awareness of the magnitude and prevalence of the issue of gender-based violence and its connection to discrimination against women. This connection was established by the CEDAW Committee in its famous General Recommendation 19, establishing that gender-based violence is a form of discrimination under Article 1 of CEDAW. Understanding the dynamics and state obligations to address discrimination and gender-based violence against women is key to grasping the nuance of human rights issues concerning women. Therefore, this chapter provides an overview of the basic principles related to discrimination and gender-based violence. These principles will be later explained in detail in future chapters in connection with issues affecting women in modern times.

## II    CEDAW AND DISCRIMINATION AGAINST WOMEN

The leading treaty in the world on discrimination against women is the Convention on the Elimination of all Forms of Discrimination against Women (hereinafter "CEDAW"). It prohibits discrimination in the areas of political and public life, nationality, education, employment, health, economic and social benefits, and marriage and family life. It addresses both direct and indirect discrimination, in the public and private spheres, in the areas of civil, political, economic, social, and cultural rights. CEDAW also mandates states to refrain from any acts of discrimination against women, and amend their current laws to prevent and respond to this problem. CEDAW moreover establishes an important connection between all rights of women and its overall prohibition of discrimination. As part of an integral strategy to address discrimination against women, state parties must adopt measures to eradicate stereotypical

---

[8]    *See generally* Beijing Declaration and Platform of Action, September 15, 1995, www.un.org/en/events/pastevents/pdfs/beijing_declaration_and_platform_for_action.pdf (last visited on September 24, 2021) (hereinafter "Beijing Declaration and Platform of Action").

[9]    For more information on the Fourth World Conference on Women and the legacy of the Beijing Platform of Action, *see* UN Women, *The Beijing Platform for Action Turns 20*, https://beijing20.unwomen.org/en/about (last visited on May 19, 2021).

[10]    *See* Beijing Platform of Action, *supra* note 8, pp. 18–108 (in which you can find a discussion of strategic objectives and needed state actions to achieve the equality of women, based on the critical areas of concern identified, including poverty, education, health, violence, armed conflict, economy, power and decision-making, institutional mechanisms, human rights, media, the environment, and the girl-child).

[11]    *See* Beijing Declaration, *supra* note 8, ¶ 14.

and cultural patterns of behavior that work to the detriment of women, and temporary special measures to address past discrimination. Excerpts from the Preamble and the main Articles of CEDAW have been included below.

**A        Convention on the Elimination of all Forms of Discrimination against Women (CEDAW)**

U.N. Doc. A/34/46, entered into force Sept. 3, 1981

*The States Parties to the present Convention,*

Noting that the Charter of the United Nations reaffirms faith in fundamental human rights, in the dignity and worth of the human person and in the equal rights of men and women,

Noting that the Universal Declaration of Human Rights affirms the principle of the inadmissibility of discrimination and proclaims that all human beings are born free and equal in dignity and rights and that everyone is entitled to all the rights and freedoms set forth therein, without distinction of any kind, including distinction based on sex,

…

Recalling that discrimination against women violates the principles of equality of rights and respect for human dignity, is an obstacle to the participation of women, on equal terms with men, in the political, social, economic and cultural life of their countries, hampers the growth of the prosperity of society and the family and makes more difficult the full development of the potentialities of women in the service of their countries and of humanity,

…

Bearing in mind the great contribution of women to the welfare of the family and to the development of society, so far not fully recognized, the social significance of maternity and the role of both parents in the family and in the upbringing of children, and aware that the role of women in procreation should not be a basis for discrimination but that the upbringing of children requires a sharing of responsibility between men and women and society as a whole,

Aware that a change in the traditional role of men as well as the role of women in society and in the family is needed to achieve full equality between men and women,

Determined to implement the principles set forth in the Declaration on the Elimination of Discrimination against Women and, for that purpose, to adopt the measures required for the elimination of such discrimination in all its forms and manifestations,

Have agreed on the following:

**PART I**
*Article I*
For the purposes of the present Convention, the term "discrimination against women" shall mean any distinction, exclusion or restriction made on the basis of sex which has the effect or purpose of impairing or nullifying the recognition, enjoyment or exercise by women, irrespective of their marital status, on a basis of equality of men and women, of human rights and fundamental freedoms in the political, economic, social, cultural, civil or any other field.

## Article 2

States Parties condemn discrimination against women in all its forms, agree to pursue by all appropriate means and without delay a policy of eliminating discrimination against women and, to this end, undertake:

(a)   To embody the principle of the equality of men and women in their national consti-
        tutions or other appropriate legislation if not yet incorporated therein and to ensure,
        through law and other appropriate means, the practical realization of this principle;
(b)   To adopt appropriate legislative and other measures, including sanctions where appro-
        priate, prohibiting all discrimination against women;
(c)   To establish legal protection of the rights of women on an equal basis with men and to
        ensure through competent national tribunals and other public institutions the effective
        protection of women against any act of discrimination;
(d)   To refrain from engaging in any act or practice of discrimination against women and to
        ensure that public authorities and institutions shall act in conformity with this obligation;
(e)   To take all appropriate measures to eliminate discrimination against women by any
        person, organization or enterprise;
(f)    To take all appropriate measures, including legislation, to modify or abolish existing
        laws, regulations, customs and practices which constitute discrimination against women;
(g)   To repeal all national penal provisions which constitute discrimination against women.

## Article 3

States Parties shall take in all fields, in particular in the political, social, economic and cultural fields, all appropriate measures, including legislation, to ensure the full development and advancement of women, for the purpose of guaranteeing them the exercise and enjoyment of human rights and fundamental freedoms on a basis of equality with men.

## Article 4

1.  Adoption by States Parties of temporary special measures aimed at accelerating de facto
    equality between men and women shall not be considered discrimination as defined in
    the present Convention, but shall in no way entail as a consequence the maintenance of
    unequal or separate standards; these measures shall be discontinued when the objectives of
    equality of opportunity and treatment have been achieved.
2.  Adoption by States Parties of special measures, including those measures contained in the
    present Convention, aimed at protecting maternity shall not be considered discriminatory.

## Article 5

States Parties shall take all appropriate measures:

(a)   To modify the social and cultural patterns of conduct of men and women, with a view
        to achieving the elimination of prejudices and customary and all other practices which
        are based on the idea of the inferiority or the superiority of either of the sexes or on
        stereotyped roles for men and women;
(b)   To ensure that family education includes a proper understanding of maternity as a social
        function and the recognition of the common responsibility of men and women in the

upbringing and development of their children, it being understood that the interest of the children is the primordial consideration in all cases.

## Article 6

States Parties shall take all appropriate measures, including legislation, to suppress all forms of traffic in women and exploitation of prostitution of women.

## PART II

### Article 7

States Parties shall take all appropriate measures to eliminate discrimination against women in the political and public life of the country and, in particular, shall ensure to women, on equal terms with men, the right:

(a)   To vote in all elections and public referenda and to be eligible for election to all publicly elected bodies;

(b)   To participate in the formulation of government policy and the implementation thereof and to hold public office and perform all public functions at all levels of government;

(c)   To participate in non-governmental organizations and associations concerned with the public and political life of the country.

## Article 8

States Parties shall take all appropriate measures to ensure to women, on equal terms with men and without any discrimination, the opportunity to represent their Governments at the international level and to participate in the work of international organizations.

## Article 9

1.  States Parties shall grant women equal rights with men to acquire, change or retain their nationality. They shall ensure in particular that neither marriage to an alien nor change of nationality by the husband during marriage shall automatically change the nationality of the wife, render her stateless or force upon her the nationality of the husband.

2.  States Parties shall grant women equal rights with men with respect to the nationality of their children.

## PART III

### Article 10

States Parties shall take all appropriate measures to eliminate discrimination against women in order to ensure to them equal rights with men in the field of education and in particular to ensure, on a basis of equality of men and women:

(a)   The same conditions for career and vocational guidance, for access to studies and for the achievement of diplomas in educational establishments of all categories in rural as well as in urban areas; this equality shall be ensured in pre-school, general, technical, professional and higher technical education, as well as in all types of vocational training;

(b)   Access to the same curricula, the same examinations, teaching staff with qualifications of the same standard and school premises and equipment of the same quality;

(c)     The elimination of any stereotyped concept of the roles of men and women at all levels and in all forms of education by encouraging coeducation and other types of education which will help to achieve this aim and, in particular, by the revision of textbooks and school programmes and the adaptation of teaching methods;

(d)     The same opportunities to benefit from scholarships and other study grants;

(e)     The same opportunities for access to programmes of continuing education, including adult and functional literacy programmes, particularly those aimed at reducing, at the earliest possible time, any gap in education existing between men and women;

(f)     The reduction of female student drop-out rates and the organization of programmes for girls and women who have left school prematurely;

(g)     The same opportunities to participate actively in sports and physical education;

(h)     Access to specific educational information to help to ensure the health and well-being of families, including information and advice on family planning.

## *Article 11*

1.  States Parties shall take all appropriate measures to eliminate discrimination against women in the field of employment in order to ensure, on a basis of equality of men and women, the same rights, in particular:

(a)     The right to work as an inalienable right of all human beings;

(b)     The right to the same employment opportunities, including the application of the same criteria for selection in matters of employment;

(c)     The right to free choice of profession and employment, the right to promotion, job security and all benefits and conditions of service and the right to receive vocational training and retraining, including apprenticeships, advanced vocational training and recurrent training;

(d)     The right to equal remuneration, including benefits, and to equal treatment in respect of work of equal value, as well as equality of treatment in the evaluation of the quality of work;

(e)     The right to social security, particularly in cases of retirement, unemployment, sickness, invalidity and old age and other incapacity to work, as well as the right to paid leave;

(f)     The right to protection of health and to safety in working conditions, including the safeguarding of the function of reproduction.

2.  In order to prevent discrimination against women on the grounds of marriage or maternity and to ensure their effective right to work, States Parties shall take appropriate measures:

(a)     To prohibit, subject to the imposition of sanctions, dismissal on the grounds of pregnancy or of maternity leave and discrimination in dismissals on the basis of marital status;

(b)     To introduce maternity leave with pay or with comparable social benefits without loss of former employment, seniority or social allowances;

(c)     To encourage the provision of the necessary supporting social services to enable parents to combine family obligations with work responsibilities and participation in public life, in particular through promoting the establishment and development of a network of child-care facilities;

    (d)    To provide special protection to women during pregnancy in types of work proved to be harmful to them.

3.   Protective legislation relating to matters covered in this article shall be reviewed periodically in the light of scientific and technological knowledge and shall be revised, repealed or extended as necessary.

### Article 12

1.   States Parties shall take all appropriate measures to eliminate discrimination against women in the field of health care in order to ensure, on a basis of equality of men and women, access to health care services, including those related to family planning.
2.   Notwithstanding the provisions of paragraph 1 of this article, States Parties shall ensure to women appropriate services in connection with pregnancy, confinement and the post-natal period, granting free services where necessary, as well as adequate nutrition during pregnancy and lactation.

### Article 13

States Parties shall take all appropriate measures to eliminate discrimination against women in other areas of economic and social life in order to ensure, on a basis of equality of men and women, the same rights, in particular:

(a)   The right to family benefits;
(b)   The right to bank loans, mortgages and other forms of financial credit;
(c)   The right to participate in recreational activities, sports and all aspects of cultural life.

### Article 14

1.   States Parties shall take into account the particular problems faced by rural women and the significant roles which rural women play in the economic survival of their families, including their work in the non-monetized sectors of the economy, and shall take all appropriate measures to ensure the application of the provisions of the present Convention to women in rural areas. …

### PART IV
### Article 15

1.   States Parties shall accord to women equality with men before the law.
2.   States Parties shall accord to women, in civil matters, a legal capacity identical to that of men and the same opportunities to exercise that capacity. In particular, they shall give women equal rights to conclude contracts and to administer property and shall treat them equally in all stages of procedure in courts and tribunals.
3.   States Parties agree that all contracts and all other private instruments of any kind with a legal effect which is directed at restricting the legal capacity of women shall be deemed null and void.
4.   States Parties shall accord to men and women the same rights with regard to the law relating to the movement of persons and the freedom to choose their residence and domicile.

## *Article 16*

1. States Parties shall take all appropriate measures to eliminate discrimination against women in all matters relating to marriage and family relations and in particular shall ensure, on a basis of equality of men and women:
   (a) The same right to enter into marriage;
   (b) The same right freely to choose a spouse and to enter into marriage only with their free and full consent;
   (c) The same rights and responsibilities during marriage and at its dissolution;
   (d) The same rights and responsibilities as parents, irrespective of their marital status, in matters relating to their children; in all cases the interests of the children shall be paramount;
   (e) The same rights to decide freely and responsibly on the number and spacing of their children and to have access to the information, education and means to enable them to exercise these rights;
   (f) The same rights and responsibilities with regard to guardianship, wardship, trustee-ship and adoption of children, or similar institutions where these concepts exist in national legislation; in all cases the interests of the children shall be paramount;
   (g) The same personal rights as husband and wife, including the right to choose a family name, a profession and an occupation;
   (h) The same rights for both spouses in respect of the ownership, acquisition, manage-ment, administration, enjoyment and disposition of property, whether free of charge or for a valuable consideration.
2. The betrothal and the marriage of a child shall have no legal effect, and all necessary action, including legislation, shall be taken to specify a minimum age for marriage and to make the registration of marriages in an official registry compulsory. …

## B    Reflections and Questions

1. There are many principles reflected in Article 1(1) of CEDAW and its definition of dis-crimination. CEDAW prohibits all distinctions, exclusions, and restrictions based on sex. This includes both direct and indirect discrimination in the political, economic, social, cultural, and civil spheres. The CEDAW Committee in its General Recommendation 28 has referred to direct discrimination as different treatment explicitly founded on sex and gender differences. Indirect discrimination instead alludes to laws, policies, programs, and practices that appear neutral, but have a discriminatory effect on women because of pre-existing inequalities.[12] What is the difference between distinctions, exclusions, and restrictions? How can it be determined that a law, policy, or practice, which appears neutral, has a disproportionate or negative impact on women?

---

[12]  *See* General Recommendation No. 28 on the Core Obligations of States Parties under Article 2 of the Convention on the Elimination of All Forms of Discrimination against Women, Committee on the Elimination of Discrimination against Women, 47th Sess., U.N. Doc. C/2010/47/GC.2, ¶ 16 (Oct. 19, 2010) (hereinafter CEDAW Committee, General Recommendation 28), discussed in section III of this chapter.

2. What is the difference between *sex* and *gender*? The text of CEDAW and its Article 1(1) contain a prohibition of discrimination on the basis of sex. The CEDAW Committee has alluded too in its General Recommendations to both sex and gender motives to discriminate. The term *sex* usually refers to the biological and physical characteristics and features that distinguish women and men, including their reproductive capacity.[13] The term *gender* is broader and refers to the roles and notions that society assigns to women and men based on their sex assigned at birth.[14] The World Health Organization has referred to five important elements that are comprehended in the concept of *gender*: relational, hierarchical, historical, contextual, and institutional.[15] Women and men are raised with norms, behaviors, and expectations of their behavior in their public and private lives based on their sex assigned at birth. Chapter 4 will also discuss how the term *gender* is now understood to include the social realities and problems faced by lesbian, bisexual, transgender, and intersex women.

3. In the case of women in particular, these gender-socially constructed roles have been used historically to place them at a disadvantage in their families, communities, and countries.[16] These roles have also impacted how most societies are structured, including legislation, policies, and practices which have treated women unequally and as second-class citizens in comparison with their male counterparts in their access to economic resources, property, credit, employment, education, health care, nationality, and other social benefits. Women's reproductive capacity and their maternity has been used frequently to relegate them to the home, unpaid work, and to limit their incursion in the employment, education, and political settings. Women's role has also been limited in decision-making, economic power structures, and reaching high political office, due to child-rearing responsibilities and unpaid work at home.[17] These historical factors underlie many of the rights contained in CEDAW.

4. The layout of the CEDAW Convention also refers to a historical concern over legal and practical barriers faced by women to exercise their citizenship rights in an autonomous way globally. Key challenges have included impediments to voting and being elected to public office; to entering into contracts; to securing independent employment and accessing higher education; to partaking in the decision-making within public institutions, employers, and organizations; limits to free expression, association, and access to information to facilitate the exercise of rights; and legal barriers to acquiring, changing, and retaining their nationality. Many of these concerns are reflected in CEDAW and its Articles 2 and 3 (and their heavy emphasis on the need for equal treatment in the laws and by public

---

[13] *See* World Health Organization, Gender, Equity, and Human Rights: Glossary of Terms and Tools, *Definition of Sex*, www.who.int/gender-equity-rights/knowledge/glossary/en/ (last visited on May 19, 2021) (hereinafter WHO Gender Glossary of Terms).

[14] *See id.* The Council of Europe Convention on preventing and combating violence against women and domestic violence also defines gender in its Article 3(c) as follows: "'gender' shall mean the socially constructed roles, behaviours, activities and attributes that a given society considers appropriate for women and men." *See* Council of Europe Convention on preventing and combating violence against women and domestic violence, Art. 3(c), May 11, 2001, C.E.T.S. No. 210 (hereinafter Istanbul Convention).

[15] *See* WHO Gender Glossary of Terms, *supra* note 13, *Definition of Gender*.

[16] For a general overview of forms of disadvantage that women and girls have faced historically, *see* Beijing Platform of Action, *supra* note 8, ¶¶ 41–209.

[17] For more discussion, *see id.*, ¶¶ 150–209.

authorities and institutions); 7 and 8 (on participation in political and public life and the right to vote); 9 (codifying the equal right of women to acquire, change, and retain their nationality); and 15 (mandating states to accord women identical legal capacity to men in legal and civil matters). In the United States, the adoption of the Nineteenth Amendment[18] of the Constitution in particular was a key historical moment in recognizing the right to vote for women and raising awareness on the limitations women faced in exercising their citizenship rights.[19]

5. Do you notice anything missing in the text of CEDAW? One of the most important historical omissions of CEDAW has been the problem of gender-based violence. Therefore, the CEDAW Committee has adopted three General Recommendations – 12, 19, and 35 – addressing the complexity of this issue and defining state obligations in this area.[20] General Recommendations 19 and 35 of the CEDAW Committee are discussed in detail in Chapter 2 of this casebook.

6. There are also ongoing discussions at the United Nations level of whether there should be a treaty solely focused on gender-based violence and separate from CEDAW. Do you think there is a need to adopt a new treaty on gender-based violence? What would be the advantages and disadvantages? What should be its main components and features?[21]

7. CEDAW is still the most reserved treaty in the world. This has challenged its adequate and prompt implementation. According to the Vienna Convention on the Law of the Treaties, states may make unilateral statements when ratifying a treaty limiting the legal effect of certain provisions.[22] Reservations, however, should not be incompatible with the object and purpose of a treaty. Should states be allowed to enter reservations to international treaties?[23] Should all universal human rights treaties be treated the same when it comes to reservations?

8. One of the most important features of CEDAW is that it delves into the family and prohibits discrimination within this cornerstone social institution. It is one of the first treaties to define a clear set of state obligations to protect members of the family. The treaty breaks convention with traditional international human rights law, piercing the veil of a mostly private and taboo institution in international affairs. Article 16 of CEDAW mandates states

---

[18]  *See* United States Constitution, Nineteenth Amendment, passed by Congress on June 4, 1919 and ratified on August 18, 1920, www.senate.gov/civics/constitution_item/constitution.htm?utm_content= buffer05951#amdt_19_(1920) (last visited on May 19, 2021).

[19]  For a detailed overview of historical challenges faced by women in the exercise of their citizenship rights in the United States and the impact of the passage of the Nineteenth Amendment, *see* Felice Batlan, *"She Was Surprised and Furious": Expatriation, Suffrage, Immigration, and the Fragility of Women's Citizenship, 1907–1940*, 15 STAN. J. C.R. & C.L. 315, 315–328 (2020).

[20]  *See* CEDAW Committee, General Recommendations 12, 19, and 35 on gender-based violence, www.ohchr.org/en/hrbodies/cedaw/pages/recommendations.aspx (last visited on May 19, 2021).

[21]  For arguments in favor of a new global treaty on gender-based violence *see* Report of the Special Rapporteur on violence against women, its causes and consequences, U.N. Doc. A/HRC/29/27' ¶¶ 6–65 (June 10, 2015).

[22]  *See* Vienna Convention on the Law of Treaties, 1155 U.N.T.S. 331, 8 I.L.M. 679, entered into force Jan. 27, 1980, Arts. 19–22.

[23]  For more reading, *see* Linda M. Keller, *Impact of States Parties' Reservations to the Convention on the Elimination of All Forms of Discrimination against Women*, MICH. ST. L. REV. 309, 315–326 (2014).

to take all appropriate measures to eliminate discrimination against women in all matters relating to marriage and family relations, and pursue the advancement of the principle of equality. These matters include decisions concerning entering or dissolving a marriage, inheritance, family name, and the number and spacing of children. Additional important language is provided by the CEDAW Committee General Recommendations 21 and 29 on the economic consequences of marriage, family relations, and its dissolution.[24] Should an international treaty be interfering with family affairs? Under which circumstances should states intervene to protect a woman from discrimination by her spouse, partner, or other family members?

9.  Do all women experience discrimination in the same way? Several factors can combine to accentuate the experience of discrimination women face on the basis of their sex and gender. These may include race, ethnicity, age, economic position, migrant status, disabilities, and being deprived of liberty, among others. The CEDAW Committee has increasingly recognized intersecting forms of discrimination which affect women in a very particular way, and expose them to forms of exclusion, inferior treatment, and gender-based violence. The problem of *intersectionality* and how it is reflected in treaties and caselaw is discussed in detail in Chapter 3 of this casebook. *Intersectionality* proposes to understand the realities faced by women with a heterogeneous lens, considering social factors which determine social disadvantage, oppression, and class differences.[25] Professor Kimberlé Crenshaw first used the term intersectionality to describe the intricacies of race and gender, and how they connect to accentuate the disadvantage of women belonging to racial groups.[26] The CEDAW Committee for its part has defined intersectionality as:

> Intersectionality is a basic concept for understanding the scope of the general obligations of States parties contained in article 2. The discrimination of women based on sex and gender is inextricably linked with other factors that affect women, such as race, ethnicity, religion or belief, health, status, age, class, caste and sexual orientation and gender identity. Discrimination on the basis of sex or gender may affect women belonging to such groups to a different degree or in different ways to men. States parties must legally recognize such intersecting forms of discrimination and their compounded negative impact on the women concerned and prohibit them. They also need to adopt and pursue policies and programmes designed to eliminate such occurrences, including, where appropriate, temporary special measures in accordance with article 4, paragraph 1, of the Convention and general recommendation No. 25.[27]

The CEDAW Committee, in its General Recommendation 28, by adopting an intersectional approach, has mandated states to adopt policies considering the intersectional burdens and

---

[24]  *See* CEDAW Committee General Recommendations 21 and 29, www.ohchr.org/EN/HRBodies/ CEDAW/Pages/Recommendations.aspx (last visited on May 19, 2021).

[25]  For more discussion of the development of the concept of intersectionality and its incorporation in the internationalman rights framework, *see* LORENA SOSA, INTERSECTIONALITY IN THE HUMAN RIGHTS LEGAL FRAMEWORK ON VIOLENCE AGAINST WOMEN; AT THE CENTER OR THE MARGINS? 7–9 (Cambridge University Press, 2017).

[26]  *See* Kimberlé Crenshaw, *Demarginalizing the Intersection of Race and Sex: A Black Feminist Critique of Antidiscrimination Doctrine, Feminist Theory and Antiracist Politics*, 1989(1) UNIVERSITY OF CHICAGO LEGAL FORUM, Article 8, 139–140, 150–167, https://chicagounbound.uchicago.edu/cgi/ viewcontent.cgi?article=1052&context=uclf.

[27]  *See* CEDAW Committee, General Recommendation 28, *supra* note 12, ¶ 18, discussed *infra*.

discrimination women face when different factors combine with their sex and gender to increase their risk to human rights violations.[28] The CEDAW Committee has also devoted many of its recent General Recommendations to address forms of intersectional discrimination, including women in conflict situations, women with refugee and asylum status, rural women, and the rights of girls.[29] Can you think of the main advantages and challenges of using the term *intersectionality* to address the human rights legal challenges faced by women? Which variables can accentuate the women's experience of discrimination?

## III    CEDAW COMMITTEE: DISCRIMINATION AGAINST WOMEN AND STATE OBLIGATIONS

CEDAW in its Article 17 established an independent monitoring body composed of 23 experts. It is part of the ten treaty-based bodies which form part of the universal system of human rights. The Committee receives and considers reports from state parties and issues concluding observations. It also offers the opportunity for civil society organizations to submit shadow reports.

The Committee can also adopt General Recommendations shedding light on the content of CEDAW dispositions. The Committee has adopted 38 General Recommendations providing important state guidance on issues such as gender-based violence, the role of women in public life, equality in marriage and family relations, temporary special measures, women migrants and those displaced, women and climate change, and other priority issues.[30]

In its General Recommendation 28, the CEDAW Committee provides its most detailed rendition of state obligations under the treaty. It delineates a number of positive and negative obligations of states to prevent, investigate, sanction, and grant reparations for discrimination against women. Some excerpts are included below.

### A    The core obligations of State parties under Article 2 of the Convention on the Elimination of All Forms of Discrimination against Women

Committee on the Elimination of Discrimination against Women, General Recommendation 28
U.N. Doc. CEDAW/C/2010/47/GC.2 (2010)

…

9. Under article 2, States parties must address all aspects of their legal obligations under the Convention to respect, protect and fulfil women's right to non-discrimination and to the enjoyment of equality. The obligation to respect requires that States parties refrain from making laws, policies, regulations, programmes, administrative procedures and

---

[28]   *See id.,* ¶ 18, discussed *infra.*
[29]   *See* CEDAW Committee General Recommendations 30, 32, 34, and 36, www.ohchr.org/EN/HRBodies/CEDAW/Pages/Recommendations.aspx (last visited May 19, 2021).
[30]   *See* General Recommendations adopted by the CEDAW Committee, www.ohchr.org/EN/HRBodies/CEDAW/Pages/Recommendations.aspx (last visited on May 19, 2021).

institutional structures that directly or indirectly result in the denial of the equal enjoyment by women of their civil, political, economic, social and cultural rights. The obligation to protect requires that States parties protect women from discrimination by private actors and take steps directly aimed at eliminating customary and all other practices that prejudice and perpetuate the notion of inferiority or superiority of either of the sexes, and of stereotyped roles for men and women. The obligation to fulfil requires that States parties take a wide variety of steps to ensure that women and men enjoy equal rights de jure and de facto, including, where appropriate, the adoption of temporary special measures in line with article 4, paragraph 1, of the Convention and general recommendation No. 25 on article 4, paragraph 1, of the Convention on the Elimination of All Forms of Discrimination against Women, on temporary special measures. This entails obligations of means or conduct and obligations of results. States parties should consider that they have to fulfil their legal obligations to all women through designing public policies, programmes and institutional frameworks that are aimed at fulfilling the specific needs of women leading to the full development of their potential on an equal basis with men.

10. States parties have an obligation not to cause discrimination against women through acts or omissions; they are further obliged to react actively against discrimination against women, regardless of whether such acts or omissions are perpetrated by the State or by private actors. Discrimination can occur through the failure of States to take necessary legislative measures to ensure the full realization of women's rights, the failure to adopt national policies aimed at achieving equality between women and men and the failure to enforce relevant laws. Likewise, States parties have an international responsibility to create and continuously improve statistical databases and the analysis of all forms of discrimination against women in general and against women belonging to specific vulnerable groups in particular. ...

13. Article 2 is not limited to the prohibition of discrimination against women caused directly or indirectly by States parties. Article 2 also imposes a due diligence obligation on States parties to prevent discrimination by private actors. In some cases, a private actor's acts or omission of acts may be attributed to the State under international law. States parties are thus obliged to ensure that private actors do not engage in discrimination against women as defined in the Convention. The appropriate measures that States parties are obliged to take include the regulation of the activities of private actors with regard to education, employment and health policies and practices, working conditions and work standards, and other areas in which private actors provide services or facilities, such as banking and housing. ...

15. The first obligation of States parties referred to in the chapeau of article 2 is the obligation to "condemn discrimination against women in all its forms". States parties have an immediate and continuous obligation to condemn discrimination. They are obliged to proclaim to their population and the international community their total opposition to all forms of discrimination against women to all levels and branches of Government and their determination to bring about the elimination of discrimination against women. The term "discrimination in all its forms" clearly obligates the State party to be vigilant in condemning all forms of discrimination, including forms that are not explicitly mentioned in the Convention or that may be emerging.

16. States parties are under an obligation to respect, protect and fulfil the right to nondiscrimination of women and to ensure the development and advancement of women in order that

they improve their position and implement their right of de jure and de facto or substantive equality with men. States parties shall ensure that there is neither direct nor indirect discrimination against women. Direct discrimination against women constitutes different treatment explicitly based on grounds of sex and gender differences. Indirect discrimination against women occurs when a law, policy, programme or practice appears to be neutral in so far as it relates to men and women, but has a discriminatory effect in practice on women because pre-existing inequalities are not addressed by the apparently neutral measure. Moreover, indirect discrimination can exacerbate existing inequalities owing to a failure to recognize structural and historical patterns of discrimination and unequal power relationships between women and men.

17. States parties also have an obligation to ensure that women are protected against discrimination committed by public authorities, the judiciary, organizations, enterprises or private individuals, in the public and private spheres. This protection shall be provided by competent tribunals and other public institutions and enforced by sanctions and remedies, where appropriate. States parties should ensure that all Government bodies and organs are fully aware of the principles of equality and non-discrimination on the basis of sex and gender and that adequate training and awareness-raising programmes are set up and carried out in this respect. …

23. States parties also agree to "pursue by all appropriate means" a policy of eliminating discrimination against women. This obligation to use means or a certain way of conduct gives a State party a great deal of flexibility for devising a policy that will be appropriate for its particular legal, political, economic, administrative and institutional framework and that can respond to the particular obstacles and resistance to the elimination of discrimination against women existing in that State party. Each State party must be able to justify the appropriateness of the particular means it has chosen and demonstrate whether it will achieve the intended effect and result. Ultimately, it is for the Committee to determine whether a State party has indeed adopted all necessary measures at the national level aimed at achieving the full realization of the rights recognized in the Convention.

## B     Reflections and Questions

1. Do you see differences between Article 2 of CEDAW and the state obligations described in General Recommendation 28? Is General Recommendation 28 binding on states? CEDAW is a universal treaty containing binding obligations for states that have joined it through ratification and/or accession. As of May 24, 2021, 189 states have ratified CEDAW. Even though CEDAW Committee General Recommendations constitute authoritative interpretations of treaty dispositions, they do not have the legal status of a treaty under international law. They can be considered sources of soft law, persuasive authority on international law, or customary international law in certain instances.[31]

2. CEDAW General Recommendation 28 discusses several layers of obligations states have to address discrimination against women. In paragraph 9, the Committee refers to the obligation to respect, requiring state parties to prevent the adoption of laws and policies which

---

[31]   For more reading, *see* COMPLIANCE AND COMMITMENT: THE ROLE OF NON-BINDING INSTRUMENTS IN THE INTERNATIONAL LEGAL SYSTEM 449–463 (Dinah Shelton, ed., Oxford University Press, 2000).

may hinder women in their full exercise of their civil, political, economic, social, and cultural rights. States are also mandated to pursue steps to eliminate customary practices which perpetuate discrimination and stereotypes against women. States are also obligated to take steps to ensure that women and men enjoy their rights on the basis of equality – in both theory and practice – in their families, communities, and countries. Which of these obligations are positive and negative in nature? Are these obligations interrelated?

3.   CEDAW General Recommendation 28 also clarifies that states have an obligation to erad- icate discrimination against women committed not only by states, but also private actors.[32] CEDAW in Article 2(e) also mandates states to adopt measures to eliminate discrimination against women by any person, organization, or enterprise. CEDAW was one of the first treaties to recognize the human rights implications of private actor activity. Discrimination against women is committed by spouses, partners, family members, employers, corpora- tions, educators, health providers, religious leaders, and many other private actors. Even though international human rights law was adopted to restrain the activity of states, there has been a growing recognition by the international community of the role a diversity of non-state actors plays in human rights violations. Should states be responsible for the actions of private actors? Which criteria should be assessed for a finding of international state responsibility for the acts of an individual, business, education, or health institution?[33]

4.   The CEDAW Committee has advanced a very extensive definition of the phrase *discrim- ination against women*, confirming in General Recommendation 28 that its protections include women discriminated against on the basis of their sexual orientation and gender identity.[34] This reflects very important developments in human rights law protecting the rights to non-discrimination, privacy, and judicial protection of women who have suffered unequal treatment due to their sexual orientation, gender identity, and expression. Can you see the advantages of having an expansive view of discrimination against women?[35]

5.   CEDAW is complemented by an Optional Protocol adopted on October 6, 1999. The Optional Protocol is a separate treaty providing the possibility for states to accept the juris- diction of the CEDAW Committee to resolve individual case complaints and assume addi- tional obligations under CEDAW. The Optional Protocol entered into force on December 22, 2000, and has been ratified by 114 state parties.[36]

---

[32]   *See supra* CEDAW Committee, General Recommendation 28, *supra* note 12, ¶¶ 10, 17.

[33]   For more reading, *see generally* Andrew Clapham, *Human Rights Obligations for Non-State Actors: Where are We Now?*, *in* DOING PEACE THE RIGHTS WAY: ESSAYS IN INTERNATIONAL LAW AND RELATIONS IN HONOR OF LOUISE ARBOUR (Fannie Lafontaine and Francoise Larocque, eds., Intersentia, 2017), https://papers.ssrn.com/sol3/papers.cfm?abstract_id=2641390.

[34]   *See supra* CEDAW Committee, General Recommendation 28, *supra* note 12, ¶ 31.

[35]   For case examples, *see* Atala Riffo & Children v. Chile, Merits, Reparations and Costs, Judgment, Inter-Am. Ct. H.R. (ser. C) No. 239, at 86–87 (Feb. 24, 2012), discussed in Chapter 4; E.B. v. France [GC], App. No. 43546/02, Eur. Ct. H.R. (2008); Christine Goodwin v. United Kingdom [GC], App. No. 28957/95, Eur. Ct. H.R. (2002), discussed in Chapter 4.

[36]   *See* Optional Protocol to the Convention on the Elimination of Discrimination against Women, G.A. Res. 54/4, annex, 54 U.N. GAOR Supp. (No. 49) at 5, U.N. Doc. A/54/49 (Vol. I) (2000), entered into force Dec. 22, 2000. *See* Status of Ratifications Interactive Dashboard, *Optional Protocol to the Convention on the Elimination of All Forms of Discrimination against Women*, https://indicators.ohchr .org/ (last visited on May 24, 2021).

6. Article 2 of the CEDAW Optional Protocol provides that communications can be submitted by individuals or groups of individuals violating CEDAW Treaty provisions. The CEDAW Committee does assess the admissibility of petitions, and considers whether domestic remedies have been exhausted. States need to be offered an opportunity to remedy the women's rights violations alleged due to the supranational nature of the international human rights system. The case decisions of the CEDAW Committee often include an overview of the facts, legal analysis and findings, as well as recommendations. Under Article 5 of the Optional Protocol, the CEDAW Committee can also issue interim measures to avoid irreparable damage. The CEDAW Committee has issued rulings on cases related to domestic violence and due diligence, access to justice, coerced sterilizations, maternal mortality, and therapeutic abortions, among other issues.[37]

7. Article 4(1) of CEDAW mandates the adoption by states of temporary special measures, with the goal of advancing the equality of men and women in our societies. The measures are intended to address past discrimination, and are part of the strategy to build societies guided by equality.[38] These measures are only meant to be temporary and should be lifted when their aims have been achieved. They are also supposed to be only part of the strategy or a multisectoral policy to address and curb discrimination against women. There is great freedom in the format and content of these measures, and states have great discretion on how to implement them at the national and local levels. Can you think of areas in which women could really benefit from temporary special measures to have more equal opportunities as compared to men?[39]

**Note: CEDAW Committee Inquiry Procedure**

Article 8 of the Optional Protocol authorizes the CEDAW Committee to investigate and document situations of systemic human rights violations. The inquiries undertaken by the CEDAW Committee have provided an important space to issue recommendations to specific states on priority issues concerning the rights of women.

In the case of Northern Ireland, the Committee visited on September 10–19, 2016, and recommended the decriminalization of abortion in all instances.[40] It also underscored the need

---

[37] For examples of case decisions adopted by the CEDAW Committee, *see* AT v. Hungary, Communication No. 002/2003, CEDAW/C/36/D/2/2003, January 26, 2005; Sahide Goetcke v. Austria, Communication No. 5/2005, CEDAW/C/39/D/5/2005, August 6, 2007; Fatma Yildirim v. Austria, Communication No. 6/2005, CEDAW/C/39/D/6/2005, October 1, 2007; AS v. Hungary, Communication No. 4/2004, CEDAW/C/36/D/4/2004, August 29, 2006; Alynne Da Silva Pimentel v. Brazil, Communication No. 17/2008, CEDAW/C/49/D/17/2008, August 10, 2011, discussed in Chapter 8; and LC v. Peru, Communication No. 22/2009, CEDAW/C/50/D/22/2009, November 4, 2011.

[38] For more discussion on temporary special measures, *see* General Recommendation No. 25 on Temporary Special Measures, Committee on the Elimination of Discrimination against Women, U.N. Doc. HRI/GEN/1/Rev. 7, ¶¶ 18–24 (2004).

[39] For more reading on the implementation of temporary special measures, *see* Asian Development Bank, Guidance Note on Gender and the Law: Temporary Special Measures to Promote Gender Equality, June 2012, at 5–8, www.adb.org/sites/default/files/institutional-document/33634/files/guidance-note -gender-and-law.pdf.

[40] *See generally* Committee on the Elimination of Discrimination against Women, *Report of the Inquiry Concerning Canada of the Committee on the Elimination of Discrimination against Women under Article 8 of the Optional Protocol to the Convention on the Elimination of All Forms of Discrimination*

for all state parties not to penalize women resorting to abortions.[41] Since then, the United Kingdom and Northern Ireland have undertaken a legal process to decriminalize abortion in Northern Ireland.[42]

The Committee also performed an inquiry related to missing and disappeared aboriginal women in Canada.[43] The Committee visited Canada on September 9–13, 2013, and emphasized in its final report the extreme nature of the violence suffered by aboriginal women, its connection with colonial and post-colonial policies, and the long-lasting socio-economic marginalization of aboriginal peoples.[44] Due to these social conditions, aboriginal women are more exposed to violence and affected by the state failure to guarantee justice in these cases.[45]

One of the most well-known inquiries completed by the CEDAW Committee was to Ciudad Juárez, Mexico, to examine the situation of missing and murdered women in this locality.[46] The CEDAW Committee visited Mexico on October 18–26, 2003, and expressed its concern over the systemic pattern of gender-based violence and killings in this locality, fueled by a culture of violence, discrimination, and impunity.[47] Among several statements, the Committee recommended to the state to integrate a gender perspective in all investigations and prevention policies to combat violence, and to adopt programs to restore the social fabric.[48]

## IV     UNIVERSAL HUMAN RIGHTS TREATIES: THE COVENANTS AND BEYOND

Even though CEDAW is the leading treaty in the world concerning the rights of women, the universal regional human rights treaties contain important dispositions that protect the rights of women to non-discrimination and equality. From these, two of the most important are the International Covenant on Civil and Political Rights (hereinafter "ICCPR") and the International Covenant on Economic, Social and Cultural Rights (hereinafter "ICESCR"). These treaties codify key rights, and both positive and negative obligations states have to

---

*against Women*, CEDAW/C/OP.8/CAN/1 (Mar. 30, 2015) (hereinafter CEDAW Committee, Inquiry Report on Canada).

[41] *See* Committee on the Elimination of Discrimination against Women, *Report of the Inquiry concerning the United Kingdom of Great Britain and Northern Ireland under Article 8 of the Optional Protocol to the Convention on the Elimination of All Forms of Discrimination against Women*, CEDAW/C/Op.8/GBR/1 (March 6, 2018), ¶ 58.

[42] *See* Henry McDonald, *Northern Ireland Confirms that Abortions Can Now Be Carried Out*, THE GUARDIAN, April 9, 2020, www.theguardian.com/world/2020/apr/09/northern-ireland-confirms-abortions-can-now-be-carried-out (last visited on September 24, 2021); Suyin Hayes, *After 158 Years U.K. Lawmakers Have Voted to Decriminalize Abortion in Northern Ireland. The Fight's Not Over Yet*, TIME, July 25, 2019, https://time.com/5634762/northern-ireland-abortion-law-impact/ (last visited on September 24, 2021).

[43] *See generally* CEDAW Committee, Inquiry Report on Canada, *supra* note 40.

[44] *See id.*, ¶¶ 201–204.

[45] *See id.*, ¶¶ 201–204.

[46] *See generally* Committee on the Elimination of all Forms of Discrimination against Women, *Report on Mexico produced by the Committee on the Elimination of Discrimination against Women under Article 8 of the Optional Protocol to the Convention, and reply from the Government of Mexico*, CEDAW/C/2005/OP.8/MEXICO (Jan. 27, 2005).

[47] *See id.*, ¶¶ 260–262, 268.

[48] *See id.*

protect, respect, and fulfill the human rights of women. The excerpts below exemplify the positive and negative obligations advanced by the ICCPR and the ICESCR.

## A    International Covenant on Civil and Political Rights

999 U.N.T.S. 171, entered into force Mar. 23, 1976

### PREAMBLE

The States Parties to the present Covenant,

Considering that, in accordance with the principles proclaimed in the Charter of the United Nations, recognition of the inherent dignity and of the equal and inalienable rights of all members of the human family is the foundation of freedom, justice and peace in the world,

Recognizing that these rights derive from the inherent dignity of the human person,

Recognizing that, in accordance with the Universal Declaration of Human Rights, the ideal of free human beings enjoying civil and political freedom and freedom from fear and want can only be achieved if conditions are created whereby everyone may enjoy his civil and political rights, as well as his economic, social and cultural rights,

Considering the obligation of States under the Charter of the United Nations to promote universal respect for, and observance of, human rights and freedoms,

Realizing that the individual, having duties to other individuals and to the community to which he belongs, is under a responsibility to strive for the promotion and observance of the rights recognized in the present Covenant,

Agree upon the following articles:

…

### Article 2

1. Each State Party to the present Covenant undertakes to respect and to ensure to all individuals within its territory and subject to its jurisdiction the rights recognized in the present Covenant, without distinction of any kind, such as race, colour, sex, language, religion, political or other opinion, national or social origin, property, birth or other status.
2. Where not already provided for by existing legislative or other measures, each State Party to the present Covenant undertakes to take the necessary steps, in accordance with its constitutional processes and with the provisions of the present Covenant, to adopt such legislative or other measures as may be necessary to give effect to the rights recognized in the present Covenant. …

### Article 3

The States Parties to the present Covenant undertake to ensure the equal right of men and women to the enjoyment of all civil and political rights set forth in the present Covenant. …

### Article 6

1. Every human being has the inherent right to life. This right shall be protected by law. No one shall be arbitrarily deprived of his life. …

*Article 7*

No one shall be subjected to torture or to cruel, inhuman or degrading treatment or punishment. In particular, no one shall be subjected without his free consent to medical or scientific experimentation.

### Article 8

1. No one shall be held in slavery; slavery and the slave-trade in all their forms shall be prohibited.
2. No one shall be held in servitude.

### Article 9

1. Everyone has the right to liberty and security of person. No one shall be subjected to arbitrary arrest or detention. No one shall be deprived of his liberty except on such grounds and in accordance with such procedure as are established by law. ...

### Article 14

1. All persons shall be equal before the courts and tribunals. In the determination of any criminal charge against him, or of his rights and obligations in a suit at law, everyone shall be entitled to a fair and public hearing by a competent, independent and impartial tribunal established by law. ...

### Article 17

1. No one shall be subjected to arbitrary or unlawful interference with his privacy, family, home or correspondence, nor to unlawful attacks on his honour and reputation. ...

### Article 18

1. Everyone shall have the right to freedom of thought, conscience and religion. ...

### Article 21

The right of peaceful assembly shall be recognized. No restrictions may be placed on the exercise of this right other than those imposed in conformity with the law and which are necessary in a democratic society in the interests of national security or public safety, public order (ordre public), the protection of public health or morals or the protection of the rights and freedoms of others.

### Article 22

1. Everyone shall have the right to freedom of association with others, including the right to form and join trade unions for the protection of his interests. ...

### Article 26

All persons are equal before the law and are entitled without any discrimination to the equal protection of the law. In this respect, the law shall prohibit any discrimination and guarantee to all persons equal and effective protection against discrimination on any ground such as race, colour, sex, language, religion, political or other opinion, national or social origin, property, birth or other status.

## Article 27
In those States in which ethnic, religious or linguistic minorities exist, persons belonging to such minorities shall not be denied the right, in community with the other members of their group, to enjoy their own culture, to profess and practise their own religion, or to use their own language.

## B    International Covenant on Economic, Social and Cultural Rights

993 U.N.T.S. 3, entered into force Jan. 3, 1976

### PREAMBLE
The States Parties to the present Covenant,

Considering that, in accordance with the principles proclaimed in the Charter of the United Nations, recognition of the inherent dignity and of the equal and inalienable rights of all members of the human family is the foundation of freedom, justice and peace in the world,

Recognizing that these rights derive from the inherent dignity of the human person,

Recognizing that, in accordance with the Universal Declaration of Human Rights, the ideal of free human beings enjoying freedom from fear and want can only be achieved if conditions are created whereby everyone may enjoy his economic, social and cultural rights, as well as his civil and political rights,

Considering the obligation of States under the Charter of the United Nations to promote universal respect for, and observance of, human rights and freedoms,

Realizing that the individual, having duties to other individuals and to the community to which he belongs, is under a responsibility to strive for the promotion and observance of the rights recognized in the present Covenant,

Agree upon the following articles:

...

## Article 2

1. Each State Party to the present Covenant undertakes to take steps, individually and through international assistance and co-operation, especially economic and technical, to the maximum of its available resources, with a view to achieving progressively the full realization of the rights recognized in the present Covenant by all appropriate means, including particularly the adoption of legislative measures.
2. The States Parties to the present Covenant undertake to guarantee that the rights enunciated in the present Covenant will be exercised without discrimination of any kind as to race, colour, sex, language, religion, political or other opinion, national or social origin, property, birth or other status. ...

### Article 3
The States Parties to the present Covenant undertake to ensure the equal right of men and women to the enjoyment of all economic, social and cultural rights set forth in the present Covenant. ...

### Article 6
The States Parties to the present Covenant recognize the right to work, which includes the right of everyone to the opportunity to gain his living by work which he freely chooses or accepts, and will take appropriate steps to safeguard this right.

### Article 7
The States Parties to the present Covenant recognize the right of everyone to the enjoyment of just and favourable conditions of work which ensure, in particular:

(a) Remuneration which provides all workers, as a minimum, with:
  (i) Fair wages and equal remuneration for work of equal value without distinction of any kind, in particular women being guaranteed conditions of work not inferior to those enjoyed by men, with equal pay for equal work; ...

### Article 9
The States Parties to the present Covenant recognize the right of everyone to social security, including social insurance.

### Article 10
The States Parties to the present Covenant recognize that:

1. The widest possible protection and assistance should be accorded to the family, which is the natural and fundamental group unit of society, particularly for its establishment and while it is responsible for the care and education of dependent children. Marriage must be entered into with the free consent of the intending spouses.
2. Special protection should be accorded to mothers during a reasonable period before and after childbirth. During such period working mothers should be accorded paid leave or leave with adequate social security benefits.

### Article 11

1. The States Parties to the present Covenant recognize the right of everyone to an adequate standard of living for himself and his family, including adequate food, clothing and housing, and to the continuous improvement of living conditions. The States Parties will take appropriate steps to ensure the realization of this right, recognizing to this effect the essential importance of international co-operation based on free consent. ...

### Article 12

1. The States Parties to the present Covenant recognize the right of everyone to the enjoyment of the highest attainable standard of physical and mental health. ...

### Article 13

1. The States Parties to the present Covenant recognize the right of everyone to education. They agree that education shall be directed to the full development of the human person-ality and the sense of its dignity, and shall strengthen the respect for human rights and

fundamental freedoms. They further agree that education shall enable all persons to partic-ipate effectively in a free society, promote understanding, tolerance and friendship among all nations and all racial, ethnic or religious groups, and further the activities of the United Nations for the maintenance of peace. …

### *Article 15*

1. The States Parties to the present Covenant recognize the right of everyone:
   (a)  To take part in cultural life;
   (b)  To enjoy the benefits of scientific progress and its applications;
   (c)  To benefit from the protection of the moral and material interests resulting from any scientific, literary or artistic production of which he is the author.

## C     Reflections and Questions

1. Under international human rights law, states have the *negative* obligation to refrain from committing human rights violations which may contravene CEDAW. States are also mandated to adopt *positive* measures exemplified in legislation, policies, programs, and services to build societies free from discrimination.[49] Consider examples of negative and positive steps that states can adopt to comply with their human rights obligations towards women. Are these obligations connected? What are their similarities and differences?

2. The International Covenant on Civil and Political Rights (hereinafter "ICCPR") contains some of the most important foundational and individual rights of the international human rights law system. It is a document very inspired by the Universal Declaration of Human Rights. The ICCPR codifies the rights to life, to be free from torture and slavery, freedom of thought and religion, the rights to free expression and association, and the obliga-tion not to discriminate against all persons, and religious and linguistic minorities. The International Covenant on Economic, Social and Cultural Rights (hereinafter "ICESCR") includes instead rights of a wider and more systemic nature in their implementation and scope, including the rights to health, social security, and education, among others. Are civil and political rights connected to economic, social, and cultural rights?[50] Consider concrete examples of the indivisibility and interconnectedness of civil, political, economic, social, and cultural rights.

3. Do you see any differences in the language of the ICCPR and the ICESCR contained in their Article 2? The International Covenant on Civil and Political Rights codifies an immediate obligation for states to respect and ensure all rights within the Covenant. The International Covenant on Economic Social and Cultural Rights instead acknowledges the

---

[49]   For more reading on positive and negative obligations under international human rights law, *see* General Comment 31 on the Nature of the General Legal Obligation Imposed on States Parties to the Covenant on Civil and Political Rights, Human Rights Committee, U.N. Doc. CCPR/C/21/Rev.1/Add.13 (2004), ¶¶ 3–16; HURST HANNUM, DINAH SHELTON, S. JAMES AND ROSA CELORIO, *Who Has Legal Obligations under International Human Rights Law?*, *in* INTERNATIONAL HUMAN RIGHTS; PROBLEMS OF LAW, POLICY, AND PRACTICE 335–461 (Wolters Kluwer Publishers, 6th ed., 2017).

[50]   For more reading, *see* Flavia Piovesan, *Social, Economic and Cultural Rights and Civil and Political Rights*, 1 SUR – INT'L J. ON HUM. RTS. 21, 21–33 (2004).

limitations in resources that states may have to immediately implement economic, social, and cultural rights. In this sense, the ICESCR reflects the principle of progressive realization in its Article 2. Nevertheless, the Committee on Economic, Social and Cultural Rights has clarified that states do have an immediate obligation to take concrete steps to fulfill the rights in the ICESCR and to not regress on advances made.[51]

4. Both the Human Rights Committee and the Economic, Social and Cultural Rights Committee have pronounced over the key nature of the obligation not to discriminate when it comes to women. The Human Rights Committee in its General Comment 28 underscores the immediate nature of pursuing the equality of men and women under Article 3 of the ICCPR and the obligation to respect and ensure the rights of women to live free from all forms of discrimination and violence. The Economic, Social and Cultural Rights Committee also adopted its General Comment 16, in which it underscores the connection between the obligations not to discriminate and to pursue equality under the ICESCR, and how these are paramount to full compliance of economic, social, and cultural rights. The ESCR Committee also discusses how these obligations are connected to all rights in the ICESCR, including the rights to work, to form trade unions, to social security, to health, and to culture.[52]

*****

The International Covenant on Civil and Political Rights is monitored by the Human Rights Committee, which is composed of independent experts who assess the quality of implementation by the state parties. States can assume additional obligations before the Human Rights Committee by ratifying the First Optional Protocol to the ICCPR, recognizing the competence of the Committee to receive individual communications from victims of human rights violations.[53]

The Committee historically has considered individual communications addressing women's rights and gender equality issues. Copied below are excerpts from a recent decision by the Human Rights Committee concerning the matter of Sharon McIvor and Jacob Grismer, affecting aboriginal women in Canada, and the equality of their rights before the law.

**D      *Sharon McIvor and Jacob Grismer***

Human Rights Committee, Views on Communication 2020/2010
CCPR/C/124/D/2020/2010 (2019)

---

[51] For more reading, *see* General Comment 3 on the Nature of States Parties' Obligations (Art. 2, para. 1, of the Covenant), Committee on Economic, Social and Cultural Rights, U.N. Doc. HRI/GEN/1/Rev.6 at 14, ¶¶ 2, 9–13 (2003).

[52] *See* General Comment 28 on the Equality of Rights between Men and Women, Human Rights Committee, U.N. Doc. CCPR/C/21/Rev.1/Add.10, ¶¶ 5–9, 18–32 (2000); General Comment 16 on the Equal Right of Men and Women to the Enjoyment of All Economic, Social and Cultural Rights (Art. 3 of the International Covenant on Economic, Social and Cultural Rights), Committee on Economic, Social and Cultural Rights, E/C.12/2005/4, ¶¶ 22–31 (2005).

[53] *See* First Optional Protocol to the International Covenant on Civil and Political Rights, General Assembly Resolution 2200A (XXI) of 16 December 1966, entry into force 23 March 1976, in accordance with Article 9, Article 1.

*This communication was presented by Sharon McIvor and her son Jacob Grismer. They are both nationals from Canada and members of the First Nations in Merritt, British Columbia. They alleged concretely before the Human Rights Committee that the granting by Canadian law of Indian Status based on the patrilineal line, to the exclusion of the matrilineal line, contravened the ICCPR and their human rights. They raised violations of their rights to non-discrimination, equality, and culture under Articles 2(1), 3(a), 26, and 27 of the ICCPR.*

7.6 The Committee recalls that the principle of equal treatment of the sexes applies by virtue of articles 2(1), 3 and 26.21. It further recalls its General Comment No. 18 on nondiscrimination, according to which the Covenant prohibits any distinction, exclusion, restriction or preference which is based on any ground including sex, and which has the purpose or effect of nullifying or impairing the recognition, enjoyment or exercise by all persons, on an equal footing, of all rights and freedoms. In the present case, the Committee notes that the Indian Act as amended in 1985, 2011 and 2017 still incorporates a distinction based on sex. It further notes that according to the State party, this distinction will be eliminated, and all persons in the maternal line will be entitled to the same status as persons in the paternal line, when the additional provision in Bill S-3 comes into force. The Committee considers, however, that at the present time, those amendments are not yet in force, and the distinction based on sex still persists in the Indian Act. The Committee further notes that the domestic courts also found that section 6 of the 1985 Indian Act was discriminatory after the 2011 amendments.

7.7 The Committee recalls its General Comment No. 18 and its jurisprudence that not every differentiation amounts to discrimination, as long as it is based on reasonable and objective criteria, in pursuit of an aim that is legitimate under the Covenant. The test for the Committee therefore is whether, in the circumstances of the present communication, the distinction based on sex in the Indian Act, as amended, meets the criteria of reasonableness, objectivity and legitimacy of aim. …

7.10　The Committee recalls its General Comment No. 23 (1994) that article 27 establishes and recognizes a right which is conferred on individuals belonging to indigenous groups and which is distinct from, and additional to, the other rights which all persons are entitled to enjoy under the Covenant. Culture manifests itself in many forms, including a particular way of life associated with the use of land resources, especially in the case of indigenous peoples, which may include such traditional activities as fishing and hunting. Positive measures of protection are, therefore, required not only against the acts of the State party itself, whether through its legislative, judicial or administrative authorities, but also against the acts of other persons within the State party.

7.11　The Committee further recalls that the prohibition on discrimination in the Covenant applies not only to discrimination in law, but also to discrimination in fact, whether practiced by public authorities, by the community, or by private persons or bodies. It further recalls that the principle of equality sometimes requires States parties to adopt temporary special measures in order to diminish or eliminate conditions that cause or help to perpetuate discrimination prohibited by the Covenant. In the present case, the State party acknowledges both that differential treatment based on status exists, and that the additional provisions of Bill S-3 that are not yet in force will entitle persons in the maternal line to the same status as those in the paternal line. The Committee also notes the State party's argument that the distinction based on sex existing in the different sub-paragraphs of section 6(1) of the 1985 Indian Act, as amended, is justified by the legitimate aim of preservation of acquired rights. However, the State party has not demonstrated how recognizing equal status for the authors under section 6(1)(a) would adversely affect the acquired rights of others. The State party therefore has failed to demonstrate that the stated aim is based on objective and reasonable grounds. The Committee accordingly concludes that the continuing distinction based on sex in section 6(1) of the Indian Act constitutes discrimination, which has impacted the right of the authors to enjoy their own culture together with the other members of their group. The Committee therefore concludes that the authors have demonstrated a violation of articles 3 and 26, read in conjunction with article 27 of the Covenant.

7.12    In the light of the previous findings, the Committee considers that it is not necessary to examine the authors' remaining claims under the Covenant.

## E      Reflections and Questions

1. Which connections can you find in the case of *Sharon McIvor and Jacob Grismer* between the civil and political rights and the economic, social, and cultural rights of women?
2. General Comment 18 of the Human Rights Committee discusses the content of the obligation not to discriminate under the International Covenant on Civil and Political Rights codified in Article 2(1). In its analysis, the Human Rights Committee adopts the CEDAW treaty definition of discrimination in Article 1 discussed earlier in this chapter, and expands it to distinctions, exclusions, restrictions and preferences motivated by race, color, national origin, and other factors. The Human Rights Committee also refers to the definition of racial discrimination advanced by the International Convention on the Elimination of All Forms of Racial Discrimination (hereinafter "CERD") in its Article 1(1), prohibiting distinctions on the basis of race, color, descent, national, and ethnic origin.[54]
3. In the matter concerning *Sharon McIvor and Jason Grismer*, the Human Rights Committee indicates that distinctions based on sex must meet the criteria of "reasonableness, objectivity, and legitimacy of aim." The test for the Committee therefore is whether in the circumstances of the present communication, the distinction based on sex in the Indian Act, as amended, meets the criteria of reasonableness, objectivity, and legitimacy of aim.[55] Can you think of any distinctions on the basis of sex that can meet these criteria?
4. The structural discrimination against indigenous women on the basis of their sex, gender, and race in Canada has garnered wide international attention and reporting. One of the most important reports was adopted by the Inter-American Commission on Human Rights after its visit to Canada to study the situation of missing and murdered aboriginal women

---

[54]   *See* General Comment 18 on Non-Discrimination, Human Rights Committee, U.N. Doc. HRI/GEN/1/Rev.1 at 26, ¶¶ 6–7 (1994); International Convention on the Elimination of All Forms of Racial Discrimination, 660 U.N.T.S. 195, entered into force Jan. 4, 1969.
[55]   *See* Human Rights Committee, *Matter of Sharon McIvor and Jason Grismer, supra* at para. 7.7.

on August 6–9 of 2013.[56] The resulting report documents how indigenous women and girls in Canada have been murdered or disappeared at a rate four times higher than the rate of representation of indigenous women in the Canadian population.[57] The report discusses as important causes the long history of discrimination against indigenous women in Canada, including obstacles to the proper recognition of their Aboriginal Status under the Indian Act, and forced enrollment in residential schools.[58] These factors contributed to the separation of indigenous women from their cultural heritage, families, and communities. Indigenous women are still affected by high levels of poverty, economic marginalization, and inadequate housing; all economic and social factors which expose them to violence.[59]

## V   DISCRIMINATION ON THE BASIS OF SEX AT THE NATIONAL LEVEL

Some of the most important work to address the rights of women is done at the national level and by domestic courts. In the case of the United States in particular, its Supreme Court has adopted a series of rulings, discussed throughout this casebook, advancing important content to the obligations not to discriminate, equality, liberty, and privacy under the United States Constitution. This national work is important as the universal and regional treaties and mechanisms discussed in this casebook are supranational, and meant to serve only as a second avenue for justice when the national institutions fail to prevent and offer an adequate remedy for women's rights violations. The administration of justice at the national level can serve as an important layer of protection for the rights of women when other state institutions and private actors perpetuate violations of women's rights.[60] This protection can occur in federal, state, city, and municipal courts, and in the civil, criminal, and administrative spheres.

As a country example, this section in particular discusses the treatment of discrimination on the basis of sex by the United States Supreme Court. The section also comments on the legacy of female jurists in United States courts and that particularly of the late Justice Ruth Bader Ginsburg.

Our discussion begins with excerpts from the decision in the case of *United States v. Virginia* by the United States Supreme Court, whose majority opinion was authored by Justice Ruth Bader Ginsburg. The case addresses the male-only admissions policy at the Virginia Military Institute. The United States sued Virginia and the Virginia Military Institute, claiming that the exclusively male admissions policy violated the Fourteenth Amendment's Equal Protection Clause. The United States presented the lawsuit in 1990, after a complaint was filed

---

[56]   Inter-American Commission on Human Rights, *Missing and Murdered Indigenous Women in British Columbia, Canada*, OEA/Ser.L/V/II. Doc. 30/14, Executive Summary.

[57]   *See id.*, ¶ 2.

[58]   *See id.*, ¶¶ 77–101.

[59]   *See id.*, ¶¶ 1–15.

[60]   For more discussion on how constitutional litigation can be used to advance gender equality issues, *see* Beverly Baines and Ruth Rubio-Marin, *Toward a Feminist Constitutional Agenda, in* THE GENDER OF CONSTITUTIONAL JURISPRUDENCE 1–21 (Beverly Baines and Ruth Rubio-Marin eds., Cambridge University Press, 2005).

with the Attorney General by a female high-school student seeking admission to the Virginia Military Institute.[61]

## A          *United States v. Virginia*

518 U.S. 515 (1996)

Justice Ginsburg delivered the opinion of the Court

… Founded in 1839, VMI is today the sole single sex school among Virginia's 15 public institutions of higher learning. VMI's distinctive mission is to produce "citizen soldiers," men prepared for leadership in civilian life and in military service. VMI pursues this mission through pervasive training of a kind not available anywhere else in Virginia. Assigning prime place to character development, VMI uses an "adversative method" modeled on English public schools and once characteristic of military instruction. VMI constantly endeavors to instill physical and mental discipline in its cadets and impart to them a strong moral code. The school's graduates leave VMI with heightened comprehension of their capacity to deal with duress and stress, and a large sense of accomplishment for completing the hazardous course.

VMI has notably succeeded in its mission to produce leaders; among its alumni are military generals, Members of Congress, and business executives. The school's alumni overwhelmingly perceive that their VMI training helped them to realize their personal goals. VMI's endowment reflects the loyalty of its graduates; VMI has the largest per student endowment of all undergraduate institutions in the Nation. …

In 1990, prompted by a complaint filed with the Attorney General by a female high school student seeking admission to VMI, the United States sued the Commonwealth of Virginia and VMI, alleging that VMI's exclusively male admission policy violated the Equal Protection Clause of the Fourteenth Amendment. …

In the two years preceding the lawsuit, the District Court noted, VMI had received inquiries from 347 women, but had responded to none of them. …

In response to the Fourth Circuit's ruling, Virginia proposed a parallel program for women: Virginia Women's Institute for Leadership (VWIL). The 4-year, state sponsored undergraduate program would be located at Mary Baldwin College, a private liberal arts school for women, and would be open, initially, to about 25 to 30 students. Although VWIL would share VMI's mission—to produce "citizen soldiers"—the VWIL program would differ, as does Mary Baldwin College, from VMI in academic offerings, methods of education, and financial resources. …

The average combined SAT score of entrants at Mary Baldwin is about 100 points lower than the score for VMI freshmen. … Mary Baldwin's faculty holds "significantly fewer Ph.D.'s than the faculty at VMI …" and receives significantly lower salaries. …While VMI offers degrees in liberal arts, the sciences, and engineering, Mary Baldwin, at the time of trial, offered only bachelor of arts degrees. … A VWIL student seeking to earn an engineering degree could gain one, without public support, by attending Washington University in St. Louis, Missouri, for two years, paying the required private tuition. …

---

[61]   *See* United States v. Virginia, 518 U.S. 515, 523 (1996).

Today's skeptical scrutiny of official action denying rights or opportunities based on sex responds to volumes of history. As a plurality of this Court acknowledged a generation ago, "our Nation has had a long and unfortunate history of sex discrimination." *Frontiero* v. *Richardson*, 411 U.S. 677, 684 (1973). Through a century plus three decades and more of that history, women did not count among voters composing "We the People"; … not until 1920 did women gain a constitutional right to the franchise. … And for a half century thereafter, it remained the prevailing doctrine that government, both federal and state, could withhold from women opportunities accorded men so long as any "basis in reason" could be conceived for the discrimination. …

In 1971, for the first time in our Nation's history, this Court ruled in favor of a woman who complained that her State had denied her the equal protection of its laws. *Reed* v. *Reed*, 404 U.S. 71, 73 (holding unconstitutional Idaho Code prescription that, among "'several persons claiming and equally entitled to administer [a decedent's estate], males must be preferred to females'"). Since *Reed*, the Court has repeatedly recognized that neither federal nor state government acts compatibly with the equal protection principle when a law or official policy denies to women, simply because they are women, full citizenship stature—equal opportunity to aspire, achieve, participate in and contribute to society based on their individual talents and capacities. …

Without equating gender classifications, for all purposes, to classifications based on race or national origin … the Court, in post-*Reed* decisions, has carefully inspected official action that closes a door or denies opportunity to women (or to men). … To summarize the Court's current directions for cases of official classification based on gender: Focusing on the differential treatment or denial of opportunity for which relief is sought, the reviewing court must determine whether the proffered justification is "exceedingly persuasive." The burden of justification is demanding and it rests entirely on the State. See *Mississippi Univ. for Women*, 458 U. S., at 724. The State must show "at least that the [challenged] classification serves 'important governmental objectives and that the discriminatory means employed' are 'substantially related to the achievement of those objectives.'" … The justification must be genuine, not hypothesized or invented *post hoc* in response to litigation. And it must not rely on overbroad generalizations about the different talents, capacities, or preferences of males and females. …

The heightened review standard our precedent establishes does not make sex a proscribed classification. Supposed "inherent differences" are no longer accepted as a ground for race or national origin classifications. See *Loving* v. *Virginia*, 388 U.S. 1 (1967). Physical differences between men and women, however, are enduring: "[T]he two sexes are not fungible; a community made up exclusively of one [sex] is different from a community composed of both." *Ballard* v. *United States*, 329 U.S. 187, 193 (1946). …

Measuring the record in this case against the review standard just described, we conclude that Virginia has shown no "exceedingly persuasive justification" for excluding all women from the citizen soldier training afforded by VMI. We therefore affirm the Fourth Circuit's initial judgment, which held that Virginia had violated the Fourteenth Amendment's Equal Protection Clause. Because the remedy proffered by Virginia—the Mary Baldwin VWIL program—does not cure the constitutional violation, *i.e.*, it does not provide equal opportunity, we reverse the Fourth Circuit's final judgment in this case. …

Single sex education affords pedagogical benefits to at least some students, Virginia emphasizes, and that reality is uncontested in this litigation. Similarly, it is not disputed that diversity among public educational institutions can serve the public good. But Virginia has not shown that VMI was established, or has been maintained, with a view to diversifying, by its categorical exclusion of women, educational opportunities within the State. In cases of this genre, our precedent instructs that "benign" justifications proffered in defense of categorical exclusions will not be accepted automatically; a tenable justification must describe actual state purposes, not rationalizations for actions in fact differently grounded. ...

In myriad respects other than military training, VWIL does not qualify as VMI's equal. VWIL's student body, faculty, course offerings, and facilities hardly match VMI's. Nor can the VWIL graduate anticipate the benefits associated with VMI's 157-year history, the school's prestige, and its influential alumni network. ...

VMI, too, offers an educational opportunity no other Virginia institution provides, and the school's "prestige"—associated with its success in developing "citizen soldiers"—is unequaled. Virginia has closed this facility to its daughters and, instead, has devised for them a "parallel program," with a faculty less impressively credentialed and less well paid, more limited course offerings, fewer opportunities for military training and for scientific specialization. ... VMI, beyond question, "possesses to a far greater degree" than the VWIL program "those qualities which are incapable of objective measurement but which make for greatness in a ... school," including "position and influence of the alumni, standing in the community, traditions and prestige." ...

A prime part of the history of our Constitution, historian Richard Morris recounted, is the story of the extension of constitutional rights and protections to people once ignored or excluded. VMI's story continued as our comprehension of "We the People" expanded ... There is no reason to believe that the admission of women capable of all the activities required of VMI cadets would destroy the Institute rather than enhance its capacity to serve the "more perfect Union."

For the reasons stated, the initial judgment of the Court of Appeals ... is affirmed, the final judgment of the Court of Appeals ... is reversed, and the case is remanded for further proceedings consistent with this opinion.

## B          Reflections and Questions

1. Former Justice Ruth Bader Ginsburg, who served in the United States Supreme Court for 27 years and passed away on September 18, 2020, was one of the most influential jurists of her generation on gender equality issues. Prior to her time in the United States Supreme Court, she became famous for litigating successfully a series of emblematic cases on sex-based discrimination. As a Justice of the United States Supreme Court, she was a leader of its liberal wing, advocating in her majority and dissenting opinions for the rights of women, racial groups, and those marginalized. She also co-founded the American Civil Liberties Union's Women's Rights Project and was a law professor. Her life story and the obstacles she faced to secure a job upon graduation from Columbia Law School due to her sex motivated much of her legal work on behalf of women.[62]

---

[62] For more reading on the legacy of the work of former Justice Ruth Bader Ginsburg in the treatment of gender equality issues by United States Courts, *see generally* Deborah Jones Merritt and David M. Lieberman, *Ruth Bader Ginsburg's Jurisprudence of Opportunity and Equality*, 104 COLUM. L. REV. 39 (2004).

2. Distinctions on the basis of sex have been historically reviewed by the United States Supreme Court with an intermediate level of scrutiny, which is not as strict as the legal standard applied to classifications on the basis of race. In *Craig v. Boren*, the United States Supreme Court established in 1976 that gender classifications must advance important governmental objectives and must be "substantially related" to the achievement of those objectives to be in accordance with the Equal Protection Clause of the Fourteenth Amendment of the U.S. Constitution. *See, Craig v. Boren*, 429 U.S. 190, 197 (1976). In *United States v. Virginia*, the United States Supreme Court established that states must advance an "exceedingly persuasive justification" to justify a gender-based distinction. Is the standard of review advanced by Justice Ginsburg and the majority opinion in *United States v. Virginia* consistent with intermediate scrutiny? Should gender-based classifications be subjected to as strict scrutiny as those based on race?

3. Reflect on the questions below related to the *United States v. Virginia* decision:
   a. Is it relevant to the discrimination analysis in this case that the Virginia Military Institute is a public institution?
   b. Do you think that this case would have had a different outcome if a military educational program of comparable quality had been available for women?
   c. Were new rights for women created by this decision?

4. The United States Supreme Court has not historically referred to international law when ruling on cases related to the human rights of women. The United States has also not ratified CEDAW. Can you think of reasons why it would be useful for the United States to ratify CEDAW? If ratified, would it be useful for United States Courts to refer to CEDAW principles and obligations? Does it matter whether international law is applied by domestic courts when ruling on cases advancing the rights of women?

5. Do female judges have a special obligation to advance women's rights in their rulings? Is a progressive notion of the content of the United States Constitution always necessary to respect and ensure human rights?

**Note and exercise: The complicated history of the Equal Rights Amendment in the United States**

Even though the United States Constitution does include the Equal Protection Clause in its Fourteenth Amendment, it is devoid of any explicit provision recognizing equality between the sexes. The complicated process of adopting an *Equal Rights Amendment* to the United States Constitution has been part of the historical struggle to achieve equal protection of the law for women in the United States. Even though the Equal Rights Amendment was first introduced by the National Woman's Party in 1923, it gained real momentum in Congress between 1971 and 1972. It was approved in 1971 by the U.S. House of Representatives and in 1972 by the United States Senate. This was a key achievement by the growing feminist movement in the United States. Conservative backlash, however, impeded final ratification of the Equal Rights Amendment, falling short of the required 38 states needed for this purpose.[63] Most recently,

---

[63] For a response to the arguments against the Equal Rights Amendment, and analysis of its potential impact on legislation which differentiates on the basis of sex, *see* Ruth Bader Ginsburg, *The Need for the Equal Rights Amendment*, 59 A.B.A. J. 1013, 1014–1019 (1973).

discussions over the potential adoption of the Equal Rights Amendment have been revived again, particularly after the *MeToo* movement, discussed in Chapter 6 of this casebook.[64] States like Nevada, Illinois, and Virginia have ratified the Equal Rights Amendment recently.[65]

Consider the implications of the potential ratification of the Equal Rights Amendment. In this regard, contemplate the following questions:

a. What do you think would be the impact of passing the Equal Rights Amendment in the work of the U.S. Supreme Court and lower courts?
b. Do you think an Equal Rights Amendment would motivate the United States Supreme Court to apply strict scrutiny to cases alleging discrimination on the basis of sex?
c. What would be the effect of the passage of the Equal Rights Amendments on current legislation?
d. Can you think of contemporary problems in the United States that are connected to discrimination against women? How do you think adoption of the Amendment would help address discrimination against women in key sectors such as education, employment, community, family, and in political life?
e. Do constitutional protection and litigation make a difference to respect, protect, and fulfill the equality of women?
f. Should the Equal Rights Amendment be limited solely to discrimination on the basis of sex? What about discrimination on the basis of gender and the concerns of LGBTI groups?

## VI    STEREOTYPES AND CULTURAL PATTERNS OF BEHAVIOR

One of the most important legacies of CEDAW is that it addresses in the text of the treaty the issue of stereotypes and socio-cultural patterns of behavior that work socially to the detriment of women. Stereotypes are referred to in Article 5 of the text of CEDAW, which posits that states should adopt measures to modify social and cultural patterns and prejudices based on stereotyped roles for men and women. Article 2(f) of CEDAW moreover mandates states to adopt measures to address existing customs and practices which constitute discrimination against women both in law and in practice. Article 10(c) additionally provides that states should eliminate stereotypes in education and teaching methods.

The CEDAW Committee has also identified as a central obligation to eliminate discrimination against women the need to address the persistence of gender-based stereotypes impacting women in the law, social structures, institutions, and in the acts of individuals.[66] How are stereotypes defined? Why are they considered harmful when it comes to women?

---

[64]    For arguments favoring the continued relevance and present need to adopt the Equal Rights Amendment, *see* Sarah M. Stephens, *At the End of Our Article III Rope: Why We Still Need the Equal Rights Amendment*, 80 BROOK. L. REV. 407–426 (2015).

[65]    For more history on the Equal Rights Amendment and present challenges, *see* Alex Cohen and Wilfred U. Codrington III, *The Equal Rights Amendment Explained*, January 23, 2020, www .brennancenter.org/our-work/research-reports/equal-rights-amendment-explained.

[66]    *See* CEDAW Committee, General Recommendation 25, Temporary Special Measures, *supra* note 38, ¶¶ 6–8.

Rebecca Cook and Simone Cusack have defined gender stereotypes as follows:

Stereotyping is part of human nature. It is the way we categorize individuals, often unconsciously into particular groups or types, in part to simplify the world around us. It is the process of ascribing to an individual general attributes, characteristics, or roles by reason only of his or her apparent membership in a particular group. Stereotyping produces generalizations or preconceptions concerning attributes, characteristics, or roles of members of a particular social group, which renders unnecessary consideration of any particular individual member's abilities, needs, wishes, and circumstances.

Stereotypes affect both men and women. However, they often have a particularly egregious effect on women. As one commentator has explained, a "useful way of examining the continued disadvantage of women is to identify the assumptions and stereotypes which have been central to the perpetuation and legitimation of women's legal and social subordination. Such assumptions have roots which stretch deep into the history of ideas, yet continue to influence the legal and social structure of modern society. Indeed, the continuity is startling, given the extent and fundamental nature of change in the political and economic context."

Stereotypes degrade women when they assign them to subservient roles in society, and devalue their attributes and characteristics. Prejudices about women's inferiority and their stereotyped roles generate disrespect and devaluation of women in all sectors of society. [67]

Gender-based violence, and its intricate link to discrimination, will be discussed in the following section. The decision below, made by the CEDAW Committee in the case of *Karen Vayag Vertido v. The Philippines*, exemplifies how gender stereotypes can negatively delay the investigation of cases of rape, and what states can do to address this human rights problem.

**A      *Karen Tayag Vertido v. Philippines* (Excerpts)**

Committee on the Elimination of Discrimination against Women
Communication No. 18, 2008, CEDAW/C/46/D/18/2008, July 16, 2010
Citations and footnotes omitted

*The author of this complaint is a woman from the Philippines who served as Executive Director of the Davao City Chamber of Commerce and Industry. She claims that the former President of the Chamber raped her on March 29, 1996. Within 48 hours, she reported this crime to the police and filed a complaint with the authorities. The case remained at the trial court level between 1997 and 2005. The Regional Court of Davao City concluded that the testimony of the complainant contained many voids and therefore could not lead to a conviction. The victim alleged before the CEDAW Committee that she was a victim of discrimination against women under Article 1 of CEDAW and that she suffered human rights violations of Articles 2(c), 2(f) and 5(a) of the Convention.*

8.2 The Committee will consider the author's allegations that gender-based myths and misconceptions about rape and rape victims were relied on by Judge Hofileña Europa in the Regional Court of Davao City in its decision, under article 335 of the Revised Penal Code of 1930, leading to the acquittal of the alleged perpetrator, and will determine whether this amounted to a violation of the rights of the author and a breach of the corresponding State

---

[67]    *See* REBECCA COOK AND SIMONE CUSACK, *Introduction*, *in* GENDER STEREOTYPING: TRANSNATIONAL LEGAL PERSPECTIVES 1–3 (University of Pennsylvania Press, 2010).

party's obligations to end discrimination in the legal process under articles 2(c), 2(f) and 5(a) of the Convention. ...

8.4 The Committee further reaffirms that the Convention places obligations on all State organs and that States parties can be responsible for judicial decisions which violate the provisions of the Convention. It notes that by articles 2(f) and 5(a), the State party is obligated to take appropriate measures to modify or abolish not only existing laws and regulations, but also customs and practices that constitute discrimination against women. In this regard, the Committee stresses that stereotyping affects women's right to a fair and just trial and that the judiciary must take caution not to create inflexible standards of what women or girls should be or what they should have done when confronted with a situation of rape based merely on preconceived notions of what defines a rape victim or a victim of gender-based violence, in general. The Committee further recalls its general recommendation No. 19 on violence against women. This general recommendation addresses the question of whether States parties can be held accountable for the conduct of non-State actors. ... States may also be responsible for private acts if they fail to act with due diligence to prevent violations of rights or to investigate and punish acts of violence. ... In the particular case, the compliance of the State party's due diligence obligation to banish gender stereotypes on the grounds of articles 2(f) and 5(a) needs to be assessed in the light of the level of gender sensitivity applied in the judicial handling of the author's case.

8.5 ... The Committee, after a careful examination of the main points that determined the judgement, notes the following issues. First of all, the judgement refers to principles such as that physical resistance is not an element to establish a case of rape, that people react differently under emotional stress, that the failure of the victim to try to escape does not negate the existence of the rape as well as to the fact that "in any case, the law does not impose upon a rape victim the burden of proving resistance". The decision shows, however, that the judge did not apply these principles in evaluating the author's credibility against expectations about how the author should have reacted before, during and after the rape owing to the circumstances and her character and personality. The judgement reveals that the judge came to the conclusion that the author had a contradictory attitude by reacting both with resistance at one time and submission at another time, and saw this as being a problem. ... It is clear from the judgement that the assessment of the credibility of the author's version of events was influenced by a number of stereotypes, the author in this situation not having followed what was expected from a rational and "ideal victim" or what the judge considered to be the rational and ideal response of a woman in a rape situation ... the Committee finds that to expect the author to have resisted in the situation at stake reinforces in a particular manner the myth that women must physically resist the sexual assault. In this regard, the Committee stresses that there should be no assumption in law or in practice that a woman gives her consent because she has not physically resisted the unwanted sexual conduct, regardless of whether the perpetrator threatened to use or used physical violence.

8.6 Further misconceptions are to be found in the decision of the Court, which contains several references to stereotypes about male and female sexuality being more supportive for the credibility of the alleged perpetrator than for the credibility of the victim. ... Other factors taken into account in the judgement, such as the weight given to the fact that the author and the accused knew each other, constitute a further example of "gender-based myths and misconceptions."

8.7 With regard to the definition of rape, the Committee notes that the lack of consent is not an essential element of the definition of rape in the Philippines Revised Penal Code. It recalls its general recommendation No. 19 of 29 January 1992 on violence against women, where it made clear, in paragraph 24(b), that "States parties should ensure that laws against family violence and abuse, rape, sexual assault and other gender-based violence give adequate protection to all women, and respect their integrity and dignity". Through its consideration of States parties' reports, the Committee has clarified time and again that rape constitutes a violation of women's right to personal security and bodily integrity, and that its essential element was lack of consent.

8.8 The Committee finally would like to recognize that the author of the communication has suffered moral and social damage and prejudices, in particular by the excessive duration of the trial proceedings and by the revictimization through the stereotypes and gender-based myths relied upon in the judgement. The author has also suffered pecuniary damages due to the loss of her job. ...

## B    Reflections and Questions

1. How are stereotypes connected to discrimination against women? Stereotypes are generalizations about women's potential, capacity, and inclination to perform certain forms of employment, tasks, and roles in a society. They can curb women's opportunities to obtain a comprehensive education at the primary, secondary, and higher education levels, and to enter specific professions that have been male-dominated. Stereotypes about women's role as caretakers have also led to societies built on women's attention to family matters involving children, the elderly, and the sick, as opposed to developing women as leaders and catalysts for change.[68]

2. Can you think of stereotypes that may benefit women?[69]

3. Do men suffer from stereotypes? Historically men have been expected in most societies to be heads of household and the lead income providers for their families. They are also expected to be masculine, strong, and assertive. These are only some examples of the stereotyped notions that men still face socially, which challenge their involvement in the caretaking and raising of their children and in partaking in home responsibilities. There is still stigma associated with men pursuing paternity leave policies and other kinds of leave to care for their children and to negotiate work schedules conducive to helping in the

---

[68]    For more reading, *see generally* Anne Marie Slaughter, *Why Women Still Can't Have It All*, THE ATLANTIC, July/August 2012 issue, www.theatlantic.com/magazine/archive/2012/07/why-women-still-cant-have-it-all/309020/; Marcia L. McCormick, *Stereotypes as Channels and the Social Model of Discrimination*, 36(1) SAINT LOUIS UNIVERSITY PUBLIC LAW REVIEW, Article 5 (2017), https://papers.ssrn.com/sol3/papers.cfm?abstract_id=3285914.

[69]    *See* Lindsay Pattison, *How Gender Stereotypes Could Actually Help Women at Work*, FORTUNE, May 9, 2017, https://fortune.com/2017/05/09/dealing-with-gender-stereotypes/.

caretaking of their families. This in turn has affected the possibility of women to work and reach decision-making positions in politics and business, among other sectors.[70]

4.  Stereotypes affect women in every realm of social life, including the family, school, employers, the health sector, and in politics. One of the areas in which women have been very negatively impacted by stereotypes is in the investigation, judgment, and sanction of cases related to gender-based violence. In its General Recommendation 33 on access to justice, the CEDAW Committee expressed its concern over stereotyping and gender bias in justice systems, and how these impede the full enjoyment of the rights of women.[71] The Committee referred in particular to the application by judges of notions of what they consider acceptable behavior for women, and criminalize those who do not conform to these standards. Stereotypes can also affect the credibility offered to women's testimonies and views in these processes, and negatively impact investigations and trials.[72]

5.  How do you ensure that the training of justice officials is effective to prevent the application of stereotypes in decision-making? As indicated earlier, one of the most complex problems that women suffer in their quest for justice for acts of discrimination and gender-based violence are forms of revictimization by justice officials, including judges, prosecutors, lawyers, investigators, and law enforcement officials in general. Justice officials can negatively affect the investigation and processing of these cases by applying preconceived notions of how women should behave, dress, and react to specific crimes, including those related to sexual violence. Preconceived notions begin early, in the home, and are later cemented in social tolerance of gender-based violence as normal. Effective training to curb gender-based violence needs to include a process, benchmarks, and forms of accountability. Education at schools, colleges, and law schools of the importance of non-discrimination and the negative influence of stereotypes is also key to eventually producing justice officials which operate free from these notions.[73]

6.  Simone Cusack and Alexandra Timmer have referred to the importance of naming stereotypes and identifying them as a social harm, in order to be able to effectively prevent and eradicate them.[74] They have discussed in their scholarship how Karen Tayag Vertido identified in her complaint a number of stereotypes that harmed her legal process, includ-

---

[70]   For more reading *see* Shelley Zalis, *The Future Of Masculinity: Overcoming Stereotypes*, FORBES, January 22, 2019, www.forbes.com/sites/shelleyzalis/2019/01/22/the-future-of-masculinity-overcoming -stereotypes/?sh=361fa9051af3; UN Women, Men Can Transform Gender Stereotypes and Inequality, Speech by UN Women Executive Director Phumzile Mlambo-Ngcuka, November 11, 2014, https://www .unwomen.org/en/news/stories/2014/11/ed-speech-at-menengage-global-symposium-india.

[71]   *See* General Recommendation 33 on Women's Access to Justice, Committee on the Elimination of Discrimination against Women, CEDAW/C/GC/33, ¶¶ 26–29 (July 23, 2015).

[72]   *See id.*

[73]   For more reading, *see* INTERNATIONAL COMMISSION OF JURISTS, WOMEN'S ACCESS TO JUSTICE FOR GENDER-BASED VIOLENCE: A PRACTITIONER'S GUIDE 233–234, 241–242 (International Commission of Jurists, 2016), www.icj.org/wp-content/uploads/2016/03/Universal-Womens-accesss-to-justice -Publications-Practitioners-Guide-Series-2016-ENG.pdf; Inter-American Commission on Human Rights, Access to Justice for Women Victims of Violence in the Americas, OEA/Ser.L/V//II. Doc. 68, ¶¶ 182–184 (Jan. 20, 2007), www.cidh.org/women/access07/tocaccess.htm.

[74]   *See* Simone Cusack and Alexandra Timmer, *Gender Stereotyping in Rape Cases: The CEDAW Committee's Decision in Vertido v The Philippines*, 11(2) HUMAN RIGHTS LAW REVIEW 7–10 (2011), https://academic.oup.com/hrlr/article-abstract/11/2/329/582590?redirectedFrom=fulltext.

ing (i) the lack of evidence that a woman physically resisted a sexual assault; (ii) women as untruthful when it comes to allegations of rape; and (iii) older men as not capable of committing rape. Karen Tayag Vertido also identified a number of "rape myths," including the notion that perpetrators of rape are all strangers, and that rape cannot occur between acquaintances.[75]

## VII    FINAL COMMENTS: CEDAW IN PRACTICE

More than forty years have passed since the adoption of CEDAW and there are still many challenges in its implementation. Even though CEDAW has been deeply influential in the reform of constitutions and laws around the world, an adequate legal framework does not guarantee effective enforcement. Political will from states is key to guaranteeing an adequate implementation of CEDAW's dispositions. It is also crucial to disseminate information of CEDAW and state obligations in all sectors of society, and in different languages. One important gain is the active participation of civil society organizations in the work of the CEDAW Committee, and many of the experts in the Committee come from civil society as well.

CEDAW is meant to protect women of different ages, cultures, races, ethnicities, sexual orientations, gender identities, socio-economic standards, and religions. There is important advocacy work devoted to promote the substantive implementation of CEDAW, the lifting of its reservations, the ratification of the Optional Protocol, and compliance with the general recommendations and case decisions adopted by the CEDAW Committee.[76]

---

[75]  *See id.*, page 8.
[76]  For more reading, *see* Lisa Gormley, *40 Years of Creativity, Striving for Women's Human Rights Across the Globe*, London School of Economics, July 12, 2019, https://blogs.lse.ac.uk/wps/2019/07/12/40-years-of-creativity-striving-for-womens-human-rights-across-the-globe/; Bandana Rana, Vice-Chair of the CEDAW Committee, Statement Marking 40th Anniversary of CEDAW, December 18, 2019, www.ohchr.org/EN/NewsEvents/Pages/DisplayNews.aspx?NewsID=25443&LangID=E.

# 2.  Gender-based violence as a form of discrimination

## I  INTRODUCTION: THE WIDESPREAD NATURE OF GENDER-BASED VIOLENCE

One of the most important omissions in the text of CEDAW is the problem of gender-based violence. Gender-based violence is one of the most serious, alarming, and prevalent human rights violations in the world. The World Health Organization and UN Women both estimate that 35 percent of women worldwide (one in three) have experienced either physical and/or sexual intimate partner violence or sexual violence by a non-partner at some point in their lives.[1]

Violence against women can be physical, psychological, and sexual. It affects women of all ages, socio-economic backgrounds, races, and ethnicities. It bears enormous social and economic costs for societies.[2]

The United Nations General Assembly adopted its Declaration on the Elimination of Violence against Women in 1993, offering a definition of violence against women as "any act of gender-based violence that results in, or is likely to result in, physical, sexual or psychological harm or suffering to women, including threats of such acts, coercion or arbitrary deprivation of liberty, whether occurring in public or in private life."[3]

The Vienna Declaration and Platform of Action, subscribed to by more than 170 states, also proclaimed the right of women and girls to live free from all forms of gender-based violence, sexual harassment, and exploitation, and the indivisibility of the human rights of women with universal human rights.[4] In 1995, the Beijing Declaration and Program of Action established that women's rights are human rights, and the priority nature of the prevention and elimination of all forms of violence against women and girls.[5]

---

[1]   *See* World Health Organization, Violence against women (who.int) (last visited on May 19, 2021); UN Women, *Facts and Figures: Ending Violence against Women*, www.unwomen.org/en/what-we-do/ending-violence-against-women/facts-and-figures (last visited on May 19, 2021).

[2]   For more reading, *see* World Bank, Brief: *Gender-Based Violence (Violence against Women and Girls)* (Sept. 25, 2019), www.worldbank.org/en/topic/socialsustainability/brief/violence-against-women-and-girls.

[3]   *See* Declaration on the Elimination of Violence against Women, G.A. Res. 48/104, 48 U.N. GAOR Supp. (No. 49) at 217, U.N. Doc. A/48/49 (1993), Article 1, discussed *infra*.

[4]   *See* Vienna Declaration, World Conference on Human Rights, Vienna, 14–25 June 1993, U.N. Doc. A/CONF.157/24 (Part I) at 20 (1993), Article 18,

[5]   *See generally* Beijing Declaration and Platform of Action, September 15, 1995, www.un.org/en/events/pastevents/pdfs/beijing_declaration_and_platform_for_action.pdf (hereinafter Beijing Declaration and Platform of Action), Numerals 14 and 29 (Beijing Declaration).

However, to date, the United Nations has not adopted a universal treaty solely dedicated to the issue of gender-based violence. To make up for this gap, the CEDAW Committee has adopted three General Recommendations to address the issue of gender-based violence and explain its connection to the prohibition of discrimination in CEDAW.[6] These recommendations, establishing as a cornerstone principle that gender-based violence is a form of discrimination against women, are discussed in the following section.

The following readings, questions, and analysis discuss the different dimensions of the problem of gender-based violence, including its nature as a human rights issue; its modern manifestations; universal and regional approaches to gender-based violence; and its extreme forms such as femicide and gender-motivated killings.

## II  GENDER-BASED VIOLENCE AS AN INTERNATIONAL HUMAN RIGHTS ISSUE

As discussed earlier, CEDAW does not cover gender-based violence in the text of the treaty. It was not until 1992 that the CEDAW Committee established an intricate link between gender-based violence and the problem of discrimination against women. The CEDAW Committee confirmed in its landmark General Recommendation 19 that all states are obligated to act promptly to prevent and eradicate gender-based violence as a form of discrimination. This was an important step towards the conceptualization of gender-based violence as a human rights violation meritorious of state action, resources, and attention. The readings below provide background and analysis on this key development for the international human rights of women

### A  CEDAW Committee, General Recommendation No. 19, Violence against Women

Committee on the Elimination of Discrimination against Women
U.N. Doc. A/47/38 (1992)

1. Gender-based violence is a form of discrimination that seriously inhibits women's ability to enjoy rights and freedoms on a basis of equality with men. ...
6. The Convention in article 1 defines discrimination against women. The definition of discrimination includes gender-based violence, that is, violence that is directed against a woman because she is a woman or that affects women disproportionately. It includes acts that inflict physical, mental or sexual harm or suffering, threats of such acts, coercion and other deprivations of liberty. Gender-based violence may breach specific provisions of the Convention, regardless of whether those provisions expressly mention violence.
7. Gender-based violence, which impairs or nullifies the enjoyment by women of human rights and fundamental freedoms under general international law or under human rights

---

[6]  *See* General Recommendations 12, 19, and 35 of the CEDAW Committee, www.ohchr.org/EN/HRBodies/CEDAW/Pages/Recommendations.aspx.

conventions, is discrimination within the meaning of article 1 of the Convention. These rights and freedoms include:

(a)   The right to life;
(b)   The right not to be subject to torture or to cruel, inhuman or degrading treatment or punishment;
(c)   The right to equal protection according to humanitarian norms in time of international or internal armed conflict;
(d)   The right to liberty and security of person;
(e)   The right to equal protection under the law;
(f)   The right to equality in the family;
(g)   The right to the highest standard attainable of physical and mental health;
(h)   The right to just and favourable conditions of work.

8. The Convention applies to violence perpetrated by public authorities. Such acts of violence may breach that State's obligations under general international human rights law and under other conventions, in addition to breaching this Convention.

9. It is emphasized, however, that discrimination under the Convention is not restricted to action by or on behalf of Governments. For example, under article 2(e) the Convention calls on States parties to take all appropriate measures to eliminate discrimination against women by any person, organization or enterprise. Under general international law and specific human rights covenants, States may also be responsible for private acts if they fail to act with due diligence to prevent violations of rights or to investigate and punish acts of violence, and for providing compensation. …

11. Traditional attitudes by which women are regarded as subordinate to men or as having stereotyped roles perpetuate widespread practices involving violence or coercion, such as family violence and abuse, forced marriage, dowry deaths, acid attacks and female circumcision. Such prejudices and practices may justify gender-based violence as a form of protection or control of women. The effect of such violence on the physical and mental integrity of women is to deprive them the equal enjoyment, exercise and knowledge of human rights and fundamental freedoms. While this comment addresses mainly actual or threatened violence the underlying consequences of these forms of gender-based violence help to maintain women in subordinate roles and contribute to the low level of political participation and to their lower level of education, skills and work opportunities. …

17. Equality in employment can be seriously impaired when women are subjected to gender-specific violence, such as sexual harassment in the workplace.

18. Sexual harassment includes such unwelcome sexually determined behaviour as physical contact and advances, sexually coloured remarks, showing pornography and sexual demand, whether by words or actions. Such conduct can be humiliating and may constitute a health and safety problem; it is discriminatory when the woman has reasonable grounds to believe that her objection would disadvantage her in connection with her employment, including recruitment or promotion, or when it creates a hostile working environment. …

23. Family violence is one of the most insidious forms of violence against women. It is prevalent in all societies. Within family relationships women of all ages are subjected to violence of all kinds, including battering, rape, other forms of sexual assault, mental and other forms of violence, which are perpetuated by traditional attitudes. Lack of economic independence forces many women to stay in violent relationships. The abrogation of their

family responsibilities by men can be a form of violence, and coercion. These forms of violence put women's health at risk and impair their ability to participate in family life and public life on a basis of equality.

24. In light of these comments, the Committee on the Elimination of Discrimination against Women recommends that:

(a)    States parties should take appropriate and effective measures to overcome all forms of gender-based violence, whether by public or private act;

(b)    States parties should ensure that laws against family violence and abuse, rape, sexual assault and other gender-based violence give adequate protection to all women, and respect their integrity and dignity. Appropriate protective and support services should be provided for victims. Gender-sensitive training of judicial and law enforcement officers and other public officials is essential for the effective implementation of the Convention;

(c)    States parties should encourage the compilation of statistics and research on the extent, causes and effects of violence, and on the effectiveness of measures to prevent and deal with violence;

(d)    Effective measures should be taken to ensure that the media respect and promote respect for women;

(e)    States parties in their reports should identify the nature and extent of attitudes, customs and practices that perpetuate violence against women and the kinds of violence that result. They should report on the measures that they have undertaken to overcome violence and the effect of those measures; …

## B        Declaration on the Elimination of Violence against Women

United Nations General Assembly Resolution 48/104 (1993)

**The General Assembly,**

Recognizing the urgent need for the universal application to women of the rights and principles with regard to equality, security, liberty, integrity and dignity of all human beings, …

Recognizing that effective implementation of the Convention on the Elimination of All Forms of Discrimination against Women would contribute to the elimination of violence against women and that the Declaration on the Elimination of Violence against Women, set forth in the present resolution, will strengthen and complement that process,

Concerned that violence against women is an obstacle to the achievement of equality, development and peace, as recognized in the Nairobi Forward-looking Strategies for the Advancement of Women, in which a set of measures to combat violence against women was recommended, and to the full implementation of the Convention on the Elimination of All Forms of Discrimination against Women,

Affirming that violence against women constitutes a violation of the rights and fundamental freedoms of women and impairs or nullifies their enjoyment of those rights and freedoms, and concerned about the long-standing failure to protect and promote those rights and freedoms in the case of violence against women,

Recognizing that violence against women is a manifestation of historically unequal power relations between men and women, which have led to domination over and discrimination against women by men and to the prevention of the full advancement of women, and that violence against women is one of the crucial social mechanisms by which women are forced into a subordinate position compared with men,

Concerned that some groups of women, such as women belonging to minority groups, indigenous women, refugee women, migrant women, women living in rural or remote communities, destitute women, women in institutions or in detention, female children, women with disabilities, elderly women and women in situations of armed conflict, are especially vulnerable to violence, …

Solemnly proclaims the following Declaration on the Elimination of Violence against Women and urges that every effort be made so that it becomes generally known and respected:

### Article 1

For the purposes of this Declaration, the term "violence against women" means any act of gender-based violence that results in, or is likely to result in, physical, sexual or psychological harm or suffering to women, including threats of such acts, coercion or arbitrary deprivation of liberty, whether occurring in public or in private life.

### Article 2

Violence against women shall be understood to encompass, but not be limited to, the following:

(a) Physical, sexual and psychological violence occurring in the family, including battering, sexual abuse of female children in the household, dowry-related violence, marital rape, female genital mutilation and other traditional practices harmful to women, non-spousal violence and violence related to exploitation;

(b) Physical, sexual and psychological violence occurring within the general community, including rape, sexual abuse, sexual harassment and intimidation at work, in educational institutions and elsewhere, trafficking in women and forced prostitution;

(c) Physical, sexual and psychological violence perpetrated or condoned by the State, wherever it occurs.

### Article 3

Women are entitled to the equal enjoyment and protection of all human rights and fundamental freedoms in the political, economic, social, cultural, civil or any other field. These rights include, inter alia:

(a) The right to life;
(b) The right to equality;
(c) The right to liberty and security of person;
(d) The right to equal protection under the law;
(e) The right to be free from all forms of discrimination;
(f) The right to the highest standard attainable of physical and mental health;
(g) The right to just and favourable conditions of work;
(h) The right not to be subjected to torture, or other cruel, inhuman or degrading treatment or punishment.

### Article 4

States should condemn violence against women and should not invoke any custom, tradition or religious consideration to avoid their obligations with respect to its elimination. States should pursue by all appropriate means and without delay a policy of eliminating violence against women and, to this end, should:

(a)     Consider, where they have not yet done so, ratifying or acceding to the Convention on the Elimination of All Forms of Discrimination against Women or withdrawing reservations to that Convention;

(b)     Refrain from engaging in violence against women;

(c)     Exercise due diligence to prevent, investigate and, in accordance with national legislation, punish acts of violence against women, whether those acts are perpetrated by the State or by private persons;

(d)     Develop penal, civil, labour and administrative sanctions in domestic legislation to punish and redress the wrongs caused to women who are subjected to violence; women who are subjected to violence should be provided with access to the mechanisms of justice and, as provided for by national legislation, to just and effective remedies for the harm that they have suffered; States should also inform women of their rights in seeking redress through such mechanisms;

(e)     Consider the possibility of developing national plans of action to promote the protection of women against any form of violence, or to include provisions for that purpose in plans already existing, taking into account, as appropriate, such cooperation as can be provided by non-governmental organizations, particularly those concerned with the issue of violence against women;

(f)     Develop, in a comprehensive way, preventive approaches and all those measures of a legal, political, administrative and cultural nature that promote the protection of women against any form of violence, and ensure that the re-victimization of women does not occur because of laws insensitive to gender considerations, enforcement practices or other interventions; …

## C     Reflections and Questions

1.  The CEDAW Committee in its General Recommendation 19 refers to gender-based violence as a form of discrimination. As discussed in this section, this has become a cornerstone principle of what are considered as international human rights law and women's rights today. This connection was key since CEDAW was silent on the issue of gender-based violence. Moreover, both the Universal Declaration of Human Rights and the International Covenant on Civil and Political Rights include a prohibition of discrimination on the basis of sex, but are also devoid of any references to gender-based violence.[7]

2.  The connection between discrimination and violence has opened the door to the development of legal standards and content pertaining to state obligations concerning gender-based

---

    [7]    *See* Universal Declaration of Human Rights, G.A. Res. 217A (III), U.N. Doc. A/810 at 71 (1948), Article 2; International Covenant on Civil and Political Rights, G.A. Res. 2200A (XXI), 21 U.N. GAOR Supp. (No. 16) at 52, U.N. Doc. A/6316 (1966), 999 U.N.T.S. 171, entered into force Mar. 23, 1976, Article 2(1).

violence. Even though the founding instruments of international human rights law prohibited discrimination on the basis of sex, international human rights law in its essence was not adopted with a gender perspective or violence against women lens.[8] Do you think that the connection between gender-based violence and discrimination against women is still useful today for the international human rights framework? Or should gender-based violence and discrimination against women be treated as separate and independent human rights issues meritorious of state attention?[9]

3.  When is violence against women considered gender-based? General Recommendation 19 of the CEDAW Committee defines gender-based violence as "violence that is directed against a woman because she is a woman or that affects women disproportionately."[10] Can you think of examples of violence against women that cannot be considered gender-based? Is it better to use the term violence against women or gender-based violence?

4.  Is the connection between gender-based violence and discrimination always clear? Can you think of instances in which acts of gender-based violence may not have discrimination as a root cause? How can you best ensure that states adequately address discrimination and gender-based violence through legislation, public policies, institutions, and programs?[11]

5.  The United Nations Declaration on the Elimination of Violence against Women is a very important historical document for several reasons. It is one of the first instruments which connects violence to important values such as liberty and dignity, and to the full exercise of the human rights of women. The Declaration also recognizes how specific groups of women can be more vulnerable to the issue of gender-based violence, which is an important precursor for the later incorporation in the international human rights framework of the issue of intersectionality. Article 2 provides one of the most important definitions of violence against women, recognizing physical, psychological, and sexual violence. In its Article 4, the Declaration also rejects the notion that customs, traditions, and religion can be invoked to justify gender-based violence. In Article 4 also, the Declaration includes explicitly the due diligence obligation of states to prevent and respond to violence against women perpetrated by both government and private actors. The principles advanced in the Declaration greatly impacted the later language which was included in the regional treaties addressing gender-based violence in the Americas, Africa, and Europe, which will be discussed in the following section.

---

[8]  For more reading, *see* Hilary Charlesworth, *Feminist Methods in International Law*, 36 STUD. TRANSNAT'L LEGAL POL'Y 159, 162–168 (2004); Hilary Charlesworth, Christine Chinkin, and Shelly Wright, *Feminist Approaches to International Law*, 85 AM. J. INT'L L. 613, 613–615, 621–634 (1991).

[9]  For more reading on advantages and challenges of the ongoing connection between gender-based violence and discrimination against women, *see* ALICE EDWARDS, VIOLENCE AGAINST WOMEN UNDER INTERNATIONAL HUMAN RIGHTS LAW, 429–442 (Cambridge University Press, 2011).

[10]  *See* CEDAW Committee, General Recommendation 19, *supra*, ¶ 6.

[11]  For more reading, *see* Julie Goldscheid, *Domestic and Sexual Violence as Sex Discrimination: Comparing American and International Approaches*, CUNY ACADEMIC WORKS 378–393 (2006), https://academicworks.cuny.edu/cgi/viewcontent.cgi?article=1160&context=cl_pubs.

# III   GENDER-BASED VIOLENCE AGAINST WOMEN

There have been ongoing debates at the United Nations level over the need for a new treaty that exclusively addresses gender-based violence. General Recommendation 19 of the CEDAW Committee has become a key reference globally for the issue of gender-based violence, but it does not have the force of a treaty. The concept of gender-based violence is also fast evolving and every day more forms are recognized that surpass the physical, psychological, and sexual violence. Among these are sexual harassment, femicides, hate speech, violence in the digital space, obstetrics violence, spiritual violence, environmental violence, political violence, among others.

The CEDAW Committee, in response to this reality, adopted in 2017 a new General Recommendation 35 underscoring the duty of states to act with due diligence to prevent, investigate, sanction, and grant reparations for acts of gender-based violence against women. Excerpts are included below.

**A      General Recommendation No. 35 on Gender-Based Violence against Women, Updating General Recommendation No. 19**

Committee on the Elimination of all Forms of Discrimination against Women
CEDAW/C/GC/35, July 14, 2017

2.   … The *opinio juris* and State practice suggest that the prohibition of gender-based violence against women has evolved into a principle of customary international law. General recommendation No. 19 has been a key catalyst for this process. …

6.   … gender-based violence against women, whether committed by States, intergovernmental organisations or non-state actors, including private persons and armed groups, remains pervasive in all countries of the world, with high levels of impunity. It manifests in a continuum of multiple, interrelated and recurring forms, in a range of settings, from private to public, including technology-mediated settings and in the contemporary globalized world it transcends national boundaries.

7.   In many states, legislation addressing gender-based violence against women remains non-existent, inadequate and/or poorly implemented. An erosion of legal and policy frameworks to eliminate gender-based discrimination or violence, often justified in the name of tradition, culture, religion or fundamentalist ideologies, and significant reductions in public spending, often as part of "austerity measures" following economic and financial crises, further weaken the state responses. In the context of shrinking democratic spaces and consequent deterioration of the rule of law, all these factors allow for the pervasiveness of gender-based violence against women and lead to a culture of impunity. …

9.   The concept of "violence against women" in general recommendation No. 19 and other international instruments and documents has emphasized that this violence is gender-based. Accordingly, this document uses the expression "gender-based violence against women", as a more precise term that makes explicit the gendered causes and impacts of the violence. This expression further strengthens the understanding of this violence as a social – rather than an individual – problem, requiring comprehensive responses, beyond specific events, individual perpetrators and victims/survivors.

10. The Committee considers that gender-based violence against women is one of the fundamental social, political and economic means by which the subordinate position of women with respect to men and their stereotyped roles are perpetuated. Throughout its work, the Committee has made clear that this violence is a critical obstacle to achieving substantive equality between women and men as well as to women's enjoyment of human rights and fundamental freedoms enshrined in the Convention. ...

12. ... discrimination against women is inextricably linked to other factors that affect their lives. The Committee's jurisprudence highlights that these may include ethnicity/race, indigenous or minority status, colour, socioeconomic status and/or caste, language, religion or belief, political opinion, national origin, marital and/or maternal status, age, urban/rural location, health status, disability, property ownership, being lesbian, bisexual, transgender or intersex, illiteracy, trafficking of women, armed conflict, seeking asylum, being a refugee, internal displacement, statelessness, migration, heading households, widowhood, living with HIV/AIDS, deprivation of liberty, being in prostitution, geographical remoteness and stigmatisation of women fighting for their rights, including human rights defenders. Accordingly, because women experience varying and intersecting forms of discrimination, which have an aggravating negative impact, the Committee acknowledges that gender-based violence may affect some women to different degrees, or in different ways, so appropriate legal and policy responses are needed. ...

14. Gender-based violence affects women throughout their life cycle and accordingly references to women in this document include girls. This violence takes multiple forms, including acts or omissions intended or likely to cause or result in death or physical, sexual, psychological or economic harm or suffering to women, threats of such acts, harassment, coercion and arbitrary deprivation of liberty. Gender-based violence against women is affected and often exacerbated by cultural, economic, ideological, technological, political, religious, social and environmental factors, as evidenced, among others, in the contexts of displacement, migration, increased globalization of economic activities including global supply chains, extractive and offshoring industry, militarization, foreign occupation, armed conflict, violent extremism and terrorism. Gender-based violence against women is also affected by political, economic and social crises, civil unrest, humanitarian emergencies, natural disasters, destruction or degradation of natural resources. Harmful practices and crimes against women human rights defenders, politicians, activists or journalists are also forms of gender-based violence against women affected by such cultural, ideological and political factors. ...

20. Gender-based violence against women occurs in all spaces and spheres of human interaction, whether public or private. These include the family, the community, the public spaces, the workplace, leisure, politics, sport, health services, educational settings and their redefinition through technology-mediated environments, such as contemporary forms of violence occurring in the Internet and digital spaces. In all these settings, gender-based violence against women can result from acts or omissions of State or non-State actors, acting territorially or extraterritorially, including extraterritorial military action of States, individually or as members of international or intergovernmental organizations or coalitions, or extraterritorial actions by private corporations. ...

23. States parties are responsible for preventing these acts or omissions by their own organs and agents – including through training and the adoption, implementation and monitoring

of legal provisions, administrative regulations and codes of conduct – and to investigate, prosecute and apply appropriate legal or disciplinary sanctions as well as provide reparation in all cases of gender-based violence against women, including those constituting international crimes, as well as in cases of failure, negligence or omission on the part of public authorities. In so doing, women's diversity and the risks of intersectional discrimination stemming from it should be taken into consideration.

## B    Reflections and Questions

1.  The CEDAW Committee in its General Recommendation 35 held that the prohibition of gender-based violence has become a principle of customary international law. The statute of the International Court of Justice in its Article 38(1)(b) lists international custom as a primary source of international law.[12] Customary international law is composed of practices and rules followed by states as law, regardless of whether they have been codified in treaties or their domestic laws. Which factors make the prohibition of gender-based violence a rule of customary international law?[13]

2.  General Recommendation 35 of the CEDAW Committee refers to gender-based violence against women. It greatly expands the coverage of the term to economic harm, forced sterilizations, the criminalization of abortion, and the abuse and mistreatment of women seeking reproductive health services and information. The CEDAW Committee also offers a detailed rendition of factors which aggravate the exposure to violence, including technology and crimes against human rights defenders and journalists. Is it useful to have an expansive definition of gender-based violence?

3.  After the adoption of General Recommendation 35, is there still a normative gap in international law concerning gender-based violence? Is there still need for a universal treaty exclusively focused on gender-based violence?[14]

4.  General Recommendation 35 of the CEDAW Committee confirms that states can be internationally responsible for gender-based violence committed by non-state actors. These include businesses and corporations. Women can suffer sexual harassment, workplace violence, and forms of different treatment in promotions and salaries.[15] At the request of the former Human Rights Commission, the United Nations appointed a Special Representative on human rights and transnational corporations and business enterprises to "identify and clarify" standards of corporate accountability for transnational corporations and business

---

[12]   *See* Statute of the International Court of Justice, 1945, Article 38(1)(b), www.icj-cij.org/en/statute.

[13]   For more reading on international customary law, *see* SEAN MURPHY, *International Law Creation, Section B: Customary International Law*, in PRINCIPLES OF INTERNATIONAL LAW (West Academic Publishing, 3rd ed., 2018).

[14]   For more reading, *see* Ronagh J.A. McQuigg, *The CEDAW Committee and Gender-Based Violence against Women: General Recommendation No. 35*, 6 INT'L HUM. RTS. L. REV. 263, 271–278 (2017); Global Rights for Women, *Time for a Change: The Need for a Binding International Treaty on Violence against Women* (2019), https://globalrightsforwomen.org/wp-content/uploads/2020/02/Time_for_a_Change-2.pdf; Report of the Special Rapporteur on violence against women, its causes and consequences, U.N. Doc. A/HRC/29/27 (June 10, 2015).

[15]   *See, for reference*, Inter-American Commission on Human Rights, *Business and Human Rights*, OEA/Ser.L/V/II CIDH/REDESCA/INF.1/19, ¶¶ 331–339 (Nov. 1, 2019).

enterprises.[16] The Special Representative appointed, Professor John Ruggie, developed a set of guiding principles highlighting the states' duty to protect human rights; the corporate responsibility to respect human rights; and access to a remedy when human rights violations occur in the context of business and human rights.[17] According to the Ruggie Principles, states are obligated to protect against human rights abuses within their territory by third parties, including business enterprises.[18] On the other hand, business enterprises have the responsibility to respect human rights by preventing harm, and act with human rights due diligence to identify and mitigate human rights impacts.[19] Is there a difference between obligations and responsibilities?

5.  The CEDAW Committee in its General Recommendation 35 refers as well to the situation of girls. Girls under 18 years old are one of the groups of women most affected by different forms of sexual, physical, and psychological violence. Violence can be perpetrated against girls in their families, communities, schools, while seeking health services, on the internet, and in religious institutions.[20] According to the U.N. Special Rapporteur on violence against women, one in three girls have been victims of rape during their lifetimes.[21] Due diligence in the case of girls entails taking into account a gender perspective, as well as important principles which guide the human rights of children, including non-discrimination and the best interests of the child; the right to be heard; and the rights to life and development.[22] Several cases have been decided and are being considered by international courts documenting the arduous road to justice faced by girls when they suffer rape, sexual violence, and other human rights violations, including revictimization, institutional violence by government authorities, and the lack of credibility for their statements.[23]

---

[16] *See* U.N. Commission on Human Rights, *Human Rights Resolution 2005/69: Human Rights and Transnational Corporations and Other Business Enterprises*, 20 April 2005, E/CN.4/RES/2005/69.

[17] *See Guiding Principles on Business and Human Rights: Implementing the United Nations "Protect, Respect, and Remedy" Framework*, Final Report of the Special Representative of the Secretary General on the Issue of Human Rights and Transnational Corporations and other Business Enterprises, John Ruggie, U.N. Doc. A/HRC/17/31 (2011), Parts I, II, and III (hereinafter Ruggie Principles).

[18] *See id.*, Section I(A), Principle 1.

[19] *See id.*, Section II(A), Principles 11–17.

[20] For more reading on the problem of violence against girls, *see* UNICEF Innocenti Research Center, A STUDY ON VIOLENCE AGAINST GIRLS 16–21 (March 9–10, 2009), www.unicef-irc.org/publications/pdf/violence_girls_eng.pdf.

[21] *See* Report of the Special Rapporteur on violence against women, its causes and consequences, Dubravka Šimonović, *Rape as a grave, systematic and widespread human rights violation, a crime and a manifestation of gender-based violence against women and girls, and its prevention*, A/HRC/47/26, ¶ 8 (April 19, 2021).

[22] For more discussion of these principles, *see* General Comment 12 on the Right to be Heard, Committee on the Rights of the Child, CRC/C/GC/12, ¶ 2 (July 20, 2009).

[23] For case examples, *see generally*, V.R.P., V.P.C. et al. v. Nicaragua, Preliminary Objections, Merits, Reparations and Costs, Judgment, Inter-Am. Ct. H.R., Series C No. 350 (March 8, 2018); Equality Now, *An Important Step Toward Accountability for Sexual Violence in Bolivia and Beyond*, November 20, 2020, www.equalitynow.org/brisa_iachr_case_referral (discussing the case of Brisa Liliana de Angulo Lozada v. Bolivia currently before the Inter-American Court of Human Rights).

# IV   REGIONAL APPROACHES TO GENDER-BASED VIOLENCE

Gender-based violence has been a key component of the work of the regional human rights protection systems in the Americas, Europe, and Africa. The three systems have adopted their own treaties outlining a set of state obligations to prevent and respond to the problem of violence against women. The three treaties define violence against women, and establish the connection between this issue and prevailing social discrimination, prejudices, and stereotypes. They foremost advance the legal standard of due diligence mandating states to prevent, investigate, sanction, and grant reparations for all acts of gender-based violence, and the duty to safeguard an adequate and effective access to justice when these acts occur. States are required to adopt legislation, public policies, programs, and collect statistics on the issue of gender-based violence. States must also have in place resources for victims, including shelters and protection orders in cases of potential imminent harm.

These regional treaties have opened a space to develop detailed jurisprudence alluding to the different components of states' negative and positive obligations to address the complex nature of violence against women. They are considered a strong complement to the universal system of statements prohibiting gender-based violence and the CEDAW Committee General Recommendations 19 and 35. Excerpts of the three regional treaties are included below.

## A        Inter-American Convention on the Punishment, Prevention, and Eradication of Violence against Women (hereinafter "Convention of Belém do Pará"), 1994

THE STATES PARTIES TO THIS CONVENTION,

RECOGNIZING that full respect for human rights has been enshrined in the American Declaration of the Rights and Duties of Man and the Universal Declaration of Human Rights, and reaffirmed in other international and regional instruments;

AFFIRMING that violence against women constitutes a violation of their human rights and fundamental freedoms, and impairs or nullifies the observance, enjoyment and exercise of such rights and freedoms;

CONCERNED that violence against women is an offense against human dignity and a manifestation of the historically unequal power relations between women and men; …

**HAVE AGREED** to the following: …

**Article 1**
For the purposes of this Convention, violence against women shall be understood as any act or conduct, based on gender, which causes death or physical, sexual or psychological harm or suffering to women, whether in the public or the private sphere.

**Article 2**
Violence against women shall be understood to include physical, sexual and psychological violence:

a. that occurs within the family or domestic unit or within any other interpersonal relationship, whether or not the perpetrator shares or has shared the same residence with the woman, including, among others, rape, battery and sexual abuse;

b.  that occurs in the community and is perpetrated by any person, including, among others, rape, sexual abuse, torture, trafficking in persons, forced prostitution, kidnapping and sexual harassment in the workplace, as well as in educational institutions, health facilities or any other place; and
c.  that is perpetrated or condoned by the state or its agents regardless of where it occurs. ...

## Article 4
Every woman has the right to the recognition, enjoyment, exercise and protection of all human rights and freedoms embodied in regional and international human rights instruments. These rights include, among others:

a.  The right to have her life respected;
b.  The right to have her physical, mental and moral integrity respected;
c.  The right to personal liberty and security;
d.  The right not to be subjected to torture;
e.  The rights to have the inherent dignity of her person respected and her family protected;
f.  The right to equal protection before the law and of the law;
g.  The right to simple and prompt recourse to a competent court for protection against acts that violate her rights;
h.  The right to associate freely;
i.  The right of freedom to profess her religion and beliefs within the law; and
j.  The right to have equal access to the public service of her country and to take part in the conduct of public affairs, including decision-making. ...

## Article 6
The right of every woman to be free from violence includes, among others:

a.  The right of women to be free from all forms of discrimination; and
b.  The right of women to be valued and educated free of stereotyped patterns of behavior and social and cultural practices based on concepts of inferiority or subordination.

## Article 7
The States Parties condemn all forms of violence against women and agree to pursue, by all appropriate means and without delay, policies to prevent, punish and eradicate such violence and undertake to:

a.  refrain from engaging in any act or practice of violence against women and to ensure that their authorities, officials, personnel, agents, and institutions act in conformity with this obligation;
b.  apply due diligence to prevent, investigate and impose penalties for violence against women;
c.  include in their domestic legislation penal, civil, administrative and any other type of provisions that may be needed to prevent, punish and eradicate violence against women and to adopt appropriate administrative measures where necessary;

d. adopt legal measures to require the perpetrator to refrain from harassing, intimidating or threatening the woman or using any method that harms or endangers her life or integrity, or damages her property;
e. take all appropriate measures, including legislative measures, to amend or repeal existing laws and regulations or to modify legal or customary practices which sustain the persistence and tolerance of violence against women;
f. establish fair and effective legal procedures for women who have been subjected to violence which include, among others, protective measures, a timely hearing and effective access to such procedures;
g. establish the necessary legal and administrative mechanisms to ensure that women subjected to violence have effective access to restitution, reparations or other just and effective remedies; and
h. adopt such legislative or other measures as may be necessary to give effect to this Convention. ...

**Article 12**
Any person or group of persons, or any nongovernmental entity legally recognized in one or more member states of the Organization, may lodge petitions with the Inter-American Commission on Human Rights containing denunciations or complaints of violations of Article 7 of this Convention by a State Party, and the Commission shall consider such claims in accordance with the norms and procedures established by the American Convention on Human Rights and the Statutes and Regulations of the Inter-American Commission on Human Rights for lodging and considering petitions.

**B    African Charter on Human and Peoples' Rights on the Rights of Women in Africa (hereinafter "Maputo Protocol"), 2003**

...

RECALLING that women's rights have been recognised and guaranteed in all international human rights instruments, notably the Universal Declaration of Human Rights, the International Covenant on Civil and Political Rights, the International Covenant on Economic, Social and Cultural Rights, the Convention on the Elimination of All Forms of Discrimination against Women and its Optional Protocol, the African Charter on the Rights and Welfare of the Child, and all other international and regional conventions and covenants relating to the rights of women as being inalienable, interdependent and indivisible human rights;

...

RECOGNISING the crucial role of women in the preservation of African values based on the principles of equality, peace, freedom, dignity, justice, solidarity and democracy;

...

CONCERNED that despite the ratification of the African Charter on Human and Peoples' Rights and other international human rights instruments by the majority of States Parties, and their solemn commitment to eliminate all forms of discrimination and harmful practices against women, women in Africa still continue to be victims of discrimination and harmful practices;
HAVE AGREED AS FOLLOWS:

**Article 1 Definitions**

For the purpose of the present Protocol:

…

(f)     "Discrimination against women" means any distinction, exclusion or restriction or any differential treatment based on sex and whose objectives or effects compromise or destroy the recognition, enjoyment or the exercise by women, regardless of their marital status, of human rights and fundamental freedoms in all spheres of life;

(g)     "Harmful Practices" means all behaviour, attitudes and/or practices which negatively affect the fundamental rights of women and girls, such as their right to life, health, dignity, education and physical integrity; …

(j)     "Violence against women" means all acts perpetrated against women which cause or could cause them physical, sexual, psychological, and economic harm, including the threat to take such acts; or to undertake the imposition of arbitrary restrictions on or deprivation of fundamental freedoms in private or public life in peace time and during situations of armed conflicts or of war;

(k)     "Women" means persons of female gender, including girls.

**Article 2 Elimination of Discrimination against Women**

1. States Parties shall combat all forms of discrimination against women through appropriate legislative, institutional and other measures. In this regard they shall:
    (a)     include in their national constitutions and other legislative instruments, if not already done, the principle of equality between women and men and ensure its effective application;
    (b)     enact and effectively implement appropriate legislative or regulatory measures, including those prohibiting and curbing all forms of discrimination particularly those harmful practices which endanger the health and general well-being of women;
    (c)     integrate a gender perspective in their policy decisions, legislation, development plans, programmes and activities and in all other spheres of life; …
2. States Parties shall commit themselves to modify the social and cultural patterns of conduct of women and men through public education, information, education and communication strategies, with a view to achieving the elimination of harmful cultural and traditional practices and all other practices which are based on the idea of the inferiority or the superiority of either of the sexes, or on stereotyped roles for women and men.

**Article 3 Right to Dignity**

1. Every woman shall have the right to dignity inherent in a human being and to the recognition and protection of her human and legal rights.
2. Every woman shall have the right to respect as a person and to the free development of her personality.
3. States Parties shall adopt and implement appropriate measures to prohibit any exploitation or degradation of women.

4.  States Parties shall adopt and implement appropriate measures to ensure the protection of every woman's right to respect for her dignity and protection of women from all forms of violence, particularly sexual and verbal violence.

**Article 4 The Rights to Life, Integrity and Security of the Person**

1.  Every woman shall be entitled to respect for her life and the integrity and security of her person. All forms of exploitation, cruel, inhuman or degrading punishment and treatment shall be prohibited.
2.  States Parties shall take appropriate and effective measures to:
    (a)  enact and enforce laws to prohibit all forms of violence against women including unwanted or forced sex whether the violence takes place in private or public;
    (b)  adopt such other legislative, administrative, social and economic measures as may be necessary to ensure the prevention, punishment and eradication of all forms of violence against women;
    (c)  identify the causes and consequences of violence against women and take appropriate measures to prevent and eliminate such violence;
    (d)  actively promote peace education through curricula and social communication in order to eradicate elements in traditional and cultural beliefs, practices and stereotypes which legitimise and exacerbate the persistence and tolerance of violence against women; …

**Article 5 Elimination of Harmful Practices**
States Parties shall prohibit and condemn all forms of harmful practices which negatively affect the human rights of women and which are contrary to recognised international standards. States Parties shall take all necessary legislative and other measures to eliminate such practices, including:

a)  creation of public awareness in all sectors of society regarding harmful practices through information, formal and informal education and outreach programmes;
b)  prohibition, through legislative measures backed by sanctions, of all forms of female genital mutilation, scarification, medicalisation and para-medicalisation of female genital mutilation and all other practices in order to eradicate them;
c)  provision of necessary support to victims of harmful practices through basic services such as health services, legal and judicial support, emotional and psychological counselling as well as vocational training to make them self-supporting;
d)  protection of women who are at risk of being subjected to harmful practices or all other forms of violence, abuse and intolerance. …

**Article 8 Access to Justice and Equal Protection before the Law**
Women and men are equal before the law and shall have the right to equal protection and benefit of the law. States Parties shall take all appropriate measures to ensure:

a)  effective access by women to judicial and legal services, including legal aid;
b)  support to local, national, regional and continental initiatives directed at providing women access to legal services, including legal aid; …

**Article 10 Right to Peace**

1. Women have the right to a peaceful existence and the right to participate in the promotion and maintenance of peace.
2. States Parties shall take all appropriate measures to ensure the increased participation of women:
   (a)   in programmes of education for peace and a culture of peace;
   (b)   in the structures and processes for conflict prevention, management and resolution at local, national, regional, continental and international levels; …

**Article 13 Economic and Social Welfare Rights**

States Parties shall adopt and enforce legislative and other measures to guarantee women equal opportunities in work and career advancement and other economic opportunities. In this respect, they shall:

a)   promote equality of access to employment;
b)   promote the right to equal remuneration for jobs of equal value for women and men;
c)   ensure transparency in recruitment, promotion and dismissal of women and combat and punish sexual harassment in the workplace;
d)   guarantee women the freedom to choose their occupation, and protect them from exploitation by their employers violating and exploiting their fundamental rights as recognised and guaranteed by conventions, laws and regulations in force;
e)   create conditions to promote and support the occupations and economic activities of women, in particular, within the informal sector; …

**Article 14 Health and Reproductive Rights**

1. States Parties shall ensure that the right to health of women, including sexual and reproductive health is respected and promoted. This includes:
   (a)   the right to control their fertility;
   (b)   the right to decide whether to have children, the number of children and the spacing of children;
   (c)   the right to choose any method of contraception;
   (d)   the right to self-protection and to be protected against sexually transmitted infections, including HIV/AIDS; …
2. States Parties shall take all appropriate measures to: …
   (c)   protect the reproductive rights of women by authorising medical abortion in cases of sexual assault, rape, incest, and where the continued pregnancy endangers the mental and physical health of the mother or the life of the mother or the foetus.

C          **Council of Europe Convention on Preventing and Combating Violence against Women and Domestic Violence (hereinafter "Istanbul Convention"), 2011**

…

Condemning all forms of violence against women and domestic violence;

Recognising that the realisation of *de jure* and *de facto* equality between women and men is a key element in the prevention of violence against women; …

Recognising the structural nature of violence against women as gender-based violence, and that violence against women is one of the crucial social mechanisms by which women are forced into a subordinate position compared with men;

Recognising, with grave concern, that women and girls are often exposed to serious forms of violence such as domestic violence, sexual harassment, rape, forced marriage, crimes committed in the name of so-called "honour" and genital mutilation, which constitute a serious violation of the human rights of women and girls and a major obstacle to the achievement of equality between women and men; …

Aspiring to create a Europe free from violence against women and domestic violence, …

## Article 1 – Purposes of the Convention

1.  The purposes of this Convention are to:
    a.  protect women against all forms of violence, and prevent, prosecute and eliminate violence against women and domestic violence;
    b.  contribute to the elimination of all forms of discrimination against women and promote substantive equality between women and men, including by empowering women;
    c.  design a comprehensive framework, policies and measures for the protection of and assistance to all victims of violence against women and domestic violence;
    d.  promote international co-operation with a view to eliminating violence against women and domestic violence;
    e.  provide support and assistance to organisations and law enforcement agencies to effectively co-operate in order to adopt an integrated approach to eliminating violence against women and domestic violence. …

## Article 2 – Scope of the Convention

1.  This Convention shall apply to all forms of violence against women, including domestic violence, which affects women disproportionately.
2.  Parties are encouraged to apply this Convention to all victims of domestic violence. Parties shall pay particular attention to women victims of gender-based violence in implementing the provisions of this Convention.
3.  This Convention shall apply in times of peace and in situations of armed conflict.

## Article 3 – Definitions

For the purpose of this Convention:

a.  "violence against women" is understood as a violation of human rights and a form of discrimination against women and shall mean all acts of gender-based violence that result in, or are likely to result in, physical, sexual, psychological or economic harm or suffering to women, including threats of such acts, coercion or arbitrary deprivation of liberty, whether occurring in public or in private life;

b. "domestic violence" shall mean all acts of physical, sexual, psychological or economic violence that occur within the family or domestic unit or between former or current spouses or partners, whether or not the perpetrator shares or has shared the same residence with the victim;

c. "gender" shall mean the socially constructed roles, behaviours, activities and attributes that a given society considers appropriate for women and men;

d. "gender-based violence against women" shall mean violence that is directed against a woman because she is a woman or that affects women disproportionately;

e. "victim" shall mean any natural person who is subject to the conduct specified in points a and b;

f. "women" includes girls under the age of 18.

## Article 4 – Fundamental rights, equality and non-discrimination

1. Parties shall take the necessary legislative and other measures to promote and protect the right for everyone, particularly women, to live free from violence in both the public and the private sphere.

2. Parties condemn all forms of discrimination against women and take, without delay, the necessary legislative and other measures to prevent it, in particular by:
   – embodying in their national constitutions or other appropriate legislation the principle of equality between women and men and ensuring the practical realisation of this principle;
   – prohibiting discrimination against women, including through the use of sanctions, where appropriate;
   – abolishing laws and practices which discriminate against women.

3. The implementation of the provisions of this Convention by the Parties, in particular measures to protect the rights of victims, shall be secured without discrimination on any ground such as sex, gender, race, colour, language, religion, political or other opinion, national or social origin, association with a national minority, property, birth, sexual orientation, gender identity, age, state of health, disability, marital status, migrant or refugee status, or other status.

4. Special measures that are necessary to prevent and protect women from gender-based violence shall not be considered discrimination under the terms of this Convention.

## Article 5 – State obligations and due diligence

1. Parties shall refrain from engaging in any act of violence against women and ensure that State authorities, officials, agents, institutions and other actors acting on behalf of the State act in conformity with this obligation.

2. Parties shall take the necessary legislative and other measures to exercise due diligence to prevent, investigate, punish and provide reparation for acts of violence covered by the scope of this Convention that are perpetrated by non-State actors.

## Article 6 – Gender-sensitive policies

Parties shall undertake to include a gender perspective in the implementation and evaluation of the impact of the provisions of this Convention and to promote and effectively implement policies of equality between women and men and the empowerment of women. ...

## Chapter III – Prevention
## Article 12 – General obligations

1. Parties shall take the necessary measures to promote changes in the social and cultural patterns of behaviour of women and men with a view to eradicating prejudices, customs, traditions and all other practices which are based on the idea of the inferiority of women or on stereotyped roles for women and men.
2. Parties shall take the necessary legislative and other measures to prevent all forms of violence covered by the scope of this Convention by any natural or legal person.
3. Any measures taken pursuant to this chapter shall take into account and address the specific needs of persons made vulnerable by particular circumstances and shall place the human rights of all victims at their centre.
4. Parties shall take the necessary measures to encourage all members of society, especially men and boys, to contribute actively to preventing all forms of violence covered by the scope of this Convention.
5. Parties shall ensure that culture, custom, religion, tradition or so-called "honour" shall not be considered as justification for any acts of violence covered by the scope of this Convention.
6. Parties shall take the necessary measures to promote programmes and activities for the empowerment of women. ...

Article 53 – Restraining or protection orders

1. Parties shall take the necessary legislative or other measures to ensure that appropriate restraining or protection orders are available to victims of all forms of violence covered by the scope of this Convention.
2. Parties shall take the necessary legislative or other measures to ensure that the restraining or protection orders referred to in paragraph 1 are:
   – available for immediate protection and without undue financial or administrative burdens placed on the victim;
   – issued for a specified period or until modified or discharged;
   – where necessary, issued on an ex parte basis which has immediate effect;
   – available irrespective of, or in addition to, other legal proceedings;
   – allowed to be introduced in subsequent legal proceedings.
3. Parties shall take the necessary legislative or other measures to ensure that breaches of restraining or protection orders issued pursuant to paragraph 1 shall be subject to effective, proportionate and dissuasive criminal or other legal sanctions.

## D      Reflections and Questions

1. The regional treaties use different terminology to address the problem of gender-based violence. The Convention of Belém do Pará refers to violence against women, and physi-

cal, sexual, and psychological harm. The Istanbul Convention alludes to violence against women, domestic violence, and gender-based violence against women. The Maputo Protocol refers to traditional harmful practices. Each treaty is a reflection of its region's culture, values, and history with international law and human rights. Is there a term that is more effective for the prevention and response to gender-based violence? Is the terminology used to address gender-based violence relevant in the design by states of legislation, public policies, programs, and services?

2. One important feature of the regional treaties is the connection that they draw between the problem of gender-based violence and other human rights. The Convention of Belém do Pará connects violence against women to the rights to life, personal integrity, liberty and security, to be free from torture, to dignity, and to participation. The Maputo Protocol also alludes to economic, social, and cultural rights such as those related to health and education. The Istanbul Convention establishes a firm link between the problems of violence against women, domestic violence, and discrimination, and offers a very expansive list of prohibited motives, including many for the first time such as sexual orientation, gender identity, age, state of health, and disability. The treaties confirm that gender-based violence greatly impairs the life plan and goals of all women, and their free enjoyment of many paramount human rights.

3. The Maputo Protocol in particular contains language reflecting an approach to the human rights of women considering the formidable impacts of armed conflicts and poverty. In its Articles 3, 5, 10, and 11, the Maputo Protocol recognizes the state obligation to protect the rights of women to dignity, to peace, and to be free from traditional harmful practices. The Maputo Protocol also has a heavy emphasis on economic, social, and cultural rights, providing in Article 13 that states should guarantee the rights of women to equal employment, economic opportunities, remuneration, and social security. The Maputo Protocol is still the only regional human rights treaty to explicitly authorize medical abortions in specific circumstances, in Article 14(2.c).[24]

4. A Committee of Independent Experts has been created to monitor the Istanbul Convention, GREVIO. It publishes reports assessing legislative and other measures adopted by state parties to enforce the Istanbul Convention. It can also initiate special inquiry procedures and adopt general recommendations on the scope of the Convention provisions. The first ten members of GREVIO were elected on May 4, 2015 for four-year terms. GREVIO is currently preparing its first General Recommendation on the application of the Istanbul Convention to violence against women taking place online and in the realm of technology.[25]

---

[24] For more background reading on the Maputo Protocol, *see* Christine Ocran, *Protocol to the African Charter on Human and Peoples' Rights on the Rights of Women in Africa*, 15 AFR. J. INT'L & COMP. L. 147 (2007); Kaniye S.A. Ebeku, *A New Dawn for African Women – Prospects of Africa's Protocol on Women's Rights*, 16 SRI LANKA J. INT'L L. 83 (2004).

[25] For more information on the work of GREVIO and its first General Recommendation, *see GREVIO to prepare its first General Recommendation on the implementation of the Istanbul Convention* (June 29, 2020), www.coe.int/en/web/istanbul-convention/-/grevio-to-prepare-its-first-general-recommendation -on-the-implementation-of-the-istanbul-convention (last visited on May 19, 2021); *About GREVIO – Group of Experts on Action against Violence against Women and Domestic Violence* (last visited on May 19, 2021).

5. The Convention of Belém do Pará is monitored by its own follow-up mechanism, MESECVI. MESECVI has a Committee of Independent Experts, appointed by states and serving in a personal capacity, which produce national and regional reports on the implementation of the Convention of Belém do Pará. The MESECVI has released an important set of hemispheric and thematic reports, general recommendations, and declarations on varied topics, including the connection between gender-based violence and sexual and reproductive rights, child pregnancy, and femicide, and political harassment.[26] The Inter-American Commission and Court of Human Rights have also issued case rulings applying Article 7 of the Convention of Belém do Pará, which will be discussed in more detail in Chapter 11.[27]

6. Despite the ongoing gravity of the problem of gender-based violence in the Americas and enforcement problems, the Convention of Belém do Pará has had a significant influence in the legislation, public policies, and programs adopted by Latin American states to address domestic violence and sexual violence.[28] It is also the most ratified regional human rights treaty in the Americas, having more state parties than the American Convention on Human Rights. The Convention of Belém do Pará only lacks the ratifications of the United States, Canada, and Cuba. Why do you think the Convention of Belém do Pará has more ratifications than the American Convention on Human Rights?

## E        Practical exercise: Comparison of regional treaties on violence against women

Review closely the text of the Inter-American Convention on the Prevention, Punishment, and Eradication of Violence against Women (Convention of Belém do Pará), the Protocol to the African Charter on Human and Peoples' Rights on the Rights of Women in Africa (Maputo Protocol), and the European Convention on Preventing and Combating Violence against Women and Domestic Violence (Istanbul Convention), included *supra*. Consider the following questions:

1. Which can be the main benefits of having a recognition in regional treaties of the prohibition of gender-based violence? Is this legal recognition needed? Please discuss the main advantages and disadvantages of having these specialized treaties.

2. These regional treaties all contain different definitions of the problem of gender-based violence. Based on your reading of these treaties, what should be the definition of gender-based violence in the present?

---

[26]   For reference, *see* MESECVI Declarations on *Femicide, Violence against Women, Sexual and Reproductive Rights, Political Harassment,* and *Gender Equality and Women's Empowerment for the Good of Humanity* (last visited on May 19, 2021), www.oas.org/en/mesecvi/library.asp#declarations.

[27]   For general reference, *see* Rosa M. Celorio, The Rights of Women in the Inter-American System of Human Rights: Current Opportunities and Challenges in Standard-Setting, 65 U. Miami L. Rev. 819 (2011).

[28]   *See* Inter-American Commission on Human Rights, Hearing, *Challenges of Protecting Women from Violence 20 Years after the Belem do Para Convention*, March 27, 2014, www.youtube.com/watch ?v=5jAAWqEKJVc; MESECVI, *Second Hemispheric Report on the Implementation of the Belém do Pará Convention* (April 2012), pp. 15–57, www.oas.org/es/mesecvi/docs/mesecvi-segundoinformeh emisferico-es.pdf.

3. The regional treaties use different terms to refer to gender-based violence and human rights obligations that are connected to this issue. They refer to it as violence against women, gender-based violence, domestic violence, and harmful practices. Which are the advantages and disadvantages of the terminology used in each of the regional treaties?

4. Do you see differences between these treaties and General Recommendations 19 and 35 of the CEDAW Committee and the U.N. Declaration on the Elimination of Violence against Women, discussed *supra*?

5. Reflect on the connection between gender-based violence and the human rights of women in general. Identify some examples and how this should be reflected in future regional treaties.

**Note: Regional treaty obligations, due diligence, and violence against women**

A cornerstone contribution of the regional human rights protection systems has been in the application of the due diligence standard to gender-based violence. This has been done through the regional treaties and jurisprudence. The Inter-American Court of Human Rights issued its landmark judgment in the case of *Velasquez Rodriguez v. Honduras*, highlighting state obligations to protect rights and to prevent, investigate, and punish any human rights violation under the American Convention.[29] This judgment greatly influenced the incorporation of the due diligence standard in the Convention of Belém do Pará and the Istanbul Convention. It has also propelled an important line of jurisprudence by both the inter-American and European systems adding content to the duty of states to act with due diligence to prevent, investigate, respond, and grant reparations for acts of gender-based violence.[30]

According to Article 7 of the Convention of Belém do Pará, due diligence entails a complementary set of duties for states to prevent, investigate, sanction, and grant reparations for acts of violence against women. These include the adoption of new legislation, the modification of cultural practices, the availability of protection orders and other measures to prevent imminent harm, and the grant of reparations. The Istanbul Convention in Articles 4, 5, and 6 mandates states to adopt legislation to protect women from violence in the public and private spheres, abolish laws and practices which discriminate against women, and prevent acts of violence from both state and non-state actors. In Articles 6, 7, 11, 12, 18, and 29 of the Istanbul Convention, the states are obligated to adopt gender-sensitive policies, data collection and research, steps to prevent violence against women and the cultural practices which fuel its repetition, protection measures against imminent harm, and the establishment of adequate remedies against perpetrators.[31]

---

[29]  *See* Velásquez Rodríguez v. Honduras, Merits, Judgment, Inter-Am. Ct. H.R. (ser. C) No. 4, ¶¶ 1–3, 159–185 (July 29, 1988).

[30]  For case examples, *see* González et al. ("Cotton Field") v. Mexico, Preliminary Objection, Merits, Reparations, and Costs, Judgment, Inter-Am. Ct. H.R. (ser. C) No. 205 (Nov. 16, 2009); Opuz v. Turkey, App. No. 33401/02, Eur. Ct. H.R. (2009).

[31]  For more reading on the due diligence standard, the role of state interventions, and its application by the regional human rights protection systems, *see* Debra J. Liebowitz and Julie Goldscheid, *Due Diligence and Gender Violence: Parsing Its Power and Its Perils*, 48 Cornell Int'l L. J. 301, 304–333 (2015); Rosa Celorio, Discrimination and the Regional Human Rights Protection Systems: The Enigma of Effectiveness, 40 U. Pa. J. Int'l L. 781, 823–826 (2019).

# V PROBLEM OF FEMICIDE AND EXTREME FORMS OF GENDER-BASED VIOLENCE

One of the most alarming forms of violence perpetrated against women are killings based on their gender. This problem is commonly referred to by the international community as *femicide*,[32] and still occurs in different regions of the world. Civil society organizations from Latin America have been some of the most active and vocal in giving visibility to these killings due to their widespread and common nature in countries such as Mexico, Guatemala, and El Salvador, among others.[33] This type of violence is fueled by a context of structural discrimination against women. The killings are often joined by forms of sexual violence and torture.

Included below are excerpts from a report adopted by the former U.N. Special Rapporteur on violence against women, its causes, and consequences, on the gravity and magnitude of the problem of gender-related killings at the global level.

## A Report of the Special Rapporteur on violence against women, its causes and consequences, Rashida Manjoo

A/HRC/20/16, May 23, 2012

14. In this report, the Special Rapporteur addresses the topic of gender-related killings of women whether they occur in the family or the community or are perpetrated or condoned by the State. Globally, the prevalence of different manifestations of such killings is increasing, and a lack of accountability for such crimes is the norm. Terms such as femicide, feminicide, honour killings and crimes of passion, among others, have been used to define such killings.

15. Rather than a new form of violence, gender-related killings are the extreme manifestation of existing forms of violence against women. Such killings are not isolated incidents that arise suddenly and unexpectedly, but are rather the ultimate act of violence which is experienced in a continuum of violence. Women subjected to continuous violence and living under conditions of gender-based discrimination and threat are always on "death row, always in fear of execution". …

16. The killings can be active or direct, with defined perpetrators, but they can also be passive or indirect. The direct category includes: killings as a result of intimate-partner violence; sorcery/witchcraft-related killings; honour-related killings; armed conflict-related kill-

---

[32] UN Women has defined *femicide* as

the intentional murder of women because they are women, but may be defined more broadly to include any killings of women or girls. Femicide differs from male homicide in specific ways. For example, most cases of femicide are committed by partners or ex-partners, and involve ongoing abuse in the home, threats or intimidation, sexual violence or situations where women have less power or fewer resources than their partner.

www.unwomen.org/en/what-we-do/ending-violence-against-women/faqs/types-of-violence (last visited on May 19, 2021).

[33] For more reading, *see* Economic Commission for Latin America and the Caribbean (ECLAC), Gender Equality Observatory for Latin America and the Caribbean, *Femicide: The Most Extreme Expression of Violence against Women*, Notes for Equality, No. 27, November 15, 2018, https://oig.cepal.org/sites/default/files/nota_27_eng.pdf.

ings; dowry-related killings; gender identity- and sexual orientation-related killings; and ethnic- and indigenous identity-related killings. The indirect category includes: deaths due to poorly conducted or clandestine abortions; maternal mortality; deaths from harmful practices; deaths linked to human trafficking, drug dealing, organized crime and gang-related activities; the death of girls or women from simple neglect, through starvation or ill-treatment; and deliberate acts or omissions by the State.

17. The discrimination and violence that is reflected in gender-related killings of women can be understood as multiple concentric circles, each intersecting with the other. These circles include structural, institutional, interpersonal and individual factors. The structural factors include macrolevel social, economic and political systems; institutional factors include formal and informal social networks and institutions; interpersonal factors include personal relationships between partners, among family members and within the community; and individual factors include personality and individual capacities to respond to violence.

18. Thus an understanding of gender-related killings requires taking into account the political, social and economic contexts within which it takes place, including the responses of men to women's empowerment; the political, legal and societal reaction to such killings; the principle of the continuum of violence; and patterns of structural discrimination and inequality that continue to form part of the reality of women's lives. It is also important to disaggregate data by factors such as race, ethnicity, education, sexual orientation and economic status, among others, to establish systemic patterns that exacerbate existing vulnerabilities.

19. Impunity for the killings of women has become a global concern. As noted by the Secretary General: "Impunity for violence against women compounds the effects of such violence as a mechanism of control. When the State fails to hold the perpetrators accountable, impunity not only intensifies the subordination and powerlessness of the targets of violence, but also sends a message to society that male violence against women is both acceptable and inevitable. As a result, patterns of violent behaviour are normalized."

\*\*\*\*\*

The problem of femicide has also propelled international courts to adopt some of the leading judgments adding content to the states' obligation to act with due diligence. Most cases of femicide end in impunity, and are not properly investigated and sanctioned by states. One of the paradigmatic cases of femicide has been the case of Ciudad Juárez, Mexico. Since 1993, hundreds of women have been reported as disappeared and murdered in this locality. The case became emblematic due to government failures in the prompt search of the victims when reported as disappeared, and in the investigation of the murders after the bodies were found. The mothers of many of the victims have become global human rights activists, seeking justice, truth, and reparations for the death of their daughters.

The Inter-American Commission on Human Rights was one of the first entities to raise awareness of this pattern of murders by visiting Ciudad Juárez, Mexico in February of 2002. By publishing its report of the visit in March of 2003, the Commission joined a variety of national entities, international agencies, Special Rapporteurs and civil society organizations in expressing their alarm over the pattern of women's disappearances and murders in the locality, and the impunity of these crimes.[34]

The Inter-American Court of Human Rights also adopted its judgment in the case of *González et al. v. Mexico* in 2009, highlighting alarming state irregularities in the investigation and sanction of three murders of women in Ciudad Juárez, Mexico. The application before the Inter-American Court of Human Rights relates to the disappearance and death of Claudia Ivette González, Esmeralda Herrera Monreal, and Laura Berenice Ramos Monárrez. They were first reported to the authorities as disappeared by their family members, and their bodies were later found in a cotton field in Ciudad Juárez on November 6, 2001. The petitioners argued before both the Inter-American Commission and Court of Human Rights that the authorities in Mexico had failed to act with due diligence to protect the life of the victims, and adequately and effectively investigate their deaths. They also claimed that the murders had taken place amidst a context in which the disappearance and murders of women had increased significantly since 1993; crimes which were for the most part not properly investigated and brought to justice. Excerpts of this judgment have been included below. In these excerpts, the Court discusses how the state failed to prevent these crimes and the effects of this failure on the rights to life, personal integrity, and liberty.

**B**       *González et al. v. Mexico* **("Cotton Field" case), Inter-American Court of Human Rights**

Preliminary Objection, Merits, Reparations and Costs, Judgment of Nov. 16, 2009. Series C No. 205

252.   The Court has established that the obligation of prevention encompasses all those measures of a legal, political, administrative and cultural nature that ensure the safeguard of human rights, and that any possible violation of these rights is considered and treated as an unlawful act, which, as such, may result in the punishment of the person who commits it, as well as the obligation to compensate the victims for the harmful consequences. It is also clear that the obligation to prevent is one of means or conduct, and failure to comply with it is not proved merely because the right has been violated.

253.   The Convention of Belém do Pará defines violence against women and its Article 7(b) obliges the States Parties to use due diligence to prevent, punish and eliminate this violence.

254.   Since 1992, CEDAW established that "States may also be responsible for private acts if they fail to act with due diligence to prevent violations of rights or to investigate and punish acts of violence, and for providing compensation." The 1993 Declaration on the Elimination of Violence against Women of the General Assembly of the United Nations urged the States to "[e]xercise due diligence to prevent, investigate and, in accordance with national legislation, punish acts of violence against women, whether those acts are perpetrated by the State or by private persons" and so did the Platform for Action of the Beijing

---

[34]   *See generally* Inter-American Commission on Human Rights, *The Situation of the Rights of Women in Ciudad Juárez, Mexico: The Right to be Free from Violence and Discrimination*, OEA/Ser.L/V/II.117, Doc. 44, March 7, 2003.

World Conference on Women. In 2006, the U.N. Special Rapporteur on violence against women stated that "[b]ased on practice and the *opinio juris* … it may be concluded that there is a norm of customary international law that obliges States to prevent and respond with due diligence to acts of violence against women …". …

258.   The foregoing reveals that States should adopt comprehensive measures to comply with due diligence in cases of violence against women. In particular, they should have an appropriate legal framework for protection that is enforced effectively, and prevention policies and practices that allow effective measures to be taken in response to the respective complaints. The prevention strategy should also be comprehensive; in other words, it should prevent the risk factors and, at the same time, strengthen the institutions that can provide an effective response in cases of violence against women. Furthermore, the State should adopt preventive measures in specific cases in which it is evident that certain women and girls may be victims of violence. This should take into account that, in cases of violence against women, the States also have the general obligation established in the American Convention, an obligation reinforced since the Convention of Belém do Pará came into force. The Court will now examine the measures adopted by the State prior to the facts of this case to comply with its obligation of prevention. …

279.   Even though the State was fully aware of the danger faced by these women of being subjected to violence, it has not shown that, prior to November 2001, it had adopted effective measures of prevention that would have reduced the risk factors for the women. Although the obligation of prevention is one of means and not of results, the State has not demonstrated that the creation of the FEIHM and some additions to its legislative framework, although necessary and revealing a commitment by the State, were sufficient and effective to prevent the serious manifestations of violence against women that occurred in Ciudad Juárez at the time of this case.

280.   Nevertheless, according to the Court's jurisprudence, it is evident that a State cannot be held responsible for every human rights violation committed between private individuals within its jurisdiction. Indeed, a State's obligation of guarantee under the Convention does not imply its unlimited responsibility for any act or deed of private individuals, because its obligation to adopt measures of prevention and protection for private individuals in their relations with each other is conditional on its awareness of a situation of real and imminent danger for a specific individual or group of individuals and the reasonable possibility of preventing or avoiding that danger. In other words, even though the juridical consequence of an act or omission of a private individual is the violation of certain human rights of another private individual, this cannot be attributed automatically to the State, because the specific circumstances of the case and the discharge of such obligation to guarantee must be taken into account.

281.   In this case, there are two crucial moments in which the obligation of prevention must be examined. The first is prior to the disappearance of the victims and the second is before the discovery of their bodies.

282.   Regarding the first moment – before the disappearance of the victims – the Tribunal finds that the failure to prevent the disappearance does not *per se* result in the State's international responsibility because, even though the State was aware of the situation of risk for women in Ciudad Juárez, it has not been established that it knew of a real and imminent danger for the victims in this case. Even though the context of this case and the State's

international obligations impose on it a greater responsibility with regard to the protection of women in Ciudad Juárez, who are in a vulnerable situation, particularly young women from humble backgrounds, these factors do not impose unlimited responsibility for any unlawful act against such women. Moreover, the Court can only note that the absence of a general policy which could have been initiated at least in 1998 – when the CNDH warned of the pattern of violence against women in Ciudad Juárez – is a failure of the State to comply in general with its obligation of prevention.

283. With regard to the second moment – before the discovery of the bodies – given the context of the case, the State was aware that there was a real and imminent risk that the victims would be sexually abused, subjected to ill-treatment and killed. The Tribunal finds that, in this context, an obligation of strict due diligence arises in regard to reports of missing women, with respect to search operations during the first hours and days. Since this obligation of means is more rigorous, it requires that exhaustive search activities be conducted. Above all, it is essential that police authorities, prosecutors and judicial officials take prompt immediate action by ordering, without delay, the necessary measures to determine the whereabouts of the victims or the place where they may have been retained. Adequate procedures should exist for reporting disappearances, which should result in an immediate effective investigation. The authorities should presume that the disappeared person has been deprived of liberty and is still alive until there is no longer any uncertainty about her fate.

284. Mexico did not prove that it had adopted reasonable measures, according to the circumstances surrounding these cases, to find the victims alive. The State did not act promptly during the first hours and days following the reports of the disappearances, losing valuable time. In the period between the reports and the discovery of the victims' bodies, the State merely carried out formalities and took statements that, although important, lost their value when they failed to lead to specific search actions. In addition, the attitude of the officials towards the victims' next of kin, suggesting that the missing persons' reports should not be dealt with urgently and immediately, leads the Court to conclude reasonably that there were unjustified delays following the filing of these reports. The foregoing reveals that the State did not act with the required due diligence to prevent the death and abuse suffered by the victims adequately and did not act, as could reasonably be expected, in accordance with the circumstances of the case, to end their deprivation of liberty. This failure to comply with the obligation to guarantee is particularly serious owing to the context of which the State was aware – which placed women in a particularly vulnerable situation – and of the even greater obligations imposed in cases of violence against women by Article 7(b) of the Convention of Belém do Pará.

285. In addition, the Tribunal finds that the State did not prove that it had adopted norms or implemented the necessary measures, pursuant to Article 2 of the American Convention and Article 7(c) of the Convention of Belém do Pará, that would have allowed the authorities to provide an immediate and effective response to the reports of disappearance and to adequately prevent the violence against women. Furthermore, it did not prove that it had adopted norms or taken measures to ensure that the officials in charge of receiving the missing reports had the capacity and the sensitivity to understand the seriousness of the phenomenon of violence against women and the willingness to act immediately.

286.   Based on the foregoing, the Court finds that the State violated the rights to life, personal integrity and personal liberty recognized in Articles 4(1), 5(1), 5(2) and 7(1) of
the American Convention, in relation to the general obligation to guarantee contained in
Article 1(1) and the obligation to adopt domestic legal provisions contained in Article 2
thereof, as well as the obligations established in Article 7(b) and 7(c) of the Convention
of Belém do Pará, to the detriment of Claudia Ivette González, Laura Berenice Ramos
Monárrez and Esmeralda Herrera Monreal.

## C       Reflections and Questions

1.  The *Cotton Field* judgment is historic in the inter-American system of human rights. It is
    the first judgment of the Inter-American Court of Human Rights that addresses compre-
    hensively due diligence and state obligations to prevent, investigate, sanction and grant
    reparations for acts of violence against women in light of the American Convention of
    Human Rights and the Convention of Belém do Pará.[35]
2.  In its *Cotton Field* judgment, the Inter-American Court of Human Rights held the state
    responsible for several violations under the American Convention and the Convention of
    Belém do Pará committed to the detriment of the three victims and their family members.
    Very prominent was the State failure to guarantee human rights by failing to act with
    the due diligence necessary to protect the rights to life, to humane treatment, to personal
    liberty and to live free from violence of the three victims. The Court also found that the
    state failed to adequately and effectively investigate their disappearances and homicides,
    and considered these obligations of a "wider scope" and implications in cases of violence
    against women. The Court moreover found violations to the rights to not discriminate
    against women on the basis of sex, and the rights to humane treatment and access to justice
    of the family members of the deceased.[36]
3.  The *Cotton Field* judgment is one of the most detailed decisions adopted by a human rights
    court shedding light on the content of the due diligence standard in cases of gender-based
    violence. It was highly influenced by the previous judgment of the Inter-American
    Court of Human Rights in the case of *Velasquez Rodriguez*, and its interpretation of the
    general guarantee of human rights under Article 1.1 of the American Convention. The
    Inter-American Court in *Cotton Field* refers to the duty of prevention as comprehensive, of
    means and not results, and entailing the adoption of legal, public policy, and institutional
    measures designed to prevent acts of violence against women. The Court also refers to
    the wider scope of the investigation of cases of killings of women, especially those taking
    place in a general context of violence. The Court also refers to judicial ineffectiveness and
    its social message of tolerance of violence against women, which promotes its repetition.
    The Court lastly refers to an obligation to act with strict due diligence to act swiftly upon

---

[35]   For more reading on the history of the women's rights jurisprudence of the inter-American system
of human rights and the significance of the *Cotton Field* judgment, *see generally* Rosa Celorio, The
Rights of Women in the Inter-American System of Human Rights, supra note 27.
[36]   For more reading, *see* Rosa Celorio, Introductory Note to the Inter-American Court of Human
Rights: *Case of Gonzalez (Cotton Field) v. Mexico*, 49 INT'L LEGAL MATERIALS 637–639 (2010).

reports of missing women in a context of disappearances and murders, in search operations during the first hours and days.

4. The *Cotton Field* judgment does leave some questions unanswered. What is a state obligation of means and not results? What does it mean to have an obligation of wide scope to investigate cases of violence against women? What is a gender perspective in the investigation of these cases? Is there a difference between due diligence and strict due diligence?[37]

5. The *Cotton Field* judgment is also known for its gender approach to reparations as a key component of the due diligence obligation in cases of violence against women. The Court alludes to the importance of "rectification" in cases of systemic and structural discrimination against women.[38] Traditional reparation schemes in international human rights law refer to restitution and the need to return victims to their position and life plans before the human rights violation occurred. In cases of gender-based violence, there is a need to change the discrimination context which promoted the human rights violations in the first place. How do you transform a context of discrimination against women?[39]

## VI   FINAL COMMENTS: GENDER-BASED VIOLENCE, THE "*METOO* MOVEMENT," AND SOCIAL PROTEST

The *MeToo* movement – which began in 2016 and will be discussed in detail in Chapter 6 – confirmed to the world the ongoing gravity of the problem of gender-based violence in the daily lives of many women. It also shed light on the different settings in which violence against women still occurs today, including employers, businesses, schools, churches, the internet, and social media. Discrimination against women is still a fixture of our societies and gender-based violence is one of the most common manifestations of this problem. The path to fully comply with CEDAW and its General Recommendations 19 and 35 in most countries is still long and arduous, with many steps and multidisciplinary strategies sorely needed. Women are still on the streets protesting and demanding change and state accountability for serious acts of gender-based violence.

International law and human rights developments have offered important standards and benchmarks for states to follow to prevent, investigate, and grant reparations for acts of gender-based violence. Many cases ruled by United Nations bodies and regional Commissions and Courts have exemplified the human rights violations women still face and issued important orders and guidelines for states to follow to resolve these problems. Which steps should

---

[37] For more reading on the legacy of the *Cotton Field* judgment, *see generally* Caroline Bettinger-López, *The Challenge of Domestic Implementation of International Human Rights Law in the Cotton Field Case*, 15 CUNY L. REV. 315 (2012); Paulina García-del Moral, *The "Formally Feminist State": A Potential New Player in the Inter-American Human Rights System*, AJIL UNBOUND, 113, 365–369 (2019), www.cambridge.org/core/journals/american-journal-of-international-law/article/formally-feminist-state-a-potential-new-player-in-the-interamerican-human-rights-system/B2 16E54395C7C94C399D96CC3440BE12.

[38] *See* Inter-Am. Ct. H.R., *Cotton Field judgment*, ¶ 450.

[39] For more reading, *see* Ruth Rubio-Marin and Clara Sandoval, *Engendering the Reparations Jurisprudence of the Inter-American Court of Human Rights: The Promise of the Cotton Field Judgment*, 33 HUMAN RIGHTS QUARTERLY 1062–1091, 1077–1089 (2011).

states prioritize to face the complex and widespread nature of gender-based violence? What is the connection between international human rights law and the national legal framework when it comes to addressing gender-based violence? What role should women play in the design of legislation, policies, and strategies to curb gender-based violence? These are all key questions in addressing gender-based violence that will be discussed in the following chapters of this casebook.

# 3.    Intersectionality and the interconnectedness of discrimination: the case of indigenous women

## I    INTRODUCTION: INTERSECTIONAL FORMS OF DISCRIMINATION AND THE EXPERIENCE OF INDIGENOUS WOMEN

One of the most important developments in the area of women's rights has been the recognition of multiple forms of discrimination that women may face due to factors combined with their sex and gender. These factors may include race, ethnic origin, age, economic position, sexual orientation and gender identity, disabilities, migration status, and deprivation of liberty, among others. Some of the women most affected by intersectional discrimination are those afro-descendent; indigenous; girls and older women; lesbian, bisexual, transgender, and intersex women; migrants and those internally displaced; women and girls living with disabilities; and women deprived of liberty in prisons and psychiatric institutions.

Many universal and regional bodies are referring to the concept of intersectionality to promote understanding of the different burdens that women may face socially that increase their risk of problems such as gender-based violence and forms of disparate treatment.[1] The term found its earlier expressions in scholarship – a development lead by Professor Kimberle Crenshaw – to describe the different layers of discrimination that women can face on the basis of their sex, gender, and race, resulting in their disadvantaged, marginalized, and inferior position in our societies.[2]

The readings in this chapter discuss treaties, reports, and individual cases which have shed light on the content of the state obligation to address and recognize intersectional forms of discrimination faced by women. The chapter also discusses concretely the situation of indigenous women as an example of a group particularly affected by discrimination on the basis of their sex, gender, indigenous origin or identity, ethnicity, race, language, and situation of poverty.[3]

---

[1]    For an overview of the incorporation of the intersectionality approach in the work of the United Nations, *see* LORENA SOSA, INTERSECTIONALITY IN THE HUMAN RIGHTS LEGAL FRAMEWORK ON VIOLENCE AGAINST WOMEN: AT THE CENTER OR THE MARGINS? 61–120 (Cambridge University Press, 2017). For a discussion of the use of the concept of intersectionality in the work of the Inter-American and European human rights systems, *see* Rosa Celorio, *Discrimination and the Regional Human Rights Protection Systems: The Enigma of Effectiveness*, 40 U. PA. J. INT'L L. 781, 814–818 (2019).

[2]    Kimberle Crenshaw, *Demarginalizing the Intersection of Race and Sex: A Black Feminist Critique of Antidiscrimination Doctrine, Feminist Theory and Antiracist Politics*, 1989(1) UNIVERSITY OF CHICAGO LEGAL FORUM, Article 8, 139–140, 150–167.

[3]    For an overview of forms of discrimination and human rights challenges faced by indigenous women and girls globally, *see* International Indigenous Women's Forum (FIMI), *Global Study in the*

An intersectional lens often requires taking into consideration the different dimensions of the experience of discrimination women face. In the case of indigenous women in particular, discrimination must be understood taking into consideration the multidimensional nature of their identity – as women and as indigenous.[4] As women, they are subjected to discrimination by both state and non-state actors, and are frequently the object of gender-based violence. As indigenous, they have an inextricable connection to their peoples, territories, natural resources, culture, and worldview. Indigenous women have faced – and still face – a history of colonialism, racism, and the dispossession of their ancestral territories. These problems are fueled and sustained by forms of structural discrimination, militarization, armed conflicts, forced migration, and internal displacement. They are also aggravated by the execution of economic projects geared towards development, investment, extraction, mining, and tourism activities in lands, territories, and natural resources that indigenous peoples use and enjoy without their free, prior, and informed consultation and consent; a problem which has very specific effects on indigenous women, their culture, and subsistence.

Based on these factors, any legislation and policies adopted to address the needs of indigenous women need to contemplate their multilayered identity and the forms of intersectional discrimination that they face. Steps to comply with universal and regional human rights treaties must be guided by a gender, indigenous women, intersectional, and intercultural perspective.[5] It is also key to interpret the prohibition of discrimination against women contained in CEDAW and other universal and regional treaties taking into consideration the rights of indigenous women to self-determination and the integrity of their territories, culture, worldview, and environment; and to consultation, consent, effective participation, and benefit sharing in matters which concern them. This weaving of rights forms the foundation and starting point for a holistic understanding of the rights of indigenous women. The violation of any of these rights constitutes intersectional discrimination against indigenous women.

Intersectional discrimination against indigenous women also needs to be understood considering both their individual and collective dimensions. In its individual dimension, indigenous women and girls suffer intersecting forms of discrimination by both state and non-state actors on the basis of their sex, gender, indigenous origin or identity, ethnicity, race, language, and situation of poverty. Racism, discriminatory stereotypes, marginalization, and gender-based violence are interrelated violations experienced by indigenous women and girls. Discrimination and gender-based violence threaten the individual autonomy, personal liberty, privacy, and integrity of all indigenous women and girls.

In its collective dimension, discrimination and gender-based violence against indigenous women and girls threaten and disrupt the spiritual life, cultural integrity and survival, and

---

*Situation of Indigenous Women and Girls* (2020), pp. 35–64, https://fimi-iiwf.org/wp-content/uploads/2020/09/GlobalStudyFIMI_20-englishRGB-2.pdf.

   [4]   For more discussion of how sex, gender, and indigenous origin can combine to increase the exposure of indigenous women to forms of discrimination and violence, *see* Inter-American Commission on Human Rights, *Indigenous Women and their Human Rights in the Americas*, OEA/Ser.L/V/II.Doc. 44/17, April 17, 2017, ¶¶ 38–41.

   [5]   For more discussion on how the fulfillment of the indigenous right to self-determination and the elimination of violence against indigenous women are connected, *see* Rauna Koukkanen, *Self-Determination and Indigenous Women's Rights at the Intersection of International Human Rights*, 34 HUMAN RIGHTS QUARTERLY 225–250, 225–227, 238–249 (2012).

social fabric of indigenous peoples and communities. They have a chilling effect on the continuance and preservation of the knowledge, culture, worldview, identity, and traditions of indigenous peoples. Failure to protect the rights to self-determination, ownership, consultation and consent, and the effective participation of indigenous women constitutes discrimination against them and their communities. Discrimination and gender-based violence against indigenous women and girls violate the human dignity of indigenous peoples and communities. As indicated in the Preamble of the United Nations Declaration on the Rights of Indigenous Peoples, the leading instrument in the world on indigenous peoples' rights, collective rights are indispensable for the existence, well-being, and integral development of indigenous peoples and indigenous women and girls.[6]

This chapter discusses the problem of intersectionality, the interconnectedness of forms of discrimination, and how these are all illustrated in the challenges faced by indigenous women.

## II   DISCRIMINATION WITH A GENDER, INDIGENOUS WOMEN, INTERSECTIONAL, AND INTERCULTURAL PERSPECTIVE[7]

The obligation to take into consideration intersectionality concerns by states has been codified at this stage in some treaties. Some examples are the Convention of Belém do Pará, discussed earlier in Chapter 2, and the Inter-American Convention against all Forms of Discrimination and Intolerance. Some examples of the treaty language used are included below.

### A   Article 9, Inter-American Convention on the Punishment, Prevention, and Eradication of Violence against Women ("Convention of Belém do Pará"), 1994

With respect to the adoption of the measures in this Chapter, the States Parties shall take special account of the vulnerability of women to violence by reason of among others, their race or ethnic background or their status as migrants, refugees or displaced persons. Similar consideration shall be given to women subjected to violence while pregnant or who are disabled, of minor age, elderly, socioeconomically disadvantaged, affected by armed conflict or deprived of their freedom.

### B   Article 1, Inter-American Convention against all Forms of Discrimination and Intolerance

For purposes of this Convention:

3. Multiple or aggravated discrimination is any preference, distinction, exclusion, or restriction based simultaneously on two or more of the criteria set forth in Article 1.1, or others

---

[6]   *See* United Nations Declaration on the Rights of Indigenous Peoples, G.A. Res. 61/295, U.N. Doc. A/RES/61/295 (Sept. 13, 2007), Preamble (hereinafter UNDRIP).

[7]   An *intercultural perspective* takes into consideration the cultural diversity of indigenous peoples, their languages, and worldview. For more reading, *see* IACHR, *Indigenous Women and their Human Rights in the Americas*, *supra* note 4, ¶¶ 151–152, 159.

recognized in international instruments, the objective or result of which is to nullify or curtail, the equal recognition, enjoyment, or exercise of one or more human rights and fundamental freedoms enshrined in the international instruments applicable to the States Parties, in any area of public or private life. …

*****

As exemplified by these treaty provisions, states have been mandated to incorporate an intersectional approach in their adoption of legislation and policies concerning women, and to eliminate multiple forms of discrimination which impair the exercise by women of all their rights in public and private life. Intersectional discrimination has been connected in treaties to indirect discrimination, temporary special measures, and forms of intolerance.

In the following report adopted by the former U.N. Special Rapporteur on indigenous peoples, Victoria Tauli Corpuz, she connects the concept of multiple forms of discrimination to the realities faced by indigenous women, and as a critical impediment to the full exercise of their civil, political, economic, social, and cultural rights.

## C     Report of the Special Rapporteur on indigenous peoples, Victoria Tauli Corpuz

A/HR/C/30/41, August 6, 2015

…

5.  Indigenous women experience a broad, multifaceted and complex spectrum of mutually reinforcing human rights abuses. That spectrum is influenced by multiple and intersecting forms of vulnerability, including patriarchal power structures; multiple forms of discrimination and marginalization, based on gender, class, ethnic origin and socioeconomic circumstances; and historical and current violations of the right to self-determination and control of resources.

6.  Despite many barriers to inclusion, indigenous leaders and advocates have made significant strides in achieving recognition of indigenous peoples' rights and perspectives, including the adoption of the United Nations Declaration on the Rights of Indigenous Peoples, the establishment of the Permanent Forum on Indigenous Issues, the mandate of the Special Rapporteur on the rights of indigenous peoples and the Expert Mechanism on the Rights of Indigenous Peoples. Indigenous women actively participated in the processes that gave birth to all those mechanisms and thus feel some ownership over the Declaration and the mechanisms. …

8.  Despite the progress made, systematic attention to the specific vulnerability of indigenous women has remained limited in relation to the scale of abuses against them. Furthermore, what international attention has been given to the issue has not sufficiently focused on the nexus between individual and collective rights, nor on how intersecting forms of discrimination and vulnerability contribute to ongoing abuses of indigenous women's rights. That has created a gap that has contributed to ongoing widespread impunity in relation to the rights of indigenous women and girls.

9.  There have been some promising signs of progress towards closing that gap, such as the efforts taken by indigenous women to empower themselves by establishing their own organizations and networks, and making their issues more visible at national and global levels. Indigenous women's participation in the United Nations world conferences on women has increased with time, the highlight being the conference in Beijing in 1995, where participants ensured references to indigenous women and achieved the adoption of the Beijing Declaration of Indigenous Women, which has served as a guiding framework in many of their subsequent efforts to build and strengthen their organizations. It must be recognized that the United Nations has established a solid gender equality and women's rights regime, which has opened up more possibilities for indigenous women to engage in debates on gender issues. Several Special Rapporteurs, including the previous rapporteurs on indigenous peoples' rights, have contributed through raising awareness of issues facing indigenous women and have made relevant recommendations. …

12. When examining the rights of indigenous women and girls, it is vital to consider the unique historical experiences of indigenous communities. Many forms of violence and abuse against indigenous women and girls have a strong intergenerational element. Violations of the broad right to self-determination of indigenous peoples are historically and currently endemic. Those have included gross and sustained assaults on the cultural integrity of indigenous peoples; denigration and non-recognition of customary laws and governance systems; failure to develop frameworks that allow indigenous peoples appropriate levels of self-governance; and practices that strip indigenous peoples of autonomy over land and natural resources. Those patterns of violations are vividly exemplified by colonization, but have also been perpetuated by post-colonial power structures and State practices. Those violations of the right to self-determination have been highly detrimental to the advancement of the rights of indigenous women and girls in a number of ways.

13. The response of indigenous communities to attacks against self-determination has, at times, additionally subjugated the rights of women. In the battle for indigenous communities to assert their right to self-determination, women's rights have often been considered divisive and external to the indigenous struggle and connected to "external values" or "Western values" that privilege individual over communal rights. Such a false dichotomy between collective and women's rights has, paradoxically, further entrenched the vulnerability of indigenous women to abuse and violence. Indigenous women are therefore stripped of their right to self-determination by both violations against their collective rights, as members of indigenous communities, and violations against their individual rights, as sub-collectives within those communities. …

38. Indigenous women have the right, to participate in public and political decision-making processes. That right stems broadly from the right to self-determination, as well as from the provisions of the Convention on the Elimination of All Forms of Discrimination against Women. However, in reality, indigenous women are often excluded from both indigenous decision-making structures and local and national political processes in States. As highlighted by the Committee on the Elimination of Discrimination against Women, there are very few indigenous women in national and local political processes and in some countries, there are none at all. Indigenous power structures and self-governance agreements tend to be patriarchal and exclude the involvement and perspectives of women.

39. Female indigenous human rights defenders have faced particular challenges when exercising their right to participate in public life. Female human rights defenders play a vital role in protecting women in indigenous communities and can be valuable resources to States in the context of balancing their duty to protect all women and the need to respect the right to self-determination and autonomy of indigenous communities. However, in a number of countries, the activities of female human rights defenders from indigenous communities have been criminalized and they have been subjected to severe forms of violence. For example, in Oaxaca, Mexico, female human rights defenders were reported to have been killed recently.

    ...

46. The issue of violence against women is indivisibly linked to the categories of rights discussed above. In fact, the endemic violations of collective, civil and political, and economic, social and cultural rights can be seen as constituting a form of structural violence against indigenous women and girls. Structural violence results in women being victimized by the realities of the circumstances of their everyday life and routinely excluded from the rights and resources otherwise guaranteed to citizens. Structural violence is interlinked and mutually reinforcing with other forms of violence, as discussed below ...

47. Indigenous women are significantly more likely to experience rape than non-indigenous women. It has been estimated that more than one in three indigenous women are raped during their lifetime. Behind these shocking statistics are multiple forms of sexual violence against indigenous women by a multitude of actors in different geographical regions. Coordinated and comparative information on sexual violence is very limited, due in part to significant underreporting and a lack of investment in disaggregated data collection that include indigenous women and communities. That makes analysis of systemic level prevalence and trends very difficult. ...

51. Indigenous women are often caught in the crossfire of conflict situations and subjected to militarized violence. Conflicts may be between different ethnic groups and may also involve government forces and business actors. Indigenous women and girls have been victims of gender-based violence in conflicts for example in Colombia, Guatemala, Mexico, Nicaragua, Peru, the Philippines and Nigeria. ...

## D       Reflections and Questions

1. Article 9 of the Convention of Belém do Pará discussed *supra* mandates states to take special account of factors which can accentuate the vulnerability of women to violence, including their race; age; refugee, displaced and/or migrant status; situation of armed conflict; for living with a disability; and due to a situation of deprivation of liberty. Article 1(1) of the OAS Convention against Discrimination and Intolerance discussed *supra* expands this list to include additional discrimination factors, including sexual orientation, gender identity and expression, socioeconomic status, and political opinions. This expansion of discrimination factors reflects the growing recognition of the international community of specific variables which increase the risk to abuse and human rights violations of many women and can intersect to intensify their discrimination experience. Do you think that consistently expanding the list of discrimination factors is a positive development for inter-

national law and the concept of intersectionality? Or is it better to focus on just a limited number of factors? Please take into account in your answer the human and financial resources limitations that states often face to adopt legislation and policies to protect the rights of women.[8]

2. The former U.N. Special Rapporteur on indigenous peoples refers to the multiple forms of discrimination that indigenous women face and the combination of factors which reinforce human rights abuses against them. Indigenous women – as other women – are impacted by gender-based discrimination, stereotypes, and violence in their private and public lives, including within their families, communities, and while pursuing employment, education, health, and justice services. However, indigenous women also have a very special link to their lands, territories, and natural resources, and these constitute an essential part of their identity.[9] Additionally, they often lack possession, title, and legal recognition of their ancestral lands and territories, which leads to poverty, barriers to accessing food and water security, and obstacles to securing the natural resources necessary for their survival. This has been fueled by a history of colonization, racism, militarization, forced migration and displacement, and armed conflicts affecting indigenous peoples; a history which has facilitated gender-based discrimination and violence against indigenous women and girls.[10] These problems have been aggravated by the implementation over indigenous territories of extractive, development, tourism, investment, mining, and other economic activities without their free, prior, and informed consultation and consent. When executing these economic activities, government and private actors enter indigenous territories and can commit violence and discrimination against indigenous women. These projects can also result in environmental degradation.[11]

3. Gender-based violence also severely affects indigenous women and girls. As indicated by the former U.N. Special Rapporteur in her report discussed *supra*, indigenous women are significantly more likely to experience rape than non-indigenous women. UN Women, UNICEF, and UNFPA have reported about violence against indigenous women concretely that while there is a growing body of evidence of the magnitude, nature, and consequences of gender-based violence globally, knowledge of its extent for indigenous women is limited and tends to vary considerably by issue and region.[12] Gender-based violence

---

[8]   For more reading on the concept of intersectionality and its advantages and limitations, *see* Sosa, *supra* note 1, pp. 7–9, 16–32.

[9]   For more discussion of the importance of land for indigenous peoples, *see* Study of the United Nations Expert Mechanism on the Rights of Indigenous Peoples, Right to Land under the United Nations Declaration on the Rights of Indigenous Peoples: A Human Rights Focus (July 15, 2020), ¶¶ 5–13.

[10]   For more discussion of key components of the right to free, prior, and informed consultation and consent, *see* Report of the Special Rapporteur on the situation of human rights and fundamental freedoms of indigenous peoples, James Anaya, *Promotion and protection of all human rights, civil, political, economic, social and cultural rights, including the right to development*, A/HRC/12/34 (2009), ¶¶ 36–57.

[11]   For more reading, *see* IACHR, *Indigenous Women and their Human Rights in the Americas*, *supra* note 4, ¶¶ 1–12, 30–50, 78–132, 185–227.

[12]   *See* UN Women, UNICEF, UNFPA, *Breaking the Silence on Violence against Indigenous Girls, Adolescents and Young Women*, May 2013, p. 4. *See also for reference*, U.N. Inter-Agency Support Group on Indigenous Peoples' Issues, *U.N. Thematic Paper on the Elimination and Responses to Violence, Exploitation and Abuse of Indigenous Girls, Adolescents and Young Women* (preparation of the World Conference on Indigenous Peoples 2014), pp. 1–2, 4–10.

against indigenous women and girls also harms collectively the spiritual, cultural, and social fabric of indigenous peoples and their communities. Violence against indigenous women is perpetrated by both state and non-state actors, including private individuals, businesses, members of armed forces, illegal groups, and others. Some forms of violence against indigenous women that have been documented are sexual violence, rape, and torture;[13] gender-based killings;[14] spiritual violence;[15] environmental violence;[16] violence connected to the implementation of extractive development projects;[17] and violence in the sphere of sexual and reproductive rights.[18]

4.  Despite this grim context, indigenous women are very active participants in their communities, countries, and at the national and international levels. They are very well organized in networks and organizations, and have very active participation in United Nations processes, as well as those of the regional human rights protection systems.[19] Indigenous women are consequential actors and knowledge-transmitters both within and outside their communities. However, as indicated in the U.N. Special Rapporteur's Report *supra* in paragraphs 38 and 39, indigenous women can be excluded from decision-making in national and local processes, as well as in their own communities and indigenous systems.

---

[13]　*See for example*, Rosendo-Cantú et al. v. Mexico, Preliminary Objection, Merits, Reparations, and Costs, Inter-Am. Ct. H.R. Series (ser. C) No. 216, ¶¶ 69–79, 107–122; Fernández Ortega et al. v. Mexico, Preliminary Objection, Merits, Reparations, and Costs, Judgment of August 30, 2010, Inter-Am. Ct. H.R., Series C No. 215, ¶¶ 77–89, 117–132.

[14]　*See, generally*, Committee on the Elimination of Discrimination against Women, *Report of the Inquiry Concerning Canada of the Committee on the Elimination of Discrimination against Women under Article 8 of the Optional Protocol to the Convention on the Elimination of All Forms of Discrimination against Women*, CEDAW/C/OP.8/CAN/1, ¶¶ 95–119 (Mar. 30, 2015) (hereinafter CEDAW Committee, Inquiry Report on Canada).

[15]　The Inter-American Commission on Human Rights has defined *spiritual violence* as taking place when "acts of violence and discrimination against indigenous women not only harm those women individually, but also negatively the collective identity of the communities to which they belong," *see* IACHR, *Indigenous Women and their Human Rights in the Americas*, *supra* note 4, ¶ 80.

[16]　The term *environmental violence* is increasingly used to refer to the many impacts that environmental harm, degradation, and pollution have on indigenous women and girls. For more reading, *see* Andrea Carmen, *Environmental Violence: Impacts on Indigenous Women and Girls, in* INDIGENOUS PEOPLES' RIGHTS AND UNREPORTED STRUGGLES: CONFLICT AND PEACE 96–97, 98–102, 104–106 (Elsa Stamatopoulou ed., Institute for the Study of Human Rights, Columbia University, 2017).

[17]　For more discussion, *see* Inter-American Commission on Human Rights, *Indigenous Peoples, Afro-Descendent Communities, and Natural Resources: Human Rights Protection in the Context of Extraction, Exploitation, and Development Activities*, OEA/Ser.L/V/II, doc. 47/15, ¶¶ 318–321 (Dec. 31, 2015), www.oas.org/en/iachr/reports/pdfs/extractiveindustries2016.pdf (hereinafter IACHR Report on Extractive Industries).

[18]　*See for example*, Inter-American Commission on Human Rights, *La CIDH emite medidas cautelares a favor de 7 mujeres embarazadas del pueblo indígena Wichí, en Formosa, Argentina*, April 16, 2021, No. 092-21, www.oas.org/es/CIDH/jsForm/?File=/es/cidh/prensa/comunicados/2021/092.asp (Precautionary Measures adopted by the IACHR to protect 7 pregnant indigenous Wichí women in Formosa, Argentina due to fears of being submitted to forced C-sections, deprivation of liberty, and separation from their babies by the government authorities).

[19]　For a discussion of achievements in the incorporation of indigenous women's issues in global agendas, *see* Report of the United Nations Permanent Forum on Indigenous Peoples, *Indigenous women and their role in the 25-year review of the implementation of the Beijing Declaration and Platform for Action*, United Nations Economic and Social Council, E/C.19/2020/8 (Jan. 30, 2020), ¶¶ 10–26.

Indigenous women's human rights defenders advocating for the defense of their lands, territories and other social causes face killings, acts of harassment, and the criminalization of their work.

5. The right to effective participation in political and public life for indigenous women is recognized in Articles 7 and 8 of CEDAW, as well as in Articles 5, 18, and 19 of the United Nations Declaration on the Rights of Indigenous Peoples. Indigenous women should be able to participate and act as leaders in consultation processes in matters which affect their communities; to run and be elected to public office; to vote; and to participate in discussion spaces concerning matters which affect them. Some key challenges which affect indigenous women today in their effective participation are low levels of education, literacy, and language constraints; lack of time due to child care and securing water and food for their communities; and limited exposure to relevant legal, political, and institutional processes.[20] The effective participation and leadership of indigenous women are key to overcome the ongoing forms of intersectional discrimination they face.

6. Despite the gravity of the intersectional discrimination faced by indigenous women, their rights have received limited attention at the international and regional levels. International law currently has well-recognized lines of legal standards and jurisprudence dedicated to both women and indigenous peoples, but these developments have barely combined to adequately reflect the multidimensional identity of indigenous women.[21] These legal developments have had as their foundation very important treaties and instruments, including CEDAW, the United Nations Declaration on the Rights of Indigenous Peoples (hereinafter "UNDRIP"), International Labour Organization Indigenous and Tribal Peoples Convention 169 (hereinafter "ILO Convention 169"), the American Convention on Human Rights, and the African Charter on Human and Peoples' Rights. Important scholars, such as Professor Rauna Kaukkanen, have advocated for a human rights framework related to indigenous women which connects the goal of self-determination with the gendered components of their human rights experience.[22] This would be an important step forward in addressing the intersectional forms of discrimination faced by indigenous women. One promising initiative is that the CEDAW Committee has embarked on a process to prepare its first General Recommendation on the rights of indigenous women and girls, building on the statements already made in its General Recommendation 34 on rural women.[23] Which would be important legal statements that the CEDAW Committee can make in its new General Recommendation on Indigenous Women and Girls? How can it best capture the forms of intersectional discrimination faced by indigenous women and the scope of state

---

[20]   For more discussion of ongoing challenges to the effective participation of indigenous women in community, national, and global processes, *see id.*, ¶¶ 28–71; FIMI, *Global Study in the Situation of Indigenous Women and Girls, supra* note 3, pp. 50–53.

[21]   For some exceptions of reports that do strive to cover the gender and indigenous components of the identity of indigenous women in universal and regional human rights protection systems, *see generally* Report of the Special Rapporteur on the rights of indigenous peoples, Victoria Tauli Corpuz, A/HR/C/30/41 (Aug. 6, 2015), discussed in this chapter, and IACHR, *Indigenous Women and their Human Rights in the Americas, supra* note 4.

[22]   *See* Koukkanen, *supra* note 5, pp. 225–227, 238–249.

[23]   *See* General Recommendation 34 on Rural Women, Committee on the Elimination of Discrimination against Women, CEDAW/C/GC/34 (2016), ¶¶ 12–15,17(c), 21, 25(e), 28–31, 33–39, 40–41, 43, 48, 50, 54, 57.

obligations? How can UNDRIP be helpful in the work of the CEDAW Committee in this
new General Recommendation?

## III      INTERSECTIONAL DISCRIMINATION AGAINST INDIGENOUS WOMEN: INDIVIDUAL CASE EXAMPLES

The cases below offer examples of the problem of intersectional discrimination against indigenous women in different realms. The case of *Cecilia Kell v. Canada* discusses this issue in
the areas of domestic violence and the right to decent housing, and how state authorities can
be perpetrators and facilitators of intersectional discrimination. The case of *Valentina Rosendo
Cantú* exemplifies the challenges that indigenous women victims of rape face to secure access
to justice after these acts occur, and the problem of militarization of territories enjoyed by
indigenous peoples.

### A      CEDAW Committee, *Cecilia Kell v. Canada*

Communication No. 19/2008
CEDAW/C/51/D/19/2008
April 27, 2012

*The facts of this case are related to an aboriginal woman – Cecilia Kell – who purchased
a house from the N.W.T. Housing Corporation with her common law partner. She suffered
domestic violence at the hands of her partner. Eventually her partner requested the N.W.T.
Housing Corporation to remove her name from the lease, making him the exclusive owner of
the property, and he evicted her from the property. She alleged before the CEDAW Committee
discrimination on the basis of sex, marital status, cultural heritage, and in the exercise of her
property rights under CEDAW.*

10.1    The Committee has considered the present communication in the light of all the infor-
         mation made available to it by the author and by the State party, as provided for in article
         7, paragraph 1, of the Optional Protocol.
10.2    In the present case, the Committee observes that the author's name was removed from
         the Assignment of Lease, making her partner, who was not a member of the aboriginal
         community, the sole owner of the property; that she lost her share in the house as a result
         of an alleged fraudulent transaction effected by her partner; that such change was impos-
         sible without action or inaction of the Northwest Territories Housing Corporation; that the
         Northwest Territories Housing Corporation was an agent of the State party; that her partner
         was serving as a director of the Housing Authority Board and therefore occupied a position
         of authority; that she was not informed by the Housing Corporation of the annulment of
         her property rights, despite the fact that she was the eligible right holder as a member of the
         Rae-Edzo community. These facts show that the author's property rights were prejudiced
         as a result of an act of a public authority acting together with her partner. The Committee
         also observes that the author was subsequently denied access to the family home by her
         partner, who changed the locks and evicted her while she was attempting to escape an
         abusive relationship and seeking protection in a battered women's shelter. The Committee
         further notes that the author's lawyer, who was assigned by the Legal Services Board,

advised her to follow the evacuation request made by her partner, and did not challenge the validity of such request. The Committee considers that the combined effect of the above facts led to discrimination against the author as defined by article 1 of the Convention. The Committee considers that the author has established a distinction based on the fact that she was an aboriginal woman victim of domestic violence, which she clearly submitted in her first lawsuit against her partner, and that such violence had the effect of impairing the exercise of her property rights. In its general recommendation No. 28, the Committee states that intersectionality is a basic concept for understanding the scope of the general obligation of States parties contained in article 2 of the Convention. The discrimination of women based on sex and gender is inextricably linked with other factors that affect women, such as race, ethnicity, religion or belief, health, status, age, class, caste, and sexual orientation and gender identity. States parties must legally recognize and prohibit such intersecting forms of discrimination and their compounded negative impact on the women concerned. Accordingly, the Committee finds that an act of intersectional discrimination has taken place against the author.

10.3    As to the author's allegation regarding violations of her rights under article 2, paragraphs (d) and (e), of the Convention, the Committee recalls that the said article calls on States parties to ensure that public authorities and institutions refrain from engaging in any act or practice of discrimination against women and to take all appropriate measures to eliminate discrimination against women by any person, organization or enterprise. Article 2, paragraph (d), of the Convention establishes an obligation for States parties not only to abstain from engaging in any act or practice of direct and indirect discrimination against women, but to ensure that any laws, policies or actions that have the effect or result of generating discrimination are abolished. Further, article 2, paragraph (e), of the Convention requires the State party to adopt measures that ensure the practical realization of the elimination of discrimination against women, which includes measures enabling women to make complaints about violations of their rights under the Convention and have effective remedies. As the author is an aboriginal woman who is in a vulnerable position, the State party is obliged to ensure the effective elimination of intersectional discrimination. ...

10.7    With respect to the author's allegations in regard to article 16, paragraph 1(h), of the Convention, the Committee takes note of the State party's submission that the author has not pointed out any property laws or customs that discriminate against married or unmarried women; any discriminatory practices or laws that interfered with her ownership, acquisition, management, administration or enjoyment of the Rae-Edzo property in particular; or any discriminatory conduct on the part of the authorities in respect of the removal of her name from the Assignment of Lease for said property. The Committee, however, observes that even though the formal eligibility criteria did not require so, the author was advised by a Tenant Relations officer of the Rae-Edzo Housing Authority that her partner's application for housing would be considered if the author's name was added to the application. The Committee also observes that the author was a victim of domestic violence, a fact which was not contested by the State party; that her partner tried to stop her from working, thus limiting her ability to lead an independent economic life; and that she was evicted from her home while seeking protection from domestic violence in a battered women's shelter. The Committee further observes that, according to the State party's submission, both the author's income and the income of her partner were taken into account in determining their eligibility under the Northern Territorial Rental Purchase Program, yet when her name was removed from the Assignment of Lease, the Northwest Territories Housing Corporation did not take her contribution into consideration or inform her of the removal. These facts considered together indicate that the rights of the author under article 16, paragraph 1(h), of the Convention have been violated. ...

**B**      *Valentina Rosendo Cantú*, **Inter-American Court of Human Rights**

Preliminary Objection, Merits, Reparations, and Costs
Judgment of August 31, 2010, Series C No. 216.

*This case is related to the rape of Valentina Rosendo Cantú – an indigenous woman and a member of the Me'phaa indigenous group in Mexico – by members of the military in the state of Guerrero. She did report her rapes before the authorities, but found significant roadblocks in her access to justice, due to the application of military justice and a health system unprepared to address cases of rape affecting indigenous women. The excerpts discuss the issue of rape as torture when committed by military members and the failure of the state of Mexico to investigate these acts.*

107.    Given that the Court has established that Mrs. Rosendo Cantú was the victim of an act of sexual violence committed by State agents, it must now determine the legal definition of this act.

108.    The Court recalls that, according to the Convention of Belém do Pará, violence against women constitutes not only a violation of human rights, but is also "an offense against human dignity and a manifestation of the historically unequal power relations between women and men" that "pervades every sector of society, regardless of class, race or ethnic group, income, culture, level of education, age or religion and strikes at its very foundation."

109.    In accordance with international case law and taking into account the provisions of the Convention, the Court has previously considered that sexual violence involves acts of a sexual nature, committed against a person without their consent, and that in addition to the physical invasion of the human body, they may include acts which do not involve penetration or even any physical contact. In particular, rape constitutes a paradigmatic form of violence against women, and its consequences go far beyond the victim herself.

110.    The Court will consider whether the facts of this case are subsumed in the definition of torture, as argued by the Commission and the representatives. To this end, the Court recalls that in the case of *Bueno Alves v. Argentina*, based on the definition established in the Convention Against Torture, the Court considered that mistreatment which meets the following conditions constitutes an act of torture: i) intentional, ii) causes severe physical or mental suffering and iii) is committed with an objective or purpose.

*i) Intentionality*

111.    Regarding the existence of an intentional act, the evidence in the case file confirms that the mistreatment was deliberately inflicted on the victim. Indeed, the Court considers it proven that one of the attackers hit Mrs. Rosendo Cantú in the abdomen with his weapon, causing her to fall to the ground and strike her head on a rock. She was then seized by the

hair, her face was scratched and, while having a weapon pointed at her, she was forcibly sexually assaulted by two soldiers while the other six watched the rape.

*ii) Severe physical or mental suffering*

112. In order to assess the severity of a victim's suffering, the Court must take into account the specific circumstances of each case. In doing so, it must consider various aspects of the treatment such as the duration, the method used or the way in which the suffering was inflicted, the potential physical and mental effects and also the status of the person who endured the suffering, including age, gender and health condition, among other personal circumstances.

113. As to the physical suffering, the Court recalls that two medical certificates were issued 12 and 23 days after the incident which provide evidence of physical injuries. The Court also has testimonial evidence indicating that after the incident Mrs. Rosendo Cantú was injured, with physical pain, for which she sought the assistance of two doctors.

114. Aside from the foregoing, the Court has established that an act of torture may be perpetrated both through acts of physical violence and acts that cause acute mental or moral suffering to the victim. In addition, this Court has recognized that rape is an extremely traumatic experience that can have severe consequences and cause significant physical and psychological damage, leaving the victim "physically and emotionally humiliated," a situation that, unlike other traumatic experiences, is difficult to overcome with the passage of time. This reveals that severe suffering of the victim is inherent to rape, even when there is no evidence of physical injuries or disease. Indeed, the after-effects of rape do not always involve physical injuries or disease. Women victims of rape also experience severe trauma and psychological and social consequences.

115. In this case, Mrs. Rosendo Cantú was subjected to an act of violence and physical control by the soldiers who intentionally perpetrated the sexual assault against her. Her vulnerability and the coercion that the soldiers exercised over her was reinforced by the participation of the other six soldiers, who were also armed, exacerbating the context of the sexual violence perpetrated against her. It is evident to the Court that the suffering endured by Mrs. Rosendo Cantú, while being forced into sexual acts against her will, with six other people observing, was of the greatest intensity, particular considering that she was a minor. The psychological and moral suffering was aggravated by the circumstances in which the rape took place, inasmuch as she could not rule out the possibility that the violence against her could be further increased by the soldiers who witnessed the rape, since that it was possible that they would also rape her. ...

*iii) Purpose*

117. In general terms, the Court considers that rape, like torture, pursues the objective of intimidating, degrading, humiliating, punishing or controlling the victim. The rape of Mrs. Rosendo Cantú took place in the context of a situation in which the soldiers were questioning the victim without obtaining the information they sought. Without denying the possibility that there were also other objectives, the Court considers it proven that in this case the rape had the specific purpose of punishing the victim because she failed to provide the required information.

118. The Court also considers that rape may constitute torture even when it consists of a single act or takes place outside State facilities. This is so because the objective and subjective elements that define an act as torture do not refer to the accumulation of acts

or to the place where the act is committed, but rather to the intention, the severity of the suffering and the purpose of the act, stipulations that have been met in this case. Based on the foregoing, the Court concludes that the rape in this case entailed a violation of Mrs. Rosendo Cantú's personal integrity, constituting an act of torture in accordance with Article 5(2) of the American Convention and Article 2 of the Convention Against Torture.

...

177.   In cases of violence against women, the general obligations established in Articles 8 and 25 of the American Convention are complemented and enhanced for States Parties by the obligations arising from the specific obligations of the Inter-American treaty of the Convention of Belém do Pará. Article 7(b) of this Convention specifically requires the States Parties to apply due diligence to prevent, punish and eradicate violence against women. Thus, when an act of violence is committed against a woman, it is particularly important that the authorities in charge of the investigation conduct it in a resolute and effective manner, taking into account society's obligation to reject violence against women and the State's obligation to eliminate it and secure the victims' trust in the State institutions for their protection.

178.   On previous occasions, this Court has defined the guiding principles that must be observed in criminal investigations into human rights violations, which include, *inter alia*: the recovery and preservation of evidence in order to assist in a potential criminal investigation of the perpetrators; identification of possible witnesses, obtaining their statements and determination of the cause, manner, place and time of the act investigated. In addition, there should be a thorough examination of the crime scene and a rigorous analysis of the evidence by competent professionals using the most appropriate procedures. In cases of violence against women, several international instruments describe and illustrate the State's obligation to investigate such acts with due diligence. For example, in the course of a criminal investigation for rape: i) the victim's statement should be taken in a safe and comfortable environment, providing privacy and trust; ii) the victim's statement should be recorded to avoid or limit the need for repetition; iii) the victim should be provided with medical, health care and psychological treatment, both on an emergency basis, and continuously if required, through an assistance protocol designed to lessen the consequences of rape; iv) a complete and detailed medical and psychological examination should be conducted immediately by suitable trained personnel, of the sex preferred by the victim insofar as this is possible, and the victim should be informed that she may be accompanied by a trusted person if she so wishes; v) the investigative tasks should be coordinated and documented and the evidence handled with care, taking sufficient samples and performing all possible tests to determine the perpetrator of the act, and obtaining other evidence such as the victim's clothing, immediate examination of the crime scene and guaranteeing the proper chain of custody of the evidence, and vi) access to free legal assistance at all stages of the proceedings should be provided for the victim.

179.   In this case, in addition to the facts acknowledged by the State, the Court considers proven the following omissions and errors in the investigations:

i)     the State had knowledge of the facts prior to the filing of the formal complaint on March 8, 2002 with the Public Prosecutor's Office, but did not immediately open an investigation, did not offer prompt medical assistance to the victim to obtain the necessary expert evidence and did not immediately file a complaint for the possible rape of an indigenous girl. ...

iv) even though she did not speak Spanish fluently at the time of the incident, Mrs. Rosendo Cantú was not provided with an interpreter, but had to be assisted by her husband; in the Court's opinion this was inappropriate because it failed to respect her cultural diversity, and failed to ensure the quality of the contents of the statement, or protect the confidentiality of the complaint. The Court considers it especially inappropriate that victim had to turn to her husband to recount the facts of the rape; ...

180. At the same time, the Court notes with particular concern that the authorities in charge of the investigation focused their efforts on repeatedly summoning Mrs. Rosendo Cantú to make statements and not on obtaining and safeguarding other evidence. The Court emphasizes that in cases of rape, insofar as possible, the investigation must try to avoid re-victimization or the re-experiencing of the profoundly traumatic experience each time the victim recalls or testifies about what happened.

181. Furthermore, the Court finds that in this case, several of the government employees who initially intervened in the complaint filed by Mrs. Rosendo Cantú showed a complete lack of motivation, sensitivity and competence. Likewise, the failure of the medical staff and officials of the Public Prosecutor's Office who initially attended the victim to use an action protocol was especially serious and had negative consequences on the assistance afforded to the victim and on the legal investigation of the rape. Regarding this aspect, the Court stresses the comments made by the expert witness Arroyo Vargas during the public hearing of the case, that in "cases of sexual violence, the minimum standards [for evidence gathering] must be immediacy and speed."

182. Based on the foregoing considerations and on the State's partial acknowledgement of responsibility, the Court concludes that the State authorities did not act with due diligence in the investigation of the rape of Mrs. Rosendo Cantú, which, in addition, exceeded a reasonable period of time. Consequently, the State violated her rights to a fair trial and to judicial protection established in Articles 8(1) and 25(1) of the American Convention, in relation to Article 1(1) thereof, and did not comply with the obligations established in Article 7(b) of the Convention of Belém do Pará, to the detriment of Mrs. Rosendo Cantú. ...

## C    Reflections and Questions

1. In the case of *Cecilia Kell v. Canada*, the CEDAW Committee refers in paragraph 10.2 to the "compounded impact" that intersecting forms of discrimination can have on the ability of indigenous women to have a dignified life. In this case, the author was an aboriginal woman, a victim of domestic violence, and of limited economic means. These factors all resulted in formidable barriers for her to exercise her right to adequate and decent housing, and to protection from domestic violence. They also heavily and negatively influenced the actions of government authorities towards her needs and demands. Which steps do you consider government authorities in this case could have taken to respond to the victim's needs with a gender, indigenous women, intersectional, and intercultural perspective? How could the government authorities have adequately and promptly complied with CEDAW?

2. Many forms of discrimination and acts of gender-based violence suffered by indigenous women are intricately connected with the legacy of colonization and the militarization of their territories. Indigenous women can suffer acts of sexual violence and rape by state and non-state actors, including members of the military; obstacles to guarantee food security, water, health, and educational services; and high levels of maternal mortality and morbidity. The Inter-American Court of Human Rights has ruled against the state of Mexico in two cases related to indigenous women – *Ines Fernandez Ortega* and *Valentina Rosendo Cantú* discussed *supra* – and held the state responsible for violations under the American Convention for their rape and torture by military members in the state of Guerrero.[24] One of the petitioners before the Court, Valentina Rosendo Cantú, whose case was discussed *supra*, was raped by military officials when she was washing clothing in a stream near her home.[25] She was 17 years old at the time of these events.[26] There was significant military presence in the state of Guerrero.[27] When you think of the obligation to act with due diligence that has been discussed throughout this casebook, which criteria should guide the prevention, investigation, and sanction of gender-based violence concerning indigenous women?

3. The judgment of *Valentina Rosendo Cantú* also illustrates the arduous road to justice for indigenous women who suffer rape and other forms of sexual violence. In this case, the rapes the petitioner suffered can be considered both institutional violence committed by state agents and a form of torture. Valentina Rosendo Cantú did report these acts before the authorities, but faced medical and justice systems unprepared to offer culturally appropriate attention and services. The Inter-American Court of Human Rights advances in this judgment key analysis which should inform a multidisciplinary approach for indigenous women in their access to justice, considering the history of gender-based violence and discrimination; racism; barriers to access lands, territories, and natural resources; and inadequate health and education services.[28] Indigenous women are routinely denied their right to a remedy and sexual violence cases often end in impunity. Some important challenges documented in ordinary justice systems are racism; the lack of culturally appropriate procedures and evidence collection; the dearth of interpreters; geographic remoteness; and the absence of timely and specialized medical care.[29] Indigenous justice systems, for their part, can be male dominated, and very influenced by gender stereotypes which are harmful

---

[24]   *See for example*, Inter-Am. Ct. H.R., Rosendo-Cantú et al. v. Mexico, *supra* note 13, ¶¶ 69–79, 107–122; Inter-Am. Ct. H.R., Fernández Ortega et al. v. Mexico, *supra* note 13, ¶¶ 77–89, 117–132.

[25]   Inter-Am. Ct. H.R., Rosendo-Cantú et al. v. Mexico, *supra* note 13, ¶¶ 70–79.

[26]   *Id.*, ¶ 72.

[27]   *Id.*, ¶ 70.

[28]   For more discussion of challenges faced by indigenous women in their access to justice, *see* Study by the Expert Mechanism of the Rights of Indigenous Peoples, *Access to Justice in the Promotion and Protection of the Rights of Indigenous Peoples*, U.N. Human Rights Council, A/HRC/EMRIP/2014/3/Rev.1, June 25, 2014, ¶¶ 35–42; IACHR, *Indigenous Women and their Human Rights in the Americas*, *supra* note 4, ¶ 138.

[29]   Report of the Special Rapporteur on the rights of indigenous peoples, *Rights of indigenous peoples*, A/HRC/42/37, ¶¶ 69–74 (August 2, 2019); s*ee* General Recommendation 33 on Women's Access to Justice, Committee on the Elimination of Discrimination against Women, CEDAW/C/GC/33, ¶¶ 61–64 (July 23, 2015).

towards indigenous women.[30] Do you think having more indigenous women judges, attorneys, experts, and health providers could make a difference in these cases? Which components should training oriented to justice officials include on the intersectional forms of discrimination faced by indigenous women?

4. Universal and regional human rights bodies have referred extensively to the right to free, prior and informed consultation of indigenous peoples in matters and decisions which concern their territories and natural resources.[31] This is a right reflected in the United Nations Declaration on the Rights of Indigenous Peoples and in other international instruments.[32] Land is a defining feature of the identity, culture, and history of indigenous peoples.[33] Accordingly, states must take special care in complying with the right to consultation in good faith, without delay, and comprehensively. Some well-accepted principles are that consultations must be undertaken before the implementation of a project; they should be respectful of the leadership and decision-making structures of indigenous peoples; they should be undertaken in good faith, including an adequate participation of authorities and other community leaders in the negotiations; adequate information should be available in all phases of project negotiations and implementations; indigenous peoples should be able to consent or not consent when large-scale projects are executed; environmental impact assessments should be undertaken and supervised by governments; and governments have an obligation to supervise and prevent harm, especially foreseeable and preventable harm by corporations and its own government-led initiatives.[34] The concept of effective participation has also been advanced as key in matters that affect indigenous peoples.[35] It is critical that indigenous women do have a leadership role in consultation processes in relation to activities which could lead to environmental harm and the degradation of their territories, and actively participate in decision-making and policies related to environmental concerns and development plans concerning their territories.

---

[30]  *Id. See also* IACHR, *Indigenous Women and their Human Rights in the Americas, supra* note 4, ¶¶ 139–149.

[31]  *See for example*, Report of the Special Rapporteur on the situation of human rights and fundamental freedoms of indigenous peoples, James Anaya, *supra* note 10, ¶¶ 36–57; Saramaka People. v. Suriname, Preliminary Objections, Merits, Reparations, and Costs, Judgment, Inter-Am. Ct. H.R. (ser. C) No. 172, ¶¶ 102, 129, 133–140 (Nov. 28, 2007); Kichwa Indigenous People of Sarayaku v. Ecuador, Merits and Reparations, Judgment Inter-Am. Ct. H.R. (ser. C) No. 245, ¶¶ 180–211 (June 27, 2012).

[32]  *See* UNDRIP, *supra* note 6, Articles 10, 11, 15, 17, 19, 28, 29, 30, 32, 36, and 38; Indigenous and Tribal Peoples Convention, June 7, 1989, 1650 U.N.T.S. 383 (hereinafter ILO Convention No. 169), Article 6(1)(a).

[33]  *See* Study of the United Nations Expert Mechanism on the Rights of Indigenous Peoples on the Right to Land under the United Nations Declaration on the Rights of Indigenous Peoples: A Human Rights Focus (July 15, 2020), ¶ 5.

[34]  *See, as reference*, Study of the United Nations Expert Mechanism on the Rights of Indigenous Peoples on free, prior and informed consent: a human rights-based approach, A/HRC/39/62 (August 10, 2018), ¶¶ 14–30; Report of the Special Rapporteur on the situation of human rights and fundamental freedoms of indigenous peoples, James Anaya, *supra* note 10, ¶¶ 36–57.

[35]  For more reading on the concept of effective participation, *see* Inter-Am. Court H.R., Kichwa Indigenous People of Sarayaku v. Ecuador, *supra* note 31, ¶¶ 201–211; Rio Declaration on Environment and Development, U.N. General Assembly, A/CONF.151/26 (Vol. I) (Aug. 12, 1992), Principle 22; U.N. Human Rights Committee, Poma Poma v. Peru, CCPR/C/95/D/1457/2006 (April 24, 2009), ¶ 7.6.

## IV     RESOLVING THE PUZZLE OF INTERSECTIONAL EQUALITY

The term intersectionality has been useful in giving a name to the different layers, factors, burdens, and disadvantages which enhance the experience of discrimination of women. Examining closely the situation of indigenous women reveals the intricate nature of this problem, often involving the study of the history of racism, colonialism, poverty, and dispossession of territories intertwined with gender considerations and impacts on them. Gender-based violence in particular can silence the spirit, voice, leadership, and incidence of indigenous women and girls, and severely impair the transmission of culture, traditions, languages, the advancement of self-determination and effective participation, and the preservation of a safe and healthy environment.

Intersectionality involves considering contextual aspects which go beyond women and gender and understanding different worldviews, cultures, traditions, and life paths. It also contemplates viewing women through a heterogeneous lens, understanding their differences.

The path is still long to the full understanding of how to best fully implement an intersectional approach, and thus how to really achieve intersectional equality. There is an increasing need to collect data and information of the specific realities of women who are indigenous; afro-descendent; girls and older; lesbian, bisexual, transgender, and intersex; living with disabilities; migrants, displaced, and stateless; and those deprived of liberty; among others. This is key to having a full picture of the intersecting factors which determine their discrimination experience and life opportunities. This information can also inform the state adoption of better legislation, policies, and programs.

Universal and regional bodies have an immense opportunity to develop detailed standards and guidelines for states of how to act with due diligence to prevent and respond to intersectional forms of discrimination. This requires leaving comfort zones and finding ways to combine and establish connections between different legal standards that have not colluded before. The new General Recommendation on Indigenous Women and Girls of the CEDAW Committee provides an invaluable opportunity to find intersections between women's rights and indigenous peoples' rights. This can propel similar analysis related to other groups of women who suffer daily the effects of multiple forms of discrimination, historical disadvantage, and social power and domination which have not worked to their benefit.

It is also key that women who live with acutely multiple forms of discrimination are actively and effectively involved in decision-making and leadership in matters which affect them at the community, local, national, and international levels. Women are paramount for the transmission and preservation of knowledge, culture, traditions, and human rights. Their voices are simply critical to resolving the puzzle of intersectional equality.

# 4. Sexual orientation and gender identity

## I INTRODUCTION: THE EVOLUTION OF GENDER EQUALITY

The international community has made great progress in developing a set of core legal standards to advance the human rights of persons historically discriminated against based on their sexual orientation and gender identity. This progress stemmed from a growing recognition of the gravity, severity, and frequency of acts of discrimination and violence perpetrated against persons and motivated by their sexual orientation and gender identity.[1]

These legal standards include the rights of lesbian, gay, bisexual, transgender, and intersex persons (hereinafter "LGBTI persons"). International, regional, and national courts have adopted a number of case decisions recognizing the rights to privacy, non-discrimination and equality, and gender expression and identity of LGBTI persons. Several national courts and international bodies have also recognized the right to marriage equality of same-sex couples. All of these legal developments have also signified important progress for the rights of women in general, especially those with non-conforming sexual orientations and gender identities.

The Yogyakarta Principles were a paramount moment for the international community in identifying a set of principles and legal obligations states must follow to protect the rights of persons of diverse sexual orientation and gender identities. The Yogyakarta Principles recognized the many human rights violations suffered by persons due to their actual or perceived sexual orientation and gender identity as a serious concern, including extrajudicial killings, torture, sexual assault and rape, and arbitrary interferences with the right to privacy.[2] The resulting Yogyakarta Principles – which were also revised and updated ten years later – establish and clarify obligations under international human rights law to protect the rights of LGBTI persons.

---

[1]  For a general overview of human rights violations faced by LGBTI persons, *see* Michael O'Flaherty, *The Yogyakarta Principles at Ten*, 33(4) NORDIC JOURNAL OF HUMAN RIGHTS, 280, 281–283 (2015); Report of the Office of the High Commissioner for Human Rights, *Discrimination and Violence against Individuals Based on their Sexual Orientation and Gender Identity*, A/HRC/29/23 (2015), ¶¶ 20–38, 43–54.

[2]  The Yogyakarta Principles, *Principles on the application of international human rights law in relation to sexual orientation and gender identity*, March 2007, Introduction, p. 6, www.icj.org/wp-content/uploads/2012/08/Yogyakarta-Principles-publication-2007-eng.pdf. *See also generally*, The Yogyakarta Principles plus 10, *Additional Principles and State Obligations on the Application of International Human Rights in Relation to Sexual Orientation, Gender Identity, Gender Expression, and Sex Characteristics to Complement Yogyakarta Principles* (Nov. 10, 2017), www.lgbti-era.org/sites/default/files/pdfdocs/A5_yogyakartaWEB-2.pdf.

International law developments have also reconceptualized and expanded which individuals can be considered women and girls, and who is protected under gender equality legal standards. General Recommendation 28 of the CEDAW Committee expressly recognizes that discrimination on the basis of sex and gender includes lesbian, bisexual, and transgender women.[3] As discussed earlier, CEDAW – and the interpretations of the CEDAW Committee – have established comprehensive obligations for states to prohibit discrimination against women, including the adoption of laws, policies, programs, and other measures to ensure compliance with the treaty.

There has also been a significant trend to recognize discrimination on the basis of sexual orientation and gender identity as implicit and prohibited factors of discrimination in universal and regional treaties. The Human Rights Committee; the Economic, Social and Cultural Rights Committee; the European Court of Human Rights; and both the Inter-American Commission and Court of Human Rights have made critical statements reading these factors as prohibited in the general discrimination clauses of the treaties that they supervise.[4] New treaties in the OAS and the Council of Europe also expressly prohibit discrimination on the basis of sexual orientation, gender identity, and expression.[5]

National courts have also had a leading role in prohibiting forms of discrimination on the basis of diverse sexual orientations and gender identities. These decisions have been grounded on rights to privacy, non-discrimination, and equal protection at the constitutional and other normative levels. Some of these decisions have also recognized a human right to marriage equality for same-sex couples. The United States Supreme Court has been a leading court in this regard, recognizing important constitutional rights for LGBTI persons which will be discussed in this chapter.

Studying discrimination on the basis of sexual orientation and gender identity in many ways takes us back to the origins of gender equality. It makes us reflect on how sex and gender are defined and how they impact, and have impacted, the situation of women in our societies. At one level, women have been historically discriminated against based on their sex assigned at birth. This discrimination has been compounded by gender and socially assigned notions and stereotypes of the roles that they should occupy in their families, employers, and in their public and private lives. Some of the most victimized women historically have been those self-identified or perceived as lesbian, bisexual, and transgender, who still suffer the brunt of

---

[3]   *See* General Recommendation No. 28 on the Core Obligations of States Parties under Article 2 of the Convention on the Elimination of All Forms of Discrimination against Women, Committee on the Elimination of Discrimination against Women, 47th Sess., U.N. Doc. C/2010/47/GC.2, ¶ 18 (Oct. 19, 2010), discussed *supra* in Chapter 1.

[4]   For examples, *see* U.N. Human Rights Committee, Toonen v. Australia, Communication No. 488/1992, U.N. Doc. CCPR/C/50/D/488/1992 (1994), ¶ 8.7, *discussed infra*; General Comment 20 on Non-discrimination in economic, social and cultural rights (Art. 2, para. 2, of the International Covenant on Economic, Social and Cultural Rights), Committee on Economic, Social and Cultural Rights, E/C.12/ GC/20 2 (July 2009), ¶ 32; Karner v. Austria, App. No. 40016/98, Eur. Ct. H.R., ¶ 37; Atala Riffo and Daughters v. Chile, Merits, Reparations and Costs, Judgment, Inter-Am. Ct. H.R. (ser. C) No. 239, at 86–87 (Feb. 24, 2012), ¶ 91.

[5]   *See, e.g.,* Inter-American Convention against all Forms of Discrimination and Intolerance, Art. 1.1, Organization of American States, June 5, 2013 (hereinafter OAS Convention on Discrimination and Intolerance); Council of Europe Convention on preventing and combating violence against women and domestic violence, May 11, 2001, C.E.T.S. No. 210, Art. 4(3) (hereinafter Istanbul Convention).

social stereotypes, stigmatization, social rejection, and violence. Core obligations related to the rights of women to live free from discrimination and gender-based violence, due diligence, privacy, and access to justice all acquire a special meaning when it comes to women who are part of LGBTI groups.

The following section discusses case rulings and other statements adopted by universal, regional, and national courts advancing the rights of LGBTI persons and the rights of women.

## II  SEXUAL ORIENTATION AND GENDER IDENTITY AS PROHIBITED FACTORS OF DISCRIMINATION

A core foundation for many of the legal developments related to sexual orientation and gender identity has been an open and flexible reading of the prohibition of discrimination in the universal and regional human rights protection treaties. A significant number of universal treaty-based organs have interpreted discrimination clauses as containing a prohibition of discrimination on the basis of sexual orientation and gender identity, including the Human Rights Committee and the Economic, Social and Cultural Rights Committee.[6] This open reading has also been applied by the European Court of Human Rights, and the Inter-American Commission and Court of Human Rights.[7] This is an important step forward by human rights bodies, as they adapt to contemporary times and needs in the area of discrimination, and become responsive to ongoing forms of discrimination against LGBTI persons and groups.

The cases discussed in this section are illustrative of this tendency. The case of *Karen Atala and Others v. Chile* below is the first judgment ever adopted by the Inter-American Court of Human Rights in the area of sexual orientation and gender identity. The case is related to a well-known judge in Chile, Karen Atala, who lost custody of her daughters due to her cohabitation with a partner of the same sex, and harmful stereotypes about maternity and diverse sexual orientations. The United States Supreme Court case of *Bostock v. Clayton County* relates to three employees who claimed that they were fired from their employers after they revealed that they were homosexual and transgender. In its landmark judgment, the United States Supreme Court ruled that Title VII of the Civil Rights Act of 1964 and its prohibition of sex discrimination applies to gay and transgender persons. When you review these two cases, compare their approaches to the reading of discrimination clauses, and the consideration of sexual orientation as a prohibited motive.

### A  *Karen Atala v. Chile*, Inter-American Court of Human Rights

Merits, Reparations and Costs, Judgment of February 24, 2012, Series C No. 239.

*The excerpts below illustrate the analysis of the Inter-American Court of Human Rights in this case of the content of Article 1(1) of the American Convention on Human Rights and its application to discrimination on the basis of sexual orientation in custody cases.*

---

[6]  *See, for example*, U.N. Human Rights Committee, Toonen v. Australia, *supra* note 4, ¶ 8.7, *discussed infra*; General Comment 20, *supra* note 4, ¶ 32.

[7]  *See, e.g.*, Eur. Ct. H.R., Karner v. Austria, *supra* note 4, ¶ 37; Inter-Am. Ct. H.R., Atala Riffo and Daughters v. Chile, *supra* note 4, ¶ 91.

83. The Court has established, as has the European Human Rights Court, that human rights treaties are living instruments, whose interpretation must go hand in hand with evolving times and current living conditions. This evolving interpretation is consistent with the general rules of interpretation set forth in Article 29 of the American Convention, as well as those established in the Vienna Convention on the Law of Treaties.

84. In this regard, when interpreting the words "any other social condition" of Article 1(1) of the Convention, it is always necessary to choose the alternative that is most favorable to the protection of the rights enshrined in said treaty, based on the principle of the rule most favorable to the human being.

85. According to Article 1(1) of the American Convention, the specific criteria by virtue of which discrimination is prohibited do not constitute an exhaustive or limitative list, but merely illustrative. Indeed, the wording of said article leaves open the criteria with the inclusion of the term "another social condition," allowing for the inclusion of other categories that have not been explicitly indicated. Consequently, the Court should interpret the term "any other social condition" of Article 1(1) of the Convention in the context of the most favorable option for the human being and in light of the evolution of fundamental rights in contemporary international law. ...

91. Bearing in mind the general obligations to respect and guarantee the rights established in Article 1(1) of the American Convention, the interpretation criteria set forth in Article 29 of that Convention, the provisions of the Vienna Convention on the Law of Treaties, and the standards established by the European Court and the mechanisms of the United Nations, the Inter-American Court establishes that the sexual orientation and gender identity of persons is a category protected by the Convention. Therefore, any regulation, act, or practice considered discriminatory based on a person's sexual orientation is prohibited. Consequently, no domestic regulation, decision, or practice, whether by state authorities or individuals, may diminish or restrict, in any way whatsoever, the rights of a person based on his or her sexual orientation.

92. With regard to the State's argument that, on the date on which the Supreme Court issued its ruling there was a lack of consensus regarding sexual orientation as a prohibited category for discrimination, the Court points out that the alleged lack of consensus in some countries regarding full respect for the rights of sexual minorities cannot be considered a valid argument to deny or restrict their human rights or to perpetuate and reproduce the historical and structural discrimination that these minorities have suffered. The fact that this is a controversial issue in some sectors and countries, and that it is not necessarily a matter of consensus, cannot lead this Court to abstain from issuing a decision, since in doing so it must refer solely and exclusively to the stipulations of the international obligations arising from a sovereign decision by the States to adhere to the American Convention.

93. A right granted to all persons cannot be denied or restricted under any circumstances based on their sexual orientation. This would violate Article 1(1) of the American Convention. This inter-American instrument proscribes discrimination, in general, including categories such as sexual orientation, which cannot be used as grounds for denying or restricting any of the rights established in the Convention. ...

94. The Court notes that in order to prove that a distinction in treatment has occurred in a particular [custody decision], it is not necessary that the decision in its entirety be based "fundamentally and solely" on the person's sexual orientation. It is sufficient to confirm that,

to a certain extent, the person's sexual orientation was taken into account, either explicitly or implicitly, in adopting a specific decision. ...

96. Regarding the context of the custody proceeding, the Court notes out that the custody claim was filed under the supposition that Ms. Atala "[was] not capable of looking after and taking care of [the three girls, given that] her new choice of sexual life together with her lesbian relationship with another woman, [were] having [...] harmful consequences on the development of these minors, since the mother ha[d] shown no interest whatsoever in looking after and protecting [...] the overall development of these girls." Therefore, in addition to other considerations, the custody process revolved around Ms. Atala's sexual orientation and the alleged effects that her living with her partner could have on the three girls. Therefore, this consideration was central to the discussion between the parties and in the main judicial decisions made during the proceeding.

97. Specifically, the Court finds that the Supreme Court of Justice of Chile invoked the following reasons as grounds for the judgment: i) the "deterioration in the social, family, and educational environment of the girls since the mother began to cohabit with her homosexual partner" and the "effects that this cohabitation could have on the psychological and emotional well-being of the daughters;" ii) the alleged "risk for the integral development of the girls from which they must be protected" due to "the potential confusion over sexual roles that could be caused in them by the absence from the home of a male father and his replacement by another person of the female gender;" iii) the alleged existence of "a situation of risk" that places them in a "vulnerable position in their social environment," due to the risk of social discrimination, iv) that Ms. Atala had allegedly put "her own interests before those of her daughters when she chose to express her homosexual status". These arguments and the language used show a link between the judgment and the fact that Ms. Atala lived with a partner of the same sex, which indicates that the Supreme Court gave significant importance to Ms. Atala's sexual orientation. ...

119. The Court considers that to justify a distinction in treatment and the restriction of a right, based on the alleged possibility of social discrimination, proven or not, that the minors might face due to their parents' situation cannot be used as legal grounds for a decision. While it is true that certain societies can be intolerant toward a person because of their race, gender, nationality, or sexual orientation, States cannot use this as justification to perpetuate discriminatory treatments. States are internationally compelled to adopt the measures necessary "to make effective" the rights established in the Convention, as stipulated in Article 2 of said Inter-American instrument, and therefore must be inclined, precisely, to confront intolerant and discriminatory expressions in order to prevent exclusion or the denial of a specific status. ...

121. On the other hand, with regard to the argument that the child's best interest might be affected by the risk of rejection by society, the Court considers that potential social stigma due to the mother or father's sexual orientation cannot be considered as a valid "harm" for the purposes of determining the child's best interest. If the judges who analyze such cases confirm the existence of social discrimination, it is completely inadmissible to legitimize that discrimination with the argument of protecting the child's best interest. In the instant case, the Court also emphasizes that Ms. Atala had no reason to suffer the consequences of the girls allegedly being discriminated against in their community due to her sexual orientation.

122.    Therefore, the Court concludes that the argument of potential social discrimination was not adequate to fulfill the declared purpose of protecting the best interest of Ms. Atala's daughters. ...

**B          *Bostock v. Clayton County*, United States Supreme Court**

590 U.S. ___ (2020)
Citations and footnotes omitted

*The following case excerpts discuss the connection between discrimination on the basis of sex, sexual orientation, and gender identity in Title VII of the Civil Rights Act of 1964.*

JUSTICE GORSUCH delivered the opinion of the Court

Sometimes small gestures can have unexpected consequences. Major initiatives practically guarantee them. In our time, few pieces of federal legislation rank in significance with the Civil Rights Act of 1964. There, in Title VII, Congress outlawed discrimination in the workplace on the basis of race, color, religion, sex, or national origin. Today, we must decide whether an employer can fire someone simply for being homosexual or transgender. The answer is clear. An employer who fires an individual for being homosexual or transgender fires that person for traits or actions it would not have questioned in members of a different sex. Sex plays a necessary and undisguisable role in the decision, exactly what Title VII forbids.

Those who adopted the Civil Rights Act might not have anticipated their work would lead to this particular result. Likely, they weren't thinking about many of the Act's consequences that have become apparent over the years, including its prohibition against discrimination on the basis of motherhood or its ban on the sexual harassment of male employees. But the limits of the drafters' imagination supply no reason to ignore the law's demands. When the express terms of a statute give us one answer and extratextual considerations suggest another, it's no contest. Only the written word is the law, and all persons are entitled to its benefit. ...

Few facts are needed to appreciate the legal question we face. Each of the three cases before us started the same way: An employer fired a long-time employee shortly after the employee revealed that he or she is homosexual or transgender—and allegedly for no reason other than the employee's homosexuality or transgender status. ...

This Court normally interprets a statute in accord with the ordinary public meaning of its terms at the time of its enactment. After all, only the words on the page constitute the law adopted by Congress and approved by the President. If judges could add to, remodel, update, or detract from old statutory terms inspired only by extratextual sources and our own imaginations, we would risk amending statutes outside the legislative process reserved for the people's representatives. And we would deny the people the right to continue relying on the original meaning of the law they have counted on to settle their rights and obligations. ...

With this in mind, our task is clear. We must determine the ordinary public meaning of Title VII's command that it is "unlawful ... for an employer to fail or refuse to hire or to discharge any individual, or otherwise to discriminate against any individual with respect to his compensation, terms, conditions, or privileges of employment, because of such individual's race, color, religion, sex, or national origin ..." To do so, we orient ourselves to the time of the statute's adoption, here 1964, and begin by examining the key statutory terms in turn before assessing their impact on the cases at hand and then confirming our work against this Court's precedents.

The only statutorily protected characteristic at issue in today's cases is "sex"—and that is also the primary term in Title VII whose meaning the parties dispute. Appealing to roughly contemporaneous dictionaries, the employers say that, as used here, the term "sex" in 1964 referred to "status as either male or female [as] determined by reproductive biology." The employees counter by submitting that, even in 1964, the term bore a broader scope, capturing more than anatomy and reaching at least some norms concerning gender identity and sexual orientation. But because nothing in our approach to these cases turns on the outcome of the parties' debate, and because the employees concede the point for argument's sake, we proceed on the assumption that "sex" signified what the employers suggest, referring only to biological distinctions between male and female.

Still, that's just a starting point. The question isn't just what "sex" meant, but what Title VII says about it. Most notably, the statute prohibits employers from taking certain actions "because of" sex. And, as this Court has previously explained, "the ordinary meaning of 'because of' is 'by reason of' or 'on account of …'" In the language of law, this means that Title VII's "because of" test incorporates the "simple" and "traditional" standard of but-for causation … That form of causation is established whenever a particular outcome would not have happened "but for" the purported cause … In other words, a but-for test directs us to change one thing at a time and see if the outcome changes. If it does, we have found a but-for cause.

This can be a sweeping standard. Often, events have multiple but-for causes. So, for example, if a car accident occurred both because the defendant ran a red light and because the plaintiff failed to signal his turn at the intersection, we might call each a but-for cause of the collision. When it comes to Title VII, the adoption of the traditional but-for causation standard means a defendant cannot avoid liability just by citing some other factor that contributed to its challenged employment decision. So long as the plaintiff's sex was one but-for cause of that decision, that is enough to trigger the law. …

As sweeping as even the but-for causation standard can be, Title VII does not concern itself with everything that happens "because of" sex. The statute imposes liability on employers only when they "fail or refuse to hire," "discharge," "or otherwise … discriminate against" someone because of a statutorily protected characteristic like sex. The employers acknowledge that they discharged the plaintiffs in today's cases, but assert that the statute's list of verbs is qualified by the last item on it: "otherwise … discriminate against." By virtue of the word otherwise, the employers suggest, Title VII concerns itself not with every discharge, only with those discharges that involve discrimination. …

From the ordinary public meaning of the statute's language at the time of the law's adoption, a straightforward rule emerges: An employer violates Title VII when it intentionally fires an individual employee based in part on sex. It doesn't matter if other factors besides the plaintiff's sex contributed to the decision. And it doesn't matter if the employer treated women as a group the same when compared to men as a group. If the employer intentionally relies in part on an individual employee's sex when deciding to discharge the employee—put differently, if changing the employee's sex would have yielded a different choice by the employer—a statutory violation has occurred. Title VII's message is "simple but momentous": An individual employee's sex is "not relevant to the selection, evaluation, or compensation of employees."

The statute's message for our cases is equally simple and momentous: An individual's homosexuality or transgender status is not relevant to employment decisions. That's because it is impossible to discriminate against a person for being homosexual or transgender without discriminating against that individual based on sex. Consider, for example, an employer with two employees, both of whom are attracted to men. The two individuals are, to the employer's mind, materially identical in all respects, except that one is a man and the other a woman. If the employer fires the male employee for no reason other than the fact he is attracted to men, the employer discriminates against him for traits or actions it tolerates in his female colleague. Put differently, the employer intentionally singles out an employee to fire based in part on the employee's sex, and the affected employee's sex is a but-for cause of his discharge. Or take an employer who fires a transgender person who was identified as a male at birth but who now identifies as a female. If the employer retains an otherwise identical employee who was identified as female at birth, the employer intentionally penalizes a person identified as male at birth for traits or actions that it tolerates in an employee identified as female at birth. Again, the individual employee's sex plays an unmistakable and impermissible role in the discharge decision. …

We agree that homosexuality and transgender status are distinct concepts from sex. But, as we've seen, discrimination based on homosexuality or transgender status necessarily entails discrimination based on sex; the first cannot happen without the second. Nor is there any such thing as a "canon of donut holes," in which Congress's failure to speak directly to a specific case that falls within a more general statutory rule creates a tacit exception. Instead, when Congress chooses not to include any exceptions to a broad rule, courts apply the broad rule. And that is exactly how this Court has always approached Title VII. "Sexual harassment" is conceptually distinct from sex discrimination, but it can fall within Title VII's sweep. Would the employers have us reverse those cases on the theory that Congress could have spoken to those problems more specifically? Of course not. As enacted, Title VII prohibits all forms of discrimination because of sex, however they may manifest themselves or whatever other labels might attach to them. …

Some of those who supported adding language to Title VII to ban sex discrimination may have hoped it would derail the entire Civil Rights Act. Yet, contrary to those intentions, the bill became law. Since then, Title VII's effects have unfolded with far-reaching consequences, some likely beyond what many in Congress or elsewhere expected.

But none of this helps decide today's cases. Ours is a society of written laws. Judges are not free to overlook plain statutory commands on the strength of nothing more than suppositions about intentions or guesswork about expectations. In Title VII, Congress adopted broad language making it illegal for an employer to rely on an employee's sex when deciding to fire that employee. We do not hesitate to recognize today a necessary consequence of that legislative choice: An employer who fires an individual merely for being gay or transgender defies the law.

The judgments of the Second and Sixth Circuits in Nos. 17-1623 and 18-107 are affirmed. The judgment of the Eleventh Circuit in No. 17-1618 is reversed, and the case is remanded for further proceedings consistent with this opinion.

It is so ordered.

## C    Reflections and Questions

1. In the case of *Karen Atala and Others*, the Inter-American Court of Human Rights interpreted the clause on "other social condition" in the prohibition of discrimination under Article 1.1 of the American Convention to include sexual orientation and gender identity as prohibited factors. This means that the American Convention identifies sex, sexual orientation, and gender identity as three distinct factors which can form the basis for a legal finding of discrimination. In *Bostock v. Clayton County*, the United States Supreme Court interpreted the Civil Rights Act and its prohibition of discrimination on the basis of sex as also protecting homosexual and transgender persons. Judge Gorsuch authored the majority opinion, in which he recognized that homosexuality and transgender status are distinct concepts from sex. However, the decision does indicate that discrimination on the basis of sexual orientation or gender identity "necessarily entails" discrimination on the basis of sex. Applying a textualist approach, Judge Gorsuch states in the opinion that discrimination on the basis of sexual orientation and gender identity cannot happen without that based on sex. Therefore, these two case rulings apply different paths to arrive at a similar conclusion. Which legal strategy do you believe is best and could advance further the protection of women historically discriminated against on the basis of their sexual orientation and gender identity?

2. The flexible reading of non-discrimination clauses has also been a fixture of the analysis of United Nations treaty-based organs related to sexual orientation and gender identity. The International Covenant on Economic, Social and Cultural Rights in its Article 2.2 mandates:

> The States Parties to the present Covenant undertake to guarantee that the rights enunciated in the present Covenant will be exercised without discrimination of any kind as to race, colour, sex, language, religion, political or other opinion, national or social origin, property, birth or other status.

The Economic, Social and Cultural Rights Committee in its General Comment 20 indicates that a flexible interpretation of the phrase "other status" in Article 2.2 is needed to reflect forms of differential treatment that lack a reasonable and objective justification.[8] The prohibition of discrimination under Article 2.2 reflects both explicitly and implicitly the experience of social groups that have suffered marginalization and are vulnerable to human rights violations. The Committee also read sexual orientation and gender identity as recognized in Article 2.2.[9] The Committee expressly indicated that persons who are transgender, transsexual, or intersex are often victims of human rights violations, in the realms of employment and education. Can you think of other factors used to discriminate which should be recognized as implicit in universal and regional human rights treaties?

3. The European Court of Human Rights has been a leading tribunal in the protection of the rights of LGBTI persons. For example, the Court recognized the rights of homosexual persons and couples to adopt and have custody of their children in the cases of *E.B. v.*

---

[8]    *See* Committee on Economic, Social and Cultural Rights, General Comment 20, *supra* note 4, ¶ 32.

[9]    *See id.*

*France* and *Salgueiro da Silva Mouta v. Portugal*;[10] found violations when persons were discharged from the Royal Navy in the United Kingdom due to their sexual orientation;[11] and rejected discrimination in property inheritance laws.[12] Many of these cases have been ruled on by the European Court of Human Rights on the basis of Article 8 and the right to respect private and family life, and Article 14 and its prohibition of discrimination. The European Court of Human Rights also ruled on the cases of *MC and AC v. Romania* and *Identoba and Others v. Georgia*, in which it found violations of the prohibition of torture and inhuman and degrading treatment in respect of state failures to protect protesters from violence perpetrated by private individuals based on hatred against homosexuals in peaceful LGBTI demonstrations, and to effectively investigate these crimes.[13]

4.  The Inter-American Commission and Court of Human Rights have also ruled on key cases on discrimination on the basis of sexual orientation, including the *Karen Atala* judgment on discrimination in custody matters discussed *supra*, and the case of *Azul Rojas Marín and Another v. Peru*.[14] The matter of *Azul Rojas Marín* relates to the alleged detention and torture of a gay man, who currently identifies as a woman and goes by the name "Azul."[15] It was alleged in the case that Azul was detained by the police in an unlawful, arbitrary, and discriminatory manner.[16] Azul was subjected to acts of physical and mental violence during her detention, including rape, owing to the perception that she was a gay man at the time.[17] The Inter-American Court reiterated in its decision that LGBTI persons have historically faced structural discrimination, stigmatization, and different forms of violence.[18] The Court refers with alarm to violence against LGBTI persons based on prejudice; a negative perception of diverse sexual orientations and gender identities; and that perpetrated to communicate messages of exclusion and subordination.[19] The Court found violations in this case to the rights to personal liberty; integrity; privacy; torture; and judicial protection and guarantees. The Inter-American Court of Human Rights also ruled on its Advisory Opinion OC-24/17, discussed *infra*, advancing a right to marriage equality and non-discrimination on the basis of sexual orientation, gender identity, and gender expression.

5.  New treaties are starting to recognize explicitly discrimination on the basis of sexual orientation and gender identity. The 2013 Inter-American Convention Against All Forms of Discrimination and Intolerance recognizes in Article 1.1 that discrimination may be

---

[10]  *For reference, see*, E.B. v. France [GC], App. No. 43546/02, Eur. Ct. H.R. (2008), ¶¶ 70–98; Salgueiro da Silva Mouta v. Portugal, App. No. 33290/96, Eur. Ct. H.R., ¶¶ 23–36 (Dec. 21, 1999).

[11]  *See, e.g.*, Lustig-Prean and Beckett v. United Kingdom, App. Nos. 31417/96 and 32377/96, Eur. Ct. H.R. ¶¶ 80–105 (Sept. 27, 1999).

[12]  *See* Eur. Ct. H.R., Karner v. Austria, *supra* note 4, ¶¶ 29–43.

[13]  M.C. v. Romania, App. No. 12060/12, Eur. Ct. H.R., ¶¶ 107–126 (April 12, 2016); Identoba and Others v. Georgia, App. No. 73235/12, Eur. Ct. H.R., ¶¶ 56–59, 65–81 (May 12, 2015).

[14]  *See generally* Azul Rojas Marín et al. v. Peru, Preliminary Objections, Merits, Reparations and Costs, Judgment, Inter-Am. Ct. H.R., Series C No. 402 (March 12, 2020).

[15]  *Id.*, ¶¶ 45, 49, 52.

[16]  *Id.*, ¶ 53.

[17]  *Id.*, ¶ 53.

[18]  *Id.*, ¶ 90.

[19]  *Id.*, ¶¶ 92, 93, 158–167.

based on sexual orientation, gender identity, and gender expression.[20] The Council of Europe Convention on preventing and combating violence against women and domestic violence also provides in its Article 4(3) that the implementation of the provisions in this Convention will be ensured without discrimination on the basis of sexual orientation and gender identity.[21]

6. The U.S. Supreme Court ruling in the case of *Bostock v. Clayton County* on June 15, 2020, was historic in establishing that employers are prohibited from discriminating against any individual on the basis of their sexual orientation or gender identity in the employment setting. The case illustrates how federal courts can offer expansive or narrow interpretations to federal statutes. In this particular instance, the Court interpreted broadly the prohibition of discrimination on the basis of sex under the landmark Civil Rights Act, granting federal judicial protection to millions of LGBTI people who are employed in the United States. The majority concluded that it is unconstitutional for sexual orientation and gender identity to be considered as factors in employment decisions, even though these factors are not explicitly mentioned in the Civil Rights Act. The decision in *Bostock* is also an important addition to the line of cases already adopted by the U.S. Supreme Court in *Obergefell v. Hodges*, discussed *infra*, guaranteeing the right to marriage equality, and *Lawrence v. Texas*, declaring the unconstitutionality of laws which prohibit private and consensual intimate activity between homosexual persons. *Bostock v. Clayton County* is a landmark decision in protecting the rights of lesbian, bisexual, and transwomen in the realm of employment.[22] Can you think of other spheres in which the rights of lesbian, bisexual, and transwomen need protection from discrimination?

## III  THE RIGHT TO PRIVACY

An important point of origin for international legal developments related to sexual orientation and gender identity was concerns linked to sodomy laws. Sodomy laws prohibit sexual relations between same-sex consenting adults. At least 66 countries still criminalize consensual same-sex sexual acts.[23] Most sodomy laws impose criminal sanctions and can entail jail time. Several individual case petitions have been presented before universal and regional human rights bodies and courts alleging that these laws contravene the rights to privacy. The resulting judgments have advanced through analysis of the duty of states not to arbitrarily interfere with the right to privacy and family life. The decisions have often connected the enjoyment

---

[20]  Inter-American Convention against all Forms of Discrimination and Intolerance, Art. 1.1, Organization of American States, June 5, 2013 (hereinafter OAS Convention on Discrimination and Intolerance).

[21]  See, Council of Europe, Convention on preventing and combating violence against women and domestic violence, Article 4(3).

[22]  Rosa Celorio, *A Glimpse of Hope from the U.S. Supreme Court: Bostock v. Clayton County*, June 30, 2020, https://blogs.cuit.columbia.edu/rightsviews/2020/06/30/a-glimpse-of-hope-from-the-u-s-supreme-court-bostock-v-clayton-county/.

[23]  For more reading, *see* International Lesbian, Gay, Bisexual, Trans and Intersex Association (ILGA World), *Report on State-Sponsored Homophobia*, 2019, pp. 197–202, https://ilga.org/downloads/ILGA_State_Sponsored_Homophobia_2019.pdf.

of the right to privacy with the obligation to prevent non-discrimination on the basis of sexual orientation and gender identity.

One interesting fact is that in several of the cases the sodomy laws were not currently enforced by the states involved. In these instances, allegations were presented indicating that their sole existence presented an imminent threat to the right to privacy and promoted prejudice and stigma towards homosexual persons.

Below are excerpts of the historic decision adopted by the United Nations Human Rights Committee in the case of *Toonen v. Australia* regarding the effect of sodomy laws in the rights to privacy and discrimination. This is followed by excerpts from the decision of the Inter-American Commission on Human Rights in the case of *Martha Lucia Alvarez Giraldo*, regarding the right to intimate visits of homosexual persons deprived of liberty.

## A        *Toonen v. Australia*, United Nations Human Rights Committee

Communication No. 488/1992, U.N. Doc. CCPR/C/50/D/488/1992 (1994)

*The author in this case challenged two provisions of the Tasmanian Criminal Code criminalizing homosexual relations between consenting adults.*

8.1 The Committee is called upon to determine whether Mr. Toonen has been the victim of an unlawful or arbitrary interference with his privacy, contrary to article 17, paragraph 1, and whether he has been discriminated against in his right to equal protection of the law, contrary to article 26.

8.2 Inasmuch as article 17 is concerned, it is undisputed that adult consensual sexual activity in private is covered by the concept of "privacy", and that Mr. Toonen is actually and currently affected by the continued existence of the Tasmanian laws. The Committee considers that Sections 122(a), (c) and 123 of the Tasmanian Criminal Code "interfere" with the author's privacy, even if these provisions have not been enforced for a decade. In this context, it notes that the policy of the Department of Public Prosecutions not to initiate criminal proceedings in respect of private homosexual conduct does not amount to a guarantee that no actions will be brought against homosexuals in the future, particularly in the light of undisputed statements of the Director of Public Prosecutions of Tasmania in 1988 and those of members of the Tasmanian Parliament. The continued existence of the challenged provisions therefore continuously and directly "interferes" with the author's privacy.

8.3 The prohibition against private homosexual behavior is provided for by law, namely, Sections 122 and 123 of the Tasmanian Criminal Code. As to whether it may be deemed arbitrary, the Committee recalls that pursuant to its General Comment 16[32] on article 17, the "introduction of the concept of arbitrariness is intended to guarantee that even interference provided for by the law should be in accordance with the provisions, aims and objectives of the Covenant and should be, in any event, reasonable in the circumstances". The Committee interprets the requirement of reasonableness to imply that any interference with privacy must be proportional to the end sought and be necessary in the circumstances of any given case.

8.4 While the State party acknowledges that the impugned provisions constitute an arbitrary interference with Mr. Toonen's privacy, the Tasmanian authorities submit that the challenged laws are justified on public health and moral grounds, as they are intended in part to prevent the spread of HIV/AIDS in Tasmania, and because, in the absence of specific limitation clauses in article 17, moral issues must be deemed a matter for domestic decision. …

8.5 As far as the public health argument of the Tasmanian authorities is concerned, the Committee notes that the criminalization of homosexual practices cannot be considered a reasonable means or proportionate measure to achieve the aim of preventing the spread of AIDS/HIV. …

8.6 The Committee cannot accept either that for the purposes of article 17 of the Covenant, moral issues are exclusively a matter of domestic concern, as this would open the door to withdrawing from the Committee's scrutiny a potentially large number of statutes interfering with privacy. It further notes that with the exception of Tasmania, all laws criminalizing homosexuality have been repealed throughout Australia and that, even in Tasmania, it is apparent that there is no consensus as to whether Sections 122 and 123 should not also be repealed. Considering further that these provisions are not currently enforced, which implies that they are not deemed essential to the protection of morals in Tasmania, the Committee concludes that the provisions do not meet the "reasonableness" test in the circumstances of the case, and that they arbitrarily interfere with Mr. Toonen's right under article 17, paragraph 1.

8.7 The State party has sought the Committee's guidance as to whether sexual orientation may be considered an "other status" for the purposes of article 26. The same issue could arise under article 2, paragraph 1, of the Covenant. The Committee confines itself to noting, however, that in its view the reference to "sex" in articles 2, paragraph 1, and 26 is to be taken as including sexual orientation. …

**B** *Martha Lucia Álvarez Giraldo*, **Inter-American Commission on Human Rights**

REPORT No. 122/18, CASE 11.656
OEA/Ser.L/V/II.169 Doc. 139
October 5, 2018

*In this case, the petitioner alleged that her rights to privacy, humane treatment, and equal protection had been violated by the denial of intimate visits with her same-sex partner while imprisoned. The excerpts below discuss the interpretation of the right to privacy by the Inter-American Commission on Human Rights in the context of sexual orientation.*

185. As for the scope of the right to a private life recognized in Article 11 of the Convention, the case law of the Inter-American Court and the Commission's decisions have established that the right to a private life should be understood in the broad sense, as encompassing all spheres of the intimate realm and autonomy of an individual, including the development of his or her identity. That being the case, the decisions a person makes regarding his or her sexual life are a fundamental part of his or her private life, as sexuality "is an integral part of the personality of every human being [and] [i]ts full development depends upon

the satisfaction of basic human needs such as the desire for contact, intimacy, emotional expression, pleasure, tenderness and love." Sexual orientation constitutes a fundamental component of an individual's private life, as are the behaviors that attend the exercise of one's sexuality consistent with one's sexual orientation. There is a "clear nexus" between sexual orientation and the development of the identity and life plan of an individual, including his or her personality and relations with other human beings; in general, a person's sexual orientation "is also linked to the notion of freedom and a person's right to self-determination and to freely choose the options and circumstances that give meaning to his or her existence, in accordance with his or her own choices and convictions."

186.     A person's sexual orientation also includes the possibility of freely expressing that sexual orientation, as part of the free development of personality that is vital to a person's life plan. Thus, factors that interfere with a woman's ability to decide matters related to the exercise of her sexuality must be free of any stereotyped notions regarding the scope and content of this aspect of her private life, especially when combined with consideration of her sexual orientation.

187.     For its part, the main purpose of the provision contained in Article 11(2) of the Convention is to protect individuals from "arbitrary or abusive" State interference in the exercise of this right, mindful that any such interference may involve elements of "injustice, unpredictability and unreasonableness."

188.     Given these considerations, the protection offered under Article 11(2) of the Convention prohibits any arbitrary or abusive State interference that affects aspects of an individual's sexual life, including his or her sexual orientation and the exercise of his or her sexuality. The European Court of Human Rights has written that States must have particularly convincing and weighty reasons to justify interference by the authorities based on a person's sexual orientation. …

189.     While the exercise of some rights of persons in the custody of the State may be affected, this does not mean that those rights are completely forfeit by the very act of deprivation of liberty; the State is the guarantor of the exercise of these rights, while the individual is subject to certain statutory and regulatory obligations that he or she must observe. While the principal element that defines the deprivation of liberty is the individual's dependence on the decisions made by the staff of the establishment where he or she is being held, the prison authorities themselves must not go beyond the ends that the deprivation of freedom is intended to serve, nor may they exceed the disciplinary authority that their office confers upon them. …

192.     Thus, the State's positive obligation to create conditions that ensure that the interpersonal relationships of persons in its custody will be maintained is because these relationships are part of their private life and privacy, a realm that is wholly their own and into which no one may intrude. The Commission therefore considers that the logical consequence of making re-socialization one of the purposes that the custodial regime is intended to serve, is that respect for a person's private life is a right whose exercise must be permitted even during incarceration; the absolute suppression of this right would undermine the resocialization purpose of sentences of incarceration delivered in the exercise of the State's punitive authority. …

199.     The Commission observes that in the present case, the petitioners alleged that the Colombian State arbitrarily and abusively interfered in Marta Álvarez' private life by

denying her a right given under domestic law, based on discriminatory prejudices regarding her sexual orientation and because she was a woman. For their part, the prison authorities who denied Marta Álvarez' request for an intimate visit, argued that the restriction of this right was a reasonable consequence of the limitations that the prison regime imposed.

200. In this regard, the IACHR reiterates its finding *supra* in the sense that the denial of the right to intimate visit to Marta Lucía Álvarez was a disproportionate restriction which contravened the Convention because the State did not prove that there was a strict causation between the limitation of the right to intimate visit and the aims indicated by the State (prison security and protection of the rights of third parties). …

201. As previously established, any restriction imposed on a prisoner's exercise of a right must be in furtherance of the ends that the prison regime itself seeks to achieve. The facts established in this case show that the prison authorities used various devices to obstruct the exercise of the right to intimate visits, driven by their own personal prejudices regarding the alleged victim's sexual orientation. …

205. Given the foregoing considerations, the Commission concludes that by having tolerated discriminatory treatment on the part of the prison and court authorities, in the form of disproportionate and unjustified interference in Marta Álvarez' private life, the State of Colombia violated Article 11(2) of the American Convention, read in conjunction with the duty of non-discrimination contained in Article 1(1) thereof. …

## C    Reflections and Questions

1. The 1994 United Nations Human Rights Committee decision in the case of *Toonen v. Australia* was one of the first ones to develop the content of the right to privacy in the realm of sexual orientation. The decision confirms that sodomy laws threaten the right to privacy of persons of non-conforming sexual orientations and gender identities, even when these are not being enforced in a specific country. The Committee makes clear that any interference with the right to privacy based on the sexual orientation of persons must meet reasonableness requirements, be proportional to the aim pursued, and be necessary under the circumstances of the given case.[24] The Committee also connected sodomy laws with discrimination on the basis of sexual orientation, prohibited by Articles 2.1 and 26 of the International Covenant on Civil and Political Rights.

2. The Human Rights Committee through its decision in *Toonen v. Australia* addressed basic human rights which are implicated when sexual orientation is exercised in the home. Many of the earlier cases related to LGBTI persons defined specific rights which were key to full enjoyment by homosexual persons – and persons of non-conforming sexual orientations and gender identities – in the private or family spheres. As discussed in earlier sections, international human rights law was originally conceived to restrain government abuse in public settings, not necessarily the family or home setting. This piercing of the veil of the home and the awareness of the need to address human rights violations in the family was really developed later with the adoption of CEDAW and other treaties. Can you think of reasons why it was important for international human rights law to also cover and be rele-

---

[24]    *See* Human Rights Committee, Toonen v. Australia, *supra* note 4, ¶ 8.3.

vant in the home setting? Think of specific human rights violations that women who are or are perceived as lesbian, bisexual, transgender, or intersex may face in the home or family setting.

3.  In the 2018 case of *Martha Lucia Álvarez Giraldo*, regarding the prohibition of same-sex intimate visits in prisons, the Inter-American Commission on Human Rights had the opportunity to shed light on the content of the right to privacy in a custody setting, beyond the home realm. The Inter-American Commission explained that the enjoyment of the right to privacy in the sphere of sexual orientation extends to the definition of a life plan based on this orientation, and the ability to express it autonomously, including the exercise of sexuality. Stereotypes and forms of intersectional discrimination based on sex, gender, and sexual orientation should not interfere with this life plan, in both in the home and social settings. According to the Inter-American Commission on Human Rights, convincing and weighty reasons need to be advanced by a state to justify and interfere with the right to privacy of persons in both the private and public settings, based on motives guided by their sexual orientation.

4.  Conversion therapies are some of the most alarming arbitrary intrusions in the lives of persons on the basis of their non-conforming sexual orientations and gender identities. The current U.N. Independent Expert on Protection against Violence and Discrimination based on Sexual Orientation and Gender Identity (hereinafter "U.N. SOGI Independent Expert") released a report on this problem on 2020.[25] In the report, he documents the prevalence of conversion therapies and interventions based on the premise that a person's sexual orientation, gender identity, and expression should be changed, or promoting that individuals do not express their sexual orientation and/or gender identity.[26] The report identifies three approaches that often guide these practices, including "psychotherapeutic, medical, and faith-based."[27] The report affirms that at least 68 countries have evidence of these therapies, and may involve corrective rape, mental health services, exorcism, and rehabilitation programs, all disproportionately affecting young people.[28] Forms of sexual violence, and physical and psychological violence can often be part of conversion therapies, including corrective rape and forced nudity; shackling; beatings; isolation; and solitary confinement.[29] Consider specific human rights that are violated by conversion therapies. How would the duty of states to act with due diligence apply to conversion therapies? How can states prevent and sanction these practices?

5.  One of the most invisible and underreported forms of discrimination and violence occurs against intersex persons. Intersex individuals are born with physical sex characteristics that do not conform to the normative definitions for male and female bodies.[30] This may

---

[25]  *See* Report of Independent Expert on protection against violence and discrimination based on sexual orientation and gender identity on Practices of "So-Called Conversion Therapy", A/HRC/44/53 (May 1, 2020).

[26]  *Id.*, ¶¶ 17, 37.

[27]  *Id.*, ¶ 41.

[28]  *Id.*, ¶¶ 24–25, 36–54.

[29]  *Id.*, ¶¶ 38–39.

[30]  *See* definition of "intersex people" in United Nations Office of the High Commissioner for Human Rights, *Born Free and Equal*, 2nd ed., 2019, p. 5, www.ohchr.org/Documents/Publications/Born_Free _and_Equal_WEB.pdf.

be apparent at birth or later in life, and intersex persons may have any sexual orientation or gender identity. Bodies like the Inter-American Commission on Human Rights have reported on very specific human rights violations faced by intersex persons for not conforming to socially accepted standards for female and male bodies.[31] These include genital normalizing surgeries, involuntary sterilization, human experimentation, lack of informed consent for medical procedures, and the denial of needed health-care services.[32] Identify ways in which the legal standards discussed in this book related to the human rights of women apply to the human rights violations faced by intersex persons.

## IV THE RIGHT TO GENDER IDENTITY AND EXPRESSION

The Yogyakarta Principles expressed their concern over serious forms of violence, exclusion, and prejudice faced by persons on the basis of their gender identity.[33] They refer in particular to the situation of persons who are or are perceived to be transgender.[34] The Yogyakarta Principles defined *gender identity* as:

> Each person's deeply felt internal and individual experience of gender, which may or may not correspond with the sex assigned at birth, including the personal sense of the body (which may involve, if freely chosen, modification of bodily appearance or function by medical, surgical or other means) and other expressions of gender, including dress, speech and mannerisms.[35]

Since then, multiple organizations have documented the alarming situation of trans persons in many countries and localities. Concerns are often related to individuals who are considered transgender or non-conforming, which means that their gender identities, expressions, and/or experiences differ from those associated with the sex they were assigned at birth.[36]

Transgender persons are often the subject of harassment; physical, psychological, and sexual violence; stereotypes; discrimination; and forms of community rejection and stigmatization.[37] They also often suffer unequal protection in the law, having scarce recognition of their diverse

---

[31] Inter-American Commission on Human Rights, *Violence against Lesbian, Gay, Bisexual, Trans and Intersex Persons in the Americas*, OAS/Ser.L/V/II.rev.1 Doc. 36, ¶ 182 (Nov. 12, 2015).

[32] *Id.*, ¶¶182–195.

[33] *See generally*, Yogyakarta Principles, *supra* note 2, Preamble; The Yogyakarta Principles plus 10, *supra* note 2.

[34] *Id.*

[35] Yogyakarta Principles, *supra* note 2, Preamble and p. 8.

[36] Human Rights Campaign Foundation, *An Epidemic of Violence: Fatal Violence against Transgender and Gender Nonconforming People in the United States in 2020*, p. 3, https://hrc-prod -requests.s3-us-west-2.amazonaws.com/FatalViolence-2020Report-Final.pdf?mtime=20201119101455 &focal=none; U.N. Office of the High Commissioner for Human Rights, *Born Free and Equal*, *supra* note 30, pp. 5–6.

[37] For more discussion on human rights violations suffered by transgender persons, *see* Report of the Independent Expert on protection against violence and discrimination based on sexual orientation and gender identity, A/73/152, July 12, 2018, ¶¶ 17–18, 25–32 (On effective measures to ensure respect of gender identity and guidance to States on how to address violence and discrimination based on gender identity).

and non-conforming identities.[38] These factors present formidable challenges for transgender persons and women to fully enjoy their civil, political, economic, social, and cultural rights.

This section discusses the landmark case of *Christine Goodwin* – ruled on by the European Court of Human Rights – on the situation of transgender women, which exemplifies the gravity and imminent nature of their human rights situation, the international law approach to this issue, and the need for increased state attention.

## A      *Christine Goodwin v. United Kingdom*, European Court of Human Rights

Application No. 28957/95, July 11, 2002
© Council of Europe, reproduced with permission

*The applicant in the case below had undergone gender reassignment surgery and lived as a woman. Even though the surgery was perfomed by the National Health Service, the law still did not recognize her gender change. She claimed she experienced different forms of harassment due to her gender change.*

76. The Court observes that the applicant, registered at birth as male, has undergone gender re-assignment surgery and lives in society as a female. Nonetheless, the applicant remains, for legal purposes, a male. This has had, and continues to have, effects on the applicant's life where sex is of legal relevance and distinctions are made between men and women, as, *inter alia*, in the area of pensions and retirement age. For example, the applicant must continue to pay national insurance contributions until the age of 65 due to her legal status as male. However, as she is employed in her gender identity as a female, she has had to obtain an exemption certificate which allows the payments from her employer to stop while she continues to make such payments herself. Though the Government submitted that this made due allowance for the difficulties of her position, the Court would note that she nonetheless has to make use of a special procedure that might in itself call attention to her status.

77. It must also be recognised that serious interference with private life can arise where the state of domestic law conflicts with an important aspect of personal identity. The stress and alienation arising from a discordance between the position in society assumed by a post-operative transsexual and the status imposed by law which refuses to recognise the change of gender cannot, in the Court's view, be regarded as a minor inconvenience arising from a formality. A conflict between social reality and law arises which places the transsexual in an anomalous position, in which he or she may experience feelings of vulnerability, humiliation and anxiety.

78. In this case, as in many others, the applicant's gender re-assignment was carried out by the national health service, which recognises the condition of gender dysphoria and provides, *inter alia*, re-assignment by surgery, with a view to achieving as one of its principal purposes as close an assimilation as possible to the gender in which the transsexual perceives that he or she properly belongs. The Court is struck by the fact that nonetheless the gender re-assignment which is lawfully provided is not met with full recognition in law, which

---

[38]   *Id.*

might be regarded as the final and culminating step in the long and difficult process of transformation which the transsexual has undergone. The coherence of the administrative and legal practices within the domestic system must be regarded as an important factor in the assessment carried out under Article 8 of the Convention. Where a State has authorised the treatment and surgery alleviating the condition of a transsexual, financed or assisted in financing the operations and indeed permits the artificial insemination of a woman living with a female-to-male transsexual (as demonstrated in the case of X., Y. and Z. v. United Kingdom, cited above), it appears illogical to refuse to recognise the legal implications of the result to which the treatment leads. ...

93. Having regard to the above considerations, the Court finds that the respondent Government can no longer claim that the matter falls within their margin of appreciation, save as regards the appropriate means of achieving recognition of the right protected under the Convention. Since there are no significant factors of public interest to weigh against the interest of this individual applicant in obtaining legal recognition of her gender re-assignment, it reaches the conclusion that the fair balance that is inherent in the Convention now tilts decisively in favour of the applicant. There has, accordingly, been a failure to respect her right to private life in breach of Article 8 of the Convention. ...

## B    Reflections and Questions

1. The decision of the European Court of Human Rights in the case of *Christine Goodwin* is a landmark in the protection of the rights of persons and women who identify or are perceived as transgender or non-conforming. The decision exemplifies the formidable barriers faced by many transgender women – those who were identified at birth as male, but now live as women – in having the law recognize their changed gender. Even though the National Health Service provided Christine Goodwin with the opportunity to have gender reassignment surgery, the law still recognized her as a man. As indicated by the Court, this exposed Christine Goodwin to sexual harassment, vulnerability, humiliation, and anxiety. The Court continues its dynamic and evolutive approach in interpreting the scope of Article 8 of the European Convention on Human Rights in matters concerning sexual orientation and gender identity, and applies a very narrow margin of appreciation.[39] In essence, the European Court of Human Rights indicates that laws should not conflict with integral aspects of personal identity. The Court did not find any "significant factors of public interest" to weigh against the interest of this applicant in securing legal recognition of her gender-reassignment.[40]

2. The well-known organization, Human Rights Campaign, released a report in 2020, documenting the widespread and endemic nature of violence against transgender and gender non-conforming people in the United States. Just in 2020, they reported at least 37 cases of fatal violence against transgender and gender non-conforming people, which is higher than

---

[39]    *See* Christine Goodwin v. United Kingdom [GC], App. No. 28957/95, Eur. Ct. H.R., ¶¶ 74–75 (2002).

[40]    *See id.*, ¶ 93.

any other year recorded by the Human Rights Campaign.[41] Between 2013 and 2020, the Human Rights Campaign has documented at least 37 cases of fatal violence against transgender and gender non-conforming people across 30 states in the United States.[42] They also underscored the epidemic and disproportionate effect of this violence on transgender women in particular and persons of color, highlighting the gender-based intersectional, racism, and discriminatory basis for many of these crimes.[43] This violence is often joined by poverty and homelessness. The report recommends in particular steps to eliminate the stigma against transgender and gender non-conforming people; the correct use of their chosen name and pronouns; the support of laws and policies which prohibit discrimination on the basis of gender identity; the need of increased representation of these voices in communities; and the demand to build inclusive communities.[44] Can you think of other measures states can take to prevent and eliminate discrimination, prejudice, and stigma against transgender persons?

3. The Inter-American Commission on Human Rights has also been one of the leading regional bodies in the world expressing concern over the forms of stigma, prejudice, violence, and harassment faced by transgender persons.[45] For example, the Inter-American Commission and its Rapporteurship on Economic, Social, Cultural, and Environmental Rights issued a report on 2020, highlighting the still-dire situation of transgender persons in the region of the Americas.[46] The report underscores violations to their rights to life; extrajudicial executions committed by state actors; killings perpetrated by non-state actors; and acts of rape and sexual violence.[47] Regarding transgender persons in particular, the report expresses concern over their low life expectancy; the legitimization by government authorities of stigma and prejudice; and exposure to extreme forms of violence and discrimination.[48] Transgender persons are often driven from their homes, leave the educational system, and have limited opportunities to join the labor market, which forces many of them to pursue sex work as an option.[49] Other challenges are unstable living situations; the lack of a family network; having to attend educational establishments governed by cisnormative disciplinary and behavioral rules; harassment and bullying; and the lack of recognition of gender changes in the law.[50] Consider steps that states can take to ensure that

---

[41] Human Rights Campaign Foundation, *An Epidemic of Violence: Fatal Violence against Transgender and Gender Nonconforming People in the United States in 2020*, Introduction and p. 2, https://hrc-prod-requests.s3-us-west-2.amazonaws.com/FatalViolence-2020Report-Final.pdf?mtime=20201119101455&focal=none.

[42] *Id.*, p. 4.

[43] *Id.*, p. 56.

[44] *Id.*, p. 64.

[45] *See, for reference*, Inter-American Commission on Human Rights, *On the occasion of International Transgender Day of Visibility, the IACHR and a UN expert urge States to guarantee the full exercise of the human rights of transgender persons*, No. 069/18 (March 29, 2018), www.oas.org/en/iachr/media _center/PReleases/2018/069.asp.

[46] *See* Inter-American Commission on Human Rights and Rapporteur on Economic, Social, Cultural, and Environmental Rights, *Report on Trans and Gender Diverse Persons and Their Economic, Social, Cultural, and Environmental Rights*, OEA/Ser.L/V/II. Doc. 239 (Aug. 7, 2020).

[47] *Id.*, ¶ 2.

[48] *Id.*, ¶ 4.

[49] *Id.*, ¶¶ 5, 6, 274–279.

[50] *Id.*, ¶¶ 171–192, 248–282.

transgender women fully enjoy their rights to non-discrimination, violence, education, and employment.

# V    MARRIAGE EQUALITY

Courts around the world have been progressing in their recognition of equal or comparable rights between heterosexual and homosexual couples in marriages, partnerships, and civil unions. An important fixture of this trend has been the increasing recognition of the right to enter into marriage of same-sex couples. Some of these decisions have occurred at the national level, spearheaded by Supreme Courts reading a right to marry and to equal protection in their national constitutions.

Below are excerpts of the United States Supreme Court decision in the case of *Obergefell v. Hodges* which recognized the right to marriage equality in the United States. The case was presented by 14 same-sex couples and two men whose partners had died.[51] They challenged laws which defined marriage between a man and a woman in Michigan, Kentucky, Ohio, and Tennessee, and argued they contravened the Fourteenth Amendment of the U.S. Constitution by denying them the right to marry.[52] The decision recognized a fundamental right to marry in the Due Process and Equal Protection Clauses of the U.S. Constitution, and how this right extends to same-sex couples.[53] The decision also requires all states to recognize same-sex marriages undertaken in other states.[54]

The *Obergefell v. Hodges* decision has been lauded by many activists and experts in the United States as a major step in the advancement of the human rights of LGBTI persons.[55] The decision is a landmark and cornerstone moment for the rights of same-sex couples in the United States.

## A    *Obergefell v. Hodges*, United States Supreme Court

576 U. S. ____ (2015)

Justice Kennedy delivered the opinion of the Court

The Constitution promises liberty to all within its reach, a liberty that includes certain specific rights that allow persons, within a lawful realm, to define and express their identity. The petitioners in these cases seek to find that liberty by marrying someone of the same sex and having their marriages deemed lawful on the same terms and conditions as marriages between persons of the opposite sex. ...

From their beginning to their most recent page, the annals of human history reveal the transcendent importance of marriage. The lifelong union of a man and a woman always has promised nobility and dignity to all persons, without regard to their station in life. Marriage

---

[51]    *See* Obergefell v. Hodges, 576 U. S. ____ (2015), p. 2.
[52]    *Id.*
[53]    *Id.*, pp. 27–28.
[54]    *Id.*, pp. 27–28.
[55]    *See, as reference*, Amnesty International, *Victory! Marriage Equality is a Right* (2015), www.amnestyusa.org/victory-marriage-equality-is-a-right/.

is sacred to those who live by their religions and offers unique fulfillment to those who find meaning in the secular realm. Its dynamic allows two people to find a life that could not be found alone, for a marriage becomes greater than just the two persons. Rising from the most basic human needs, marriage is essential to our most profound hopes and aspirations.

The centrality of marriage to the human condition makes it unsurprising that the institution has existed for millennia and across civilizations. Since the dawn of history, marriage has transformed strangers into relatives, binding families and societies together … It is fair and necessary to say these references were based on the understanding that marriage is a union between two persons of the opposite sex.

That history is the beginning of these cases. The respondents say it should be the end as well. To them, it would demean a timeless institution if the concept and lawful status of marriage were extended to two persons of the same sex. Marriage, in their view, is by its nature a gender-differentiated union of man and woman. This view long has been held—and continues to be held—in good faith by reasonable and sincere people here and throughout the world.

The petitioners acknowledge this history but contend that these cases cannot end there. Were their intent to demean the revered idea and reality of marriage, the petitioners' claims would be of a different order. But that is neither their purpose nor their submission. To the contrary, it is the enduring importance of marriage that underlies the petitioners' contentions. This, they say, is their whole point. Far from seeking to devalue marriage, the petitioners seek it for themselves because of their respect—and need—for its privileges and responsibilities. And their immutable nature dictates that same-sex marriage is their only real path to this profound commitment.

The cases now before the Court involve other petitioners as well, each with their own experiences. Their stories reveal that they seek not to denigrate marriage but rather to live their lives, or honor their spouses' memory, joined by its bond.

The ancient origins of marriage confirm its centrality, but it has not stood in isolation from developments in law and society. The history of marriage is one of both continuity and change. That institution—even as confined to opposite-sex relations—has evolved over time. …

These new insights have strengthened, not weakened, the institution of marriage. Indeed, changed understandings of marriage are characteristic of a Nation where new dimensions of freedom become apparent to new generations, often through perspectives that begin in pleas or protests and then are considered in the political sphere and the judicial process. …

Under the Due Process Clause of the Fourteenth Amendment, no State shall "deprive any person of life, liberty, or property, without due process of law." The fundamental liberties protected by this Clause include most of the rights enumerated in the Bill of Rights … In addition these liberties extend to certain personal choices central to individual dignity and autonomy, including intimate choices that define personal identity and beliefs. …

The identification and protection of fundamental rights is an enduring part of the judicial duty to interpret the Constitution. That responsibility, however, "has not been reduced to any formula …" Rather, it requires courts to exercise reasoned judgment in identifying interests of the person so fundamental that the State must accord them its respect … That process is guided by many of the same considerations relevant to analysis of other constitutional provisions that set forth broad principles rather than specific requirements. History and tradition guide and discipline this inquiry but do not set its outer boundaries … That method respects our history and learns from it without allowing the past alone to rule the present.

The nature of injustice is that we may not always see it in our own times. The generations that wrote and ratified the Bill of Rights and the Fourteenth Amendment did not presume to know the extent of freedom in all of its dimensions, and so they entrusted to future generations a charter protecting the right of all persons to enjoy liberty as we learn its meaning. When new insight reveals discord between the Constitution's central protections and a received legal stricture, a claim to liberty must be addressed.

Applying these established tenets, the Court has long held the right to marry is protected by the Constitution … It cannot be denied that this Court's cases describing the right to marry presumed a relationship involving opposite-sex partners. The Court, like many institutions, has made assumptions defined by the world and time of which it is a part … This was evident in *Baker* v. *Nelson*, 409 U. S. 810, a one-line summary decision issued in 1972, holding the exclusion of same-sex couples from marriage did not present a substantial federal question.

Still, there are other, more instructive precedents. This Court's cases have expressed constitutional principles of broader reach. In defining the right to marry these cases have identified essential attributes of that right based in history, tradition, and other constitutional liberties inherent in this intimate bond … And in assessing whether the force and rationale of its cases apply to same-sex couples, the Court must respect the basic reasons why the right to marry has been long protected. …

This analysis compels the conclusion that same-sex couples may exercise the right to marry. The four principles and traditions to be discussed demonstrate that the reasons marriage is fundamental under the Constitution apply with equal force to same-sex couples.

A first premise of the Court's relevant precedents is that the right to personal choice regarding marriage is inherent in the concept of individual autonomy. …

Choices about marriage shape an individual's destiny. …

As all parties agree, many same-sex couples provide loving and nurturing homes to their children, whether biological or adopted. And hundreds of thousands of children are presently being raised by such couples … Most States have allowed gays and lesbians to adopt, either as individuals or as couples, and many adopted and foster children have same-sex parents … This provides powerful confirmation from the law itself that gays and lesbians can create loving, supportive families.

Excluding same-sex couples from marriage thus conflicts with a central premise of the right to marry. Without the recognition, stability, and predictability marriage offers, their children suffer the stigma of knowing their families are somehow lesser. …

The limitation of marriage to opposite-sex couples may long have seemed natural and just, but its inconsistency with the central meaning of the fundamental right to marry is now manifest. With that knowledge must come the recognition that laws excluding same-sex couples from the marriage right impose stigma and injury of the kind prohibited by our basic charter. …

… No union is more profound than marriage, for it embodies the highest ideals of love, fidelity, devotion, sacrifice, and family. In forming a marital union, two people become something greater than once they were. As some of the petitioners in these cases demonstrate, marriage embodies a love that may endure even past death. It would misunderstand these men and women to say they disrespect the idea of marriage. Their plea is that they do respect it, respect it so deeply that they seek to find its fulfillment for themselves. Their hope is not to be condemned to live in loneliness, excluded from one of civilization's oldest institutions. They ask for equal dignity in the eyes of the law. The Constitution grants them that right.

The judgment of the Court of Appeals for the Sixth Circuit is reversed.

Chief Justice Roberts, with whom Justice Scalia and Justice Thomas join, dissenting
Petitioners make strong arguments rooted in social policy and considerations of fairness. They contend that same-sex couples should be allowed to affirm their love and commitment through marriage, just like opposite-sex couples. That position has undeniable appeal; over the past six years, voters and legislators in eleven States and the District of Columbia have revised their laws to allow marriage between two people of the same sex.

But this Court is not a legislature. Whether same-sex marriage is a good idea should be of no concern to us. Under the Constitution, judges have power to say what the law is, not what it should be. The people who ratified the Constitution authorized courts to exercise "neither force nor will but merely judgment ..."

Although the policy arguments for extending marriage to same-sex couples may be compelling, the legal arguments for requiring such an extension are not. The fundamental right to marry does not include a right to make a State change its definition of marriage. And a State's decision to maintain the meaning of marriage that has persisted in every culture throughout human history can hardly be called irrational. In short, our Constitution does not enact any one theory of marriage. The people of a State are free to expand marriage to include same-sex couples, or to retain the historic definition.

Today, however, the Court takes the extraordinary step of ordering every State to license and recognize same-sex marriage. Many people will rejoice at this decision, and I begrudge none their celebration. But for those who believe in a government of laws, not of men, the majority's approach is deeply disheartening. Supporters of same-sex marriage have achieved considerable success persuading their fellow citizens—through the democratic process—to adopt their view. That ends today. Five lawyers have closed the debate and enacted their own vision of marriage as a matter of constitutional law. Stealing this issue from the people will for many cast a cloud over same-sex marriage, making a dramatic social change that much more difficult to accept.

The majority's decision is an act of will, not legal judgment. The right it announces has no basis in the Constitution or this Court's precedent. The majority expressly disclaims judicial "caution" and omits even a pretense of humility, openly relying on its desire to remake society according to its own "new insight" into the "nature of injustice ..." As a result, the Court invalidates the marriage laws of more than half the States and orders the transformation of a social institution that has formed the basis of human society for millennia, for the Kalahari Bushmen and the Han Chinese, the Carthaginians and the Aztecs. Just who do we think we are? ...

Understand well what this dissent is about: It is not about whether, in my judgment, the institution of marriage should be changed to include same-sex couples. It is instead about whether, in our democratic republic, that decision should rest with the people acting through their elected representatives, or with five lawyers who happen to hold commissions authorizing them to resolve legal disputes according to law. The Constitution leaves no doubt about the answer ...

If you are among the many Americans—of whatever sexual orientation—who favor expanding same-sex marriage, by all means celebrate today's decision. Celebrate the achievement of a desired goal. Celebrate the opportunity for a new expression of commitment to a partner. Celebrate the availability of new benefits. But do not celebrate the Constitution. It had nothing to do with it.

I respectfully dissent.

## B    Reflections and Questions

1. An important precursor to *Obergefell v. Hodges* was the landmark ruling of *Lawrence v. Texas*, 539 U.S. 558 (2003), in which the United States Supreme Court declared unconstitutional laws prohibiting homosexual activity between consenting adults. The United States Supreme Court focused its analysis on *Lawrence v. Texas* on conceptions of liberty and freedom under the Due Process Clause of the Fourteenth Amendment, and how the Constitution protects individuals from unwarranted government intrusions. In the majority opinion, the Court referred to how:

   > Liberty protects the person from unwarranted government intrusions into a dwelling and other private places. In our tradition the State is not omnipresent in the home. And there are other spheres of our lives and existence, outside the home, where the State should not be a dominant presence. Freedom extends beyond spatial bounds. Liberty presumes an autonomy of self that includes freedom of thought, belief, expression, and certain intimate conduct ... The instant case involves liberty of the person both in its spatial and in its more transcendent dimensions. ...[56]
   > The petitioners are entitled to respect for their private lives. The State cannot demean their existence or control their destiny by making their private sexual conduct a crime. Their right to liberty under the Due Process Clause gives them the full right to engage in their conduct without intervention of the government. The Texas statute furthers no legitimate state interest which can justify its intrusion into the personal and private life of the individual ..."[57]

   The majority opinion in *Lawrence v. Texas* was also authored by Justice Kennedy, widely respected for his opinions advancing the rights of persons discriminated for their sexual orientation.

2. Notice in *Obergefell v. Hodges* the incorporation of the Equal Protection Clause in the Supreme Court's analysis of the Fourteenth Amendment and the concepts of rights, liberty, autonomy, and marriage under the United States Constitution. Compare the Majority Opinion in *Obergefell v. Hodges* with the Dissenting Opinion authored by Chief Justice John Roberts. What should be the role of courts and legislatures in deciding matters related to rights, family, and gender equality issues? Which should be the guiding criteria for courts to intervene in matters related to family and marriage?

3. The Supreme Court in *Obergefell* also refers to the role of courts in advancing human rights and rejecting forms of injustice. The Supreme Court refers in particular to how constitutional interpretation by the courts should protect rights, even when those rights are not yet protected in the law or in society as a whole. The democratic processes should not violate human rights.[58] In essence, individuals should be able to access courts to ensure the full enjoyment of their human rights, and do not need to wait for legislative change to see

---

[56]  Lawrence v. Texas, 539 U. S. _____ (2003), Majority Opinion, p. 1.
[57]  Lawrence v. Texas, 539 U. S. _____ (2003), Majority Opinion, p. 18.
[58]  *Id.*, pp. 24–25.

their rights protected.[59] Should courts be protecting human rights not protected already by the law? What should be the role of courts in human rights protection and the protection of the rights of women?

4. Even though *Obergefell* does not refer to international law, in many ways it advances principles already recognized by regional human rights protection systems in the area of marriage equality. For example, the Inter-American Court of Human Rights, in its Advisory Opinion 24/17, highlights the rights of homosexual persons to have recognition of their family relationships free from all forms of discrimination. [60] This requires states to ensure the right to marry to same sex-couples as a guarantee of equal dignity to persons historically the subject of discrimination. [61] The Inter-American Court of Human Rights, as well as the European Court of Human Rights, have also defined the notion of family in a non-traditional way, and how this institution should respond to the evolution of times in legal interpretation and analysis.[62] Can you think of ways that national courts – such as the United States Supreme Court – would benefit from referring to international law principles in judgments related to gender equality and the rights of women?

## VI    CONCLUSIONS: WHAT LIES AHEAD FOR LGBTI ISSUES AND WOMEN'S RIGHTS

The increasing protection of the rights of LGBTI persons by universal, regional, and national courts and entities signals an important expansion in the human rights of women. It is a necessary and welcomed development, and flexible legal interpretations are key for increased protection of lesbian, trans, bisexual, and intersex women. This development has also offered the international, regional, and national communities the opportunity to redefine the concept of women as beneficiaries of protection, adding important layers concerning their sexuality, identity, personal liberty, autonomy, and life plans. Today discrimination on the basis of sexual orientation and gender identity are fixtures of international law, and signal the wide scope and potential for future legal developments in the area of gender equality.

There are some key areas of development for legal standards in the future related to LGBTI persons. One of them is the opportunity that both universal and regional entities have to process individual case petitions in this area of the law, exemplifying for states what full LGBTI protection should look like at the national, local, and community levels. National courts have a leading role and voice here, interpreting national constitutions as protecting against discrimination on the basis of sexual orientation and gender identity; even when legal instruments even when legal instruments are not explicit. National courts also have a key role

---

[59]   *Id.*, pp. 24–25.
[60]   Inter-Am. Court H.R., Gender identity, and equality and non-discrimination with regard to same-sex couples. State obligations in relation to change of name, gender identity, and rights deriving from a relationship between same-sex couples (interpretation and scope of Articles 1(1), 3, 7, 11(2), 13, 17, 18 and 24, in relation to Article 1, of the American Convention on Human Rights), Advisory Opinion OC-24/17, ¶¶ 200–229 (Nov. 24, 2017), Series A No. 24.
[61]   *Id.*
[62]   *See* Schalk and Kopf v. Austria, App. No. 30142/04, Eur. Ct. H.R., ¶¶ 87–95 (June 24, 2010); Inter-Am. Court H.R., Advisory Opinion 24/17, *supra* note 60, ¶¶ 173–199; Inter Am. Court H.R., Atala Riffo and Daughters v. Chile, *supra* note 4, ¶¶ 141–146.

in the identification, development, and protection of rights, even when society still does not perceive this need for protection. Laws, public policies, and programs at the national and local levels also need to reflect the needs, voices, and demands of LGBTI communities and women.

It is also key to work at the social and community levels to address the prejudice, stigma, discrimination, and ongoing violence that still affect persons who are gay, lesbian, transgender, intersex, and those who defy social expectations with their sexual orientation, gender identity and expression, and sex characteristics. This is key to the full diversity and inclusion of our societies, and for the full respect, protection, and fulfillment of the rights of women. The representation and leadership also of women of diverse and non-conforming sexual orientations and gender identities is also paramount to the recognition of their needs in laws, public policies, and programs, and in society as a whole.

# 5. Women and times of emergency: the case of COVID-19

## I INTRODUCTION: TIMES OF EMERGENCY AND THEIR BURDENS ON WOMEN

During 2020–2021, the world was affected by the coronavirus pandemic.[1] The virus was first detected in Wuhan, China, and quickly spread to more than 200 countries around the world. On March 11, 2020, the World Health Organization called the outbreak a global pandemic, urging states to adopt prompt measures to stop the spread of the virus.[2]

As of May 24, 2021, there have been 166,984,785 global cases confirmed, and 3,466,670 deaths.[3] Just in the United States, there have been 32,947,548 cases and 587,342 deaths.[4]

In order to prevent further contagion, countries implemented a number of measures, including orders to shelter in place for all persons, curfews, and lockdowns; social distancing; the wearing of masks in public; and the closing of all businesses and schools. Most international flights were cancelled and borders were closed. Public life and mass gatherings stopped. Social interactions became virtual and limited. Millions of persons and their families were confined to their homes for months at a time. Hospitals became overburdened and thousands of health workers were on the front lines risking their lives every day to fight for the survival of those affected. Nursing homes, prisons, and health institutions became breeding grounds for the virus, causing numerous casualties. In simple words, life as we knew it stopped.

The COVID-19 pandemic is not the first major public health emergency to have a deep global impact. Another well-known pandemic of wide scope was the 1918 Spanish Flu, which affected approximately 500 million people globally, resulting in the death of close to 50

---

[1]    By the publication date of this book, the world is still reeling from the effects of the COVID-19 pandemic.

[2]    *See* World Health Organization, WHO Director-General's opening remarks at the media briefing on COVID-19 (11 March 2020), www.who.int/director-general/speeches/detail/who-director-general-s-opening-remarks-at-the-media-briefing-on-covid-19---11-march-2020.

[3]    *See* John Hopkins University & Medicine, Coronavirus Resource Center, *COVID-19 Case Tracker*, https://coronavirus.jhu.edu/map.html (last visited on May 24, 2021).

[4]    *See* Center for Diseases Control and Prevention, *United States COVID-19 Cases and Deaths by State*, https://covid.cdc.gov/covid-data-tracker/#cases_casesinlast7days (last visited on May 24, 2021).

million individuals.[5] More recently, other health events that gripped the world's attention were the HIV/AIDS virus[6] and the Ebola outbreak.[7]

The onset and development of the COVID-19 pandemic exemplifies the magnitude and human impact of times of emergency. COVID-19 was in general a formidable challenge for states and a test to the rule of law. States were forced to find immediate ways to control the spread of the virus, while at the same time preserving governance and human rights. Times of crisis greatly threaten the continuity of the work of national institutions; access to information, accountability, transparency, and freedom of speech; and access to justice. The COVID-19 pandemic also aggravated in many ways the inequality in our societies. Many persons, groups, and collectivities around the world still suffer daily forms of discrimination due to their sex, gender, race, ethnic background, age, and income status, among other variables. These groups were also overrepresented in the death rates from the COVID-19 virus, and faced significant delays in access to the new COVID-19 vaccines.[8]

Human rights violations in general accentuate in times of crisis. The coronavirus pandemic was no exception. Organizations such as Human Rights Watch promptly reported concerns over human rights issues in the state response to the coronavirus pandemic, including the lack of availability of accurate information on COVID-19; barriers to accessing needed health services, especially affecting marginalized populations; the imposition of quarantines and lockdowns of wide scope and unlimited length; travel bans and restrictions affecting asylum seekers and migrants; discrimination and xenophobia; lack of prevention measures in prisons, immigration detention centers, and other residential institutions affecting the elderly and those living with disabilities; and obstacles to accessing protective equipment for health workers.[9]

Women were also disproportionally impacted by the coronavirus pandemic. Even though all of humanity was affected by COVID-19, women suffered the burden in a very specific way. Women workers were suddenly at home full-time, caring for their children, the elderly, and the sick. They had to become immediately both virtual employees and teachers to do home schooling for their children. They were disproportionately affected by unemployment and the fluctuations in the economy. Women are overly represented in the informal economic sector, which resulted in many of them losing their livelihoods and living in poverty conditions.

---

[5] For more history and resources on the 1918 Spanish Flu, *see* Centers for Disease Control and Prevention, *1918 Pandemic (H1N1 virus)*, www.cdc.gov/flu/pandemic-resources/1918-pandemic-h1n1 .html (last visited on May 24, 2021).

[6] For more reading on the history of the HIV/AIDS epidemic, *see* World Health Organization, *Why the HIV epidemic is not over*, www.who.int/news-room/spotlight/why-the-hiv-epidemic-is-not-over (last visited on May 24, 2021).

[7] For a discussion of key moments in the Ebola outbreak, *see* Centers for Disease Control and Prevention, *2014–2016 Ebola Outbreak in West Africa*, www.cdc.gov/vhf/ebola/history/2014-2016 -outbreak/index.html (last visited on May 24, 2021).

[8] For more reading on these issues, *see* Don Bambino Geno Tai, Aditya Shah, Chyke A. Doubeni, Irene G. Sia, and Mark L. Wieland, *The Disproportionate Impact of COVID-19 on Racial and Ethnic Minorities in the United States*, 72(4) CLINICAL INFECTIOUS DISEASES 703–706 (2021), https://academic .oup.com/cid/article/72/4/703/5860249; Christina Morales, *Black and Latino Americans confront many challenges to vaccinations*, N.Y. TIMES, February 18, 2021, www.nytimes.com/2021/02/18/world/us -coronavirus-vaccine-minorities.html.

[9] *See* Human Rights Watch, *Human Rights Dimensions of COVID-19*, May 19, 2020, www.hrw.org/ news/2020/03/19/human-rights-dimensions-covid-19-response.

Orders restricting women to their homes also greatly increased their exposure to domestic violence and other forms of harm by their partners and family members. COVID-19 also curbed the ability of women to access needed sexual and reproductive health services, and access to health services in general. All these burdens were particularly heavy on women affected by poverty and a low-income status, and those who were elderly, indigenous, afro-descendent, migrants, and deprived of their liberty. Women from these groups have faced acute forms of discrimination historically, and the coronavirus worsened their risk and exposure.

Women were tested in the coronavirus pandemic and this modern emergency in their resilience, stamina, and survival skills. All of their human rights were challenged in some way during this crisis. Women, however, were also key to addressing the pandemic. Women constituted a large component of the health workers who were risking their lives daily to fight the disease and care for those affected. Some of the most visible country leaders fighting the pandemic were women, and with successful results. Women also compose a large group of the journalists, human rights defenders, and researchers who were bringing information daily to the public of the magnitude and spread of COVID-19. In the author's view, this is a moment with an important legacy in the way we perceive the development and effectiveness of human rights norms concerning women, and how they are applied when our humanity is tested. It is a moment that allowed us to see women as multidimensional beings, in many roles beyond victimhood, as political leaders, doctors, nurses, teachers, and heads of household.

This chapter explores the effects of the coronavirus pandemic on women and the worsening of discrimination and gender-based violence in times of emergency. The chapter also addresses state obligations to respect, protect, and fulfill the rights of women in times of crisis, and the gender perspective needed to adequately prevent and respond to structural problems such as discrimination and violence against women. Lastly, the chapter highlights the role of women as leaders and decision-makers in shaping policy, legislation, and government responses in times of emergency.

## II    DISCRIMINATION AND GENDER-BASED VIOLENCE DURING COVID-19

As discussed in Chapter 1, one of the most serious challenges women still face is discrimination, both systemic and structural. Discrimination comes in many forms, including disparate treatment in the family, employment, education, health services, and different areas of public and private life. Women can also suffer intersectional forms of discrimination, based on their sex, gender, race, ethnic background, income status, age, and other factors. As discussed in Chapter 2, one of the most extreme forms of discrimination is gender-based violence, still a widespread and alarming human rights issue affecting women and girls. These problems are aggravated during times of emergency.

All the factors that have historically exposed women to human rights violations, including stereotypes, expectations of the social roles that they should perform in society, and the unequal division of responsibilities within households, are accentuated in moments of crisis and unrest. As an example of this issue, the following readings discuss the impact of the COVID-19 pandemic on discrimination and violence against women.

**A       United Nations Secretary General, Policy Brief: The Impact of COVID-19 on Women**

April 9, 2020, pp. 2–3

The year 2020, marking the twenty-fifth anniversary of the Beijing Platform for Action, was intended to be ground-breaking for gender equality. Instead, with the spread of the COVID-19 pandemic even the limited gains made in the past decades are at risk of being rolled back. The pandemic is deepening pre-existing inequalities, exposing vulnerabilities in social, political and economic systems which are in turn amplifying the impacts of the pandemic.

Across every sphere, from health to the economy, security to social protection, the impacts of COVID-19 are exacerbated for women and girls simply by virtue of their sex:

- Compounded economic impacts are felt especially by women and girls who are generally earning less, saving less, and holding insecure jobs or living close to poverty.
- While early reports reveal more men are dying as a result of COVID-19, the health of women generally is adversely impacted through the reallocation of resources and priorities, including sexual and reproductive health services.
- Unpaid care work has increased, with children out-of-school, heightened care needs of older persons and overwhelmed health services.
- As the COVID-19 pandemic deepens economic and social stress coupled with restricted movement and social isolation measures, gender-based violence is increasing exponentially. Many women are being forced to "lockdown" at home with their abusers at the same time that services to support survivors are being disrupted or made inaccessible.
- All of these impacts are further amplified in contexts of fragility, conflict, and emergencies where social cohesion is already undermined and institutional capacity and services are limited.

…

COVID-19 is not only a challenge for global health systems, but also a test of our human spirit. Recovery must lead to a more equal world that is more resilient to future crises. Fiscal stimulus packages and emergency measures to address public health gaps have been put in place in many countries to mitigate the impacts of COVID-19. It is crucial that all national responses place women and girls – their inclusion, representation, rights, social and economic outcomes, equality and protection – at their center if they are to have the necessary impacts. This is not just about rectifying long-standing inequalities but also about building a more just and resilient world. It is in the interests of not only women and girls but also boys and men. Women will be the hardest hit by this pandemic but they will also be the backbone of recovery in communities. Every policy response that recognizes this will be the more impactful for it. To achieve this, the policy brief emphasizes three cross-cutting priorities:

1) ENSURE WOMEN'S EQUAL REPRESENTATION IN ALL COVID-19 RESPONSE PLANNING AND DECISION-MAKING. Evidence across sectors, including economic planning and emergency response, demonstrates unquestioningly that policies that do not consult women or include them in decision-making are simply less effective, and can even do harm. Beyond individual women, women's organizations who are often on the front line of response in communities should also be represented and supported.

2)    DRIVE TRANSFORMATIVE CHANGE FOR EQUALITY BY ADDRESSING THE CARE ECONOMY, PAID AND UNPAID. In the formal economy care jobs, from teachers to nurses, are underpaid in relation to other sectors. In the home, women perform the bulk of care work, unpaid and invisible. Both are foundational to daily life and the economy but are premised on and entrench gendered norms and inequalities.

3)    TARGET WOMEN AND GIRLS IN ALL EFFORTS TO ADDRESS THE SOCIO-ECONOMIC IMPACT OF COVID-19. It will be important to apply an intentional gender lens to the design of fiscal stimulus packages and social assistance programmes to achieve greater equality, opportunities, and social protection.

…

**B      Violence against women as the "shadow pandemic"**

Statement by Phumzile Mlambo-Ngcuka, Executive Director of UN Women
April 6, 2020

With 90 countries in lockdown, four billion people are now sheltering at home from the global contagion of COVID-19. It's a protective measure, but it brings another deadly danger. We see a shadow pandemic growing, of violence against women.

As more countries report infection and lockdown, more domestic violence helplines and shelters across the world are reporting rising calls for help. In Argentina, Canada, France, Germany, Spain, the United Kingdom, and the United States, government authorities, women's rights activists and civil society partners have flagged increasing reports of domestic violence during the crisis, and heightened demand for emergency shelter. Helplines in Singapore and Cyprus have registered an increase in calls by more than 30 per cent …

Confinement is fostering the tension and strain created by security, health, and money worries. And it is increasing isolation for women with violent partners, separating them from the people and resources that can best help them. It's a perfect storm for controlling, violent behavior behind closed doors. And in parallel, as health systems are stretching to breaking point, domestic violence shelters are also reaching capacity, a service deficit made worse when centers are repurposed for additional COVID-response.

Even before COVID-19 existed, domestic violence was already one of the greatest human rights violations. In the previous 12 months, 243 million women and girls (aged 15–49) across the world have been subjected to sexual or physical violence by an intimate partner. As the COVID-19 pandemic continues, this number is likely to grow with multiple impacts on women's wellbeing, their sexual and reproductive health, their mental health, and their ability to participate and lead in the recovery of our societies and economy.

Wide under-reporting of domestic and other forms of violence has previously made response and data gathering a challenge, with less than 40 per cent of women who experience violence seeking help of any sort or reporting the crime. Less than 10 per cent of those women seeking help go to the police. The current circumstances make reporting even harder, including limitations on women's and girls' access to phones and helplines and disrupted public services like police, justice and social services. These disruptions may also be compromising the care and support that survivors need, like clinical management of rape, and mental health and psycho-social support. They also fuel impunity for the perpetrators. In many countries the law is not on women's side; 1 in 4 countries have no laws specifically protecting women from domestic violence. …

COVID-19 is already testing us in ways most of us have never previously experienced, providing emotional and economic shocks that we are struggling to rise above. The violence that is emerging now as a dark feature of this pandemic is a mirror and a challenge to our values, our resilience and shared humanity. We must not only survive the coronavirus, but emerge renewed, with women as a powerful force at the center of recovery. …

## C	Reflections and Questions

1. The readings in this section exemplify the broad scope of the problems and challenges that can be faced by women during a time of emergency. One of the most affected areas during the COVID-19 pandemic has been women's home life. Women have historically suffered discrimination in the family and have assumed most of the caretaking of children and the elderly, even when they have a work life outside the home. This situation was aggravated by COVID-19. COVID-19 forced many women to assume home teaching of their children, due to the closing of schools and their transition to online teaching. Many women also needed additional child care since they are essential workers that cannot work from home. Which human rights obligations do states have under CEDAW to support women in the transition to home school teaching and with child care?[10]

2. According to General Comment 22 of the Economic, Social and Cultural Rights Committee, reproductive and sexual rights health services for women should be accessible, affordable, and of quality. The General Comment confirms also that the enforcement of the right to sexual and reproductive health is affected by social determinants of health, including social inequality and the unequal distribution of decision-making and resources on the basis of gender, ethnic origin, age, disability, and other factors. How can states guarantee accessibility, affordability, and quality of sexual and reproductive health services for women during times of emergency? How is this connected to the situation of women health workers and protections they need from COVID-19, and other associated risks?[11]

3. Many women who work in the informal sector have been negatively impacted by COVID-19 due to the closing of businesses and social distancing measures. Women in the informal sector have also not benefited from the state relief measures designed to counter the effects of COVID-19. Which measures can states adopt to ensure that women working in the informal sector have adequate financial relief due to loss of income produced by a pandemic?[12]

---

[10] For more reading, see Helen Lewis, *The Coronavirus is a Disaster for Feminism: Pandemics Affect Men and Women Differently*, THE ATLANTIC (March 19, 2020), www.theatlantic.com/international/archive/2020/03/feminism-womens-rights-coronavirus-covid19/608302/.

[11] For more reading, *see* General Comment 22 on the Right to Sexual and Reproductive Health, Article 12 of the International Covenant on Economic, Social and Cultural Rights, Committee on Economic, Social and Cultural Rights, E/C.12/GC/22 (May 2, 2016), ¶¶ 8, 11–21.

[12] For more reading, *see* Rachel Moussié and Silke Staab, UN Women, *Three Ways to Contain COVID-19's impact on informal women workers* (May 18, 2020), https://data.unwomen.org/features/three-ways-contain-covid-19s-impact-informal-women-workers.

4. One of the main concerns related to the situation of women during COVID-19 has been the alarming rates of domestic violence. Orders to shelter in place and lockdowns have forced women to stay in their homes for prolonged periods of time with partners and spouses who are perpetrators of domestic violence. In many regions of the world, there have been increases in the reporting of domestic violence incidents.[13] Shelters and courts – who have traditionally served as important places for women affected by domestic violence – have been closed or operating to a modified schedule. This situation has promoted that states should adopt alternative measures to report domestic violence incidents, including the development of new hotlines, and the possibility of reporting via WhatsApp and in pharmacies.[14]

## III    STATE OBLIGATIONS DURING PUBLIC EMERGENCIES: UNIVERSAL TREATIES

In times of emergency, states have an international law duty to protect the health, life, and personal integrity of their population. However, even in moments of crisis, there are a number of overarching human rights obligations and rule of law principles that still apply, including the duty to ensure that all state restrictions of any human rights are justified by the principles of legality, necessity, and proportionality, and are temporary. States are also obligated to act with due diligence to prevent, investigate, sanction, and grant reparations for human rights violations, and ensure a functioning justice system that holds persons accountable. States must also guarantee the respect, protection, and fulfillment of the rights to be free from discrimination and violence, and that health services of quality and affordability are accessible to all.

Below are excerpts of comments and statements adopted by United Nations treaty-based organs highlighting specific state obligations and legal standards which should guide human rights restrictions during states of emergency.

### A    Article 4: States of Emergency, Human Rights Committee

General Comment 29
CCPR/C/21/Rev.1/Add.11 (August 31, 2001)

2. Measures derogating from the provisions of the Covenant must be of an exceptional and temporary nature. Before a State moves to invoke article 4, two fundamental conditions must be met: the situation must amount to a public emergency which threatens the life of the nation, and the State party must have officially proclaimed a state of emergency. The latter requirement is essential for the maintenance of the principles of legality and rule of law at times when they are most needed. When proclaiming a state of emergency with con-

---

[13]    For more reading, *see for example*, International Rescue Committee, *IRC Data Shows an Increase in Reports of Gender-Based Violence Across Latin America* (June 9, 2020), www.rescue.org/press-release/irc-data-shows-increase-reports-gender-based-violence-across-latin-america.

[14]    For more reading, *see for example*, United Nations High Commissioner for Human Rights, *COVID-19 and Women's Human Rights: Guidance*, April 15, 2020, www.ohchr.org/documents/issues/women/covid-19_and_womens_human_rights.pdf.

sequences that could entail derogation from any provision of the Covenant, States must act within their constitutional and other provisions of law that govern such proclamation and the exercise of emergency powers; it is the task of the Committee to monitor the laws in question with respect to whether they enable and secure compliance with article 4. In order that the Committee can perform its task, States parties to the Covenant should include in their reports submitted under article 40 sufficient and precise information about their law and practice in the field of emergency powers.

3. Not every disturbance or catastrophe qualifies as a public emergency which threatens the life of the nation, as required by article 4, paragraph 1. During armed conflict, whether international or non-international, rules of international humanitarian law become applicable and help, in addition to the provisions in article 4 and article 5, paragraph 1, of the Covenant, to prevent the abuse of a State's emergency powers. The Covenant requires that even during an armed conflict measures derogating from the Covenant are allowed only if and to the extent that the situation constitutes a threat to the life of the nation. If States parties consider invoking article 4 in other situations than an armed conflict, they should carefully consider the justification and why such a measure is necessary and legitimate in the circumstances. On a number of occasions, the Committee has expressed its concern over States parties that appear to have derogated from rights protected by the Covenant, or whose domestic law appears to allow such derogation in situations not covered by article 4.

4. A fundamental requirement for any measures derogating from the Covenant, as set forth in article 4, paragraph 1, is that such measures are limited to the extent strictly required by the exigencies of the situation. This requirement relates to the duration, geographical coverage and material scope of the state of emergency and any measures of derogation resorted to because of the emergency. Derogation from some Covenant obligations in emergency situations is clearly distinct from restrictions or limitations allowed even in normal times under several provisions of the Covenant. Nevertheless, the obligation to limit any derogations to those strictly required by the exigencies of the situation reflects the principle of proportionality which is common to derogation and limitation powers. Moreover, the mere fact that a permissible derogation from a specific provision may, of itself, be justified by the exigencies of the situation does not obviate the requirement that specific measures taken pursuant to the derogation must also be shown to be required by the exigencies of the situation. In practice, this will ensure that no provision of the Covenant, however validly derogated from will be entirely inapplicable to the behaviour of a State party. When considering States parties' reports the Committee has expressed its concern over insufficient attention being paid to the principle of proportionality. …

7. Article 4, paragraph 2, of the Covenant explicitly prescribes that no derogation from the following articles may be made: article 6 (right to life), article 7 (prohibition of torture or cruel, inhuman or degrading punishment, or of medical or scientific experimentation without consent), article 8, paragraphs 1 and 2 (prohibition of slavery, slave-trade and servitude), article 11 (prohibition of imprisonment because of inability to fulfil a contractual obligation), article 15 (the principle of legality in the field of criminal law, i.e. the requirement of both criminal liability and punishment being limited to clear and precise provisions in the law that was in place and applicable at the time the act or omission took place, except in cases where a later law imposes a lighter penalty), article 16 (the recogni-

tion of everyone as a person before the law), and article 18 (freedom of thought, conscience and religion). The rights enshrined in these provisions are non-derogable by the very fact that they are listed in article 4, paragraph 2. …

8.  According to article 4, paragraph 1, one of the conditions for the justifiability of any derogation from the Covenant is that the measures taken do not involve discrimination solely on the ground of race, colour, sex, language, religion or social origin. …

## B          Guidance Note on CEDAW and COVID-19, CEDAW Committee

April 22, 2020

The Committee on the Elimination of Discrimination against Women (the Committee) expresses deep concern about exacerbated inequalities and heightened risks of gender-based violence and discrimination faced by women due to the current COVID-19 crisis and calls on States to uphold the rights of women and girls.

While many States consider restrictions on freedom of movement and physical distancing necessary to prevent contagion, such measures may disproportionately limit women's access to health care, safe shelters, education, employment and economic life. The effects are aggravated for disadvantaged groups of women and women in conflict or other humanitarian situations.

States parties to the Convention on the Elimination of All Forms of Discrimination against Women (the Convention) have an obligation to ensure that measures taken to address the COVID-19 pandemic do not directly or indirectly discriminate against women and girls. States parties also have an obligation to protect women from, and ensure accountability for, gender-based violence, enable women's socio-economic empowerment and guarantee their participation in policy and decision making in all crisis responses and recovery efforts …

In particular, the Committee calls on States parties to:

1.  **Address the disproportionate impact of the pandemic on women's health.** Gender bias in the allocation of resources and diversion of funds during pandemics worsen existing gender inequalities, often to the detriment of women's health needs. Women's disproportionate burden of caring for children at home and for sick or older family members as well as their high representation in the health workforce expose women to an increased risk of contracting COVID-19. States parties must address women's increased health risk through preventive measures and by ensuring access to early detection and treatment of COVID-19. States parties should also protect women health workers and other frontline workers from contagion through measures such as the dissemination of necessary precautionary information and adequate provision of personal protective equipment as well as psychosocial support.

2.  **Provide sexual and reproductive health as essential services.** States parties must continue to provide gender-responsive sexual and reproductive health services, including maternity care, as part of their COVID-19 response. Confidential access to sexual and reproductive health information and services such as modern forms of contraception, safe abortion and post-abortion services and full consent must be ensured to women and girls at all times, through toll-free hotlines and easy-to-access procedures such as online prescrip-

tions, if necessary free of charge. States parties should raise awareness about the particular risks of COVID-19 for pregnant women and women with pre-existing health conditions. They should provide manuals for health workers guiding strict adherence to prevention of infection, including for maternal health, during pregnancy, at-birth and the post-delivery period.

3. **Protect women and girls from gender-based violence.** During confinement, women and girls are at increased risk of domestic, sexual, economic, psychological and other forms of gender-based violence by abusive partners, family members, and care persons, and in rural communities. States parties have a due diligence obligation to prevent and protect women from, and hold perpetrators accountable for, gender-based violence against women. They should ensure that women and girls who are victims or at risk of gender-based violence, including those living in institutions, have effective access to justice, particularly to protection orders, medical and psycho-social assistance, shelters and rehabilitation programmes. National response plans to COVID-19 should prioritize availability of safe shelters, hotlines and remote psychological counselling services and inclusive and accessible specialized and effective security systems, including in rural communities, and address women's mental health issues, which stem from violence, social isolation and related depression. States parties should develop protocols for the care of women not admitted to such services due to their exposure to COVID-19, which includes safe quarantine and access to testing.

4. **Ensure equal participation of women in decision-making.** Governments, multilateral institutions, the private sector and other actors should ensure women's equal representation, including through women's rights organizations, meaningful participation and leadership in the formulation of COVID-19 response and recovery strategies, including social and economic recovery plans, at all levels and recognize women as significant agents for societal change in the present and post COVID-19 period. …

7. **Adopt targeted measures for disadvantaged groups of women.** States parties should uphold the SDG principle of 'Leave no one behind' promoting inclusive approaches in their legislative, policy and other measures. During the COVID-19 pandemic, they should reinforce measures to support disadvantaged or marginalized groups of women. …

## C    Reflections and Questions

1. Article 4(2) of the International Covenant on Civil and Political Rights explicitly indicates that no derogation will be accepted from a number of rights. These include the right to life codified in Article 6; the prohibition of torture or cruel, inhuman or degrading treatment in Article 7; and freedom of thought, conscience, and religion in Article 18. What is the difference between these rights and other human rights contained in the ICCPR?[15]

2. The CEDAW Committee in its Guidance Note on point 7 calls for "inclusive approaches in their legislative, policy and other measures" for women during the COVID-19 and other pandemics. How do you include the voices and an intersectional approach in the adoption

---

[15]   *See* Audrey Lebret, *COVID-19 Pandemic and Derogation to Human Rights*, 7(1) Journal of Law and Biosciences (May 4, 2020), https://academic.oup.com/jlb/article/7/1/lsaa015/5828398.

of legislation, programs, and services during public emergencies? How do you ensure that women are integrated in the response to COVID-19?[16]

3. COVID-19 has also worsened the gender digital divide, as will be discussed in more detail in Chapter 13. Women and girls – especially those from low-income and marginalized groups, and living in rural areas – face key barriers to access technology crucial to continuing schooling, performing work functions, and participating in social affairs and decision-making. Some of the challenges are high costs to access the internet and low computer availability. Women are also exposed to newer forms of violence in the digital and cyberworld, including bullying and hate speech.[17]

4. One of the groups of most concern regarding the impact of COVID-19 has been women deprived of liberty. Unsanitary prison conditions, overcrowding, and challenges to accessing adequate health care have been reported as some of the main contributors to the spread of COVID-19 in prisons. Which measures do you think can be adopted to protect those deprived of liberty from the spread of COVID-19?[18]

## IV    REGIONAL HUMAN RIGHTS PROTECTION SYSTEMS AND COVID-19

The regional human rights protection systems for Europe and the Americas have been adopting important statements highlighting the need to protect all human rights during the COVID-19 pandemic, including those of women and girls. These statements have been issued taking into consideration the rights and obligations contained in the leading treaties governing these systems, including the European Convention on Human Rights and the American Convention on Human Rights. The following readings illustrate the regional interpretations of state obligations and their scope in times of emergency to respect the rights of women and girls.

---

[16]    For more discussion, *see* Lowy Institute, The Interpreter, *Why Gender Matters in the Impact and Recovery from COVID-19*, March 20, 2020, www.lowyinstitute.org/the-interpreter/why-gender-matters-impact-and-recovery-covid-19; Organisation of Economic Co-operation and Development (hereinafter OECD), *Women at the Core of the Fight against COVID-19 Crisis*, Policy Brief (2020), Introduction and pp. 14–24, https://read.oecd-ilibrary.org/view/?ref=127_127000-awfnqj80me&title=Women-at-the-core-of-the-fight-against-COVID-19-crisis.

[17]    For more reading, *see* UN Women Executive Director Phumzile Mlambo-Ngcuka and Plan International CEO Anne-Birgitte Albrectsen, *We Cannot Allow COVID-19 to Reinforce the Gender Digital Divide*, May 6, 2020, https://www.unwomen.org/en/news/stories/2020/5/op-ed-ed-phumzile-covid-19-and-the-digital-gender-divide; United Nations Educational, Scientific, and Cultural Organization (UNESCO) and Broadband Commission for Sustainable Development, Working Group on the Digital Gender Divide, *Recommendations for action: bridging the gender gap in Internet and broadband access and use*, Executive Summary and pp. 18–44 (March 2017), www.broadbandcommission.org/Documents/publications/WorkingGroupDigitalGenderDivide-report2017.pdf.

[18]    For more reading, *see* European Committee for the Prevention of Torture and Inhuman or Degrading Treatment or Punishment (CPT), *Statement of principles relating to the treatment of persons deprived of their liberty in the context of the coronavirus disease (COVID-19) pandemic* (March 20, 2020), https://rm.coe.int/16809cfa4b; Office of the High Commissioner for Human Rights and World Health Organization, March 2020, Inter-Agency Standing Committee (hereinafter IASC), *Interim Guidance on COVID-19: Focus on Persons Deprived of Their Liberty* (March 27, 2020), https://interagencystandingcommittee.org/other/iasc-interim-guidance-covid-19-focus-persons-deprived-their-liberty.

**A** **Respecting democracy, rule of law, and human rights in the framework of the COVID-19 sanitary crisis: A toolkit for member states**

Council of Europe
SG/Inf(2020)11, April 7, 2020
© Council of Europe, Reproduced with Permission

The extent of measures taken in response to the current COVID-19 threat and the way they are applied considerably vary from one state to another in different points of time. While some restrictive measures adopted by member states may be justified on the ground of the usual provisions of the European Convention on Human Rights (Convention) relating to the protection of health (see Article 5 paragraph 1e, paragraph 2 of Articles 8 to 11 of the Convention and Article 2 paragraph 3 of Protocol No 4 to the Convention), measures of exceptional nature may require derogations from the states' obligations under the Convention. It is for each state to assess whether the measures it adopts warrant such a derogation, depending on the nature and extent of restrictions applied to the rights and freedoms protected by the Convention. The possibility for states to do so is an important feature of the system, permitting the continued application of the Convention and its supervisory machinery even in the most critical times.

Any derogation will be assessed by the European Court of Human Rights (Court) in cases that will be brought before it. The Court has granted states a large margin of appreciation in this field: "It falls in the first place to each Contracting State, with its responsibility for 'the life of [its] nation', to determine whether that life is threatened by a 'public emergency' and, if so, how far it is necessary to go in attempting to overcome the emergency. By reason of their direct and continuous contact with the pressing needs of the moment, the national authorities are in principle in a better position than the international judge to decide both on the presence of such an emergency and on the nature and scope of derogations necessary to avert it. In this matter Article 15 § 1 (…) leaves those authorities a wide margin of appreciation."

A derogation is also subject to formal requirements: the Secretary General of the Council of Europe, being the depository of the Convention, must be fully informed of the measures taken, of the reasons therefore, and of the moment these measures have ceased to operate …

Certain convention rights do not allow for any derogation: the right to life, except in the context of lawful acts of war (Article 2), the prohibition of torture and inhuman or degrading treatment or punishment (Article 3), the prohibition of slavery and servitude (Article 4§1) and the rule of "no punishment without law" (Article 7). There can be no derogation from abolishment of death penalty…

A derogation under Article 15 is not contingent on the formal adoption of the state of emergency or any similar regime at the national level. At the same time, any derogation must have a clear basis in domestic law in order to protect against arbitrariness and must be strictly necessary to fighting against the public emergency. States must bear in mind that any measures taken should seek to protect the democratic order from the threats to it, and every effort should be made to safeguard the values of a democratic society, such as pluralism, tolerance and broadmindedness. While derogations have been accepted by the Court to justify some exceptions to the Convention standards, they can never justify any action that goes against the paramount Convention requirements of lawfulness and proportionality. …

The principle of non-discrimination is highly relevant in the current context. When assessing whether derogating measures were "strictly required" under Article 15 of the Convention, the Court examines whether the measures discriminate unjustifiably between different categories of persons. Also, certain forms of discrimination can amount to degrading treatment proscribed by Article 3, a non-derogable provision. Moreover, the fact of not taking into account the specific needs of persons belonging to a disadvantaged group may result in discrimination. The prohibition of discrimination may thus entail obligations to take positive measures to achieve substantive equality. ...

## B      Pandemic and human rights in the Americas

Inter-American Commission on Human Rights
Resolution 1/2020, April 24, 2020

## A. INTRODUCTION
The Americas and the world are now facing an unprecedented global health emergency caused by the pandemic of the COVID-19 virus. Central to the measures taken by the States to address and contain the virus should be full respect for human rights.

The COVID-19 pandemic may seriously affect the full exercise of people's human rights because of the severe risks to life, health and personal safety that it poses, and may have an immediate, mid and long-term impact on societies as a whole, and on particularly vulnerable individuals and groups.

The Americas are the region of highest inequality on the planet, characterized by profound social divides where poverty and extreme poverty are problems that cut across all countries of the region, along with the lack of or poor access to drinking water and sanitation, food insecurity, environmental pollution and the lack of adequate housing. Added to this are high rates of informal sector jobs and meager incomes that adversely impact a large number of people in the region, and that make the socioeconomic impact of COVID-19 of even greater concern. All of this prevents or makes it difficult for millions of people to take basic measures to prevent the disease, mainly when it affects people who are in a particularly vulnerable situation.

The region is also characterized by high rates of generalized violence and particularly violence based on gender, race or ethnicity, and by the persistence of scourges such as corruption and impunity. In addition, citizens of the region are exercising their right of social protest in a context of disproportionate use of force, as well as acts of violence and vandalism; severe crises in the prisons that are touching the vast majority of countries; and the profoundly worrying expansion of the phenomenon of migration, forced internal displacement, refugees and stateless persons, and structural discrimination against particularly vulnerable groups.

In this context, the pandemic poses even more significant challenges for the countries of the Americas, both in terms of health policies and measures, and in their economic capacities, to enable them to set in motion measures to address and contain the virus. These measures are urgently needed to protect their peoples under international human rights law adequately.

The pandemic is also having different, intersectional impacts on the realization of the economic, social, cultural and environmental rights of certain groups that are particularly vulnerable. It is therefore essential that policies be adopted to effectively prevent contagion, as well as social security measures and access to public health care systems that can provide timely, affordable diagnosis and treatment, and give comprehensive, non-discriminatory physical and mental health care to people in a particularly vulnerable situation.

...

**Women [Recommendations for States]**

49. Include a gender perspective, based on an intersectional approach, in all government responses to contain the pandemic, taking into account the different contexts and conditions that could increase the vulnerability to which women are exposed, such as, inter alia, economic difficulties, age, status as a migrant or displaced person, disability, incarceration, ethnic or racial origin, sexual orientation, and gender identity and/or expression.

50. Ensure that women hold decision-making positions in committees and working groups that may be set up in response to the COVID-19 health crisis, and ensure that a gender perspective is included in the design, implementation, execution and monitoring of measures and policies adopted in response to this health crisis. In particular, incorporate a cross-cutting gender perspective, in light of the context and conditions that magnify the effects of the crisis, such as economic difficulties, status as a migrant or displaced person, incarceration, and ethnic or racial origin, among other things.

51. Enhance services that provide a response to gender violence, particularly violence within the family and sexual violence during confinement. Reformulate the traditional response mechanisms by adopting alternative channels for communication and strengthening community networks to expand complaint mechanisms and protection orders during the period of confinement. Also, develop protocols for care, and build the capacities of security officers and justice personnel involved in the investigation and punishment of acts of violence within the family. Distribute guidance on the management of such cases to all government institutions.

52. Offer differentiated care to female health care professionals working as front-line responders to the COVID-19 health crisis. In particular, offer them adequate resources to help them do their job, mental health care, and means of reducing their double workload as professionals and as homemakers.

53. Guarantee the availability and continuation of sexual and reproductive health services during the pandemic crisis, and particularly step-up comprehensive sex education measures and the distribution via accessible media of information in readily understandable language to reach the broad diversity of women. …

## C     Reflections and Questions

1.  One of the most important areas of human rights concern during the COVID-19 pandemic is related to the rights to participation, access to information, liberty, expression, and association. Many states imposed orders to shelter in place, lockdowns, and curfews which limited the ability to form mass gatherings and to discuss issues in a social setting. Can you think how these limitations impacted women in particular? Can women be disproportionately affected by restrictions during a public emergency even if they are not gender-specific?

2.  Both the universal and regional human rights protection systems have alluded to the element of necessity in their COVID-19 guidelines, and how any restrictions to human

rights must be justified by need. Which criteria should be considered in determining the need for human rights restrictions during a public emergency?[19]

3.  The right to life is at the center of any state response to a public emergency. International standards have been adopted affirming the negative and positive obligations that states have to protect the right to life. States have a negative obligation to prevent the arbitrary deprivation and loss of life. They also have a positive obligation to facilitate the conditions for the right to life to be properly respected and fulfilled; which entails ensuring that persons can lead a dignified life and form their own life plans. Therefore, states are first mandated during pandemics to adopt prompt and reasonable steps to curb contagion and prevent foreseeable loss of life. In a second dimension, states also have the duty to protect the life of health workers, human rights defenders, protesters, and journalists. In a third dimension, states have a duty to ensure the continuity of key services for women in the area of sexual and reproductive health, including access to obstetrics and gynecology services, contraception methods, and elements to make informed and autonomous decisions. How can states reconcile these three obligations during a public emergency? How is this obligation applicable to the situation of women and the different roles they perform in a pandemic?[20]

4.  The Inter-American Commission on Human Rights underscores how the Americas is the region of the world most affected by inequality. It is also one of the most diverse regions in the world. It integrates many racial and ethnic groups, languages, and nationalities. It has high numbers of indigenous populations, for example. Indigenous peoples in the Americas have faced a history of discrimination, exclusion, and marginalization. They are still fighting daily to see their rights to self-determination, consultation, their territories, national resources, non-discrimination, and effective participation fully respected. They also face inequalities and obstacles in access to basic economic, social, and cultural rights such as access to health care, water, food security, and formal employment. Indigenous women – as is discussed in Chapter 3 – face an increased risk of violations of their human rights due to their status as indigenous and their sex and gender. There is emerging data illustrating that indigenous peoples were disproportionately affected by COVID-19. What do you think is the role of international law, human rights law standards, indigenous self-governance structures, and community responses in countering and mitigating the effects of COVID-19 on indigenous peoples? How do you ensure that state policies include a gender, indigenous women, intersectional, and intercultural perspective in all public policies when addressing a public emergency such as COVID-19?[21]

---

[19]   *See for reference*, United Nations High Commissioner for Human Rights, *COVID-19: States should not abuse emergency measures to suppress human rights – UN experts* (March 16, 2020), www .ohchr.org/EN/NewsEvents/Pages/DisplayNews.aspx?NewsID=25722&LangID=E.

[20]   *See* Anand Grover, former U.N. Special Rapporteur on the right of everyone to the enjoyment of the highest attainable standard of physical and mental health, and Ximena Casas, Women's Rights Researcher at Human Rights Watch, *Protecting Women's Reproductive Health during a Pandemic* (March 12, 2020), www.hrw.org/news/2020/05/12/protecting-womens-reproductive-health-during -pandemic; Jonathan Cooper, *Dignity, the Right to Life, and the Coronavirus*, Oxford Human Rights Hub (March 23, 2020), https://ohrh.law.ox.ac.uk/dignity-the-right-to-life-and-the-coronavirus/.

[21]   *See* Report of the Special Rapporteur on the rights of indigenous peoples, José Francisco Calí Tzay, *Rights of indigenous peoples*, A/75/185, pp. 16–49 (July 20, 2020); Canadian Feminist Alliance for International Action (FAFIA) and Dr. Pamela Palmater, Chair in Indigenous Governance at Ryerson

**D        Practical exercise: Analysis of COVID-19 restrictions with a human rights perspective**

During 2020–2021, countries in Europe and the Americas had to implement a series of restrictions to the activities of their populations to contain the spread of COVID-19. Some of the measures included the following:

(1)    strict orders to shelter in place, quarantines, and curfews;
(2)    directives to close schools, businesses, and places of employment;
(3)    social distancing measures in public places;
(4)    the suspension of international flights; and
(5)    the restriction of the entry of foreigners to their countries.

Review the compatibility of these measures with the European Convention on Human Rights and the American Convention on Human Rights. In your analysis, consider the following aspects:

- individual human rights that could be at stake;
- possible criteria to justify the restriction of rights;
- groups of the population that can be negatively affected or can derive a benefit from these measures, including women and girls;
- the existence or non-existence of alternative measures to fulfill the same objective;
- additional information from states that may be needed to evaluate these measures.

# V        WOMEN AS LEADERS IN TIMES OF CRISIS

Women shone as political leaders during the COVID-19 pandemic. Countries that had women leaders fared better in COVID-19 contagion statistics and in mortality rates. Some important examples were the leaders of Germany, New Zealand, and Taiwan.[22] The COVID-19 pandemic and its response have strengthened the case for female leadership.

Many media outlets have been documenting how women may possess traits which are advantageous for leadership during times of public emergencies. Women were also at the helm of some of the most important international organizations confronting this crisis, including the United Nations High Commissioner for Human Rights. CEDAW in its Articles 7 and 8 mandates states to adopt all measures at their disposal to ensure that women can effectively participate in the policymaking process of their countries, hold public office, and perform public duties at all levels of government.

The following readings illustrate the role of women leaders during the COVID-19 pandemic, and what this may mean for female leadership in times of future crisis.

---

University, *Impact of the COVID-19 Pandemic on Indigenous Women and Girls in Canada*, pp. 4–10 (June 19, 2020), http://fafia-afai.org/wp-content/uploads/2020/06/P.-Palmater-FAFIA-Submission -COVID19-Impacts-on-Indigenous-Women-and-Girls-in-Canada-June-19-2020-final.pdf.

[22]    For more discussion, *see* Supriya Garikipati and Uma Kambhampati, *Women Leaders are Better at Fighting the Pandemic*, VoxEU CEPR (June 21, 2020), .

A          **COVID-19 and women's leadership: from an effective response to building back better**

UN Women, 2020

### Women are leading the way

Women are Heads of State and Government in only 21 countries worldwide, but their leadership has been lauded for its greater effectiveness in managing the COVID-19 health crisis. Women Heads of Government in Denmark, Ethiopia, Finland, Germany, Iceland, New Zealand and Slovakia are being recognized for the rapidity of the response they are leading, which has not only included measures to 'flatten the curve'—such as confinement measures, social distancing and widespread testing—but also the transparent and compassionate communication of fact-based public health information. In countries such as Canada, Ethiopia, India and Madagascar, women medical and health experts are increasingly found in leadership positions and taking the lead in daily press briefings and public service announcements. Women mayors across the world, from Banjul (the Gambia) to Barcelona (Spain), have been highly visible in responding to the pandemic and are sharing their experiences in online forums.

The leadership styles of women leaders in the COVID-19 response have been described as more collective than individual, more collaborative than competitive and more coaching than commanding. It is noteworthy that in 2019—prior to the pandemic—nearly half of the world's population (47 per cent) believed that men made better political leaders than women. Today, lower COVID-19 death rates and effective virus containment policies in countries led by women are disproving the discriminatory social norms driving these beliefs. …

New burdens risk further hindering women's participation. During the pandemic, many women are shouldering additional domestic and care work at home and are facing threats related to the virus and its effects, which may negatively impact their ability to participate fully in public life. Measures should be taken to address these burdens, including through the provision of protective equipment for women who work in their communities, access to information and funding and changes in working practices. For example, if parliaments are deciding on new procedures to deliberate and take decisions during the pandemic, they should take into account the needs of women legislators and staff, who may have more care duties at home but should still be involved in passing emergency laws, allocating resources and scrutinizing government spending. …

The many existing examples of women who are leading effective and inclusive responses to the pandemic should encourage governments, elected officials and UN agencies to propel more women into decision-making processes and support more gender-balanced institutions. While governments have the most visible role in facilitating women's equal representation and participation in decision-making, parliamentarians and local elected officials—as well as UN agencies, non-governmental organizations (NGOs) and the private sector—all have a role to play. …

## B   Inter-American Model Law on the Prevention, Punishment and Eradication of Violence against Women in Political Life[23]

Follow-Up Mechanism to the Convention of Belém do Pará – MESECVI
Organization of American States

This law represents the first regional effort to define the problem of political violence against women by incorporating the inter-American and international legal framework; as well as to identify responsible bodies and action guidelines in relation to prevention, care, punishment and redress of this violence, including the role of the National Machineries for Women. In addition, it seeks to determine what type of acts of political violence should be sanctioned, distinguishing between serious and very serious offenses, and criminal offenses, indicating the punishments that can be applied.

Among the main contributions of this norm is the consecration of the right of women to a political life free from violence and the definition of the concept of violence against women in the political life, following the definitions established in the Belém do Pará Convention and by the CEDAW Committee in its General Recommendation No. 19 (1992). The key to the definition of political violence against women is found in the expression "based on gender." The concept thus encompasses any manifestation of violence in the political sphere directed against women by virtue of their being women, or disproportionately affecting women, the purpose or result of which is to fully or partially prevent women from enjoying their political rights. Thus, this violence is produced by the fact of being a woman and participating in public and political space, bearing in mind that it is not the physical space where the violence takes place that defines it, but rather the power relations that exist in that space.

In keeping with the provisions of the Convention, the Model Law also distinguishes the areas in which political violence, such as: the private or family sphere when a partner prevents a woman from voting or from accessing the polls; the public sphere, referring to the violence that can occur, for example, in a political party, a neighborhood association or through communications media; and at the level of the State, as is the case of violence perpetrated by persons in government positions …

One of the most innovative aspects of the Model Law is the establishment of the link between political violence against women and the achievement of political parity, taking as a reference the work of the CIM in this area. This perspective was embodied in the Declaration on Political Harassment and Violence against Women, which states that the problem of political violence against women shows that the achievement of political parity in democracy is not exhausted by the adoption of quotas or electoral parity, but requires a comprehensive approach that ensures, on the one hand, the equal access of women and men to all State institutions and political organizations, and on the other, to ensure that the conditions in the exercise are free from discrimination and violence against women at all levels and spaces of political life. …

### Chapter I General Provisions

### Article 3. Definition of violence against women in the political life

---

[23]   Property of the General Secretariat of the Organization of American States; reproduced with permission. All rights reserved.

For the effects of this law, "violence against women in the political life" shall be understood as any action, conduct or omission, carried out directly or through third parties that, based on gender, causes harm or suffering to a woman or to various women, which has the effect or purpose of impairing or nullifying the recognition, enjoyment or exercise by women of their political rights.

Violence against women in the political life may include, but is not limited to, physical, sexual, psychological, moral, economic or symbolic violence. ...

### Article 5. Spheres of violence
Violence against women in the political life has as its object or result undermining or nullifying the recognition, enjoyment or exercise of women's political rights and can take place:

a)    Within the family or domestic unit or in any other interpersonal relationship.
b)    In any public sphere, including all public, private, and mixed organizations such as political parties; trade unions; communications media and social networks.
c)    That is perpetrated or condoned by the state, or its agents regardless of where it occurs.

### Article 6. Manifestations of violence against women in the political life
Violence against women in the political life shall be understood, among other actions, as any conduct, action or omission that, based on gender:

a)    (Femicide) Cause, or may cause, the violent death of women because of their participation or political activity.
b)    Physically attacks one or several women with the effect or purpose of reducing or nullifying their political rights.
c)    Sexually attacks one or several women, or provokes an abortion, with the effect or purpose of reducing or nullifying their political rights.
d)    Involves unwanted sexual proposals, touching, approaching, or invitations that influence the political aspirations of women and the conditions and environment where political and public activity takes place.
e)    Threatens, frightens or intimidates, in any way, one or several women and/or their families with the effect or purpose of nullifying her political rights, including resignation of the position or function that they hold or exercise, or to which they postulate. ...

### C       Reflections and Questions

1.  As the reading from UN Women indicates *supra*, even though women have been lauded for their leadership during the COVID-19 pandemic, many steps are still needed to ensure that they are fully represented in decision-making processes during times of crisis. Some of the recommendations to improve the situation by UN Women are that governments at all levels should ensure gender balance in all decision-making spaces related to COVID-19; the harnessing of existing gender equality institutions and mechanisms in the pandemic response; ensuring that gender equality concerns are incorporated in the design and implementation of national COVID-19 policy responses and budgets; improving access to public information for women and their organizations; and supporting the work of

women's organizations in the response to COVID-19.[24] Can you think of other steps that states should take to ensure that women are fully represented in decision-making processes during times of emergency?

2. There are a series of important goals and concepts related to the participation of women in public and political life that have been identified by universal and regional human rights bodies. One is the concept of *effective participation*, alluding to not only the numeric nature of women's inclusion in politics, but also their ability to influence key decision-making.[25] Participation has been differentiated from *representation*, which refers more to the actual reflection of women's needs and priorities in legislation, policies, programs, and other measures.[26] *Parity* has also become an important goal of the international community, promoting that women should be represented numerically and in a balanced way in comparison to their male counterparts.[27] Parity also requires an articulated approach to ensure that women have equality in access to all state institutions, organizations, and have the conditions to exercise their political life free from all forms of discrimination and stereotypes. These goals are particularly key in issues concerning peace, and security, the resolution of armed conflicts, and transitional justice; processes in which women still have limited participation.[28] How do you think that the concepts of effective participation, representation, and parity are related? Do you always need the effective participation of women to achieve adequate representation of gender issues? Do women always need to sit in the negotiation table to be represented?

3. One of the most important challenges that women face to exercise their political rights, be elected, and stay in public office is *political violence*. Political violence can be in the form of physical, psychological, and sexual violence and harassment, and can result in killings and the ceasing of political activities.[29] Political violence can be perpetrated by both

---

[24] UN Women, *COVID-19 and Women's Leadership: From an Effective Response to Building Back Better* (2020), pp. 5–7.

[25] For more discussion, *see* U.N. Working Group on the Issue of Discrimination against Women in Law and in Practice, *Report on Women's Equal, Full, and Effective Participation in Political and Public Life in the Context of Democracy and Human Rights, including in Times of Political Transition*, ¶¶ 37–44 (2013), http://idsn.org/wp-content/uploads/user_folder/pdf/New_files/UN/SP/HRC23_Report_UN_WG_discrimination_against_women_in_law_and_practice.pdf.

[26] For a discussion of the link between the concepts of participation, representation, inclusive, and representative democracies, *see* Inter-American Commission on Human Rights, *The Road to Substantive Democracy: Women's Political Participation in the Americas*, Executive Summary, OEA/Ser.L/V/II. Doc. 79 (April 18, 2011).

[27] For a connection between the problem of gender-based violence and political parity, *see* Follow-Up Mechanism to the Convention of Belém do Pará (MESECVI), *Declaration on Political Harassment and Violence against Women*, p. 8, www.oas.org/es/mesecvi/docs/DeclaracionViolenciaPolitica-EN.pdf. The goal of gender balance in governmental bodies and entities was also identified as a needed state action in the Beijing Platform of Action. *See* Beijing Declaration and Platform of Action, September 15, 1995, ¶ 190(a), www.un.org/en/events/pastevents/pdfs/Beijing_Declaration_and_Platform_for_Action.pdf (hereinafter Beijing Declaration and Platform of Action).

[28] As a relevant reference, *see* U.N. S.C. Res. 1325, S/RES/1325 (October 31, 2000).

[29] For more reading on the forms, causes, and consequences of political violence, *see* U.N. Special Procedures, U.N. High Commissioner for Human Rights, and UN Women, *Violence against Women in Politics, Expert Group Meeting Report & Recommendations*, March 8–9, 2018, New York, pp. 7–15, www.unwomen.org/en/digital-library/publications/2018/9/egm-report-violence-against-women-in-politics.

government and private actors to impede women from exercising their rights to vote, to be elected to office, to hold political positions, and to be leaders of human rights organizations. As the MESECVI Model Law indicates, the problem of political violence tends to be more acute at the local level. One of the complexities of the problem of political violence is the wide range of actors that may be involved, including husbands, partners, community members, elected officials, and political parties, just to name a few. Political violence and harassment can also occur in the digital and social media setting, as women increasingly use the internet to influence public and political life, as will be discussed in Chapter 13. Another key challenge is that the problem of political violence is not yet reflected in the legislation of most countries. This casebook has discussed the duty of states to act with due diligence towards all forms of gender-based violence. Which steps can states take to prevent, investigate, sanction, and grant reparations towards acts of political violence? What can political parties and communities do to prevent and address this problem?

4. Can you think of qualities that help women be effective leaders during times of emergency? News reports and studies have highlighted women's empathy, compassion, participatory styles, and emotional intelligence as key aspects. Are these stereotypes about women leaders? Can men also have these qualities in leadership? Remember the discussion on stereotypes in Chapter 1.[30]

5. Are all women leaders the same? What qualities do they share or not share? Compare the styles of Jacinda Ardern, President of New Zealand; Angela Merkel, Chancellor of Germany; and Tsa Ing-wen, President of Taiwan.[31]

6. Women are participating more in politics every day. They hold positions as presidents, legislators, and judges in many countries. However, women still face many challenges to reach real decision-making positions in their countries, and important barriers, such as family responsibilities; lack of day care options; limited campaign funding and resources; resistance from political parties; and stereotypes and double standards of women's leadership.[32] The CEDAW Committee calls on states in its Article 7 to eliminate discrimination in the political and public life of their countries, and ensure that women participate on an equal footing with men in voting during elections, in the formulation of government policy, and in participation in non-governmental organizations. In this regard, the CEDAW Committee and the Inter-Parliamentary Union issued a joint call on March 8, 2021 for National Action Plans to Achieve Gender Parity by 2030.[33] They recommended the inclusion of specific targets in national action plans, including gender parity goals achieving

---

[30] For more reflections, *see* Andreas Kluth, *Women Have Been Better Leaders than Men during the Pandemic*, Bloomberg Opinion (August 26, 2020), www.bloomberg.com/opinion/articles/2020-08-26/female-leaders-such-as-ardern-merkel-have-handled-coronavirus-better-than-men.

[31] *See* Shelley Zalis, NBC News, *In the COVID-19 Era, Female Leaders are Shining – Here's Why* (June 9, 2020), www.nbcnews.com/know-your-value/feature/covid-19-era-female-leaders-are-shining-here-s-why-ncna1227931.

[32] For good statistics on this issue, *see* Inter-Parliamentary Union and UN Women, *Women in Politics: 2019*, https://www.unwomen.org/en/digital-library/publications/2019/03/women-in-politics-2019-map. *See also*, U.N. News, *Political Participation of Women Suffering Serious Regression, UN General Assembly President Warns* (March 12, 2019), https://news.un.org/en/story/2019/03/1034521.

[33] *See Joint Call by the United Nations Committee on the Elimination of Discrimination against Women and the Inter-Parliamentary Union for National Action Plans to achieve gender parity by 2030*, International Women's Day (March 8, 2021), www.ipu.org/iwd-2021-statement.

equal representation of men and women; the repeal of laws which discriminate against women; the adoption of laws to prevent and criminalize gender-based violence against women in politics; to mobilize media formats and technological tools; and to incentivize political parties. Men still hold most political power globally, including in key institutions such as the executive, legislative, and judicial branches of government; political parties; and the media. What is the role of men in achieving the targets identified by CEDAW and the IPU?

## VI    CONCLUSIONS: THE LONG-TERM EFFECTS OF COVID-19 ON THE HUMAN RIGHTS OF WOMEN

COVID-19 has been a watershed moment which has deeply impacted the lives of women globally. It has illustrated the need for more adequate and equal access to child care, technology, economic relief, and participation spaces during times of crisis. It has also offered the international community the opportunity to see women in all their roles – as leaders, workers, mothers, health providers, journalists, human rights defenders, and researchers. It is a moment that has made us reconceptualize the way international law applies to the daily lives of women, especially in times of crisis. COVID-19 has also worsened the situation of discrimination and gender-based violence, and had a formidable impact on women already at increased exposure to human rights violations, including those deprived of liberty, those indigenous and afro-descendent, and those low-income and most marginalized.

COVID-19 can also end up transforming the way women work, lead, care for their children, and use technology in the future. International law can provide an important roadmap and structure for these transformations, and can itself evolve to respond to contemporary times and the realities and challenges posed by COVID-19.

# 6.   Due diligence in the contemporary world: the era of *MeToo*, non-state actors, and social protest

## I   INTRODUCTION: THE INTRICATE NATURE OF DUE DILIGENCE AND STATE RESPONSIBILITY IN THE ERA OF *METOO*

The *MeToo* movement flourished in 2017, when millions of women joined in revealing their experiences of sexual violence in both public and private spaces. Many famous women publicly denounced rape, sexual violence, and harassment perpetrated by high-profile executives and powerful personalities in the media and the Hollywood industry, among other sectors. Various leading figures lost their positions and industry influence due to accusations from many women of patterns of sexual violence and harassment.[1] The *MeToo* movement started in the United States and became a global phenomenon.[2]

The *MeToo* movement was also joined by social protests and campaigns in many countries, demanding the eradication of gender-based violence and justice for these crimes. Women have been on the streets seeking change and accountability for ongoing violence.[3]

The *MeToo* movement and this wave of social protests shed light on the ongoing nature and wide scope of the problem of gender-based violence. It also confirmed the important role of private actors in perpetrating and tolerating acts of violence against women, in particular in the workplace. These tendencies also revealed that most cases of gender-based violence still end in impunity with perpetrators largely unsanctioned, which fuels the repetition of these crimes. Even though there has been an important wave of universal and regional treaties promoting better state responses to gender-based violence, as well as legislation, public policies, and programs, these have been largely ineffective in preventing and eradicating this serious problem.[4]

---

[1]   For more reading, *see* MeToo, *History & Inception*, 2020, https://metoomvmt.org/get-to-know-us/history-inception/ (last visited on May 19, 2021).

[2]   For more discussion, *see* THE WASHINGTON POST, *#MeToo is at a crossroads in America. Around the world, it's just beginning* (May 8, 2020), www.washingtonpost.com/opinions/2020/05/08/metoo-around-the-world/.

[3]   For examples, *see* Isabel Kennon and Grace Valdevitt, *Women Protest for their Lives: Fighting Femicide in Latin America*, Atlantic Council (Feb. 24, 2020), www.atlanticcouncil.org/blogs/new-atlanticist/women-protest-for-their-lives-fighting-femicide-in-latin-america/.

[4]   Jeni Klugman, *Gender Based Violence and the Law*, Background Paper for World Development Report 2017, ¶¶ 1–4, 6–40, https://pubdocs.worldbank.org/en/232551485539744935/WDR17-BP-Gender-based-violence-and-the-law.pdf.

This poses the question of what happens after the *MeToo* movement? How can we achieve real prevention of gender-based violence? How can the administration of justice be adequate and effective in investigating and sanctioning the acts denounced through the *MeToo* movement? How can we build societies and cultures guided by respect for women and the fostering of their life plans and full potential? How can we fulfill the promise of the due diligence standard? These are all questions that are explored in this chapter.

## II   DUE DILIGENCE: PREVENTION, INVESTIGATION, SANCTION, AND REPARATIONS

Due diligence at this stage has found expression in treaties, declarations, resolutions, and national legislation. It is a well-known benchmark of state responsibility for acts of gender-based violence. Universal and regional human rights mechanisms have defined it in theory as the obligation to prevent, investigate, sanction, and grant reparations. Many universal and regional bodies, as well as scholars and experts, have been trying to define the content of what it means to prevent, investigate, sanction, and grant reparations, and the scope of these obligations for states. States are required to organize their entire structure to act with due diligence to prevent and respond to gender-based violence. However, there is still great discussion of the scope and reach of these state obligations and how to make them effective. The *MeToo* movement confirmed that the path to full compliance with the due diligence standard is long and challenging. These are issues discussed in the following two readings.

**A     Report of the Special Rapporteur on violence against women, its causes, and consequences, Yakin Erturk, *The due diligence standard as a tool for the elimination of violence against women***

E/CN.4/2006/61, January 20, 2006

*Summary*
… The 1993 Declaration on the Elimination of Violence against Women as well as other international instruments adopted the concept of due diligence, in relation to violence against women, as a yardstick to assess whether the State has met its obligation. Under the due diligence obligation, States have a duty to take positive action to prevent and protect women from violence, punish perpetuators of violent acts and compensate victims of violence. However, the application of the due diligence standard, to date, has tended to be State-centric and limited to responding to violence when it occurs, largely neglecting the obligation to prevent and compensate and the responsibility of non-State actors.

The current challenge in combating violence against women is the implementation of existing human rights standards to ensure that the root causes and consequences of violence against women are tackled at all levels from the home to the transnational arena. The multiplicity of forms of violence against women as well as the fact that this violence frequently occurs at the intersection of different types of discrimination makes the adoption of multifaceted strategies to effectively prevent and combat this violence a necessity.

In this regard, the potential of the due diligence standard is explored at different levels of intervention: individual women, the community, the State and the transnational level. At each level, recommendations for relevant actors are highlighted. The report concludes that if we continue to push the boundaries of due diligence in demanding the full compliance of States with international law, including to address the root causes of violence against women and to hold non-State actors accountable for their acts of violence, then we will move towards a conception of human rights that meets our aspirations for a just world free of violence. ...

*Prevention*

38. As a general rule, States have sought to discharge their due diligence obligations of prevention of violence against women through the adoption of specific legislation, the development of awareness-raising campaigns and the provision of training for specified professional groups. The forms of violence covered by these interventions include; domestic violence, sexual assault, trafficking, "honour crimes" and sexual harassment. These programmes tend to view violence against women as a stand-alone issue and there are relatively few examples of linkages being made between violence and other systems of oppression. ...

*Protection*

47. There are many measures undertaken by States in terms of their due diligence obligation to protect, which consist mainly of provision of services to women, such as telephone hotlines, health care, counselling centres, legal assistance, shelters, restraining orders and financial aid to victims of violence. According to government reports, shelters are generally run by NGOs with State or external donor funding. In certain States, protective services are given a legislative basis either within formally adopted action plans or strategies on violence against women or within legislation on domestic violence. This does not appear to be the norm, however, and most countries include protective mechanisms in their programmes on violence against women without stipulating the legal bases for these services. ...

50. The obligation to investigate and appropriately punish acts of violence against women with due diligence has, in the main, been seen by States as an obligation to adopt or modify legislation while reinforcing the capacities and powers of police, prosecutors and magistrates. A number of States noted recent amendments to their criminal codes in order to modify or repeal discriminatory provisions and to ensure that violent acts are met with appropriate punishments. As mentioned previously, some States have adopted specific legislation on domestic violence and trafficking which establish new criminal offences and often provide for the creation of specialized investigatory or prosecutorial units. ...

*The potential of the due diligence standard*

74. The current understanding and application of the due diligence standard as well as the gaps and challenges identified above highlight the need to re-imagine the standard so that it responds more effectively to violence against women. The major potential that I see for expanding the due diligence framework lies (a) in the full implementation of generalized obligations of prevention and compensation, and in the effective realisation of existing obligations to protect and punish, and (b) in the inclusion of relevant non-State actors as the bearers of duties in relation to responding to violence against women. ...

76. Therefore, in exercising due diligence to effectively implement human rights law – in order to prevent, protect, prosecute and provide compensation with regard to violence against women – States and other relevant actors must use multiple approaches in intervening at different levels: the individual, community, State and the transnational arena. …

## B     *Opuz v. Turkey*, European Court of Human Rights

App. 33401/02, June 6, 2009
© Council of Europe, reproduced with permission
Citations and footnotes omitted

*In this case, the applicant filed a number of complaints with the authorities for at least eight assaults perpetrated by her ex-husband, H.O., involving threats, beatings, and murder attempts. The complaints were later withdrawn by the applicant and the investigations were discontinued. H.O. eventually shot the applicant's mother on March 11, 2002 resulting in her death. H.O. was convicted and sentenced to life imprisonment, but was eventually released. The appeal proceedings were still pending before the Court of Cassation in Turkey. The excerpts below are related to the Court's analysis of the right to life under Article 2 and the prohibition of discrimination under Article 14 of the European Convention on Human Rights and their applicability to cases of domestic violence.*

128.   The Court reiterates that the first sentence of Article 2 § 1 enjoins the State not only to refrain from the intentional and unlawful taking of life, but also to take appropriate steps to safeguard the lives of those within its jurisdiction. This involves a primary duty on the State to secure the right to life by putting in place effective criminal-law provisions to deter the commission of offences against the person backed up by law-enforcement machinery for the prevention, suppression and punishment of breaches of such provisions. It also extends in appropriate circumstances to a positive obligation on the authorities to take preventive operational measures to protect an individual whose life is at risk from the criminal acts of another individual.

129.   Bearing in mind the difficulties in policing modern societies, the unpredictability of human conduct and the operational choices which must be made in terms of priorities and resources, the scope of the positive obligation must be interpreted in a way which does not impose an impossible or disproportionate burden on the authorities. Not every claimed risk to life, therefore, can entail for the authorities a Convention requirement to take operational measures to prevent that risk from materialising. For a positive obligation to arise, it must be established that the authorities knew or ought to have known at the time of the existence of a real and immediate risk to the life of an identified individual from the criminal acts of a third party and that they failed to take measures within the scope of their powers which, judged reasonably, might have been expected to avoid that risk. Another relevant consideration is the need to ensure that the police exercise their powers to control and prevent crime in a manner which fully respects the due process and other guarantees which legitimately place restraints on the scope of their action to investigate crime and bring offenders to justice, including the guarantees contained in Articles 5 and 8 of the Convention.

130. In the opinion of the Court, where there is an allegation that the authorities have violated their positive obligation to protect the right to life in the context of their above-mentioned duty to prevent and suppress offences against the person, it must be established to its satisfaction that the authorities knew or ought to have known at the time of the existence of a real and immediate risk to the life of an identified individual or individuals from the criminal acts of a third party and that they failed to take measures within the scope of their powers which, judged reasonably, might have been expected to avoid that risk. Furthermore, having regard to the nature of the right protected by Article 2, a right fundamental in the scheme of the Convention, it is sufficient for an applicant to show that the authorities did not do all that could be reasonably expected of them to avoid a real and immediate risk to life of which they have or ought to have knowledge. This is a question which can only be answered in the light of all the circumstances of any particular case. ...

133. Turning to the circumstances of the case, the Court observes that the applicant and her husband, H.O., had a problematic relationship from the very beginning. As a result of disagreements, H.O. resorted to violence against the applicant and the applicant's mother therefore intervened in their relationship in order to protect her daughter. She thus became a target for H.O., who blamed her for being the cause of their problems. ...

135. Furthermore, the victims' situations were also known to the authorities and the mother had submitted a petition to the Diyarbakır Chief Public Prosecutor's Office, stating that her life was in immediate danger and requesting the police to take action against H.O. However, the authorities' reaction to the applicant's mother's request was limited to taking statements from H.O. about the mother's allegations. Approximately two weeks after this request, on 11 March 2002, he killed the applicant's mother.

136. Having regard to the foregoing, the Court finds that the local authorities could have foreseen a lethal attack by H.O. While the Court cannot conclude with certainty that matters would have turned out differently and that the killing would not have occurred if the authorities had acted otherwise, it reiterates that a failure to take reasonable measures which could have had a real prospect of altering the outcome or mitigating the harm is sufficient to engage the responsibility of the State. Therefore, the Court will next examine to what extent the authorities took measures to prevent the killing of the applicant's mother. ...

137. The Government claimed that each time the prosecuting authorities commenced criminal proceedings against H.O., they had to terminate those proceedings, in accordance with the domestic law, because the applicant and her mother withdrew their complaints. In their opinion, any further interference by the authorities would have amounted to a breach of the victims' Article 8 rights. The applicant explained that she and her mother had had to withdraw their complaints because of death threats and pressure exerted by H.O.

138. The Court notes at the outset that there seems to be no general consensus among States Parties regarding the pursuance of the criminal prosecution against perpetrators of domestic violence when the victim withdraws her complaints. Nevertheless, there appears to be an acknowledgement of the duty on the part of the authorities to strike a balance between a victim's Article 2, Article 3 or Article 8 rights in deciding on a course of action. In this connection, having examined the practices in the member States, the Court observes that there are certain factors that can be taken into account in deciding to pursue the prosecution:

- the seriousness of the offence;
- whether the victim's injuries are physical or psychological;
- if the defendant used a weapon;
- if the defendant has made any threats since the attack;
- if the defendant planned the attack;
- the effect (including psychological) on any children living in the household;
- the chances of the defendant offending again;
- the continuing threat to the health and safety of the victim or anyone else who was, or could become, involved;
- the current state of the victim's relationship with the defendant and the effect on that relationship of continuing with the prosecution against the victim's wishes;
- the history of the relationship, particularly if there had been any other violence in the past; and
- the defendant's criminal history, particularly any previous violence. …

143.   In the Court's opinion, it does not appear that the local authorities sufficiently considered the above factors when repeatedly deciding to discontinue the criminal proceedings against H.O. Instead, they seem to have given exclusive weight to the need to refrain from interfering with what they perceived to be a "family matter". Moreover, there is no indication that the authorities considered the motives behind the withdrawal of the complaints. This is despite the applicant's mother's indication to the Diyarbakır Public Prosecutor that she and her daughter had withdrawn their complaints because of the death threats issued and pressure exerted on them by H.O. It is also striking that the victims withdrew their complaints when H.O. was at liberty or following his release from custody. …

153.   Moreover, the Court concludes that the criminal-law system, as applied in the instant case, did not have an adequate deterrent effect capable of ensuring the effective prevention of the unlawful acts committed by H.O. The obstacles resulting from the legislation and failure to use the means available undermined the deterrent effect of the judicial system in place and the role it was required to play in preventing a violation of the applicant's mother's right to life as enshrined in Article 2 of the Convention. The Court reiterates in this connection that, once the situation has been brought to their attention, the national authorities cannot rely on the victim's attitude for their failure to take adequate measures which could prevent the likelihood of an aggressor carrying out his threats against the physical integrity of the victim. There has therefore been a violation of Article 2 of the Convention. …

199.   The Court has established that the criminal-law system, as operated in the instant case, did not have an adequate deterrent effect capable of ensuring the effective prevention of unlawful acts by H.O. against the personal integrity of the applicant and her mother and thus violated their rights under Articles 2 and 3 of the Convention.

200.   Bearing in mind its finding above that the general and discriminatory judicial passivity in Turkey, albeit unintentional, mainly affected women, the Court considers that the violence suffered by the applicant and her mother may be regarded as gender-based violence which is a form of discrimination against women. Despite the reforms carried out by the Government in recent years, the overall unresponsiveness of the judicial system and impunity enjoyed by the aggressors, as found in the instant case, indicated that there was insufficient commitment to take appropriate action to address domestic violence. …

202.  In view of the above, the Court concludes that there has been a violation of Article 14 of the Convention, read in conjunction with Articles 2 and 3, in the instant case.

## C    Reflections and Questions

1.  Former U.N. Special Rapporteur Yakin Erturk underscores the need for multifaceted strategies to fully realize the promise of the due diligence standard in the realm of gender-based violence. She discusses in particular the different levels of intervention needed to accomplish this goal, including working with individual women, the community, the state, and the transnational level. Can you think of examples of multifaceted strategies to be implemented in these different areas?[5]

2.  The former U.N. Special Rapporteur also discusses the importance of prevention to address gender-based violence effectively. Prevention entails the adoption of legislation, programs, and awareness-raising campaigns, and a well-functioning justice system to sanction crimes. Even though some regions of the world, like the Americas, have adopted extensive legislation to address the different dimensions of gender-based violence, this problem is still widespread around the world. A variety of existing laws address concretely the problems of domestic violence, gender-based violence, femicide, and feminicide. The adoption of legislation in itself, however, has proven insufficient to curb forms of gender-based violence. Which steps do you believe can make legislation more effective at the national level to prevent and respond to gender-based violence?[6]

3.  The former U.N. Special Rapporteur also discusses the state-centric nature of the analysis of the due diligence standard to date. Different universal and regional bodies have identified the need to explore the due diligence standard for gender-based violence committed by non-state actors. Many of the case decisions reviewed in this textbook, including *Opuz v. Turkey* discussed *supra*, involve acts of gender-based violence perpetrated by private actors. Gender-based violence is perpetrated by private individuals and in the context of corporations, international organizations, non-governmental entities, religious institutions, and transnational entities. Some of these non-state actors, such as corporations and businesses, have more members, population, and financial power than states themselves. Should these non-state actors be held to the same standard of due diligence responsibility as states? Should states be held responsible for the acts of non-state actors?[7]

4.  *Opuz v. Turkey* exemplifies the relationship of the rights to life and to be free from torture, inhuman, and degrading treatment with the duty to act with due diligence to address gender-based violence. In order to safeguard these rights, government authorities must act

---

[5]  For good examples, *see* U.N. Secretary General, *Report on Intensification of efforts to eliminate all forms of violence against women and girls*, A/75/274, July 30, 2020, ¶¶ 7–9, 12–34, https://undocs .org/en/A/75/274; Rashida Manjoo, *The Continuum of Violence against Women and the Challenges of Effective Redress*, 1(1) INT'L. HUM. RTS. L. REV. 16–29 (2012).

[6]  For more reading, *see* Rosa Celorio, *Having Strong Gender-Based Violence Laws Isn't Enough*, AMERICAS QUARTERLY (October 21, 2020), https://americasquarterly.org/article/having-strong-gender -violence-laws-isnt-enough/.

[7]  For more reading, *see* HURST HANNUM, DINAH SHELTON, S. JAMES AND ROSA CELORIO, *Who Has Legal Obligations under International Human Rights Law?*, *in* INTERNATIONAL HUMAN RIGHTS; PROBLEMS OF LAW, POLICY, AND PRACTICE (Wolters Kluwer Publishers, 6th ed., 2017).

promptly, exhaustively, and use all available means to prevent, investigate, and sanction acts of domestic violence. The Court highlights the knowledge requirement, which is particularly important when complaints have been submitted before the authorities. The Court goes as far as indicating that authorities may be considered to have known of imminent acts of domestic violence even when the complaints have been withdrawn by the victims. Domestic violence victims can withdraw complaints due to death threats and economic dependence on the aggressor. The European Court of Human Rights holds that government authorities still have an obligation to protect victims of domestic violence, even when they withdraw their complaints. Can this be contrary to a woman's autonomy and privacy?[8]

5. The *Opuz v. Turkey* judgment was historic for the European Court of Human Rights in recognizing the connection between gender-based violence and discrimination. Even though this link has been the hallmark of developments in the area of international law concerning gender equality issues, the European Court of Human Rights had been largely silent on this issue. It is also noteworthy that the European Court of Human Rights in this case referred to international precedent from the CEDAW Committee and the Inter-American Commission on Human Rights highlighting this important connection.[9]

## III THE *METOO* MOVEMENT: TURNING THE INVISIBLE VISIBLE

One of the most important achievements of the *MeToo* movement is that it brought to light the experiences of violence against women of all ages, races, and income levels. It also incorporated the widespread nature of gender-based violence into daily conversation and the news. It was in many ways a very catalytic moment for women globally, joined with a call for prevention, action, and accountability. The movement propelled a reflection of how social institutions need to be transformed to prevent gender-based violence, including the need to establish reporting avenues for these acts, to respect the credibility of the victims, and to sanction these crimes. The readings below discuss the impact of this movement and its legacy.

### A   Confronting Sexual Violence, Demanding Equality

International Women's Day Statement, United Nations Women's Human Rights Experts
Geneva, Tuesday, March 6, 2018

A time to pay tribute to women
For more than a hundred years, the world has commemorated International Women's Day. Each year this Day presents an occasion to celebrate the progress on the road of women's right to equality. It is an occasion to be reminded that the road remains long and full of obstacles.

---

[8]   For more reading, *see* Cheryl Hannah, *Health, Human Rights, and Violence against Women and Girls: Broadly Redefining Affirmative State Duties after Opuz v. Turkey*, 34 HASTINGS INT'L & COMP. L. REV. 127, 136–147 (2011); Rosa Celorio, *Introductory Note to the European Court of Human Rights: Opuz v. Turkey*, 48 INT'L LEGAL MATERIALS 907–908 (2009).

[9]   For more reading, *see* Opuz v. Turkey, App. No. 33401/02, Eur. Ct. H.R., ¶¶ 72–86 (2009); Sarah Murphy, *Domestic Violence as Sex Discrimination: Ten Years since the Seminal European Court of Human Rights Decision in Opuz v. Turkey*, 51 N.Y.U. J. INT'L L. & POL. 1347, 1347–1357 (2019).

It is a time to pay tribute to the countless women throughout history who have dared to stand up, to protest, and to say no to discrimination against women and girls and one of its worst manifestations: violence. Their courage and revolt have been the driving force behind the progress made.

This year we seize this moment to pay tribute to the brave women who have spoken out against sexual harassment and other forms of sexual violence which they have been subjected to at the hands of abusive men who enjoyed impunity made possible by environments which normalise such violence. Through their courageous actions, these women have launched a global movement of women breaking the silence on sexual harassment and all other forms of sexual violence too often tolerated.

We also seize the moment to honour all those women who endure violence in silence because their voices are not heard, or they are threatened for speaking out. We honour the domestic workers in the confines of private homes in a foreign land, the migrant women and asylum seekers on the move, women who struggle to feed their children, and women who are deprived of liberty. We pledge our support through our respective mandates.

A universal plague

It is the voices of so many individual women, together, that has created this powerful move-ment which has swept much of the globe, building on decades of advocacy from women's rights movements demanding an end to violence against women. The individual stories of being subjected to sexual violence have painted a collective picture of our society. The ques-tion being asked is no longer whether to believe the woman, but rather what is wrong with our society. How can sexual violence exercised against women exist on such a massive and endemic scale in a time of peace and in the most ordinary places of life: work places, schools, universities, on the streets, in public transportation, and at home? From North to South, from East to West, sexual violence crosses lines of culture, religion, ideology, stages of economic development and touches women of all social backgrounds and in all professional settings, whether it is in political parties, financial institutions, or the media and entertainment industry, academic institutions and the humanitarian field. It happens in the family. It is truly a universal plague.

Concentration of power

The universal nature of sexual violence against women and girls is only a reflection of centu-ries of domination and oppression of one sex over the other, which has kept women in a sec-ondary place, long excluded from public life and from positions of power. The consequences of this inequality linger on today and resurge forcefully at times where we see women are scarcely represented in national and global political and economic decision-making bodies, but concentrated in precarious employment and often paid less. We see women who live in situations of dependence, economically and professionally, for existence and for advancement. Women experience life, from childhood to old age, as inferior and disadvantaged rather than as equals. They are held back by deeply entrenched but often invisible forces, be they political, economic, cultural, or religious. We see the undying will for control over women's bodies and their autonomy, and the tendency of seeing women as objects. In so many spheres of life, there is still a concentration of power and entitlement in the hands of men and the abuse of this power through sexual violence.

A significant moment

History will tell what a pivotal moment this movement is for women's rights. Women, with the power of their loud and clear voices, individually and collectively, have always been the active driving forces for social and cultural change. We have a moment now where the shame and fear have shifted from the victims to the side of abusers and perpetrators of sexual violence, who have to face the consequences of their unacceptable behaviour in many cases and criminal acts in others. The all-powerful are no longer the untouchable who can enjoy impunity with peace of mind. Their ability to buy silence and cover-up is being questioned and their power of intimidation is starting to evaporate. We have a moment where the complacence of others and the indifference of our institutions are no longer accepted without challenge. Blaming the victim can no longer be the automatic response to sexual violence.

This is a transformative moment, a liberating and an empowering moment. By speaking out at this scale, women are shaking centuries-old established discriminatory norms which normalise, accept and justify sexual violence against women and have constrained women in well-defined roles of inferiority and subordination. This is what is so significant about the moment. It is no longer just about individuals, it is about society. It is not about so-called morals and honour, it is about women's rights as human rights. It is the system of the concentration of power and domination that is being challenged.

Making it a truly global movement

We need to maintain the momentum to make it a truly global movement which reaches all the women and girls in places where breaking silence on violence against women is still taboo and where women have little resort to justice and no choice other than carrying the burden of shame and blame. It is in these places, far away from the spotlights of international media, that the voices of women need to be heard and must be heard.

History has also taught us that full equality for women everywhere will continue to be a long struggle. Every step forward in the direction of women's independence and equality has encountered push-backs from an alliance of conservative forces. It has been 70 years since women's right to equality was enshrined in the Universal Declaration of Human Rights and nearly 40 years since a ground-breaking comprehensive international treaty on women's rights, the Convention on the Elimination of All Forms of Discrimination against Women, came into existence. Waiting for another hundred years to achieve equality is unacceptable, as is rolling back our hard fought gains.

The existence of law and policy in combating sexual harassment and other forms of sexual violence is important but not sufficient. Equality between women and men is a struggle of humanity, a struggle for both men and women. In the face of sexual violence and discrimination, everyone is concerned and everyone needs to act.

**B      Allison Page and Jacqueline Arcy, # *MeToo and the Politics of Collective Healing: Emotional Connection as Contestation***

COMMUNICATION, CULTURE AND CRITIQUE, 1–16 (2019)
Reproduced with permission from Oxford University Press
Citations and footnotes omitted

In 2006, Tarana Burke first used MeToo to create solidarity among survivors of sexual violence, developing her vision of "empowerment through empathy" specifically to support fellow survivors of color. Emphasizing the intersections between racialized and gendered violence, Burke began the MeToo movement to address the lack of support resources for survivors of color, particularly in the U.S. south. For Burke, the affective potential of connecting survivors to one another uses "the power of empathy to stomp out shame" and, further, addresses sexual violence as an epidemic that cannot be solved through momentary spurts of public attention and outcry.

More than a decade later, the viral spread of the #MeToo hashtag began in October 2017 in response to a tweet by white actress Alyssa Milano, soliciting widespread documentation of the extent of sexual violence: "If all the women and men who have been sexually harassed, assaulted or abused wrote 'me too' as a status, we might give people a sense of the magnitude of the problem. #metoo." Within the first 24 hours, there were more than 12 million social media posts from people using the hashtag to share personal stories of abuse and harassment, and to convey words of support for survivors. By the end of 2017, there were over 6.5 million tweets with the hashtag. In an unsurprising maneuver—occluding and expunging the work of women of color—media sources were quick to credit Milano and other white, female celebrities with founding the movement, erasing Burke's efforts and initial vision. Feminist and antiracist activists have raised concerns about the erasure of Burke and other women of color from the #MeToo movement. We share this critique, and are thus interested in theorizing how the particular emotions expressed on digital media—including rage, pain, and solidarity—work toward Burke's original project of mass healing and ending sexual violence through a restorative approach that does not bolster the prison-industrial complex.

In this article, we argue that the affective economy of #MeToo aligns with Burke's ongoing vision by focusing on collective healing and care. #MeToo participants engaging in emotional care work—affective labor done in service to others—have created digital support networks that provide a foundation for a politics of care that is antithetical to a punishment model reliant on surveillance, policing, and imprisonment, which destroys communities, sidelines survivors, and devalues healing. The caring labor involved in these ephemeral exchanges fosters connection and support: feelings that are crucial to healing. We define a politics of care as a transformative and holistic framework that attends to, rather than erases, the emotional aspects of survivorship and creates a foundation for restorative justice. We therefore see the collective expression of rage, pain, and solidarity as a potential tool for building a politics of care that could supersede a reliance on the state and the logics of incarceration.

The #MeToo movement, therefore, suggests an alternative to popular and carceral feminisms, which dominate digital spaces and contemporary feminist politics. Emphasizing individual empowerment and visibility over collectivity and structural change, popular feminism, which has flourished alongside "popular misogyny," predominantly views consumer culture as the locus of resistance. Unsurprisingly, #MeToo has been commodified—there are MeToo necklaces to accompany tote bags bearing slogans about empowerment—and used to justify punitive measures akin to carceral feminism, which is a strand of feminism that relies on and collaborates with the carceral state and promotes incarceration, surveillance, and increased policing as a feminist solution to sexual and gender violence. Neither formation emphasizes collective care nor centers healing, both of which are central to restorative justice. By contrast, the #MeToo movement's focus on healing and connection twists the digital attention economy's logics of quantification and visibility in ways that exceed capital …

… #MeToo offers a basis for restorative justice through its emphasis on centering survivors and care, rather than punishment; simply put, this is a prerequisite for establishing alternative modes of justice and reparation. These are not new ideas, and scholars and activists working on prison abolition, in particular, have long theorized a world where justice does not equal incarceration. By looking to the state, carceral feminism seeks solutions to gender-based and sexual violence at the very site of violence for many, including people of color, trans and queer people, and poor people. Carceral logics inform and uphold rape culture: as such, the prison will never undo it. Yet as Ruth Wilson Gilmore makes plain, prison abolition requires forging new ways of being, not just abolishing old ones. The values of restorative justice—including care, repair, and healing—are the same that infuse the ways that #MeToo has been taken up online. In its current iteration, #MeToo is not an example of restorative justice, but rather contributes to an emotional framework required of alternatives to carcerality by centering care and healing. According to anti-prison activist Vicki Law, the "criminal punishment system" is incapable of addressing healing "because the survivor has nothing to do with it." #MeToo is thus one small slice of a much larger cultural shift needed to transform justice …

## C    Reflections and Questions

1. One of most important discussion points that has emerged from the *MeToo* movement is how to develop adequate and effective avenues to report cases of gender-based violence. Historically, women have faced many challenges to report acts of sexual violence and harassment in the workplace and other sectors, including voids in and the inadequate functioning of complaint mechanisms, potential stigma, a perceived lack of credibility, and reprisals. The problem has been particularly acute as many gender-based violence acts are perpetrated by male high-level figures, executives, decision-makers, and supervisors. Highly influenced by the *MeToo* movement, in 2019 the International Labour Organization adopted a new Convention Concerning the Elimination of Violence and Harassment in the World of Work.[10] The Convention recognizes that gender-based violence and harassment in the employment setting are human rights violations and a threat to the goals of equality and decent work.[11] In Article 10, the new ILO Convention mandates states to ensure easy and safe access to reporting mechanisms in cases of workplace violence and harassment, including protection against reprisals for those who submit complaints. What do you think are important features of reporting mechanisms for gender-based violence?[12]

2. An area of study after the *MeToo* movement is access to justice and the steps needed to ensure that cases of gender-based violence are adequately sanctioned. Most cases of gender-based violence still end in impunity, sending a social message that acts of

---

[10]    *See* International Labor Convention 190, Convention Concerning the Elimination of Violence and Harassment in the World of Work, adopted in Geneva, June 21, 2019, www.ilo.org/wcmsp5/groups/public/---ed_norm/---relconf/documents/meetingdocument/wcms_711570.pdf.

[11]    *See id.*, Preamble and Article 1(b).

[12]    For more reading, *see* Human Rights Watch, *Two Years after MeToo#: New Treaty Anchors Workplace Protections* (December 20, 2019), www.hrw.org/news/2019/12/20/two-years-after-metoo-new-treaty-anchors-workplace-protections.

gender-based violence will be socially tolerated, which fuels their repetition. Even after *MeToo*, and as will be discussed in section IV of this chapter, there are still many women protesting in the streets to demand accountability for gender-based crimes. According to the CEDAW Committee, a proper access to justice for gender-based violence is "multidimensional"; encompassing the guarantee of remedies for victims and an administration of justice system that is available, accessible, and of good quality. The CEDAW Committee has also underscored important obstacles to an adequate and effective access to justice, including the high concentration of courts and quasi-judicial bodies in cities and their non-availability in rural areas; the financial resources needed to access courts; the intricate nature and length of legal proceedings; the scarcity of high-quality legal advice; and judgments which are not gender sensitive. A state review of existing legislative frameworks to ensure that they do not discriminate against women in theory and in practice is also paramount.[13]

3. Many women have come forward during the *MeToo* movement and shared their stories of gender-based violence. What do you think could be the best ways to promote accountability for these crimes and access to justice? Which kinds of remedies would be the most effective to address cases of gender-based violence – criminal, civil or administrative? How can employer harassment and discrimination policies and laws be reviewed to facilitate access to justice?[14]

4. As Allison Page and Jacqueline Arcy discuss in their article, the *MeToo* movement also offers the opportunity to reflect on the concept of justice for cases of gender-based violence. Much of the emphasis has been on criminal sanctions for these crimes. As discussed earlier, a wide variety of legislation has been adopted providing for criminal penalties and civil sanctions for these crimes, but these acts still continue occurring on an endemic scale. This provokes the question of whether approaches more oriented towards collective healing, care, and restorative justice may be important to explore to effectively address gender-based violence and prevent its recurrence. This is key due to the disproportionate and negative effects of incarceration policies on racial groups and those socially disadvantaged. As discussed throughout this book, justice and accountability are important hallmarks of the due diligence obligation of states towards violence against women. Which do you think could be five principles to guide conceptions of justice to address cases of gender-based violence in the future? How can restorative justice, collective healing, and care be incorporated in the due diligence response by states to gender-based violence?

5. Another important aspect raised in the article by Allison Page and Jacqueline Arcy is the role of technology when it comes to addressing gender-based violence. As is discussed in Chapter 13 of this book, technology is now a fixture in the daily lives of many women, and a key vehicle for their effective participation socially. However, the digital space, the internet, and social media outlets can be important settings for acts of violence against women.

---

[13]  *See* General Recommendation 33 on Women's Access to Justice, Committee on the Elimination of Discrimination against Women, CEDAW/C/GC/33, ¶¶ 1, 13, and 21 (July 23, 2015).

[14]  For more reading, *see* Elizabeth C. Tippett, *The Legal Implications of the MeToo Movement*, 57 MINNESOTA LAW REVIEW 237–272, 288–298 (2018), https://scholarship.law.umn.edu/cgi/viewcontent.cgi?article=1056&context=mlr; Time's Up, *Turning Pain into Action: Ensuring Safe Work for All*, https://timesupnow.org/work/safety/turning-pain-into-action-ensuring-safe-work-for-all/ (last visited on May 19, 2021).

Technology may be critical as well for the effective prevention, reporting, and sanctioning of gender-based violence and in the pursuit of justice for these crimes. Can you think of creative ways to use technology to address and prevent gender-based violence?

6. How do you prevent *MeToo*? How do you change the behavior of employers? The Time's Up Legal Defense Fund was created in January of 2018 to address workplace harassment. It works with the National Women's Law Center Fund and the Time's Up Foundation, and connects victims to attorneys, supports them with legal fees, and provides media assistance. The Fund supports many low-income employees who suffer sexual harassment and other forms of sexual violence in the workplace. This initiative is backed by more than 300 women in the entertainment business in the United States and has a network of 700 attorneys supporting victims.[15]

7. As transformative labor practices, Time's Up has recommended several steps to employers to prevent sexual harassment and ensure a safe working environment. They have called on employers to establish anonymous reporting avenues and educate employees about how to use these; to consistently monitor workplace conditions through the use of climate surveys; to create a complaint mechanism for reprisals; to hold investigations with independent entities; and to be consistent in disciplinary measures.[16] Other recommendations include creating an Ombudsperson figure to receive complaints, and to complete investigations even when the alleged harasser resigns or retires. Employers should also reevaluate existing policies and enforce training and cultural changes that prevent the repetition of sexual harassment. Inclusion and diversity should also be important hiring goals. Employers should also revisit provisions in employment contracts – such as non-disclosure agreements, confidentiality clauses, and arbitration requirements that protect alleged harassers. They also recommend placing alleged harassers on leave and relieving them of supervisory duties when claims meet a baseline of credibility. Employers should also publicly announce that they will take seriously allegations of harassment and retaliation. What other measures do you think employers can adopt to ensure a workplace free from sexual harassment?

8. The stories of sexual harassment of many women of different races and ethnicities have also been brought to light during the *MeToo* movement. Many women from diverse racial groups are often marginalized and low-income, which increases their exposure to sexual harassment in the workplace. They are also frequently absent from discussions and in the identification of measures to end sexual harassment. Many activists and scholars are advocating for a transformation of the workplace culture with an intersectional approach, considering the experiences of African-American, Latinx, Indigenous, and women from other racial and historically discriminated groups.[17] Many of their violence stories are

---

[15] For more information, *see Our Story: TIME'S UP was born when women said "enough is enough"*, https://timesupnow.org/about/our-story/ (last visited on May 19, 2021).

[16] For more reading, *see* Time's Up, *Leading with Transparency: Recommended Practices for Employers When a High-Profile Individual Is Accused of Sexual Harassment* (October 21, 2019), https://timesupfoundation.org/recommended-practices-for-employers-when-a-high-profile-individual-is -accused-of-sexual-harassment/.

[17] Trina Jones and Emma E. Wade, *Me Too: Race, Gender, and Ending Workplace Sexual Harassment*, 27 DUKE J. GENDER L. & POL'Y 203, 206–214 (2020); Jessica Prois and Carolina Moreno,

still hidden and underreported. They have a crucial role in the finding of solutions to the alarming problem of gender-based violence.

## IV    NON-STATE ACTORS AND DUE DILIGENCE

Non-state actors have an active role in the human rights issues that women still face today. Acts of gender-based violence and discrimination are committed by private individuals in many settings, including the family; the workplace; and in education, health, and religious institutions. Many private actors are involved in perpetrating gender-based violence, including individuals, family members, businesses, international organizations, religious institutions, illegal groups, and users of social media platforms, among others. Some of these private actors have more members, resources, and influence than states themselves.

As discussed previously, the current international human rights law system was conceived to restrain state authority towards the individual. It has served to define important state obligations to protect the human rights of all, including women. States are required to refrain from committing violations to the rights to life, to personal integrity, and to be free from torture and inhuman and degrading treatment.

However, the contemporary world contains many non-state actors whose actions have negative repercussions on women's life, integrity, dignity, privacy, and life plans. What are the obligations of states to supervise and regulate the actions of these non-state actors? Should non-state actors be held accountable in the same way as states when they commit human rights violations against women? Should states bear international responsibility for harm committed by non-state actors? These are questions explored by the case, reflections, and questions below.

### A    Excerpts from *Jessica Lenahan (Gonzalez et al. v. United States)*

Inter-American Commission on Human Rights
No. 80/11, Case 12.626 (2011)
Citations and footnotes omitted

*This case is related to the domestic violence faced by Jessica Lenahan and the tragic deaths of her three daughters due to the non-enforcement of her restraining order. The Inter-American Commission on Human Rights discusses in the excerpts below the United States' affirmative obligation to act with due diligence under the American Declaration, and its relevance for cases of domestic violence against women.*

115.    The Commission begins analyzing this first question by underscoring its holding at the admissibility stage, that according to the well-established and long-standing jurisprudence and practice of the inter-American human rights system, the American Declaration is recognized as constituting a source of legal obligation for OAS member states, including those States that are not parties to the American Convention on Human Rights. These

---

*The MeToo Movement Looks Different for Women of Color. Here are 10 Stories*, Huff Post (January 2, 2018), www.huffpost.com/entry/women-of-color-me-too_n_5a442d73e4b0b0e5a7a4992c.

obligations are considered to flow from the human rights obligations of Member States under the OAS Charter. Member States have agreed that the content of the general principles of the OAS Charter is contained in and defined by the American Declaration, as well as the customary legal status of the rights protected under many of the Declaration's core provisions.

116.   The inter-American system has moreover held that the Declaration is a source of international obligation for all OAS member states, including those that have ratified the American Convention. The American Declaration is part of the human rights framework established by the OAS member states, one that refers to the obligations and responsibilities of States and mandates them to refrain from supporting, tolerating or acquiescing in acts or omissions that contravene their human rights commitments.

117.   As a source of legal obligation, States must implement the rights established in the American Declaration in practice within their jurisdiction. The Commission has indicated that the obligation to respect and ensure human rights is specifically set forth in certain provisions of the American Declaration. International instruments in general require State parties not only to respect the rights enumerated therein, but also to ensure that individuals within their jurisdictions also exercise those rights. The continuum of human rights obligations is not only negative in nature; it also requires positive action from States. …

120.   In light of these considerations, the Commission observes that States are obligated under the American Declaration to give legal effect to the obligations contained in Article II of the American Declaration. The obligations established in Article II extend to the prevention and eradication of violence against women, as a crucial component of the State's duty to eliminate both direct and indirect forms of discrimination. In accordance with this duty, State responsibility may be incurred for failures to protect women from domestic violence perpetrated by private actors in certain circumstances. …

138.   The undisputed facts of this case show that Jessica Lenahan possessed a valid restraining order at the time of the events, initially granted by the justice system on a temporary basis on May 21, 1999, and then rendered permanent on June 4, 1999. The terms of the temporary order included both Jessica Lenahan and her daughters as beneficiaries and indicated expressly that "physical or emotional harm" would result if Simon Gonzales was not excluded from their home. When the order was rendered permanent, Jessica Lenahan was granted temporary sole physical custody of her three daughters. Simon Gonzales was also granted parenting time under the terms of the protection order, under certain conditions. Simon Gonzales' time with his daughters during the week was restricted to a "mid-week dinner visit" that Simon Gonzales and Jessica Lenahan had to previously arrange "upon reasonable notice." …

141.   The Commission considers that the issuance of this restraining order and its terms reflect that the judicial authorities knew that Jessica Lenahan and her daughters were at risk of harm by Simon Gonzales. The petitioners have construed this order before the Commission as a judicial determination of that risk upon breach of its terms; an allegation uncontested by the State. The order precludes even the parties from changing the terms by agreement, since only the relevant Court can change this order.

142.   The Commission considers that the issuance of a restraining order signals a State's recognition of risk that the beneficiaries would suffer harm from domestic violence on the part of the restrained party, and need State protection. This recognition is typically the product

of a determination from a judicial authority that a beneficiary – a woman, her children and/ or other family members – will suffer harm without police protection. The United States itself acknowledges in its pleadings that it has adopted a series of measures at the federal and state levels to ensure that protection orders are effectively implemented by the police, since they represent an assessment of risk and a form of State protection.

143.   Therefore, the Commission considers that the State's recognition of risk in this domestic violence situation through the issuance of a restraining order – and the terms of said order – is a relevant element in assessing the human rights implications of the State's action or inaction in responding to the facts presented in this case. It is a key component in determining whether the State authorities should have known that the victims were in a situation of imminent risk of domestic violence upon breach of the terms of the order. It is also an indicator of which actions could have been reasonably expected from the authorities. …

146.   In this case, it is undisputed that Jessica Lenahan had eight contacts with the Castle Rock Police Department throughout the evening of June 22$^{nd}$ and the morning of June 23$^{rd}$ of 1999, and that during each of these contacts she informed the Castle Rock Police Department that she held this restraining order. She also informed them that she did not know the whereabouts of her daughters, that they were very young girls, and that she was afraid they had been picked up by their father without notice, along with their friend.

147.   Therefore, in this case the CRPD was made aware that a restraining order existed. Knowing that this restraining order existed, they would have reasonably been expected to thoroughly review the terms of the order to understand the risk involved, and their obligations towards this risk. According to the requirements of the order itself, the CRPD should have promptly investigated whether its terms had been violated. If in the presence of probable cause of a violation, they should have arrested or sought a warrant for the arrest of Simon Gonzales as the order itself directed. This would have been part of a coordinated protection approach by the State, involving the actions of its justice and law enforcement authorities. …

150.   Based on a thorough review of the record, the Commission considers that the CRPD failed to undertake the mentioned investigation actions with the required diligence and without delay. Its response can be at best characterized as fragmented, uncoordinated and unprepared; consisting of actions that did not produce a thorough determination of whether the terms of the restraining order at issue had been violated. …

## B     Reflections and Questions

1. In the *Jessica Lenahan* decision, the Inter-American Commission on Human Rights holds that the United States has a positive and affirmative duty under international human rights law to protect victims of domestic violence from potential harm by private individuals. In essence, in this case, the IACHR considered that police and other government authorities should have adopted all reasonable steps to adequately enforce her restraining order and protect her daughters in response to her repeated calls. This case was previously ruled upon by the United States Supreme Court – *Castle Rock v. Gonzales* – which held that police officers have discretion of when to enforce a restraining order. In the past, the U.S. Supreme Court has been hesitant to hold the government accountable for failures to protect

persons from harm created by non-state actors.[18] Review the IACHR *Jessica Lenahan* decision and compare its analysis on affirmative obligations with the U.S. Supreme Court decision in *Castle Rock v. Gonzales*. Which approach to positive obligations can be most protective of future domestic violence victims? Would you have argued the case of *Castle Rock v. Gonzales* differently before the United States Supreme Court?

2. One of the most important challenges that women face today is the lack of adequate enforcement of restraining orders, which women can request to receive state protection from domestic violence. In many countries, the police are resistant to enforcing restraining and other types of protection orders under the assumption that domestic violence matters are private and should be resolved in the home. Victims also frequently lack credibility when they report potential violations of the protection order. Many women and their children have died from intimate partner violence due to the non-enforcement of protection orders.[19]

3. Efforts to implement the *Jessica Lenahan* decision have illustrated the importance of the state and local levels to achieve the domestic enforcement of case decisions adopted by supranational human rights protection systems. Domestic enforcement of international human rights law is not only a matter of national concern and the involvement of states, cities, and municipalities can be critical. Over 30 municipalities in the United States have adopted resolutions invoking the Inter-American Commission on Human Rights' decision in the *Jessica Lenahan* case and freedom from domestic violence as a human right.[20] Moreover, at least six jurisdictions in the United States have adopted ordinances based on CEDAW.[21] The first of these was adopted in San Francisco in 1998, offering a broad definition of discrimination; providing for equal access of women to health care, employment, economic, and educational opportunities and the need to address violence against women and girls; and emphasizing the importance of reviewing city policies and programs to eradicate discrimination in areas including services, budgeting, and employment.[22] Can you think of advantages at the local level that favor the implementation of international human rights law legal standards related to discrimination against women?

---

[18] *See generally, for reference*, Castle Rock v. Gonzales, 545 U.S. 748 (2005); DeShaney v. Winnebago County, 489 U.S. 189 (1989).

[19] *See, for reference*, Kate Ballou, *Failure to Protect: Our Civil System's Chronic Punishment of Victims of Domestic Violence*, 31 NOTRE DAME J.L. ETHICS & PUB. Pol'y 355, 355–367 (2017).

[20] For more discussion of implementation efforts related to the *Jessica Lehanan* decision adopted by the Inter-American Commission on Human Rights, *see* Caroline Bettinger-López, *Introduction: Jessica Lenahan (Gonzales) v. United States: Implementation, Litigation, and Mobilization Strategies*, 21 AM. U. J. GENDER SOC. POL'Y & L. 207, 225–228 (2012); Kristina Puga, NBC News, *Home Truth Shows a Mother's Fight for Justice After Her Husband Killed Their 3 Daughters* (October 3, 2018), www.nbcnews.com/news/latino/home-truth-shows-mother-s-fight-justice-after-her-husband-n915981.

[21] For more discussion and examples of CEDAW-based ordinances in U.S. municipalities, *see* Columbia Law School, Human Rights Institute, *Gender Equity Through Human Rights: Local Efforts to Advance the Status of Women and Girls in the United States*, January 2017, pp. 8–11, https://web.law.columbia.edu/sites/default/files/microsites/human-rights-institute/gender_equity_through_human_rights_for_publication.pdf.

[22] *See* City and County of San Francisco Municipal Code, Administrative Code, *Chapter 33A: Local Implementation of the United Nations Convention on the Elimination of All Forms of Discrimination against Women* (CEDAW), Sections 33A.1(c) and 33A.2(d), https://sfgov.org/dosw/cedaw-ordinance.

4.  International courts have frequently held that a state must have known of potential harm created by a non-state actor in order to be found accountable for a failure to protect. Many of these cases have been connected to the rights to life and to be free from torture, and the victims and/or their family members had reported ongoing violence before state authorities. Do you think states should still be held accountable for unreported private harm? What if the state knew of a context of frequent violence against women perpetrated by non-state actors?[23]

5.  The United Nations Ruggie Principles define a set of responsibilities that businesses must abide by to prevent human rights violations. One of the responsibilities is to do no harm when they are conducting corporate activities. Under Principle 11, business enterprises should respect human rights. This entails businesses adopting measures to prevent, mitigate, and remedy adverse human rights impacts. Principle 22 also establishes that businesses have the responsibility of ensuring access to remedies by victims when harm does occur. Under Principle 1, states for their part are mandated to protect against human rights abuses by third parties. States also have the correlative obligation under Principle 2 to set out obligations for businesses to respect human rights, especially when they are operating abroad and in other countries. The U.N. Ruggie Principles use the term *responsibilities* instead of *obligations* when it comes to corporate entities. The U.N. Ruggie Principles do frame these responsibilities as part of the due diligence standard. There are many issues women can confront in the workplace and in the business context which are related to human rights, including sex and pregnancy-based discrimination, the gender pay gap, sexual harassment, and forms of gender-based violence. Do you think that corporate entities should have more responsibilities to prevent and protect from harm against women based on the due diligence standard? How do you think these principles would apply in the context of sex discrimination, sexual harassment, and gender-based violence and pay gaps in the workplace?[24]

6.  Other regional human rights protection systems have delved into the question of the scope of state responsibility over the activities of businesses which could be harmful and threaten human rights. The Inter-American System of Human Rights in particular has published a number of regional reports related to businesses, extractive industries, and human rights. In these reports, the approach has been more affirmative when it comes to the state obligations, including a clear mandate to proactively supervise the activities of businesses as a measure to adequately prevent harm. This mandate to supervise and monitor extends to labor practices which can be harmful to women, including dangerous working conditions,

---

[23]   *See for example*, Eur. Ct. H.R., Opuz v. Turkey, *supra* note 9, ¶¶ 128–202; González et al. ("Cotton Field") v. Mexico, Preliminary Objection, Merits, Reparations, and Costs, Judgment, Inter-Am. Ct. H.R. (ser. C) No. 205, ¶¶ 258–286 (Nov. 16, 2009).

[24]   *See Guiding Principles on Business and Human Rights: Implementing the United Nations "Protect, Respect, and Remedy" Framework*, Final Report of the Special Representative of the Secretary General on the Issue of Human Rights and Transnational Corporations and Other Business Enterprises, John Ruggie, U.N. Doc. A/HRC/17/31 (2011), Pillars 1 and 2 and Principles 1, 2, 11, 22 (hereinafter Ruggie Principles); U.N. Working Group on Business and Human Rights, *Gender Dimensions of the Guiding Principles on Business and Human Rights* (2019), pp. 9–11, 20–21, and 34–35, www.undp.org/publications/gender-dimensions-guiding-principles-business-and-human-rights.

deficient health standards, forms of violence and harassment, and the application of gender stereotypes which hurt women's professional progression.[25]

# V   SOCIAL PROTEST TO ENFORCE DUE DILIGENCE

The *MeToo* movement in many ways has been joined by many forms of social protest and mobilization campaigns. Much of this mobilization has taken place on the streets at the local, national, regional, and global levels. Thousands of women have been on the streets demanding an end to violence against women, its recognition as a serious and alarming human rights violation, the reform of existing legislation, and accountability for these crimes. Local, national, regional, and global civil society organizations have led the way along with women of all ages, races, ethnicities, and social classes.

You may ask yourself, how is this all connected to international and human rights law governing the rights of women? Protest may be a way for women to exercise their autonomy, voices, demands, and human rights concerns. The mobilization has included important themes, colors, symbols, music, and catchphrases. Shared below is a reading related to the global social protest efforts around the song *Un violador en tu camino* (*A Rapist in Your Path* in English), written and performed by Las Tesis in Chile.[26] All of the street demonstrations in different continents inspired by this song illustrate the contemporary forms of social protest advocating for accountability for acts of gender-based violence and the transformation of our societies.

**A       Paula Serafini, *"A Rapist in Your Path", Transnational Feminist Protest and Why (and How) Performance Matters***

23(2) European Journal of Cultural Studies 290–295, 292–294
Reproduced with permission from Sage Publications
Citations and footnotes omitted

…

There is a long history of performance as a form of political action. Performance art and social mobilisation have a tendency to feed off each other, and indeed several forms of performance art find their origins in performative political action. Such is the case with feminist performance in the United States, whose lineage is to the guerrilla theatre and university uprisings of feminist movements in the 1960s and 1970s (which in turn built on the civil rights movement). But while it is widely acknowledged that instances of bodies in assembly and collective art making can give voice to powerful emotions and feelings of collective empowerment, it is also

---

[25]   For more reading, *see* Inter-American Commission on Human Rights, Rapporteur on Economic, Social, Cultural, and Environmental Rights, *Empresas y Derechos Humanos* [Business and Human Rights], OEA/Ser.L/V/II CIDH/REDESCA/INF.1/19, ¶¶ 97–103, 331–339 (Nov. 1, 2019), www.oas.org/es/cidh/informes/pdfs/EmpresasDDHH.pdf; Inter-American Commission on Human Rights, *Indigenous Peoples, Afro-Descendent Communities, and Natural Resources: Human Rights Protection in the Context of Extraction, Exploitation, and Development Activities*, OEA/Ser.L/V/II. Doc. 47/15, ¶¶ 98–105, 318–321 (Dec. 31, 2015), www.oas.org/en/iachr/reports/pdfs/ExtractiveIndustries2016.pdf.

[26]   For more reading, *see* Gaby Hinsliff, *"The rapist is you!": Why a Chilean protest chant is being sung around the world*, The Guardian, February 3, 2020, https://www.theguardian.com/society/2020/feb/03/the-rapist-is-you-chilean-protest-song-chanted-around-the-world-un-iolador-en-tu-camino.

worth considering the internal politics of such forms of action if we want to understand why and how performance can enact change.

In performance actions, it is often the case that artistic and political objectives are understood as being in tension with each other. Groups are constantly negotiating what it is that they want the performance to achieve as a political intervention, on one hand, and what they want it to achieve as a work of art on the other. Sometimes, the creative and aesthetic possibilities of performance are not seen as powerful ends in themselves, but rather as mere instruments for achieving particular political objectives. Other times, it is assumed that art is intrinsically transformative, and that a performance of artistic quality has the potential for personal and collective transformation, as an expression that is different and separate from activist tactics and strategies, and which therefore has its own distinctive value and purpose. It is, however, when the artistic and political objectives of a performance are understood as being complementary rather than contradictory or competing, that performances have a better chance of being transformative on different levels, from the individual experience of participants to the collective and the structural. In other words, the most powerful performances tend to be those that adopt a prefigurative approach that considers art as a medium for social and political action, and activism as a social, creative practice.

Art activism thus becomes an aesthetic–political practice through which we can build specific ways of relating to each other and acting collectively towards achieving social and political transformations. Because of the understanding of art and activism it puts forward, and the forms of agency and action it facilitates, *Un violador en tu camino* can be read as a case of prefigurative art activism.

*Un violador en tu camino* displays an ethos of collective ownership and horizontality; it was conceived by Las Tesis with the aim of enacting some of the transformative theories of feminist thought – in this case, specifically Rita Segato's work on rape as a moralising and political act of domination. But the performance action came into being and evolved with the social protests in Chile and women's responses to the violence experienced at the hands of the police, and continued to develop and shift as it travelled the world. Each new enactment similarly involves no distinction between artist and participant, given that the collective that created the first performance has no presence or say in how it is interpreted and taken on by different groups. While in each particular case there is a person or group that takes it upon themselves to organise a local version of the performance, this has tended to follow the dynamics of grassroots organising rather than those of institutional, participatory art. As such, the organising processes are more open and porous, even when, due to practical reasons, one or more people take on a coordinating and facilitating role. In order to achieve horizontal participation, the lyrics and steps of the performance are deliberately easy to learn, making full participation accessible to most. At the same time, the potential for adaptation of *Un violador en tu camino* has been crucial to its accessibility, giving rise to performances where wheelchair users join the frontlines, and others where participants maintain the basic choreography while reproducing the lyrics in sign language.

But, despite its simplicity and fluidity, the combination of words and movement performed simultaneously by rows of participants – sometimes in the hundreds – is aesthetically stunning, and affectively moving. The song puts into words that which has been silent for too long: It is the system that is killing us. It is the government officials and police officers. It is the judges. It is you. Participants in the performance are speaking truth to power in a collective act of denunciation that marks a point of no return: We are no longer silenced, and you are no longer shielded. The result of this approach is a performance that allows participants to feel empowered as political subjects through an instance of political and artistic participation. Their bodies in the street are simultaneously demarcating a feminist space of political action and of collective creative expression. Through their song and their movements they are protesting, but they are also enacting a series of values such as sorority and (transnational) solidarity, horizontality, collectivity and the accessibility of both political and artistic participation. …

*Un violador en tu camino* is thus a powerful, prefigurative performance action because it mobilises participants and appeals to audiences as a sharp denunciation of violence, a demonstration of collective, prefigurative political action, a visually impressive composition and a song that stays in our heads and our hearts. …

## B     Reflections and Questions

1.  Ongoing social protest to advance the human rights of women – particularly reflected in campaigns such as *Ni Una Menos*[27] (*Not One Woman Less* in English) – serves as a staggering reminder of the dire problems of gender-based violence and discrimination, and the ongoing repetition and impunity of these crimes. It is also interesting to note that many of the protests are coming from middle-income and low-income countries, or what is considered the Global South, but have been echoed globally. The human rights challenges faced by women still have a universal nature, and the road to full compliance with due diligence principles and obligations is still very arduous. It will be interesting to see whether these protests help build more sustained coalitions and movements to demand better functioning administration of justice systems, and a better legislative and policy response to gender-based violence and discrimination in general. The problems have been worsened in many ways by the COVID-19 pandemic. Several organizations have reported increases in reports of gender-based violence during the pandemic. The work to advance the rights of women, prevent violence, and bring perpetrators to justice will be ongoing in the post COVID-19 world.[28]

2.  One of the most important motivations for social protests in regions such as Latin America has been the widespread nature of femicides and feminicides – namely gender-motivated killings of women. Latin America is considered one of the most violent regions of the world, especially for women. These crimes are often left in impunity, often joined by

---

[27]   For more reading on the *Ni Una Menos* mobilization, *see* Anya Prusa, Beatriz Garcia Nice, and Olivia Soledad, *"Not One Wom[a]n Less, Not One More Death": Feminist Activism and Policy Responses in Gender-Based Violence in Latin America*, GEORGETOWN JOURNAL OF INTERNATIONAL AFFAIRS (August 12, 2020), https://gjia.georgetown.edu/2020/08/12/not-one-women-less-not-one-more -death-feminist-activism-and-policy-responses-to-gender-based-violence-in-latin-america/.

[28]   For reference, *see* International Rescue Committee, *IRC Data Shows an Increase in Gender-Based Violence across Latin America* (June 9, 2020), www.rescue.org/press-release/irc-data-shows-increase -reports-gender-based-violence-across-latin-america; United Nations High Commissioner for Refugees, *Gender-Based Violence on the Rise during Lockdowns* (November 25, 2020), www.unhcr.org/en-us/ news/stories/2020/11/5fbd2e774/gender-based-violence-rise-during-lockdowns.html.

significant irregularities in their investigation, judgment, and sanction. What cultural and social structural changes do you think can be implemented to prevent these crimes?[29]

3.  Social protests can have results for women. In Argentina, abortion during the first 14 weeks of pregnancy was legalized as recently as December 30, 2020, after extensive civil society mobilization and street demonstrations. The demands were symbolized by the color green and handkerchiefs. The legalization was celebrated as a major achievement for women's rights all over the world, and is sure to resonate in the rest of the Americas region.[30]

## VI     CONCLUSIONS: THE LONG ROAD TO GUARANTEE EFFECTIVE DUE DILIGENCE IN CASES OF GENDER-BASED VIOLENCE

As this chapter has demonstrated, full due diligence and the adequate prevention and sanction of gender-based violence and discrimination against women are still a distant dream. Even though important achievements and gains have been made in areas such as legislation and public policies, the ongoing problem of violence against women reveals the need for more proactive responses and multidisciplinary strategies from state and non-state actors to end this problem. One in three women will still suffer acts of violence in their lifetime, and many of these crimes will go unsanctioned. Much action is needed to ensure that the promise of the due diligence standard and the universal and regional human rights instruments and treaties prohibiting gender-based violence and mandating prompt state action are fully implemented.

However, what we have seen with the *MeToo* movement and the recent social protests is that women want to be active participants in the finding of solutions to the problems of gender-based violence and discrimination. They do not want to be passive beneficiaries of legislation and policies that do not respond to their needs and demands in a patriarchy driven world. Women want to be policymakers, leaders, decision-makers, and active participants in the process of designing strategies that promote a better implementation of the due diligence standard in their countries. This is part of their autonomy, dignity, and life choices. Through sharing their stories, and their marches, protests, statements, songs, and language, they are saying "enough," and it is time to move forward to a world really free from all types of violence and discrimination against women.

As the above readings indicate, the COVID-19 pandemic has paralyzed the world in many ways and impacted efforts to protect the human rights of women. At the same time, the pandemic has also opened up an opportunity to reflect on key features for a world post crisis. Women's leadership will undoubtedly be part of this new context, and social protest illustrates the need for more spaces for women to voice their demands and have an influence in decision-making. Women constitute more than half of the world's population and have different ages, races, ethnicities, economic situations, and social backgrounds. But one important

---

[29]   For more reading, *see* Economic Commission for Latin America and the Caribbean (ECLAC), Gender Equality Observatory for Latin America and the Caribbean, *Femicide: The Most Extreme Expression of Violence against Women*, Notes for Equality, No. 27, November 15, 2018, https://oig.cepal.org/sites/default/files/nota_27_eng.pdf.

[30]   *See* Daniel Politi and Ernesto Londoño, *Argentina Legalizes Abortion, a Milestone in a Conservative Region*, N.Y. TIMES, December 30, 2020, www.nytimes.com/2020/12/30/world/americas/argentina-legalizes-abortion.html.

characteristic that binds all women is their experience of gender-based violence and discrimination. This is illustrated in the global and widespread nature of social protest demanding accountability and a better government response to these problems.

Women will be key players in the post-COVID-19 world, and the due diligence standard and international human rights law provide a good roadmap and goal to work towards.

# 7. The challenging road to equality and the pursuit of non-discrimination

## I    INTRODUCTION: DISCRIMINATION ON THE BASIS OF SEX AND LEGAL TENDENCIES

As discussed in Chapter 1, the recognition of discrimination against women was paramount to the development of international law today as focused on the rights of women. CEDAW prohibits discrimination against women in all of its forms and dimensions, and contains an explicit mandate for states to adopt legislation, policies, and programs to fully eradicate and prevent this problem. CEDAW also contains in Article 1 the leading definition in the world of discrimination against women, and proscribes restrictions, exclusions, and different treatment on the basis of sex. According to the important precedent set by the CEDAW Committee, women should enjoy equal social opportunities and conditions, as compared to men, to succeed and influence decision-making in our societies.

The international and national understanding of discrimination against women has greatly evolved. Discrimination and equality are still terms in development. In the past few decades, new terminology and concepts have been identified to name the different forms of discrimination faced by women. These terms include vulnerability, stereotypes, and intersectionality, among others. United Nations bodies and regional commissions and courts have also set important content and benchmarks for states to follow in terms of state obligations, including the duty to address both direct and indirect forms of discrimination, and the obligation to act with due diligence. Many tribunals are reviewing different treatment in legislation and court judgments towards women with intense scrutiny, applying both strict and intermediate reviews to these distinctions.[1]

Despite these advances, forms of discrimination against women are still very widespread around the world. Women suffer the negative effects of gender stereotypes, racism, forms of hate speech, and different treatment in employment, education, health, and other settings. As discussed earlier, violence against women and girls is still one of the most serious and widespread global problems faced. Discrimination occurs at the hands of both state and non-state actors in these contexts. This reality raises the question of which steps are needed to make existing legal standards, developed at the regional, national, and local levels, more impactful.[2]

---

[1]    *See as reference*, Dimitrina Petrova, *Implementing Anti-Discrimination Law and the Human Rights Movement*, 17(1) HELSINKI MONITOR 19, 19–25, 31–33 (2006); Jarlath Clifford, *Equality*, *in* THE OXFORD HANDBOOK OF INTERNATIONAL HUMAN RIGHTS (Dinah Shelton ed., Oxford University Press, 2013).

[2]    *See as reference*, World Economic Forum, *Global Gender Gap Report* 5–6, 8–27 (2020).

This chapter focuses on the evolving nature of discrimination against women, including existing challenges. The sections discuss terminology and legal developments that seem promising in the path towards eradicating this problem, and ways to move forward. One important question this chapter posits is whether the existing universal and regional standards related to discrimination against women are sufficient to address the alarming and changing nature of this problem and its manifestations today. Overall, it ponders which measures can have a meaningful impact in the daily lives of women when it comes to eradicating discrimination.

## II     VULNERABILITY AND STEREOTYPES

The concept of vulnerability has been used by different regional human rights protection systems to identify a diversity of sectors and groups of the population which are at an increased risk of discrimination and other human rights violations. Women have been among those identified as particularly "vulnerable" to discrimination and gender-based violence, due to differentiated and disadvantaged treatment historically. The term has been used to develop lines of jurisprudence in the regional protection systems in both Europe and the Americas, for example.

The identification of a group as vulnerable has also been often combined with its recognition as the subject of negative stereotypes. As discussed earlier in Chapter 1 of this book, stereotypes are preconceived notions of the social roles of either sex. In the case of women, stereotypes about their social role and functions have been used to relegate them to the home, and impede the full development of their life plans and aspirations.

The readings below exemplify how approaches related to the concepts of vulnerability and stereotypes have been reflected in the jurisprudence of both the European and American regional human rights protection systems. Professors Lourdes Peroni and Alexandra Timmer discuss how an approach guided by "vulnerability" has been developed by the European Court of Human Rights. The European Court of Human Rights ruling in the case of *Carvalho Pinto de Sousa Mourais v. Portugal* illustrates how stereotypes regarding women's sexuality can represent an important barrier to fully accessing justice in a case of medical malpractice. The Inter-American Court of Human Rights judgment in the matter of *Gonzalez Lluy et al. v. Ecuador* shows how the terms vulnerability and stereotypes can be applied to legally characterize the discrimination and realities faced by a young girl living with HIV due to a negligent blood transfusion. Lastly, the case of *BS v. Spain*, ruled on by the European Court of Human Rights exemplifies how vulnerabilities and intersections based on sex and race can accentuate the exposure of afro-descendent women to institutional violence by government authorities, and the obligation to investigate the racist motives which fuel these acts in the first place.

**A**     **Lourdes Peroni and Alexandra Timmer, *Vulnerable Groups: The Promise of an Emerging Concept in European Human Rights Convention Law***

11(4) INTERNATIONAL JOURNAL OF CONSTITUTIONAL LAW, 1056–1059, 1061–1065 (2013) © Oxford University Press, reproduced with permission
Citations and footnotes omitted

Though each and every move of the European Court of Human Rights is intensely followed these days, one recent development in the front lines of its reasoning has so far escaped scholarly attention: the emergence of the concept of vulnerable groups. ...

The Strasbourg Court originally used this concept in relation to the Roma minority. "[A]s a result of their turbulent history," the Court has held, "the Roma have become a specific type of disadvantaged and vulnerable minority" in need of special protection. In recent years, the concept has gained legal momentum when the Court started to regard people with mental disabilities as a "particularly vulnerable group in society, who have suffered considerable discrimination in the past." The Court has further expanded the list of vulnerable groups to asylum seekers and people living with HIV. ...

Vulnerability is a concept fraught with paradox. To start with, the concept is in common use but its meaning is imprecise and contested. Confusing, complex, vague, ambiguous are but a few of the labels scholars across disciplines have used to refer to it. ...

A central paradox of vulnerability is that it is both universal and particular. Both of these features arise in the first place from our embodiment: as embodied beings we are all vulnerable, but we experience this vulnerability uniquely through our individual bodies. The centrality of the corporeal dimension of vulnerability is reflected in the term's etymology: the term stems from the Latin *vulnus*, which means, "wound." Turning first to the meaning of vulnerability in the universal sense, it comes as no surprise that harm and suffering feature centrally in most accounts of vulnerability. ...

Thus, as vulnerable subjects we are constantly susceptible to harm. Harm, of course, comes in many varieties that intersect and reinforce one another. Injuries can be bodily, moral, psychological, economic and institutional, just to mention a few. These different forms of harm already hint at the ways in which vulnerability is particular (as well as universal). Our "different forms of embodiment" and our different positions within "webs of economic and institutional relationships" mean that each of us experiences vulnerability uniquely. Martha Fineman points out that the experience of vulnerability "is greatly influenced by the quality and quantity of resources we possess or can command."

Recently, however, theorists have moved towards an understanding of vulnerability that expands beyond (universal and particular) suffering, to encompass positive aspects. Human vulnerability is generative of suffering, so the argument runs, but also of empathy, pleasure, innovation, social institutions, intimacy and social-connectedness. Martha Fineman argues that this generative capacity of vulnerability "presents opportunities for innovation and growth, creativity, and fulfillment. It makes us reach out to others, form relationships, and build institutions." Indeed, Fineman insists that we need to re-conceptualize vulnerability in this positive manner in order to get rid of the stigmatizing effects otherwise attached to the term. ...

Before moving on to the case law analysis, it bears standing still for a moment and consider what kind of role vulnerability has so far played in the human rights context. At first sight, human rights lawyers suffer less from the is/ought dilemma precisely because they can refer to the human rights corpus, which in essence lays down the rule that abuse of human embodied vulnerability is prohibited. However, as we shall see, critically minded human rights scholars have shown that the story is not that straightforward. The relationship between vulnerability and human rights is a contested terrain. ...

The rapid development of the concept of vulnerable groups in recent high-profile judgments of the Strasbourg case law raises several basic questions. How has the Court evoked the concept of group vulnerability? And, are there any risks associated to the Court's characterization and deployment of the concept? Based on these questions, this section offers a critical assessment of the Court's formulation and use of the concept. …

The concept of vulnerable groups was introduced in 2001, in *Chapman v. the United Kingdom*, to refer to the Roma minority. The case involved a Roma woman who was evicted from her own land because she stationed her caravan there without a planning permission. The Court rejected the applicant's alleged violation of the right to respect for her minority lifestyle (Article 8 ECHR). It also dismissed her discrimination complaint (Article 14 ECHR). The applicant's argument was that the UK government prevented her from pursuing a lifestyle that she viewed as central to her cultural tradition: living and travelling in a caravan. …

In this early formulation, the vulnerability of Roma seems to arise primarily from the group's minority status and from the lack of consideration of its minority lifestyle in the planning and decision-making processes. Group vulnerability does not, however, play a key role in the Court's proportionality reasoning. In fact, Ms. Chapman loses the case, mostly as a result of the large margin of appreciation left to states when it comes to the implementation of planning policies, in this case, environmental regulations. Notwithstanding this, *Chapman*'s articulation of vulnerability already puts in place the elements that will shape the Court's later formulations of "vulnerable groups": belonging to a group (in this case, the Roma minority) whose vulnerability is partly constructed by broader societal, political, and institutional circumstances (in this case, power differentials and a planning framework unresponsive to the needs arising from a way of life different from that of the majority). …

In the years following *Chapman*, the Court has broadened and refined the concept's content and scope. As we will discuss, the Court has not only reaffirmed the vulnerability of Roma in different contexts and for a mix of other reasons; it has also extended the list of "vulnerable groups" to persons with mental disabilities, people living with HIV, and asylum seekers. However, what exactly ties all these groups together is still not entirely clear, as the Court has not (yet) fully developed a coherent set of indicators to determine what renders a group vulnerable. To be sure, in all the cases, the Court draws on European or international human rights reports and resolutions to determine what it is that makes groups vulnerable. These references, however, serve to confirm rather than to establish group vulnerability.

Based on a close reading of the case law, our understanding is that the concept of group vulnerability, as used by the Court, has three characteristics: it is relational, particular, and harm-based. The Court's account of group vulnerability is first of all *relational*. As already transpired from *Chapman*, the Court locates vulnerability not in the individual alone but rather in her wider social circumstances. The Court's notion of vulnerable groups is thus relational because it views the vulnerability of certain groups as shaped by social, historical, and institutional forces. In other words, the Court links the individual applicant's vulnerability to the social or institutional environment, which originates or sustains the vulnerability of the group she is (made) part of. The emphasis on context inherent in the relational character of the Court's understanding of group vulnerability is in line with contemporary analyses that use vulnerability as a critical tool. …

**B**     *Carvalho Pinto de Sousa Mourais v. Portugal,* **European Court of Human Rights**

Application No. 17484/15, July 25, 2017
© Council of Europe, reproduced with permission
Citations and footnotes omitted

*In the following case, the applicant underwent a surgical procedure for a gynecological disease, which resulted in several ailments, including severe pain, the loss of sense in her reproductive organs, and the inability to sustain sexual relations. The applicant became depressed, suicidal, and isolated. The applicant sought damages unsuccessfully before the domestic courts. The section below discusses her allegations and the Court's assessment of violations to the prohibition of discrimination under Article 14 of the European Convention on Human Rights, in connection with the right to private and family life under Article 8.*

44. The Court has established in its case-law that in order for an issue to arise under Article 14, there must be a difference in treatment of persons in analogous or relevantly similar situations. Such a difference in treatment is discriminatory if it has no objective and reasonable justification; in other words, if it does not pursue a legitimate aim or if there is no reasonable relationship of proportionality between the means employed and the aim sought to be realised. Contracting States enjoy a certain margin of appreciation in assessing whether and to what extent differences in otherwise similar situations justify a difference in treatment … The notion of discrimination within the meaning of Article 14 also includes cases where a person or group is treated, without proper justification, less favourably than another, even though the more favourable treatment is not called for by the Convention. …

45. Article 14 does not prohibit all differences in treatment, but only those differences based on an identifiable, objective or personal characteristic, or "status", by which individuals or groups are distinguishable from one another. It lists specific grounds which constitute "status" including, *inter alia*, sex, race and property. The words "other status" have generally been given a wide meaning, and their interpretation has not been limited to characteristics which are personal in the sense that they are innate or inherent … In this regard, the Court has recognised that age might constitute "other status" for the purposes of Article 14 of the Convention … although it has not, to date, suggested that discrimination on grounds of age should be equated with other "suspect" grounds of discrimination. …

46. The Court further reiterates that the advancement of gender equality is today a major goal for the member States of the Council of Europe and very weighty reasons would have to be put forward before such a difference of treatment could be regarded as compatible with the Convention … In particular, references to traditions, general assumptions or prevailing social attitudes in a particular country are insufficient justification for a difference in treatment on the grounds of sex. For example, in a case concerning the bearing of a woman's maiden name after marriage, it considered that the importance attached to the principle of non-discrimination prevented States from imposing traditions that derive from the man's primordial role and the woman's secondary role in the family … The Court has also considered that the issue with stereotyping of a certain group in society lies in the fact that it prohibits the individualised evaluation of their capacity and needs. …

47. Lastly, as concerns the burden of proof in relation to Article 14 of the Convention, the Court reiterates that once the applicant has demonstrated a difference in treatment, it is for the Government to show that it was justified. ...

(b)    Application of those principles to the instant case ...

52. The Court acknowledges that in deciding claims related to non-pecuniary damage within the framework of liability proceedings, domestic courts may be called upon to consider the age of claimants, as in the instant case. The question at issue here is not considerations of age or sex as such, but rather the assumption that sexuality is not as important for a fifty-year-old woman and mother of two children as for someone of a younger age. That assumption reflects a traditional idea of female sexuality as being essentially linked to child-bearing purposes and thus ignores its physical and psychological relevance for the self-fulfilment of women as people. Apart from being, in a way, judgmental, it omitted to take into consideration other dimensions of women's sexuality in the specific case of the applicant. In other words, in the instant case the Supreme Administrative Court made a general assumption without attempting to look at its validity in the specific case of the applicant herself, who was fifty at the time of the operation at issue. ...

53. In the Court's view, the wording of the Supreme Administrative Court's judgment when reducing the amount of compensation in respect of non-pecuniary damage cannot be regarded as an unfortunate turn of phrase, as asserted by the Government. It is true that in lowering the amount the Supreme Administrative Court also took it for granted that the pain suffered by the applicant was not new. Nevertheless, the applicant's age and sex appear to have been decisive factors in the final decision, introducing a difference of treatment based on those grounds ... This approach is also reflected in the decision of the Supreme Administrative Court to lower the amount awarded to the applicant in respect of the costs of a maid on the grounds that she "probably only needed to take care of her husband" given her children's age at the material time. ...

54. In the Court's view, those considerations show the prejudices prevailing amongst the judiciary in Portugal, as pointed out in the report of 29 June 2015 by the UN Human Rights Council's Special Rapporteur on the Independence of Judges and Lawyers ... They also confirm the observations and concerns expressed by the Permanent Observatory on Portuguese Justice regarding the prevailing sexism within judicial institutions in its report of November 2006 on domestic violence. ...

56. In view of the foregoing considerations, the Court concludes that there has therefore been a violation of Article 14 of the Convention taken in conjunction with Article 8. ...

## C    *Gonzalez Lluy et. al v. Ecuador*, **Inter-American Court of Human Rights**

Preliminary Objections, Merits, Reparations and Costs, Judgment of September 1, 2015, Series C No. 298
Citations and footnotes omitted

*The case below is related to Talía Gabriela Gonzalez Lluy who became infected with HIV as a result of a blood transfusion at the Azuay Red Cross Bank. She was three years old at the time. The petitioners alleged before the Inter-American Court that the state failed in its duty to appropriately supervise the activities of private health services and that these acts had not been properly investigated by the state with due diligence. The following section discusses the intersectional discrimination and stigma that Talía suffered in school for living with HIV.*

275.    According to the United Nations, discrimination resulting from being a person living with HIV "is not only wrong in itself but also creates and sustains conditions leading to societal vulnerability to infection by HIV, including lack of access to an enabling environment that will promote behavioral change and enable people to cope with HIV." On this point, the *International Guidelines on HIV/AIDS and Human Rights* of the OHCHR and UNAIDS mention the promotion of supportive and enabling environments for people living with HIV.

276.    In this case, the problems of the adaptability of the environment are revealed, among other matters, by the problems face by Talía after her expulsion from the Zoila Aurora Palacios School. The Lluy family had to look for schools that were far away to avoid the treatment that was harming Talía. ...

277.    Looking for schools so that Talía could complete her education was very complicated, because the different schools advised each other of the child's medical condition. Teresa Lluy indicated that when she went to a new school to enroll Talía "they already knew about [Talía and they] were not even allowed to enter [before they] were told that there were no places available and that [they] should leave ..."

282.    Given the precarious financial situation of Talía's family and the stigma associated with her illness, she did not receive a stable education in a single educational establishment. ...

284.    As can be seen, in different situations within the educational environment, both Talía and her family faced a climate hostile to the illness. In this regard, taking into account that, under the United Nations Convention on the Rights of Persons with Disabilities, "persons with disabilities are part of human diversity and humanity," the educational establishment were bound to provide an educational environment that would accept and celebrate that diversity. The Court considers that the need for Talía Gonzales Lluy, her family, and some of her teachers to hide the fact that Talía was living with HIV or to hide in order to accede to and remain within the education system constituted a disregard for the value of human diversity. The education system was called upon to help Talía and her family talk about HIV without having to hide it, and to help her retain the highest possible self-esteem as a result of her environment and, to a great extent, to educate the other students and teachers about the meaning of diversity and the need to safeguard the principle of non-discrimination in every sphere. ...

285.    The Court notes that discrimination against Talía has been associated with factors such as being a woman, a person living with HIV, a person with disabilities, and a minor, and also her socio-economic status. These aspects made her more vulnerable and exacerbated the harm that she suffered. ...

288.    The Court notes that certain groups of women suffer discrimination throughout their life based on more than one factor combined with their gender, which increases their risk of enduring acts of violence and other violations of their human rights. In this regard, the Special Rapporteur on violence against women, its causes and consequences, has established that: "[d]iscrimination based on race, ethnicity, national origin, ability, socio-economic class, sexual orientation, gender identity, religion, culture, tradition and other realities often intensifies acts of violence against women." In the case of women

with HIV/AIDS, the gender perspective provides a way of understanding living with the illness in the context of the "roles and expectations that affect peoples' lives, choices and interactions (particularly in terms of sexual feelings, desires and behaviors)."

289.   In this case, statements that have not been contested by the State illustrate the impact that the Lluy family's situation of poverty had on the approach to Talía's HIV… These statements have also explained the discrimination in the educational environment associated with how, in a prejudiced and stigmatizing way, Talía Gonzales Lluy was considered a risk for her classmates, not only when she was expelled from the Zoila Aurora Palacios School, but at other time when she tried to access the education system. In addition, as regards employment, the Court notes that Teresa Lluy was dismissed from her job owing to the stigma of having a daughter with HIV and, subsequently, in other jobs she obtained, she was also dismissed owing to Talía's status as a person living with HIV. …

290.   The Court notes that, in Talía's case, numerous factors of vulnerability and risk of discrimination intersected that were associated with her condition as a minor, a female, a person living in poverty, and a person living with HIV. The discrimination experienced by Talía was caused not only by numerous factors, but also arose from a specific form of discrimination that resulted from the intersection of those factors; in other words, if one of those factors had not existed, the discrimination would have been different. Indeed, the poverty had an impact on the initial access to health care that was not of the best quality and that, to the contrary, resulted in the infection with HIV. The situation of poverty also had an impact on the difficulties to gain access to the education system and to lead a decent life. Subsequently, because she was a child with HIV, the obstacles that Talía suffered in access to education had a negative impact on her overall development, which is also a differentiated impact taking into account the role of education in overcoming gender stereotypes. As a child with HIV, she required greater support from the State to implement her life project. As a woman, Talía has described the dilemmas she feels as regards future maternity and her interaction in an intimate relationship, and has indicated that she has not had appropriate counseling. In sum, Talía's case illustrates that HIV-related stigmatization does not affect everyone in the same way and that the impact is more severe on members of vulnerable groups.

291.   Based on all the foregoing, the Court concludes that Talía Gonzales Lluy suffered discrimination derived from her situation as a person living with HIV, a child, a female, and living in conditions of poverty. Consequently, the Court considers that the Ecuadorian State violated the right to education of Talía Gonzales Lluy contained in Article 13 of the Protocol of San Salvador, in relation to Articles 19 and 1(1) of the American Convention. …

## D      European Court of Human Rights, *BS v. Spain*

App. No. 47159/08, July 24, 2012
© Council of Europe, reproduced with permission
Citations and footnotes omitted

*In the following case, the applicant – an afro-descendent woman – alleged that while she worked as a prostitute police officers targeted her based on racial motives. This resulted in acts of physical and psychological violence. The excerpts below discuss the Court's assessment of violations of the prohibition of discrimination under Article 14 of the European Convention on Human Rights, in connection with the right to a remedy contained in Article 3.*

48. The applicant also alleged that she had been discriminated against as evidenced by the racist remarks made by the police officers, namely, "get out of here you black whore". She submitted that other women in the same area carrying on the same activity but with a "European phenotype" had not been stopped by the police. ...

58. The Court considers that where the State authorities investigate violent incidents, they have an additional obligation to take all reasonable measures to identify whether there were racist motives and to establish whether or not ethnic hatred or prejudice may have played a role in the events. Admittedly, proving racial motivation will often be extremely difficult in practice. The respondent State's obligation to investigate possible racist overtones to a violent act is an obligation to use best endeavours and not absolute. The authorities must do what is reasonable in the circumstances to collect and secure the evidence, explore all practical means of discovering the truth and deliver fully reasoned, impartial and objective decisions, without omitting suspicious facts that may be indicative of racially induced violence ... Lastly, the Court reiterates that the onus is on the Government to produce evidence establishing facts that cast doubt on the victim's account. ...

59. Furthermore, the authorities' duty to investigate the existence of a possible link between racist attitudes and an act of violence is an aspect of their procedural obligations arising under Article 3 of the Convention, but may also be seen as implicit in their responsibilities under Article 14 of the Convention to secure respect without discrimination for the fundamental value enshrined in Article 3. Owing to the interplay of the two provisions, issues such as those in the present case may fall to be examined under one of the two provisions only, with no separate issue arising under the other, or may require examination under both Articles. This is a question to be decided in each case on its facts and depending on the nature of the allegations made. ...

60. In the instant case the Court has already observed that the Spanish authorities violated Article 3 of the Convention by failing to carry out an effective investigation into the incident. It considers that it must examine separately the complaint that there was also a failure to investigate a possible causal link between the alleged racist attitudes and the violent acts allegedly perpetrated by the police against the applicant. ...

61. The Court notes that in her complaints of 21 and 25 July 2005 the applicant mentioned the racist remarks allegedly made to her by the police, such as "get out of here you black whore", and submitted that the officers had not stopped and questioned other women carrying on the same activity but having a "European phenotype". Those submissions were not examined by the courts dealing with the case, which merely adopted the contents of the reports by the Balearic Islands chief of police without carrying out a more thorough investigation into the alleged racist attitudes.

62. In the light of the evidence submitted in the present case, the Court considers that the decisions made by the domestic courts failed to take account of the applicant's particular vulnerability inherent in her position as an African woman working as a prostitute. The authorities thus failed to comply with their duty under Article 14 of the Convention taken

in conjunction with Article 3 to take all possible steps to ascertain whether or not a discriminatory attitude might have played a role in the events.

63. There has accordingly been a violation of Article 14 of the Convention taken in conjunction with Article 3 in its procedural aspect. ...

## E    Reflections and Questions

1. There has been an evolution of the terminology used to describe specific forms of discrimination faced by women and their risk of human rights violations. One of them has been the concept of *vulnerability*, which has been used by both the regional protection systems for the Americas and Europe to identify women as particularly exposed to problems such as domestic violence and human rights violations in the education and health settings.[3] It has also been a beneficial strategy, leading to lines of jurisprudence particularly focused on women's needs. Vulnerability is a controversial term though, which runs the danger of perpetuating the perception of women as victims, rather than as potential agents of leadership, change, and decision-making in our societies. As also discussed throughout this book, women have been very visible leaders in recent times of crisis and every day they hold more decision-making and influential positions. Can you think of ways to reconcile the vulnerability approach with legal standards that promote women's leadership and autonomy in decision-making? Do you think terminology in general is important when it comes to addressing discrimination against women?[4] Do you see any connections between the concept of vulnerability and the intersectionality of forms of discrimination discussed in Chapter 3?

2. Professors Peroni and Timmer discuss in their article criteria to consider a group vulnerable. Among these is the group's history of discrimination and disadvantage; their minority status; and their susceptibility to harm. Some of the examples mentioned in their article are the Roma minority in Europe, persons living with HIV, individuals with disabilities, and asylum seekers. Can you think of other groups that meet these criteria? Do you think all women meet the criteria to be considered vulnerable? Should there be other considerations and/or criteria involved in considering a group as vulnerable or susceptible to discrimination and violence?[5]

3. Is it good for international human rights to have many groups identified as vulnerable? Every day the international community identifies more groups as vulnerable or in a vulnerable position to human rights violations. Among those recently identified by the universal system of human rights and regional protection systems are older persons, persons with disabilities, and persons belonging to LGBTI groups. For example, the regional human rights protection system for the Americas has had a significant growth in its Rapporteurships

---

[3]    For more reading on tendencies in the regional human rights protection systems in the area of discrimination and the question of effectiveness, *see* Rosa Celorio, *Discrimination and the Regional Human Rights Protection Systems: The Enigma of Effectiveness*, 40 U. PA. J. INT'L L. 784–790, 798–809 (2019).

[4]    For more reading, *see* Martha Albertson Fineman, *Vulnerability and Inevitable Inequality*, 4 OSLO L. REV. 133, 134–135, 142–143, 146–149 (2017).

[5]    Alexander H.E. Morawa, *"Vulnerability" as a Concept in International Human Rights Law*, 10 JOURNAL OF INTERNATIONAL RELATIONS AND DEVELOPMENT 139–55, 139–147 (2003).

developed to protect the rights of vulnerable groups, including women; children; LGBTI persons; afro-descendent persons and indigenous peoples; persons deprived of liberty, human rights defenders; and older persons. A specialized treaty solely devoted to older persons was adopted by the Organization of American States in 2015. Is the increasing recognition of vulnerable groups advantageous for international human rights law? Can you think of steps needed to make sure that states properly protect the human rights of all these persons identified as vulnerable?[6]

4. The European Court of Human Rights judgment in the case of *Carvalho Pinto de Sousa Mourais v. Portugal* discusses negative stereotypes regarding a women's sexuality after fifty. In this particular matter, the stereotype of women's sexuality being limited to the child-bearing years was applied by the Portuguese judiciary to limit the damages awarded in this medical malpractice case. One of the most important effects of social stereotypes of the gender roles of women in society is that they can be permeated in the activity of the judiciary, representing an important barrier to treat women's cases as important and in an expeditious way. The judiciary often reflects prevailing social discrimination against women in our societies. This illustrates the need to incorporate education in law schools and in judicial training about the right of women to live free from all forms of discrimination. It is useful to train judges, prosecutors, public defenders, and all attorneys on this important value early on.[7]

5. The Inter-American Court of Human Rights case related to *Gonzalez Lluy v. Ecuador* exemplifies the gravity of the discrimination faced by girls living with HIV in education systems. In this particular case, a three-year old was infected with HIV due to a negligent blood transfusion. She was later expelled from school and suffered different kinds of discrimination in this setting. Look at paragraph 290 *supra*, on how the Court refers to both vulnerability and intersectionality in its description of the factors that drove the discrimination faced by Talía Gonzalez Lluy in the education system, including her status as a woman and as a girl, person living with HIV, individual with disabilities, and socio-economic status. The Inter-American Court also refers to HIV-related stigmatization and how it worsens in the case of vulnerable groups.[8]

6. The case of *BS v. Spain* exemplifies how courts sometimes recognize the vulnerability and intersecting forms of discrimination that women can face due to their sex and race, without using the terms "vulnerability," "intersectionality," and/or "multiple forms of discrimination." In this particular case, an afro-descendent woman claims that she was targeted for police violence and hate speech based on a combination of sexism and racism. The national administration of justice authorities in Spain failed to properly investigate whether these

---

[6] Inter-American Commission on Human Rights, *Strategic Plan 2017–2021*, pp. 30–36, www.oas .org/en/iachr/mandate/StrategicPlan2017/docs/StrategicPlan2017-2021.pdf; Inter-American Convention on Protecting the Human Rights of Older Persons, adopted on June 15, 2015, entered into force on January 11, 2017, U.N. Registration 02/27/2017 No. 54318, www.oas.org/en/sla/dil/inter_american _treaties_A-70_human_rights_older_persons_signatories.asp.

[7] For reading on judicial training experiences at the national level, *see* Beatriz Kohen, *Gender Training for the Judiciary in Argentina*, 21 INT'L J. LEGAL PROF. 333, 335–343 (2014).

[8] For more reading on the rights of girls living with HIV/AIDS, *see* General Comment 3 on HIV/AIDS and the Rights of the Child, Committee on the Rights of the Child, CRC/GC/2003/3, ¶¶ 1–3, 5–14 (March 17, 2003).

acts of police harassment and violence were motivated by racism, in contravention of Article 14 of the European Convention on Human Rights. The case is viewed as a potential precursor to the development of more concrete analysis on the problem of intersectionality by the European Court of Human Rights, which has been shy of doing so.[9]

7. Many factors can impact the effectiveness of existing legal standards adopted at the regional and universal levels to curb the problem of discrimination. These include the lack of political will by states to comply with its individual case decisions; and the scarcity of human and financial resources. Discrimination also occurs at the rural and local levels; areas in which it is very difficult for international law to really make a difference and have an impact. Can you think of ways to make universal and regional human rights bodies more effective in addressing discrimination against women? Can you think of examples of collaboration universal and regional bodies can have with national entities in addressing discrimination against women?[10]

## Note: The problem of police violence in the United States and its effects on African-American women: The case of Breonna Taylor

The United States has had a very well-known history of structural and systemic racial discrimination and racism which endures until today. One of the most heart-wrenching components of this history is the widespread problem of police killings of afro-descendent persons. Just in 2020, the police killing of George Floyd paralyzed the United States and motivated thousands to protest on the streets and demand prompt attention to the ongoing problem of racial violence and discrimination in the United States.[11] In many ways, the killing of George Floyd brought renewed attention to the problem of racial discrimination in the United States and placed the issue at the center of the presidential campaigns during 2020.

Many police violence cases have resulted from the use of excessive and unjustified force, and have ended in impunity. The most publicized cases have been of men and young boys, including Trayvon Martin, Eric Gardner, Michael Brown, and George Floyd, among many others.[12]

African-American women have also fallen victim to the problem of police killings in the United States. One of the most visible cases during 2020 was the tragic death of Breonna Taylor. On March 13, 2020, three police officers broke into Breonna Taylor's apartment and

---

[9]  For more reading, *see* Lourdes Peroni, *Racial Discrimination in Strasbourg (Part II): Intersectionality and Context*, Strasbourg Observers, https://strasbourgobservers.com/2012/10/17/racial-discrimination-in-strasbourg-part-ii-intersectionality-and-context/.

[10]  *See* Press Release, *Joint Call of United Nations Rapporteurs, Committees, and Regional Mechanisms in Africa, the Americas, and Europe, International Day on the Elimination of Violence against Women* (Nov. 22, 2017), www.oas.org/en/iachr/media_center/PReleases/2017/188.asp.

[11]  For more reading, *Why The Killing of George Floyd Sparked an American Uprising*, TIME, June 4, 2020, https://time.com/5847967/george-floyd-protests-trump/.

[12]  *See, for reference*, WASHINGTON POST, *Fatal Force (Police Shootings Database)*, updated February 18, 2021, www.washingtonpost.com/graphics/investigations/police-shootings-database/; BBC News, *Breonna Taylor: Timeline of black deaths caused by police*, January 6, 2021, www.bbc.com/news/world-us-canada-52905408; Jeffrey A. Fagan and Alexis D. Campbell, *Race and Reasonableness in Police Killings*, 100 BOSTON UNIVERSITY LAW REVIEW 951 (2020); Columbia Public Law Research Paper No. 14-655 (2020), pp. 954–60, 980–999.

shot her. The police officers forced their entry into her apartment as part of an investigation focused on drug dealing operations. No drugs were found in her apartment. Breonna Taylor was 26 years old at the time of her death. She was a medical worker and emergency room technician.[13]

The killing of Breonna Taylor demonstrates that the problem of violence against women is often connected to vulnerabilities, stereotypes, and intersectional discrimination aggravated by racism, historical disadvantage, and inferior treatment. Her case is also paradigmatic of the problem of impunity that negatively affects the investigation, judgment, and sanction of cases of violence against women. To date, no police officers have been convicted for the killing of Breonna Taylor.

## III    STRICT SCRUTINY

Tribunals around the world are reviewing distinctions and forms of differentiated treatment which affect women with intense scrutiny. According to CEDAW and prevailing discrimination law jurisprudence, any different treatment afforded to any of the sexes should be adequately justified by the states supporting these distinctions. As the cases below illustrate, different treatment in the law can affect both women and men similarly situated in the areas of employment, parental leave, and other realms. In general, these distinctions need to be justified by a legitimate government aim, they need to be reasonable and objective, and be proportional to the end sought.

The following cases show how different regional courts have applied the strict scrutiny standard to distinctions in the law affecting both women and men, and the criteria they have used to evaluate the government objectives.

**A**      ***María Eugenia Morales de Sierra v. Guatemala*, Inter-American Commission on Human Rights**

Report No. 4/01, Case 11.625
January 19, 2001
Citations and footnotes omitted

*In the case below, the petitioners alleged that the Civil Code of Guatemala discriminated against women by assigning different responsibilities to the spouses within marriage. The following excerpts discuss the Inter-American Commission on Human Rights' analysis regarding the rights to equality and non-discrimination under the American Convention.*

36. The Commission observes that the guarantees of equality and non-discrimination underpinning the American Convention and American Declaration of the Rights and Duties of Man reflect essential bases for the very concept of human rights. As the Inter-American Court has stated, these principles "are inherent in the idea of the oneness in dignity and

---

[13]    Richard A. Oppel Jr., Derrick Bryson Taylor, and Nicholas Bogel-Burroughs, *What to Know About Breonna Taylor's Death*, N.Y. TIMES, January 6, 2021, www.nytimes.com/article/breonna-taylor-police.html.

worth of all human beings." Statutory distinctions based on status criteria, such as, for example, race or sex, therefore necessarily give rise to heightened scrutiny. What the European Court and Commission have stated is also true for the Americas, that as "the advancement of the equality of the sexes is today a major goal," ... "very weighty reasons would have to be put forward" to justify a distinction based solely on the ground of sex.

37. The gender-based distinctions under study have been upheld as a matter of domestic law essentially on the basis of the need for certainty and juridical security, the need to protect the marital home and children, respect for traditional Guatemalan values, and in certain cases, the need to protect women in their capacity as wives and mothers. However, the Court of Constitutionality made no effort to probe the validity of these assertions or to weigh alternative positions, and the Commission is not persuaded that the distinctions cited are even consistent with the aims articulated. For example, the fact that Article 109 excludes a married woman from representing the marital union, except in extreme circumstances, neither contributes to the orderly administration of justice, nor does it favor her protection or that of the home or children. To the contrary, it deprives a married woman of the legal capacity necessary to invoke the judicial protection which the orderly administration of justice and the American Convention require be made available to every person.

38. By requiring married women to depend on their husbands to represent the union – in this case María Eugenia Morales de Sierra – the terms of the Civil Code mandate a system in which the ability of approximately half the married population to act on a range of essential matters is subordinated to the will of the other half. The overarching effect of the challenged provisions is to deny married women legal autonomy. The fact that the Civil Code deprives María Eugenia Morales de Sierra, as a married woman, of legal capacities to which other Guatemalans are entitled leaves her rights vulnerable to violation without recourse.

39. In the instant case the Commission finds that the gender-based distinctions established in the challenged articles cannot be justified, and contravene the rights of María Eugenia Morales de Sierra set forth in Article 24. These restrictions are of immediate effect, arising simply by virtue of the fact that the cited provisions are in force. As a married woman, she is denied protections on the basis of her sex which married men and other Guatemalans are accorded. The provisions she challenges restrict, *inter alia*, her legal capacity, her access to resources, her ability to enter into certain kinds of contracts (relating, for example, to property held jointly with her husband), to administer such property, and to invoke administrative or judicial recourse. They have the further effect of reinforcing systemic disadvantages which impede the ability of the victim to exercise a host of other rights and freedoms. ...

## B    *Konstantin Markin v. Russia*, **European Court of Human Rights**

App. No. 30078/06, March 22, 2012
© Council of Europe, reproduced with permission
Citations and footnotes omitted

*The following case analyzes the refusal of domestic authorities in Russia to grant the applicant parental leave because he is male. The analysis of the European Court of Human Rights in the following case excerpts is undertaken under Article 14 of the European Court of Human Rights, in conjunction with the right to private and family life under Article 8.*

124.   As the Court has consistently held, Article 14 complements the other substantive provisions of the Convention and its Protocols. It has no independent existence since it has
effect solely in relation to "the enjoyment of the rights and freedoms" safeguarded thereby.
Although the application of Article 14 does not presuppose a breach of those provisions
– and to this extent it is autonomous – there can be no room for its application unless the
facts at issue fall within the ambit of one or more of them. The prohibition of discrimination enshrined in Article 14 thus extends beyond the enjoyment of the rights and freedoms
which the Convention and the Protocols thereto require each State to guarantee. It applies
also to those additional rights, falling within the general scope of any Convention Article,
for which the State has voluntarily decided to provide. This principle is well entrenched in
the Court's case-law. ...

125.   The Court has also held that not every difference in treatment will amount to a violation
of Article 14. It must be established that other persons in an analogous or relevantly similar
situation enjoy preferential treatment and that this distinction is discriminatory ... A difference of treatment is discriminatory if it has no objective and reasonable justification; in
other words, if it does not pursue a legitimate aim or if there is not a reasonable relationship
of proportionality between the means employed and the aim sought to be realised. ...

126.   The Contracting States enjoy a certain margin of appreciation in assessing whether and
to what extent differences in otherwise similar situations justify a difference in treatment
... The scope of the margin of appreciation will vary according to the circumstances, the
subject matter and its background ... but the final decision as to the observance of the
Convention's requirements rests with the Court. Since the Convention is first and foremost
a system for the protection of human rights, the Court must however have regard to the
changing conditions in Contracting States and respond, for example, to any emerging
consensus as to the standards to be achieved. ...

127.   The Court further reiterates that the advancement of gender equality is today a major
goal in the member States of the Council of Europe and very weighty reasons would have
to be put forward before such a difference of treatment could be regarded as compatible
with the Convention ... In particular, references to traditions, general assumptions or prevailing social attitudes in a particular country are insufficient justification for a difference
in treatment on grounds of sex. For example, States are prevented from imposing traditions
that derive from the man's primordial role and the woman's secondary role in the family.
...

131.   The Court observes that the applicant, being a serviceman, had no statutory right to
three years' parental leave, while servicewomen were entitled to such leave. It must therefore first consider whether the applicant was in an analogous situation to servicewomen.

132.   The Court has already found that, in so far as parental leave and parental leave allowances are concerned, men are in an analogous situation to women. Indeed, in contrast to
maternity leave which is intended to enable the woman to recover from the childbirth and
to breastfeed her baby if she so wishes, parental leave and parental leave allowances relate
to the subsequent period and are intended to enable a parent concerned to stay at home to
look after an infant personally. ...

138.   Turning now to the circumstances of the present case, the Court notes that the Government advanced several arguments to justify the difference in treatment between servicemen and servicewomen as regards entitlement to parental leave. The Court will examine them in turn.

139.   Firstly, as regards the argument relating to the special social role of women in the raising of children, the Court observes that already in the *Petrovic v. Austria* case … it noted the gradual evolution of society towards a more equal sharing between men and women of responsibilities for the upbringing of their children. In that case the Court did not consider it possible to find that a distinction on the basis of sex with respect to parental leave allowances, which had existed in Austria in the 1980s, was in violation of Article 14 taken in conjunction with Article 8. …

140.   The relevant international and comparative-law material demonstrates that the evolution of society – which began in the 1980s as acknowledged in the *Petrovic* case – has since significantly advanced. It shows that in a majority of European countries, including in Russia itself, the legislation now provides that parental leave may be taken by civilian men and women, while the countries limiting the parental leave entitlement to women are in a small minority. …

142.   Similarly, the difference in treatment cannot be justified by reference to traditions prevailing in a certain country. The Court has already found that States may not impose traditional gender roles and gender stereotypes. Moreover, given that under Russian law civilian men and women are both entitled to parental leave and it is the family's choice to decide which parent should take parental leave to take care of the new-born child, the Court is not convinced by the assertion that Russian society is not ready to accept similar equality between men and women serving in the armed forces.

143.   The Court concludes from the above that the reference to the traditional distribution of gender roles in society cannot justify the exclusion of men, including servicemen, from the entitlement to parental leave. The Court agrees with the Chamber that gender stereotypes, such as the perception of women as primary child-carers and men as primary breadwinners, cannot, by themselves, be considered to amount to sufficient justification for a difference in treatment, any more than similar stereotypes based on race, origin, colour or sexual orientation.

144.   Nor is the Court persuaded by the Government's second argument, namely that the extension of the parental leave entitlement to servicemen would have a negative effect on the fighting power and operational effectiveness of the armed forces, while the granting of parental leave to servicewomen does not entail such risk because in the armed forces women are less numerous than men. …

151.   In view of the foregoing, the Court considers that the exclusion of servicemen from the entitlement to parental leave, while servicewomen are entitled to such leave, cannot be said to be reasonably or objectively justified. The Court concludes that this difference in treatment, of which the applicant was a victim, amounted to discrimination on grounds of sex.

152.   There has therefore been a violation of Article 14 taken in conjunction with Article 8.

## C      Reflections and Questions

1.  In the *María Eugenia Morales de Sierra* case, the Inter-American Commission on Human Rights discusses in paragraph 36 how "weighty reasons" are needed to justify distinctions on the basis of sex between similarly situated persons. In this particular case, those similarly situated are wives and husbands in the family, and the Civil Code of Guatemala assigned explicitly different roles for the spouses in and out of the home. The IACHR looked in particular at whether the distinction was justified by a legitimate government aim, whether it was objective and reasonable, and whether it was proportional to the end sought. The IACHR rejected the Guatemalan Constitutional Court argument that these distinctions were designed to protect women and their role in the family. The IACHR also went as far as indicating that this unjustified different treatment left women with increased exposure to and risk of gender-based violence. Can you think of cases in which distinctions in the law between women and men may be adequately justified by a government aim?[14]

2.  In the case of *Konstantin Markin v. Russia*, the European Court of Human Rights also reviews a legal distinction in the awarding of parental leave between men and women with a strict scrutiny standard. Do you see any difference between the application of the standard in the *Konstantin Markin* judgment with the *María Eugenia Morales de Sierra* ruling?

3.  In paragraph 126 of the *Konstantin Markin* judgment *supra*, the Court discusses the margin of appreciation that European states have when it comes to reviewing the legality of distinctions between similarly situated persons, and the consideration of any evidence of consensus among European states of how to address these at the national level. Do you think the application of this margin of appreciation affected the result of this case?[15]

4.  In the *Konstantin Markin* case *supra*, the European Court of Human Rights alludes in paragraph 132 to how stereotypes can be the basis of distinctions in the law between men and women. In this particular case, the distinction is between military service men and women and their access to parental leave. The government had justified the sole availability of parental leave to women on the basis of the presupposed special and biological connection between women and their children, particularly right after birth. The European Court of Human Rights rejected this notion and considered both men and women as similarly placed when it came to parental leave. Stereotypical notions cannot be used to justify a government objective. Note as well how the European Court of Human Rights focuses on the impact of social advances in reviewing these distinctions. In paragraph 140 *supra*, the European Court of Human Rights refers in particular to the tendency in European countries of moving towards a more egalitarian sharing among men and women of child-rearing responsibilities and the increasing role of men as caretakers in this capacity.

---

[14]   For examples of temporary special measures that may be justified to advance the participation of women in political decision-making positions, *see* Social Science Research Council, Working Paper, Mona Lena Brook, *Gender and Elections: Temporary Special Measures Beyond Quotas* (February 2015), pp. 1–3, 4–24.

[15]   For a discussion of the discrimination-focused jurisprudence of the European Court of Human Rights, and the application of the margin of appreciation doctrine, *see* Oddny Mjoll Arnardottir, *The Differences That Make a Difference: Recent Developments on the Discrimination Grounds and the Margin of Appreciation under Article 14 of the European Convention on Human Rights*, 14 Hum. Rts. L. Rev. 647, 648–663 (2014).

As the European Court of Human Rights does frequently in its jurisprudence, it takes into consideration the legal changes and advances in European states in its interpretation of the content and scope of the European Convention on Human Rights and in this particular case Article 14 and its prohibition of discrimination.[16]

## IV HATE SPEECH AND GENDER IDEOLOGY

There has been important progress towards advancement of the rights of women at the national level and in many regions of the world. There are many countries at the moment with legislation, policies, and programs designed to build societies free from all forms of discrimination, and mechanisms to prevent and adequately respond to gender-based violence. Every day there are more women in leadership and decision-making positions, including presidents, prime ministers, senators and parliamentarians, judges, executives, journalists, and human rights defenders. Women and girls have also become important influencers and voices in the digital space, and in the transition to a virtual world.

Even though this is important social progress, there has been important backlash towards women and girls in these roles. Some of the backlash has been in the form of hate speech for defying the socially predetermined roles of women as relegated to the family, with the goal of silencing and curtailing the active role women have in our societies. Hate speech can be part of a gender backlash movement – sometimes referred to as gender ideology[17] – meant to drive a return to patriarchalism, and a narrow understanding of the content of women's and gender equality. Gender ideology can be in the form of opposition to advances in the recognition of rights for persons historically discriminated against on the basis of sexual orientation and gender identity, and sexual and reproductive rights. This section examines the problem of hate speech, forms of gender backlash, and what they mean for the future of the rights of women to live free from discrimination.

**A        Council of Europe, Commissioner for Human Rights, *Hate Speech Against Women Should be Specifically Tackled* (2014)[18]**

© Council of Europe, reproduced with permission

---

[16]    For more reading on the potential impact of the *Konstantin Markin* ruling in the gender discrimination jurisprudence of the European Court of Human Rights, *see* Alexandra Timmer, *Konstantin Markin v. Russia: Gender Justice in Strasbourg*, Strasbourg Observers (March 22, 2012), https://strasbourgobservers.com/2012/03/22/gender-justice-in-strasbourg/#more-1492. For a discussion of the discrimination jurisprudence of the European Court of Human Rights, *see* Janneke Gerards, *The Discrimination Grounds of Article 14 of the European Convention on Human Rights*, 13 HUM. RTS. L. REV. 99, 100–103, 116–113 (2013).

[17]    For more reading on gender ideology tendencies, *see* Human Rights Watch, *Breaking the Buzz Word: Fighting the Gender Ideology Myth*, www.hrw.org/world-report/2019/essay/breaking-the-buzzword.

[18]    *See* Council of Europe, Commissioner for Human Rights, *Hate Speech Against Women Should be Specifically Tackled* (2014), https://www.coe.int/en/web/commissioner/-/hate-speech-against-women-should-be-specifically-tackl-1.

In May 2013, a campaign led notably by Women, Action and the Media and the Everyday Sexism Project attracted global public attention to the issue of social media content promoting violence against women. Such content included the photograph of a well-known singer with a bloodied and beaten face with a caption celebrating her boyfriend's assault. The campaign prompted Facebook to react and update its policies on hate speech, which now take better account of an often-neglected type of hate speech, that targeting women.

Such hate speech is proliferating, notably on the Internet, with daily calls for violence against women and threats of murder, sexual assault or rape.

Arguably, the most famous case is that of Malala Yousafzai, the young Pakistani girl who, after surviving an assassination attempt prompted by her stance for women's rights, had to withstand a hostile campaign on the Internet. Malala is now a symbol of women's struggle worldwide, including in Europe. Recent cases, in fact, remind us that if we believe that hate speech against women is not a European problem, we are profoundly wrong.

A few days ago, for example, an investigation was opened in the UK against two police officers who used denigrating language against a 19-year old woman who intended to lodge a complaint for domestic violence.

In Italy, the speaker of Parliament, Laura Boldrini, has been the target of repeated hate speech since she was sworn in, including recently when the leader of the 5-Star Movement, a political group which obtained a quarter of the votes in last year's legislative elections, published a clearly misogynistic post on his blog, which was picked up by his social media account and those used by his MPs, and which generated violent, insulting comments against her. Numerous are also the cases of female journalists all over Europe who have been the target of explicit gender-based threats. Many of them felt obliged to leave the blogosphere.

These are just few examples of a much broader, underestimated phenomenon that needs to be urgently tackled. …

**A clear signal**

Freedom of expression is a fundamental right which must be protected, but it is not an absolute right. There are limits which apply, in particular with regard to hate speech.

Hate speech against women is a long-standing, though underreported problem in Europe that member states have the duty to fight more resolutely.

It is necessary that legal and political tools be in place to firmly condemn it and prosecute the perpetrators. As the world celebrates International Women's Day on March 8, political and opinion leaders in Europe should send a signal to the public which clearly shows that violent discourse against women has no place in a democratic society and will not be tolerated.

**B      Tanya Katerí Hernández, *Hate Speech and the Language of Racism in Latin America: A Lens for Reconsidering Global Hate Speech Restrictions and Legislation Models***

32 U. PA. J. INT'L L. 805, 807–826 (2010–2011), reproduced with permission
Citations and footnotes omitted
…

"Hate speech expresses, advocates, encourages, promotes or incites hatred of a group of individuals distinguished by a particular feature or set of features," whom are targeted for hostility. While the English language term "hate speech" is often used as a term of art within

Latin American legal publications, commentators appear to use "hate speech" and "discurso del odio" interchangeably. Regardless of which term is used, it is a concept that is globally understood and widely prohibited.

The significant harms hate speech incites have engendered a widespread international consensus that it should be illegal. When hate speech is permitted to be propagated, it encourages a social climate in which particular groups are denigrated and their discriminatory treatment is accepted as normal. Even the presumably free speech absolutist United States has come to implicitly acknowledge the hate speech infringements on equality through employment discrimination laws regarding racial and sexual harassment.

Hate speech creates discord in the community, harms the target group, and infringes upon equality. For instance, the knowledge that anti-Semitic hate propaganda was clearly connected to the rise of Nazism informed the development of international laws against hate speech. Discourse analysis and philosophy scholars have similarly noted that racism is taught and legitimated through public discourse.

In addition, hate speech imposes direct health harms on racialized groups. In short, hate speech directly implicates a nation-state's pursuit of racial equality. In fact, political discourse and elections become healthier and more moderate in jurisdictions that enact hate speech legislation such as Britain, Germany, Austria, the Netherlands, India, and post-apartheid South Africa. Of course as an empirical matter, it may instead be that the egalitarian nature of the societies is what first creates the moderate political discourse that leads to hate speech legislation. Nevertheless, such jurisdictions chose to enact hate speech legislation because there is little social value in racist speech whose basic purpose is to degrade others, deny them their identity as human beings, exclude them from the entitlements of the basic social and constitutional covenant, and expose them to violence. By denying human dignity to some people, hate speech attacks the very basis of democratic systems.

Yet, it should be noted that the regulation of hate speech can be viewed as a danger to democracy. This alternative vision of hate speech regulation as a harm arises out of the concern that regulation is a form of censorship that can hinder expressive platforms for advocating racial equality, and thus lead to selective prosecution targeted at unpopular political minorities. The history of the Civil Rights Movement in the United States is emblematic of the importance of having unfettered free speech rights to demonstrate, march, and express dissident perspectives about the existence of white supremacy and need for social justice. Indeed, the First Amendment of the U.S. Constitution has historically enabled civil rights proponents to articulate their political speech even when socially unpopular. ...

## C     Reflections and Questions

1.  International law today has very developed legal standards related to freedom of expression. There are also a number of universal and regional mechanisms created to address freedom of expression, including Special Rapporteurships at the United Nations and the Inter-American Commission on Human Rights solely devoted to this issue. Existing human rights treaties also contain vast provisions protecting the right to freedom of expression, including Article 19 of the International Covenant on Civil and Political Rights, Article 10

of the European Convention on Human Rights, Article 9 of the African Charter on Human and Peoples' Rights, and Article 13 of the American Convention on Human Rights.[19]

2.  The Human Rights Committee has indicated concretely that Article 19 (paragraph 2) of the ICCPR requires state parties to guarantee fully the right to freedom of expression, which includes the "right to seek, receive and impart information and ideas of all kinds regardless of frontiers."[20] This includes expression which may be considered "deeply offensive."[21] According to the Human Rights Committee, Article 19 (paragraph 3) of the ICCPR states that any restrictions to the right to freedom of expression must be provided for in the law, be justified by legitimate state aims, must be grounded on necessity, and be carefully tailored to the end pursued.[22] Considering these international law principles, when can speech considered motivated by hatred be regulated and/or restricted? How can the requirements of legality, necessity, and proportionality be applied to regulate hate speech? What should be the criteria guiding these restrictions?

3.  There has been rising global concern over forms of hate speech in the last decade. Hate speech can occur online and offline, and can involve the dissemination of ideas and messages which promote animosity towards women and girls, racial, minority, and ethnic groups, human rights defenders, journalists, migrants, refugees, and other groups. Several well-known country leaders have used political rhetoric founded on hatred to reach high politically elected office and incentivize social violence. It is often used against human rights defenders and leaders when they advocate for causes which are not popular socially, are opposed by given groups of the population, or threaten large economic interests. For example, it has been well documented how social media platforms have been used to incite violence and hate speech against the Rohingya minority in Myanmar.[23]

4.  Due to the ongoing gravity of the problem of hate speech, in 2020 the United Nations released a specialized strategy and plan of action to address this issue.[24] The strategy document alludes to hate speech, xenophobia, racism, and intolerance as social dividers and forms of extreme discrimination nationally and around the world.[25] The strategy defines hate speech as "any kind of communication in speech, writing or behaviour, that attacks or uses pejorative or discriminatory language with reference to a person or a group on the

---

[19]  *See, for reference*, Agnès Callamard, *Introduction: Regardless of Frontiers? Global Freedom of Expression Norms for a Troubled World, in* REGARDLESS OF FRONTIERS: GLOBAL FREEDOM OF EXPRESSION IN A TROUBLED WORLD 5–13 (Lee C. Bollinger and Agnès Callamard, eds., Columbia University Press, 2021).

[20]  *See* General Comment 34 on Article 19: Freedoms of Opinion and Expression, Human Rights Committee, CCPR/C/GC/34, ¶ 11 (Sept. 12, 2011).

[21]  *See id.*, ¶ 11.

[22]  *See id.*, ¶¶ 24–27, 33–36.

[23]  For more reading on hate speech worldwide, *see Joint open letter on concerns about the global increase in hate speech*, signed by 26 United Nations Special Rapporteurs, Independent Experts, and Working Groups, September 23, 2019, www.ohchr.org/EN/NewsEvents/Pages/DisplayNews.aspx?NewsID=25036&LangID=E.; Alexandra Stevenson, *Facebook admits it was used to incite violence in Myanmar*, N.Y. TIMES, November 6, 2018, www.nytimes.com/2018/11/06/technology/myanmar-facebook.html.

[24]  *See, generally*, United Nations, *United Nations Strategy and Plan of Action on Hate Speech*, September 2020, www.un.org/en/genocideprevention/documents/advising-and-mobilizing/Action_plan_on_hate_speech_EN.pdf.

[25]  *Id.*, p. 3.

basis of who they are, in other words, based on their religion, ethnicity, nationality, race, colour, descent, gender or other identity factor."[26]

The U.N. strategy also affirms how hate speech is intimately connected to violence and undermines sustainable development efforts. The execution of this strategy has been entrusted to a United Nations Working Group on Hate Speech, which includes the coordinated efforts of 16 United Nations agencies, Country Teams, Peace Operations, and Political Missions.[27] States are considered those mainly responsible for preventing and countering hate speech, in accordance with international law and human rights law.[28]

The United Nations' strategy mandates state action in three categories of hate speech, including "direct or public incitement to genocide" and "advocacy of national, racial and religious hatred that constitutes incitement to discrimination, hostility or violence," which are prohibited by international law; forms of hate speech which may need to be prohibited in accordance with the requirements of legality, legitimate aim, need, and proportionality; and instances in which legal restrictions should not be imposed on expressions which are offensive, shocking or disturbing.[29] The severity of the speech can be assessed on the basis of six criteria: (i) the legal, political, social, and economic context; (ii) the position or status of the speaker in society; (iii) the state of mind of the speaker; (iv) the nature and style of the expression; (v) reach of expression; and (vi) degree of risk of harm.[30] The United Nations' strategy also encourages both state and non-state actors to adopt comprehensive approaches to hate speech, including the enactment of measures, policies, and practices advocating for tolerance and social awareness.[31] Consider five ways in which the United Nations' strategy to address hate speech can be applied to that motivated by gender-based violence and discrimination.

5. The European Court of Human Rights has ruled on important cases related to hate speech in the area of sexual discrimination and what can constitute permissible restrictions to the right to freedom of expression protected by Article 10 of the European Convention on Human Rights. For example, in the case of *Vejdeland & Others v. Sweden*, the European Court of Human Rights examined a matter in which applicants distributed leaflets in an upper secondary school which contained denigrating language based on sexual orientation.[32] The applicants considered that their conviction by the Supreme Court for agitation against a national or ethnic group interfered with their right to freedom of expression under Article 10 of the European Convention.[33] The applicants denied that the leaflets were intended to motivate hateful acts against persons on the basis of their sexual orientation.[34] The European Court of Human Rights found that the interference with the right to freedom of expression in this case was prescribed by law, necessary in a democratic society, and

---

[26] *Id.*, p. 8.
[27] *Id.*, p. 3.
[28] *Id.*, p. 5.
[29] *Id.*, p. 5.
[30] *Id.*, pp. 17–18.
[31] *Id.*, p. 15.
[32] *See Vejdeland & Others v. Sweden*, App. No. 1813/07, Eur. Ct. H. R., ¶¶ 7–17, 41–60 (Feb. 9, 2012).
[33] *Id.*, ¶¶ 21, 23–60.
[34] *Id.*, ¶¶ 7–17, 41–60.

proportional. The Court held that discrimination on the basis of sexual orientation is as serious as discrimination based on race, origin, or color, and inciting to hatred does not necessarily need to include a call to violence or other criminal acts to be prohibited by law.[35] The Court also considered that the leaflets were left in lockers of young people who are at an "impressionable and sensitive age" and had no possibility to decline or accept them.[36]

6. Two of the most affected regions by gender ideology tendencies have been Latin America and Europe. Gender ideology forms of expression have been used by conservative groups to criticize the advancement of the rights of women and girls, in particular those related to sexual and reproductive rights, and progress on behalf of LGBTI individuals and groups. A resonating theme is the call to return to traditional family values, and a denomination of feminist tendencies as radical and contrary to religious tenets.[37]

## V    CONCLUSIONS: TOWARDS THE AUTONOMY AND LEADERSHIP OF WOMEN FROM A HUMAN RIGHTS PERSPECTIVE

This chapter has focused on the contours and complexity of the problem of discrimination against women. The international community has progressed in the development of terminology identifying the forms of discrimination and inferior treatment faced by women, and the definition of state obligations to prevent and eradicate them. Key terms such as vulnerability, stereotypes, and intersectionality when properly used can provide an important perspective for states of critical issues that need to be addressed in their national and local policies.

Legal standards underscore crucial steps for states to take at the national level to comply with international law and connect it with the national and local realities. Discrimination is an area in progress, and there is an urgent need for more legal standards in areas such as technology and social media; stereotypes in education; hate speech and violence; temporary special measures in education and employment; strict scrutiny for different treatment which is harmful to women; and the implementation of the concept of gender parity in political participation and other key social areas. Legal standards need to adapt and reflect the modern manifestations of the problem of discrimination.

The challenge now is how to contextualize and implement theoretical concepts at the national level, to ensure that they really have a positive impact on women's daily lives. On this road, it is key to incorporate women from different races, ethnicities, income levels, and social conditions so they can have an important voice in the development of legislation, policies,

---

[35]   *Id.,* ¶ 55.

[36]   *Id.,* ¶ 56.

[37]   For more reading on gender ideology tendencies, *see* Eliza Apperly, *Why Europe's Far Right Is Targeting Gender Studies,* THE ATLANTIC, June 15, 2019, www.theatlantic.com/international/archive/ 2019/06/europe-far-right-target-gender-studies/591208/; Maxine Molineaux, *The Battle Over Gender Ideology,* INTERNATIONAL POLITICS AND SOCIETY, August 12, 2017, www.ips-journal.eu/regions/latin -america/the-battle-over-gender-ideology-2472/; Sonia Correa, *Gender Ideology: Tracking its Origins and Meanings in Current Gender Politics,* London School of Economics Department of Gender Studies, https://blogs.lse.ac.uk/gender/2017/12/11/gender-ideology-tracking-its-origins-and-meanings-in-current -gender-politics/.

programs, and local measures which are destined to advance their human rights. This is key to advancing women's leadership, autonomy, and dignity. It is also paramount to achieving the effectiveness of any international law and national measures dedicated to the prevention and eradication of discrimination.

# 8. Sexual and reproductive rights: a gender equality and international law approach

## I  INTRODUCTION: SEXUAL AND REPRODUCTIVE RIGHTS AS WOMEN'S RIGHTS

This chapter centers on the sexual and reproductive rights of women, including an overview of contemporary developments, challenges, and advances. It reviews in particular important foundational documents to what we understand are women's rights related to sexuality, reproduction, and the right to the highest attainable standard of health in this area, including the Cairo Programme of Action adopted in 1994. An important foundational pillar to women's sexual and reproductive rights are their rights to decide freely and responsibly on the number, spacing, and timing of their children. Women also have the right to access the information, education, means, and services necessary to make these decisions, and to adopt them free from all forms of violence, coercion, discrimination, and gender stereotypes.

As indicated in the Cairo Programme of Action, sexual and reproductive rights are a combination of both classical and specialized rights recognized at the universal, regional, and national levels. At the very core of sexual and reproductive rights are the rights to life, health, personal integrity, liberty, freedom of expression, privacy, non-discrimination, and freedom from violence, among others.

It is important to underscore that sexual and reproductive rights are an integral part of the human rights of women discussed throughout this casebook. Many of the state obligations analyzed are intricately connected with full compliance with sexual and reproductive rights, including the rights of women to have a dignified life; to personal integrity; to access scientific progress; to live free from all forms of intersectional discrimination and violence; the obligation of states to act with due diligence to protect all human rights; and the right to access adequate and effective judicial remedies when human rights violations occur. Many paramount values and principles are also part of the backbone of women's sexual and reproductive rights, including reproductive autonomy, dignity, liberty, privacy, informed consent, effective participation, and bodily integrity. There are many ongoing debates today regarding the content of sexual and reproductive rights, and social controversy driven by ideological, moral, and religious considerations.

Key legal standards related to sexual and reproductive rights have been adopted by United Nations treaty-based and charter-based organs; case decisions and judgments have been issued by the regional human rights protection systems in Europe, the Americas, and Africa, and by diverse national courts. Some of those most affected by sexual and reproductive rights restrictions today are women from low-income groups; women who belong to racial and ethnic minorities; girls under the age of 18; lesbian, bisexual, transgender, and intersex women; women deprived of liberty; women with disabilities; and migrants, refugees, and those displaced, as will be discussed throughout this chapter. Important benchmarks regarding sexual and reproductive rights have been identified in the Sustainable Development Goals, including the reduction of maternal mortality and the guarantee of universal access to sexual and reproductive health-care services and rights.[1]

This chapter delves into key areas related to the sexual and reproductive rights of women, including accessibility, affordability, and quality; the regulation of abortion; maternal health, mortality, and morbidity; and the content of the right to life and assisted reproductive technologies. Some of the issues explored in this chapter are important content in the state obligations to guarantee adequate services women need to ensure their sexual and reproductive health; the role of gender stereotypes and forms of discrimination as barriers to the offer of reproductive health services; how age, race, and income level can function as challenges to access key sexual and reproductive health services; rights related to abortion and the impact of legal restrictions; the ongoing problems of maternal mortality and morbidity; the concept of reproductive autonomy and its exercise regarding assisted reproductive technologies; the elements of informed consent; and the connection of gender-based violence to the exercise of sexual and reproductive rights.

## II    ACCESSIBILITY, AFFORDABILITY, AND QUALITY OF SEXUAL AND REPRODUCTIVE HEALTH SERVICES

The Cairo Programme of Action was the result of the International Conference on Population and Development, held in Egypt on September 5–13, 1994. It was adopted by 179 governments and underscored sexual and reproductive health as a fundamental component of the human rights of women. The Programme of Action was also historic in connecting gender equality and the empowerment of women with the goal of advancing social development and population policies. Many of the principles advanced by the Cairo Programme of Action still constitute the backbone of the content of sexual and reproductive rights. The Cairo Programme of Action in particular has informed the identification of elements to ensure the accessibility, affordability, and quality of sexual and reproductive health services.

Included below are key excerpts of the Cairo Programme of Action. This is followed by General Comment 22 of the Economic, Social and Cultural Rights Committee, which provides an overview of important guiding principles for the guarantee of the right to sexual and reproductive health under Article 12 of the International Covenant on Economic, Social and Cultural Rights.

### A    Programme of Action of the International Conference on Population and Development

A/CONF.171113/Rev.1, Cairo, September 5–13, 1994

---

[1]    For more reading, *see* U.N. General Assembly, *Transforming our World: The 2030 Agenda for Sustainable Development Goals*, A/RES/70/1 (Oct. 21, 2015), Goals 3.1, 3.7, and 5.6; Natalia Kanem, Executive Director of the United Nations Population Fund, *Sexual and Reproductive Health and Rights: The Cornerstone of Sustainable Development*, https://www.un.org/en/chronicle/article/sexual -and-reproductive-health-and-rights-cornerstone-sustainable-development.

7.2 Reproductive health is a state of complete physical, mental and social well-being and not merely the absence of disease or infirmity, in all matters relating to the reproductive system and to its functions and processes. Reproductive health therefore implies that people are able to have a satisfying and safe sex life and that they have the capability to reproduce and the freedom to decide if, when and how often to do so. Implicit in this last condition are the right of men and women to be informed and to have access to safe, effective, affordable and acceptable methods of family planning of their choice, as well as other methods of their choice for regulation of fertility which are not against the law, and the right of access to appropriate health-care services that will enable women to go safely through pregnancy and childbirth and provide couples with the best chance of having a healthy infant. In line with the above definition of reproductive health, reproductive health care is defined as the constellation of methods, techniques and services that contribute to reproductive health and well-being by preventing and solving reproductive health problems. It also includes sexual health, the purpose of which is the enhancement of life and personal relations, and not merely counselling and care related to reproduction and sexually transmitted diseases.

7.3 Bearing in mind the above definition, reproductive rights embrace certain human rights that are already recognized in national laws, international human rights documents and other consensus documents. These rights rest on the recognition of the basic right of all couples and individuals to decide freely and responsibly the number, spacing and timing of their children and to have the information and means to do so, and the right to attain the highest standard of sexual and reproductive health. It also includes their right to make decisions concerning reproduction free of discrimination, coercion and violence, as expressed in human rights documents. In the exercise of this right, they should take into account the needs of their living and future children and their responsibilities towards the community. The promotion of the responsible exercise of these rights for all people should be the fundamental basis for government- and community-supported policies and programmes in the area of reproductive health, including family planning. As part of their commitment, full attention should be given to the promotion of mutually respectful and equitable gender relations and particularly to meeting the educational and service needs of adolescents to enable them to deal in a positive and responsible way with their sexuality. Reproductive health eludes many of the world's people because of such factors as: inadequate levels of knowledge about human sexuality and inappropriate or poor-quality reproductive health information and services; the prevalence of high-risk sexual behaviour; discriminatory social practices; negative attitudes towards women and girls; and the limited power many women and girls have over their sexual and reproductive lives. Adolescents are particularly vulnerable because of their lack of information and access to relevant services in most countries. Older women and men have distinct reproductive and sexual health issues which are often inadequately addressed. …

7.6 All countries should strive to make accessible through the primary health-care system, reproductive health to all individuals of appropriate ages as soon as possible and no later than the year 2015. Reproductive health care in the context of primary health care should, inter alia, include: family-planning counselling, information, education, communication and services; education and services for prenatal care, safe delivery and post-natal care, especially breast-feeding and infant and women's health care; prevention and appropriate treatment of infertility; abortion as specified in paragraph 8.25, including prevention of abortion and the management of the consequences of abortion; treatment of reproductive tract infections; sexually transmitted diseases and other reproductive health conditions; and information, education and counselling, as appropriate, on human sexuality, reproductive health and responsible parenthood. Referral for family-planning services and further diagnosis and treatment for complications of pregnancy, delivery and abortion, infertility, reproductive tract infections, breast cancer and cancers of the reproductive system, sexually transmitted diseases, including HIV/AIDS should always be available, as required. Active discouragement of harmful practices, such as female genital mutilation, should also be an integral component of primary health care, including reproductive health-care programmes.

7.7 Reproductive health-care programmes should be designed to serve the needs of women, including adolescents, and must involve women in the leadership, planning, decision-making, management, implementation, organization and evaluation of services. Governments and other organizations should take positive steps to include women at all levels of the health-care system.

7.8 Innovative programmes must be developed to make information, counselling and services for reproductive health accessible to adolescents and adult men. Such programmes must both educate and enable men to share more equally in family planning and in domestic and child-rearing responsibilities and to accept the major responsibility for the prevention of sexually transmitted diseases. Programmes must reach men in their workplaces, at home and where they gather for recreation. Boys and adolescents, with the support and guidance of their parents, and in line with the Convention on the Rights of the Child, should also be reached through schools, youth organizations and wherever they congregate. Voluntary and appropriate male methods for contraception, as well as for the prevention of sexually transmitted diseases, including AIDS, should be promoted and made accessible with adequate information and counselling.

7.9 Governments should promote much greater community participation in reproductive health-care services by decentralizing the management of public health programmes and by forming partnerships in cooperation with local non-governmental organizations and private health-care providers. All types of non-governmental organizations, including local women's groups, trade unions, cooperatives, youth programmes and religious groups, should be encouraged to become involved in the promotion of better reproductive health.

7.10   Without jeopardizing international support for programmes in developing countries, the international community should, upon request, give consideration to the training, technical assistance, short-term contraceptive supply needs and the needs of the countries in transition from centrally managed to market economies, where reproductive health is poor and, in some cases, deteriorating. Those countries, at the same time, must themselves give higher priority to reproductive health services, including a comprehensive range of contraceptive means, and must address their current reliance on abortion for fertility regulation by meeting the need of women in those countries for better information and more choices on an urgent basis.

7.11   Migrants and displaced persons in many parts of the world have limited access to reproductive health care and may face specific serious threats to their reproductive health and rights. Services must be particularly sensitive to the needs of individual women and adolescents and responsive to their often-powerless situation, with particular attention to those who are victims of sexual violence. ...

B      **Committee on Economic, Social and Cultural Rights, General Comment 22,**
       ***On the Right to sexual and reproductive health (article 12 of the International***
       ***Covenant on Economic, Social and Cultural Rights)***

E/C.12/GC/22
May 2, 2016

5.  The right to sexual and reproductive health entails a set of freedoms and entitlements. The freedoms include the right to make free and responsible decisions and choices, free of violence, coercion and discrimination, regarding matters concerning one's body and sexual and reproductive health. The entitlements include unhindered access to a whole range of health facilities, goods, services and information, which ensure all people full enjoyment of the right to sexual and reproductive health under article 12 of the Covenant. ...

11. The right to sexual and reproductive health is an integral part of the right of everyone to the highest attainable physical and mental health. Following the elaboration in the Committee's general comment No. 14, comprehensive sexual and reproductive health care contains the four interrelated and essential elements described below.

**Availability**

12. An adequate number of functioning health-care facilities, services, goods and programmes should be available to provide the population with the fullest possible range of sexual and reproductive health care. This includes ensuring the availability of facilities, goods and services for the guarantee of the underlying determinants of the realization of the right to sexual and reproductive health, such as safe and potable drinking water and adequate sanitation facilities, hospitals and clinics.

13. Ensuring the availability of trained medical and professional personnel and skilled providers who are trained to perform the full range of sexual and reproductive health-care services is a critical component of ensuring availability. Essential medicines should also be available, including a wide range of contraceptive methods, such as condoms and emergency contraception, medicines for abortion and for post-abortion care, and medicines, including generic medicines, for the prevention and treatment of sexually transmitted infections and HIV.

14. Unavailability of goods and services due to ideologically based policies or practices, such as the refusal to provide services based on conscience, must not be a barrier to accessing services. An adequate number of health-care providers willing and able to provide such services should be available at all times in both public and private facilities and within reasonable geographical reach.

**Accessibility**

15. Health facilities, goods, information and services related to sexual and reproductive health care should be accessible to all individuals and groups without discrimination and free

from barriers. As elaborated in the Committee's general comment No. 14, accessibility includes physical accessibility, affordability and information accessibility.

## Physical accessibility

16. Health facilities, goods, information and services related to sexual and reproductive health care must be available within safe physical and geographical reach for all, so that persons in need can receive timely services and information. Physical accessibility should be ensured for all, especially persons belonging to disadvantaged and marginalized groups, including, but not limited to, persons living in rural and remote areas, persons with disabilities, refugees and internally displaced persons, stateless persons and persons in detention. When dispensing sexual and reproductive services to remote areas is impracticable, substantive equality calls for positive measures to ensure that persons in need have communication and transportation to such services.

## Affordability

17. Publicly or privately provided sexual and reproductive health services must be affordable for all. Essential goods and services, including those related to the underlying determinants of sexual and reproductive health, must be provided at no cost or based on the principle of equality to ensure that individuals and families are not disproportionately burdened with health expenses. People without sufficient means should be provided with the support necessary to cover the costs of health insurance and access to health facilities providing sexual and reproductive health information, goods and services.

## Information accessibility

18. Information accessibility includes the right to seek, receive and disseminate information and ideas concerning sexual and reproductive health issues generally, and also for individuals to receive specific information on their particular health status. All individuals and groups, including adolescents and youth, have the right to evidence-based information on all aspects of sexual and reproductive health, including maternal health, contraceptives, family planning, sexually transmitted infections, HIV prevention, safe abortion and post-abortion care, infertility and fertility options, and reproductive cancer. ...

## Acceptability

20. All facilities, goods, information and services related to sexual and reproductive health must be respectful of the culture of individuals, minorities, peoples and communities and sensitive to gender, age, disability, sexual diversity and life-cycle requirements. However, this cannot be used to justify the refusal to provide tailored facilities, goods, information and services to specific groups.

## Quality

21. Facilities, goods, information and services related to sexual and reproductive health must be of good quality, meaning that they are evidence-based and scientifically and medically appropriate and up-to-date. This requires trained and skilled health-care personnel and scientifically approved and unexpired drugs and equipment. The failure or refusal to incor-

porate technological advances and innovations in the provision of sexual and reproductive health services, such as medication for abortion, assisted reproductive technologies and advances in the treatment of HIV and AIDS, jeopardizes the quality of care.

## Non-discrimination and equality

22. Article 2 (2) of the Covenant provides that all individuals and groups shall not be discriminated against and shall enjoy equal rights. All individuals and groups should be able to enjoy equal access to the same range, quality and standard of sexual and reproductive health facilities, information, goods and services, and to exercise their rights to sexual and reproductive health without experiencing any discrimination.

23. Non-discrimination, in the context of the right to sexual and reproductive health, also encompasses the right of all persons, including lesbian, gay, bisexual, transgender and intersex persons, to be fully respected for their sexual orientation, gender identity and intersex status. Criminalization of sex between consenting adults of the same gender or the expression of one's gender identity is a clear violation of human rights. Likewise, regulations requiring that lesbian, gay, bisexual transgender and intersex persons be treated as mental or psychiatric patients, or requiring that they be "cured" by so-called "treatment", are a clear violation of their right to sexual and reproductive health. State parties also have an obligation to combat homophobia and transphobia, which lead to discrimination, including violation of the right to sexual and reproductive health. ...

## Intersectionality and multiple discrimination

30. Individuals belonging to particular groups may be disproportionately affected by intersectional discrimination in the context of sexual and reproductive health. As identified by the Committee, groups such as, but not limited to, poor women, persons with disabilities, migrants, indigenous or other ethnic minorities, adolescents, lesbian, gay, bisexual, transgender and intersex persons, and people living with HIV/AIDS are more likely to experience multiple discrimination. Trafficked and sexually exploited women, girls and boys are subject to violence, coercion and discrimination in their everyday lives, with their sexual and reproductive health at great risk. Also, women and girls living in conflict situations are disproportionately exposed to a high risk of violation of their rights, including through systematic rape, sexual slavery, forced pregnancy and forced sterilization. Measures to guarantee non-discrimination and substantive equality should be cognizant of and seek to overcome the often-exacerbated impact that intersectional discrimination has on the realization of the right to sexual and reproductive health. ...

## C     Reflections and Questions

1. The Cairo Programme of Action in its point 7.3 highlights the multidimensional nature of the recognition and codification of sexual and reproductive rights. Its language can be understood to indicate that sexual and reproductive rights are a combination of those recognized in universal, regional, and national instruments. This includes treaties, declarations, and resolutions. For example, some rights which can be considered pertinent and related to women's sexuality and reproduction have already been recognized by

the International Covenant on Civil and Political Rights (hereinafter "ICCPR") and the International Covenant on Economic, Social and Cultural Rights (hereinafter "ICESCR"). These include the rights to non-discrimination (Article 2), to equality and equal protection of the laws (Articles 3 and 26), to life (Article 6), to be free from torture (Article 8), to personal liberty (Article 9), to private and family life (Article 17), the right to freedom of expression (Article 19), and the right to participation (Article 25); all protected rights under the ICCPR.[2] The ICESCR also protects the rights to education (Article 13) and health (Article 19),[3] and CEDAW prohibits discrimination against women in the field of health care (Article 12).[4]

2. There are also important examples of the recognition of the more specialized components of sexual and reproductive rights at the regional level. The Maputo Protocol mandates states in Article 14 to ensure that the right to health of women, including their sexual and reproductive health, is protected. This includes ensuring the respect for the right of women to control their own fertility; the right to decide whether to have children, and the number and spacing of children; the right to choose any method of contraception; the right to be protected against sexually transmitted infections; and the right to have family planning education.[5] Article 14 also mandates states to authorize medical abortions to protect the reproductive rights of women in cases of "sexual assault, rape, incest, and where the continued pregnancy endangers the mental and physical health of the mother or the life of the mother or the foetus."[6] At the OAS level, the Follow-up Mechanism to the Convention of Belém do Pará – the MESECVI – adopted a Declaration on September 19, 2014, mandating states to take important steps including incorporating sexual and reproductive rights training in their educational systems; guaranteeing women access to health services free from discrimination; and to exercise due diligence in the eradication of gender stereotypes which may hinder the ability of women and girls to properly access information and services integral to their sexual and reproductive rights.[7]

---

[2]   *See* International Covenant on Civil and Political Rights, G.A. Res. 2200A (XXI), 21 U.N. GAOR Supp. (No. 16) at 52, U.N. Doc. A/6316 (1966), 999 U.N.T.S. 171, entered into force Mar. 23, 1976, Articles 2, 3, 6, 8, 9, 17, 19, 25, and 26, www.ohchr.org/en/professionalinterest/pages/ccpr.aspx.

[3]   *See* International Covenant on Economic, Social and Cultural Rights, G.A. Res. 2200A (XXI), 21 U.N. GAOR Supp. (No. 16) at 49, U.N. Doc. A/6316 (1966), 993 U.N.T.S. 3, entered into force Jan. 3, 1976, Articles 13 and 19, www.ohchr.org/en/professionalinterest/pages/cescr.aspx.

[4]   *See* Convention on the Elimination of All Forms of Discrimination against Women (CEDAW), G.A. Res. 34/180, 34 U.N. GAOR Supp. (No. 46) at 193, U.N. Doc. A/34/46, entered into force Sept. 3, 1981,Article 12.

[5]   *See* Protocol to the African Charter on Human and Peoples' Rights on the Rights of Women in Africa, Adopted by the 2nd Ordinary Session of the Assembly of the Union, Maputo, CAB/LEG/66.6 (Sept. 13, 2000); reprinted in 1 Afr. Hum. Rts. L.J. 40, entered into force Nov. 25, 2005 (hereinafter Maputo Protocol), Article 14(1)(a–g).

[6]   *See* Maputo Protocol, Article 14(2)(c). *See also generally*, African Commission on Human and Peoples' Rights, *General Comment No. 2 on Article 14.1 (a), (b), (c) and (f) and Article 14. 2(a) and (c) of the Protocol to the African Charter on Human and Peoples' Rights on the Rights of Women in Africa*, www.achpr.org/legalinstruments/detail?id=13.

[7]   *See* OAS, MESECVI, *Declaration on Violence against Women, Girls and Adolescents and their Sexual and Reproductive Rights*, OEA/Ser.L/II.7.10, MESECVI/CEVI/DEC.4/14, pp. 3–7 (Sept. 19, 2014).

3. Some of the newer country constitutions globally reflect important sexual and reproductive rights. For example, the Constitution of Ecuador – adopted in 2008 – in its Article 332 commits to the guarantee of the reproductive rights of workers, including the prohibition of employment termination due to pregnancy, lactation, or any discrimination on the basis of reproductive capacity.[8] The Constitution of Bolivia – adopted in 2009 – guarantees in Article 66 the right of both women and men to exercise both their sexual and reproductive rights.[9] The Constitution of South Africa – adopted in 1996 – guarantees to everyone in its Article 27 the right to have access to reproductive health-care services.[10] Should sexual and reproductive rights be protected at the constitutional level? Is this legal recognition needed at the national level? Or is legislation sufficient?

4. Women and girls globally face important barriers to adequately access sexual and reproductive health services. These include geographic distance and the lack of presence of gynecological services in rural areas; services that are plagued with financial and human resource limitations; linguistic differences; the dearth of culturally appropriate services; and the scarce information and high cost of the services available. Women and girls can also suffer mistreatment from doctors and other medical personnel who hold stereotyped notions of their ability to make decisions concerning their health, sexuality, and reproduction. These barriers tend to be formidable for afro-descendent and indigenous women, and women of low income means. Challenges can be very acute for adolescent girls, who often lack adequate education of where to seek important information and services related to contraceptives and sexually transmitted diseases.[11]

5. The Cairo Programme of Action defined *reproductive health* in its paragraph 7.2 referred to *supra*. The World Health Organization has defined *sexual health* instead as follows:

> Sexual health is a state of physical, emotional, mental and social well-being in relation to sexuality; it is not merely the absence of disease, dysfunction or infirmity. Sexual health requires a positive and respectful approach to sexuality and sexual relationships, as well as the possibility of having pleasurable and safe sexual experiences, free of coercion, discrimination and violence. For sexual health to be attained and maintained, the sexual rights of all persons must be respected, protected and fulfilled. (World Health Organization and Human Reproduction Programme: Research for Impact, *Sexual health and its linkages to reproductive health: an operational approach* (2017), p. 3)

When you look at these definitions, which are the main similarities and differences? How are reproductive and sexual health connected to each other? In preparing your answers, identify five human rights that are connected to both sexual and reproductive health.

6. There have been a number of cases before international and regional bodies related to women who faced important obstacles in their access to needed health-care services due

---

[8]     Constitution of Ecuador, October 20, 2008, Article 332, https://pdba.georgetown.edu/Constitutions/Ecuador/english08.html.
[9]     Constitution of Bolivia, 2009, Article 66, www.constituteproject.org/constitution/Bolivia_2009.pdf.
[10]    Constitution of South Africa, 1996, with amendments through 2012, Article 27, www.constituteproject.org/constitution/South_Africa_2012.pdf?lang=en.
[11]    *See, as reference, Nairobi Statement on ICPD25: Accelerating the Promise* (2019), pp. 1–7, www.nairobisummiticpd.org/content/icpd25-commitments.

to their reproductive capacity. Several of these cases have centered on important obstacles to access abortions in countries in which abortion is legal under certain circumstances. For example, in the case of *Paulina del Carmen Ramírez Jacinto*, ruled as a friendly settlement by the Inter-American Commission on Human Rights, the petitioner was a 14-year-old victim of rape who became pregnant as a result.[12] She attempted to obtain an abortion – which was legal at the time in Mexico – but faced noteworthy obstacles from public officials and medical personnel to have the procedure performed. These included offering Paulina Ramírez Jacinto and her mother inaccurate information about the medical effects of an abortion, and trying to dissuade them with information related to the Catholic Church and its principles. All of this information ended up dissuading the mother from agreeing to the procedure. The petitioners presented the case before the Inter-American Commission on Human Rights as emblematic of girls and women who are forced into motherhood after rape by facing important barriers to exercising their legitimate right to a legal abortion in Mexico.[13]

7. As indicated by General Comment 22 of the Committee on Economic, Social and Cultural Rights, there are groups of women who face acute forms of discrimination and gender-based violence in their access to sexual and reproductive health services. Among these are women from low-income groups; women who belong to racial and ethnic minorities; girls; lesbian, bisexual, transgender, and intersex women; women deprived of liberty; women with disabilities; and women migrants. Intersectional discrimination concerns are very prevalent in the offer of sexual and reproductive health services. Racism, gender stereotypes, and forms of arbitrary and disparate treatment can also be very present in the attitudes of medical personnel. This mistreatment can also lead to forms of psychological, physical, and sexual violence.[14]

8. A new United States government administration assumed office on January 20, 2021, with the leadership of President Joseph Robinette Biden, Jr. and Vice-President Kamala Harris. Since the beginning of their mandate, the administration has taken proactive steps to reenter the world stage and collaborate in the advancement of the rights of women and their sexual and reproductive rights. For example, on January 28, 2021, President Biden adopted a *Memorandum on Protecting Women's Health at Home and Abroad*, underscoring the need for women in the United States and abroad to have access to the health care that they need, including reproductive health care.[15] This memorandum repeals what is known as the *Mexico City Policy* or *Global Gag Rule*, which restricts non-governmental organizations that receive U.S. global assistance funding from offering any services and/ or information related to abortion. The memorandum also restores funding to the United

---

[12] *See generally*, Paulina del Carmen Ramírez Jacinto v. Mexico, Petition 161-02, Inter-Am. Comm'n H.R., Report No. 21/07 (March 9, 2007).

[13] *See id.*, ¶¶ 9–16.

[14] For more reading, *see* Michelle Lokot and Yeva Avakyan, *Intersectionality as a Lens to the COVID-19 Pandemic: Implications for Sexual and Reproductive Health in Development and Humanitarian Contexts*, 28(1) SEXUAL AND REPRODUCTIVE HEALTH MATTERS 41–43 (2020), https://www.tandfonline.com/doi/full/10.1080/26410397.2020.1764748.

[15] *See* White House, *Memorandum on Protecting Women's Health at Home and Abroad* (Jan. 28, 2021), www.whitehouse.gov/briefing-room/presidential-actions/2021/01/28/memorandum-on-protecting-womens-health-at-home-and-abroad/.

Nations Population Fund, which supports reproductive health care for women and girls in more than 150 countries. On February 8, 2021, the Biden-Harris Administration also announced its intention to reengage with the United Nations Human Rights Council, as part of a new foreign policy approach guided by democracy, human rights, and equality.[16] Can you think of important steps that the United States government can pursue to advance the respect for and guarantee of the sexual and reproductive rights of women in the United States and globally? How can the government promote the accessibility, availability, affordability, and quality of sexual and reproductive health services both in the United States and abroad?

**Note: Sexual and reproductive rights activism and the work of human rights defenders**

One of the most active components of human rights defenders' work is the advancement of sexual and reproductive rights. There are many organizations working today to ensure that women have unhindered access to sexual and reproductive health services, safe abortion, contraception and family planning methods, and adequate health care before, during, and after their pregnancies. Human rights defenders are also working to end all forms of discrimination on the basis of sexual orientation, gender identity, and gender expression. These organizations and networks are national, regional, and international.[17]

Sexual and reproductive rights continue to be very polarizing issues in most societies. This has led to many human rights organizations and individuals, working to advance these issues, facing acts of harassment and violence by many state and non-state actors, including those directed towards their family members.[18] Some of these acts include the criminalization of their activities; the delegitimization of their discourse; threatening their life and integrity; arbitrary and unjustified detentions; and psychological, physical, and sexual violence. Several of these acts have led to killings and other tragic results.[19] The United Nations Rapporteurship on Human Rights Defenders, as well as the Inter-American Commission on Human Rights, have been very active in denouncing acts of criminalization, harassment, and violence faced by women human rights defenders in general.[20]

---

[16] *See* Press Statement, Antony J. Blinken, Secretary of State, February 8, 2021, *U.S. Decision to Reengage with the U.N. Human Rights Council*, https://geneva.usmission.gov/2021/02/08/us-decision-to-reengage-with-the-un-human-rights-council/.

[17] For more discussion, *see* Cynthia Soohoo and Diana Hortsch, *Who Is A Human Rights Defender? An Essay on Sexual and Reproductive Rights Defenders*, 65 U. MIAMI L. REV. 981, 987–998 (2011).

[18] *See* Women Human Rights Defenders International Coalition, *Global Report on the Situation of Women Human Rights Defenders* (2012), pp. 89–107.

[19] *See* United Nations, *Women human rights defenders must be protected, say UN experts*, International Women Human Rights Defenders Day (Nov. 29, 2018), www.ohchr.org/en/NewsEvents/Pages/DisplayNews.aspx?NewsID=23943&LangID=E; U.N. Human Rights Council, Report of the Special Rapporteur on the situation of human rights defenders, Margaret Sekaggya, A/HRC/25/55, ¶¶ 98–101 (Dec. 23, 2013).

[20] *See* United Nations, *Women human rights defenders face worsening violence, warns UN human rights expert* (Feb. 28, 2019), www.ohchr.org/EN/NewsEvents/Pages/DisplayNews.aspx?NewsID=24232&LangID=E; Report of U.N. Rapporteur on the situation of human rights defenders, Michel Forst, A/HRC/40/60 (Jan. 10, 2019), ¶¶ 35–57, 79–82; Inter-American Commission on Human Rights, *Criminalization of the Work of Human Rights Defenders*, OEA/Ser.L/V/II. Doc. 49/15 (Dec. 31, 2015), ¶¶ 161–172.

Women who work as defenders face intersectional discrimination and an enhanced risk of human rights violations. They are subjected to stereotypes of how women should behave socially, which can translate into backlash against their leadership and assertive work. The causes they advance can also be controversial, especially in contexts of crisis and armed conflicts. International courts have declared that states have a duty to act with due diligence to prevent and protect women human rights defenders from harm, especially in armed conflict contexts and settings of risk. This entails creating safe social conditions for women human rights defenders to be able to fully exercise their rights and advance their social causes. Acts of delegitimization, violence, and discrimination perpetrated against women human rights defenders have a social chilling effect, dissuading society from defending human rights. Women human rights defenders should also have adequate access to judicial protection and guarantees when they suffer threats to their life, integrity, and work.[21]

## III    THE REGULATION OF ABORTION

According to the World Health Organization (hereinafter "WHO"), 73.3 million induced (safe and unsafe) abortions occurred worldwide each year between 2015 and 2019.[22] Three out of four abortions are unsafe.[23] The WHO also reports that every year 4.7–13.2 percent of maternal deaths can be considered the result of unsafe abortion. [24] The WHO moreover estimates that approximately 68,000 women die globally every year as a result of unsafe induced abortions.[25]

The fact that abortion is prohibited does not mean that women refrain from subjecting themselves to unsafe abortions. The complete prohibition of abortion is closely linked to the problem of maternal mortality. Many international mechanisms and experts have devoted a high level of attention to abortion restrictions due to their impact on public health and the problem of maternal mortality.[26]

The Center for Reproductive Rights reported in 2019 that abortion is still fully criminalized in at least 26 countries and that 90 million women of reproductive age live in these countries.[27] Close to 50 countries have liberalized their abortion laws since the adoption of the Cairo Programme of Action in 1994.[28] The countries that have liberalized abortion either authorize it within the first trimester of pregnancy, or permit abortions under specific grounds. Noteworthy

---

[21]   For an example of a case decided by an international court advancing the protection of women human rights defenders, *see* Yarce et al. v. Colom., Preliminary Objection, Merits, Reparations and Costs, Inter-Am. Ct. H.R. (ser. C), No. 326, ¶¶ 1–2, 138–202, 271–277 (Nov. 22, 2016).

[22]   World Health Organization (hereinafter WHO), *Preventing Unsafe Abortion: Key Facts* (Sept. 25, 2020), www.who.int/news-room/fact-sheets/detail/preventing-unsafe-abortion.

[23]   *See id.*

[24]   *See id.*

[25]   WHO, *Unsafe Abortion. The Preventable Pandemic*, Panel 1: Key Messages, pp. 2–3, www.who .int/reproductivehealth/topics/unsafe_abortion/article_unsafe_abortion.pdf.

[26]   For example, *see* United Nations, *Unsafe abortion is still killing tens of thousands women around the world – UN rights experts warn*, International Safe Abortion Day (Sept. 28, 2016), www.ohchr.org/ en/NewsEvents/Pages/DisplayNews.aspx?NewsID=20600&LangID=E.

[27]   Center for Reproductive Rights, *The World's Abortion Laws Map, 2019*, https://reproductiverights .org/sites/default/files/documents/World-Abortion-Map.pdf.

[28]   Center for Reproductive Rights, *By the Numbers: The Legal Status of Abortion Worldwide*, p. 1, https://reproductiverights.org/sites/default/files/documents/World-Abortion-Map-ByTheNumbers.pdf.

grounds for exceptions are when an abortion is needed to save the life of a woman; when an abortion is required due to health or therapeutic reasons; when a pregnancy is the result of rape; in cases of fetal anomalies; and for socio-economic reasons.[29] One recent example is Argentina, which liberalized its abortion law on January 14, 2021, to permit abortions during the first 14 weeks of pregnancy. Argentina is one of the leading countries in South America in terms of geographical area, population, and influence.[30]

The regulation of abortion is a highly polarizing and contentious issue in most societies. Those who advance pro-life positions argue that the unborn or the fetus has life, and therefore it is entitled to legal protection, and pregnancies should not be terminated under any circumstances. Those who are pro-choice consider instead that a woman should have the right to terminate a pregnancy, especially during the first 12 weeks of pregnancy, and in cases of rape, when a therapeutic abortion is needed, and in cases of fetal malformations. Much of the debate is centered on the scope and limits of the right to life, when does life begin, and the decision-making autonomy of women over their bodies and reproductive life.[31]

There are some areas of emerging consensus in international law with regard to rights related to abortion which will be discussed in this section, including the need to legally authorize therapeutic abortions to respect and ensure women's rights to life, personal integrity, health, and to non-discrimination. Sexual violence victims should also have access to services that they need to mitigate the effects of the harm suffered, including information about legal abortion services and the applicability of exceptions. Laws that prohibit abortions categorically tend to be discriminatory towards women, because they restrict health services that only women need because of their reproductive capacity. Prevention is also key and women should have quality education and information available on contraception and family planning methods to make informed choices and avoid unwanted pregnancies.

National and regional court decisions have begun to shed light on the content of the rights to life, to health, to privacy, and non-discrimination in the context of abortion. This chapter discusses in particular two landmark decisions related to the issue of abortion. The first decision was adopted by the United States Supreme Court in the case of *Roe v. Wade*, legalizing the practice of abortion in the United States during the first trimester of pregnancy. The second decision was adopted by the European Court of Human Rights in the case of *VO v. France*, in which the Court offered a narrow interpretation of the right to life under the European Convention on Human Rights, limiting its reach to born persons.

This chapter reflects on the impact of these national and international decisions, the state of international law related to the practice of abortion, and the rights of women and girls in this context.

---

[29]   Guttmacher Institute, *Abortion Worldwide 2017: Uneven Progress and Unequal Access*, pp. 14–19, www.guttmacher.org/sites/default/files/report_pdf/abortion-worldwide-2017.pdf.

[30]   Center for Reproductive Rights, *In Historic Victory, Argentina Legalizes Abortion* (Jan. 15, 2021), https://reproductiverights.org/story/historic-vote-argentina-legalize-abortion.

[31]   For more reading, *see* Mary Ziegler, *Both sides in the abortion fight now claim to be for women's equality: How the abortion debate has evolved*, THE WASHINGTON POST, Jan. 24, 2020, www .washingtonpost.com/outlook/2020/01/24/both-sides-abortion-fight-now-claim-be-womens-equality/.

## A  *Roe v. Wade*, 410 U.S. 113 (1973)

United States Supreme Court
Citations and footnotes omitted

*In this case, Jane Roe challenged the constitutionality of Texas statutes prohibiting abortion. She claimed the statutes were vague and violated her right to personal privacy protected by the First, Fourth, Fifth, Ninth, and Fourteenth Amendments of the United States Constitution. She alleged in particular that she was unmarried and pregnant, and wanted access to a safe and legal abortion.*

We forthwith acknowledge our awareness of the sensitive and emotional nature of the abortion controversy, of the vigorous opposing views, even among physicians, and of the deep and seemingly absolute convictions that the subject inspires. One's philosophy, one's experiences, one's exposure to the raw edges of human existence, one's religious training, one's attitudes toward life and family and their values, and the moral standards one establishes and seeks to observe, are all likely to influence and to color one's thinking and conclusions about abortion. In addition, population growth, pollution, poverty, and racial overtones tend to complicate and not to simplify the problem.

Our task, of course, is to resolve the issue by constitutional measurement, free of emotion and of predilection. We seek earnestly to do this, and, because we do, we have inquired into, and in this opinion place some emphasis upon, medical and medical-legal history and what that history reveals about man's attitudes toward the abortion procedure over the centuries. …

The principal thrust of appellant's attack on the Texas statutes is that they improperly invade a right, said to be possessed by the pregnant woman, to choose to terminate her pregnancy. Appellant would discover this right in the concept of personal "liberty" embodied in the Fourteenth Amendment's Due Process Clause; or in personal, marital, familial, and sexual privacy said to be protected by the Bill of Rights or its penumbras or among those rights reserved to the people by the Ninth Amendment. Before addressing this claim, we feel it desirable briefly to survey, in several aspects, the history of abortion, for such insight as that history may afford us, and then to examine the state purposes and interests behind the criminal abortion laws.

It perhaps is not generally appreciated that the restrictive criminal abortion laws in effect in a majority of States today are of relatively recent vintage. Those laws, generally proscribing abortion or its attempt at any time during pregnancy except when necessary to preserve the pregnant woman's life, are not of ancient or even of common law origin. Instead, they derive from statutory changes effected, for the most part, in the latter half of the 19th century.

The State has a legitimate interest in seeing to it that abortion, like any other medical procedure, is performed under circumstances that ensure maximum safety for the patient. This interest obviously extends at least to the performing physician and his staff, to the facilities involved, to the availability of after-care, and to adequate provision for any complication or emergency that might arise. The prevalence of high mortality rates at illegal "abortion mills" strengthens, rather than weakens, the State's interest in regulating the conditions under which abortions are performed. Moreover, the risk to the woman increases as her pregnancy continues. Thus, the State retains a definite interest in protecting the woman's own health and safety when an abortion is proposed at a late stage of pregnancy.

The third reason is the State's interest – some phrase it in terms of duty – in protecting prenatal life. Some of the argument for this justification rests on the theory that a new human life is present from the moment of conception. The State's interest and general obligation to protect life then extends, it is argued, to prenatal life. Only when the life of the pregnant mother herself is at stake, balanced against the life she carries within her, should the interest of the embryo or fetus not prevail. Logically, of course, a legitimate state interest in this area need not stand or fall on acceptance of the belief that life begins at conception or at some other point prior to live birth. In assessing the State's interest, recognition may be given to the less rigid claim that as long as at least potential life is involved, the State may assert interests beyond the protection of the pregnant woman alone. ...

It is with these interests, and the eight to be attached to them, that this case is concerned.

The Constitution does not explicitly mention any right of privacy. In a line of decisions, however, the Court has recognized that a right of personal privacy, or a guarantee of certain areas or zones of privacy, does exist under the Constitution. In varying contexts, the Court or individual Justices have, indeed, found at least the roots of that right in the First Amendment; in the Fourth and Fifth Amendments; or in the concept of liberty guaranteed by the first section of the Fourteenth Amendment. These decisions make it clear that only personal rights that can be deemed "fundamental" or "implicit in the concept of ordered liberty," are included in this guarantee of personal privacy. They also make it clear that the right has some extension to activities relating to marriage. ...

This right of privacy, whether it be founded in the Fourteenth Amendment's concept of personal liberty and restrictions upon state action, as we feel it is, or, as the District Court determined, in the Ninth Amendment's reservation of rights to the people, is broad enough to encompass a woman's decision whether or not to terminate her pregnancy. The detriment that the State would impose upon the pregnant woman by denying this choice altogether is apparent. Specific and direct harm medically diagnosable even in early pregnancy may be involved. Maternity, or additional offspring, may force upon the woman a distressful life and future. Psychological harm may be imminent. Mental and physical health may be taxed by child care. There is also the distress, for all concerned, associated with the unwanted child, and there is the problem of bringing a child into a family already unable, psychologically and otherwise, to care for it. In other cases, as in this one, the additional difficulties and continuing stigma of unwed motherhood may be involved. All these are factors the woman and her responsible physician necessarily will consider in consultation.

On the basis of elements such as these, appellant and some amici argue that the woman's right is absolute and that she is entitled to terminate her pregnancy at whatever time, in whatever way, and for whatever reason she alone chooses. With this we do not agree. Appellant's arguments that Texas either has no valid interest at all in regulating the abortion decision, or no interest strong enough to support any limitation upon the woman's sole determination, are unpersuasive. The Court's decisions recognizing a right of privacy also acknowledge that some state regulation in areas protected by that right is appropriate. ...

We, therefore, conclude that the right of personal privacy includes the abortion decision, but that this right is not unqualified, and must be considered against important state interests in regulation.

We note that those federal and state courts that have recently considered abortion law challenges have reached the same conclusion. A majority, in addition to the District Court in the present case, have held state laws unconstitutional, at least in part, because of vagueness or because of overbreadth and abridgment of rights. ... Others have sustained state statutes. ...

Although the results are divided, most of these courts have agreed that the right of privacy, however based, is broad enough to cover the abortion decision; that the right, nonetheless, is not absolute, and is subject to some limitations; and that, at some point, the state interests as to protection of health, medical standards, and prenatal life, become dominant. We agree with this approach.

Where certain "fundamental rights" are involved, the Court has held that regulation limiting these rights may be justified only by a "compelling state interest ..." and that legislative enactments must be narrowly drawn to express only the legitimate state interests at stake. ...

The Constitution does not define "person" in so many words. Section 1 of the Fourteenth Amendment contains three references to "person." The first, in defining "citizens," speaks of "persons born or naturalized in the United States." The word also appears both in the Due Process Clause and in the Equal Protection Clause. "Person" is used in other places in the Constitution: in the listing of qualifications for Representatives and Senators, Art. I, § 2, cl. 2, and § 3, cl. 3; in the Apportionment Clause, Art. I, § 2, cl. 3; in the Migration and Importation provision, Art. I, § 9, cl. 1; in the Emolument Clause, Art. I, § 9, cl. 8; in the Electors provisions, Art. II, § 1, cl. 2, and the superseded cl. 3; in the provision outlining qualifications for the office of President, Art. II, § 1, cl. 5; in the Extradition provisions, Art. IV, § 2, cl. 2, and the superseded Fugitive Slave Clause 3; and in the Fifth, Twelfth, and Twenty-second Amendments, as well as in §§ 2 and 3 of the Fourteenth Amendment. But in nearly all these instances, the use of the word is such that it has application only post-natally. None indicates, with any assurance, that it has any possible pre-natal application.

All this, together with our observation, supra, that, throughout the major portion of the 19th century, prevailing legal abortion practices were far freer than they are today, persuades us that the word "person," as used in the Fourteenth Amendment, does not include the unborn. This is in accord with the results reached in those few cases where the issue has been squarely presented ...

This conclusion, however, does not of itself fully answer the contentions raised by Texas, and we pass on to other considerations.

The pregnant woman cannot be isolated in her privacy. She carries an embryo and, later, a fetus, if one accepts the medical definitions of the developing young in the human uterus. ... The situation therefore is inherently different from marital intimacy, or bedroom possession of obscene material, or marriage, or procreation, or education, with which Eisenstadt and Griswold, Stanley, Loving, Skinner, and Pierce and Meyer were respectively concerned. As we have intimated above, it is reasonable and appropriate for a State to decide that, at some point in time another interest, that of health of the mother or that of potential human life, becomes significantly involved. The woman's privacy is no longer sole and any right of privacy she possesses must be measured accordingly.

Texas urges that, apart from the Fourteenth Amendment, life begins at conception and is present throughout pregnancy, and that, therefore, the State has a compelling interest in protecting that life from and after conception. We need not resolve the difficult question of when life begins. When those trained in the respective disciplines of medicine, philosophy, and theology are unable to arrive at any consensus, the judiciary, at this point in the development of man's knowledge, is not in a position to speculate as to the answer.

It should be sufficient to note briefly the wide divergence of thinking on this most sensitive and difficult question. There has always been strong support for the view that life does not begin until live birth. ...

In areas other than criminal abortion, the law has been reluctant to endorse any theory that life, as we recognize it, begins before live birth, or to accord legal rights to the unborn except in narrowly defined situations and except when the rights are contingent upon live birth. ...

In view of all this, we do not agree that, by adopting one theory of life, Texas may override the rights of the pregnant woman that are at stake. We repeat, however, that the State does have an important and legitimate interest in preserving and protecting the health of the pregnant woman, whether she be a resident of the State or a nonresident who seeks medical consultation and treatment there, and that it has still another important and legitimate interest in protecting the potentiality of human life. These interests are separate and distinct. Each grows in substantiality as the woman approaches term and, at a point during pregnancy, each becomes "compelling."

With respect to the State's important and legitimate interest in the health of the mother, the "compelling" point, in the light of present medical knowledge, is at approximately the end of the first trimester. This is so because of the now-established medical fact ... that, until the end of the first trimester mortality in abortion may be less than mortality in normal childbirth. It follows that, from and after this point, a State may regulate the abortion procedure to the extent that the regulation reasonably relates to the preservation and protection of maternal health. Examples of permissible state regulation in this area are requirements as to the qualifications of the person who is to perform the abortion; as to the licensure of that person; as to the facility in which the procedure is to be performed, that is, whether it must be a hospital or may be a clinic or some other place of less-than-hospital status; as to the licensing of the facility; and the like.

This means, on the other hand, that, for the period of pregnancy prior to this "compelling" point, the attending physician, in consultation with his patient, is free to determine, without regulation by the State, that, in his medical judgment, the patient's pregnancy should be terminated. If that decision is reached, the judgment may be effectuated by an abortion free of interference by the State.

With respect to the State's important and legitimate interest in potential life, the "compelling" point is at viability. This is so because the fetus then presumably has the capability of meaningful life outside the mother's womb. State regulation protective of fetal life after viability thus has both logical and biological justifications. If the State is interested in protecting fetal life after viability, it may go so far as to proscribe abortion during that period, except when it is necessary to preserve the life or health of the mother.

Measured against these standards, Art. 1196 of the Texas Penal Code, in restricting legal abortions to those "procured or attempted by medical advice for the purpose of saving the life of the mother," sweeps too broadly. The statute makes no distinction between abortions performed early in pregnancy and those performed later, and it limits to a single reason, "saving" the mother's life, the legal justification for the procedure. The statute, therefore, cannot survive the constitutional attack made upon it here. ...

**B**      *VO v. France*

European Court of Human Rights
Application No. 53924/00, July 8, 2004
© Council of Europe, reproduced with permission

*In this case, the applicant was forced to undergo a therapeutic abortion due to medical neg-
ligence. She unsuccessfully filed a criminal complaint at the national level alleging unintentional homicide. She alleged before the European Court of Human Rights that the absence of
a criminal remedy in the French legal system to sanction the unintentional homicide of a fetus
contravened the right to life under Article 2 of the European Convention on Human Rights.
Below are excerpts of the Court's analysis of the scope of the right to life under Article 2.*

81. The special nature of the instant case raises a new issue. The Court is faced with a woman
    who intended to carry her pregnancy to term and whose unborn child was expected to be
    viable, at the very least in good health. Her pregnancy had to be terminated as a result of
    an error by a doctor and she therefore had to have a therapeutic abortion on account of
    negligence by a third party. The issue is consequently whether, apart from cases where the
    mother has requested an abortion, harming a foetus should be treated as a criminal offence
    in the light of Article 2 of the Convention, with a view to protecting the foetus under that
    Article. This requires a preliminary examination of whether it is advisable for the Court
    to intervene in the debate as to who is a person and when life begins, in so far as Article 2
    provides that the law must protect "everyone's right to life".

82. As is apparent from the above recapitulation of the case-law, the interpretation of Article
    2 in this connection has been informed by a clear desire to strike a balance, and the
    Convention institutions' position in relation to the legal, medical, philosophical, ethical
    or religious dimensions of defining the human being has taken into account the various
    approaches to the matter at national level. This has been reflected in the consideration
    given to the diversity of views on the point at which life begins, of legal cultures and of
    national standards of protection, and the State has been left with considerable discretion in
    the matter … It follows that the issue of when the right to life begins comes within the
    margin of appreciation which the Court generally considers that States should enjoy in this
    sphere, notwithstanding an evolutive interpretation of the Convention, a "living instrument
    which must be interpreted in the light of present-day conditions …" The reasons for that
    conclusion are, firstly, that the issue of such protection has not been resolved within the
    majority of the Contracting States themselves, in France in particular, where it is the
    subject of debate … and, secondly, that there is no European consensus on the scientific
    and legal definition of the beginning of life. …

84. At European level, the Court observes that there is no consensus on the nature and status
    of the embryo and/or foetus … although they are beginning to receive some protection
    in the light of scientific progress and the potential consequences of research into genetic
    engineering, medically assisted procreation or embryo experimentation. At best, it may
    be regarded as common ground between States that the embryo/foetus belongs to the
    human race. The potentiality of that being and its capacity to become a person – enjoying
    protection under the civil law, moreover, in many States, such as France, in the context of

inheritance and gifts, and also in the United Kingdom ... require protection in the name of human dignity, without making it a "person" with the "right to life" for the purposes of Article 2. ...

85. Having regard to the foregoing, the Court is convinced that it is neither desirable, nor even possible as matters stand, to answer in the abstract the question whether the unborn child is a person for the purposes of Article 2 of the Convention ("*personne*" in the French text). As to the instant case, it considers it unnecessary to examine whether the abrupt end to the applicant's pregnancy falls within the scope of Article 2, seeing that, even assuming that that provision was applicable, there was no failure on the part of the respondent State to comply with the requirements relating to the preservation of life in the public-health sphere. With regard to that issue, the Court has considered whether the legal protection afforded the applicant by France in respect of the loss of the unborn child she was carrying satisfied the procedural requirements inherent in Article 2 of the Convention.

86. In that connection, it observes that the unborn child's lack of a clear legal status does not necessarily deprive it of all protection under French law. However, in the circumstances of the present case, the life of the foetus was intimately connected with that of the mother and could be protected through her, especially as there was no conflict between the rights of the mother and the father or of the unborn child and the parents, the loss of the foetus having been caused by the unintentional negligence of a third party. ...

88. The Court reiterates that the first sentence of Article 2, which ranks as one of the most fundamental provisions in the Convention and also enshrines one of the basic values of the democratic societies making up the Council of Europe ... requires the State not only to refrain from the "intentional" taking of life, but also to take appropriate steps to safeguard the lives of those within its jurisdiction. ...

89. Those principles apply in the public-health sphere too. The positive obligations require States to make regulations compelling hospitals, whether private or public, to adopt appropriate measures for the protection of patients' lives. They also require an effective independent judicial system to be set up so that the cause of death of patients in the care of the medical profession, whether in the public or the private sector, can be determined and those responsible made accountable. ...

94. In conclusion, the Court considers that in the circumstances of the case an action for damages in the administrative courts could be regarded as an effective remedy that was available to the applicant. Such an action, which she failed to use, would have enabled her to prove the medical negligence she alleged and to obtain full redress for the damage resulting from the doctor's negligence, and there was therefore no need to institute criminal proceedings in the instant case.

95. The Court accordingly concludes that, even assuming that Article 2 was applicable in the instant case ... there has been no violation of Article 2 of the Convention.

## C    Reflections and Questions

1. *Roe v. Wade* is one of the most consequential decisions ever decided by the United States Supreme Court. The Court recognized a constitutional right for women to terminate their pregnancies, in a legal environment and historical backdrop in which most abortions were prohibited by states. The Court also advances in *Roe v. Wade* a trimester and a graduality

framework, in which the state interest in regulating the practice of abortion increases as the pregnancy progresses. The United States Supreme Court has had the opportunity to review many other state laws and statutes setting limits to the practice of abortion and has upheld to date the holding of *Roe v. Wade*.[32]

2. A recent example of the United States Supreme Court treatment of abortion matters took place in *June Medical Services v. Russo*.[33] In this 2020 decision, the United States Supreme Court considered unconstitutional a Louisiana statute that required doctors performing abortions to have admitting privileges at a hospital within 30 miles of the place where they perform these procedures.[34] The Court held that the Louisiana law imposed undue burdens on a woman's constitutional right to choose an abortion by posing substantial obstacles and offering no significant health benefits. The Court largely based its decision on its previous holding in the similar case of *Whole Women's Health v. Hellerstedt*. Note that the ruling of the United States Supreme Court in *June Medical Services v. Russo* had four dissenting opinions, which reflects the Court's ongoing division of opinion when it comes to abortion matters and restrictions imposed by states.[35]

3. The United States Supreme Court decision in *Roe v. Wade* is still highly controversial. Judicial positions related to abortion issues and the holding of *Roe v. Wade* are heavily scrutinized when the Senate reviews new presidential nominees to hold seats as justices in the United States Supreme Court.[36] Do you think moral, ideological, or religious positions concerning abortion should matter in the appointment of new judges?

4. In *Roe v. Wade*, the United States Supreme Court recognizes the right to privacy under the Due Process of the Fourteenth Amendment of the Constitution and how this right includes abortion decisions. The right to privacy is not mentioned in the Constitution. Leading attorneys and scholars have made the argument that *Roe v. Wade* should have considered the discriminatory nature of restrictions related to abortion, instead of focusing so heavily on the right to privacy.[37] Who are the most affected by abortion laws? Is this a privacy matter? Is this a discrimination or equality issue? Is this a health concern? How would you have decided this case?

5. Leading organizations in the United States are advocating for the adoption of specific federal legislation that safeguards access to abortion care in every state. The Women's Health Protection Act (2019) is a federal legislative project which purports to protect abortion care from restrictions which may be contrary to *Roe v. Wade*, including abortion bans prior to viability; requirements that doctors provide medically accurate information

---

[32] For more reading on the legal history of abortion and its treatment by United States courts, *see* MARY ZIEGLER, ABORTION AND THE LAW IN AMERICA: ROE V. WADE TO THE PRESENT 11–26, 88–120 (Cambridge University Press, 2020).

[33] *See generally*, June Medical Services LLC v. Russo, 591 US ___ (2020).

[34] *See generally*, June Medical Services LLC v. Russo, 591 US ___ (2020).

[35] *See* June Medical Services LLC v. Russo, 591 US ___ 1–3, 16–40 (2020); Concurring Opinion by Chief Justice John Roberts, Dissenting Opinions by Justices Clarence Thomas, Samuel Alito, Neil Gorsuch, and Brett Kavanaugh.

[36] NEW YORK TIMES, *Barrett's Record: A Conservative Who Would Push the Supreme Court to the Right*, November 2, 2020, www.nytimes.com/article/amy-barrett-views-issues.html.

[37] Alisha Haridasani Gupta, *Why Ruth Bader Ginsburg Wasn't All That Fond of Roe v. Wade*, NEW YORK TIMES, September 21, 2020, www.nytimes.com/2020/09/21/us/ruth-bader-ginsburg-roe-v-wade.html.

to women seeking abortions; and state-mandated medical procedures and protocols such as submitting women to ultrasounds and to long waiting periods.[38] The Bill has been introduced in the House of Representatives by Congresspersons Judy Chu, Lois Frankle, and Marcia Fudge, and in the Senate by Senators Richard Blumenthal and Tammy Baldwin. Do you think it is better to authorize abortions by courts or by means of federal legislation? Weigh the pros and cons of each approach.

6. One of the groups of most concern in respect of abortion restrictions are girls under 18 who need these services due to rape and incest. Some of these cases have garnered global attention. One important example is the case of *Mainumby* from Paraguay, relating to a ten-year-old girl who became pregnant in 2015 due to sexual violence committed by her mother's partner.[39] Her mother requested the termination of her pregnancy from medical staff and a board of medical personnel recommended this alternative due to the young age of Mainumby and the high-risk nature of her pregnancy, but the recommendations were not followed through. Mainumby eventually gave birth to her daughter. The legislation in Paraguay at the time only authorized abortions in high-risk cases for the mother. The Inter-American Commission on Human Rights adopted precautionary measures, urging the state of Paraguay to protect the rights to life and personal integrity of Mainumby, by following the practices and policies recommended by the World Health Organization in these kinds of cases.[40]

7. In the case of *LC v. Peru*, the CEDAW Committee also reviewed the case of a victim of sexual abuse at the age of 13.[41] She became pregnant as a result and attempted suicide by jumping from a building. Surgery was recommended and scheduled by medical personnel to prevent LC from becoming permanently disabled, but was postponed due to potential harm to the fetus. Abortion at the time was legal in Peru to avoid serious and permanent harm to the health of the mother, but not in cases of rape. LC eventually suffered a miscarriage and did not receive the recommended surgery for three and a half months. She is paralyzed from the neck down and had to abandon her treatment due to lack of economic means. The CEDAW Committee found that the state violated Article 12 and the right to health by failing to provide LC with access to an effective and accessible procedure to qualify for a therapeutic abortion and the spinal surgery that she needed. The CEDAW Committee also expressed its alarm over stereotypes suggesting that the protection of the fetus should prevail over the health of the mother, and the lack of legislation in Peru legalizing abortion in cases of rape.[42]

---

[38] For more reading, *see* Act for Women, *The Women's Health Protection Act*, https://actforwomen .org/the-womens-health-protection-act/ (last visited on May 19, 2021); Center for Reproductive Rights, *Annual Report, 2020*, https://annualreport.reproductiverights.org/?_ga=2.203375378.2046961045 .1615488897-334195324.1614696553.

[39] *See, generally*, Inter-American Commission on Human Rights, *Precautionary Measures adopted in the case of Mainumby*, Resolution 22/2015, www.oas.org/es/cidh/decisiones/pdf/2015/mc178-15-es .pdf.

[40] *See id.*, Inter-American Commission on Human Rights, *Precautionary Measures adopted in the case of Mainumby*.

[41] *See, generally*, CEDAW Committee, LC v. Peru, Communication No. 22/2009, CEDAW/C/50/D/22/200.

[42] *See id.*, ¶¶ 1–2.15, 8.6–10.

# IV    MATERNAL HEALTH, MORTALITY, AND MORBIDITY

The reduction of global maternal mortality has been included as an important target in Sustainable Development Goal 3.[43] State governments globally have committed to reducing the global maternal mortality ratio to less than 70 per 100,000 live births by 2030.[44] However, the rates of maternal mortality are still exceedingly high. According to the World Health Organization, every day in 2017 approximately 810 women died from maternal health complications, including preventable causes related to pregnancy and childbirth.[45] A high percentage of these maternal deaths – 94 percent – occur in low- and lower-middle-income countries, but developed countries are not an exception to this problem.[46] Adolescent girls in particular – between the ages of 10 and 14 – face in particular an enhanced risk to complications and deaths resulting from pregnancy.[47]

Maternal health has been identified by both United Nations and regional mechanisms as a crucial area of attention to see the rights of women fully respected, protected, and fulfilled. Many rights have been identified as at play in guaranteeing that women have adequate health care during their pregnancies and the post-partum period. This area of women's rights is intricately connected with the rights to life, personal integrity, health, non-discrimination, and freedom from violence. Key principles such as autonomy, dignity, and privacy are also relevant to the protection of the rights of women to safe motherhood. Women who suffer intersectional discrimination and systemic forms of exclusion, such as those afro-descendent, indigenous, deprived of liberty, with disabilities, and migrants, are particularly affected by formidable barriers to adequately access the health-care services they need during their reproductive lives.[48]

This section discusses the case of *Alyne Da Silva Pimentel Teixeira*, decided by the CEDAW Committee, as emblematic of maternal deaths, and the violations of the rights to life, health, and non-discrimination of an afro-descendent woman who sought and received inadequate obstetric health services.

## A    *Alyne Da Silva Pimentel Teixeira v. Brazil*, CEDAW Committee

Communication No. 17/2008
CEDAW/C/49/D/17/2008
August 10, 2011

---

[43]   For more reading, *see* U.N. General Assembly, *Transforming our World: The 2030 Agenda for Sustainable Development Goals*, A/RES/70/1, October 21, 2015, Goal 3.1 and ¶ 26.

[44]   *See id.*, Goal 3.1 and ¶ 26.

[45]   *See* World Health Organization, *Maternal Mortality* (Sept. 19, 2019), www.who.int/news-room/fact-sheets/detail/maternal-mortality.

[46]   *Id.*

[47]   *Id.*

[48]   For more reading, *see Trends in Maternal Mortality: 2000–2017*, Estimates by WHO, UNICEF, UNFPA, World Bank Group and the United Nations Population Division, Executive Summary, https://apps.who.int/iris/bitstream/handle/10665/327596/WHO-RHR-19.23-eng.pdf?ua=1;    Inter-American Commission on Human Rights, *Access to Maternal Health Care Services from a Human Rights Perspective*, OEA/Ser.L/V/II. Doc. 69, 7 June 2010, Introduction, ¶¶ 1–21, www.oas.org/en/iachr/women/docs/pdf/saludmaternaeng.pdf.

*This case is related to Alyne da Silva Pimentel Teixeira, an afro-descendent woman from Brazil, who sought medical services from a private health center due to medical issues connected to her pregnancy. She was six months pregnant at the time. She died from complications resulting from low quality health care.*

...

7.1 The [CEDAW] Committee has considered the present communication in the light of all the information made available to it by the author and by the State party, as provided for in article 7, paragraph 1, of the Optional Protocol.

7.2 The author claims that Ms. da Silva Pimentel Teixeira's death constitutes a violation of her right to life and health, under articles 2 and 12, in conjunction with article 1, of the Convention, as the State party did not ensure appropriate medical treatment in connection with pregnancy and did not provide timely emergency obstetric care, hence infringing the right to non-discrimination based on gender, race and socio-economic background. In order to review these allegations the Committee first has to consider whether the death was "maternal". It will then consider whether the obligations under article 12, paragraph 2, of the Convention, according to which State parties shall ensure to women appropriate services in connection with pregnancy, confinement and the post-natal period, have been met in this case. Only after these considerations will the Committee review the other alleged violations of the Convention.

7.3 Although the State party argued that Ms. da Silva Pimentel Teixeira's death was non-maternal and that the probable cause of her death was digestive haemorrhage, the Committee notes that the sequence of events described by the author and not contested by the State party, as well as expert opinion provided by the author, indicate that her death was indeed linked to obstetric complications related to pregnancy. Her complaints of severe nausea and abdominal pain during her sixth month of pregnancy were ignored by the health centre, which failed to perform an urgent blood and urine test to ascertain whether the foetus had died. The tests were done two days later, which led to a deterioration of Ms. da Silva Pimentel Teixeira's condition. The Committee recalls its general recommendation No. 24, in which it states that it is the duty of State parties to ensure women's right to safe motherhood and emergency obstetric services, and to allocate to these services the maximum extent of available resources. It also states that measures to eliminate discrimination against women are considered to be inappropriate in a health-care system which lacks services to prevent, detect and treat illnesses specific to women. In the light of these observations, the Committee also rejects the argument of the State party that the communication did not contain a casual link between Ms. da Silva Pimentel Teixeira's gender and the possible medical errors committed, but that the claims concerned a lack of access to medical care related to pregnancy. The Committee therefore is of the view that the death of Ms. da Silva Pimentel Teixeira must be regarded as maternal.

7.4 The Committee also notes the author's allegation concerning the poor quality of the health services provided to her daughter, which not only included the failure to perform a blood and urine test, but also the fact that the curettage surgery was only carried out 14 hours after labour was induced in order to remove the afterbirth and placenta, which had not been fully expelled during the process of delivery and could have caused the haemorrhaging and ultimately death. The surgery was done in the health centre, which was not adequately equipped, and her transfer to the municipal hospital took eight hours, as the hospital refused to provide its only ambulance to transport her, and her family was not able to secure a private ambulance. It also notes that her transfer to the municipal hospital without her clinical history and information on her medical background was ineffective, as she was left largely unattended in a makeshift area in the hallway of the hospital for 21 hours until she died. The State party did not deny the inappropriateness of the service nor refute any of these facts. Instead it admitted that Ms. da Silva Pimentel Teixeira's vulnerable condition required individualized medical treatment, which was not forthcoming due to a potential failure in the medical assistance provided by a private health institution, caused by professional negligence, inadequate infrastructure and lack of professional preparedness. The Committee therefore concludes that Ms. da Silva Pimentel Teixeira has not been ensured appropriate services in connection with her pregnancy.

7.5 The State party argued that the inappropriateness of the service is not imputable to it, but to the private health-care institution. It stated that the allegations revealed a number of poor medical practices attributable to a private institution that led to Ms. da Silva Pimentel Teixeira's death. It acknowledged shortcomings in the system used to contract private health services and, by extension, the inspection and control thereof. The Committee therefore notes that the State is directly responsible for the action of private institutions when it outsources its medical services, and that furthermore, the State always maintains the duty to regulate and monitor private health-care institutions. In line with article 2(e) of the Convention, the State party has a due diligence obligation to take measures to ensure that the activities of private actors in regard to health policies and practices are appropriate. In this particular case, the State party's responsibility is strongly anchored in the Brazilian Constitution (articles 196–200) which affirms the right to health as a general human right. The Committee therefore concludes that the State party has failed to fulfil its obligations under article 12, paragraph 2, of the Convention. …

7.6 The Committee notes that the author claims that the lack of access to quality medical care during delivery is a systematic problem in Brazil, especially with regard to the way human resources are managed in the Brazilian health system. The Committee also takes note of the argument of the State party that specific medical care was not denied because of an absence of public policies and measures within the State party, as there are a number of policies in place to address the specific needs of women. The Committee refers to its general recommendation No. 28 (2010) on the core obligations of States parties under article 2 of the Convention and notes that the policies of the State party must be action- and result-oriented as well as adequately funded. Furthermore, the policy must ensure that there are strong and focused bodies within the executive branch to implement such policies. The lack of appropriate maternal health services in the State party that clearly fails to meet the specific, distinctive health needs and interests of women not only constitutes a violation of article 12, paragraph 2, of the Convention, but also discrimination against women under article 12, paragraph 1, and article 2 of the Convention. Furthermore, the lack of appropriate maternal health services has a differential impact on the right to life of women.

7.7 The Committee notes the author's claim that Ms. da Silva Pimentel Teixeira suffered from multiple discrimination, being a woman of African descent and on the basis of her socio-economic background. In this regard, the Committee recalls its concluding observations on Brazil, adopted on 15 August 2007, where it noted the existence of de facto discrimination against women, especially women from the most vulnerable sectors of society such as women of African descent. It also noted that such discrimination was exacerbated by regional, economic and social disparities. The Committee also recalls its general recommendation No. 28 (2010) on the core obligations of States parties under article 2 of the Convention, recognizing that discrimination against women based on sex and gender is inextricably linked to other factors that affect women, such as race, ethnicity, religion or belief, health, status, age, class, cast, and sexual orientation and gender identity. The Committee notes that the State party did not rule out that discrimination might have contributed to some extent, but not decisively, to the death of the author's daughter. The State party also acknowledged that the convergence or association of the different elements described by the author may have contributed to the failure to provide necessary and emergency care to her daughter, resulting in her death. In such circumstances, the Committee concludes that Ms. da Silva Pimentel Teixeira was discriminated against, not only on the basis of her sex, but also on the basis of her status as a woman of African descent and her socio-economic background. …

**B      Reflections and Questions**

1. The CEDAW Committee in the case of *Alyne Da Silva Pimentel Teixeira* determines that the death is maternal and that the victim died from obstetric complications. The Committee also identifies a right to safe motherhood, comprehended within the right to health and connected to the prohibition of discrimination. This is important as the right to non-discrimination is always an obligation of immediate effect for states. The Committee also underscores how the lack of appropriate health services has a differential impact on women, and can be particularly jarring in the case of afro-descendent women and those of low-income positions. All these problems were compounded by the fact that no judicial proceedings had been initiated in this case to establish responsibility for the death of the victim, despite significant efforts from her family members. Another key aspect of the *Alyne Da Silva Pimentel Teixeira* case is the state obligation to act with due diligence to supervise and prevent maternal deaths in the actions of private health institutions.[49]

2. African-American women are among the groups most affected by maternal mortality issues. This is the case even in the United States. The Commonwealth Fund has reported that the maternal death ratio for African-American women in the United States (37.1 per 100,000 pregnancies) is 2.5 times the ratio for white women (14.7) and three times the ratio for Hispanic women (11.8).[50]

3. The Office of the United Nations High Commissioner for Human Rights (OHCHR) has published technical guidance offering examples of the role of governments and their

---

[49]   *See, in particular*, Alyne Da Silva Pimentel Teixeira v. Brazil, *supra*, paras. 7.3, 7.7–7.8, Recommendation 2(a).

[50]   *See* The Commonwealth Fund, Issue Brief and Report, *Maternal Mortality in the United States: A Primer* (Dec. 16, 2020), www.commonwealthfund.org/publications/issue-brief-report/2020/dec/maternal-mortality-united-states-primer#:~:text=Highlights,after%20the%20day%20of%20birth.

minimum obligations in meeting their accessibility, affordability, and quality obligations to prevent maternal mortality and morbidity.[51] In this capacity, the OHCHR has underscored the need for states to employ the maximum available resources to ensure the accessibility, availability, and quality of maternal health-care services. This requires deliberate, concrete and targeted steps and the prevention of any retrogressive measures in relation to sexual and reproductive health.[52] How can it be measured that states are assigning and investing the maximum available resources in maternal health services? Can you think of indicators that may be useful for this purpose?

4. One key area that is affecting women in the area of maternal health is the problem of sterilizations without informed consent. Violence is intricately connected with many violations of sexual and reproductive rights. Psychological, physical, and sexual violence can occur in health settings and in the provision of care and services. A very common form of gender-based violence is forced sterilizations, which occur without obtaining the free, prior, and informed consent of the woman patient. A great deal of this violence is founded on negative gender stereotypes of a woman's ability to make decisions related to her health, family planning, and reproductive life. A number of cases have been decided at the international level illustrating the way in which sterilizations may occur without consent, and their human rights repercussions. In the case of *IV v. Bolivia*, the Inter-American Court of Human Rights found the state responsible for human rights violations when a bilateral tubal ligation was performed on a woman without her informed consent at a hospital, leading to the permanent loss of her reproductive capacity.[53] The Court stressed that informed consent should be secured before any medical procedures take place; free from any kind of pressure; and should include full information of the lasting effects of the procedure involved.[54] The European Court of Human Rights has also considered cases related to the forced sterilization of Roma women, who often suffer this form of discrimination and mistreatment in health-care institutions.[55] Forced sterilizations violate the rights of women to be free from gender-based violence and discrimination, to personal integrity, privacy, and reproductive autonomy, and to access to information.

## V    THE RIGHT TO LIFE AND ASSISTED REPRODUCTIVE TECHNOLOGIES

There have been important developments concerning international legal standards governing the use of assisted reproductive technologies by women and couples in conceiving children. Many of these cases have been related to the banning or restriction of *in vitro* fertilization

---

[51]   *See generally* United Nations High Commissioner for Human Rights, Report before United Nations General Assembly and Human Rights Council, *Technical Guidance on the application of a human rights-based approach to the implementation of policies and programmes to reduce preventable maternal morbidity and mortality*, A/HRC/21/22 (July 2, 2012).

[52]   *See id.*, ¶¶ 20–21. For a general overview of the problem of maternal mortality and general state measures needed, *see* ¶¶ 3–7, 11–25, 53–80.

[53]   *See* I.V. v. Bolivia, Preliminary Objections, Merits, Reparations and Costs, Inter-Am. Ct. H.R., Series C, No. 32, ¶¶ 142–220 (Nov. 30, 2016).

[54]   *Id.*

[55]   *See* VC v. Slovakia, App. No. 18968/07, Eur. Ct. H.R., ¶¶ 130–155 (Nov. 8, 2011).

techniques (hereinafter "*in vitro* fertilization" or "IVF") and the use of donor ova and sperm. Important concepts for women's rights have been advanced in these cases, including reproductive autonomy, personal liberty, and dignity. The cases allude in detail to the content of cornerstone state obligations in this area, including the rights to privacy and family life, personal integrity, non-discrimination, and to access the benefits of scientific progress.

Copied below are excerpts of the Inter-American Court of Human Rights decision in the case of *Artavia Murillo*, concerning the restriction of *in vitro* fertilization in Costa Rica. This was the first decision of the Inter-American Court of Human Rights that centered on the sexual and reproductive rights of women.

A        ***Artavia Murillo v. Costa Rica*, Inter-American Court of Human Rights**

Preliminary Objections, Merits, Reparations and Costs
Judgment of November 28, 2012, Series C No. 257
Citations and footnotes omitted

*This case is related to a challenge to the prohibition on IVF in Costa Rica, by means of a ruling of the Constitutional Chamber of the Supreme Court of Justice. The challenge was brought forth by 14 couples who could only conceive by means of IVF. The Supreme Court of Justice of Costa Rica had justified the prohibition on the need to protect the life of embryos under Article 4(1) of the American Convention on Human Rights. The excerpts below discuss the scope of the right to life under Article 4(1) of the American Convention on Human Rights.*

158.    … [T]he Court observes that the Constitutional Chamber's judgment included a concept of absolute protection of the life of the embryo, because it stated that "since the right is declared in favor of everyone, without exception – any exception or limitation destroys the very content of the right – it must be protected for those who are born and also for the unborn." Despite the foregoing, the Constitutional Chamber indicated that "advances in science and biotechnology are so rapid that the technique could be improved in such a way that the concerns that have been indicated disappear"; thus the Chamber stated that "it [should be expressly recorded that, not even by norm of legal rank, is it possible to authorize legally [the] application of [IVF], at least, […] while its scientific development remains at its current stage and entails the conscious damage to human life." …

172.    To date, the Court's case law has not ruled on the disputes that have arisen in this case with regard to the right to life. In cases of extrajudicial executions, enforced disappearances and deaths that can be attributed to the failure of the States to adopt measures, the Court has indicated that the right to life is a fundamental human right, the full enjoyment of which is a prerequisite for the enjoyment of all other human rights. Based on this fundamental role assigned to it in the Convention, States have an obligation to create the conditions to ensure that no violations of that right occur. The Court has also indicated that the right to life presupposes that no one may be arbitrarily deprived of his life (negative obligation) and that the States must adopt all appropriate measures to protect and preserve the right to life (positive obligation) of all those who are subject to their jurisdiction. This includes adopting the necessary measures to create an adequate regulatory framework that

deters any threat to the right to life and safeguards the right to have access to conditions that ensure a decent life.

173.    In the instant case, the Constitutional Chamber considered that these and other aspects of the right to life require the absolute protection of the embryo within the framework of the inviolability of life from conception ... To determine whether an obligation of absolute protection exists in those terms, the Court proceeds to analyze the scope of Articles 1(2) and 4(1) of the American Convention in relation to the terms "person," "human being," "conception" and "in general." The Court reiterates its case law according to which a provision of the Convention must be interpreted in good faith, according to the ordinary meaning to be given to the terms of the treaty and their context, and bearing in mind the object and purpose of the American Convention, which is the effective protection of the human person, as well as by an evolutive interpretation of international instruments for the protection of human rights. Within this framework, the Court will now make an interpretation that is: (i) in accordance with the ordinary meaning of the terms; (ii) systematic and historic; (iii) evolutive, and (iv) of the object and purpose of the treaty. ...

176.    In this case the Court observes that the concept of "person" is a legal term that is analyzed in many of the domestic legal systems of the States Parties. However, for the purposes of the interpretation of Article 4(1), the definition of person stems from the mentions made in the treaty with regard to "conception" and to "human being," terms whose scope should be assessed based on the scientific literature.

177.    The Court notes that the Constitutional Court chose one of the scientific positions on this issue to define as of when it was considered that life began. On this basis, the Constitutional Court understood that conception would be the moment when the egg is fertilized and assumed that, as of that moment, a person existed who held the right to life.

178.    In this regard, in the instant case, the parties also forwarded as evidence a series of scientific articles and expert opinions that will be used in the following paragraphs to determine the scope of the literal interpretation of the terms "conception," "person" and "human being." In addition, the Court will refer to the literal meaning of the expression "in general" in Article 4(1) of the Convention.

179.    The Court underlines that the evidence in the case file shows that IVF has transformed the discussion on how the phenomenon of "conception" is understood. Indeed, IVF has revealed that some time may elapse between the fusion of the egg and the spermatozoid and implantation. Therefore, the definition of "conception" accepted by the authors of the American Convention has changed. Prior to IVF, the possibility of fertilization occurring outside a woman's body was not contemplated scientifically.

180.    The Court observes that in the current scientific context there are two different interpretations of the term "conception." One school of thought understands "conception" as the moment of union, or fertilization of the egg by the spermatozoid. Fertilization results in the creation of a new cell: the zygote. Certain scientific evidence considers the zygote as a human organism that contains the necessary instructions for the development of the embryo. Another school of thought understands "conception" as the moment when the fertilized egg is implanted in the uterus. The implantation of the fertilized egg in the mother's uterus allows the new cell, the zygote, to connect with the mother's circulatory system, providing it with access to all the hormones and other elements necessary for the embryo's development. ...

183.   However, in addition to these two possible hypotheses on the moment at which "conception" should be understood to occur, the parties have presented a different thesis regarding the moment when it is believed that the embryo reaches a sufficient degree of maturity to be considered a "human being." Some hold the view that life begins with fertilization, recognizing the zygote as the first corporal manifestation of the continuing process of human development, while others consider that the starting point for the development of the embryo, and subsequently of its human life, is its implantation in the uterus where it has the capacity to add its genetic potential to the mother's potential. Moreover, others emphasize that life begins when the nervous system develops. ...

185.   Regarding the dispute as to when human life begins, the Court considers that this is a question that has been assessed in different ways from a biological, medical, ethical, moral, philosophical and religious perspective, and it concurs with domestic and international courts that there is no one agreed definition of the beginning of life. Nevertheless, it is clear to the Court that some opinions view a fertilized egg as a complete human life. Some of these opinions may be associated with concepts that confer certain metaphysical attributes on embryos. Such concepts cannot justify preference being given to a certain type of scientific literature when interpreting the scope of the right to life established in the American Convention, because this would imply imposing specific types of beliefs on others who do not share them.

186.   Despite the foregoing, the Court considers that it is appropriate to define how to interpret the term "conception" in relation to the American Convention. In this regard, the Court underscores that the scientific evidence agrees in making a difference between two complementary and essential moments of embryonic development: fertilization and implantation. The Court observes that it is only after completion of the second moment that the cycle is concluded, and that conception can be understood to have occurred. Taking into account the scientific evidence presented by the parties in this case, the Court notes that, even though, once the egg has been fertilized, this gives rise to a different cell with sufficient genetic information for the potential development of a "human being," the fact is that if this embryo is not implanted in a woman's body its possibilities of development are nil. If an embryo never manages to implant itself in the uterus, it could not develop, because it would not receive the necessary nutrients, nor would it be in a suitable environment for its development. ...

187.   Thus, the Court considers that the term "conception" cannot be understood as a moment or process exclusive of a woman's body, given that an embryo has no chance of survival if implantation does not occur. Proof of this is that it is only possible to establish whether or not pregnancy has occurred once the fertilized egg has been implanted in the uterus, when the hormone known as "chorionic gonadotropin" is produced, which can only be detected in a woman who has an embryo implanted in her. Prior to this, it is impossible to determine whether the union between the egg and a spermatozoid occurred within the body or whether this union was lost prior to implantation. In addition, it has already been pointed out that when Article 4 of the American Convention was drafted the dictionary of the *Real Academia* differentiated between the moment of fertilization and the moment of conception, understanding conception as implantation. When drafting the relevant provisions in the American Convention, the moment of fertilization was not mentioned.

188. Furthermore, with regard to the expression "in general," the *Diccionario de la Real Academia Española* states that this means "in common, generally" or "without specifying or individualizing anything." According to the structure of the second phrase of Article 4(1) of the Convention, the term "in general" is related to the expression "from the moment of conception." The literal interpretation indicates that the expression relates to anticipating possible exceptions to a particular rule. The other methods of interpretation would suggest the meaning of a provision that contemplates exceptions.

189. Taking the above into account, the Court understands the word "conception" from the moment at which implantation occurs, and therefore considers that, before this event, Article 4 of the American Convention cannot be applied. In addition, the term "in general" infers exceptions to a rule, but the interpretation in keeping with the ordinary meaning does not allow the scope of those exceptions to be specified. ...

222. The expression "every person" is used in numerous articles of the American Convention and the American Declaration. When analyzing these articles, it is not feasible to maintain that an embryo is the holder of and exercises the rights established in each of these articles. Also, taking into account, as indicated previously, that conception can only take place within a woman's body ... it can be concluded with regard to Article 4(1) of the Convention, that the direct subject of protection is fundamentally the pregnant woman, because the protection of the unborn child is implemented essentially through the protection of the woman, as revealed by Article 15(3)(a) of the Protocol of San Salvador, which obliges the States Parties "to provide special care and assistance to mothers during a reasonable period before and after childbirth," and article VII of the American Declaration, which establishes the right of all women, during pregnancy, to special protection, care, and aid.

223. Consequently, the Court concludes that the historic and systematic interpretation of precedents that exist in the inter-American system confirms that it is not admissible to grant the status of person to the embryo. ...

227. The reports of the Committee on the Elimination of Discrimination against Women (hereinafter also "CEDAW") makes it clear that the fundamental principles of equality and non-discrimination require that precedence be given to protecting the rights of pregnant women over the interest of protecting the life in formation. In the case of *L.C. v. Peru*, the Committee found the State responsible for violating the rights of a girl who was denied a crucial surgical operation, based on the excuse that she was pregnant, giving priority to the fetus over the mother's health. In view of the fact that the continuation of the pregnancy represented a grave danger for the young woman's physical and mental health, the Committee concluded that denying her a therapeutic abortion and postponing the operation constituted gender-based discrimination and a violation of her right to health and non-discrimination.

228. The Committee also expressed its concern over the potential of anti-abortion laws to jeopardize women's rights to life and health. The Committee has established that the total ban on abortion, as well as its criminalization under certain circumstances, violates the provisions of the Convention. ...

## B    Reflections and Questions

1. International and regional courts in general have refrained from extending right to life protections to unborn persons, as illustrated by the *VO v. France* case discussed in section III
   of this chapter.[56] They have also stayed away from discussions related to when life begins.[57]
   One important exception was the Inter-American Court of Human Rights decision in the
   case of *Artavia Murillo v. Costa Rica*, discussed *supra*, in which the Court interpreted the
   meaning of the term "conception" in Article 4.1 of the American Convention which reads:
   "Every person has the right to have his life respected. This right shall be protected by law
   and, in general, from the moment of conception. No one shall be arbitrarily deprived of
   his life." The Constitutional Court of Costa Rica had justified its prohibition of IVF in
   the country as a measure to protect the right to life of the embryos under Article 4.1 of
   the American Convention on Human Rights. The Inter-American Court of Human Rights
   discussed the different scientific interpretations of the term conception. One interpretation
   is that "conception" occurs when the egg is fertilized by the spermatozoid. The second
   interpretation is that "conception" takes place instead when the fertilized egg is implanted
   in the uterus. The Inter-American Court boldly interpreted that conception begins after
   implantation, since an embryo has no chance of survival if implantation does not occur.
   The Court held in general that the protection of the right to life under Article 4.1 is not
   absolute and must be balanced with the rights of women.[58] Do you think that courts should
   be offering judicial opinions of when life begins? What criteria should courts use to assess
   scientific evidence in their rulings?
2. The Inter-American Court of Human Rights in the *Artavia Murillo* case largely bases its
   holding on the elements which integrate the reproductive autonomy of women and the
   weighing of interests involved in determining the reach of the right to life protection under
   the American Convention on Human Rights. The Court provides a very thorough analysis
   of the connection of all these essential sexual and reproductive rights, including the rights
   to private and family life; the concept of liberty and self-direction, dignity and personal
   autonomy; and the right of women to access the benefits of scientific progress. The Court
   also underscores that in the weighing of the interests involved in this case – including
   those of the unborn and embryos – the rights of women have a preferred stature according
   to CEDAW and its equality and non-discrimination principles. Therefore, total bans on
   IVF constitute disproportionate and unnecessary restrictions of rights contained in the
   American Convention on Human Rights. In essence, there is a need to take into consideration competing rights in applying Article 4.1 of the American Convention.[59] Can you
   think of rights contained in the American Convention which may be in conflict with the
   protection of the right to life under Article 4.1 of the American Convention? Which criteria
   should guide the weighing of the different interests involved?

---

[56]  *See* European Court of Human Rights, VO v. France, *supra*, ¶¶ 84–86.

[57]  *See, e.g.*, Baby Boy v. United States, Case 2.141, Inter-Am. Comm'n H.R., Resolution 23/81, Case
2.141, March 6, 1981, ¶¶ 18–19.

[58]  *See* Artavia Murillo et al. ("In vitro fertilization") v. Costa Rica, Preliminary Objections, Merits,
Reparations and Costs, Inter-Am. Ct. H.R. (ser. C) No. 257, ¶ 175–264 (Nov. 28, 2012).

[59]  *See id.*, ¶¶ 142–150, 227, 274–316.

3. The European Court of Human Rights has also ruled on cases related to restrictions linked to assisted reproduction techniques. One important ruling was in the case of *SH and Others v. Austria*, in which the Court assesses the human rights implications of legal restrictions of the use of ova and sperm donation for IVF techniques.[60] In the ruling, the Court focuses largely on whether these restrictions interfered with the right to private life, were necessary in a democratic society, and exceeded the margin of appreciation afforded to state parties to the Convention. The Court weighed heavily the moral and ethical issues involved in the regulation of assisted reproduction techniques and what it perceived as a lack of common ground among European states in this area. The Court also took into consideration that homologous artificial procreation methods involving the use of ova and sperm from the spouses or cohabiting couples were still permitted under the Act, and that there was no prohibition on going abroad to perform IVF procedures.[61] Ultimately, the Court did not find a violation of Article 8 and the right to private life under the European Convention on Human Rights. The Court also refrained from reviewing this application under the right to non-discrimination under Article 14 of the European Convention on Human Rights.[62] Do you agree with the reasoning of the European Court of Human Rights in the case of *SH and Others*? Can you identify specific rights which may be violated by a prohibition on the use of donor sperm and ova donation for IVF and other assisted reproduction techniques?

## VI   CONCLUSIONS: DISTANCE BETWEEN THE THEORY AND THE PRACTICAL APPLICATION OF SEXUAL AND REPRODUCTIVE RIGHTS TODAY

Twenty-six years after the Cairo Programme of Action was adopted, full compliance with the sexual and reproductive rights of women is still a distant dream. Even though a large number of legal standards have been developed giving content and advancing the sexual and reproductive rights of women, the road is arduous when it comes to their practical application.

Many women and girls globally still face formidable barriers to access sexual and reproductive health services; contraceptives and family planning methods; and basic sex education and information to make choices vital to their health, bodies, and reproductive lives. Maternal mortality and morbidity rates continue to be high in many countries, and both women and girls face significant obstacles to access legal and safe abortions. Forms of discrimination, stereotypes, and violence are still fixtures of the provision of health services. The situation is particularly alarming when it comes to women who are afro-descendent, indigenous, girls and older persons, members of LGBTI groups, living with disabilities, deprived of liberty, migrants, and low-income. Armed conflicts, pandemics, civil unrest, and times of crisis are important threats to the availability of basic sexual and reproductive health services that women and girls still need. Advances are not guaranteed to be sustainable, and the backlash and controversy over basic women's human rights in this arena is concerning. The promises of Cairo on sexual and

---

[60]   *See generally* SH and Others v. Austria, App. No. 57813/00, Eur. Ct. H.R., ¶¶ 91–97, 100–118 (Nov. 3, 2011).

[61]   *See id.*

[62]   *Id.*, ¶¶ 119–120.

reproductive rights and of Beijing on the advancement of the rights of women in all areas are still pending.

The present and future development and implementation of legislation, policies, and programs related to sexual and reproductive health should be guided by important legal standards and advances set at the universal and regional levels in this area. The accomplishment of Sustainable Development Goal 5 on gender equality is intricately connected with the safeguarding of women's and girls' sexual and reproductive rights. The fulfillment of this goal demands taking into consideration key values, including the autonomy, liberty, dignity, and privacy of women and girls. It also entails prioritizing the effective participation and leadership of women and girls in the design of initiatives which affect them, and have them as intended beneficiaries. This will be particularly key in the post-COVID-19 world; after having an opportunity to reset, reimagine, and conceive of new societies, women and girls should be key in shaping their present and future regarding sexual and reproductive health.

# 9.   Economic, social, and cultural rights of women

## I   INTRODUCTION: THE ECONOMIC AUTONOMY AND DIGNIFIED LIFE OF WOMEN

Access by women to economic resources is an important variable in the protection of their human rights. Economic autonomy, the ability to secure decent and quality employment, and an education of quality can be paramount for women to make free and informed decisions over their life plans. These principles have been recognized by both universal and regional human rights bodies for the full respect for and guarantee of the right to a dignified life of women. However, many women lack financial independence; depend on the informal economy for employment or are unemployed; and are devoid of the means necessary to have significant influence and decision-making in their families, communities, and societies. This in turn exposes many women to situations of discrimination and gender-based violence in their homes and in different public settings. Barriers to secure employment and low educational levels are also important impediments to women to reaching decision-making and leadership positions.[1]

These issues are at the heart of the economic, social, and cultural rights of women. As discussed in Chapter 1, the International Covenant on Economic, Social and Cultural Rights has codified a number of fundamental rights in the areas of education, employment, social security, health, food, and others. These are crucial facilitators for the exercise of the rights of women in general, and are key preconditions for the exercise of civil and political rights. Even though civil and political rights were separated from economic, social, and cultural rights at the time of the adoption of the covenants, it is important to keep in mind that they were conceived as indivisible, and both sets of rights were contained in the foundational document of the human rights system, the Universal Declaration of Human Rights.[2]

A complex aspect of compliance with economic, social, and cultural rights has always been the language of the Covenant when it comes to state obligations. As referred to previously, the Covenant explicitly characterizes state obligations as progressive in nature, subjecting state compliance to the maximum available resources. This language is different from that contained in the International Covenant on Civil and Political Rights, which makes its obliga-

---

[1]   *See, for reference*, WORLD ECONOMIC FORUM, GLOBAL GENDER GAP REPORT 5–6 (2020), www3 .weforum.org/docs/WEF_GGGR_2020.pdf; Inter-American Commission on Human Rights, *The Work, Education, and Resources of Women: The Road to Equality in Guaranteeing Economic, Social, and Cultural Rights*, Executive Summary, OEA/Ser.L/V/II.143 Doc. 59 (Nov. 3, 2011), www.oas.org/en/ iachr/women/docs/pdf/WomenDESC2011.pdf.

[2]   Universal Declaration of Human Rights, G.A. Res. 217A (III), U.N. Doc. A/810 at 71 (1948), Articles 1–27, www.un.org/en/about-us/universal-declaration-of-human-rights.

tions of immediate effect.[3] However, the Committee on Economic, Social and Cultural Rights has made very clear that several specific obligations related to the Covenant are immediate in nature, including the obligation to take steps to comply with its provisions; to ensure the satisfaction of sufficient levels of each right; the principle of non-regression; and the duties to not discriminate and to guarantee equality.[4]

There are still many lingering challenges which impede the adequate enforcement of the provisions of the International Covenant on Economic, Social and Cultural Rights, including lack of political will and adequate budgeting from states; the treatment of economic, social, and cultural rights as second generation rights to civil and political rights; the systemic and wide nature of the rights to education, health, social security, food, and water, among others; and the need for indicators of adequate compliance with both the immediate and progressive obligations under the Covenant.[5]

It is important to note since the onset that economic, social, and cultural rights are not only based on legal instruments and norms. The international community has identified very important goals to ensure the sustainable development of our societies, and these constitute an important backbone to the fulfillment of the economic, social, and cultural rights of women today. Most noteworthy are the Sustainable Development Goals, discussed in earlier chapters. In the 2030 Agenda for Sustainable Development, 193 countries recognized in its Preamble the problem of poverty as a critical global challenge and its eradication as a requirement for sustainable development.[6] A total of 17 goals were identified and 169 targets, including ending poverty and hunger (Goals 1 and 2); ensuring good health and well-being (Goal 3); offering education of quality (Goal 4); achieving gender equality (Goal 5) and reducing inequality (Goal 10); achieving decent work and economic growth (Goal 8); among others.[7] The 2030 Agenda expressly states that these goals and targets seek to advance not only sustainable development, but also human rights, gender equality, and the empowerment of women and girls in the economic, social, and environmental spheres.[8]

This chapter will explore how state obligations and goals related to economic, social, and cultural rights are applicable to the situation of women and girls in particular. As examples, this chapter will delve in particular into the challenge of securing decent and quality employment; state human rights obligations towards women in the context of business; and the content of the rights to food, water security, and health. Chapter 10 will discuss in more detail women's rights concerning the environment and climate change.

---

[3]    Compare Article 2.1 of the International Covenant on Economic, Social and Cultural Rights with Article 2(1) and (2) of the International Covenant on Civil and Political Rights.

[4]    General Comment 3 on the Nature of States parties' obligations (Fifth session, 1990), Committee on Economic, Social and Cultural Rights, U.N. Doc. E/1991/23, annex III at 86 (1991), ¶¶ 1–12; General Comment 20 on Non-discrimination in economic, social and cultural rights (art. 2, para. 2, of the International Covenant on Economic, Social and Cultural Rights), Committee on Economic, Social and Cultural Rights, ¶¶ 7–9, E/C.12/GC/20 2 (July 2009).

[5]    For a good reference on contemporary challenges in the enjoyment of economic, social, and cultural rights, *see* United Nations, *The Sustainable Development Goals Report 2020*, ¶¶ 24–55, https://unstats.un.org/sdgs/report/2020/The-Sustainable-Development-Goals-Report-2020.pdf.

[6]    U.N. General Assembly, *Transforming Our World: The 2030 Agenda for Sustainable Development Goals*, A/RES/70/1 (October 21, 2015), p. 1.

[7]    *See id.*, pp. 14–27.

[8]    *See id.*, p. 1.

## II    THE PUZZLE OF PROGRESSIVE AND IMMEDIATE OBLIGATIONS: ECONOMIC, SOCIAL, AND CULTURAL RIGHTS

As indicated previously, the International Covenant on Economic, Social and Cultural Rights identified a number of progressive and immediate obligations states have to advance the protection of the rights of women in key areas such as education, employment, health, social security, and food. The Committee on Economic, Social and Cultural Rights has made clear that the prohibition of non-discrimination and the guarantee of equality permeate and are applicable to all Covenant provisions and that these obligations are always of immediate effect.[9]

The language of the International Covenant on Economic, Social and Cultural Rights has served as a reference for different regional treaties in Africa, the Americas, and Europe governing this area of the law. In regions of the world such as Africa and the Americas, economic, social, and cultural rights have become a fixture of national policies and discourse, and an important component of policy agendas and litigation before international bodies.[10]

The first part of this section includes and discusses examples of regional treaty provisions related to economic, social, and cultural rights. The second part discusses General Comment 16 of the Economic, Social and Cultural Rights Committee, which advances key principles which should govern the application of the principle of non-discrimination in the enforcement of economic, social, and cultural rights to the benefit of women.

### A    African Charter on Human and Peoples' Rights (Banjul Charter)

*Article 14*
The right to property shall be guaranteed. It may only be encroached upon in the interest of public need or in the general interest of the community and in accordance with the provisions of appropriate laws.

*Article 15*
Every individual shall have the right to work under equitable and satisfactory conditions, and shall receive equal pay for equal work.

*Article 16*

1. Every individual shall have the right to enjoy the best attainable state of physical and mental health.
2. States Parties to the present Charter shall take the necessary measures to protect the health of their people and to ensure that they receive medical attention when they are sick.

---

[9]    Committee on Economic, Social and Cultural Rights, General Comment 20, *supra* note 4, ¶¶ 7–9.

[10]    *See for reference*, Tara J. Melish, *Rethinking the "Less as More" Thesis: Supranational Litigation of Economic, Social and Cultural Rights in the Americas*, 39 N.Y.U. J. INT'L L. & POL. 171, 274–287 (2006); Manisuli Ssenyonjo, *The Influence of the International Covenant on Economic, Social and Cultural Rights in Africa*, 64 NETH. INT. LAW REV. 259–289, 262–273 (2017).

## *Article 17*

1. Every individual shall have the right to education.
2. Every individual may freely, take part in the cultural life of his community.
3. The promotion and protection of morals and traditional values recognized by the community shall be the duty of the State. …

## *Article 21*

1. All peoples shall freely dispose of their wealth and natural resources. …

## *Article 22*

1. All peoples shall have the right to their economic, social and cultural development with due regard to their freedom and identity and in the equal enjoyment of the common heritage of mankind.
2. States shall have the duty, individually or collectively, to ensure the exercise of the right to development.

## *Article 24*
All peoples shall have the right to a general satisfactory environment favorable to their development.

## B          American Convention on Human Rights

### Article 26. Progressive Development
The States Parties undertake to adopt measures, both internally and through international cooperation, especially those of an economic and technical nature, with a view to achieving progressively, by legislation or other appropriate means, the full realization of the rights implicit in the economic, social, educational, scientific, and cultural standards set forth in the Charter of the Organization of American States as amended by the Protocol of Buenos Aires.

## C          Additional Protocol to the American Convention on Human Rights in the Area of Economic, Social and Cultural Rights (Protocol of San Salvador)

### *Article 1 Obligation to Adopt Measures*
The States Parties to this Additional Protocol to the American Convention on Human Rights undertake to adopt the necessary measures, both domestically and through international cooperation, especially economic and technical, to the extent allowed by their available resources, and taking into account their degree of development, for the purpose of achieving progressively and pursuant to their internal legislations, the full observance of the rights recognized in this Protocol. …

### *Article 2 Obligation to Enact Domestic Legislation*

If the exercise of the rights set forth in this Protocol is not already guaranteed by legislative or other provisions, the States Parties undertake to adopt, in accordance with their constitutional processes and the provisions of this Protocol, such legislative or other measures as may be necessary for making those rights a reality.

### Article 3 Obligation of Nondiscrimination

The State Parties to this Protocol undertake to guarantee the exercise of the rights set forth herein without discrimination of any kind for reasons related to race, color, sex, language, religion, political or other opinions, national or social origin, economic status, birth or any other social condition. …

### Article 6 Right to Work

1. Everyone has the right to work, which includes the opportunity to secure the means for living a dignified and decent existence by performing a freely elected or accepted lawful activity. …

### Article 8 Trade Union Rights

1. The States Parties shall ensure:
    a. The right of workers to organize trade unions and to join the union of their choice for the purpose of protecting and promoting their interests. As an extension of that right, the States Parties shall permit trade unions to establish national federations or confederations, or to affiliate with those that already exist, as well as to form international trade union organizations and to affiliate with that of their choice. The States Parties shall also permit trade unions, federations and confederations to function freely. …

### Article 9 Right to Social Security

1. Everyone shall have the right to social security protecting him from the consequences of old age and of disability which prevents him, physically or mentally, from securing the means for a dignified and decent existence. In the event of the death of a beneficiary, social security benefits shall be applied to his dependents. …

### Article 10 Right to Health

1. Everyone shall have the right to health, understood to mean the enjoyment of the highest level of physical, mental and social well-being. …

### Article 11 Right to a Healthy Environment

1. Everyone shall have the right to live in a healthy environment and to have access to basic public services. …

### *Article 12 Right to Food*

1. Everyone has the right to adequate nutrition which guarantees the possibility of enjoying the highest level of physical, emotional and intellectual development. ...

### *Article 13 Right to Education*

1. Everyone has the right to education.
2. The States Parties to this Protocol agree that education should be directed towards the full development of the human personality and human dignity and should strengthen respect for human rights, ideological pluralism, fundamental freedoms, justice and peace. ...

### *Article 14 Right to the Benefits of Culture*

1. The States Parties to this Protocol recognize the right of everyone:
    a.    To take part in the cultural and artistic life of the community;
    b.    To enjoy the benefits of scientific and technological progress;
    c.    To benefit from the protection of moral and material interests deriving from any scientific, literary or artistic production of which he is the author. ...

### *Article 19 Means of Protection*

...

5. Any instance in which the rights established in paragraph a) of Article 8 and in Article 13 are violated by action directly attributable to a State Party to this Protocol may give rise, through participation of the Inter-American Commission on Human Rights and, when applicable, of the Inter-American Court of Human Rights, to application of the system of individual petitions governed by Article 44 through 51 and 61 through 69 of the American Convention on Human Rights. ...

### D        European Social Charter

### Article 1 – The right to work

With a view to ensuring the effective exercise of the right to work, the Contracting Parties undertake:

1. to accept as one of their primary aims and responsibilities the achievement and maintenance of as high and stable a level of employment as possible, with a view to the attainment of full employment;
2. to protect effectively the right of the worker to earn his living in an occupation freely entered upon;
3. to establish or maintain free employment services for all workers;
4. to provide or promote appropriate vocational guidance, training and rehabilitation.

### Article 2 – The right to just conditions of work

With a view to ensuring the effective exercise of the right to just conditions of work, the Contracting Parties undertake:

1. to provide for reasonable daily and weekly working hours, the working week to be progressively reduced to the extent that the increase of productivity and other relevant factors permit;
2. to provide for public holidays with pay;
3. to provide for a minimum of four weeks' annual holiday with pay;
4. to eliminate risks in inherently dangerous or unhealthy occupations, and where it has not yet been possible to eliminate or reduce sufficiently these risks, to provide for either a reduction of working hours or additional paid holidays for workers engaged in such occupations. …

### Article 4 – The right to a fair remuneration

With a view to ensuring the effective exercise of the right to a fair remuneration, the Parties undertake:

1. to recognise the right of workers to a remuneration such as will give them and their families a decent standard of living;
2. to recognise the right of workers to an increased rate of remuneration for overtime work, subject to exceptions in particular cases;
3. to recognise the right of men and women workers to equal pay for work of equal value. …

### Article 8 – The right of employed women to protection of maternity

With a view to ensuring the effective exercise of the right of employed women to the protection of maternity, the Parties undertake:

1. to provide either by paid leave, by adequate social security benefits or by benefits from public funds for employed women to take leave before and after childbirth up to a total of at least fourteen weeks;
2. to consider it as unlawful for an employer to give a woman notice of dismissal during the period from the time she notifies her employer that she is pregnant until the end of her maternity leave, or to give her notice of dismissal at such a time that the notice would expire during such a period. …

### E    Reflections and Questions

1. The African Charter on Human and Peoples' Rights has a very expansive coverage of economic, social and cultural rights, especially when compared to the American Convention on Human Rights and the European Convention on Human Rights.[11] It covers some of the

---

[11] For reading on the coverage of economic, social, and cultural rights in the African Charter on Human and Peoples' Rights and its effects on women, *see* Adetoun O. Ilumoka, *African Women's Economic, Social, and Cultural Rights – Toward a Relevant Theory and Practice, in* HUMAN RIGHTS OF WOMEN: NATIONAL AND INTERNATIONAL PERSPECTIVES 307–325 (Rebecca Cook ed., University of Pennsylvania Press, 1994).

classic rights contained in the International Covenant on Economic, Social and Cultural Rights, including the rights to work (Article 15), health (Article 16), and education (Article 17). It also codifies a set of new rights in this area, including to freely dispose of wealth and natural resources (Article 21), the right to development (Article 22), and to a generally satisfactory environment (Article 24). In several of the Articles, the African Charter refers to the individual and collective nature of these rights (see for example Article 21). Even though not explicitly referred to by the African Charter, the African Commission has interpreted that the Charter does also reflect the rights to food and water.[12] Can you reconcile individual and collective rights? Could they ever be in conflict? Which steps do you think are necessary for the adequate implementation of collective rights?

2. The African Charter does not refer explicitly to the principle of progressive realization. However, the African Commission has indicated that this principle does guide the implementation of the economic, social, and cultural rights contained in the African Charter, which entails that states move "expeditiously and effectively" towards the full realization of these rights.[13] According to the African Commission, states must implement "reasonable and measurable" plans, including realistic benchmarks and time frames.[14] The African Commission also considers some obligations of immediate effect, including the duty to take concrete and deliberate steps to implement these rights; the prohibition of retrogressive actions; the guarantee of minimum essential levels of each right contained in the Charter; and the obligation to prevent discrimination in the enjoyment of economic, social, and cultural rights.[15] The African Commission has greatly emphasized the importance of taking into account vulnerable and disadvantaged groups in states' steps to respect, protect, and fulfill economic, social, and cultural rights. It has also mandated states to adopt measures to prevent and mitigate the psychological and physical effects of survivors of different forms of gender-based violence; the adequate sanction of the perpetrators; and the training of the health and law enforcement personnel to promote the humane treatment of victims.[16]

3. As opposed to the African Charter on Human and Peoples' rights, the American Convention on Human Rights only includes one Article that alludes concretely to economic, social, and cultural rights. Article 26 mandates state parties to adopt measures to achieve progressively the full realization of economic, social, and cultural rights. The vagueness and generality of this disposition has led to many legal debates in the Inter-American Commission on Human Rights and the Inter-American Court of Human Rights over its content, reach, and justiciability to individual cases. Both the Inter-American Commission and Court on Human Rights have been hesitant historically to find states individually responsible under Article 26 for failures to respect and ensure different economic, social, and cultural rights

---

[12]    African Commission on Human and Peoples' Rights, *Principles and Guidelines on the Implementation of Economic, Social and Cultural Rights in the African Charter on Human and Peoples' Rights*, www.achpr.org/public/Document/file/English/achpr_instr_guide_draft_esc_rights_eng.pdf, ¶¶ 83, 87.

[13]   *See id.*, ¶ 13.

[14]   *See id.*, ¶ 14.

[15]   *See id.*, ¶¶ 14 and 16–20.

[16]   *See id.*, point ii, p. 28; ¶¶ 31–38, 55, sections f–h, i–p; ¶ 67, sections x–kk.

claims.[17] It was not until recently that the Inter-American Court of Human Rights ruled on its first cases finding violations under Article 26. For example, the Inter-American Court of Human Rights found in its 2020 ruling in the case of the *Employees of the Fireworks Factory of Santo Antônio de Jesus v. Brazil*[18] – discussed *infra* – that the state failed to ensure the right to just and favorable conditions of work without discrimination to afro-descendent women and girl workers who were harmed and killed in an explosion in a fireworks factory in violation of the rights established under Articles 26 and 24 of the American Convention, in relation to Article 1(1) of the same instrument. Moreover, in the 2020 judgment in the case of *Lhaka Honhat Association v. Argentina*,[19] the Court concluded that Argentina violated Article 26 of the American Convention by failing to prevent harmful third-party activities in indigenous territories, resulting in the degradation of the environment due to livestock and illegal logging activities, and obstacles to accessing water storage facilities.

4. The Protocol of San Salvador does provide more explicit coverage to economic, social, and cultural rights as illustrated *supra*, but only allows justiciability for individual case petitions presented before the Inter-American Commission and Court under Article 8(a) on trade union rights and Article 13 on the right to education. The Protocol has been more prominently featured in the judgments and opinions adopted by the Inter-American Court of Human Rights recently. For example, in the case of *Gonzalez Lluy v. Ecuador*, discussed in Chapter 7, the Inter-American Court found Ecuador internationally responsible for the stigma, prejudices, and discrimination suffered by the three-year-old victim in the education system for living with HIV.[20] The Court considered that the discrimination suffered by Talía Gonzalez Lluy was intersectional, due to her situation as a person living with HIV, a child, a woman, and for being affected by poverty.[21] The Court concretely found violations of her right to education under Article 13 of the Protocol of San Salvador, in relation to Articles 19 and 1(1) of the American Convention.[22] As discussed throughout this casebook, the American Convention on Human Rights is the leading human rights treaty in the Americas. The Protocol of San Salvador instead is a specialized treaty solely devoted to economic, social, and cultural rights. Does it matter under which of these treaties the Inter-American Court of Human Rights finds human rights violations concerning economic, social, and cultural issues?

---

[17]  For a description of the early tendencies of the Inter-American Commission on Human Rights and the Inter-American Court of Human Rights in its jurisprudence in the area of economic, social, and cultural rights, *see* Tara Melish, *The Inter-American Commission on Human Rights: Defending Social Rights Through Case-Based Petitions*, pp. 348–361 and *The Inter-American Court of Human Rights: Beyond Progressivity*, pp. 388–405, *in* Social Rights Jurisprudence: Emerging Trends In International And Comparative Law (Malcolm Langford ed., Cambridge University Press, 2008).

[18]  *See* Employees of the Fireworks Factory of Santo Antônio de Jesus v. Brazil, Preliminary Objections, Merits, Reparations and Costs' Judgment, Inter-Am. Ct. H.R., Series C No. 407, ¶ 203.

[19]  Indigenous Communities of the Lhaka Honhat Association (Our Land) v. Argentina, Merits, Reparations and Costs, Judgment, Inter-Am. Ct. H.R. Series C No. 400 ¶ 289 (February 6, 2020).

[20]  Gonzales Lluy et al. v. Ecuador, Preliminary Objections, Merits, Reparations and Costs, Inter-Am. Ct. H.R., Series C No. 298, ¶¶ 234–291 (Sept. 1, 2015).

[21]  *See id.*, ¶¶ 290–291.

[22]  *See id.*, ¶ 291.

5. The European Convention on Human Rights is exclusively devoted to civil and political rights. Economic, social, and cultural rights in the Council of Europe are addressed by the European Social Charter, adopted in 1961 and revised in 1996.[23] The European Social Charter has a heavy emphasis on the right to work, just working conditions, rights in the area of maternity for employed women, and the right to dignity at work (see for example, Articles 1–4, 8, 26), and other key rights in the areas of health, social security, and education (see for example Articles 7, 11, and 12). The Charter also protects the rights of specific groups such as persons living with disabilities (Article 15) and the elderly (Article 23). It is important to note that ratification of the Charter is not mandatory for Council of Europe member states. They can also select which provisions of the Charter to accept. Only 36 member states of the Council of Europe have ratified the Revised European Social Charter. Are there any important rights related to economic, social, and cultural issues which affect women that you see are missing from the European Social Charter?

6. On the basis of Articles 24 and 25 of the 1961 European Social Charter, a European Committee of Social Rights was established to monitor the implementation of the Charter.[24] The Committee includes a state reporting system and a collective complaints mechanism. With regard to individual complaints, only 16 states have accepted the jurisdiction of the Committee to hear individual and collective complaints. Under the 1995 Additional Protocol to the European Social Charter Providing for a System of Collective Complaints, complaints can be filed by trade unions, international and national employer organizations, and international non-governmental organizations. What advantages do you see in allowing not only individual, but also collective complaints? How would these advantages be applicable to women?

7. The European Union has also adopted the Charter of Fundamental Rights of the European Union, which has extensive coverage of economic, social, and cultural rights. Among the rights protected are the rights to dignity (Article 1); to education (Article 14); to engage in work (Article 15); to property (Article 17); cultural, religious, and linguistic diversity (Article 22); fair and just working conditions (Article 31); social security (Article 34); and health care (Article 35).[25] The Charter is binding on EU member states since the entry into force of the Treaty of Lisbon in December of 2009. The content of the Charter is interpreted by the European Court of Justice. The European Convention on Human Rights is also interpreted by the European Court of Justice.[26] The European Union and the Council of Europe have undertaken a process for the EU to secure accession to the European

---

[23] *See generally* European Social Charter (Revised), European Treaty Series No. 163, Strasbourg, 3.V.1996.

[24] For more information on the work of the European Committee of Social Rights, *see* www.coe.int/en/web/european-social-charter/european-committee-of-social-rights (last visited on May 19, 2021).

[25] *See Charter of Fundamental Rights of the European Union*, 2000 O.J. (C 364) 1 (Dec. 7, 2000), Articles 1, 17, 22, 28, 31–32, 34–35, 37.

[26] For a history of the work of the European Court of Justice in the area of human rights, *see* Elizabeth F. Defeis, *Human Rights and the European Court of Justice: An Appraisal*, 31(5) FORDHAM INTERNATIONAL LAW JOURNAL, Article 2, https://ir.lawnet.fordham.edu/cgi/viewcontent.cgi?article=2110&context=ilj.

Convention on Human Rights, in order to promote consistency between the EU law and the Convention system.[27]

***** 

As discussed earlier, the Committee on Economic, Social and Cultural Rights has identified non-discrimination and the guarantee of equality as one of the obligations of immediate effect under the International Covenant on Economic, Social and Cultural Rights.[28] This entails states eliminating all forms of intersectional discrimination, stereotypes, and disparate and arbitrary treatment which can pose formidable barriers for women to fully exercise and enjoy all of their rights in the areas of health, education, employment, social security, food and water, and other realms. It demands immediate steps to ensure accessibility, affordability, and quality of services; the adoption of legislation, public policies, and programs; as well as ensuring the guarantee of judicial remedies when human rights violations occur.

General Comment 16 copied below identifies steps needed from states to adequately ensure non-discrimination and the pursuit of equality in the respect, protection, and fulfillment of the economic, social, and cultural rights of women.

## F      Human Rights Committee, General Comment 16

Twenty-third session, 1988, Compilation of General Comments and General Recommendations Adopted by Human Rights Treaty Bodies, U.N. Doc. HRI/GEN/1/Rev.1 at 21 (1994)

19. States parties' obligation to protect under Article 3 of the ICESCR includes inter alia, the respect and adoption of constitutional and legislative provisions on the equal right of men and women to enjoy all human rights and the prohibition of discrimination of any kind. …
20. States parties have an obligation to monitor and regulate the conduct of non-state actors to ensure that they do not violate the equal right of men and women to enjoy economic, social and cultural rights. …
21. The obligation to fulfill requires States parties to take steps to ensure that in practice, men and women enjoy their economic, social and cultural rights on a basis of equality. Such steps should include: … the adoption of temporary special measures to accelerate women's equal enjoyment of their rights, gender audits, and gender-specific allocation of resources.
22. Article 3 is a cross-cutting obligation and applies to all of the rights stated in Articles 6 to 15 of the Covenant. It requires addressing gendered social and cultural prejudices, provid-ing for equality in the allocation of resources and promoting the sharing of responsibilities in the family, community and public life. The examples provided in the following para-

---

[27]   Council of Europe and European Commission, *The EU's accession to the European Convention on Human Rights: Joint statement on behalf of the Council of Europe and the European Commission*, September 29, 2020, https://search.coe.int/directorate_of_communications/Pages/result_details.aspx?ObjectId=09000016809fbd51.

[28]   *See* Committee on Economic, Social and Cultural Rights, General Comment 20, *supra* note 4, ¶¶ 7–9.

graphs may be taken as guidance on the ways in which Article 3 applies to other rights in the Covenant, but are not intended to be exhaustive.

23. Article 6(1) of the Covenant requires States parties to safeguard the right of everyone to the opportunity to gain a living by work which is freely chosen or accepted and to take the necessary steps to achieve the full realization of this right. Implementing Article 3 in relation to Article 6 requires inter alia, that, in law and in practice, men and women have equal access to jobs at all levels and all occupations and that vocational training and guidance programmes, in both the public and private sectors, provide men and women with the skills, information and knowledge necessary for them to benefit equally from the right to work.

24. Article 7(a) of the Covenant requires States parties to recognize the right of everyone to enjoy just and favourable conditions of work and to ensure among other things, fair wages and equal pay for work of equal value. Article 3 in relation to Article 7 requires, inter alia, that the State party identifies and eliminates the underlying causes of pay differentials, such as gender-biased job evaluation or the perception that productivity differences between men and women exist. ...

25. Article 8(1)(a) of the Covenant requires States parties to ensure the right of everyone to form and join trade unions of his or her choice. Article 3 in relation to Article 8 requires allowing men and women to organize and join trade workers associations, that address their specific concerns. In this regard, particular attention should be given to domestic workers, rural women, women working in female-dominated industries and women working at home, who are often deprived of this right.

26. Article 9 of the Covenant requires that States parties recognize the right of everyone to social security, including social insurance, and to equal access to social services. Implementing Article 3 in relation to Article 9 requires, inter alia, equalizing the compulsory retirement age for both men and women; ensuring that women receive the equal benefit of public and private pension schemes; and guaranteeing adequate maternity leave for women, paternity leave for men, and parental leave for both men and women.

27. Article 10(1) of the Covenant requires that States parties recognize that the widest possible protection and assistance should be accorded to the family, and that marriage must be entered into with the free consent of the intending spouses. Implementing Article 3 in relation to Article 10 requires States parties, inter alia, to provide victims of domestic violence, who are primarily female, with access to safe housing, remedies and redress of physical, mental and emotional damage. ...

28. Article 11 of the Covenant requires States parties to recognize the right of everyone to an adequate standard of living for him/herself and his/her family, including adequate housing (11(1)) and adequate food (11(2)). Implementing Article 3 in relation to Article 11(1) requires that women have a right to own, use or otherwise control housing, land and property on an equal basis with men, and to access necessary resources to do so. Implementing Article 3 in relation to Article 11(2) also requires States parties, inter alia, to ensure that women have access to, or control over, means of food production, and actively address customary practices under which women are not allowed to eat until the men are fully fed, or are only allowed less nutritious food.

29. Article 12 of the Covenant requires States parties to undertake steps towards the full realization of the right of everyone to the enjoyment of the highest attainable standard of phys-

ical and mental health. The implementation of Article 3 in relation to Article 12 requires, at a minimum, the removal of legal and other obstacles that prevent men and women from accessing and benefiting from healthcare on a basis of equality. This includes, inter alia, addressing the ways in which gender roles affect access to determinants of health, such as water and food; the removal of legal restrictions on reproductive health provisions; the prohibition of female genital mutilation; and the provision of adequate training for health care workers to deal with women's health issues.

30. Article 13(1) of the Covenant requires States parties to recognize the right of everyone to education and in 13(2)(a), that primary education shall be compulsory and available free to all. Implementing Article 3 in relation to Article 13 requires, inter alia, the adoption of legislation and policies to ensure the same admissions criteria for boys and girls in all levels of education. …

31. Article 15(1)(a) and (b) of the Covenant require States parties to recognize the right of everyone to take part in cultural life and to enjoy the benefits of scientific progress. Implementing Article 3 in relation to Article 15(1)(a) and (b) requires, inter alia, overcoming institutional barriers and other obstacles, such as those based on cultural and religious traditions, which prevent women from fully participating in cultural life, science education and scientific research, and directing resources to scientific research relating to the health and economic needs of women on an equal basis with those of men. …

## G    Reflections and Questions

1. General Comment 16 refers in its paragraph 20 to state obligations to monitor the activity of non-state actors which can impede the enjoyment of the economic, social, and cultural rights of women. Consider which non-state actors may be involved in violations of the rights of women in the areas of education, employment, health, food, and water. What might be the best ways for a state to monitor and supervise their activities?[29]

2. General Comment 16 *supra* also refers in its paragraph 21 to temporary special measures as part of the state strategy to advance the economic, social, and cultural rights of women. As discussed previously, temporary special measures may be adopted in many formats in legislation, policies, and programs – both in the public and private sectors – including quotas, numerical targets, forms of preferred treatment, and diversity and inclusion-driven recruitment and promotions.[30] The international community now not only discusses temporary special measures, but also the goal of parity for women, as discussed in Chapter 5, due to the increasing emphasis on the importance of women reaching decision-making and

---

[29]   For more reading on non-state actors and economic, social, and cultural rights, *see* Manisuli Ssenyonjo, *Non-State Actors and Economic, Social, and Cultural Rights, in* Economic, Social, and Cultural Rights in Action 109–135 (Mashood Baderin and Robert McCorquodale eds., Oxford University Press, 2007).

[30]   For examples of temporary special measures which can be adopted in the field of economic, social, and cultural rights *see* Christine Chinkin, *Gender and Economic, Social, and Cultural Rights, in* Economic, Social, and Cultural Rights in International Law: Contemporary Issues and Challenges 156–157 (Eibe Riedel, Gilles Giacca, and Christophe Golay eds., Oxford University Press, 2014); Christine Chinkin, *The Protection of Economic, Social, and Cultural Rights Post-Conflict,* pp. 25–26, www2.ohchr.org/english/issues/women/docs/Paper_Protection_ESCR.pdf.

leadership goals. How do you reconcile the adoption of temporary special measures with the progressive nature of most economic, social, and cultural rights? How can they be an effective part of a strategy to advance the economic, social, and cultural rights of women in the long term?

3. With regard to education, many advances have been documented internationally in the access of women and girls to education at the primary and higher education levels. However, the problem of gender-based violence continues to be alarming in educational institutions. Women and girls frequently face forms of harassment and physical, sexual, and psychological violence by their peers and teachers. Some of these incidents have tragic results.[31] The Inter-American Court of Human Rights recently ruled on its decision in the case of *Guzmán Albarracín et. al.* – discussed in Chapter 11 – in which a young girl committed suicide after sustaining a sexual relationship and suffering acts of sexual violence from the vice principal of her school for more than a year.[32] Paola Albarracín was between 14 and 16 years old at the time of the events.[33] The Court considered that this case occurred in the context of a relationship of "power and trust," perpetrated by an authority figure at the school, and by a public official towards a girl in a vulnerable situation.[34] The Court held that Paola Albarracín's rights to life, personal integrity, private life, and to education were violated under Articles 4(1), 5(1) and 11 of the American Convention; Article 13 of the Protocol of San Salvador, in relation to Articles 1(1) and 19 thereof; and Articles 7.a, 7.b and 7.c of the Belém do Pará Convention, to the detriment of Paola del Rosario Guzmán Albarracín.[35]

4. The problem of child marriage has also been well documented internationally. The CEDAW Committee and the Committee on the Rights of the Child (hereinafter "CRC") have defined an *early marriage*, as one in which one of the parties is under 18 years old.[36] Both the CEDAW and CRC Committees consider early marriages as forced and a harmful practice, due to the inability of one or more of the entering parties to provide full, free, and informed consent.[37] According to the organization Girls Not Brides, every year 12 million girls are married globally before the age of 18.[38] Significant variables contributing to this problem are poverty, social insecurity, the notion that women are inferior to men, and lack

---

[31] *See* UNICEF, *25 years of uneven progress: Despite gains in education, world still a violent, highly discriminatory place for girls*, March 4, 2020, www.unicef.org/press-releases/25-years-uneven-progress-despite-gains-education-world-still-violent-highly.

[32] *See* Guzmán Albarracín et al. v. Ecuador, Merits, Reparations and Costs, Judgment, Inter-Am. Ct. H.R., Series C No. 405 (June 24, 2020).

[33] *See id.,* ¶ 122.

[34] *See id.,* ¶¶ 127–170.

[35] *See id.,* ¶¶ 167–168.

[36] For more discussion, *see* Committee on the Elimination of Discrimination against Women, *Joint general recommendation No. 31 of the Committee on the Elimination of Discrimination against Women/ General comment No. 18 of the Committee on the Rights of the Child on harmful practices*, CEDAW/C/ GC/31-CRC/C/GC/18, ¶ 20.

[37] *Id.,* ¶¶ 20–24.

[38] Girls Not Brides, *About Child Marriage*, www.girlsnotbrides.org/about-child-marriage/ (last visited on May 19, 2021).

of education.[39] Some important results of child marriage are the incidence of domestic violence, rape within marriage, obstacles to accessing employment and education, and health challenges related to early pregnancies.[40]

## III     DECENT AND QUALITY EMPLOYMENT: THE SITUATION OF WOMEN

One of the areas in which women suffer the most human rights violations is in the realm of employment. Women every day are entering the workforce in larger numbers, but they are not necessarily having full careers and reaching decision-making and leadership positions. Some of the problems which account for this problem are the gender pay gap; the lack of sufficient protection during pregnancy; intersectional discrimination and stereotypes; and the unequal division of childcare responsibilities in the home. Women often have to work in unhealthy and unsafe labor conditions, and are frequently victims of harassment and violence by their colleagues and supervisors. Work–life balance is still a challenge and our social structures are still not set up to facilitate women succeeding in the workplace.

This section discusses a number of cases and treaties which allude to these ongoing challenges for women in the workplace.

### A     *Ledbetter v. Goodyear Tire & Rubber Co.*

550 U.S. 618 (2007)
Citations and footnotes omitted

*This case is related to the pay-related discrimination Lilly Ledbetter suffered while working for respondent Goodyear Tire and Rubber during 1979–1998 and her efforts to secure a remedy.*

[Lilly Ledbetter] sought review of the following question: "Whether and under what circumstances a plaintiff may bring an action under Title VII of the Civil Rights Act of 1964 alleging illegal pay discrimination when the disparate pay is received during the statutory limitations period, but is the result of intentionally discriminatory pay decisions that occurred outside the limitations period." …

In light of disagreement among the Courts of Appeals as to the proper application of the limitations period in Title VII disparate-treatment pay cases, we granted certiorari. …

Title VII of the Civil Rights Act of 1964 makes it an "unlawful employment practice" to discriminate "against any individual with respect to his compensation … because of such individual's … sex …" An individual wishing to challenge an employment practice under this provision must first file a charge with the EEOC. Such a charge must be filed within a specified period (either 180 or 300 days, depending on the State) "after the alleged unlawful

---

[39]   International Women's Health Coalition, *The Facts on Child Marriage*, https://iwhc.org/resources/facts-child-marriage/ (last visited on May 19, 2021).
[40]   Equality Now, *What Are the Long-Term Impacts of Child Marriage? Your Questions Answered*, May 17, 2019, www.equalitynow.org/long_term_impacts_child_marriage (last visited on May 19, 2021).

employment practice occurred," and if the employee does not submit a timely EEOC charge, the employee may not challenge that practice in court.

In addressing the issue whether an EEOC charge was filed on time, we have stressed the need to identify with care the specific employment practice that is at issue ... Ledbetter points to two different employment practices as possible candidates. Primarily, she urges us to focus on the paychecks that were issued to her during the EEOC charging period (the 180-day period preceding the filing of her EEOC questionnaire), each of which, she contends, was a separate act of discrimination. Alternatively, Ledbetter directs us to the 1998 decision denying her a raise, and she argues that this decision was "unlawful because it carried forward intentionally discriminatory disparities from prior years ..." Both of these arguments fail because they would require us in effect to jettison the defining element of the legal claim on which her Title VII recovery was based.

Ledbetter asserted disparate treatment, the central element of which is discriminatory intent. ...

However, Ledbetter does not assert that the relevant Goodyear decisionmakers acted with actual discriminatory intent either when they issued her checks during the EEOC charging period or when they denied her a raise in 1998. Rather, she argues that the paychecks were unlawful because they would have been larger if she had been evaluated in a nondiscriminatory manner prior to the EEOC charging period ... Similarly, she maintains that the 1998 decision was unlawful because it "carried forward" the effects of prior, uncharged discrimination decisions. In essence, she suggests that it is sufficient that discriminatory acts that occurred prior to the charging period had continuing effects during that period. ...

Ledbetter's arguments here—that the paychecks that she received during the charging period and the 1998 raise denial each violated Title VII and triggered a new EEOC charging period—cannot be reconciled with Evans, Ricks, Lorance, and Morgan. Ledbetter, as noted, makes no claim that intentionally discriminatory conduct occurred during the charging period or that discriminatory decisions that occurred prior to that period were not communicated to her. Instead, she argues simply that Goodyear's conduct during the charging period gave present effect to discriminatory conduct outside of that period ... But current effects alone cannot breathe life into prior, uncharged discrimination; as we held in Evans, such effects in themselves have "no present legal consequences ..." Ledbetter should have filed an EEOC charge within 180 days after each allegedly discriminatory pay decision was made and communicated to her. She did not do so, and the paychecks that were issued to her during the 180 days prior to the filing of her EEOC charge do not provide a basis for overcoming that prior failure. ...

Ledbetter, finally, makes a variety of policy arguments in favor of giving the alleged victims of pay discrimination more time before they are required to file a charge with the EEOC. Among other things, she claims that pay discrimination is harder to detect than other forms of employment discrimination. We are not in a position to evaluate Ledbetter's policy arguments, and it is not our prerogative to change the way in which Title VII balances the interests of aggrieved employees against the interest in encouraging the "prompt processing of all charges of employment discrimination ..." and the interest in repose. Ledbetter's policy arguments for giving special treatment to pay claims find no support in the statute and are inconsistent with our precedents. We apply the statute as written, and this means that any unlawful employment practice, including those involving compensation, must be presented to the EEOC within the period prescribed by statute.

For these reasons, the judgment of the Court of Appeals for the Eleventh Circuit is affirmed.

JUSTICE GINSBURG, with whom JUSTICE STEVENS, JUSTICE SOUTER, and JUSTICE BREYER join, dissenting.

Lilly Ledbetter was a supervisor at Goodyear Tire and Rubber's plant in Gadsden, Alabama, from 1979 until her retirement in 1998. For most of those years, she worked as an area manager, a position largely occupied by men. Initially, Ledbetter's salary was in line with the salaries of men performing substantially similar work. Over time, however, her pay slipped in comparison to the pay of male area managers with equal or less seniority. By the end of 1997, Ledbetter was the only woman working as an area manager and the pay discrepancy between Ledbetter and her 15 male counterparts was stark: Ledbetter was paid $3,727 per month; the lowest paid male area manager received $4,286 per month, the highest paid, $5,236. …

Title VII proscribes as an "unlawful employment practice" discrimination "against any individual with respect to his compensation … because of such individual's race, color, religion, sex, or national origin." An individual seeking to challenge an employment practice under this proscription must file a charge with the EEOC within 180 days "after the alleged unlawful employment practice occurred …"

Ledbetter's petition presents a question important to the sound application of Title VII: What activity qualifies as an unlawful employment practice in cases of discrimination with respect to compensation. One answer identifies the pay-setting decision, and that decision alone, as the unlawful practice. Under this view, each particular salary-setting decision is discrete from prior and subsequent decisions, and must be challenged within 180 days on pain of forfeiture. Another response counts both the pay-setting decision and the actual payment of a discriminatory wage as unlawful practices. Under this approach, each payment of a wage or salary infected by sex-based discrimination constitutes an unlawful employment practice; prior decisions, outside the 180-day charge-filing period, are not themselves actionable, but they are relevant in determining the lawfulness of conduct within the period. The Court adopts the first view, but the second is more faithful to precedent, more in tune with the realities of the workplace, and more respectful of Title VII's remedial purpose. …

Pay disparities, of the kind Ledbetter experienced, have a closer kinship to hostile work environment claims than to charges of a single episode of discrimination. Ledbetter's claim, resembling Morgan's, rested not on one particular paycheck, but on "the cumulative effect of individual acts …" Initially in line with the salaries of men performing substantially the same work, Ledbetter's salary fell 15 to 40 percent behind her male counterparts only after successive evaluations and percentage-based pay adjustments … Over time, she alleged and proved, the repetition of pay decisions undervaluing her work gave rise to the current discrimination of which she complained. Though component acts fell outside the charge-filing period, with each new paycheck, Goodyear contributed incrementally to the accumulating harm. …

The realities of the workplace reveal why the discrimination with respect to compensation that Ledbetter suffered does not fit within the category of singular discrete acts "easy to identify." A worker knows immediately if she is denied a promotion or transfer, if she is fired or refused employment. And promotions, transfers, hirings, and firings are generally public events, known to co-workers. When an employer makes a decision of such open and definitive character, an employee can immediately seek out an explanation and evaluate it for pretext.

Compensation disparities, in contrast, are often hidden from sight. It is not unusual, decisions in point illustrate, for management to decline to publish employee pay levels, or for employees to keep private their own salaries ... Tellingly, as the record in this case bears out, Goodyear kept salaries confidential; employees had only limited access to information regarding their colleagues' earnings. ...

In light of the significant differences between pay disparities and discrete employment decisions of the type identified in Morgan, the cases on which the Court relies hold no sway. ...

Specifically, Ledbetter's evidence demonstrated that her current pay was discriminatorily low due to a long series of decisions reflecting Goodyear's pervasive discrimination against women managers in general and Ledbetter in particular. ...

Yet, under the Court's decision, the discrimination Ledbetter proved is not redressable under Title VII. Each and every pay decision she did not immediately challenge wiped the slate clean. Consideration may not be given to the cumulative effect of a series of decisions that, together, set her pay well below that of every male area manager. Knowingly carrying past pay discrimination forward must be treated as lawful conduct. Ledbetter may not be compensated for the lower pay she was in fact receiving when she complained to the EEOC. Nor, were she still employed by Goodyear, could she gain, on the proof she presented at trial, injunctive relief requiring, prospectively, her receipt of the same compensation men receive for substantially similar work. ...

For the reasons stated, I would hold that Ledbetter's claim is not time barred and would reverse the Eleventh Circuit's judgment.

## B        Maternity Protection Convention, 2000 (No. 183)

International Labour Organization

### Preamble
Noting the need to revise the Maternity Protection Convention (Revised), 1952, and the Maternity Protection Recommendation, 1952, in order to further promote equality of all women in the workforce and the health and safety of the mother and child, and in order to recognize the diversity in economic and social development of Members, as well as the diversity of enterprises, and the development of the protection of maternity in national law and practice, and ...

Taking into account the circumstances of women workers and the need to provide protection for pregnancy, which are the shared responsibility of government and society ...

### *Article 1*
For the purposes of this Convention, the term *woman* applies to any female person without discrimination whatsoever and the term *child* applies to any child without discrimination whatsoever.

### *Article 2*

1. This Convention applies to all employed women, including those in atypical forms of dependent work. ...

### *HEALTH PROTECTION*

*Article 3*

Each Member shall, after consulting the representative organizations of employers and workers, adopt appropriate measures to ensure that pregnant or breastfeeding women are not obliged to perform work which has been determined by the competent authority to be prejudicial to the health of the mother or the child, or where an assessment has established a significant risk to the mother's health or that of her child.

## MATERNITY LEAVE
*Article 4*

1. On production of a medical certificate or other appropriate certification, as determined by national law and practice, stating the presumed date of childbirth, a woman to whom this Convention applies shall be entitled to a period of maternity leave of not less than 14 weeks.
2. The length of the period of leave referred to above shall be specified by each Member in a declaration accompanying its ratification of this Convention. …
4. With due regard to the protection of the health of the mother and that of the child, maternity leave shall include a period of six weeks' compulsory leave after childbirth, unless other-wise agreed at the national level by the government and the representative organizations of employers and workers.
5. The prenatal portion of maternity leave shall be extended by any period elapsing between the presumed date of childbirth and the actual date of childbirth, without reduction in any compulsory portion of postnatal leave.

## LEAVE IN CASE OF ILLNESS OR COMPLICATIONS
*Article 5*

On production of a medical certificate, leave shall be provided before or after the maternity leave period in the case of illness, complications or risk of complications arising out of pregnancy or childbirth. The nature and the maximum duration of such leave may be specified in accordance with national law and practice.

## BENEFITS
*Article 6*

1. Cash benefits shall be provided, in accordance with national laws and regulations, or in any other manner consistent with national practice, to women who are absent from work on leave referred to in Articles 4 or 5.
2. Cash benefits shall be at a level which ensures that the woman can maintain herself and her child in proper conditions of health and with a suitable standard of living.
3. Where, under national law or practice, cash benefits paid with respect to leave referred to in Article 4 are based on previous earnings, the amount of such benefits shall not be less than two-thirds of the woman's previous earnings or of such of those earnings as are taken into account for the purpose of computing benefits. …

## *Article 7*

1. A Member whose economy and social security system are insufficiently developed shall be deemed to be in compliance with Article 6, paragraphs 3 and 4, if cash benefits are provided at a rate no lower than a rate payable for sickness or temporary disability in accordance with national laws and regulations. …

## EMPLOYMENT PROTECTION AND NON-DISCRIMINATION
### *Article 8*

1. It shall be unlawful for an employer to terminate the employment of a woman during her pregnancy or absence on leave referred to in Articles 4 or 5 or during a period following her return to work to be prescribed by national laws or regulations, except on grounds unrelated to the pregnancy or birth of the child and its consequences or nursing. The burden of proving that the reasons for dismissal are unrelated to pregnancy or childbirth and its consequences or nursing shall rest on the employer.
2. A woman is guaranteed the right to return to the same position or an equivalent position paid at the same rate at the end of her maternity leave.

## *Article 9*

1. Each Member shall adopt appropriate measures to ensure that maternity does not constitute a source of discrimination in employment, including – notwithstanding Article 2, paragraph 1 – access to employment. …

## BREASTFEEDING MOTHERS
### *Article 10*

1. A woman shall be provided with the right to one or more daily breaks or a daily reduction of hours of work to breastfeed her child.
2. The period during which nursing breaks or the reduction of daily hours of work are allowed, their number, the duration of nursing breaks and the procedures for the reduction of daily hours of work shall be determined by national law and practice. These breaks or the reduction of daily hours of work shall be counted as working time and remunerated accordingly …

C       *Case of the Employees of the Fireworks Factory of Santo Antônio de Jesus v. Brazil*

Inter-American Court of Human Rights
Preliminary Objections, Merits, Reparations and Costs, Judgment of July 15, 2020, Series C No. 407
Citations and footnotes omitted

*This case is related to an explosion in a private fireworks factory in Santo Antônio de Jesus, Brazil, killing 60 people, including 19 girls. The Inter-American Commission on Human*

*Rights claimed before the Inter-American Court of Human Rights that the state had failed to adequately protect the right to safe working conditions of the workers. The excerpts below discuss the scope of the right to work under inter-American instruments.*

148.   First, the Court recalls that the explosion that this case refers to occurred in a privately-owned fireworks factory and that the State cannot be considered responsible for every human rights violation committed by private individuals within its jurisdiction. Therefore, the Court must examine the particular circumstances of the case and the implementation of the obligation to ensure rights in order to establish whether the State can be attributed with international responsibility in the specific case.

149.   In this regard, the Court recalls that the State had the obligation to ensure the rights recognized in the American Convention and that this entailed the adoption of the necessary measures to prevent possible violations. Previously, it determined that the manufacture of fireworks is a dangerous activity; thus, in this case, the State was obliged to regulate, supervise and oversee that the working conditions were safe in order to prevent occupational accidents caused by the handling of dangerous materials. …

161.   The right to just and favorable conditions of work has been recognized in different international instruments in addition to the OAS Charter and the American Declaration. Within the inter-American system, Article 7 of the Additional Protocol to the American Convention on Human Rights in the Area of Economic, Social and Cultural Rights "Protocol of San Salvador" (hereinafter "Protocol of San Salvador") establishes that "[t]he States Parties to this Protocol recognize that the right to work to which the foregoing article refers presupposes that everyone shall enjoy that right under just, equitable, and satisfactory conditions, which the States Parties undertake to guarantee in their internal legislation, particularly with respect to: […] (e) Safety and hygiene at work." …

174.   Taking into account the facts and the particularities of this case, the Court concludes that this right means that the worker must be able to carry out his work in adequate conditions of safety, hygiene and health that prevent occupational accidents, and this is especially relevant in the case of activities that involve significant risk to the life and integrity of the workers. …

175.   As already indicated, Brazil had the obligation to ensure just and favorable conditions of work as described in the preceding paragraph. However, the workers of the factory of "Vardo dos Fogos" worked in precarious, unhealthy and unsafe conditions, in sheds located in fields that did not meet even the minimum standards of safety for carrying out a dangerous activity and that did not meet the conditions that would have avoided or prevented occupational accidents. They never received any information on safety measures, or work-related protection equipment. And all this took place without the State exercising any supervision or oversight actions to verify the working conditions of those employed in the fireworks factory, or taking any action to prevent accidents, even though domestic law characterized the activities carried out in the factory as especially dangerous. …

177.   The Court has verified that several children and adolescents worked in the fireworks factory. Thus, of the 60 people who died, 19 were girls and one was a boy, the youngest of whom was 11 years of age. Meanwhile, the survivors included a girl and two boys who were between 15 and 17 years of age. …

188.    In the instant case, the Commission argued that there was a connection between the State's failure to comply with its obligations and the situation of poverty faced in the municipality of Santo Antônio de Jesus, so that the situation of poverty of the fireworks factory workers had resulted in the violation of their right to just and favorable conditions of work without discrimination. This would indicate that the case involves an alleged structural discrimination for reasons of poverty. In this regard, the Court notes that the presumed victims were individuals who, on account of the structural discrimination based on their situation of poverty, were unable to access any other source of income and had to accept employment in conditions of vulnerability that disregarded the mandates of the American Convention and that exposed them to victimization.

189.    Thus, the fact that an especially dangerous economic activity had been set up in the area was related to the poverty and marginalization of the population that lived, and still lives, there. For the inhabitants of the districts in which the workers of the fireworks factory lived, the work they were offered there was not only the main, but also the only, employment option because they had very low levels of schooling and literacy; they were also perceived as being rather untrustworthy and were therefore unable to obtain other employment. In this regard, the United Nations Guiding Principles on extreme poverty and human rights recognize that "persons living in poverty experience unemployment, underemployment, unreliable casual labour, low wages and unsafe and degrading working conditions."

190.    In addition to the structural discrimination due to the presumed victim's poverty status, the Court considers that various structural disadvantages coalesced around them and had an impact on their victimization. These disadvantages were both economic and social, and also related to certain groups of individuals. In other words, there was a convergence of factors of discrimination. The Court has referred to this concept explicitly or tacitly in various judgments and has referred to different categories in this regard.

191.    That said, in this case, the intersection of factors of discrimination increased the comparative disadvantages of the presumed victims. Thus, the presumed victims shared specific factors of discrimination suffered by those living in poverty, women, and Afro-descendants, but they also suffered a specific form of discrimination owing to the confluence of all these factors and, in some cases, because they were pregnant, because they were girls, or because they were girls and pregnant. In this regard, it is important to stress that the Court has established that pregnancy may constitute a situation of particular vulnerability and, in some cases of victimization, pregnancy may result in a differentiated violation. ...

200.    In this specific case, the Court has determined that the workers of the fireworks factory were part of a discriminated or marginalized group because they were in a situation of structural poverty and also most of them were Afro-descendant women and girls. However, the State failed to take any measure that could be assessed by the Court as a way of addressing or seeking to reverse the situation of structural poverty and marginalization of the fireworks factory workers based on the factors of discrimination that coalesced in this case. ...

203.    In sum, the Court finds that the situation of poverty of the presumed victims, added to the intersectional factors of discrimination described above that exacerbated the condition of vulnerability: (i) facilitated the installation and operation of a factory dedicated to

a particularly dangerous activity, without any oversight of the hazardous activity or the occupational health and safety conditions by the State, and (ii) led the presumed victims to accept work that jeopardized their life and integrity and that of their underage children. In addition, (iii) the State failed to take measures to ensure material equality in the right to work for a group of women who were marginalized and faced discriminated [*sic*]. This situation signifies that, in this case, the State failed to ensure the right to just and favorable conditions of work, without discrimination, as well as the right to equality established in Articles 24 and 26, in relation to Article 1(1) of the Convention.

## D    Reflections and Questions

1. On January 29, 2009, the Lilly Ledbetter Fair Pay Act of 2009 was signed into law by then United States President Barack Obama. The Act amended Title VII of the Civil Rights Act of 1964 by establishing that the 180-day statute of limitations for pay discrimination claims resets with each new paycheck relevant to the action. Therefore, the law addressed the *Ledbetter v. Goodyear Tire & Rubber Co.* United States Supreme Court judgment *supra*, which had held that the statute of limitations for these types of claims began on the date of the discriminatory wage decision and not on the date of the latest paycheck. The law also prohibits all discriminatory compensation decisions. The adoption of this statute illustrates the effects that court decisions and dissident opinions can have on the adoption of future legislation advancing the rights of women in the workplace and the elimination of the gender pay gap in employment.[41] Which approach to gender pay discrimination claims do you prefer – the one advanced by the US Supreme Court Decision or the later federal statute? Do you agree with the dissenting opinion advanced by Justice Ginsburg in the *Ledbetter v. Goodyear Tire & Rubber Co.* US Supreme Court decision?

2. Adequate legal protection for women during their pregnancies, after childbirth, and during the lactation period is paramount to the adequate enjoyment of the right to decent and quality work. It is also vital for women to preserve their employment, continue in the work-place, and reach senior positions. The Maternity Protection Convention 183 was adopted in 2000 by the International Labour Organization to advance protection for women workers during pregnancy and the lactation period.[42] Article 14.1 provides that women should be entitled to a period of maternity leave of no less than 14 weeks. According to the International Labour Organization, the majority of countries in the world adhere to or

---

[41]  For more reading, *see* Lilly Ledbetter Fair Pay Act of 2009, www.govinfo.gov/content/pkg/ PLAW-111publ2/html/PLAW-111publ2.htm; US Equal Employment Opportunity Commission, *Notice Concerning the Lilly Ledbetter Fair Pay Act of 2009*, www.eeoc.gov/statutes/notice-concerning-lilly -ledbetter-fair-pay-act-2009 (last visited on May 19, 2021).

[42]  The ILO has adopted several treaties related to maternity leave, including Maternity Convention 183 (2000); Maternity Protection Convention 1919 (No. 3); and the Maternity Protection Convention (Revised) 1952 (No. 103). For more information, *see* ILO, *International Labour Standards on Maternity Protection*, www.ilo.org/global/standards/subjects-covered-by-international-labour-standards/maternity -protection/lang--en/index.htm. The ILO has also adopted the Workers with Family Responsibilities Convention 1981 (No. 156), www.ilo.org/dyn/normlex/en/f?p=NORMLEXPUB:12100:0::NO::P12100 _ILO_CODE:C156.

exceed the 14-week standard period of maternity leave.[43] Many countries also provide cash benefits to women during their maternity leave through national social security schemes.[44] According to Article 6 of the Maternity Convention 183, the cash benefits paid during the maternity leave period should be at least two-thirds of a woman's previous income. These cash benefits should ensure that a woman and her children can have an adequate standard of living and health conditions during the maternity leave period. Legislation has been adopted in many countries to protect women, their employment, and their right to live free from discrimination during pregnancy and its aftermath.[45] Most international organizations are now recommending a combination of maternity, paternity, parental, and adoption leave benefits to ensure a more balanced division of childcare responsibilities in the home and a better work–life balance.[46] What do you think are the benefits and disadvantages of maternity leave policies?

3. Despite the leave advances highlighted in point 2, the United States still lacks federal national legislation mandating paid maternity leave for all employees.[47] Employees do have the option to take unpaid leave under the Family and Medical Leave Act for 12 weeks.[48] As of October 1, 2020, federal government employees may now be eligible for paid parental leave for up to 12 weeks.[49] A group of US employers does provide maternity leave to their women employees, but many fail to do so.[50] States such as California, Connecticut, Massachusetts, and New York have adopted their own paid family leave laws.[51] The Pregnancy Discrimination Act does prohibit employers from firing, refusing to hire, or denying a woman a promotion due to pregnancy.[52] Do you think that the United States government should adopt federal legislation mandating paid maternity and paternity

---

[43]  INTERNATIONAL LABOUR ORGANIZATION, MATERNITY AND PATERNITY AT WORK: LAW AND PRACTICE ACROSS THE WORLD 9–12 (2014), www.ilo.org/wcmsp5/groups/public/---dgreports/---dcomm/---publ/documents/publication/wcms_242615.pdf.

[44]  *See id.*, pp. 20–30.

[45]  *See id.*, pp. 76–86.

[46]  Directive (EU) 2019/1158 of the European Parliament and of the Council, June 20, 2019, Preamble Points 19–31, Articles 4–6; IACHR, *The Work, Education, and Resources of Women, supra* note 1, ¶¶ 145–160; ILO Maternity Protection Recommendation, 2000 (No. 191), *Section on Related Types of Leave*, Point 10, www.ilo.org/dyn/normlex/en/f?p=NORMLEXPUB:12100:::NO:12100:P12100_ILO_CODE:R191:NO.

[47]  *See* Pew Research Center, *Among 41 countries, only U.S. lacks paid parental leave* (Dec. 16, 2019), www.pewresearch.org/fact-tank/2019/12/16/u-s-lacks-mandated-paid-parental-leave/.

[48]  US Department of Labor, *Family and Medical Leave Act*, www.dol.gov/agencies/whd/fmla (last visited on May 19, 2021).

[49]  US Department of Commerce, *Paid Parental Leave for Federal Employees*, www.commerce.gov/hr/paid-parental-leave-federal-employees (last visited on May 19, 2021).

[50]  *See* Institute for Women's Policy Research, *Maternity Leave in the United States: Paid Parental Leave Is Still Not Standard, Even Among the Best U.S. Employers* (August 2007), https://iwpr.org/wp-content/uploads/2020/09/A131.pdf.

[51]  *See* National Partnership of Women and Families, *Expecting Better: A State-by-State Analysis of Parental Leave Programs*, pp. 14–19, 21, 27–28, 33, www.leg.state.nv.us/App/NELIS/REL/79th2017/ExhibitDocument/OpenExhibitDocument?exhibitId=29512&fileDownloadName=0330ab266_ParentalLeaveReportMay05.pdf.

[52]  *See* US Equal Employment Opportunity Commission, The Pregnancy Discrimination Act of 1978, www.eeoc.gov/statutes/pregnancy-discrimination-act-1978.

leave in all employers? What should be the length of the leave provided for? Should the grant of maternal, paternity, and parental leave be mandatory for private employers?

4. The case of the *Fireworks Factory Workers*, *supra*, exemplifies the unsafe labor conditions that many women and girls can be subjected to in the private sector. This is often the product of the lack of options for decent and quality employment and high levels of poverty. As the Inter-American Court of Human Rights explains, there are many human rights involved in the guarantee of labor conditions that are safe and healthy, including the rights to life, personal integrity, work, special protection of children, non-discrimination and equality, and judicial protection and guarantees. The Inter-American Court of Human Rights in this case found violations of the rights to equality (Article 24) and economic, social, and cultural rights (Article 26) for failures of the state to appropriately regulate, supervise, and oversee the activity of a private company and its working conditions. This case really exemplifies the situation of structural discrimination and poverty that many afro-descendent girls face and the lack of employment options.[53] Nineteen of those killed by the firework factory explosion were girls under 18 years old.[54] Can you think of ways to integrate an intersectional discrimination approach to employee protection in the workplace, considering variables like race, ethnicity, age, and economic position?[55]

5. Women are increasingly key members of the workforce and compose a large percentage of college graduates.[56] However, they are still facing very important challenges to balance work demands and their lives at home. Many women still bear the main responsibility for raising and caring for their children, and barriers to access affordable childcare. Some social barriers that have been documented are the professional value afforded to face time and hours in the office; the wage gap and the lack of opportunities for promotions; school schedules; prevailing social stereotypes relegating women to the home and to lower-ranked positions in the workplace; the lack of supporting partners and family members; and the unequal division of family responsibilities.[57] At the same time, the work that women perform in the home is frequently undervalued. CEDAW and other universal and regional human rights treaties mandate states to create the social conditions for women to be able to find decent and quality employment, to stay in the workplace, and to rise to

---

[53] *See* Inter-Am. Ct. H.R., *Employees of the Fireworks Factory*, discussed *supra*, ¶ 191.

[54] *See id.*, ¶ 177.

[55] For more reading *see* Natalia Brigagao, *Workers of the Fireworks Factory of Santo Antônio de Jesus and their family members vs. Brazil and why we need to talk about socioeconomic gender inequality*, Oxford Human Rights Hub (July 18, 2019), https://ohrh.law.ox.ac.uk/workers-of-the-fireworks-factory-of-santo-antonio-de-jesus-and-their-family-members-vs-brazil-and-why-we-need-to-talk-about-socioeconomic-gender-inequality/.

[56] *See* Study International, *Women are outnumbering men at a record high in universities worldwide* (March 7, 2018), www.studyinternational.com/news/record-high-numbers-women-outnumbering-men-university-globally/; Jon Marcus, *Why Men Are the New College Minority*, The Atlantic (Aug. 8, 2017), www.theatlantic.com/education/archive/2017/08/why-men-are-the-new-college-minority/536103/.

[57] For more reading, *see* Caryl Rivers and Rosalind C. Barnett, *8 Big Problems for Women in the Workplace*, Chicago Tribune (May 18, 2016), www.chicagotribune.com/opinion/commentary/ct-women-pay-gap-workplace-equality-perspec-0519-jm-20160518-story.html.

decision-making and leadership positions.[58] There is a great deal of literature available on this issue, including commentary, articles, and books by high-profile women documenting their experiences of leadership.[59] Many of these women have voiced the challenges they have faced to wage successful careers, raise their children, and balance work with their personal demands.[60] Can you think of important social changes needed for women to be able to enter the workforce in higher numbers? Consider also strategies to facilitate women rising to leadership and decision-making positions in employment. Do you think temporary special measures could be useful?

6. One of the employment areas with the greatest development in legal standards in recent years has been business and human rights. The United Nations adopted the UN Ruggie Principles – discussed in Chapter 6 – but regional human rights protection systems have also been issuing case decisions and reports offering authorized interpretations of the content of regional human rights treaties when it comes to state obligations vis-à-vis corporations that operate in their territories and the human rights responsibilities of the corporations themselves. One area of analysis has been women. Many human rights violations have been documented which affect women, including forms of discrimination and stereotypes which discourage their long-term stay in the workforce and limit their options to secure promotions and leadership positions.[61] Other important problems are unhealthy working conditions and hours; pay differentials as compared to their male counterparts; discrimination on the basis of pregnancy; sexual and labor harassment; and physical, psychological, and sexual violence. Women are often also part of indigenous groups and human rights defenders which are opposing development, tourism, investment, and extractive industry projects implemented without free, prior, and informed consultation and consent. Many of the projects are harmful to the environment and threaten important sources of livelihood and survival for the indigenous peoples affected.[62]

---

[58]   For more reading *see* CEDAW, Article 11; CEDAW Committee General Recommendations 13 (equal remuneration for work of equal value) and 17 (measurement and quantification of the unremunerated domestic activities of women and their recognition in the GNP), www.ohchr.org/en/hrbodies/cedaw/pages/recommendations.aspx; General Comment 18 on the Right to Work, Committee on Economic, Social and Cultural Rights, E/C.12/GC/186 (February 2006), ¶ 13.

[59]   For more reading *see generally*, Anne Marie Slaughter, *Why Women Can't Still Have It All*, THE ATLANTIC (August 21, 2012), www.theatlantic.com/magazine/archive/2012/07/why-women-still-cant-have-it-all/309020/; SHERYL SANDBERG, LEAN IN: WOMEN, WORK, AND THE WILL TO LEAD (Deckle Edge, 2013).

[60]   *Id.*

[61]   *See* discussion in U.N. Working Group on Business and Human Rights, *Gender Dimensions of the Guiding Principles on Business and Human Rights*, A/HRC/41/43, May 23, 2019, ¶¶ 1–42.

[62]   For more reading, *see* INTERNATIONAL LABOUR ORGANIZATION, UN WOMEN AND EUROPEAN UNION, EMPOWERING WOMEN AT WORK: COMPANY POLICIES AND PRACTICES FOR GENDER EQUALITY 30–38 (2020), www.ilo.org/wcmsp5/groups/public/---ed_emp/---emp_ent/---multi/documents/publication/wcms_756721.pdf; Inter-American Commission on Human Rights, *Business and Human Rights* (Informe Empresas y Derechos Humanos: Estándares Interamericanos), OEA/Ser.L/V/II CIDH/REDESCA/INF.1/19 (Nov. 1, 2019), ¶¶ 331–339; Inter-American Commission on Human Rights, *Indigenous Peoples, Afro-Descendent Communities, and Natural Resources: Human Rights Protection in the Context of Extraction, Exploitation, and Development Activities*, OEA/Ser.L/V/II. Doc. 47/15, ¶¶ 167–169 (Dec. 31, 2015) (Hereinafter Report on Extractive Industries).

7. Women are also frequently underrepresented in management positions in corporations and businesses. In the United States for example, 37 women are CEOs of Fortune 500 companies, that is, for only 7.4 percent of businesses in the ranking.[63] Some reasons advanced for this pattern are few professional opportunities for women to advance to decision-making positions; the lack of professional networking and contacts; and the home demands that women still face.[64] Greater gender diversity in leadership improves business results and there has been a consistent demand for a reform of employment policies favoring women's inclusion and means to balance their work and home lives.[65] Career mentoring and professional development programs have also proven key for women to reach higher-level positions in corporations and businesses. Can you think of concrete steps that businesses can pursue to promote women reaching management and leadership positions?

8. The United Nations Working Group on Business and Human Rights refers to three gender windows to implement the Ruggie Principles, including non-discrimination; a gender perspective; and the consideration of additional legal standards.[66] These windows demand that businesses take into account human rights impacts; the risks faced by women; and the continued monitoring of their effectiveness. Businesses are also called to take into consideration important universal human rights standards, such as CEDAW and other universal and regional treaties. Transformative measures are also key to change discriminatory and stereotyped patterns of behavior which impede women's advancement and development in the workplace. Many businesses have created departments and initiatives to address social responsibility and human rights issues, as well as oversight boards, to prevent adverse human rights impacts in their operations, and to foster accountability and remedies when such impacts do occur.[67]

## IV    FOOD, WATER SECURITY, AND HEALTH

As discussed earlier, the United Nations Committee on Economic, Social and Cultural Rights has referred to a minimum set of core obligations states need to guarantee for its population. This includes basic accessibility to food, water security, and health services which are vital for survival and for a dignified life for many individuals and groups. These also should be of

---

[63] For more reading, *see* Emma Hinchliffe, *The number of female CEOs in the Fortune 500 hits an all-time record*, FORTUNE (May 18, 2020), https://fortune.com/2020/05/18/women-ceos-fortune-500 -2020/.

[64] For more reading, *see* Herminia Ibarra, Robin J. Ely, and Deborah M. Kolb, *Women Rising: The Unseen Barriers*, HARVARD BUSINESS REVIEW, September 2013, https://hbr.org/2013/09/women-rising -the-unseen-barriers; FORBES, *15 Biggest Challenges Women Leaders Face and How to Overcome Them* (Feb. 26, 2018), www.forbes.com/sites/forbescoachescouncil/2018/02/26/15-biggest-challenges-women -leaders-face-and-how-to-overcome-them/?sh=654e2acc4162.

[65] For more reading, *see* INTERNATIONAL LABOUR ORGANIZATION, THE BUSINESS CASE FOR CHANGE, Executive Summary, pp. 19–25, 60–75, www.ilo.org/wcmsp5/groups/public/---dgreports/---dcomm/-- -publ/documents/publication/wcms_700953.pdf.

[66] *See* discussion in U.N. Working Group on Business and Human Rights, *Gender Dimensions of the Guiding Principles on Business and Human Rights*, *supra* note 61, ¶¶ 36–38.

[67] *See* Office of High Commissioner for Human Rights, *Business and Human Rights: A Progress Report*, Part III: *Business Takes the Lead*, pp. 15–22, www.ohchr.org/Documents/Publications/ BusinessHRen.pdf.

quality, acceptable, and affordable. Systems established to guarantee food, water, and health offerings should also be free from any kind of intersectional discrimination, and fully available for populations in both urban and rural areas, and of high- and low-income status.

Specific Sustainable Development Goals have been devoted to these specific basic needs, including the end of hunger and achieving food security (Goal 2), ensuring availability and sustainable management of water and sanitation for all (Goal 7), and the guarantee of healthy lives and well-being for all ages (Goal 3).[68]

Unfortunately, according to the World Food Programme, of the 690 million people who suffer food insecurity in the world, 60 percent are women and girls.[69] Women also confront formidable barriers to have sustained access to water that is safe and of adequate quality.[70] As discussed in Chapter 8, many women confront obstacles to accessing adequate health services, especially women who are low-income, afro-descendent, and indigenous.[71]

This section discusses some of the universal and regional human rights treaties and standards governing the rights to food, water, and health, and ongoing challenges for women.

**A      *Women's Rights and the Right to Food***

Report of the Special Rapporteur on the Right to Food, Olivier De Schutter
A/HRC/22/50, December 24, 2012

4. [The] various forms of discrimination against women and girls are human rights violations that States have a duty to combat. They affect directly the right to food of women and girls. They also have impacts on the right to food of others through three pathways. First, discrimination against pregnant women and women of child-bearing age has intergenerational consequences. Maternal and child undernutrition affects the learning performance of children, and their incomes as adults thus depend on the quality of their nutrition as young infants, during the 1,000-day window during pregnancy and until the second birthday. The disadvantage of poor nutrition during pregnancy or early childhood is also carried over from one generation to the next: a woman who has been poorly fed as an infant will have children with a lower birthweight.

5. Second, socially constructed gender roles and the weak bargaining position of women within households result in a situation in which they may not be able to decide to which priorities the household budget should go. Yet, because men are currently insufficiently sensitized to the importance of caring for children and for their nutrition needs in particular, the nutrition, health and education of children significantly improve when women are enabled to make such decisions. ...

---

[68]  *See* U.N. General Assembly, *Transforming Our World: The 2030 Agenda for Sustainable Development Goals*, *supra* note 6, Goals 2, 3, and 7.
[69]  *See* World Food Programme USA, #WomenAreHungrier, www.wfpusa.org/explore/wfps-work/who-wfp-serves/women-hunger/ (last visited on May 19, 2021).
[70]  *See* UN Water, Eliminating Discrimination and Inequalities in Access to Water and Sanitation 10–13 (Oct. 27, 2015) www.unwater.org/publications/eliminating-discrimination-inequalities-access-water-sanitation/.
[71]  *See* United Nations, *Sustainable Development Goals Report 2020*, *supra* note 5, pp. 28–31.

6. Third, discrimination against women as food producers is not only a violation of their rights, it also has society-wide consequences, because of the considerable productivity losses entailed. Access to productive resources such as land, inputs, technology and services are decisive in explaining the difference in yields between male and female small-holders; the greater ability for men to command labor, both from (unremunerated) family members and from other members of the community, also plays a role. Evidence suggests that countries where women lack land ownership rights or access to credit have on average 60 per cent and 85 per cent more malnourished children, respectively. Moreover, according to a recent review, 79 per cent of existing studies on fertilizer, seed varieties, tools, and pesticide use concluded that men have higher access to these inputs. ...

7. Access to food can be secured (i) by obtaining incomes from employment or self-employment; (ii) by social transfers; or (iii) by own production, for individuals who have access to land and other productive inputs. This report examines how, at each of these levels, women face discrimination and marginalization, with negative impacts both for them and for society as a whole. Rural women in particular deserve greater attention in food security strategies: they fare worse than rural men and urban women and men on all development indicators. ...

9. Women are disproportionately represented in the "periphery" part of the workforce that coexists with the "core" segment of permanently employed farmworkers. This "periphery" segment of the workforce is made of unskilled workers, often without a formal contract of employment, and their work is often seasonal or temporary (or classified as such even when it is in fact continuous). The main reason why women are disproportionately represented in this segment is because they have fewer alternative options and are thus easier to exploit. ...

14. Women's access to employment in the industry or the services sectors of the economy requires improved access to education for girls; and infrastructural and services investments that relieve women from part of the burden of the household chores that women shoulder disproportionately. ...

22. The right to social security, as guaranteed under the International Covenant on Economic, Social and Cultural Rights, includes access to health care; benefits and services to persons without work-related income due to sickness, disability, maternity, employment injury, unemployment, old age or death of a family member, including contributory or non-contributory pensions for all older persons; family and child support sufficient to cover food, clothing, housing, water and sanitation; survivor and orphan benefits. The Special Rapporteur observes that, in many cases, the specific situation of women is not considered in the design and implementation of programmes. ...

29. Due to prevalent societal norms and gender roles, their higher average levels of education, and the fact that they are less constrained, men are often better placed to seize opportunities arising from employment creation in the industry and services sectors. The result is that, with some exceptions (e.g. women migration for household work), men tend to migrate first from rural areas, for longer periods and to further destinations. Women stay behind in the village – especially relatively older women, beyond 35 years of age, who are poorly educated and less independent – to take care of the children and the elderly, and increasingly, also to tend the family plot of land. Data in this area are often imprecise and difficult to interpret, partly because of the lack of gender-disaggregated data, as much of women's

contribution to "subsistence" agriculture goes unreported in official statistics, and because the share of women's employment in agriculture varies from crop to crop and from activity to activity – ploughing, for instance, remains predominantly a task performed by men. Nonetheless, overall, this feminization of agriculture is well documented.

30. Concerns have been expressed about the impact that the feminization of agriculture may have on local food security, given the obstacles women face which negatively affect their productivity. Indeed, women often have little legal protection or rights to property ownership, and they face cultural and social norms that hinder their ability to improve productivity. How can these challenges be met? In the longer term, improving education for women and expanding opportunities for them in off-farm employment are key. But for the large number of women who depend on agriculture, including, increasingly, urban and periurban agriculture, it is equally important – and urgent – to improve women's opportunities to thrive as producers. Gender-sensitive agricultural policies are required, consistent with guideline 8.6 of the Right to Food Guidelines concerning women's full and equal participation in the economy and the right of women to inherit and possess land and other property, and access to productive resources, including credit, land, water and appropriate technologies. …

32. Women face multiple forms of discrimination in accessing land. As regards land that is inherited, laws in many countries still discriminate against women, and even when the discriminatory elements are removed, the laws are often circumvented under the pressure of social and cultural norms. …

39. A human rights-based strategy to address gender discrimination against women includes four complementary requirements. It must relieve women of the burdens of household chores; it must be empowering and challenge the existing division of roles; it must systematically aim at taking into account gender in existing food security strategies; and, as regards governance, it must be part of a multisectoral and multi-year effort, including independent monitoring of progress towards certain targets. …

## B      Guidelines on the Right to Water in Africa

African Commission on Human and Peoples' Rights
Adopted during the 26th Extra-Ordinary Session of the African Commission on Human and Peoples' Rights held from 16 to 30 July 2019, in Banjul, The Gambia

2.2 States shall pursue, through an integrated water strategy, the realization of the right to water and all other water-related human rights, such as the right to life, the right to survival and development of children, the right to economic, social and cultural development, the right to food, the right to livelihood, the right to health, the right to education, the right to a satisfactory environment and the right to sanitation. …

3.1 All rights, including the right to water, are of immediate application to States upon ratification of the Charter.

3.2 States shall respect, protect, promote and fulfil the right to water exercised individually, in association with others or within a community or group. No hierarchy is accorded to any of these duties and all shall be protected through administrative and judicial remedies.

3.3 States shall take deliberate, concrete and targeted steps to move as expeditiously and effectively as possible towards the goal of full realisation of the right to water, using the maximum available resources. …

4.1 States shall mobilise available resources in order to respect, protect, promote and fulfill the right to water.

4.2 To that end, States should mobilise financial and non-financial resources, including technical and human resources and prioritise resources that are more sustainable and allow greater responsiveness to domestic needs and accountability to their people.

4.3 When a State claims that it has failed to realise the right to water, due to whatever reason such as economic constraints or adjustments, it shall show that it has allocated all available resources towards the realization of human rights, including the right to water. …

5.1 States shall ensure a non-discriminatory participation to all stakeholders in the water sector, as well as equal access to water and water facilities and services. States shall take positive measures to ensure that vulnerable and marginalized groups and groups with special needs, including cultural, spiritual and religious needs, participate in the water sector and have access to water. …

5.2. In accordance with Article 2 of the African Charter, States shall prohibit any discrimination hindering access to water on the grounds of age, race, ethnic origin, colour, sex, gender, sexual orientation, language, religion, political or any other opinion, national and social origin, economic status, birth, health status or other status. Discrimination includes any conduct or omission that has the purpose or effect of nullifying or impairing the equal access to and enjoyment of economic, social and cultural rights.

5.3 Gender equality and the protection of women's and girls' rights shall receive particular attention in the water sector. …

22.1 States shall take action to reduce the disproportionate burden and amount of time women bear in water collection.

22.2 States shall guarantee safe access to water for women and girls at any time of the day and strengthen customary and statutory institutions and mechanisms for defending or protecting women's rights to water.

22.3 States shall pay particular attention to alleviate difficulties encountered by rural women in accessing water who have to pay fees in some countries affected by desertification. …

## C      Reflections and Questions

1. The right to food and its implementation with a gender perspective is a multilayered obligation for states. As indicated in the UN Special Rapporteur's report *supra* (paragraph 39), this requires a human rights-oriented strategy to address structural discrimination against women, including lessening the home workload for women, the transformation of the existing division of roles in the family, the consideration of women in food security strategies, and the monitoring of the progress achieved. Important variables are the inter-generational nature of the problems, ongoing discrimination against women as food producers, the feminization of agriculture, and the burdens carried by women in the care economy. Access to land is still an ongoing issue, worsened by the discrimination still prevalent in inheritance laws. The situation of rural women, indigenous, afro-descendent,

and low-income women is particularly dire in securing the accessibility, acceptability, affordability, and quality of food.[72]

2.  Both regional and universal mechanisms have begun giving content to the right to a dignified life, which reaches beyond the prohibition of arbitrary deprivations of life. The Human Rights Committee has recently stated that the right to life should not be interpreted narrowly, and extends to situations in which there is no loss of life.[73] Therefore, the right also provides that individuals should live their life with dignity.[74] The Human Rights Committee has affirmed that states have a duty under the right to life to ensure access without delay to food, water, and health care, including the development of strategic and contingency plans.[75] The Inter-American Court of Human Rights also advanced a right to a dignified life in its judgment in the case of *Yakye Axa Indigenous Community v. Paraguay*, in which it held that states have a duty to guarantee minimum living conditions, and take positive and concrete measures to ensure the right to a decent life, especially in the case of persons in a situation of vulnerability or at risk of human rights violations.[76] This case addressed the consequences of dispossession of traditional lands by the Yakye Axa indigenous peoples, and the formidable obstacles they faced to access needed natural resources to practice traditional subsistence activities, including hunting, fishing, and gathering. At the time of the events, the members of the Yakye Axa Community also did not have access to adequate housing with basic services such as clean water and access to health care.[77] Can you think of other components to the right to a decent life? Please consider elements in particular that would facilitate women having autonomy in pursuing their life plans and having all their needs met.[78]

3.  In its Guidelines, the African Commission on Human and Peoples' Rights refers in paragraph 2.2 *supra* to an integrated water strategy for the realization of the right to water. This strategy includes the mobilization of resources to ensure the respect and fulfillment of the right to water, especially for women inhabiting rural areas. The African Commission also alludes to the right to water as a right of immediate application, as with the other provisions in the African Charter on Human and Peoples' Rights.[79] The right to water has not been explicitly codified in either the International Covenant on Economic, Social and Cultural Rights or the regional human rights treaties. However, both universal and regional entities have recognized its existence and expressed their concerns over disruptions of water

---

[72] For more reading, *see* General Recommendation 34 on the Rights of Rural Women, CEDAW/C/GC/34, CEDAW Committee, ¶¶ 37, 60–61, 63–66; Christine Chinkin and Shelley Wright, *The Hunger Trap: Women, Food, and Self-Determination*, 14 MICH. J. INT'L L. 262, 264–287 (1993).

[73] *See* United Nations Human Rights Committee, General Comment 36 on Article 6: The Right to Life, U.N. Human Rights Committee, CCPR/C/GC/36, ¶ 7, (Sept. 3, 2019).

[74] *See id.*, ¶ 3.

[75] See *id.*, ¶ 26.

[76] Yakye Axa Indigenous Community v. Paraguay, Merits, Reparations and Costs, Judgment, Inter-Am. Ct. H.R, Series C No. 125, ¶¶ 162–176 (June 17, 2005).

[77] *Id.*, ¶¶ 164–165.

[78] For more reading on developments related to the right to a dignified life, *see* Thomas M. Antkowiak, *A "Dignified Life" and the Resurgence of Social Rights*, 18 NW. J. HUM. RTS. 1, 16–39 (2020).

[79] African Commission on Human and Peoples' Rights, *Guidelines on the Right to Water in Africa*, *supra*, para. 3.1.

supply, shortages, and the barriers to the accessibility of safe, acceptable, sufficient, and affordable water.[80] State obligations related to the right to water have been analyzed under the lens of the rights to life, personal integrity, health, non-discrimination, and rights over territories and natural resources.[81] Disruptions in water supply and quality issues have been associated with climate change and natural disasters, extractive activities, armed conflicts, and the deficient sanitary conditions of prisons.[82]

4. Many of the challenges identified in the readings *supra* in respect of access to food, water, and adequate health services are particularly acute in the case of indigenous women. Many indigenous women live in remote areas, in which they face difficult obstacles to accessing quality food, water, health-care services, and needed economic resources.[83] This can increase maternal mortality rates, the onset of diseases and malnutrition, and pose important barriers to accessing sexual and reproductive health services of quality; including instances of obstetric violence, forced sterilizations, and culturally inappropriate treatment.[84] The implementation of extractive projects without consultation, and ongoing threats from both state and non-state actors to their lands and territories often cause disruptions and unclean water supplies, and can serve as an impediment to hunting and other activities important for food security. Indigenous peoples have a right under international law to self-determination and self-governance, which means that indigenous peoples and communities globally have produced important knowledge and strategies as to how to address these economic, social, and cultural rights issues.[85] It is important for states to tap into this knowledge and best practices produced in indigenous peoples and communities in addressing threats to full enjoyment of the rights to food, water, and health of indigenous

---

[80]   *General Comment 15 on the Right to Water*, Committee on Economic, Social and Cultural Rights, ¶¶ 2–6 E/C.12/2002/11 (reading a right to water into Article 11.1 of the International Covenant on Economic, Social and Cultural Rights); Inter-American Commission on Human Rights, Chapter IV.A., *Access to Water in the Americas*, Annual Report 2015, ¶¶ 26–28 (indicating that although the right to water is not expressly recognized in the inter-American system, several of its instruments codify a series of rights linked to access to water, its availability, quality, and accessibility without discrimination).

[81]   *See for example*, Sawhoyamaxa Indigenous Community v. Paraguay, Merits, Reparations and Costs, Judgment, Inter-Am. Ct. H.R., Series C No. 146, ¶¶ 73, 148–178 (March 29, 2006); Diaguita Agricultural Communities of Huasco-Altinos and the Members Thereof, Petition 415-07, Inter-Am. Comm'n H.R., Report No. 141/09, ¶¶ 7–17, 56–63 (Dec. 30, 2009).

[82]   World Bank Group, *High and Dry: Climate Change, Water, and the Economy*, 2016, Executive Summary, pp. 1–7, www.worldbank.org/en/topic/water/publication/high-and-dry-climate-change-water -and-the-economy.

[83]   *See, for reference*, Inter-American Commission on Human Rights, *Indigenous Women and their Human Rights in the Americas*, OEA/Ser.L/V/II.Doc. 44/17, April 17, 2017, ¶¶ 185–218; Food and Agriculture Organization of the United Nations, *FAO Leader Calls for End to "Triple Discrimination" Against Indigenous Women* (January 12, 2018), www.fao.org/news/story/en/item/1095135/icode/.

[84]   *See, for reference*, United Nations, Report of Expert Mechanism on Indigenous Peoples, *Right to health and indigenous peoples with a focus on children and youth*, A/HRC/33/57, ¶¶ 60–66 (August 10, 2016); UNFPA and CHIRAPAC, *Recommendations of the UN Permanent Forum on Indigenous Issues regarding Sexual and Reproductive Health and Rights & Gender-Based Violence: Report on Progress and Challenges*, April 2018, pp. 30–39, www.unfpa.org/sites/default/files/pub-pdf/UNFPA_PUB_2018 _EN_human_rights_report.pdf.

[85]   *See, for reference*, United Nations Declaration on the Rights of Indigenous Peoples, G.A. Res. 61/295, U.N. Doc. A/RES/61/295 Articles 3–4, 9, 11–12, 26, and 34 (Sept. 13, 2007) (hereinafter UNDRIP).

women. Indigenous women are vital for the food and water security of their communities, and are pillars in the sustainability of their culture, language, and worldview. This is part of the content of important principles such as effective participation and consultation, and the finding of adequate solutions.

## Note: Human rights related to menstruation

There has been increasing documentation of human rights concerns about menstruation. The United Nations Populations Fund (hereinafter "UNFPA") has characterized menstruation as a human rights issue in itself.[86] UNFPA has highlighted the obstacles that women and girls can face to secure basic information pertinent to their menstrual health, supplies, and medicines for period pain. UNFPA has also documented how the beginning of the menstrual cycle for young girls can expose them to child marriages and social stigma. It can also constitute an important barrier to girls attending school and securing a long-term education.

A number of United Nations experts called on the international community on March 8, 2019, to eradicate the taboo regarding menstrual health, and to ensure that discrimination and stereotypes are eliminated.[87] The experts also expressed their concern over the consideration of menstruating women and girls as "contaminated and impure," and the restrictions they suffer in respect of attending religious and cultural ceremonies, cooking, and engaging in community activities. Many women around the world live in conditions in which they lack the privacy and hygiene necessary during their menstrual cycles. This situation is particularly alarming for girls that live in poverty and in armed conflict situations.

It is important to note that several human rights can be at issue when it comes to the forms of discrimination, stigma, and stereotypes that women and girls can face associated with their menstrual cycles. These include their rights to a dignified life; personal integrity; to non-discrimination and equality; to health, water and sanitation; to education; to employment; to dignity; and to effective participation, among others. Menstrual health is a basic and corner-stone component of the economic, social, and cultural rights, and the sexual and reproductive health of girls and women. This means that states have an obligation to act without delay and with due diligence to safeguard the basic information, sanitation needs, and privacy conditions needed by girls and women during their menstrual cycles.[88]

---

[86]  *See* United Nations Population Fund, *Menstruation is not a girls' or women's issue – it's a human rights issue* (May 28, 2019), www.unfpa.org/news/menstruation-not-girls-or-womens-issue-%E2%80%93-its-human-rights-issue.

[87]  United Nations, International Women's Day, March 8, 2019, *Women's menstrual health should no longer be a taboo, say UN human rights experts*, https://www.ohchr.org/EN/NewsEvents/Pages/DisplayNews.aspx?NewsID=24256&LangID=E.

[88]  For more reading, *see* Human Rights Watch and Wash United, *Understanding Menstrual Hygiene Management and Human Rights*, 2017, pp. 5–16, www.hrw.org/sites/default/files/news_attachments/mhm_practitioner_guide_web.pdf.

# V    CONCLUSIONS: WOMEN AND ACCESS TO RESOURCES

Economic, social, and cultural rights is one of the areas of the human rights of women in which more work needs to be done. Women and girls are still alarmingly affected by poverty and challenging barriers to seeing their rights to access and control economic resources, work, education, food, water, and health duly respected and protected. The adequate fulfillment of these rights is key not only to full compliance with economic, social, and cultural rights, but also civil and political rights. Many of the Sustainable Development Goals and the ongoing discussions related to the need for women in decision-making and leadership positions depend on their increased access to the resources, education, and employment opportunities necessary to access these spaces.

It is important that states keep in mind the interdependent nature of civil and political rights with economic, social, and cultural matters in their legislation, public policies, and programs. Understanding the connection between violations of economic, social, and cultural rights, the problem of discrimination, and the need to eradicate gender-based violence are also key. Indicators, monitoring mechanisms, and other ways to assess effectiveness with the economic, social, and cultural rights are also paramount to their full compliance. States need to be guided by the immediate obligations to adopt concrete and deliberate steps to fulfill these rights, the principle of non-regression, the duty to ensure those minimum core obligations, and the overarching duty to live free from discrimination and all forms of violence. It is important to continue keeping the lens not only on state actor obligations, but also the implications of private actor activities which may be harmful and in contravention of human rights.

This is an area also of the international human rights of women that affects particularly indigenous and afro-descendent women, rural women, women belonging to minority groups, and those of low-income and living in poverty. Economic autonomy and effective participation are important facilitators of rights that should not be underestimated.

Economic, social, and cultural rights are also deeply connected with issues concerning the environment, climate change, and natural disasters, which will be discussed in the following chapter.

# 10. Women, the environment, and climate change

## I INTRODUCTION: EXAMINING ENVIRONMENTAL LAW ISSUES WITH A GENDER AND HUMAN RIGHTS LENS

Environmental issues are currently at the forefront of international attention and debate. Much of this is due to well-known natural disasters, documented cases of environmental degradation and harm, and the increasing awareness and concern over the problem of climate change.

In this sense, the safety and health of the environment was identified in the 2030 Agenda for Sustainable Development as one of the three leading dimensions of sustainable development.[1] Several SDG goals are devoted to the environment, including Goal 13, which highlights the need to take urgent action to combat climate change and its effects; Goal 14, which calls us to conserve and use sustainably the oceans, seas, and marine resources for sustainable development; and Goal 15, which refers to the need to promote sustainable use of territorial ecosystems, to sustainably manage forests, to combat desertification, and to halt and reverse land degradation and biodiversity loss.[2]

Moreover, the international community adopted in 2015 the Paris Climate Change Agreement.[3] By joining the Paris Agreement, states commit to addressing the adverse impacts of climate change by limiting global peaking of greenhouse gas emissions, reinforcing adaptation and mitigation efforts, and implementing nationally determined contributions.[4] Leading superpowers like the United States and China joined the Paris Agreement at the time of its adoption.[5]

An important propeller of the international visibility of environmental concerns and their legal implications was the adoption of the Rio Declaration on the Environment and Development in 1992, as a result of the United Nations Conference on this issue.[6] The Rio Declaration – through 27 guiding principles – underscored environmental protection as key

---

[1]   United Nations General Assembly, *Transforming our World: The 2030 Agenda for Sustainable Development Goals*, A/RES/70/1 (Oct. 21, 2015), p. 1.

[2]   *Id.*, Goals 13, 14 and 15.

[3]   G.A. Res. 1/CP.21, Paris Agreement, Art. 2(1)(a)–(b) (Dec. 12, 2015); Historic Paris Agreement on Climate Change: 195 Nations Set Path to Keep Temperature Rise Well Below 2 Degrees Celsius, U.N. Climate Change (UNCC) (Dec. 13, 2015), https://unfccc.int/news/finale-cop21.

[4]   *See*, Paris Agreement, *supra* note 3, Arts. 4, 6, 7, 8, 9, 11–14.

[5]   As of May 19, 2021, the Paris Agreement has 191 state parties and 195 signatories. *See* Status of Treaties: 7.d Paris Agreement, U.N. Treaty Collection, https://treaties.un.org/Pages/ViewDetails.aspx ?src=TREATY&mtdsg_no=XXVII-7-d&chapter=27&clang=_en (last visited on May 19, 2021).

[6]   *See* United Nations General Assembly, Rio Declaration on the Environment and Development, A/CONF.151/26 (Vol. I), August 12, 1992, www.un.org/en/development/desa/population/migration/ generalassembly/docs/globalcompact/A_CONF.151_26_Vol.I_Declaration.pdf.

to sustainable development; advocated for state protection of the environment; promoted the principle of do no harm to the environment; and prioritized the need for individuals to participate in decision-making related to environmental issues.[7]

At this stage of international law, environment issues are governed by an interplay of hard and soft sources, recognizing a right to a healthy environment and the relevance of a range of civil, political, economic, social, and cultural rights to environmental concerns. A number of substantive and procedural obligations inherent to this right have been identified by international courts and human rights bodies, which will be discussed in the chapter. This is one of the areas of greatest legal development in international law and human rights today. Key experts and mechanisms have been created to address environmental law issues from a human rights perspective, including a United Nations Special Rapporteurship on human rights and the environment.

There has also been increasing documentation of the impact of environmental issues on the enjoyment and exercise of the rights of women. Due to the historical discrimination that women have faced, and still face, women bear many of the burdens and negative impacts of natural disasters, environmental degradation, and climate change. These include barriers to accessing safe and quality food and water, and adequate health-care services and housing; the dearth of opportunities for employment and sources of livelihood; high levels of maternal mortality and morbidity; and limits to accessing needed renewable energy, technology, education, and information. In general, natural disasters and environmental harm aggravate the existing unequal treatment faced by women and intersectional discrimination on the basis of sex, gender, race, language, economic position, age, disabilities, and other factors. Women are also at increased risk of gender-based violence in many of these scenarios. Even though women are some of the most affected by environmental events, they are often absent from decision-making processes and plans as to how to address, adapt, and mitigate the adverse effects of these incidents.[8]

This chapter discusses the current state of international law today concerning the environment and its links with the human rights of women. It provides an overview of key elements for the protection, respect, and fulfillment of the right to a healthy environment for women, and illustrates many of the contemporary challenges. This chapter also discusses climate change as a priority global issue, and its effects on women. The readings, reflections, and questions included cover the content of the cornerstone rights to live free from discrimination and gender-based violence in the context of environmental issues. Relevant principles to environmental concerns are also reviewed, including life, integrity, dignity, autonomy, access to information, participation, and adaptation.

---

[7]   *See id.*, Principles 1–27.

[8]   For a general overview of the gender dimensions of climate change issues, *see* Georgetown Institute for Women, Peace, and Security, *Women and Climate Change: Impact and Agency in Human Rights, Security, and Economic Development* (2015), pp. 19–44, https://giwps.georgetown.edu/wp-content/uploads/2017/09/Women-and-Climate-Change.pdf.

## II      THE RIGHT TO A SAFE AND HEALTHY ENVIRONMENT

Even though environmental concerns have become an important fixture of national and international discussions, the right to a safe and healthy environment has not been codified in any global human rights treaty. This is a void that has been consistently recognized by the U.N. Special Rapporteur on human rights and the environment. Mandate holders have called in particular on the United Nations to adopt steps to recognize a universal right to a safe, clean, healthy, and sustainable environment, with substantive and procedural components.[9] On October of 2021, the United Nations Human Rights Council finally formally recognized the right to a safe, clean, healthy, and sustainable environment as a human right." The footnote can be the following: U.N. Human Rights Council Resolution, The Human Rights to a Safe, Cleah, Healthy, and Sustainable Environment, A/HRC/48.L/23.1/Rev.1, October 5, 2021.

It is important to note though that the right to a safe and healthy environment has indeed been recognized in several regional treaties. These include the African Charter on Human and Peoples' Rights, the Protocol of San Salvador, the European Union Charter of Fundamental Rights, and the Arab Charter on Human Rights.[10] However, only the African Charter on Human and Peoples' Rights authorizes explicitly the presentation of individual case petitions invoking this Article before the African Commission and Court of Human Rights.

This vacuum has prompted universal and regional bodies to examine environmental concerns through the lens of general civil, political, economic, social, and cultural rights. The rights to life, integrity, dignity, health, property, non-discrimination, food, and water, and to live free from violence have been consistently connected with instances of environmental degradation and harm. Many of the individual cases examined have dealt with investment, development, and extraction projects executed in the territories of indigenous people without free, prior, and informed consent, and cases in which the states involved have failed to protect individuals and groups from environmental harm, even though this harm was imminent and known.[11]

Recently both universal and regional entities have been producing analyses and shedding light on the content of the right to a safe and healthy environment as an individual and independent right, which can be violated by states in the absence of due diligence and other human rights obligations. The readings below offer examples of the statements adopted recently by the U.N. Special Rapporteur on human rights and the environment, and the Inter-American

---

[9]    *See for example*, Report of the Special Rapporteur on the issue of human rights obligations relating to the enjoyment of a safe, clean, healthy and sustainable environment, John H. Knox, II. Framework principles on human rights and the environment, A/HRC/37/59 (Jan. 24, 2018), ¶¶ 14–16, discussed *infra*.

[10]    For relevant regional treaty dispositions providing for a right to safe and healthy environment, *see* African Charter on Human and Peoples' Rights, Article 24; the Protocol of San Salvador, Article 11; the European Union Charter of Fundamental Rights, Article 37; and the Arab Charter on Human Rights (2004), Article 38.

[11]    *See as an example and generally*, Kichwa Indigenous People of Sarayaku v. Ecuador, Merits and Reparations, Judgment Inter-Am. Ct. H.R. (ser. C) No. 245, ¶¶ 180–211 (June 27, 2012); African Commission on Human and Peoples' Rights, The Social and Economic Rights Action Center (SERAC) v. Nigeria, Communication 155/96 (2001), ¶¶ 1–9, 43–69; and Guerra and Others v. Italy (116/1996/735/932), Eur. Ct. H.R., ¶¶ 12–27, 56–60 (Feb. 19, 1998).

Court of Human Rights on the components and elements of an autonomous right to a healthy environment.

| A | **Report of the Special Rapporteur on the issue of human rights obligations relating to the enjoyment of a safe, clean, healthy and sustainable environment, John H. Knox** |

A/HRC/37/59
January 24, 2018
…

**II. Framework principles on human rights and the environment**

…

10. … The framework principles and commentary provide a sturdy basis for understanding and implementing human rights obligations relating to the environment, but they are in no sense the final word. The relationship between human rights and the environment has countless facets, and our understanding of it will continue to grow for many years to come. These framework principles do not purport to describe all of the human rights obligations that can be brought to bear on environmental issues today, much less attempt to predict those that may evolve in the future. The goal is simply to describe the main human rights obligations that apply in the environmental context, in order to facilitate their practical implementation and further development. To that end, the Special Rapporteur urges States, international organizations and civil society organizations to disseminate and publicize the framework principles, and to take them into account in their own activities. …

11. An unusual aspect of the development of human rights norms relating to the environment is that they have not relied primarily on the explicit recognition of a human right to a safe, clean, healthy and sustainable environment – or, more simply, a human right to a healthy environment. Although this right has been recognized, in various forms, in regional agreements and in most national constitutions, it has not been adopted in a human rights agreement of global application, and only one regional agreement, the African Charter on Human and Peoples' Rights, provides for its interpretation in decisions by a review body.

12. Treaty bodies, regional tribunals, special rapporteurs and other international human rights bodies have instead applied human rights law to environmental issues by "greening" existing human rights, including the rights to life and health. As the mapping report explained and the framework principles demonstrate, this process has been quite successful, creating an extensive jurisprudence on human rights and the environment. In retrospect, this development is not as surprising as it may have seemed when it first began, over two decades ago. Environmental harm interferes with the full enjoyment of a wide spectrum of human rights, and the obligations of States to respect human rights, to protect human rights from interference and to fulfil human rights apply in the environmental context no less than in any other.

13. Explicit recognition of the human right to a healthy environment thus turned out to be unnecessary for the application of human rights norms to environmental issues. At the same time, it is significant that the great majority of the countries in the world have recognized the right at the national or regional level, or both. Based on the experience of the countries that have adopted constitutional rights to a healthy environment, recognition of

the right has proved to have real advantages. It has raised the profile and importance of environmental protection and provided a basis for the enactment of stronger environmental laws. When applied by the judiciary, it has helped to provide a safety net to protect against gaps in statutory laws and created opportunities for better access to justice. Courts in many countries are increasingly applying the right, as is illustrated by the interest in the regional judicial workshops held by the United Nations Environment Programme and the Special Rapporteur.

14. On the basis of this experience, the Special Rapporteur recommends that the Human Rights Council consider supporting the recognition of the right in a global instrument. ...

15. States may be understandably reluctant to recognize a "new" human right if its content is uncertain. To be sure that a right will be taken seriously, it is important to be clear about its implications. The Special Rapporteur notes that one of the primary goals of his work on the mandate has been to clarify what human rights law requires with respect to environmental protection, including through the mapping project and these framework principles. As a result, the "human right to a healthy environment" is not an empty vessel waiting to be filled; on the contrary, its content has already been clarified, through recognition by human rights authorities that a safe, clean, healthy and sustainable environment is necessary for the full enjoyment of the human rights to life, health, food, water, housing and so forth...

### Annex: Framework principles on human rights and the environment

*Framework principle 1*     States should ensure a safe, clean, healthy and sustainable environment in order to respect, protect and fulfil human rights.

*Framework principle 2*     States should respect, protect and fulfil human rights in order to ensure a safe, clean, healthy and sustainable environment.

4.  Human rights and environmental protection are interdependent. A safe, clean, healthy and sustainable environment is necessary for the full enjoyment of human rights, including the rights to life, to the highest attainable standard of physical and mental health, to an adequate standard of living, to adequate food, to safe drinking water and sanitation, to housing, to participation in cultural life and to development, as well as the right to a healthy environment itself, which is recognized in regional agreements and most national constitutions. At the same time, the exercise of human rights, including rights to freedom of expression and association, to education and information, and to participation and effective remedies, is vital to the protection of the environment.

5.  The obligations of States to respect human rights, to protect the enjoyment of human rights from harmful interference, and to fulfil human rights by working towards their full realization all apply in the environmental context. States should therefore refrain from violating human rights through causing or allowing environmental harm; protect against harmful environmental interference from other sources, including business enterprises, other private actors and natural causes; and take effective steps to ensure the conservation and sustainable use of the ecosystems and biological diversity on which the full enjoyment of human rights depends. While it may not always be possible to prevent all environmental harm that interferes with the full enjoyment of human rights, States should undertake due

diligence to prevent such harm and reduce it to the extent possible, and provide for remedies for any remaining harm. …

*Framework principle 3*     States should prohibit discrimination and ensure equal and effective protection against discrimination in relation to the enjoyment of a safe, clean, healthy and sustainable environment.

7.  The obligations of States to prohibit discrimination and to ensure equal and effective protection against discrimination apply to the equal enjoyment of human rights relating to a safe, clean, healthy and sustainable environment. States therefore have obligations, among others, to protect against environmental harm that results from or contributes to discrimination, to provide for equal access to environmental benefits and to ensure that their actions relating to the environment do not themselves discriminate.
8.  Discrimination may be direct, when someone is treated less favourably than another person in a similar situation for a reason related to a prohibited ground, or indirect, when facially neutral laws, policies or practices have a disproportionate impact on the exercise of human rights as distinguished by prohibited grounds of discrimination. In the environmental context, direct discrimination may include, for example, failing to ensure that members of disfavoured groups have the same access as others to information about environmental matters, to participation in environmental decision-making, or to remedies for environmental harm (framework principles 7, 9 and 10). In the case of transboundary environmental harm, States should provide for equal access to information, participation and remedies without discriminating on the basis of nationality or domicile.
9.  Indirect discrimination may arise, for example, when measures that adversely affect ecosystems, such as mining and logging concessions, have disproportionately severe effects on communities that rely on the ecosystems. Indirect discrimination can also include measures such as authorizing toxic and hazardous facilities in large numbers in communities that are predominantly composed of racial or other minorities, thereby disproportionately interfering with their rights, including their rights to life, health, food and water. Like directly discriminatory measures, such indirect differential treatment is prohibited unless it meets strict requirements of legitimacy, necessity and proportionality. More generally, to address indirect as well as direct discrimination, States must pay attention to historical or persistent prejudice against groups of individuals, recognize that environmental harm can both result from and reinforce existing patterns of discrimination, and take effective measures against the underlying conditions that cause or help to perpetuate discrimination. In addition to complying with their obligations of nondiscrimination, States should take additional measures to protect those who are most vulnerable to, or at particular risk from, environmental harm (framework principles 14 and 15).

*Framework principle 4*     States should provide a safe and enabling environment in which individuals, groups and organs of society that work on human rights or environmental issues can operate free from threats, harassment, intimidation and violence.

10. Human rights defenders include individuals and groups who strive to protect and promote human rights relating to the environment. Those who work to protect the environment on

which the enjoyment of human rights depends are protecting and promoting human rights as well, whether or not they self-identify as human rights defenders. They are among the human rights defenders most at risk, and the risks are particularly acute for indigenous peoples and traditional communities that depend on the natural environment for their subsistence and culture. ...

## B     The Environment and Human Rights, Inter-American Court of Human Rights

Advisory Opinion OC-23/17 of November 15, 2017, Series A No. 23
Citations and footnotes omitted

56. Under the inter-American human rights system, the right to a healthy environment is established expressly in Article 11 of the Protocol of San Salvador:
    1.    Everyone shall have the right to live in a healthy environment and to have access to basic public services.
    2.    The States Parties shall promote the protection, preservation, and improvement of the environment.
57. It should also be considered that this right is included among the economic, social and cultural rights protected by Article 26 of the American Convention, because this norm protects the rights derived from the economic, social, educational, scientific and cultural provisions of the OAS Charter, the American Declaration of the Rights and Duties of Man (to the extent that the latter "contains and defines the essential human rights referred to in the Charter") and those resulting from an interpretation of the Convention that accords with the criteria established in its Article 29. The Court reiterates the interdependence and indivisibility of the civil and political rights, and the economic, social and cultural rights, because they should be understood integrally and comprehensively as human rights, with no order of precedence, that are enforceable in all cases before the competent authorities.
58. The Court underscores that the right to a healthy environment is recognized explicitly in the domestic laws of several States of the region, as well as in some provisions of the international *corpus iuris*, in addition to the aforementioned Protocol of San Salvador, such as the American Declaration on the Rights of Indigenous Peoples; the African Charter on Human and Peoples' Rights; the ASEAN Human Rights Declaration, and the Arab Charter on Human Rights.
59. The human right to a healthy environment has been understood as a right that has both individual and also collective connotations. In its collective dimension, the right to a healthy environment constitutes a universal value that is owed to both present and future generations. That said, the right to a healthy environment also has an individual dimension insofar as its violation may have a direct and an indirect impact on the individual owing to its connectivity to other rights, such as the rights to health, personal integrity, and life. Environmental degradation may cause irreparable harm to human beings; thus, a healthy environment is a fundamental right for the existence of humankind. ...
62. The Court considers it important to stress that, as an autonomous right, the right to a healthy environment, unlike other rights, protects the components of the environment, such as forests, rivers and seas, as legal interests in themselves, even in the absence of the

certainty or evidence of a risk to individuals. This means that it protects nature and the environment, not only because of the benefits they provide to humanity or the effects that their degradation may have on other human rights, such as health, life or personal integrity, but because of their importance to the other living organisms with which we share the planet that also merit protection in their own right. In this regard, the Court notes a tendency, not only in court judgments, but also in Constitutions, to recognize legal personality and, consequently, rights to nature. …

64. That said and as previously mentioned, in addition to the right to a healthy environment, damage to the environment may affect all human rights, in the sense that the full enjoyment of all human rights depends on a suitable environment. Nevertheless, some human rights are more susceptible than others to certain types of environmental damage. The rights especially linked to the environment have been classified into two groups: (i) rights whose enjoyment is particularly vulnerable to environmental degradation, also identified as substantive rights (for example, the rights to life, personal integrity, health or property), and (ii) rights whose exercise supports better environmental policymaking, also identified as procedural rights (such as the rights to freedom of expression and association, to information, to participation in decision-making, and to an effective remedy). …

66. The Court considers that the rights that are particularly vulnerable to environmental impact include the rights to life, personal integrity, private life, health, water, food, housing, participation in cultural life, property, and the right to not be forcibly displaced. Without prejudice to the foregoing, according to Article 29 of the Convention, other rights are also vulnerable and their violation may affect the rights to life, liberty and security of the individual, and infringe on the obligation of all persons to conduct themselves fraternally, such as the right to peace, because displacements caused by environmental deterioration frequently unleash violent conflicts between the displaced population and the population settled on the territory to which it is displaced. Some of these conflicts are massive and thus extremely grave.

67. The Court also bears in mind that the effects on these rights may be felt with greater intensity by certain groups in vulnerable situations. It has been recognized that environmental damage "will be experienced with greater force in the sectors of the population that are already in a vulnerable situation"; hence, based on "international human rights law, States are legally obliged to confront these vulnerabilities based on the principle of equality and non-discrimination." Various human rights bodies have recognized that indigenous peoples, children, people living in extreme poverty, minorities, and people with disabilities, among others, are groups that are especially vulnerable to environmental damage, and have also recognized the differentiated impact that it has on women. In addition, the groups that are especially vulnerable to environmental degradation include communities that, essentially, depend economically or for their survival on environmental resources from the marine environment, forested areas and river basins, or run a special risk of being affected owing to their geographical location, such as coastal and small island communities. In many cases, the special vulnerability of these groups has led to their relocation or internal displacement. …

123. States are bound to comply with their obligations under the American Convention with due diligence. The general concept of due diligence in international law is typically associated with the possible responsibility of a State in relation to obligations with respect to its

conduct or behavior, as opposed to obligations requiring results that entail the achievement of a specific objective. The duty of a State to act with due diligence is a concept whose meaning has been determined by international law and has been used in diverse fields, including international humanitarian law, the law of the sea, and international environmental law. In international human rights law, the duty to act with due diligence has been examined in relation to economic, social and cultural rights, regarding which States commit to take "all appropriate measures" to achieve, progressively, the full effectiveness of the corresponding rights. In addition, as this Court has emphasized, the duty to act with due diligence also corresponds, in general, to the State obligation to ensure the free and full exercise of the rights recognized in the American Convention to all persons subject to their jurisdiction, according to which States must take all appropriate measures to protect and preserve the rights recognized in the Convention, and to organize all the structures through which public authority is exercised so that they are able to ensure, legally, the free and full exercise of human rights.

124. Most environmental obligations are based on this duty of due diligence. The Court reiterates that an adequate protection of the environment is essential for human well-being, and also for the enjoyment of numerous human rights, particularly the rights to life, personal integrity and health, as well as the right to a healthy environment itself. ...

## C    Reflections and Questions

1. As discussed in previous chapters, women are still facing many forms of unequal treatment and gender-based violence in our societies. These are worsened by different kinds of environmental disasters and hazards, environmental degradation and the problem of climate change, which will be discussed in more detail in the next section. Women have also yet to partake extensively in decision-making concerning environmental legislation, policies, plans, and responses. As also discussed in previous chapters, many cases have been ruled on by both global and regional human rights bodies recognizing and advancing the rights to life, integrity, privacy, non-discrimination, and to live free from violence, and economic, social, and cultural rights; and many of these rights are already codified in treaties. Given the history of women and the protection of human rights, do you think it would be advantageous for women to have more treaty-based recognition of the right to a healthy and safe environment? Or do you think women's rights claims related to the environment should be reviewed mostly under the rights already developed and recognized by universal and regional bodies?

2. Many threats to the environment today are coming from non-state actors. Non-state actors can be in the form of corporations, businesses, and individuals who implement development, tourism, investment, mining, and extractive economic projects. These projects may result in deforestation, contamination of water sources, the loss of biodiversity, pollution, and land degradation.[12] These projects can be implemented with the authorization of the

---

[12] For more reading on the adverse impacts of different extractive industry activities on women, *see* United Nations Interagency Framework Team for Preventive Action, Extractive Industries and Conflict, Section on Gender Specific Impacts, pp. 17–18, www.un.org/en/land-natural-resources-conflict/pdfs/GN_Extractive.pdf; IACHR, Indigenous Peoples, Afro-Descendent Communities, and Natural Resources:

government or can be illegal. Those frequently affected by these projects are indigenous peoples and afro-descendent communities who live in areas rich in natural resources. Many of these economic activities are implemented without proper supervision and regulation from the states involved. Environmental impact assessments are a key form of regulation, designed to detect potential harm and negative effects of these projects, and the sharing of information of these reports to the groups which may be the most harmed. These economic activities are also frequently implemented without the free, prior, and informed consultation and consent of the indigenous peoples and afro-descendent communities who will be affected.

3. As mentioned by the Inter-American Court of Human Rights in its advisory opinion, there are a number of substantive and procedural obligations that have been identified with regards to a right to a healthy environment. The substantive obligations are related to the content of rights that are typically impacted by environmental degradation and harm, including the rights to life, personal integrity, health, and property. The procedural obligations are more preconditions and facilitators for ensuring that the right to a healthy environment is adequately implemented, including creating the conditions for freedom of expression and association, access to information, to an adequate remedy, and effective participation. It is understood that due diligence when it comes to environmental matters encompasses all of these obligations, as well as the precautionary principle, which entails taking preventive measures to avoid harm to the environment, even when there is no scientific certainty that this damage will occur. There is also a need for international cooperation. All environmental state action should also be guided by the cornerstone prohibitions of discrimination and non-violence against women.[13]

4. It is important to highlight relevant statements from different geographic regions related to the right to a healthy environment and progress in the development of additional treaties. For example, the Working Group created by the OAS to monitor compliance with the Protocol of San Salvador has identified five key obligations to adequately implement the right to a healthy environment, including i) the guarantee of a healthy environment free from discrimination; ii) to ensure basic public services free from discrimination; iii) to promote environmental protection; iv) to foster environmental conservation; and v) to motivate the improvement of the environment.[14] The Working Group has also emphasized the elements of availability, accessibility, sustainability, acceptability, and adaptability.[15] The Council of Europe has also produced important statements urging all state parties to respect and ensure the right to a healthy environment, and calling on the Committee of Ministers to begin work on a legal text on human rights and the environment.[16] What would

---

Human Rights Protection in the Context of Extraction, Exploitation, and Development Activities, OEA/Ser.L/V/II. Doc. 47/15 31 (Dec. 31 2015), pp. 167–169 (hereinafter Extractive Industries).

[13] For more discussion of the substantive and procedural content of environmental rights, *see* Dinah L. Shelton, *Developing Substantive Environmental Rights*, 1 J. HUM. RTS. & ENV'T. 89, 90–107 (2010).

[14] OAS, WORKING GROUP OF THE PROTOCOL OF SAN SALVADOR, *Second Group of Rights, The Right to a Healthy Environment*, in PROGRESS INDICATORS FOR MEASURING RIGHTS UNDER THE PROTOCOL OF SAN SALVADOR (2nd ed., 2015), ¶ 26, www.oas.org/en/sedi/pub/progress_indicators.pdf.

[15] *Id.*, ¶¶ 30–34.

[16] Council of Europe, Council of Europe Statement Ahead of World Environmental Day, June 4, 2020, www.coe.int/en/web/human-rights-rule-of-law/-/beyond-covid-19-human-rights-can-help-save-the-planet.

be advantages of having additional treaty recognition of the right to a safe and healthy environment at the regional level? Can you see disadvantages as well? What should be the components of new regional treaties addressing these issues?

5.  The regional human rights protection systems have also ruled important individual cases related to environmental concerns. Some of these individual cases have centered on violations to the right to a healthy environment, particularly in Africa, and in the other systems they have been ruled on invoking the general rights involved in leading regional treaties. An illustrative example is the case of *SERAC and the Center for Economic and Social Rights v. Nigeria*, in which the African Commission on Human and Peoples' Rights examined a communication claiming that government oil production operations – in consortiums with private corporations – had caused environmental degradation and health problems harming the Ogoni peoples and their lands.[17] The African Commission ruled in favor of the applicants, advancing legal analysis concerning the content of the right to a healthy environment under Article 24 of the African Charter on Human and Peoples' Rights, combined with the right to health also protected under Article 16.[18] The ailments included the contamination of water, soil, and air resulting in skin infections, gastrointestinal and respiratory health issues, and increased risk of cancers, neurological and reproductive problems.[19] The communication specified that the Nigerian government had condoned and facilitated these violations by placing the legal and military powers of the state at the disposal of the oil companies; failing to monitor the operations of the oil companies involved; and withholding information from Ogoni communities on the dangers created by these oil activities.[20]

6.  The European Court of Human Rights in *Lopez Ostra v. Spain* also examined an application alleging that she and her family in Lorca had suffered violations of their rights to a private and family life under Article 8 of the European Convention on Human Rights, due to the state of Spain's failure to protect them from environmental pollution and waste caused by a plant in their town.[21] The plant's activities produced gas fumes, smells, and contamination resulting in many health problems for the residents of Lorca.[22] The Court sided with the applicants and indicated that severe environmental pollution may challenge well-being; the full enjoyment of home, private, and family life; and endanger health.[23]

7.  One of the areas of key concern regarding the environment and human rights has been the precarious nature of the human rights defenders advancing these causes. Many human rights defenders advancing environmental causes have lost their lives and suffered acts of harassment, violence, and criminalization for opposing logging, investment, development, tourism, extractive, and mining projects. One of the most known cases is that of Berta Cáceres, who was a globally known environmental and indigenous peoples activist in Honduras, who also co-founded the Council of Popular and Indigenous Organizations in

---

[17]  African Commission on Human and Peoples' Rights, The Social and Economic Rights Action Center (SERAC) v. Nigeria, Communication 155/96 (2001), Summary of the Facts, ¶¶ 1–9.

[18]  *Id.*, ¶¶ 50–54 and Holding.

[19]  *Id.*, ¶ 2.

[20]  *Id.*, ¶¶ 1–9.

[21]  Lopez Ostra v. Spain, App. No. 16798/90, Eur. Ct. H.R., ¶¶ 7–9 (Dec. 9, 1994).

[22]  *Id.*, ¶ 8.

[23]  *Id.*, ¶¶ 44–58.

Honduras (COPINH). She was assassinated by armed intruders in her home on March 2, 2016. At the time of her murder, Berta Cáceres was still the beneficiary of precautionary measures granted by the Inter-American Commission on Human Rights in 2009. She worked to advance the environmental rights of the Lenca indigenous peoples and actively led a campaign to protect the Gualcarque River in the department of Santa Barbara in Honduras, in which there were plans to install the Aqua Zarca Hydroelectric Dam. She actively denounced the lack of free, prior, and informed consultation and consent in the plans to install this dam. She and other COPINH members had been victims of many threats, acts of violence, harassment, and forms of criminalization for their advocacy activities.[24]

8. New treaties have been adopted in recent years to codify and address specific legal obligations concerning the environment. One well-known effort was the adoption of the Regional Agreement on Access to Information, Public Participation, and Justice in Environmental Matters in Latin America and the Caribbean, better known as the Escazú Agreement.[25] The agreement stems from the United Nations Conference on Sustainable Development (Rio + 20) and was adopted in Escazú, Costa Rica, on March 4, 2018 under the auspices of the United Nations Economic Commission for Latin America and the Caribbean (ECLAC).[26] The agreement codifies important human rights language, including the right of all persons to have access to information in the realm of the environment in a timely and appropriate way; to participate in decisions concerning their lives and their environment; and to access justice when human rights violations have occurred.[27] The agreement also recognizes in a groundbreaking fashion the important work of human rights defenders in advancing environmental causes, and through Article 9 states commit to guaranteeing safe and enabling conditions for their work.[28] States also commit themselves to preventing, investigating, and sanctioning attacks on human rights defenders working on environmental matters. The agreement recognizes key guiding principles, including non-discrimination and equality, transparency and accountability, the principle of non-regression and progressive realization, the precautionary principle, and the focus of intergenerational equity.[29]

9. One of the groups of women hardest hit by environmental disasters, degradation, harm, and climate change is indigenous women. Indigenous women are the transmitters of culture, knowledge, history, and tradition in their communities. They have a special relationship with their land, environment, and natural resources. They have a multidimensional view of their identity – not only as women, but also as indigenous, and view their present and future as intimately tied to the enjoyment of their territories. As discussed in Chapter 3, they have both an individual and collective view of their human rights, and the full respect

---

[24] For more reading, *see* IACHR Condemns the Killing of Berta Cáceres in Honduras, Press Release No. 024/16, (March 4, 2016), www.oas.org/en/iachr/media_center/PReleases/2016/024.asp.

[25] *See generally*, U.N. Economic Commission for Latin America and the Caribbean (ECLAC), Regional Agreement on Access to Information, Public Participation and Justice in Environmental Matters in Latin America and the Caribbean, 2018, ¶¶ 11–37, https://repositorio.cepal.org/bitstream/handle/11362/43583/1/S1800428_en.pdf.

[26] *Id.*, Preface, pp. 7–9.

[27] *Id.*, Articles 5, 6, 7, 8.

[28] *Id.*, Article 9.

[29] *Id.*, Article 3.

for their rights to self-determination and free and prior consultation and consent are key pillars to the full protection of their women's rights.[30] Many indigenous women live in rural communities, which feel profound impacts from extreme weather events and hazards. These can severely affect their access to basic needs in terms of water, food, seeds, and health; restrict important sources of livelihood; and their reach of natural resources for medicinal purposes. Environmental harm can also cause formidable disruption in the cultural fabric and traditions of their communities. Even though indigenous women possess important knowledge of how to face adversity and address the adverse consequences of climate change and hold important leadership positions in their communities, this is rarely recognized by states in the legislative and planning efforts to confront environmental concerns.[31]

10. Many issues faced today by indigenous women and the contamination and degradation of their territories have been framed by several experts as forms of *environmental violence*.[32] The term "environmental violence" is increasingly used to refer to the many impacts that environmental harm, degradation, and pollution have on indigenous women and girls. The implementation of economic activities in indigenous territories which result in environmental harm can be considered a form of violence due to the close relationship indigenous women have with their lands and natural resources. Land is key to their physical and spiritual life, and to transmit culture and traditions. Transgressions of their lands can also be linked to increased exposure to sexual violence, domestic violence, trafficking, and other harms. Environmental pollution and degradation can contribute to numerous health problems for indigenous women, including illnesses, cancers, disabilities, and other ailments. The full respect for the rights to consultation and consent are paramount to any state's due diligence efforts to prevent, investigate, and grant reparations for incidents of environmental violence against women.

## III    THE EFFECTS OF CLIMATE CHANGE ON WOMEN

The SDG 2030 agenda identified as its Goal 13 the need to take urgent action to combat climate change and its effects.[33] It mandates states to incorporate climate-change measures in their national policies, strategies, and planning, and to develop strong capacities for resilience and adaptation.[34] States also commit to improve their human and institutional capacities

---

[30]    *See for reference*, Report of the Special Rapporteur on indigenous peoples, Victoria Tauli Corpuz, A/HR/C/30/41 (August 6, 2015), ¶¶ 5–60; Inter-American Commission on Human Rights, *Indigenous Women and their Human Rights in the Americas*, OEA/Ser.L/V.II Doc. 44/17 (April 17, 2017), ¶¶ 37–50.

[31]    *See as reference*, International Indigenous Women's Forum (FIMI), *Global Study on the Situation of Indigenous Women and Girls* (2020), pp. 61–64, https://fimi-iiwf.org/wp-content/uploads/2020/09/GlobalStudyFIMI_20-englishRGB-2.pdf.

[32]    For more reading on the history of the term "environmental violence" and its manifestations for indigenous women, *see* Andrea Carmen, *Environmental Violence: Impacts on Indigenous Women and Girls*, *in* INDIGENOUS PEOPLES' RIGHTS AND UNREPORTED STRUGGLES: CONFLICT AND PEACE 96–97, 98–102, 104–106 (E. Stamatopoulou ed., Institute for the Study of Human Rights, Columbia University, 2017).

[33]    *See*, U.N. General Assembly, *Transforming our World: The 2030 Agenda for Sustainable Development Goals*, *supra* note 1, Goal 13.

[34]    *Id.*, Goals 13.1 and 13.2.

for mitigation, adaptation, impact reduction, and early warning systems related to climate change.[35] Therefore, the goals of adaptation, mitigation, and resilience towards climate change issues are reflected in both universal treaties – such as the Paris Agreement discussed *supra* – and major global consensus documents seeking to advance sustainable development and the eradication of poverty, a safe and healthy environment, and gender equality.

Climate change has both human and nature-driven causes. Many organizations have reported consistently on the connections between climate change and human-propelled greenhouse gas emissions, which are important contributors to natural disasters and hazards, extreme weather events, droughts, heatwaves, floods, rising sea levels, and the spread of diseases.[36] Climate variability is a fixture now in many parts of the world, illustrated by unusual weather, rising temperatures, and fluctuations in water supply and quality.[37] The United Nations Intergovernmental Panel on Climate Change has painted a very concerning picture, documenting how global warming will likely reach 1.5°C between 2030 and 2052, which will adversely affect health, food security, water quality and availability, threats to livelihoods, and forms of development and economic growth.[38]

Climate change exacerbates the inequality and discrimination faced by women in society and increases their risk of different human rights violations.[39] This is particularly acute in the case of women who live in poverty conditions and rural areas, and those who are indigenous, afro-descendent, elderly, children, migrants, or living with disabilities, among others. There has been an increasing awareness in the international community of the gender dimensions of climate change and the importance of international and human rights law in the definition of state obligations to respect, protect, and fulfill the human rights of women affected by this dire problem.[40] This is key, as women face the brunt of many of the adverse effects of climate change, including often insurmountable barriers to food security; inconsistent water supplies; natural disaster-driven losses; high levels of maternal mortality and morbidity; and an increased risk of all forms of gender-based violence. Even though women are some of the most affected by climate change, they are often absent from climate-related policymaking and responses.

The readings below illustrate some important state obligations and principles related to addressing the adverse effects of climate change with a gender and intersectional perspective.

---

[35]  *Id.*, Goal 13.3.

[36]  World Bank Group, World Development Report: Development and Climate Change 1–35 (2010), https://openknowledge.worldbank.org/handle/10986/4387; Intergovernmental Panel on Climate Change (IPCC), Climate Change 2014: Impacts, Adaption, and Vulnerability – Technical Summary, 37–54 (2015).

[37]  *See for reference*, World Bank Group, Turn Down the Heat: Confronting the New Climate Normal 13–18 (2014).

[38]  *See* Intergovernmental Panel on Climate change (IPCC), Global Warming of 1.5 – Summary for Policy Makers (2018), pp. 6–12, www.ipcc.ch/sr15/chapter/spm/ (hereinafter Global Warming of 1.5°C).

[39]  For more reading, *see* U.N. Chronicle, Balgis Osman-Elasha, *Women … In the Shadow of Climate Change*, www.un.org/en/chronicle/article/womenin-shadow-climate-change#:~:text=Women%20have %20limited%20access%20to,able%20to%20confront%20climate%20change.

[40]  *See* Keina Yoshida and Lina Cespedes, *Climate Change Is a Women's Human Rights Issue*, July 4, 2019, https://blogs.lse.ac.uk/wps/2019/07/04/climate-change-is-a-womens-human-rights-issue/.

A      **Gender-Related Dimensions of Disaster Risk Reduction in the Context of Climate Change**

CEDAW Committee, General Recommendation 37
CEDAW/C/GC/3, February 7, 2018

1. Climate change is exacerbating the risks and impact of disasters globally by increasing the frequency and severity of weather and climate hazards, which heightens the vulnerability of communities to these hazards. Scientific evidence shows that human-caused changes in climate are now responsible for a large proportion of extreme weather events around the world. The human rights consequences of these disasters are apparent in political and economic instability, growing inequality, declining food and water security and in increased threats to health and livelihoods. While climate change affects everyone, those countries and populations, including people living in poverty, young people and future generations, who have contributed least to climate change are most vulnerable to its impact.

2. Women, girls, men and boys are affected differently by climate change and disasters, with many women and girls experiencing greater risks, burdens and impacts. Situations of crisis exacerbate pre-existing gender inequalities and also compound intersecting forms of discrimination against, inter alia, women living in poverty, indigenous women, women belonging to ethnic, racial, religious and sexual minorities, women with disabilities, women refugees and asylum seekers, internally displaced, stateless and migrant women, rural women, single women, adolescents and older women, who are often affected disproportionately compared to men or other women.

3. In many contexts, gender inequalities limit the control that women and girls have over decisions governing their lives as well as their access to resources such as food, water, agricultural inputs, land, credit, energy, technologies, education, health, adequate housing, social protection and employment. As a result of these inequalities, women and girls are more likely to be exposed to disaster-induced risks and losses related to their livelihoods and they are less able to adapt to changes in climatic conditions. While climate change mitigation and adaptation programmes may provide new employment and livelihood opportunities in sectors such as agricultural production, sustainable urban development and clean energies, failure to address the structural barriers faced by women in accessing their rights will increase gender-based inequalities and intersectional forms of discrimination.

4. Women and girls have higher levels of mortality and morbidity in situations of disaster. Gender-based economic inequalities mean that women, and female-headed households in particular, are at a higher risk of poverty and more likely to live in inadequate housing in urban and rural areas of low land value that are vulnerable to the impact of climate-related events such as floods, storms, avalanches, earthquakes, landslides and other hazards. Women and girls in conflict situations are particularly exposed to risks associated with disasters and climate change. The higher levels of mortality and morbidity among women during and following disasters are also a result of inequalities they face in access to adequate health care, food and nutrition, water and sanitation, education, technology and information. In addition, the failure to engage in gender-responsive disaster planning and implementation means that protective facilities and infrastructures such as early warning mechanisms, shelters and relief programmes have frequently neglected the specific

accessibility needs of diverse groups of women, including women with disabilities, older women and indigenous women.

5. Women and girls also face a heightened risk of gender-based violence during and following disasters. In the absence of social protection schemes and in situations where there is food insecurity, coupled with impunity for gender-based violence, women and girls are often exposed to sexual violence and exploitation as they attempt to access food and other basic needs for family members and themselves. In camps and temporary settlements, the lack of physical security, as well as the lack of safe and accessible infrastructures, including drinking water and sanitation, also result in increased levels of gender-based violence against women and girls. Women and girls with disabilities are at particular risk of gender-based violence and sexual exploitation during and following disasters due to discrimination based on physical limitations and barriers to communication, as well as the inaccessibility of basic services and facilities. Domestic violence, early and/or forced marriage, human trafficking and forced prostitution are also more likely to occur during and following disasters.

6. The vulnerability and exposure of women and girls to disaster risk and climate change are economically, socially and culturally constructed and can be reduced. Such vulnerability may vary with different disasters and across geographical and socio-cultural contexts.

7. The categorization of women and girls as passive "vulnerable groups" in need of protection from the impact of disasters is a negative gender stereotype that fails to recognize the important contributions to disaster risk reduction, post-disaster management and climate change mitigation and adaptation strategies that women are already making. Well-designed disaster risk reduction and climate change initiatives that provide for women's full and effective participation can advance substantive gender equality and women's empowerment, while ensuring that sustainable development, disaster risk reduction and climate change objectives are achieved. It should be underlined that gender equality is a pre-condition for the realization of sustainable development goals. …

25. Several cross-cutting principles and provisions of the Convention are of crucial importance for guiding legislation, policies, plans of action, programmes, budgets and other measures in relation to disaster risk reduction and climate change.

26. States parties should ensure that all policies, legislation, plans, programmes, budgets and other activities related to disaster risk reduction and climate change are gender responsive and grounded in human-rights based principles including;

   (a)  Equality and non-discrimination, with priority being accorded to the most marginalized groups of women and girls, such as those from indigenous, racial, ethnic and sexual minority groups, women and girls with disabilities, adolescents, older women, single women, female-headed households, widows, women and girls living in poverty in both rural and urban settings, women in prostitution, and internally displaced, stateless, refugee, asylum seeking and migrant women;

   (b)  Participation and empowerment, through the adoption of effective processes and the allocation of necessary resources to ensure that diverse groups of women have opportunities to participate in every stage of policy development, implementation and monitoring at each level of government from the local to the national, regional and international levels;

(c) Accountability and access to justice, which require the provision of appropriate and accurate information and mechanisms to ensure that all women and girls whose rights have been directly and indirectly affected by disasters and climate change are provided with adequate and timely remedies.

27. These three key general principles – equality and non-discrimination, participation and empowerment, accountability and access to justice – are fundamental to ensuring that all interventions related to disaster risk reduction in the context of climate change are implemented in accordance with the Convention. ...

B      Rosa Celorio, *Several Steps Forward, One Backward: Climate Change, Latin America, and Human Rights Resilience*, Maryland Journal of International Law

34 Md. J. Int'l L. 96, 133–137 (2020)

*This article discusses the implications of the 2017 U.S. withdrawal from the Paris Agreement for Latin American countries. The author urges Latin American governments to continue prioritizing action to address and respond to climate change, as an alarming global problem, despite the U.S. withdrawal. The article also posits that international human rights law and the work of the regional human rights protection system in the Americas can be useful in the design of legislation, policy, and regulatory measures to adapt, mitigate, and respond to the adverse effects of climate change. The excerpts below discuss the components of a gender perspective in efforts to address, adapt, and mitigate the effects of climate change.*

... Strategies from Latin American countries to address climate change should take into consideration all of the gender equality legal standards developed by the regional and universal system of human rights. This is key as women compose more than half of the population in the Americas.

It is well accepted internationally at this stage that women have and still suffer forms of discrimination in all social sectors and the family. Several well-known international organizations have also documented how one in three women around the world are and will be victims of gender-based violence and Latin America is no exception. Women are also highly vulnerable to poverty and to live in rural areas. Extreme weather events and natural disasters exacerbate and tap into this history of discrimination and gender-based violence, making women more vulnerable to the adverse effects of climate change. There is already an international recognition that gender equality and a gender perspective are key in climate change efforts. It is important however that the international community and bodies define in more detail what a gender perspective is to climate change efforts.

For the author, a gender perspective includes several factors. One is considering the historical discrimination that women have faced and still suffer socially. Another is taking into consideration the social drivers of this discrimination, including stereotypes and general tolerance of disadvantaged treatment. The third is understanding how intimately connected the problems of gender-based violence and discrimination are, and how one fuels the other. The fourth is understanding how state institutional failures and a culture of silence promotes the recurrence of gender-based violence and discrimination. Fifth, a gender perspective also comprehends understanding the specific social burdens and inequalities women are subjected to and the ongoing challenges to develop their life plans and to access decision-making roles in the family, education, employment, health, and economic development of their countries. Sixth, it is important to understand that the experience of every woman is different and that important variables can aggravate the gender-based discrimination and violence experience women can be exposed to, including race, ethnicity, age, and income.

Problems such as gender-based violence and discrimination against women tend to worsen in times of crisis and unrest. Climate-change related events such as extreme natural disasters and shortages can be particularly challenging for women due to this preexisting history of discrimination, violence, inequality, and social tolerance of disadvantage. They can also pose formidable barriers for women to participate in key decisions concerning adaptation, mitigation, and recovery efforts related to the adverse effects of climate change.

There is a great deal that has already been stated by the inter-American human rights system on violence and discrimination against women that is very applicable to defining the content of a gender perspective and gender-sensitive approach to climate change. One of the virtues of the inter-American system is also the range of regional and specialized treaties that it has available. Every day the definition of violence against women under the leading regional treaty of the Inter-American system is expanded. The author hopes that bodies such as the Inter-American Commission and Court begin processing individual case petitions related to women who experience harm, discrimination, and gender-based violence in contexts affected by environmental degradation and climate change effects and develop important legal standards in this realm.

According to contemporary standards related to gender-based violence and discrimination, states have a comprehensive set of obligations mandating the organization of the entire structure to act with due diligence to prevent and respond to these problems. Due diligence mandates preventing foreseeable harm and granting reparations when it occurs. It also entails from states the adoption of legislation, policies, programs, and services. The responsibilities of states also permeate the supervision and regulation of private and non-state actor activity. States are also obligated to consider the particular risk to human rights violations that some women may experience due to their race, ethnic background, age, and income status. ...

The CEDAW Committee has made a very important contribution to international understanding of what a gender-specific approach to climate change should look like. The CEDAW Committee on its General Recommendation 37 indicated how climate change and its adverse effects have an enhanced effect on pre-existing gender inequalities and aggravate forms of discrimination faced by women living in poverty, indigenous women, women belonging to ethnic, racial, religious and sexual minority groups, women with disabilities, refugee and asylum-seeking women; those internally displaced, stateless, and migrants, unmarried women, and adolescents and older women. The CEDAW Committee also expressed how gender inequalities generally limit the control and access women and girls have to resources such as food, water, agricultural input, land, credit, energy, technology, education, health services, adequate housing, social protection and employment. This in turn exposes them to disaster induced risks and changes in climatic conditions. The CEDAW Committee concedes that climate mitigation and adaptation programs in sectors such as agricultural production, sustainable urban development, and clean energy can provide jobs for women, but failure to address the structural barriers women face in general to enjoy their rights can increase gender-based inequalities and intersecting forms of discrimination.

According to the CEDAW Committee, state interventions designed to curb fossil fuel use, greenhouse gas emissions, and the harmful environmental effects of extractive industries, should incorporate a human rights and gender approach. This includes respecting and advancing the principles of equality, non-discrimination, participation, empowerment, access to justice, transparency, and the rule of law.

Very prominent in both the work of the Inter-American system and the universal mechanisms are a range of principles mandating the full participation of women in consultation processes and adequate access to information to exercise their human rights. There should also be government spaces open for women to participate and have a real voice in policy-making, and this extends to climate-related concerns. Issues such as access to health services, water, and food all have an important link to the sexual and reproductive rights of women, and it is important for governments to take this into account in their climate change actions and ambition. Women should be active participants in climate policy negotiations at the international and national levels.

It is virtually impossible to address the negative impacts of climate change without women fully incorporated in initiatives geared towards adaptation, mitigation, recovery, and response.
…

## C    Reflections and Questions

1. On January 20, 2021, President Joe Biden announced the return of the United States to the Paris Climate Change Agreement and the identification of the issue of climate change as a central priority of this administration.[41] President Biden also signed a number of orders to address climate change domestically and internationally, including the incorporation of climate change as key in U.S. and foreign policy efforts; underscoring U.S. leadership in global ambition and efforts to reduce global emissions; the launch of a process to determine the United States nationally determined contribution under the Paris Agreement; directing the Secretary of the Interior to pause entering into new oil and natural gas leases on public lands or offshore waters; and formalizing a commitment to advance environmental justice and the addressing of the disproportionate health, environmental, economic, and climate impacts of disadvantaged communities.[42] President Biden also created the position of U.S. Special Presidential Envoy for Climate, a White House Office of Domestic Climate Policy,

---

[41]  *See for reference*, White House, Paris Climate Agreement (Jan. 20, 2021), www.whitehouse.gov/briefing-room/statements-releases/2021/01/20/paris-climate-agreement/.

[42]  The White House, President Biden Takes Executive Actions to Tackle the Climate Crisis at Home and Abroad, Create Jobs, and Restore Scientific Integrity Across Federal Government (Jan. 27, 2021), www.whitehouse.gov/briefing-room/statements-releases/2021/01/27/fact-sheet-president-biden-takes-executive-actions-to-tackle-the-climate-crisis-at-home-and-abroad-create-jobs-and-restore-scientific-integrity-across-federal-government/.

and a National Climate Task Force composed of 21 federal agencies and departments, among other important steps towards institutionalizing climate change priorities.[43]

This is a significant change in policy from the former U.S. administration led by President Donald Trump. On June 1, 2017, former President Donald Trump had declared the intention to withdraw from the Paris Agreement.[44] The decision was met with global alarm, with many leaders criticizing the United States' decision and expressing their will to continue working on compliance with the Paris Agreement dispositions.[45] As an example, 200 countries gathered in Katowice, Poland, during December 3–14, 2018, and agreed upon a rule book to guide implementation of the Paris Agreement.[46] The United Nations Climate Change Conferences also continued after the U.S. withdrawal, including meetings of the parties to the Paris Agreement (CMA), overseeing its implementation.[47]

What do you think can be the main benefits of the United States rejoining the Paris Agreement, both domestically and internationally? Do you see any disadvantages? Is the Paris Agreement sufficient to address climate change concerns?

2. The Paris Agreement is largely silent on gender equality issues. The Preamble does mention that state parties should take into consideration gender equality issues and the empowerment of women in their efforts to address climate change.[48] The CEDAW Committee, numerous experts, and organizations have called for more gender-responsive climate action and ambition. An important foundation for this call has been the Gender Action Plan developed under the U.N. Framework Convention on Climate Change. The efforts have drawn attention to the disparate impact of climate change issues on women, and the need to increase women's representation in the follow-up to the Paris Agreement and the U.N. Framework Convention on Climate Change. These efforts have also under-scored the need for women and gender considerations to be properly reflected in climate policies, plans, and actions.[49]

---

[43] Council on Foreign Relations, Biden's Climate Change Policy: Why His Special Envoy Role Matters (Dec. 10, 2020), www.cfr.org/in-brief/biden-climate-change-policy-why-climate-envoy -matters.

[44] White House, President Trump Announces U.S. Withdrawal from the Paris Climate Accord (June 1, 2017), www.whitehouse.gov/articles/president-trump-announces-u-s-withdrawal-paris-climate -accord/.

[45] *See, e.g.*, Laura Smith-Spark, World Leaders Condemn Trump's Decision to Quit Paris Climate Deal, CNN (June 3, 2017), www.cnn.com/2017/06/02/world/us-climate-world-reacts; Jonathan Watts and Kate Connolly, *World Leaders React After Trump Rejects Paris Climate Deal*, THE GUARDIAN, June 1, 2017, www.theguardian.com/environment/2017/jun/01/trump-withdraw-paris-climate-deal-world -leaders-react.

[46] *See* COP 24 Katowice Poland Rule Book, United Nations Climate Chance Conference, The Katowice Rulebook – Main Principles of the Document (May 6, 2019), https://cop24.gov.pl/news/news -details/news/the-katowice-rulebook-main-principles-of-the-document/.

[47] *See, for example*, United Nations Climate Change, About the United Nations Climate Change Conference, December 2019, https://unfccc.int/about-the-un-climate-change-conference-december -2019.

[48] *See* Paris Agreement, *supra* note 3, Preamble.

[49] *See for example*, United Nations Climate Change, Bonn Conference Urges More Gender-Responsive Climate Action (July 11, 2019), https://unfccc.int/news/bonn-conference-urges-more-gender-responsive -climate-action; International Institute for Environment and Development (IIED), Advancing Gender

3. Climate change issues and their adverse effects can involve a number of important substantive human rights for women, including the rights to a safe and healthy environment,
   to a dignified life, integrity, health, food, water, housing, and the rights to live free from
   discrimination and violence. Procedural rights related to the right to a safe and healthy
   environment are also key, including to freedom of expression, association, information, to
   work as human rights defenders, and to free, prior, and informed consultation and consent.
   Basic economic, social, and cultural rights obligations are also key, including the guarantee of sufficient and core levels of the rights to health, food, and water, and the accessibility, affordability, and quality of these services. Judicial protection and guarantees are
   also relevant when human rights violations related to climate change issues occur. Which
   other human rights do you consider could be violated in climate change driven events with
   adverse impacts for women and girls?

4. The obligation to act with due diligence is also applicable to states and non-state actors
   when it comes to the human-driven causes of climate change, including efforts without
   delay to reduce greenhouse emissions; adaption and mitigation efforts to extreme weather
   events and natural disasters; to prevent foreseeable forms of environmental harm and
   degradation from the implementation of logging, investment, development, and extractive
   projects by both state and non-state actors; and to respect, protect, and fulfill the rights
   to life and personal integrity of women human rights defenders who are advocating for
   environmental causes. Many of the due diligence components of the right to a safe and
   healthy environment enumerated by the Inter-American Court of Human Rights Advisory
   Opinion, 23/17, discussed *supra*, can be pertinent to address climate challenges, including
   the regulation, supervision, and monitoring of activities which may result in environmental degradation; the establishment of contingency and early warning plans for extreme
   weather events; the mitigation of environmental damage when it has occurred; and the
   investigation, sanction, and grant of remedies for human rights violations in this context.
   States are also obligated to create spaces in which women can voice their concerns over
   climate variability and its impacts, and create the conditions for women to effectively participate in the development of legislation, national plans, policies, and programs designed
   to address climate change. Which criteria can you use to distinguish between the natural
   and the human-driven causes of climate change? What do you believe should be the main
   components of a gender perspective with due diligence in respect of climate action and
   ambition?

5. Even though the regional human rights protection systems have yet to rule concretely on
   cases on climate change issues, they have been setting important conditions for future
   individual case petitions in this area. For example, the African Commission on Human and
   Peoples' Rights adopted a resolution on climate change issues, calling on states to advance
   the rights to a generally satisfactory environment, to development, and to health.[50] The
   resolution concretely encourages member states to strengthen regional and international
   cooperation for climate action, with a human rights perspective and to adopt protection

---

Equality in the Post-2020 Climate Regime, October 2015, https://pubs.iied.org/sites/default/files/pdfs/
migrate/17313IIED.pdf.
[50]  *See* African Commission on Human and Peoples' Rights, Resolution on Climate Change and
Human Rights in Africa, ACHPR/Res.342(LVIII)2016, www.achpr.org/sessions/resolutions?id=381.

measures on behalf of children, women, older persons, persons with disabilities, indigenous peoples, and minorities from the effects of natural disasters and armed conflicts.

6. The European Court of Human Rights just admitted its first case related to climate change. In the case of Duarte Agostinho and Others v. Portugal and Others, it is alleged that global greenhouse gas emissions from 33 member states of the Council of Europe are contributing to the harms produced by global warming and climate change.[51] The petition was brought by six Portuguese children and young people, with support from Global Legal Action Network, claiming that their generation will be particularly harmed by the effects of climate change and these states' contribution to climate change.[52] The petition alleges in particular that these states have contributed to climate change in the following ways: by permitting release of emissions in their national territories and offshore areas; by allowing the export of fossil fuels extracted on their territory; by authorizing the import of goods the production of which involves the release of emissions into the atmosphere; and by enabling entities within their jurisdiction to contribute to the release of emissions overseas.[53] The applicants specify that they are already harmed by climate change in their respiratory and cardiovascular health from increased heat and air pollution, reflected in reduced energy levels and difficulty sleeping. They allege that these ailments will continue affecting both themselves in the present and the children they have. The petition has been admitted by the European Court of Human Rights under the rights to life (Article 2), private and family life (Article 8), the prohibition of discrimination (Article 14), the prohibition of torture and inhuman treatment (Article 3), and the right to property (Article 1, Protocol 1 of the Convention).[54] Can you think of potential case petitions that could be presented by women and girls before regional human rights courts raising issues related to climate change? Which human rights, treaties, and instruments would you invoke?

7. The Inter-American Commission on Human Rights has issued a number of press releases and convoked hearings on climate change issues. One of its best-known press releases on this issue called on states to address climate change issues with a holistic and human rights approach, and expressed concern over the harmful effects of climate change, including deaths and the displacement of individuals and communities because of natural disasters, cyclones, tornadoes, heat waves, and droughts.[55] The Inter-American Commission on Human Rights also referred to challenges to accessing healthy drinking water, safeguarding food security, and the negative impact of these problems on women, children, indigenous peoples, rural communities, the elderly, and persons living in poverty. In the aftermath to the devastating Hurricane Maria in Puerto Rico, the Inter-American Commission moreover

---

[51] For more discussion of this case, *see* Corina Heri, *The ECtHR's Pending Climate Change Case: What's Ill-Treatment Got To Do With It?* (Dec. 22, 2020), www.ejiltalk.org/the-ecthrs-pending-climate-change-case-whats-ill-treatment-got-to-do-with-it/.

[52] Application in the case of Duarte Agostinho and Others v. Portugal and Others, https://youth4climatejustice.org/wp-content/uploads/2020/12/Application-form-annex.pdf.

[53] *Id.*, p. 6.

[54] *See* Duarte Agostinho and Others v. Portugal and Others (communicated case) – 39371/20, Eur. Ct. H.R. (Dec. 2020), https://hudoc.echr.coe.int/eng#{%22itemid%22:[%22002-13055%22]}.

[55] *See* Inter-American Commission on Human Rights, IACHR Expresses Concern regarding Effects of Climate Change on Human Rights (Dec. 2, 2015), www.oas.org/en/iachr/media_center/preleases/2015/140.asp.

called on the United States to undertake measures to mitigate, adapt, and support communities in addressing the risks and damage associated with climate change and natural disasters.[56] The Inter-American Commission, however, did not open for processing a petition submitted in December of 2005 by the Inuit Circumpolar Council seeking to hold the United States responsible for failing to limit greenhouse gas emissions in the Arctic region. The petition alleged concretely that climate change in the Arctic region disproportionately affected the Inuit, and threatened their health, lives, land rights, and livelihoods. However, the Commission has another opportunity to rule on climate issues on the basis of a petition presented in 2021 by the Haitian children in Cité de Soleil.[57] The petition alleges that toxic trash disposal in the residential district of Cité de Soleil in Port-au-Prince is harming the health of children; damage which will be exacerbated by climate change, environmental displacement, and waterborne diseases. The petition was presented under the rights of the child (Article 19); to dignity (Article 11); to live in a healthy environment (Articles 4 and 26); and to judicial protection (Article 25) of the American Convention. How would you rule on this new petition presented by the Haitian children in Cité de Soleil? Can you think of specific human rights repercussions of the harm alleged on Haitian girls?

8. The problem of gender-based violence is also intricately connected to climate change issues.[58] When extreme weather events and natural disasters occur, women are very prone to lose their housing; basic access to food, water, and health services; and their sources of livelihood. All of this makes women more prone and vulnerable to acts of sexual, psychological, and physical violence. When droughts occur, women need to walk further to obtain water and secure food, which exposes them to different forms of gender-based violence. Extreme weather events can also worsen stress and produce the breakdown of family dynamics leading to violence against women and girls in the home. The violence can be at the hands of both state and non-state actors. Can you think of steps that states can adopt to prevent, investigate, sanction, and grant reparations with due diligence for acts of gender-based violence connected to the adverse impacts of climate change?

9. The Paris Agreement refers in its Preamble to the concept of *climate justice* and the need to take action to address climate change.[59] The term "climate justice" acknowledges in many ways the differentiated impacts that climate variability can have on those affected by poverty, historical disadvantage, discrimination.[60] There has been a surge in international litigation related to climate change that has been framed as an effort to obtain climate justice

---

[56]    *See* Inter-American Commission on Human Rights, IACHR Expresses Deep Concern about the Human Rights Situation in Puerto Rico (Jan. 18, 2018), www.oas.org/en/iachr/media_center/preleases/2018/004.asp.

[57]    *See* Petition filed before the Inter-American Commission on Human Rights Seeking to Redress Violations of the Rights of Children in Cité Soleil, Haiti, Professors James R. May and Erin Daly (Representatives) (Feb. 4, 2021), http://climatecasechart.com/climate-change-litigation/wp-content/uploads/sites/16/non-us-case-documents/2021/20210204_13174_petition.pdf.

[58]    For more reading *see* United Nations Development Programme, Why Climate Change Fuels Violence against Women (Jan. 28, 2020), www.undp.org/content/undp/en/home/blog/2020/why-climate-change-fuels-violence-against-women.html.

[59]    *See* Paris Agreement, *supra* note 3, Preamble.

[60]    Daisy Simmons, Yale Climate Connections, *What is Climate Justice?* (July 29, 2020), https://yaleclimateconnections.org/2020/07/what-is-climate-justice/; Sustainable Development Goals, Climate Justice (May 31, 2019), www.un.org/sustainabledevelopment/blog/2019/05/climate-justice/.

for these populations. In the now emblematic Netherlands Supreme Court decision in the case of the *Urgenda Foundation v. State of the Netherlands*, an environmental group, the Urgenda Foundation, and 900 Dutch citizens sued the government for failing to do more to prevent climate change.[61] In its final judgment, the Supreme Court affirmed the decisions of the district court and Court of Appeal in ordering the state to reduce greenhouse gases by the end of 2020 by at least 25 percent compared to 1990.[62] The Court makes mention of the effects of global warming, including extreme heat; drought; the disruption of ecosystems; the jeopardy of food supply; and the rise in sea levels from the melting of glaciers and the polar ice caps. [63] The Court invokes concretely the rights to life (Article 2) and to private and family life (Article 8) as imposing a positive obligation on states to prevent imminent and known hazards affecting large groups of persons, including environmental hazards and those related to climate change.[64]

## IV    CONCLUSIONS: ADVOCACY ON HUMAN RIGHTS, WOMEN, AND THE ENVIRONMENT

It is a noteworthy advance that the international community is prioritizing issues concerning climate change; the safety and health of the environment; and the importance of protecting our natural resources, ecosystems, and biodiversity from all forms of harm. This chapter has discussed a number of universal and regional treaties – including the Paris Agreement – which serve as an important legal backbone for efforts to advance the right to a safe and healthy environment; the adequate response and adaptation to, and mitigation of, the adverse effects of climate change; and the goals of a dignified life and sustainable development.

In this context, more legal standards, statements, and benchmarks are needed to facilitate women's voices and needs being taken fully into consideration. Women bear the consequences of many environmental challenges and are key to the effective design of laws, policies, and plans to respond, adapt, and mitigate. This is critical in the case of indigenous and afro-descendent women, and other groups of women who suffer deeply the negative impacts of climate change and forms of environmental harm.

The principles of non-discrimination and to live free from gender-based violence, as well as important concepts such as environmental violence and climate justice, need more discussion and development to reflect the specific realities of women. There is room to expand and define the contours of due diligence in international human rights law concerning the environment, including the obligations to prevent, investigate, sanction, and grant reparations. Much work also needs to be done with both state and non-state entities, as many private actors, especially corporate ones, often execute economic activities that threaten women's access to food, water, health services, forms of livelihood, life, and integrity. A further conceptualization of the right to a safe and healthy environment, and the content of the rights to life, personal integrity, dignity, health, food, water, non-discrimination, and gender-based violence are key

---

[61] *See* Netherlands Supreme Court, Urgenda Foundation v. State of the Netherlands, Section 2: Assumptions and Facts, www.urgenda.nl/wp-content/uploads/ENG-Dutch-Supreme-Court-Urgenda-v -Netherlands-20-12-2019.pdf.

[62] *See id.*, Section 5: Do Articles 2 and 8 ECHR oblige the State to take measures?

[63] *See id.*

[64] *See id.*

ingredients in this process. This begs the question; is this an area of the law in which we need more rights, or are the ones that we have sufficient? How do you incorporate a gender and intersectional perspective into current efforts to address environmental harms and hazards?

Concerns related to the environment bind us all. They affect all countries and individuals on Earth. They are a connecting point across cultures, languages, races, sex and genders, and histories. A safe and healthy environment is key to the present, but also the future well-being of the human person. Human rights were conceptualized as a body of laws to reduce human suffering and advance dignity and peace. A safe and healthy environment and its protection with due diligence is part of the equation to achieve the goals of the human rights system, the well-being, and the right to a dignified life of all women and girls.

# 11. Women and the regional human rights protection systems

## I INTRODUCTION: THE RELATIONSHIP BETWEEN THE UNIVERSAL AND REGIONAL HUMAN RIGHTS PROTECTION SYSTEMS: THE SITUATION OF WOMEN

The regional human rights protection systems have developed an important body of work related to the rights of women and gender equality issues. Some of the key advances in legal standards in this area are happening in the more established protection systems in the Americas, Europe, and Africa. In these three regions of the world, important treaties and mechanisms have been adopted and established by states with pertinence to the rights of women to live free from discrimination and violence, but also a range of civil, political, economic, social, and cultural rights. Every day women and girls are becoming more prominent in the case decisions, jurisprudence, statements, and activities of these regional human rights protection systems. The seeds have also been established for regional protection systems to develop in Asia and the Middle East, including the adoption of important declarations and treaties alluding to the rights of women.

Many of the existing regional systems have been developed in tandem with the universal system of human rights. The American Declaration of the Rights and Duties of Man was adopted on May 2, 1948, approximately six months before the Universal Declaration of Human Rights, which was adopted on December 10, 1948.[1] The American and African systems in particular refer extensively to universal treaties, instruments, and legal standards in their work.

Many historical factors propelled the development of regional human rights protection systems, including the lengthy history of multilateralism and the wave of repressive regimes which affected Latin America in the 1970s and 1980s; the intense human suffering and devastating loss connected to two World Wars and the Holocaust in Europe; and the post-colonization demand for self-determination and political stability, and the need to eliminate racism in Africa. In essence, regional human rights protection systems, and their instruments and mechanisms, reflect the history, politics, and culture of said regions. The 1990s in particular were a key moment for regional human rights protection systems in the area of women's rights, with the adoption in 1994 of the first regional treaty solely devoted to violence against women, the Convention of Belém do Pará, followed by the drafting of the Maputo

---

[1] *See* Universal Declaration of Human Rights, G.A. Res. 217A (III), U.N. Doc. A/810 at 71 (1948); American Declaration of the Rights and Duties of Man, O.A.S. Res. XXX, adopted by the Ninth International Conference of American States (1948).

Protocol in 1995 – both treaties discussed in Chapter 2. These treaty initiatives were heavily influenced in their language and dispositions by important universal developments, including the adoption of CEDAW in 1979, the CEDAW Committee General Recommendation 19 considering gender-based violence as a form of discrimination in 1992, and the Universal Declaration on Violence against Women in 1993; all discussed *supra* in Chapters 1 and 2.

In the present, the regional human rights protection systems have all issued important judgments, case decisions, general comments, and reports related to different aspects connected to the rights of women. This work has shed light on key state obligations, including due diligence; access to justice; the rights to live free from discrimination, violence, and torture; the rights of LGBTI persons; reproductive autonomy, personal liberty, and sexual and reproductive rights; and the rights to health, water, food, education, and employment; among other areas which will be discussed in this section. One of the most important challenges that regional human rights protection systems face today is responding to modern times and contemporary developments related to the human rights of women, and how these are impacted by pandemics, the surge of technology and social media, the environment, ongoing concerns over racial discrimination and racism, among other areas. The systems also face effectiveness challenges, human and financial limitations, and increasing political pressure, interference, and backlash from the states which created them.

This chapter discusses the work, case decisions, and statements adopted by the Americas, Europe, and African regional human rights protection systems that are illustrative of these tendencies in the area of women's rights. The chapter also delves into emerging work and approaches in Asia and the Middle East that are relevant to women and gender equality issues.

## II   INTER-AMERICAN SYSTEM OF HUMAN RIGHTS

The inter-American system of human rights has been created within the framework of the Organization of American States (hereinafter "OAS"). The OAS is composed of 35 member states from Latin America, the Caribbean, the United States, and Canada. Therefore, it includes a very intricate collection of cultures, languages, and legal regimes which are reflected in its workings. The leading treaty of the inter-American system of human rights is the American Convention on Human Rights, which codifies many key civil and political rights for women, including the rights to life, personal integrity, non-discrimination, dignity, private and family life, judicial protection and guarantees, and freedom of expression, association, information, and participation, among others.[2]

The American Convention on Human Rights also established an important enforcement machinery in the form of the Inter-American Commission on Human Rights (hereinafter "Inter-American Commission") and the Inter-American Court of Human Rights (hereinafter "Inter-American Court").[3] The Inter-American Commission functions as a quasi-judicial body entrusted with a protection and promotion mandate, including the capacity to process individual case decisions; the adoption of precautionary measures; the conduct of on-site and in-loco visits; the convoking of public hearings with different state and non-state actors in the region;

---

[2]   *See* American Convention on Human Rights, Arts. 1–26, Nov. 22, 1969, O.A.S.T.S. No. 36, 1144 U.N.T.S. 123 (hereinafter American Convention).
[3]   *See id.*, Articles 34–69.

and the publication of regional and country reports related to different facets of human rights.[4] The Inter-American Court of Human Rights for its part is a very strong court with contentious and advisory jurisdiction, which has adopted more than 400 rulings in its history, in addition to provisional measures and advisory opinions.[5]

The inter-American system of human rights became very preeminent in the Americas for its work connected with repressive regimes, exemplified by its well-known visit to Argentina in 1979 to document human rights abuses and forced disappearances occurring in the country at the time.[6] Much of the work that the Inter-American System has become known for is related to forced disappearances, amnesty laws, freedom of expression, torture, and the rights of groups particularly exposed to human rights violations, including women and indigenous peoples. In the present, the system still faces key challenges concerning increased political pressure from states; the backlog of petitions; human and financial shortages; and the lack of universal ratification of the American Convention on Human Rights and other leading treaties.[7] Major problems that plague the system are fragile democracies, weak administration of justice systems, and corruption; extensive violence and citizen insecurity; and large economic class differences and the problem of poverty.[8]

In this historical and present backdrop, the adoption of the Convention of Belém do Pará in 1994 propelled the ruling of an extensive line of cases and jurisprudence by both the Inter-American Commission and Court advancing key standards related to discrimination and violence against women and girls, the content of the due diligence obligation, and access to justice when these acts occur. This line of cases has been enriched by a series of recent decisions in which the Inter-American Court of Human Rights has made bold statements regarding the rights to education, health, and work, as well as sexual and reproductive rights and LGBTI rights.

This section discusses some emblematic case decisions and provisional measures adopted by both the Inter-American Commission and Court which exemplify legal tendencies related to the human rights of women and gender equality.

## A     *Maria da Penha Maia Fernandez*

Inter-American Commission on Human Rights
Report No. 54/01, Case 12.051, April 16, 2001
Citations and footnotes omitted

---

[4]   Inter-American Commission on Human Rights, *Annual Report 2019*, Introduction and Activities of the IACHR during 2019, www.oas.org/en/iachr/docs/annual/2019/TOC.asp.

[5]   *See id.*

[6]   Inter-American Commission on Human Rights, *Report on the Situation of Human Rights in Argentina*, OEA/Ser.L/V/II.49 (April 11, 1980), Introduction. *See also* HURST HANNUM, DINAH SHELTON, S. JAMES AND ROSA CELORIO, *Human Rights in the Americas, in* INTERNATIONAL HUMAN RIGHTS; PROBLEMS OF LAW, POLICY, AND PRACTICE 860–867 (Wolters Kluwer Publishers, 6th ed., 2017).

[7]   For a discussion of achievements and challenges which still affect the inter-American system of human rights, *see* Monica Pinto, *The Role of the Inter-American Commission and the Court of Human Rights in the Protection of Human Rights: Achievements and Contemporary Challenges*, 20(2) HUM. RTS. BRIEF 34–38 (2013).

[8]   *See id.*

*This case is related to the sequence of domestic violence acts suffered by Maria da Penha Maia Fernandes at the hands of her then husband. Her case was before the Brazilian judicial authorities for 17 years without a proper sanction of the aggressor. Copied below are excerpts of the analysis by the Inter-American Commission on Human Rights of this case under the Convention of Belém do Pará.*

53. The Convention of Belém do Pará is an essential instrument that reflects the great effort made to identify specific measures to protect the right of women to a life free of aggression and violence, both outside and within the family circle. ...

55. The impunity that the ex-husband of Mrs. Fernandes has enjoyed and continues to enjoy is at odds with the international commitment voluntarily assumed by the State when it ratified the Convention of Belém do Pará. The failure to prosecute and convict the perpetrator under these circumstances is an indication that the State condones the violence suffered by Maria da Penha, and this failure by the Brazilian courts to take action is exacerbating the direct consequences of the aggression by her ex-husband. Furthermore, as has been demonstrated earlier, that tolerance by the State organs is not limited to this case; rather, it is a pattern. The condoning of this situation by the entire system only serves to perpetuate the psychological, social, and historical roots and factors that sustain and encourage violence against women.

56. Given the fact that the violence suffered by Maria da Penha is part of a general pattern of negligence and lack of effective action by the State in prosecuting and convicting aggressors, it is the view of the Commission that this case involves not only failure to fulfill the obligation with respect to prosecute and convict, but also the obligation to prevent these degrading practices. That general and discriminatory judicial ineffectiveness also creates a climate that is conducive to domestic violence, since society sees no evidence of willingness by the State, as the representative of the society, to take effective action to sanction such acts.

57. The Commission must consider, in relation to Articles 7(c) and (h), the measures taken by the State to eliminate the condoning of domestic violence. The Commission notes the positive measures taken by the current administration towards that objective, in particular the establishment of special police stations, shelters for battered women, and others. However, in this case, which represents the tip of the iceberg, ineffective judicial action, impunity, and the inability of victims to obtain compensation provide an example of the lack of commitment to take appropriate action to address domestic violence. Article 7 of the Convention of Belém do Pará seems to represent a list of commitments that the Brazilian State has failed to meet in such cases.

58. In light of the foregoing, the Commission holds the view that this case meets the conditions for domestic violence and tolerance on the part of the State, defined in the Convention of Belém do Pará, and that the State is liable for failing to perform its duties set forth in Articles 7(b), (d), (e), (f), and (g) of that Convention in relation to rights protected therein, among them, the right to a life free of violence (Article 3), the right of a woman to have her life, her physical, mental, and moral integrity, her personal safety, and personal dignity respected, to equal protection before and of the law, and to simple and prompt recourse to a competent court for protection against acts that violate her rights (Articles 4(a), (b), (c), (d), (e), (f), and (g)). ...

# B  *Case of Guzmán Albarracín et al. v. Ecuador*

Inter-American Court of Human Rights
Merits, Reparations and Costs, Judgment of June 24, 2020. Series C, No. 405

*The case below is related to the sexual abuse suffered by Paola del Rosario Guzmán Albarracín at her public school, at the hands of her vice-principal. She was between 14 and 16 years old at the time of the events. She eventually committed suicide. The excerpts below discuss the content of the rights to non-violence, personal integrity, and private life in an educational setting, and the reinforced duty of protection towards girls.*

109.    The rights to personal integrity and to private life, recognized in Articles 5 and 11 of the American Convention, entail certain freedoms, including sexual freedom and control over one's own body. These rights may be exercised by adolescents in the measure that they develop the capacity and maturity to do so.

110.    In addition, Article 3 of the Belém do Pará Convention establishes the right of every woman to a life free from violence.

111.    In this regard, the Court finds it necessary to stress that the concept of "violence" used to examine the State's responsibility in this case is not limited to physical violence, but also includes "any act or conduct, based on gender, which causes death or physical, sexual or psychological harm or suffering to women, whether in the public or the private sphere," pursuant to Article 1 of the Belém do Pará Convention. Article 6 of the same treaty establishes that the right of every woman to be free from violence includes her right to "be free from all forms of discrimination" and to "be valued and educated free of stereotyped patterns of behavior and social and cultural practices based on concepts of inferiority or subordination." Similarly, Article 2 of that international instrument specifically mentions sexual harassment in educational institutions as a form of violence against women.

112.    Article 7 of the Belém do Pará Convention also imposes specific obligations on States to pursue policies to prevent violence "by all appropriate means and without delay," and to "refrain from engaging in any act or practice of violence against women" and "ensure that their authorities [and] officials" act in conformity with this obligation. They must also "apply due diligence to prevent, investigate and impose penalties" for such conduct, and take all appropriate measures, including legislative and administrative or other measures to "prevent, punish and eradicate violence against women." …

122.    According to the facts of the case, for more than one year, Paola del Rosario Guzmán Albarracín had a sexual relationship with the vice principal of her school when she was between 14 and 16 years old. …

129.    As a first element, it is important to stress that from the circumstances of this case it is clear that Paola's subjection to a sexual relationship with the vice principal occurred within the context of his position and role at the school. This implies that he acted as a public official, which compromises the State's responsibility.

130.    The vice principal was not only an adult man who had sexual relations with a girl under 18, with whom he had an age difference of nearly 40 years; he also had a role of power and a duty of care in relation to her. Obviously, this aspect is central to the case because, as an academic authority at Paola's school, he was required not only to respect the girl's

rights, but also, in his role as educator, he should have offered her guidance and education in a manner consistent with her rights and ensured that these were protected. Their sexual liaison also took place in the context of a clearly unequal relationship, in which the vice principal, as an academic authority, enjoyed a situation of superiority *vis-à-vis* a female student.

131.    Thus, the vice principal obtained a sexual relationship by taking advantage of his position of power and trust. This is obvious, in concrete terms, because the evidence indicates that the sexual acts between the vice principal and Paola began as a condition for him to help her so that she would pass the school year. In that situation, and in the context of harmful gender stereotypes that tend to blame the victim, the vice principal was able to exercise power and take advantage of a relationship of trust in order to normalize acts that were improper and injurious to the adolescent's rights. ...

135.    Furthermore, these acts occurred in a context in which Paola's vulnerability as an adolescent girl was heightened by a situation, which was not exceptional, of a lack of effective actions to prevent sexual violence in schools and address institutional tolerance.

136.    It has already been noted that sexual harassment and abuse in schools was a "known problem" and yet, at the time of the facts, no effective measures were taken to prevent and punish this behavior. The State also admitted that, at that time, there were no adequate public policies for preventing such behavior or for reporting, investigating and punishing acts of sexual violence in educational institutions. ...

140.    In the instant case, Paola did not receive the education that would have enabled her to understand the sexual violence inherent in the acts to which she was subjected and did not have access to an institutional system that would have supported her in coping with or reporting that situation. To the contrary, this violence was validated, normalized and tolerated by the institution.

141.    The violence to which Paola was subjected also entailed a form of discrimination. As mentioned previously, gender-based violence and violence against women are a form of discrimination prohibited by Article 1(1) of the American Convention. Sexual violence against girls not only reflects a prohibited form of discrimination based on gender, but can also be discriminatory based on age. ...

143.    Based on the facts examined so far, the Court concludes that Paola del Rosario Guzmán Albarracín was subjected, for more than one year, to sexual harassment, abuse and sexual intercourse by the vice principal of her school. This was a situation in which serious acts of sexual violence were committed against her in an educational establishment, by a public official who took advantage of his position of power and authority and of the victim's vulnerability, violating her right, as an adolescent woman, to live a life free from violence as well as her right to education. The violence Paola suffered was not an isolated incident; rather, it occurred within a structural context in which various factors of discrimination intersected, namely, the gender and age of the victim. Furthermore, this situation was tolerated by the State authorities, who failed to take adequate measures to address sexual violence in schools and to provide her with education on her sexual and reproductive rights, thereby increasing her situation of vulnerability.

144.    The above situation implies, on the one hand, a direct violation of Paola's rights owing to the sexual violence committed against her and, on other, the tolerance of such violence by the State authorities. In both cases, this conduct shows that the State failed in its obliga-

tion to respect Paola's rights. Furthermore, as the State partially admitted, it did not fulfill its duty to ensure those rights because it failed to adopt measures to prevent and address sexual violence. …

## C    Reflections and Questions

1. The case of *Maria da Penha Maia Fernandez* was the first decision ever decided by the Inter-American Commission on Human Rights applying the Convention of Belém do Pará and the due diligence standard to domestic violence against women. In *Maria da Penha Maia Fernandez*, the Inter-American Commission finds the state of Brazil responsible for violations under both the American Convention and the Convention of Belém do Pará for failing to act with due diligence to prosecute and convict the perpetrator of the acts in this case and for the overall ineffectiveness of the justice system in sanctioning domestic violence. This case is part of the first set of decisions adopted by the Inter-American Commission on Human Rights that delved into discrimination and violence against women, due diligence, access to justice, and freedom from rape as torture when perpetrated by public officials.[9]

2. The adoption of legal standards concerning women in the inter-American system has been gradual and slow, only propelled after 1995 by the entry into force of the Convention of Belém do Pará.[10] The Inter-American Court of Human Rights, however, has characterized itself as adopting a number of ground-breaking and bold judgments in the area of women's rights. A major area of legal standards development has been violence against women and its forms, illustrated by the case of *Guzman Albarracín et al.* discussed *supra*. The leading case of the Inter-American Court of Human Rights in this area – *Cotton Field*, discussed in Chapter 2, adopted in 2009 – refers in detail to state obligations to prevent, investigate, judge, and sanction cases related to missing and murdered women and girls in known contexts of structural risk, unsafety, and discrimination against women.

3. Legal standards related to violence against women adopted by the Inter-American Court of Human Rights have evolved significantly in recent cases. In the Inter-American Court of Human Rights case of the *Women victims of sexual torture in Atenco v. Mexico*, adopted in November 28, 2018, the Court held the state of Mexico responsible for the illegal and arbitrary detention of 11 women, and the sexual, physical, and psychological attacks perpetrated by state agents during their arrest, transfer, and arrival at the detention center.[11] The Court referred for the first time to the concept of "sexual torture," considering that the

---

[9]    For more reading on the development of women's rights standards in the inter-American system of human rights in individual cases, *see* Rosa M. Celorio, The Rights of Women in the Inter-American System of Human Rights: Current Opportunities and Challenges in Standard-setting, 65 U. MIAMI L. REV. 819 (2011); Inter-American Commission on Human Rights, *Standards and Recommendations: Violence and Discrimination against Women and Girls*, OEA.Ser.L/V/II. Doc. 233 (Nov. 14, 2019), www.oas.org/en/iachr/reports/pdfs/ViolenceWomenGirls-Annex1.pdf.

[10]    For more discussion on challenges which affected the development of women's legal standards in the inter-American system of human rights, *see* Patricia Palacios Zuloaga, *The Path to Gender Justice in the Inter-American Court of Human Rights*, 17 TEX. J. WOMEN & L. 227, 246–275 (2008).

[11]    *See* Women Victims of Sexual Torture in Atenco v. Mexico, Merits, Reparations and Costs, Inter-Am. Ct. H.R., Series C, No. 371, ¶¶ 1, 75–112 (Nov. 28, 2018).

attacks occurred while women were under state custody, and were used by state agents as a weapon for repressive social control during protests.[12] In the judgment in the case of *Linda Loaiza Lopez v. Venezuela*, the Court also had the opportunity to delve into issues concerning sexual violence, rape, and gender-based violence.[13] The case relates to Linda Loaiza Lopez, who at the age of 18 suffered severe and extreme acts of violence at the hands of a private individual, who kept her confined to his apartment, including forms of sexual violence and rape.[14] The case developed the concept of sexual slavery in light of the obligations of the American Convention on Human Rights, alluding to the total control the aggressor had over the victims' autonomy and movements, his ongoing threats, his exercise of power over her sexuality, the repeated acts of sexual violence, and the perpetration of extremely humiliating acts.[15]

4. The case of *Guzman Albarracin et. al.* is emblematic of the recent tendency of the Inter-American Court of Human Rights to focus on human rights violations affecting the rights of girls in particular. In this case, the Court offers a detailed analysis of the widespread exposure of girls to sexual violence and harassment in schools, and how this violence can be perpetrated by figures of authority with power and control over the victims. The Court emphasizes the intricate nature of the obligation to prevent and protect girls from violence in educational institutions, especially those public ones, and in instances in which the state knew of the frequent occurrence of this problem. The Inter-American Court of Human Rights has also ruled on cases in which girl victims of sexual violence and their families have faced significant obstacles to access justice[16] and there are pending cases which offer the opportunity to expand legal developments on behalf of girls and their human rights.[17]

5. The Inter-American Court of Human Rights judgment in the case of *Paola Albarracin v. Ecuador* illustrates a more recent line of cases adopted by the Court delving into issues related to economic, social, and cultural rights; discrimination on the basis of sexual orientation and gender identity; and sexual and reproductive rights. In the case of *Gonzalez Lluy v. Ecuador* – discussed in Chapter 7 – the Court also found the state of Ecuador responsible for violating the rights to education of the child of Talía Gonzales Lluy due to the intersectional discrimination she faced in the education system for living with HIV, as a child, a female, and of low-income status. The Inter-American Court moreover advanced key standards concerning the rights of afro-descendent women and girls to decent, quality, and safe working conditions in the case of the *Workers in the Fireworks Factory in San Antonio de Jesus and their Families v. Brazil*, discussed *supra* in Chapter 9. The Court also

---

[12] *See id.*, ¶¶ 188–209, 338–339, 390 – subset 9.

[13] *See* López Soto et al. v. Venezuela, Merits, Reparations and Costs, Judgment, Inter-Am. Ct. H.R., Series C, No. 362, ¶¶ 1, 172–182 (Sept. 26, 2018).

[14] *Id.*

[15] *Id.*

[16] *See generally* V.R.P., V.P.C. et al. v. Nicaragua, Preliminary Objections, Merits, Reparations and Costs, Judgment, Inter-Am. Ct. H.R., Series C, No. 350 (March 8, 2018).

[17] *See* Equality Now, *The Inter-American Court of Human Rights to hear landmark case on endemic sexual violence of adolescent girls in Bolivia* (Aug. 11, 2020), www.equalitynow.org/inter_american _court_of_human_rights_landmark_case_bolivia (discussing the submission by the Inter-American Commission on Human Rights of the case of Brisa Liliana de Ángulo Lozada related to Bolivia before the Inter-American Court of Human Rights).

offered a very flexible reading to Article 1.1 of the American Convention and its prohibition of discrimination to also include sexual orientation and gender identity in its landmark
case of *Karen Atala and Others*, discussed *supra* in Chapter 4. In the cases of *Artavia
Murillo* and *IV*, as discussed in Chapter 8, the Court also advanced critical analysis related
to the importance of reproductive autonomy, personal liberty, privacy, non-discrimination,
and combatting gender stereotypes in the regulation of assisted reproductive techniques
and the informed consent needed before medical procedures.

6.  An important area of innovation for the Inter-American System in the area of women's
    rights has been in the context of precautionary and provisional measures adopted by both
    the Commission and the Court. Many of these measures have been granted to protect the
    rights to life and personal integrity of women human rights defenders.[18] However, recently
    a number of measures have been issued in the area of sexual and reproductive rights,
    mandating states to adopt urgent steps to provide health services and procedures needed
    by women during their pregnancies, including those related to abortion. For example, in
    the *Matter of B. (El Salvador)*, the Court considered a request for provisional measures in
    which the petitioner was 26 weeks pregnant and had been diagnosed with an anencephalic
    fetus with low survival chances.[19] A medical hospital committee had recommended the
    ending of the pregnancy, but abortion is prohibited in El Salvador in all circumstances.[20]
    Based on these considerations, the Inter-American Court of Human Rights ordered the
    state to guarantee urgently that all medical personnel involved would adopt the necessary
    medical measures to safeguard her rights to life, personal integrity, and health, and avoid
    irreparable damage.[21] According to Article 63(2) of the American Convention and Article
    25 of the Inter-American Commission Rules of Procedure, provisional and precautionary
    measures can be adopted in cases of gravity, urgency, and irreparable damage. Consider
    how the elements of gravity, urgency, and irreparable damage were met in *Matter of B.*

7.  Both the Inter-American Commission and the Court have faced historical problems to ensure
    the representation and selection of women to positions as Commissioners and Judges. OAS
    member states nominate candidates to these positions and the candidates have in general
    been male. It was not until 2018 that the Inter-American Commission on Human Rights
    elected its first composition with a majority of women.[22] The Inter-American Commission
    just elected in 2021 its first leadership board composed of only female Commissioners[23]
    and its first woman Executive Secretary[24] for a number of years. A regional campaign has

---

[18]  For a recent example, see, Inter-American Commission on Human Rights, *IACHR Extends
Precautionary Measures in Favor of 17 Women Human Rights Defenders in Nicaragua* (Dec. 27, 2019),
www.oas.org/en/iachr/media_center/PReleases/2019/338.asp.

[19]  *See* Inter-American Court of Human Rights, Provisional Measures, Matter of B., El Salvador,
Order of the Inter-American Court of Human Rights of May 29, 2013, ¶ 8.

[20]  *Id.*

[21]  *Id.*, ¶¶ 12–16, 17.

[22]  *See* Inter-American Commission on Human Rights, *Composition*, www.oas.org/en/iachr/mandate/
composition.asp (last visited on May 19, 2021).

[23]  *See* Inter-American Commission on Human Rights, *The IACHR Elected its Leadership Board
for 2021* [La CIDH eligió su Junta Directiva para el 2021; translation by the author], www.oas.org/en/
IACHR/jsForm/?File=/es/cidh/prensa/comunicados/2021/073.asp.

[24]  Inter-American Commission on Human Rights, *IACHR selects Tania Reneaum Ponzi for
Executive Secretary* (May 4, 2021), www.oas.org/en/IACHR/jsForm/?File=/en/iachr/media_center/
PReleases/2021/115.asp.

been launched throughout the Americas to promote women holding leadership positions in universal and regional bodies – GQUAL.[25] Can you think of steps that can be adopted to promote more women being nominated as candidates to hold positions as commissioners and judges in the inter-American system of human rights? Why do you think it is important to have women in leadership positions in international bodies?

## III    EUROPEAN SYSTEM OF HUMAN RIGHTS

The heart of the European system of human rights is in the Council of Europe. In 1949, ten European countries adopted the statute of the Council of Europe, which identified human rights, the rule of law, and the pursuit of peace, justice and international cooperation as the key goals since its inception.[26] The leading work of the Council of Europe is done by the European Court of Human Rights, based in Strasbourg, which is a full-time court.[27] The foundational document of the work of the Court is the European Convention on Human Rights, the leading treaty of its kind in Europe, adopted in 1950, which covers a range of civil and political rights in the areas of life; private and family life; the prohibition of torture, inhuman and degrading treatment; equality in access to justice; liberty of expression; and non-derogation, among other areas.[28] All member states of the Council of Europe are state parties to the European Convention on Human Rights.

An important and distinguishing characteristic of the European Court of Human Rights is the ability of individuals to present petitions directly before the Court, which is different from the regional protection system in the Americas. The Court is also permanent, full-time, and better resourced than the courts in the regional protection systems in Africa and the Americas. The European Convention provided for the creation of a Committee of Ministers, which has been an instrumental institution in supervising and promoting the follow-up of judgments of the European Court of Human Rights.[29] The European Court has also had a continued evolution in its methods of work, eliminating the former European Commission on Human Rights through Protocol 11 in 1994 and creating the full-time European Court to address the backlog of individual case petitions and make the system more effective.[30] Protocol 16, which entered into force on August 1, 2018, allows the highest courts of European Convention state parties to request advisory opinions from the European Court of Human Rights on principles relating to the interpretation of the Convention.[31] The Court has also become very well known for its

---

[25]  For more reading on the GQUAL Campaign, *see* GQUAL, About the Campaign, www .gqualcampaign.org/about-gqual/ (last visited on May 19, 2021).

[26]  *See* Statute of Council of Europe, 1949, Articles 1(b) and 3, https://rm.coe.int/1680306052.

[27]  *See generally*, European Court of Human Rights, *Annual Report 2020*, www.echr.coe.int/ Documents/Annual_report_2020_ENG.pdf.

[28]  *See* European Convention for the Protection of Human Rights and Fundamental Freedoms, Arts. 2–15, 54, Nov. 4, 1950, C.E.T.S. No. 5, 213 U.N.T.S. 222, as amended by the provisions of Protocol No. 14. (C.E.T.S. No. 194) as from its entry into force on June 1, 2010 (hereinafter European Convention).

[29]  *See id.,* Article 46.

[30]  *See generally* Protocol 11 to the Convention for the Protection of Human Rights and Fundamental Freedoms, Restructuring the Control Machinery Thereby, 1994, www.echr.coe.int/Documents/Library _Collection_P11_ETS155E_ENG.pdf.

[31]  *See generally* Council of Europe, Protocol No. 16 to the Convention for the Protection of Human Rights and Fundamental Freedoms, No. 214 (2013), https://rm.coe.int/CoERMPublicCommonSearc hServices/DisplayDCTMContent?documentId=0900001680084832.

evolutive interpretation of the European Convention on Human Rights; its doctrine of margin of appreciation considering the legal practices and tendencies in European countries in its rulings; identifying a minimum body of legal standards that European states should respect; and its efforts to advance the rule of law as a priority.

It is important to note that even though the European Union did not have human rights as one of its main objectives, its European Court of Justice has issued a number of rulings related to human rights issues and the European Convention on Human Rights. It has also adopted the Charter of Fundamental Rights of the European Union, which has more extensive coverage of economic, social, and cultural rights.[32]

European countries are currently facing important human rights challenges, which constitute the backdrop for the situation of women and girls in this region. They are grappling with the legacy of the COVID-19 pandemic and engaging in efforts to address nationalist policies, hate speech, and discrimination against racial groups and minorities. Ongoing concerns are the strength and transparency of democratic institutions; challenges to the rule of law and administration of justice; the global migration crisis and the treatment of refugees; and cultural and religious diversity. The European Union has also dealt with the recent exit of the United Kingdom from the EU and the impact of this decision on multilateralism in Europe.

Violence against women and girls in the region continues to be a serious and alarming problem, illustrated by the passage of the Istanbul Convention. The Istanbul Convention, as discussed in Chapter 2, is one of the most detailed and comprehensive treaties prohibiting violence against women, and mandating states to act with due diligence to prevent, investigate, and sanction these acts, with a gender and victim's perspective.

The European Court of Human Rights has issued a number of key judgments in areas concerning gender-based violence, sexual and reproductive rights, and LGBTI rights. This section discusses the case of *MC v. Bulgaria*, about the judicial investigation of cases of rape, followed by reflections and questions of the historical work of the European system of human rights in the area of women.

## A    *MC v. Bulgaria*, European Court of Human Rights

Application No. 39272/98, December 4, 2003
© Council of Europe, reproduced with permission
Citations and footnotes omitted

*The case is related to the rape of a 14-year-old girl, and the consideration of judicial authorities of the elements of force and resistance in the investigation of these acts. In the excerpts below, the European Court of Human Rights considers the elements and circumstances that should be taken into account by justice systems in the investigation of rape cases.*

154.    In respect of the means to ensure adequate protection against rape, States undoubtedly enjoy a wide margin of appreciation. In particular, perceptions of a cultural nature, local circumstances and traditional approaches are to be taken into account.

---

[32]    *See* Charter of Fundamental Rights of the European Union, 2000 O.J. (C 364) 1 (Dec. 7, 2000),

155. The limits of the national authorities' margin of appreciation are nonetheless circumscribed by the Convention provisions. In interpreting them, since the Convention is first and foremost a system for the protection of human rights, the Court must have regard to the changing conditions within Contracting States and respond, for example, to any evolving convergence as to the standards to be achieved.

156. The Court observes that, historically, proof of physical force and physical resistance was required under domestic law and practice in rape cases in a number of countries. The last decades, however, have seen a clear and steady trend in Europe and some other parts of the world towards abandoning formalistic definitions and narrow interpretations of the law in this area.

157. Firstly, it appears that a requirement that the victim must resist physically is no longer present in the statutes of European countries. ...

163. In international criminal law, it has recently been recognised that force is not an element of rape and that taking advantage of coercive circumstances to proceed with sexual acts is also punishable. The International Criminal Tribunal for the former Yugoslavia has found that, in international criminal law, any sexual penetration without the victim's consent constitutes rape and that consent must be given voluntarily, as a result of the person's free will, assessed in the context of the surrounding circumstances. While the above definition was formulated in the particular context of rapes committed against the population in the conditions of an armed conflict, it also reflects a universal trend towards regarding lack of consent as the essential element of rape and sexual abuse.

164. As submitted by the intervener, the evolving understanding of the manner in which rape is experienced by the victim has shown that victims of sexual abuse – in particular, girls below the age of majority – often provide no physical resistance because of a variety of psychological factors or because they fear violence on the part of the perpetrator.

165. Moreover, the development of law and practice in that area reflects the evolution of societies towards effective equality and respect for each individual's sexual autonomy.

166. In the light of the above, the Court is persuaded that any rigid approach to the prosecution of sexual offences, such as requiring proof of physical resistance in all circumstances, risks leaving certain types of rape unpunished and thus jeopardising the effective protection of the individual's sexual autonomy. In accordance with contemporary standards and trends in that area, the member States' positive obligations under Articles 3 and 8 of the Convention must be seen as requiring the penalisation and effective prosecution of any non-consensual sexual act, including in the absence of physical resistance by the victim. ...

175. Turning to the particular facts of the applicant's case, the Court notes that, in the course of the investigation, many witnesses were heard and an expert report by a psychologist and a psychiatrist was ordered. The case was investigated and the prosecutors gave reasoned decisions, explaining their position in some detail.

176. The Court recognises that the Bulgarian authorities faced a difficult task, as they were confronted with two conflicting versions of the events and little "direct" evidence. The Court does not underestimate the efforts made by the investigator and the prosecutors in their work on the case.

177. It notes, nonetheless, that the presence of two irreconcilable versions of the facts obviously called for a context-sensitive assessment of the credibility of the statements made and for verification of all the surrounding circumstances. Little was done, however, to test

the credibility of the version of the events proposed by P. and A. and the witnesses called by them. ...

178.   The Court thus considers that the authorities failed to explore the available possibilities for establishing all the surrounding circumstances and did not assess sufficiently the credibility of the conflicting statements made.

179. It is highly significant that the reason for that failure was, apparently, the investigator's and the prosecutors' opinion that, since what was alleged to have occurred was a "date rape", in the absence of "direct" proof of rape such as traces of violence and resistance or calls for help, they could not infer proof of lack of consent and, therefore, of rape from an assessment of all the surrounding circumstances. ...

180.   Furthermore, it appears that the prosecutors did not exclude the possibility that the applicant might not have consented, but adopted the view that in any event, in the absence of proof of resistance, it could not be concluded that the perpetrators had understood that the applicant had not consented. ...

181.   The Court considers that, while in practice it may sometimes be difficult to prove lack of consent in the absence of "direct" proof of rape, such as traces of violence or direct witnesses, the authorities must nevertheless explore all the facts and decide on the basis of an assessment of all the surrounding circumstances. The investigation and its conclusions must be centred on the issue of non-consent.

182.   That was not done in the applicant's case. The Court finds that the failure of the authorities in the applicant's case to investigate sufficiently the surrounding circumstances was the result of their putting undue emphasis on "direct" proof of rape. Their approach in the particular case was restrictive, practically elevating "resistance" to the status of defining element of the offence. ...

## B    Reflections and Questions

1. *MC v. Bulgaria* is a landmark decision of the European Court of Human Rights regarding the elements that can be considered in a finding of rape in a criminal case. The European Court of Human Rights alludes to the positive obligation that member states of the European Convention on Human Rights have to enact criminal legislation to effectively investigate, prosecute, and sanction cases of rape. There is discussion of the trend in both European countries and international courts to not consider victim resistance or force as elements of the crime. The emphasis should be on lack of consent instead. In this sense, it is key to investigate the circumstances surrounding rape, including in the case of adolescent girls. This all signals a move in international jurisprudence favoring more the autonomy and equality of women and girls, and a more comprehensive understanding of the complexity of rape. The Court also illustrates the importance of state practices, international tendencies, and the need to consider changing conditions when analyzing and applying the margin of appreciation doctrine. The European Court of Human Rights in this case found violations of Articles 3 and 8 of the European Convention on Human Rights. It did decide not to examine the complaint under Article 14 of the European Convention on Human Rights and its prohibition of discrimination. The chapters in this book have discussed the intricate link between gender-based violence and discrimination against women. In your view, was it necessary to rule this case also applying the right to non-discrimination under

Article 14 of the ECHR? Do you think this case should have been examined under the due diligence standard, as in the *Maria da Penha* case discussed *supra*?

2. Domestic violence has been an important area of jurisprudence adopted by the European Court of Human Rights. The Court has underscored in several cases the duty of states to act with due diligence to protect women and children who suffer these acts, and adopt steps to prevent, investigate, and sanction domestic violence. The obligation of prevention is particularly key when authorities knew that the women and children at issue had already faced attacks and threats from the aggressor.[33] The European Court of Human Rights has interpreted this obligation to prevent acts of domestic violence of broad scope and relevant even when the victims involved have withdrawn their complaints.[34] Ongoing and continuing acts of domestic violence may amount to violations of the rights to life, to privacy, and to the prohibition of ill-treatment and torture under the European Convention on Human Rights.[35] They can also constitute a form of discrimination.[36] In the leading case of *Opuz v. Turkey* in particular – discussed in Chapter 6 *supra* – the European Court of Human Rights referred expressly to the obligation to act with due diligence and its development in the inter-American system of human rights.[37]

3. The analysis of the European Court of Human Rights under the prohibition of non-discrimination under Article 14 has been limited, due to the ancillary and complementary nature of the clause with other Articles in the Convention.[38] Differently from the inter-American system of human rights, many of the cases related to discrimination on the basis of sex and gender equality adopted by the European Court of Human Rights have lacked an extensive analysis under Article 14 of the European Convention. Some important exceptions are the recent cases of *Carvalho Pinto de Sousa Mourais v. Portugal* and *Konstantin Markin v. Russia*, discussed *supra* in Chapter 7, which do hold states responsible for different treatment on the basis of sex under Article 14 in connection with Article 8 of the European Convention. Protocol 12 was adopted in 2000 to offer states an opportunity to assume more comprehensive obligations under the European Convention on Human Rights in the area of non-discrimination.[39] Article 1 of the Protocol extends the prohibition of discrimination to and an autonomous right not to be discriminated against under the European Convention.[40] The European Court of Human Rights first ruled on a case applying Article 1 of Protocol 12 in *Sejdić and Finci v. Bosnia and Herzegovina*.[41]

---

[33] For example, *see* Talpis v. Italy, App. No. 41237/14, Eur. Ct. H.R., ¶¶ 95-125, (2017); Kontrová v. Slovakia, App. No. 7510/04, Eur. Ct. H.R., ¶¶ 46-55 (2007).

[34] *See* Opuz v. Turkey, App. No. 33401/02, Eur. Ct. H.R., ¶¶ 128–153 (2009).

[35] *See id.*

[36] *See id.*, ¶¶ 177–202.

[37] *See id.*, ¶¶ 83–86.

[38] For background reading on the nature of Article 14 of the European Convention on Human Rights, *see* European Court of Human Rights, *Guide on Article 14 of the European Convention on Human Rights and on Article 1 of Protocol No. 12 to the Convention*, pp. 6–9 (updated on Dec. 30, 2020), www.echr.coe.int/Documents/Guide_Art_14_Art_1_Protocol_12_ENG.pdf.

[39] *See* Council of Europe, Protocol 12 to the Convention for the Protection of Human Rights and Fundamental Freedoms, European Treaty Series, No. 177, 2000.

[40] *See id.*, Articles 1 and 2.

[41] *See* Sejdić and Finci v. Bosnia and Herzegovina, App. Nos. 27996/06 and 34836/06, Eur. Ct. H.R., ¶¶ 38–56 (Dec. 22, 2009).

In this case, the European Court of Human Rights found Bosnia and Herzegovina responsible under Article 14 of the European Convention and Article 1 of Protocol 12 for racial discrimination when the applicants were ineligible to stand for election to the House of Peoples and the Presidency on the basis of their Roma and Jewish origins.[42]

4. Historically the European Court of Human Rights has not adopted many Advisory Opinions. The Council of Europe adopted Protocol No. 16 to the European Convention in 2013, offering high domestic courts the opportunity to request advisory opinions from the European Court on legal questions related to the interpretation of the Convention.[43] The first advisory opinion decided by the European Court of Human Rights was requested by the French Court of Cassation and considered the parental rights, under French law, of intended mothers to children born abroad through a surrogacy arrangement.[44] In its decision of April 10, 2019, the European Court established that intended mothers, whether biological or not, should have the possibility of securing legal recognition in France of their relationship with the child when the intended (and biological) father has been legally recognized, and where the intended mother is identified as the legal mother in the foreign birth certificate. This is different from the Inter-American Court of Human Rights, which has used its advisory opinion competency extensively, especially to discuss legal matters which may be the object of division, polarization, or controversy in the Americas region.[45] Can you see a benefit in developing legal standards by the European Court of Human Rights through the issuance of Advisory Opinions, as opposed to individual case applications? How can both mechanisms complement each other to advance the human rights of women in member states of the Council of Europe?

5. One of the most important doctrines applied by the European Court of Human Rights has been that of margin of appreciation, affording states the discretion to adopt measures destined to comply with the European Convention. When ruling on matters related to the human rights of women and other areas, the Court typically will look at the practices of European states to determine whether there is a consensus or divergence in the applicable law. In a way, the application of the doctrine calls for a close relationship with Council of Europe states and their institutions, and respect for national practices. The broad or narrow margin of appreciation will depend on the subject matter reviewed by the European Court of Human Rights. For example, issues related to the protection of life, torture, and the prohibition of non-discrimination tend to have a more limited margin of appreciation.[46] An interesting line of cases to study from the Court is that related to sexual and reproductive

---

[42]   *Id.*

[43]   *See* Council of Europe, Protocol No. 16, *supra* note 31.

[44]   *See Advisory opinion concerning the recognition in domestic law of a legal parent–child relationship between a child born through a gestational surrogacy arrangement abroad and the intended mother*, requested by the French Court of Cassation, Eur. Ct. H.R. [GC], Request No. P16-2018-001, ¶¶ 35–59 (April 10, 2019).

[45]   For a comprehensive discussion of the Advisory Opinions practice of the Inter-American Court of Human Rights, *see generally* Thomas Buergenthal, *The Advisory Practice of the Inter-American Human Rights Court*, 79(1) Am. J. Int'l L. 1–27 (1985). For recent examples of Advisory Opinions adopted by the Inter-American Court of Human Rights, see *Advisory Opinions*, www.corteidh.or.cr/opiniones _consultivas.cfm?lang=en (last visited on May 19, 2021).

[46]   For an overview of the use, benefits, and limitations of the margin of appreciation doctrine by the European Court of Human Rights, *see* Janneke Gerards, *Margin of Appreciation and Incrementalism*

rights, in which the margin of appreciation has been interpreted as broad in cases related to the regulation of abortion,[47] and narrow in cases related to access to information connected to sexual and reproductive rights services, sexual orientation, and gender identity.[48] The American and African regional human rights protection systems do not apply the margin of appreciation doctrine in their rulings, affording very limited deference to national practices, and heavy consideration to universal standards. What do you think are the pros and cons of applying the margin of appreciation doctrine in cases related to the human rights of women and girls?

6. As discussed earlier, an important feature of the European Court of Human Rights is the ability of any person, non-governmental organization, or group of individuals to present applications directly before the Court alleging violations of the European Convention on Human Rights.[49] This is different from the regional human rights protection systems in the Americas, in which petitions need to be presented first before the Inter-American Commission. Can you think of advantages and disadvantages of having direct access to a human rights court?

7. Even though the European Court of Justice in the European Union is not a human rights court, it does review human rights matters and issues concerning women. For example, in the case of *Pensionsversicherungsanstalt v. Kleist*,[50] adopted by the European Court of Justice in 2010, the European Court examined the legality of a termination policy which affected a woman employed as a chief physician for the pension insurance institution. Mrs. Kleist was terminated pursuant to a policy by the pension insurance institution applying to all employees, whether female or male, upon reaching their retirement age. The applicant argued that the termination policy was discriminatory because it mandated women to retire five years earlier than their male counterparts, when women had the right to draw their pensions.[51] After finishing the domestic proceedings, the Austrian Supreme Court referred the case to the European Court of Justice with the question of whether the policy discriminated on the basis of sex. The European Court of Justice held that the policy directly discriminated on the basis of sex, which could not be justified by the objective of promoting the employment of younger persons.[52] The Court interpreted in particular Council Directive 76/207/EEC of February 9, 1976 (as amended), related to the implementation of the principle of equal treatment for men and women regarding access to employment, vocational training and promotion, and working conditions.[53]

---

*in the Case Law of the European Court of Human Rights*, 18 HUMAN RIGHTS LAW REVIEW 495–515, 495–506 (2018).

[47]   *See for example* A, B, C v. Ireland, App. No. 25579/05, Eur. Ct. H.R., ¶¶ 229–241 (Dec. 10, 2010); VO v. France, App. No. 53924/00, Eur. Ct. H.R., ¶¶ 81–95 (July 8, 2004).

[48]   *See for example* P. and S. v. Poland, App. No. 57375/08, ¶¶ 128–137 (Oct. 30, 2012); A.P. Garcon and Nicot v. France, App. Nos. 79885/12/52471/13 and 52596/13, ¶¶ 92–135 (April 6, 2017).

[49]   *See* European Convention for the Protection of Human Rights and Fundamental Freedoms, *supra* note 28, Article 24.

[50]   *See* European Court of Justice, Pensionsversicherungsanstalt v. Kleist (2010), https://curia.europa.eu/juris/document/document.jsf?docid=83840&doclang=EN.

[51]   *See id.*, ¶¶ 3–18.

[52]   *See id.*, ¶¶ 19–46.

[53]   *See id.*, ¶¶ 1 and 3.

# IV   AFRICAN SYSTEM OF HUMAN RIGHTS

An important multilateral effort from Africa connected to its human rights approach was the former Organization of African Unity (hereinafter "OAU"). The OAU was established on May 25, 1963, to promote unity and solidarity among African states, to address colonization, and to safeguard the sovereignty and integrity of member states. An OAU Charter was adopted upholding the doctrine of non-interference with independent states and respect for territorial integrity. The OAU strengthened the regional cooperation and discussion among African states related to human rights issues, but did not create a human rights enforcement mechanism.

The OAU was eventually replaced by the African Union on September 9, 1999, which was created to address the continent's ongoing social, economic, and political problems.[54] It also advanced stronger human rights language and the need to consolidate democratic institutions and culture in its Constitutive Act.[55] The AU has 55 member states and among its goals are to further the strong link between democracy and human rights protection, and to prevent unconstitutional changes in government propelled by dictatorships, ongoing conflicts, and military coups d'état.

The African Charter on Human and Peoples' Rights (hereinafter "African Charter") was adopted under the OAU in 1981, reflecting in its dispositions the importance of civil, political, economic, social, and cultural rights for African countries and their connection with freedom, equality, justice, and dignity.[56] As discussed earlier in this book, the African Charter is one of the leading treaties in the world on the issue of collective and peoples' rights advancing an understanding of human rights that reaches beyond the individual. The African Charter provided for the creation of an African Commission on Human and Peoples' Rights, based in Banjul, Gambia, with the goals of protecting and promoting human and peoples' rights, and interpreting the scope of the African Charter.[57] An African Court on Human and Peoples' Rights was also established by means of a Protocol to the African Charter on Human and Peoples' Rights and it is based in Arusha, Tanzania.[58]

Both the African Commission and the African Court of Human Rights have made important statements related to the rights of women which will be discussed in this section. A cornerstone treaty and basis has been the Maputo Protocol, discussed *supra* in Chapter 2, advancing the recognition of an extensive range of human rights for women in Africa, including the rights to dignity and peace, the overall prohibition of harmful practices, and the recognition of a range of civil, political, economic, social, and cultural rights.

This chapter discusses these legal developments as well as complex issues affecting the African system of human rights today.

---

[54]   *See* About the African Union, https://au.int/en/overview (last visited on May 19, 2021).

[55]   *See* African Union, *Constitutive Act*, Preamble, Article 3(h) and Article 4 (l)–(n), https://au.int/sites/default/files/pages/34873-file-constitutiveact_en.pdf.

[56]   *See* African Charter on Human and Peoples' Rights, adopted June 27, 1981, OAU Doc. CAB/LEG/67/3 rev. 5, 21 I.L.M. 58 (1982), entered into force Oct. 21, 1986, Articles 2–24.

[57]   *Id.*, Articles 30–58.

[58]   Protocol to the African Charter on Human and Peoples' Rights on the Establishment of an African Court on Human and Peoples' Rights, https://au.int/sites/default/files/treaties/36393-treaty-0019_-_protocol_to_the_african_charter_on_human_and_peoplesrights_on_the_establishment_of_an_african_court_on_human_and_peoples_rights_e.pdf.

A       **General Comment No. 2 on Article 14.1.a), (b), (c), and (f) and Article 14.2.a) and (c) of the Protocol to the African Charter on Human and Peoples' Rights on the Rights of Women in Africa**

African Commission on Human and Peoples' Rights

**Introduction**

1. The Treaty Monitoring Bodies around human rights-related conventions generally use General Comments as a tool for the interpretation and development of the provisions of relevant international legal instruments so as to guide the States in implementing their obligations. The jurisdiction of the African Commission on Human and Peoples' rights (the Commission) results from Article 45.1.b) of the African Charter on Human and Peoples' rights (African Charter), which entitles it to "formulate and develop rules and principles that address legal problems regarding the enjoyment of human and peoples' rights." As a legal instrument complementary to the African Charter, the Protocol to the African Charter on Human and Peoples' Rights on the Rights of Women in Africa (the Protocol) also falls under the Commission's interpretative jurisdiction. …

3. Aware of its commitment to promote gender equality and the need to eliminate all forms of discrimination against women, the African Union adopted the Protocol in 2003. For purposes of this instrument, which entered into force in 2005, "women" is understood as persons of female sex including girls, including women and girls living with a disability. …

19. Only a very low percentage of abortions practiced in Africa are safely conducted. As a result of this state of facts, unsafe abortions remain a factor in preventable maternal mortality. Furthermore, they are for women who undergo them a persistent disability factor which is often not listed as such. It has been demonstrated that in a context where national laws allow therapeutic abortion when it proves necessary, and where health services are available, accessible, acceptable and of good quality, the prevalence as well as the complications arising from unsafe abortions are generally lower than in countries where the legal conditions for abortion are restricted.

20. The Protocol puts on State parties the obligation to protect women's reproductive rights, particularly by authorizing safe abortion in the cases listed in Article 14.2.c). In addition, the Maputo Plan of Action urges Governments to adopt legal policies and frameworks so as to reduce cases of unsafe abortion, as well as to develop and implement national action plans in order to mitigate the prevalence of unintended pregnancies and unsafe abortions. …

23. The rights to exercise control over one's fertility, to decide one's maternity, the number of children and the spacing of births, and to choose a contraception method are inextricably linked, interdependent and indivisible.

24. The right to dignity enshrines the freedom to make personal decisions without interference from the State or non-State actors. The woman's right to make personal decisions involves taking into account or not the beliefs, traditions, values and cultural or religious practices, and the right to question or to ignore them.

25. The right to health care without discrimination requires State parties to remove impediments to the health services reserved for women, including ideology or belief-based barri-

ers. Administrative laws, policies and procedures of health systems and structures cannot restrict access to family planning/contraception on the basis of religious beliefs.

26. The right to freedom from being subjected to discrimination prohibits any deprivation concerning access to family planning/contraception services by health care providers for reasons of conscientious objection. While it is true that they may invoke conscientious objection to the direct provision of the required services, State parties must ensure that the necessary infrastructure is set up to enable women to be knowledgeable and referred to other health care providers on time. …

27. Administrative laws, policies, procedures and practices, as well as socio-cultural attitudes and standards that impede access to contraception/family planning violate the woman's right to life, non-discrimination and health, in that they deprive her of her decision-making power and force her to undergo early pregnancy, unsafe or unwanted pregnancy, with as consequence, the temptation to seek unsafe [abortion] at the risk of her health and her life. …

41. Article 14.1. a), b), c) and f) and Article and (c) impose four general obligations on State parties, like several provisions on human rights: respect, protect, promote and fulfill rights thereof.

42. The obligation to respect rights requires State parties to refrain from hindering, directly or indirectly, women's rights and to ensure that women are duly informed on family planning/contraception and safe abortion services, which should be available, accessible, acceptable and of good quality.

43. The obligation to protect requires State parties to take the necessary measures to prevent third parties from interfering with the enjoyment of women's sexual and reproductive rights. Particular attention must be given to prevention, as regards the interference of third parties concerning the rights of vulnerable groups such as adolescent girls, women living with disabilities, women living with HIV and women in situations of conflict. The obligation entails the formulation of standards and guidelines containing the precision that the consent and involvement of third parties, including but [not] limited to, parents, guardians, spouses and partners, is not required when adult women and adolescent girls want to access family planning/contraception and safe abortion services in the cases provided for in the Protocol.

44. The obligation to promote obliges State parties to create the legal, economic and social conditions that enable women to exercise their sexual and reproductive rights with regard to family planning/contraception and safe abortion, as well as to enjoy them. An essential step towards eliminating stigmatization and discrimination related to reproductive health includes, but is not limited to, supporting women's empowerment, sensitizing and educating communities, religious leaders, traditional chiefs and political leaders on women's sexual and reproductive rights as well as training health-care workers.

45. The obligation to fulfil rights requires that State Parties adopt relevant laws, policies and programs that ensure the fulfilment de jure and de facto of women's sexual and reproductive rights, including the allocation of sufficient and available resources for the full realization of those rights. …

**B**     *APDF and IHRDA v. Republic of Mali*, **African Court of Human Rights**

Application No. 046/2016
Judgment, May 11, 2018

*The applicants in this case alleged that the Family Code in Mali violated the Maputo Protocol and CEDAW regarding the minimum age and consent to marry, inheritance, and harmful practices. The following excerpts include the African Court's analysis of the allegations concerning child marriage and consent to marry.*

71. Article 2 of the Children's Charter defines a child as "every human being below the age of 18 years".
72. Article 4(1) stipulates that "In all actions concerning the child undertaken by any person or authority the best interests of the child shall be the primary consideration."
73. Article 21 of the same Charter stipulates that: "State parties ... shall take all appropriate measures to eliminate harmful social and cultural practices ... and those customs and practices discriminatory to the child on the grounds of sex or other status."
74. Article 6(b) of the Maputo Protocol provides that: "states Parties shall ensure that women and men enjoy equal rights and are regarded as equal partners in marriage. They shall enact appropriate national legislative measures to guarantee that: b) the minimum age of marriage for women shall be 18 years. ..."
75. The Court notes that the afore-mentioned provisions focus on the obligation for States to take all appropriate measures to abolish negative practices and customs as well as practices discriminatory to children born out of wedlock for reasons of their gender, especially measures to guarantee the minimum age for marriage at 18 years. ...
77. The Court also notes that Article 281 of the impugned Family Code effectively sets the marriage age at 18 for men and 16 for women. Furthermore, the Article also includes the possibility for the administrative authorities to grant special exemption for girls to be married at 15 years for "compelling reasons".
78. The Court holds in conclusion that it lies with the Respondent State to guarantee compliance with the minimum age of marriage, which is 18 years, and the right to non-discrimination; that having failed to do so, the Respondent State has violated Article 6(b) of the Maputo Protocol and Articles 2, 4(1) and 21 of the Children's Charter. ...
89. Article 6(a) of the Maputo Protocol stipulates that: "states parties shall ensure that women and men enjoy equal rights and are regarded as equal partners in marriage. They shall enact appropriate national legislative measures to guarantee that: a) no marriage shall take place without the free and full consent of both parties."
90. The Court notes that the Maputo Protocol in its Articles 2(1)(a) and 6 and CEDAW in its Articles 10 and 16 set down the principles of free consent in marriage.
91. The Court also notes that despite the fact that the said instruments are ratified by Mali, the extant Family Code envisages the application of Islamic law (Article 751) and entitles religious ministers to celebrate marriages, but does not require them to verify the free consent of the parties.
92. Furthermore, while sanctions are prescribed against the civil status officer for non-verification of the consent of the parties, no sanction is provided against a religious

minister who does not comply with this obligation. Verification of consent given orally and in person is required before the civil status officer in accordance with Article 287 of the Family Code, whereas this obligation to verify is not required of a religious minister. …

94. The Court further notes that the way in which a religious marriage takes place in Mali poses serious risks that may lead to forced marriages and perpetuate traditional practices that violate international standards which define the precise conditions regarding age of marriage and consent of the parties, for a marriage to be valid.

95. The Court notes that, in the procedure for celebration of marriage, the impugned law allows for the application of religious and customary laws on the consent to marriage. It also allows for different marriage regimes depending on whether it is celebrated by a civil officer or a religious minister – practices not consistent with international instruments, namely: the Maputo Protocol and CEDAW.

## C    Reflections and Questions

1. General Comment 2 is an example of the use of the competency of the African Commission on Human and Peoples' Rights to interpret the content of the African regional treaties. In General Comment 2, the African Commission underscores the important nature of the Maputo Protocol for the advancement of women's rights in Africa and its authorization of safe and therapeutic abortions under Article 14.2).c). The General Comment also advances groundbreaking analysis related to the rights of women, including a more solid connection between dignity and the fulfillment of sexual and reproductive rights; the need to address traditions, values, and cultural practices to promote full compliance with these rights; and the specific identification of third parties as perpetrators, including parents, guardians, spouses and partners.[59] However, the interpretation of the Maputo Protocol is not always in harmony with universal standards. For example, in paragraph 3, the African Commission defines "women" as only comprehending women and girls. This can be understood to exclude lesbian, bisexual, transgender, and intersex women, which have been recognized by the CEDAW Committee as included in the prohibition of discrimination on the basis of sex by the CEDAW Committee.[60]

2. The *APDF and IHRDA v. Republic of Mali* decision is the first one adopted by the African Court of Human Rights on issues concerning women. It contains important analysis related to the provisions governing child marriage and consent to marriage in the Maputo Protocol and other African treaties. The decision is an important step forward in the work of the African Court of Human Rights. The Court has also adopted recent groundbreaking case rulings, covering issues such as the prohibition of the death penalty – *Ally Rajabu v. Tanzania*[61] – and the rights of indigenous peoples – *African Commission on Human*

---

[59]    *See* African Commission on Human and Peoples' Rights, General Comment 2, *supra*, ¶¶ 19–20, 24 and 43.

[60]    *See* General Recommendation No. 28 on the Core Obligations of States Parties under Article 2 of the Convention on the Elimination of All Forms of Discrimination against Women, Committee on the Elimination of Discrimination against Women, 47th Sess., U.N. Doc. C/2010/47/GC.2 (Oct. 19, 2010), ¶ 18.

[61]    *See for reference*, African Court of Human Rights, Ally Rajabu and Others v. Tanzania, App. No. 007 12015, Judgment (Nov. 28, 2019), www.african-court.org/cpmt/storage/app/uploads/public/5f5/ 63d/f99/5f563df99fbc7507699184.pdf.

*and Peoples' Rights v. Republic of Kenya.*[62] However, it is of great concern that only 30 states which belong to the African Union have ratified the Protocol establishing the Court and only a small fraction of these recognize the competency of the Court to receive cases directly from NGOs and individuals.[63] Important states like Tanzania, Côte d'Ivoire, and Benin withdrew their declarations recognizing the competency of the African Court in 2019 and 2020, and Rwanda in 2016.[64] Amnesty International has referred to the lack of cooperation between states; to the continued political pressure from them towards the African system bodies; and the need to take steps to reduce their backlog as important barriers to the effectiveness of the African Court and the other mechanisms of the African system of human rights.[65]

3. The African Commission on Human and Peoples' Rights is the quasi-judicial organ of the African system of human rights, containing 11 elected member commissioners. The African Commission has available a number of important mechanisms with potential for the advancement of the human rights of women, including Special Rapporteurs on women, extrajudicial executions, freedom of expression, human rights defenders, prison conditions, refugees and those internally displaced. The Africa Commission also has working groups on indigenous peoples; economic, social, and cultural rights; and the death penalty. The African Commission can also receive and examine state party reports, communications, conduct on-site visits, and adopt General Comments containing interpretive guidance on the specific obligations of state parties in the implementation of the African regional human rights treaties, including the Maputo Protocol.[66]

4. The African Charter emphasizes both the individual and collective dimensions of the rights of women. Individual rights usually refer to the impacts and effects of human rights violations in the dignity, identity, and life plans of individual persons. Collective rights usually refer to the interdependence and interconnectedness of human persons, their communities, and societies, and how human rights violations have effects not only on individuals, but on the groups and peoples they belong to. Is a collective rights approach favorable to the advancement of the human rights of women? Can you think of instances in which individual and collective rights cannot be reconciled and may be in conflict?

---

[62] *See for reference*, African Court of Human Rights, African Commission on Human and Peoples' Rights v. Republic of Kenya, App. No. 006/2012 (May 26, 2017), www.african-court.org/en/images/Cases/Judgment/Application%20006-2012%20-%20African%20Commission%20on%20Human%20and%20Peoples%E2%80%99%20Rights%20v.%20the%20Republic%20of%20Kenya..pdf.

[63] List of Signatures, Ratifications, and Accessions, *Protocol on the Establishment of an African Court on Human and Peoples' Rights*, https://au.int/sites/default/files/treaties/36393-sl-protocol_to_the_african_charter_on_human_and_peoplesrights_on_the_estab.pdf (last visited on May 19, 2021).

[64] For more reading, *see* Nicole de Silva and Micha Plagis, *A Court in Crisis: African States' Increasing Resistance to Africa's Human Rights Court*, OpinioJuris (May 19, 2020), https://opiniojuris.org/2020/05/19/a-court-in-crisis-african-states-increasing-resistance-to-africas-human-rights-court/.

[65] AMNESTY INTERNATIONAL, *Executive Summary*, *in* THE STATE OF AFRICAN REGIONAL HUMAN RIGHTS BODIES AND MECHANISMS 41–42, 51 (2019–2020), www.amnesty.org/en/documents/afr01/3089/2020/en/.

[66] For more reading on the work of the African Commission on Human and Peoples' Rights on the rights of women, *see* AFRICAN UNION COMMISSION, UN HIGH COMMISSIONER FOR HUMAN RIGHTS, AND UN WOMEN, WOMEN'S RIGHTS IN AFRICA, 11–13, 46, 49–50, 52, 54–55 (2016), https://au.int/sites/default/files/newsevents/workingdocuments/32590-wd-womensrightsinafrica_singlepages-1.pdf.

**D        Practical exercise: Democracy and human rights**

As discussed previously, the African Union has advanced in its work a strong link between the consolidation of democracy and human rights protection. Contemplate the following questions regarding this connection:

- Are you in agreement with the link between democracy and human rights protection?
- Can there be human rights protection in other types of government regimes?
- Does a democracy always guarantee the protection of human rights?
- Are all democracies the same?
- Is democracy a precondition for the protection of women's and girls' rights?
- How can a democracy be truly inclusive and participatory?

# V        OTHER REGIONAL HUMAN RIGHTS APPROACHES

Even though the Americas, Europe, and Africa have the most formal regional human rights protection systems, other regions of the world have adopted important instruments and institutions which could be promising for the future for the advancement of the rights of women.

In the case of Asia, there is an emerging regional human rights protection system, developed under ASEAN (Association of Southeast Asian Nations), which was formed on August 8, 1967, as a forum of cooperation on matters of peace, stability, progress, and prosperity in the region.[67] ASEAN member states have undertaken common efforts to attain economic growth and political cooperation, and adopted a number of declarations identifying a set of common values. The principles of sovereignty, equality, territorial integrity, non-interference, consensus, and unity in diversity are part of the ASEAN constituting Charter.[68] After the Twenty-Sixth ASEAN Ministerial Meeting in Singapore on July 23–24, 1993, ASEAN member states identified the need for a common approach to human rights from ASEAN countries.[69]

Important steps to developing a common approach were the creation of the ASEAN Intergovernmental Commission on Human Rights[70] on October 23, 2009, and the adoption of an ASEAN Human Rights Declaration[71] on November 18, 2012. The ASEAN Declaration reaffirms the respect, promotion, and protection of human rights, and recognizes many civil, political, economic, social, and cultural rights contained in the international covenants.[72] It is important to note that the work of ASEAN in the area of human rights has been mostly oriented towards promotion, and does not include the establishment of protection mechanisms or an individual case petition system. Important historical issues that have impeded Asia from developing a more consolidated system have been the more limited history of regional cooperation; the emphasis on non-interference and sovereignty; and the vast diversity of

---

[67]    *See* About ASEAN, https://asean.org/asean/about-asean/ (last visited on May 19, 2021).

[68]    *See* ASEAN Charter, Preamble and Articles 1–5, www.aseankorea.org/files/upload/pdf/asean _charter10.pdf.

[69]    *See* 1993 Joint Communique of the 26th ASEAN Ministerial Meeting, July 24, 1993, ¶¶ 16–18, https://cil.nus.edu.sg/wp-content/uploads/formidable/18/1993-26th-AMMJC.pdf.

[70]    *See* About AICHR, https://aichr.org/about-aichr-2/ (last visited on May 19, 2021).

[71]    *See* ASEAN Human Rights Declaration, November 18, 2012, https://asean.org/asean-human -rights-declaration/.

[72]    *See id.*, points 10–38.

languages, cultures, legal systems, and religious traditions in the region.[73] Most countries in Asia, however, have ratified CEDAW and the Convention on the Rights of the Child, which are reflected in the declarations discussed in this section.

It is important to mention also the taking of a number of steps by countries in the Middle East under the Arab League to develop a common regional approach to human rights.[74] A key moment was the adoption of an Arab Charter on Human Rights in 1994, which was later revised in 2004, and recognizes a range of civil, political, economic, social, and cultural rights.[75] This effort has been complemented by the creation of an Arab Commission on Human Rights[76] and an Arab Human Rights Committee.[77]

As an example, this section discusses an important declaration adopted by ASEAN related to violence against women, and then presents reflections and questions on the potential implications of these emerging regional approaches for the rights of women.

A      Declaration on the Elimination of Violence against Women in the ASEAN Region

June 13, 2014

**RECALLING** the Declaration on the Elimination of Violence against Women adopted by the United Nations General Assembly in its Resolution 48/104 of 20 December 1993, and the Convention on the Elimination of all Forms of Discrimination against Women;

**CONCERNED** that violence against women is an obstacle to the achievement of equality, development and peace, as embodied in the Beijing Declaration and Platform for Action adopted in September 1995 by the Fourth World Conference on Women and reiterated in the twenty-third special session of the General Assembly, entitled "Women 2000: Gender Equality, Development and Peace for the 21st Century";

**DESIRING** to intensify the aims and purposes of the ASEAN Declaration (Bangkok Declaration) of 1967, the Declaration of ASEAN Concord of 1976, the Manila Declaration of 1987, the Declaration of the Advancement of Women in the ASEAN Region of 1988 and the Ha Noi Plan of Action of 1998;

**RECOGNISING** that violence against women both violates and impairs their human rights and fundamental freedoms, limits their access to and control of resources and activities, and impedes the full development of their potential;

DO HEREBY DECLARE THAT:

---

[73]   For more reading, *see generally* Mathew Davies, *The ASEAN Synthesis: Human Rights, Non-Intervention, and the ASEAN Human Rights Declaration*, 14 Geo. J. Int'l Aff. 51 (2013).

[74]   For an overview of the history and challenges of the Arab human rights system and a comparison with the other regional human rights protection systems, *see* Armis Sadri, *The Arab Human Rights System: Achievements and Challenges*, 23(7) Int. J. Hum. Rights 1166–1182, 1168–1175 (2019).

[75]   *See* League of Arab States, Arab Charter on Human Rights (May 22, 2004), https://digitallibrary .un.org/record/551368?ln=en.

[76]   For more general information, *see* Arab Commission on Human Rights, http://achr.eu/old/newa0 .htm.

[77]   For examples of the work of the Arab Human Rights Committee, *see* Rawa Ghazy Almakky, *Regionalization of Human Rights: A Critique of the Arab Human Rights Committee*, 1 Asian Y.B. Hum. Rts. & Human. L. 222, 223–224, 232–239 (2017).

In the context of strengthening regional cooperation, collaboration and coordination for the purpose of eliminating violence against women in the region, each Member Country, either individually or collectively, in ASEAN shall endeavour to fully implement the goals and commitments made related to eliminating violence against women and monitor their progress as follows:

1. To encourage greater regional and bilateral cooperation in the systematic research, collection, analysis and dissemination of data, including disaggregated by sex, age, and other relevant information, on the extent, nature and consequences of violence against women and girls, and on the impact and effectiveness of policies and programmes for combating violence against women;

2. To promote an integrated and holistic approach to eliminate violence against women by formulating mechanisms focusing on the four areas of concerns of violence against women, namely, providing services to fulfill the needs of survivors, formulating and taking appropriate responses to offenders and perpetrators, understanding the nature and causes of violence against women and changing societal attitudes and behaviour;

3. To encourage gender mainstreaming to eliminate all forms of violence against women through policies and programmes as well as systems, procedures and processes;

4. To enact and, where necessary, reinforce or amend domestic legislation to prevent violence against women, to enhance the protection, healing, recovery and reintegration of victims/survivors, including measures to investigate, prosecute, punish and where appropriate rehabilitate perpetrators, and prevent re-victimization of women and girls subjected to any form of violence, whether in the home, the workplace, the community or society or in custody;

5. To take all necessary measures to eliminate all forms of discrimination against women and to empower women and strengthen their economic independence and to protect and promote the full enjoyment of all human rights and fundamental freedoms in order to allow women and girls to protect themselves against violence;

6. To intensify efforts to develop and/or improve existing legislative, educational, social measures and support services aimed at the prevention of violence against women, including adoption and monitoring the implementation of laws, the dissemination of information, active involvement with community-based players, and the training of legal, judicial, enforcement officers, social workers and health personnel;

7. To strengthen collaboration between and among countries, through bilateral, regional and international cooperation for resource mobilisation and technical exchange programmes, including sharing of best practices and experience in raising awareness, developing advocacy programmes on preventing and tackling violence against women;

8. To support initiatives undertaken by women's organisations and non-governmental and community-based organisations on the elimination of violence against women and to establish and/or strengthen networking as well as collaborative relationships with these organisations, and with public and private sector institutions.

**B        Reflections and Questions**

1. In the context of ASEAN, one of the human rights situations with the most global attention at the moment concerns the Rohingya Muslim minority in Myanmar, which is a Buddhist-majority country. The Rohingya have been identified by the United Nations as one of the most discriminated-against ethnic groups in the world.[78] They have been subjected to deadly armed attacks by the government and its forces; the burning and destruction of their villages and homes; the widespread rape of women and girls; forms of sexual and gender-based violence; and forced displacement.[79] All these actions have been called a form of genocide, war crimes, and crimes against humanity by several entities.[80] A massive number of refugees have fled to Bangladesh and other countries.[81] On January 23, 2020, the International Court of Justice ordered Myanmar to protect Rohingya Muslims from military violence and genocide.[82] Myanmar is part of ASEAN. If the ASEAN Human Rights Commission had an individual case petition system, how could a case related to the human rights violations perpetrated against the Rohingya by Myanmar be presented? Which human rights would you invoke? What would be the main human rights violations alleged for the acts of rape, sexual violence, and gender-based violence that are occurring? Would having a regional treaty make a difference to your allegations?

2. The Arab Charter on Human Rights has been criticized since its first adoption in 1994 for failing to conform to universal human rights standards.[83] It was revised in 2004, but its language still raises concerns over its masculine approach; the recognition of Islam as the only religion; its consideration of Zionism as a form of racism and discrimination; its conservative stance on equality within the family and its definition of a family as only between men and women; the limited scope of its prohibition of violence against women and children; the application of the death penalty to children; and its treatment of

---

[78]    *See* United Nations, *Rohingya cannot become "forgotten victims," says UN chief urging world to step up support* (July 11, 2018), https://news.un.org/en/story/2018/07/1014421.

[79]    *See* United Nations High Commissioner for Human Rights (OHCHR), *Report on the Situation of Human Rights of Rohingya Muslim minority and other minorities in Myanmar*, A/HRC/43/18 (Jan. 27, 2020), ¶¶ 4–24; United Nations, *Detailed Findings of the Independent International Fact-Finding Mission on Myanmar*, U.N. Doc. A/HRC/42/CRP.5, 16 September 2019, ¶¶ 107–140, 156–170, 176–180, 481–519, 528–534.

[80]    *See* OHCHR, *Report on the Situation of Human Rights of Rohingya Muslim minority*, *supra* note 79, ¶ 4; United Nations, Detailed Findings of the Independent International Fact-Finding Mission on Myanmar, *supra* note 79, ¶¶ 214–233.

[81]    *See* Rick Noack, *Bangladesh begins relocating Rohingya refugees to remote island, despite human rights concerns*, THE WASHINGTON POST, Dec. 4, 2020, www.washingtonpost.com/world/2020/12/04/rohingya-bangladesh-refugees-island-bhasan-char/.

[82]    *See* International Court of Justice, Reports of Judgments, Advisory Opinions, and Orders Application of the Convention on the Prevention and Punishment of the Crime of Genocide (The Gambia v. Myanmar), Request for the Indication of Provisional Measures, Order of January 23, 2020, ¶¶ 64–84, www.icj-cij.org/public/files/case-related/178/178-20200123-ORD-01-00-EN.pdf.

[83]    *See for example*, United Nations News, *Arab rights charter deviates from international stand-ards, says UN official* (Jan. 30, 2008), https://news.un.org/en/story/2008/01/247292-arab-rights-charter -deviates-international-standards-says-un-official#:~:text=UN%20High%20Commissioner%20for %20Human%20Rights%20Louise%20Arbour,while%20human%20rights%20are%20universal%2C %20%E2%80%9Cregional%20systems%20.

non-citizens.[84] Membership of the Arab League is not determined by geographic location, and the countries do not necessarily have a common position towards human rights and the human rights of women.[85] Why is it important for regional human rights treaties to conform to and be in harmony with universal human rights standards?

3. One situation of great concern in the Middle East has been the documented systemic rape by ISIS – the Islamic State of Iraq and Syria – of women from the Yazidi ethnic and religious minority.[86] One of the survivors, Nadia Murad, won the Nobel Peace Prize in 2018 for her efforts to end the use of sexual violence as a weapon of war and armed conflict.[87] ISIS fighters have imposed a radical and extremist agenda in the territories occupied, including dress codes; rape and sexual slavery; beatings; and the assignment of strict gender roles for women in the home.[88] The obstacles to the legal prosecution and accountability of gender-based crimes such as the ones perpetrated by ISIS have been documented.[89] As discussed throughout this chapter, the more established regional human rights protection systems have ruled a number of noteworthy cases related to different facets of the human rights of women. Can these case decisions motivate and fuel international efforts to prosecute gender-based crimes? Which conditions need to be in place for gender-based crimes to be adequately prosecuted? Does it make a difference who perpetrated the crimes – either a state actor or a non-state actor?

## VI CONCLUSIONS: REGIONAL ADAPTATION TO THE NEW PROBLEMS FACED BY WOMEN

At this stage, the regional human rights protection systems in the Americas, Europe, and Africa in particular have developed a very important body of work related to the human rights of women. Many treaties, case decisions, reports, and statements can be found detailing state obligations related to discrimination against women and gender-based violence; the rights of women to education, employment, health, food, and water; their sexual and reproductive

---

[84] *See* Mervat Rishwami, *The Revised Charter on Human Rights: A Step Forward?*, 5(2) HUMAN RIGHTS LAW REVIEW 364–376 (2005).

[85] For more reading on ways in which the Arab Charter on Human Rights could be used as a tool to promote the human rights of women, *see generally* Ahmed Almutawa and Konstantinos Magliveras, *Enforcing Women's Rights under the Arab Charter on Human Rights 2004*, INT. J. HUM. RIGHTS (2020), www.tandfonline.com/doi/abs/10.1080/13642987.2020.1822334?journalCode=fjhr20. For an overview of discussions related to a potential Arab Charter on the Rights of Women, *see* Business Wire, *Federal National Council Launches Arab Charter on Women's Rights in Cooperation With Arab Parliament*, October 8, 2019, www.businesswire.com/news/home/20191008005832/en/Federal-National-Council -Launches-Arab-Charter-on-Women%E2%80%99s-Rights-in-Cooperation-With-Arab-Parliament.

[86] *See* Rukmini Callimachi, *ISIS Enshrines a Theology of Rape*, N.Y. TIMES, Aug. 13, 2015, www .nytimes.com/2015/08/14/world/middleeast/isis-enshrines-a-theology-of-rape.html.

[87] *See* The Nobel Prize, *Nadia Murad: Facts, the Nobel Peace Prize 2018*, www.nobelprize.org/ prizes/peace/2018/murad/facts/.

[88] For more discussion, *see* Lisa Davis, *Reimagining Justice for Gender-Based Crimes at the Margins: New Legal Strategies for Prosecuting Isis Crimes Against Women and LGBTIQ Persons*, 24(3) WILLIAM MARY J. WOMEN LAW 522–533 (2018).

[89] For a detailed discussion of the prevailing gravity of gender-based crimes and barriers to their prosecution, even with the adoption of the Rome Statute and the work of the International Criminal Court, *see id.*, pp. 513–547.

health; and other key areas. The Americas and Europe have also taken the lead in the adoption of jurisprudence related to discrimination on the basis of sexual orientation and gender identity and expression. These legal standards are a very important complement to developments at the universal level, and constitute a key guide for states of how to respect, protect, and fulfill the rights of women at the national and local levels.

Regional human rights protection systems today face formidable challenges in the effectiveness and compliance of their case rulings. Increased political pressure, the withdrawal of key states, financial limitations, and case backlogs are all common to the regions and their mechanisms. Every day states are more resistant to international supervision and accountability, particularly in the realm of individual case petitions. The promise of multilateralism has been very shaken in the past ten years with nationalist tendencies, racist discourse and xenophobia, as well as anti-human rights discourse. All these variables do affect the impact of these systems in key areas for the rights of women.

It is essential that these systems find creative ways to address these institutional challenges. The systems also need to adapt to modern times and continue pronouncing and developing legal benchmarks considering new issues faced by women in the context of pandemics, technology and social media, the environment and climate change, and forms of backlash against gender equality issues. The gendered, intersectional, and intercultural lens to these emerging issues is paramount to the success of these systems in the future. The participation and election of women Commissioners and Judges, and the protection and legitimacy of the work of women human rights defenders, are also critical tendencies to continue and sustain.

# 12. Women, culture, and religion

## I    INTRODUCTION: RECONCILING THE RIGHTS OF WOMEN, CULTURE, AND RELIGION

The exercise of culture and religion are a part of the identity, daily life, and upbringing of many women. The rights to take part in cultural life and the freedom to adopt and manifest a religion or belief are well accepted in international human rights law. However, the legal standards related to the human rights of women have a very intricate and complex relationship with culture and religion. This is an area that tests the notion of the universality, indivisibility, and interdependence of human rights, and this section focuses on potential conflicts and ways to reconcile these rights.

At the universal level, the right of everyone to take part in cultural life has been codified in Article 15.1(a) of the International Covenant on Economic, Social and Cultural Rights. According to General Comment 21 of the Economic, Social and Cultural Rights Committee, women have the freedom to take part in cultural life, and states should refrain from arbitrarily interfering with the exercise of cultural practices.[1] States are also mandated to ensure preconditions for participation, facilitation, and the promotion of cultural life.[2] However, cultural diversity and traditions cannot be invoked to justify human rights violations committed against women.[3] Harmful practices, including those connected to customs and traditions, such as female genital mutilation and child marriage, run contrary to the right to culture.[4]

For its part, the right to freedom of thought, conscience, and religion is codified in Article 18.1 of the International Covenant on Civil and Political Rights. According to General Comment 22 of the Human Rights Committee, the freedom to manifest a religion or belief (or to not have one) can be exercised individually, in the community, and privately.[5] The right includes worship, observance, practice, and teaching.[6] It includes customs such as the wearing of distinctive clothing or head coverings, dietary regulations, participation in rituals, and the use of specific language.[7] The right also entails steps from states to ensure freedom from coer-

---

[1]    *See* General Comment 21 on the Right of Everyone to Take Part in Cultural Life (Art. 15, para. 1(a), of the International Covenant on Economic, Social and Cultural Rights), Committee on Economic, Social and Cultural Rights, E/C.12/GC/21 (Dec. 21, 2009), ¶ 6.

[2]    *Id.*, ¶ 6.

[3]    *Id.*, ¶ 18.

[4]    *Id.*, ¶ 64.

[5]    *See* General Comment No. 22 on Article 18: Freedom of Thought, Conscience or Religion, U.N. Human Rights Committee, CCPR/C/21/Rev.1/Add.4 (July 30, 1993), ¶ 4.

[6]    *Id.*, ¶ 4.

[7]    *Id.*, ¶ 4.

cion, violence, and discrimination on the basis of religion.[8] In the case of states in which there is an officially established religion comprising the majority of the population, there should be no discrimination or violence perpetrated against non-believers or those who exercise other religions.[9]

Despite these precedents, there are times in which religion and culture are incompatible with the international law governing the rights of women. For example, there are religions which prohibit women from becoming religious leaders; the use of contraceptive methods, abortion, and assisted-reproductive techniques; and to exercise their diverse sexual orientations and gender identities. Women have the right to take part in these religions, but the tenets of the religions themselves run contrary to well-accepted women's rights. Sometimes religious principles are also interpreted in extreme and fundamentalist ways, resulting in major threats to the rights of women and forms of gender-based violence. All of the major world religions have served as settings for gender-based violence and discrimination against women and LGBTI groups, including Buddhism, Christianity, Hinduism, Islam, and Judaism. How can you reconcile religion, culture, and women? How can these conflicts be addressed? How can culture and religion be part of the advancement of the human rights of women?

The idea of this chapter is not to vilify culture and religion, nor to portray them as categorically harmful to the rights of women. Culture and religion indeed have historically served as facilitators of human rights violations, but they can also be important vehicles for the leadership, integrity, autonomy, identity, spirituality, and life plan of women. This chapter explores the complex nature and relationship between women, religion, and culture, ways to reconcile rights in this area, and state human rights obligations. At the core, the chapter discusses the question of what are universality, interdependence, and indivisibility of human rights in this intricate area of the law.

## II    THE COMPLEX RELATIONSHIP BETWEEN WOMEN AND RELIGION

There are many religions around the world. Women play a diversity of roles in religious institutions. Women can be believers and practitioners, participants in community activities, join specific orders, and be religious leaders in some. Women also have an important role as faith transmitters in their families and communities.

Religion has a relationship of contrasts with women. It can be a source of hope, spirituality, values, resilience during hardship, and a conveyor of human dignity. However, religious principles and tenets can be contradictory with reproductive autonomy, privacy, personal liberty, and effective participation. This chapter will not single out specific religions, on the understanding that most in some way or other can be limiting to the human rights of women.[10]

Despite these complexities, religion can be a key part of the lives and identities of women. It is very difficult to secure the full enjoyment of human rights, without respecting the exercise

---

[8]    *Id.*, ¶ 8

[9]    *Id.*, ¶ 9.

[10]    For more discussion on the conflicts between organized religions and the human rights of women, *see* SUSAN DELLER ROSS, *Conflicting Human Rights Under International Law: Freedom of Religion Versus Women's Equality Rights*, *in* WOMEN'S HUMAN RIGHTS: THE INTERNATIONAL AND COMPARATIVE LAW CASE BOOK 115–152 (University of Pennsylvania Press, 2008).

of the freedom to manifest religion or belief. Therefore, how can the rights to exercise religion and the rights of women be reconciled?

One of the areas of most incompatibility and concern is when religious principles are invoked to justify gender-based violence, harmful practices, and the inferior treatment of women, girls, and LGBTI groups in the laws, policies, and daily life. The report below adopted by the United Nations Special Rapporteur on freedom of religion or belief discusses this problem and state obligations in this area.

A    **Report of the Special Rapporteur on freedom of religion or belief, Ahmed Shaheed, *Gender-based violence and discrimination in the name of religion or belief***

A/HRC/43/48
August 24, 2020

…

7.  [There] is considerable evidence that, in all regions of the world, actors citing religious justifications for their actions have advocated to Governments and to the broader public for the preservation or imposition of laws and policies that directly or indirectly discriminate against women, girls and LGBT+ persons. In every region of the world, the Special Rapporteur has identified laws enacted with the aim of mandating standards of conduct purportedly demanded by a particular religion that effectively deny women and other individuals the right to equality and non-discrimination on the basis of their sex, sexual orientation or gender identity. Furthermore, laws identified as intended to protect the right of all individuals to manifest their religion or belief have been applied in a manner that has resulted in discrimination in practice on the same bases. Governments in all regions of the world have also failed to uphold their obligation to protect people from gender-based violence and discrimination perpetrated against them by private individuals or entities claiming a religious justification for their actions and to sanction the perpetrators of such acts. Gender-based violence and discrimination are being perpetuated both in the public sphere and by and within religious communities and entities. …

14. To date, much attention regarding gender-based discrimination in the name of religion or belief has focused on practices such as female genital mutilation, marital rape, early and forced marriage, and polygamy, all of which are rightly condemned as harmful traditional practices by the human rights community. At the same time, consultation participants across four regions also noted the increasing use of religion or belief to deny reproductive health and sexual rights, to criminalize protected conduct and deny the equal personhood of LGBT+ persons, or to undermine the right to freedom of religion or belief to women, girls and LGBT+ persons.

15. The Special Rapporteur shares the concern expressed by other United Nations human rights mechanisms about legislation in force in many countries that imposes standards of conduct allegedly prescribed by a religion or belief on the entire society and that have the effect of discriminating against women, girls and LGBT+ persons. Through the consultations held in preparing the present report, a number of additional such cases were identified

and the Special Rapporteur's attention was drawn to the significant role of religious actors and groups in mobilizing Governments to adopt such legislation. ...

17. The Special Rapporteur draws particular attention to discriminatory legal provisions in personal status and family laws that are informed by interpretations of religious traditions. As recently noted by the Secretary-General, discrimination in personal status and family laws can prevent women from leaving violent relationships and have a significant bearing on their safety and well-being, as well as numerous other rights. Across regions, participants in the consultations for the present study highlighted examples wherein Governments either enforce religious principles that promote gender-based violence and/or discrimination against women and girls through personal status or family law, or delegate authority in administrating personal status rights and affairs regulated by family law to religious communities. Despite recent reforms to the "guardianship system", women and girls in Saudi Arabia continue to face systematic discrimination in law and in practice in several areas and are inadequately protected against gender-based violence. Denominational family law in Israel, to which there is no civil alternative, permits divorce only with the consent of the husband, which reportedly can coerce women to forfeit property or custody of children. Although Tunisia stands out in the Middle East and North Africa Region for many of its protections for the human rights of women and girls, the Personal Status Code of 1956, rooted in an interpretation of Islam, requires further amendment to guarantee gender equality in inheritance rights.

18. Participants in the consultations on South and South-East Asia reported that, in many countries, Governments have advanced efforts to combat gender-based violence and discrimination, such as by criminalizing marital rape, mandating written consent for marriage from all parties and specifying a minimum age for marriage. Some States, however, delegate legal authority to minority religious communities to respect pluralism and multiculturalism, but do so in ways that dilute gender equality norms. For example, the Muslim Marriage and Divorce Act of Sri Lanka, which, unlike national legal provisions for non-Muslim women, does not identify a minimum age requirement or require a woman to consent to marriage, leaving Muslim women and girls unprotected by national provisions.
    ...

26. The Special Rapporteur and other special procedure mandate holders have also expressed concern about the imposition of restrictive garments or "modest" dress codes by laws inspired by religious beliefs and the impact of such measures on the ability of women and girls to enjoy their human rights. In 2019, in a communication to the Government of the Islamic Republic of Iran, the Special Rapporteur, along with other special procedure mandate holders, expressed concern about the Government's compulsory veil legislation and the reported arrest, enforced disappearance and arbitrary detention of women's human rights defenders who protested against it. In that communication, special procedure mandate holders recalled a recent recommendation to the Government to reject any cultural or religious practice that violated human rights and the principle of equality or prevented the establishment of an egalitarian society free of gender-based discrimination.

27. In other instances, consultation participants noted that some States had opted to limit religious practices such as wearing headscarves or full-face veils in public – attire predominantly worn by Muslim women – in their efforts to combat gender-based discrimination, but without sufficient attention to the self-understanding and agency of women. Critics of

such policies have noted the danger that such policies posed to the right to freedom of religion or belief, along with myriad other rights, noting that efforts to combat gender-based discrimination often failed to incorporate freedom of religion or belief and forced individuals to choose between their faith and national protections for human rights.

28. The Special Rapporteur notes that, in a number of countries around the world, Governments continue to maintain partial or total bans on access to abortion, and religious figures have both encouraged those measures and advocated against efforts to reform the laws. At the consultations on Latin America, it was asserted that discriminatory religious edicts informed laws and policies that restricted sexual and reproductive rights in the region, including, but not limited to, partial or total bans on access to abortion and contraception, prohibitions on assisted reproductive technologies and gender reassignment surgery, and limits on the provision of evidence-based sexuality education. …

32. In many States, religious communities and institutions are assuming an increasingly important role in the social, political and economic affairs of those countries; some are playing a critical part in the promotion and realization of human rights – including the right to freedom of religion or belief – while others are advancing protections for their religious commitments at the expense of the human rights of others both within and outside their communities. Critically in some societies, some religious institutions promote and perpetuate interpretations of religious tenets to promote gender-based violence and discrimination against women, girls and LGBT+ persons, including physical, sexual and psychological harm.

33. The Special Rapporteur is deeply concerned by numerous reports he has received, and by information provided to other United Nations human rights mechanisms, alleging that religious interest groups are engaged in campaigns characterizing rights advocates working to combat gender-based discrimination as "immoral" actors, seeking to undermine society by espousing "a gender ideology" that is harmful to children, families, tradition and religion. Invoking religious tenets, as well as pseudoscience, such actors argue for the defence of traditional values rooted in interpretations of religious teachings about the social roles for men and women in accordance with their alleged naturally different physical and mental capacities, often calling upon Governments to enact discriminatory policies. Other special procedures and participants in consultations across regions have also documented the activities of increasingly well-coordinated groups that are reportedly misusing freedom of religion or belief across continents in the media, through litigation and political campaigns to counter human rights in the name of religion or belief. …

## B    Reflections and Questions

1. Can you think of ways to reconcile the rights of women with the right to exercise and practice religion? Please identify five concrete examples.
2. The report from the U.N. Special Rapporteur on freedom of religion or belief carefully reviews the different layers and examples of forms of gender-based discrimination and violence still perpetrated against women, girls, and LGBTI groups invoking religion. The report discusses issues concerning discriminatory legislation – on its text and application – related to personal status and family laws, including those imposing norms of conduct for women; modest dress codes; and those denying equal personhood to LGBTI persons.

Key challenges are in the area of sexual and reproductive rights, limiting access to contraception alternatives, abortion, and the necessary education to make informed sexual health decisions. Harmful practices such as female genital mutilation, marital rape, early marriage, and polygamy are still widespread globally. Religious principles are still used to discredit the work of human rights defense, thereby having a chilling effect. An important challenge is the limited role of women and LGBTI groups in influencing the development of religious principles, dogma, and tenets which govern most institutionalized religions. Which steps can religions adopt to promote change and reform to prevent the use of their dogma and tenets to perpetrate acts of gender-based violence and discrimination? How can they ensure the effective participation of women and LGBTI groups in the development of religious principles?

3. It is important to note that religion can be official and institutionalized as part of a state, or be organized at the private institutional and community levels. The human rights challenges described by the U.N. Special Rapporteur's Report take place in countries in which one religion is state-sponsored or official, but also when religion is organized at the private or community level. The challenges are not only outward, but also inward in terms of violence perpetrated within the religious institutions themselves against their members and parishioners. Probably the best-known scandal was the one revealing the long history of the Catholic Church and its priests concerning sexual violence and the rape of children and nuns, with no criminal sanction or judicial accountability for these crimes.[11] There have also been increased calls for other religions to recognize internal cases of sexual abuse.[12] What can states do to prevent, supervise, and regulate the activity of private religious institutions that is harmful to women and girls? What can organized religions do to effectively prevent and sanction acts of gender-based violence that occur internally within their institutions? What should be the main components of access to justice in these kinds of cases?

4. Both the universal system of human rights and the regional human rights protection systems have expressed their concern over the widespread nature and gravity of the problem of female genital mutilation (hereinafter "FGM"). According to UNICEF, at least 200 million girls and women alive today in 31 countries have undergone FGM.[13] The CEDAW Committee has identified FGM as a harmful practice, and defined it as the partial or whole removal of the external genitalia or female genital organs of women and girls due to non-medical or non-health reasons. It can also be referred to female circumcision or female

---

[11]  For reporting on these issues, *see* Matt Carroll, Sacha Pfeiffer, and Michael Rezendes (Globe Spotlight Team), *Church allowed abuse by priest for years*, BOSTON GLOBE, Jan. 6, 2002, www .bostonglobe.com/news/special-reports/2002/01/06/church-allowed-abuse-priest-for-years/cSH fGkTIrAT25qKGvBuDNM/story.html; Jason Horowitz, *Sexual Abuse of Nuns, Longstanding Church Scandal Emerges from Shadows*, N.Y. TIMES, Feb. 6, 2019, www.nytimes.com/2019/02/06/world/ europe/pope-francis-sexual-abuse-nuns.html.

[12]  *See As a Muslim woman, it's my duty to speak out about the sexual abuse I survived as a child*, THE INDEPENDENT, Dec. 6, 2017, www.independent.co.uk/voices/sexual-abuse-metoo-muslim-woman -its-my-duty-to-speak-out-a8094796.html; Sanitsuda Ekachai, *Temples no longer safe for children*, BANGKOK POST, Oct. 30, 2019, www.bangkokpost.com/opinion/opinion/1782969/temples-no-longer -safe-for-children.

[13]  *See* UNICEF, *Female Genital Mutilation* (February 2020), https://data.unicef.org/topic/child -protection/female-genital-mutilation/.

genital cutting.[14] This practice has immediate and long-term health consequences, including severe pain, shock, and complications during childbirth.[15] The CEDAW Committee has advanced four elements to identify a practice as harmful, including (a) resulting in the denial of integrity of the victims involved; (b) their harmful and discriminatory nature; (c) that they are considered traditional and predicated on male dominance and the inequality of women; and (d) that they are imposed on women and children without the full, prior, and informed consent of the victim.[16] The CEDAW Committee has advocated for a holistic framework to prevent, sanction, and eliminate FGM and other harmful practices like child marriage, polygamy, and honor crimes.[17]

5. The United Nations General Assembly adopted a resolution on March 5, 2013, calling states to intensify global efforts to eliminate female genital mutilations. The resolution calls on states to increase their efforts at non-formal and informal education to ensure that many actors work together to eliminate this problem, including government officials, community and religious leaders, parents, and communities.[18] The Maputo Protocol, discussed in Chapter 2, also prohibits FGM in Article 5(b) as a harmful practice, mandating states to proactively address this problem by adopting legislative measures, public awareness initiatives, formal and informal education and outreach, and the necessary health services.

6. One of the complex aspects of a problem like FGM is the hidden nature of this practice and how it is driven by informal social norms of the limited and subservient role that women and girls should have in their families and societies. Many cases of FGM are underreported and performed at the community level. The available statistics are only part of a problem that is much larger. International human rights law refers to the obligations states have to act with due diligence to prevent, investigate, and sanction forms of gender-based violence such as FGM. How can a state adequately prevent FGM, when it happens at the community level and in silence? How can states work with religions, cultural leaders, and communities to prevent FGM, identify cases, and collect information?[19]

7. Religious fundamentalism is one of the most important threats faced by women's human rights today. It is key to understanding that fundamentalism is different from religion itself, and is often based on an extreme interpretation of religious dogma or tenets by a minority group. The U.N. Special Rapporteurship in the field of cultural rights has used the term fundamentalism for actors using "a putatively religious discourse" and extremism "for

---

[14] *See* Joint General Recommendation No. 31 of the Committee on the Elimination of Discrimination against Women/General Comment No. 18 of the Committee on the Rights of the Child on harmful practices, Committee on the Elimination of Discrimination against Women (hereinafter CEDAW Committee) and Committee on the Rights of the Child (hereinafter Committee on the Rights of the Child), CEDAW/C/GC/31-CRC/C/GC/18, ¶ 19 (Nov. 14, 2014).

[15] *Id.*

[16] *Id.*, ¶ 16.

[17] *Id.*, ¶¶ 31–87.

[18] *See* U.N. General Assembly Resolution, *Intensifying global efforts for the elimination of female genital mutilations*, A/RES/67/146, ¶ 2 (March 5, 2013).

[19] For more reading on potential strategies to address FGM, *see* UNICEF, Technical Note: *Gender Transformative Approaches for the Elimination of Female Genital Mutilation* (2020), pp. 8–11, www .unicef.org/media/86391/file/FGM-Mainstreaming-Gender-Equality-2020-v2.pdf.

movements with other bases."[20] The Rapporteurship has identified and linked versions and manifestations of fundamentalism in all of the major world religions.[21] The Rapporteurship has expressed concern over fundamentalist discourse harmful to women premised on the values of purity and modesty; the curtailing of freedom of artistic expression and scientific freedom; gender ideology advancing patriarchal notions; a complete rejection of equality between the sexes; the denial of women and leadership in religion; and the condemnation of diverse sexual and non-conforming sexual orientations and gender identities.[22] Secularism and the separation of church and state have been identified as paramount to ending fundamentalist ideologies which are harmful to women.[23] The U.N. Rapporteurship has mandated states to openly challenge religious fundamentalism with human rights discourse; to protect women from forms of coercion, violence, and discrimination stemming from fundamentalism; and to safeguard the legitimacy of women human rights defenders in light of growing fundamentalist rhetoric.[24]

8. It is important to note that fundamentalist discourse often claims to be advancing culture and religion, but instead serves to inhibit the exercise of these rights, and many others. One area in which religious fundamentalism has had very negative effects is in advancing legal and policy restrictions on sexual and reproductive rights.[25] Which elements should determine whether a specific religious principle or church policy is fundamentalist? How do you differentiate between fundamentalism and religion itself? Is this difference relevant when it comes to gender equality issues?

## C      Practical exercise: Religion and women

This section discusses the right to manifest religion, and potential conflicts and connections with the human rights of women. Please consider the following questions:

- Does religion challenge or advance women's rights?
- What is the difference between religious fundamentalism and religion?
- Do you think women have an inferior status in religion?
- Is religion always incompatible with women's rights?
- Do you think there are ways to find connections between the rights of women and freedom of religion?

---

[20]   *See* Report of the Special Rapporteur in the field of cultural rights, Karima Bennoune, *Cultural rights*, A/72/155, ¶ 4 (July 17, 2017).

[21]   *Id.*, ¶ 14.

[22]   *Id.*, ¶¶ 7, 14, 67–87.

[23]   *Id.*, ¶ 11.

[24]   *Id.*, ¶¶ 25, 27, 32–40.

[25]   For more discussion on the impact of religious fundamentalism on the protection of the sexual and reproductive rights of women, *see* Rayah Feldman and Kate Clark, *Women, Religious Fundamentalism and Reproductive Rights*, 4(8) REPRODUCTIVE HEALTH MATTERS 12–20 (1996); Marge Berer and T.K. Sundari Ravindran, *Fundamentalism, Women's Empowerment and Reproductive Rights*, 4(8) REPRODUCTIVE HEALTH MATTERS 7–10 (1996). For a concrete and recent example, *see* Ruby Mellen, *Mexico Is Taking Steps Toward Legalizing Abortion. But Across Latin America, Restrictions Remain Widespread*, THE WASHINGTON POST, Oct. 4, 2019, www.washingtonpost.com/world/2019/10/04/mexico-is-taking-steps-toward-legalizing-abortion-across-latin-america-restrictions-are-widespread/.

- Do you think existing universal and regional human rights instruments provide answers?
- What is the role of the state towards religious groups?
- Which kinds of measures can religious groups adopt to be in harmony with the human rights of women?

## III RELIGIOUS WEAR FROM A HUMAN RIGHTS PERSPECTIVE

The global and regional human rights protection systems have had the opportunity to assess individual cases related to the legality of national bans on headscarves and face veil coverings as religious symbols, with important repercussions on the rights of women. The most well-known case decisions have been adopted by the European Court of Human Rights and the U.N. Human Rights Committee, examining the human rights implications of bans adopted in Turkey and France. Restrictions on headscarves not only have effects on the enjoyment of the freedom to manifest one's own religion, but also impact the autonomy, privacy, personal liberty, integrity, and the right to non-discrimination of the women affected.

The approach of the European Court of Human Rights has been to afford a very wide margin of appreciation to states in the adoption of these bans considering the importance of the principle of secularism; the protection of public safety and order; the need to establish conditions for "living together"; and the absence of a European consensus in this area. The Human Rights Committee instead has considered these bans an arbitrary and unjustified interference with the freedom to manifest religion, and a form of intersectional discrimination against women on the basis of gender and religion.

Two emblematic decisions with different approaches are discussed below.

### A European Court of Human Rights, *Leyla Şahin v. Turkey*

Grand Chamber
Application No. 44774/98, November 10, 2005
© Council of Europe, reproduced with permission
Citations and footnotes omitted

*This case relates to a female medical student who claimed that the Turkish ban on Islamic headscarfs in institutions of higher education constituted an unjustified interference with her right to freedom of religion and to manifest her religion. The excerpts below illustrate the European Court of Human Rights treatment of this ban under Article 9 of the European Convention on Human Rights.*

75. The Court must consider whether the applicant's right under Article 9 was interfered with and, if so, whether the interference was "prescribed by law", pursued a legitimate aim and was "necessary in a democratic society" within the meaning of Article 9 § 2 of the Convention. …

104. The Court reiterates that, as enshrined in Article 9, freedom of thought, conscience and religion is one of the foundations of a "democratic society" within the meaning of the Convention. This freedom is, in its religious dimension, one of the most vital elements that go to make up the identity of believers and their conception of life, but it is also a precious

asset for atheists, agnostics, sceptics and the unconcerned. The pluralism indissociable from a democratic society, which has been dearly won over the centuries, depends on it. That freedom entails, *inter alia*, freedom to hold or not to hold religious beliefs and to practise or not to practise a religion. ...

106.   In democratic societies, in which several religions coexist within one and the same population, it may be necessary to place restrictions on freedom to manifest one's religion or belief in order to reconcile the interests of the various groups and ensure that everyone's beliefs are respected. This follows both from paragraph 2 of Article 9 and the State's positive obligation under Article 1 of the Convention to secure to everyone within its jurisdiction the rights and freedoms defined therein.

107.   The Court has frequently emphasised the State's role as the neutral and impartial organiser of the exercise of various religions, faiths and beliefs, and stated that this role is conducive to public order, religious harmony and tolerance in a democratic society. It also considers that the State's duty of neutrality and impartiality is incompatible with any power on the State's part to assess the legitimacy of religious beliefs or the ways in which those beliefs are expressed, and that it requires the State to ensure mutual tolerance between opposing groups. Accordingly, the role of the authorities in such circumstances is not to remove the cause of tension by eliminating pluralism, but to ensure that the competing groups tolerate each other. ...

108.   Pluralism, tolerance and broadmindedness are hallmarks of a "democratic society". Although individual interests must on occasion be subordinated to those of a group, democracy does not simply mean that the views of a majority must always prevail: a balance must be achieved which ensures the fair and proper treatment of people from minorities and avoids any abuse of a dominant position. ...

109.   Where questions concerning the relationship between State and religions are at stake, on which opinion in a democratic society may reasonably differ widely, the role of the national decision-making body must be given special importance ... This will notably be the case when it comes to regulating the wearing of religious symbols in educational institutions, especially in view of the diversity of the approaches taken by national authorities on the issue. It is not possible to discern throughout Europe a uniform conception of the significance of religion in society, and the meaning or impact of the public expression of a religious belief will differ according to time and context. Rules in this sphere will consequently vary from one country to another according to national traditions and the requirements imposed by the need to protect the rights and freedoms of others and to maintain public order. Accordingly, the choice of the extent and form such regulations should take must inevitably be left up to a point to the State concerned, as it will depend on the specific domestic context.

110.   This margin of appreciation goes hand in hand with a European supervision embracing both the law and the decisions applying it. The Court's task is to determine whether the measures taken at national level were justified in principle and proportionate. In delimiting the extent of the margin of appreciation in the present case, the Court must have regard to what is at stake, namely the need to protect the rights and freedoms of others, to preserve public order and to secure civil peace and true religious pluralism, which is vital to the survival of a democratic society. ...

112.   The interference in issue caused by the circular of 23 February 1998 imposing restrictions as to place and manner on the rights of students such as Ms Şahin to wear the Islamic
headscarf on university premises was, according to the Turkish courts, based in particular
on the two principles of secularism and equality.

113.   In its judgment of 7 March 1989, the Constitutional Court stated that secularism, as
the guarantor of democratic values, was the meeting point of liberty and equality. The
principle prevented the State from manifesting a preference for a particular religion or
belief; it thereby guided the State in its role of impartial arbiter, and necessarily entailed
freedom of religion and conscience. It also served to protect the individual not only against
arbitrary interference by the State but from external pressure from extremist movements.
The Constitutional Court added that freedom to manifest one's religion could be restricted
in order to defend those values and principles.

114.   As the Chamber rightly stated, the Court considers this notion of secularism to be consistent with the values underpinning the Convention. It finds that upholding that principle,
which is undoubtedly one of the fundamental principles of the Turkish State which are in
harmony with the rule of law and respect for human rights, may be considered necessary
to protect the democratic system in Turkey. An attitude which fails to respect that principle
will not necessarily be accepted as being covered by the freedom to manifest one's religion
and will not enjoy the protection of Article 9 of the Convention. …

116.   Having regard to the above background, it is the principle of secularism, as elucidated
by the Constitutional Court, which is the paramount consideration underlying the ban on
the wearing of religious symbols in universities. In such a context, where the values of
pluralism, respect for the rights of others and, in particular, equality before the law of men
and women are being taught and applied in practice, it is understandable that the relevant
authorities should wish to preserve the secular nature of the institution concerned and so
consider it contrary to such values to allow religious attire, including, as in the present case,
the Islamic headscarf, to be worn.

117.   The Court must now determine whether in the instant case there was a reasonable
relationship of proportionality between the means employed and the legitimate objectives
pursued by the interference.

118.   Like the Chamber, the Grand Chamber notes at the outset that it is common ground
that practising Muslim students in Turkish universities are free, within the limits imposed
by the constraints of educational organisation, to manifest their religion in accordance
with habitual forms of Muslim observance. In addition, the resolution adopted by Istanbul
University on 9 July 1998 shows that various other forms of religious attire are also forbid-
den on the university premises.

119.   It should also be noted that, when the issue of whether students should be allowed
to wear the Islamic headscarf surfaced at Istanbul University in 1994 in relation to the
medical courses, the Vice-Chancellor reminded them of the reasons for the rules on dress.
Arguing that calls for permission to wear the Islamic headscarf in all parts of the university
premises were misconceived and pointing to the public-order constraints applicable to
medical courses, he asked the students to abide by the rules, which were consistent with
both the legislation and the case-law of the higher courts.

120.   Furthermore, the process whereby the regulations that led to the decision of 9 July
1998 were implemented took several years and was accompanied by a wide debate

within Turkish society and the teaching profession. The two highest courts, the Supreme Administrative Court and the Constitutional Court, have managed to establish settled case-law on this issue. It is quite clear that throughout that decision-making process the university authorities sought to adapt to the evolving situation in a way that would not bar access to the university to students wearing the veil, through continued dialogue with those concerned, while at the same time ensuring that order was maintained and in particular that the requirements imposed by the nature of the course in question were complied with.

121.   In that connection, the Court does not accept the applicant's submission that the fact that there were no disciplinary penalties for failing to comply with the dress code effectively meant that no rules existed. As to how compliance with the internal rules should have been secured, it is not for the Court to substitute its view for that of the university authorities. By reason of their direct and continuous contact with the education community, the university authorities are in principle better placed than an international court to evaluate local needs and conditions or the requirements of a particular course. Besides, having found that the regulations pursued a legitimate aim, it is not open to the Court to apply the criterion of proportionality in a way that would make the notion of an institution's "internal rules" devoid of purpose. Article 9 does not always guarantee the right to behave in a manner governed by a religious belief and does not confer on people who do so the right to disregard rules that have proved to be justified.

122.   In the light of the foregoing and having regard to the Contracting States' margin of appreciation in this sphere, the Court finds that the interference in issue was justified in principle and proportionate to the aim pursued.

123.   Consequently, there has been no breach of Article 9 of the Convention.


**B**      *Matter of Sonia Yaker*, **United Nations Human Rights Committee**

Views on Communication No. 2747/2016
CCPR/C/123/D/2747/2016
December 7, 2018

*The case is related to a Muslim woman who wears a niqab (full face veil) and was prosecuted and convicted for this reason in France. She challenged the ban under Article 18 of the International Covenant on Civil and Political Rights and the right to freedom of thought, conscience, and religion.*

8.3 The Committee recalls its general comment No. 22, in which it stated that the freedom to manifest religion or belief may be exercised either individually or in community with others and in public or private. The observance and practice of religion or belief may include not only ceremonial acts, but also such customs as the wearing of distinctive clothing or head coverings. The author's statement that the wearing of the full veil is customary for a segment of the Muslim faithful and that it concerns the performance of a rite and practice of a religion is not in question. It is also undisputed that Act No. 2010-1192, prohibiting garments intended to conceal the face in public, is applicable to the niqab worn by the author, who as a result is forced to renounce the clothing that corresponds to her religious approach or risk penalties. Accordingly, the Committee considers that the ban introduced under the Act constitutes a restriction or limitation of the author's freedom to manifest her beliefs or religion – by wearing her niqab – within the meaning of article 18(1) of the Covenant.

8.4 The Committee must therefore determine whether this restriction is authorized by article 18(3) of the Covenant. The Committee recalls that article 18(3) permits restrictions on the freedom to manifest religion or belief only if limitations are prescribed by law and are necessary to protect public safety, order, health or morals, or the fundamental rights and freedoms of others. The Committee also recalls that paragraph 3 of article 18 is to be strictly interpreted: restrictions are not allowed on grounds not specified there, even if they would be allowed as restrictions to other rights protected in the Covenant, such as national security. Limitations may be applied only for those purposes for which they were pre-scribed and must be directly related and proportionate to the specific need on which they are predicated. Restrictions may not be imposed for discriminatory purposes or applied in a discriminatory manner.

8.5 In the present case, the Committee notes that it is undisputed that the prohibition against wearing the niqab falls clearly within the scope defined under article 1 of Act No. 2010-1192. It is therefore incumbent upon the Committee to assess whether the restriction, which is prescribed by law, pursues a legitimate objective, is necessary for achieving that objective, and is proportionate and non-discriminatory.

8.6 The Committee notes that the State party has indicated two objectives that the Act is intended to pursue, namely the protection of public order and safety, and the protection of the rights and freedoms of others.

8.7 With respect to protection of public order and safety, the State party contends that it must be possible to identify all individuals when necessary to avert threats to the security of persons or property and to combat identity fraud. The Committee recognizes the need for States, in certain contexts, to be able to require that individuals show their faces, which might entail one-off obligations for individuals to reveal their faces in specific circumstances of a risk to public safety or order, or for identification purposes. The Committee observes, however, that the Act is not limited to such contexts, but comprehensively prohibits the wearing of certain face coverings in public at all times, and that the State party has failed to demonstrate how wearing the full-face veil in itself represents a threat to public safety or order that would justify such an absolute ban. Nor has the State party provided any public safety justification or explanation for why covering the face for certain religious purposes – i.e., the niqab – is prohibited, while covering the face for numerous other purposes, including sporting, artistic, and other traditional and religious purposes, is allowed. The Committee further observes that the State party has not described any context, or provided any example, in which there was a specific and significant threat to public order and safety that would justify such a blanket ban on the full-face veil. No such threats are described in the statement of purpose of Act No. 2010-1192 or in the National Assembly resolution of 11 May 2010, which preceded the adoption of the Act.

8.8 Even if the State party could demonstrate the existence of a specific and significant threat to public safety and order in principle, it has failed to demonstrate that the prohibition con-tained in Act No. 2010-1192 is proportionate to that objective, in view of its considerable impact on the author as a woman wearing the full-face veil. Nor has it attempted to demonstrate that the ban was the least restrictive measure necessary to ensure the protection of the freedom of religion or belief.

8.9 With regard to the second objective presented by the State party, understood as the protection of the fundamental rights and freedoms of others under article 18(3), the Committee notes the State party's argument based on the concept of "living together" or respect for the minimum requirements of life in society, public spaces being the main place in which social life happens and people come into contact with others. According to the State party, showing one's face signals a person's readiness to be identified as an individual by the other party and not to "unfairly" conceal one's frame of mind, this being "the minimum degree of trust that is essential for living together in an egalitarian and open society". The Committee also notes the author's claim that the legislature did not clearly define such an objective, either in the Act itself or in the statement of purpose. The Committee recognizes it may be in a State's interest to promote sociability and mutual respect among individuals, in all their diversity, in its territory, and thus that the concealment of the face could be perceived as a potential obstacle to such interaction.

8.10    However, the Committee observes that the protection of the fundamental rights and freedoms of others requires identifying what specific fundamental rights are affected, and the persons so affected. Article 18(3) exceptions are to be interpreted strictly and not applied in the abstract. In the present case, the Committee observes that the concept of "living together" is very vague and abstract. The State party has not identified any specific fundamental rights or freedoms of others that are affected by the fact that some people present in the public space have their face covered, including fully veiled women. ...

8.12    In the light of the foregoing, the Committee considers that the State party has failed to demonstrate that the limitation of the author's freedom to manifest her religion or beliefs, through the wearing of the niqab, was necessary and proportionate within the meaning of article 18(3) of the Covenant. The Committee therefore concludes that the ban introduced by Act No. 2010-1192 and the conviction of the author under said Act for wearing the niqab violated the author's rights under article 18 of the Covenant. ...

8.15    The Committee notes that the State party has provided no explanation why the blanket prohibition on the author's veil is reasonable or justified, in contrast to the exceptions allowable under the Act. The Committee further notes that the blanket ban on the full-face veil introduced by the Act appears to be based on the assumption that the full veil is inherently discriminatory and that women who wear it are forced to do so. While acknowledging that some women may be subject to family or social pressures to cover their faces, the Committee observes that the wearing of the full veil may also be a choice – or even a means of staking a claim – based on religious belief, as in the author's case. The Committee further considers that the prohibition, rather than protecting fully veiled women, could have the opposite effect of confining them to their homes, impeding their access to public services and exposing them to abuse and marginalization. Indeed, the Committee has previously stated its concern that the Act's ban on face coverings in public places infringes the freedom to express one's religion or belief, has a disproportionate impact on the members of specific religions and on girls, and that the Act's effect on certain groups' feeling of exclusion and marginalization could run counter to the intended goals. ...

## C     Reflections and Questions

1. Do you agree with the European Court of Human Rights judgment in the case of *Leyla Şahin v. Turkey*? Do you think the Court should have ruled differently and why?

2. Consider all the different kinds of headscarves and face coverings that women can wear, including those connected, and those unrelated to the Muslim faith. Do all these coverings have the same messages for you? Does it make a difference in your analysis whether women are wearing these coverings voluntarily, or as part of a religious or cultural mandate?

3. The case of *Leyla Şahin v. Turkey* in particular illustrates the significant influence of the doctrine of margin of appreciation in the work of the European Court of Human Rights. It also corroborates the regional value afforded to the principles of secularism, democracy, and the messages associated with religious symbols.[26] The Court also discusses in paragraph 108 *supra* the importance of pluralism, tolerance, and broadmindedness as hallmarks of a democratic society. Can you reconcile the banning of headscarves and face coverings connected with the Muslim faith with the pluralism and multiculturalism needed in a democratic society?

4. Consider also the arguments of the European Court of Human Rights in the case of *Leyla Şahin v. Turkey* regarding the need to advance gender equality as support for implementing this ban on headscarves and coverings. Do you think gender equality considerations justify the imposition of a prohibition on headscarves and face coverings? Do you think the analysis is different if at issue is a full face covering such as a burqa or niqab worn as a religious and cultural mandate?

5. The European Court of Human Rights also considered a later case – *S.A.S. v. France* – in which the state argued that the ban on face and full body coverings at issue was necessary to establish the conditions for persons to live together in a society.[27] In its final decision, the European Court of Human Rights ruled on behalf of the state and did give weight to the argument that the face plays an important role in social interaction, and how concealing the face with a veil may breach the rights of others to live in a space of socialization which makes living together easier.[28] When living in a society, there are moments and settings in which the physical identification of a person may be necessary, including hospitals, schools, employment, and law enforcement. Is there a way to legalize the wearing of burqas and niqabs, and also meet these social needs?

6. Consider the different women's rights which can be affected by a ban on headscarves or face coverings. In the case of *Leyla Şahin v. Turkey*, the applicant was attending medical school and had to conclude her studies at a different university institution instead, outside of Turkey. She considered wearing the headscarf at issue as a religious mandate. Therefore, it can be argued that the ban restricted her accessibility to higher education of quality, and therefore the full enjoyment of her right to education. Think of all the civil,

---

[26] For a detailed discussion of the Leyla Şahin v. Turkey judgment, the principle of secularism, and the regulation of headscarves, *see* Karima Benoune, *Secularism and Human Rights: A Contextual Analysis of Headscarves, Religious Expression and Women's Equality Under International Law*, 45 COLUM. J. TRANSNAT'L. L. 367, 367–426, 377–397 (2007).

[27] *See* S.A.S. v. France [GC], App. No. 43835/11, ¶¶ 23–159 (July 1, 2014).

[28] *Id.*, ¶ 122.

political, economic, social, and cultural rights that are discussed throughout this casebook with pertinence to women. Can you think of other human rights of women that are affected by bans on religious headscarves and face coverings which affect women?

7.   The Human Rights Committee decision in the case of *Matter of Sonia Yaker* in many ways offers a counter view to the European Court of Human Rights approach to the prohibition of face coverings. The Committee sees this case as a non-discrimination issue, and advances the notion that any sort of different treatment of face coverings grounded on the Muslim faith needs to be justified by reasonableness, objectivity, and legitimacy. It considered this case in particular as one related to indirect and intersectional discrimination,[29] by imposing a restriction which disproportionately affected the author as a Muslim woman who chose to wear a veil; and established an arbitrary distinction between her and others who wear other face coverings. The Committee acknowledges also that some women wear the veil by choice, and that the sanctions were criminal in nature. Overall, the Committee found that insufficient justifications had been advanced by the state. Please consider the strengths and weaknesses of this approach by the U.N. Human Rights Committee. Do you prefer this approach over that of the European Court of Human Rights? Should the European Court of Human Rights cases have been examined also under a non-discrimination lens? Do you think the European Court of Human Rights cases would have reached the same result if they had been examined under Article 14 of the European Convention on Human Rights and its prohibition of discrimination?

## IV    WOMEN AND CULTURE

Culture is at the heart of the identity and integrity of most women. Women can relate to culture as participants, creators, and artists. Women often are the ones entrusted with transmitting culture in their families and communities. Women also can play a vital leadership and autonomous role in reshaping and transforming cultural norms, attitudes, and stereotypes which are harmful.

As indicated earlier in this chapter, culture can be a facilitator of human rights violations, but also an enabler of human rights protection. States have the obligation to respect, protect, and fulfill the right to culture, which means preventing any state and/or non-state entities from interfering with the right of women to take part in cultural life. States also need to prevent culture being invoked as a justification for human rights violations affecting women and girls.

This section and the reading below discuss ways in which gender and culture are related in the area of the human rights of women.

---

[29]   For more discussion of the Matter of Sonia Yaker case in light of the problem of intersectional discrimination, *see* Monika Zalnieriute and Catherine Weiss, *Reconceptualizing Intersectionality in Judicial Interpretation: Moving Beyond Formalistic Accounts of Discrimination on Islamic Covering Prohibitions*, 35(1) BERKELEY JOURNAL OF GENDER, LAW AND JUSTICE 71–90, 79–86 (2020), UNSW Law Research Paper No. 20-01 (Nov. 21, 2019), https://papers.ssrn.com/sol3/papers.cfm?abstract_id= 3514948.

**A**      **Report of the Special Rapporteur in the field of cultural rights, Farida Shaheed,** *Enjoyment of cultural rights of women on an equal basis with men*

A/67/287
August 10, 2012

…

3. Gender, culture and rights intersect in intricate and complex ways. The tendency to view culture as largely an impediment to women's human rights is both oversimplistic and problematic. By attributing self-propelling agency to "culture" independent of the actions of human beings, it diverts attention from specific actors, institutions, rules and regulations, keeping women subordinated within patriarchal systems and structures. It also renders invisible women's agency in both reproducing and challenging dominant cultural norms and values. Nevertheless, many practices and norms that discriminate against women are justified by reference to culture, religion and tradition, leading experts to conclude that "no social group has suffered greater violation of its human rights in the name of culture than women" and that it is "inconceivable" that a number of such practices "would be justified if they were predicated upon another protected classification such as race". The use of discourses of cultural relativism to challenge the universal legitimacy and applicability of human rights norms is a serious concern.

4. The Special Rapporteur wishes to stress that "the critical issue, from the human rights perspective, is not whether and how religion, culture and tradition prevail over women's human rights, but how to arrive at a point at which women own both their culture (and religion and tradition) and their human rights". "The struggle for women's human rights is not against religion, culture, or tradition." Cultures are shared outcomes of critical reflection and continuous engagements of human beings in response to an ever-changing world. The task at hand is to identify how human rights in general, and equal cultural rights in particular, can enable women "to find paths through which we may view tradition with new eyes, in such a way that it will not violate our rights and restore dignity to … women … [and] change those traditions which diminish our dignity".

5. The realization of women's cultural rights is closely dependent on the enjoyment of other rights. The reverse is also true. Situated at the juncture of civil and political rights, on the one hand, and economic, social and cultural rights, on the other, women's equal cultural rights are transformative: they are empowering rights, providing important opportunities for the realization of other human rights. This report proposes to shift the paradigm from one that views culture merely as an obstacle to women's rights to one that seeks to ensure equal enjoyment of cultural rights; such an approach also constitutes a critical tool for the realization of all their human rights. …

12. Gender equality analyses consistently emphasize women's diverse identities and related implications. The Beijing Declaration adopted at the Fourth World Conference on Women, for example, acknowledges, in paragraph 32, that women and girls face multiple barriers "because of such factors as their race, age, language, ethnicity, culture, religion or disability or because they are indigenous people". "Intersectional" identities oblige women to deal with multiple and many-layered forms of oppression simultaneously. For example, Traveller women in Ireland face "triple discrimination — as Travellers, as women, and as

Traveller women"; more in contact with settled people than men, women are more likely to confront racism from outsiders while being blamed by other Travellers if they speak out against negative internal practices, which is perceived as speaking against the community. A dualistic "either/or" perspective on identity cannot account for the interacting, intersecting and shifting positions of domination and subordination that the same person occupies because of her varied identities.

13. Recognizing and protecting multiple identities helps to resist and overcome political forces, in particular identity politics, which seek to deny any possibility of pluralism within self and society, as well as gender equality.

14. People must be able to thrive "both as an individual and as a member of larger communities". Stressing that "women's full participation in the cultural and political life of the state" is undermined by "the systematic denial of their political, economic, social, civil and other legal rights", scholars insist that human rights must focus on ensuring "personhood" for women, which is both individualistic and relational. This resonates with the notion of "citizen participation" advanced by gender equality advocates and scholars, for example, in Latin America. One obstacle to such participation is that cultural rights have been the "poor cousins" of economic and social rights, receiving scant attention at the national and international levels. Women's cultural inequality, coupled with economic and social inequalities, "makes it difficult, if not impossible, for them to exercise their civil and political rights, to enjoy personal autonomy and to participate in the political life of their community or country". ...

24. Three principal and interrelated components of the right to take part in cultural life elaborated by the Committee on Economic, Social and Cultural Rights and the Special Rapporteur are: (a) participation in; (b) access to; and (c) contribution to cultural life. The Special Rapporteur has further elaborated that this includes the right to access and enjoy tangible and intangible heritage. Some key elements with regard to women are as follows.

25. Participation covers not only the right of individuals to act freely, to choose one's own identity and to manifest one's own cultural practices, but also the right not to participate in specific traditions, customs and practices, particularly those that infringe on human rights and dignity. ...

28. From a human rights perspective, participation must ensure decision-making. Women must enjoy the freedom to create new communities of shared cultural values around any markers of identity they want to privilege, new cultural meanings and practices without fear of punitive actions, including any form of violence. ...

30. Access covers, inter alia, the right of everyone to know, understand and benefit from the cultural heritage and cultural life of their own communities as well as that of other communities. Accessing and enjoying cultural heritage implies the ability, inter alia, to know, understand, enter, visit, make use of, maintain, exchange and develop cultural heritage; to contribute to the identification, interpretation and development of cultural heritage, as well as to the design and implementation of preservation/safeguard policies and programmes. ...

31. Equal cultural rights would ensure women's ability to seek proactively knowledge and creative human expressions, scientific knowledge, applications and technologies and to widen their horizon, including beyond the cultural communities in which they are born and raised. Women must be able to access cultural goods and resources, institutions and

infrastructure that enable them to follow a specific way of life, including in the areas of leisure, sports, culture and education.

32. Information and communication technologies, including the Internet, are especially important for accessing information, establishing and developing contacts with persons with similar views beyond primary communities, as well as expressing oneself and contributing one's own knowledge and ideas.

33. Equal contribution to cultural life entails the ability to use imagination and intellect in both experiencing and producing works and events of one's own choice: spiritual and material, intellectual and emotional, including in all forms of artistic creativity, for example music and literature. Equally important is being able to engage in critical reflection to form conceptions of, and contribute to establishing, key values, norms and standards. Women must have the freedom to undertake scientific research, be recognized as knowledge holders and be able to contribute to the scientific enterprise without encumbrances. ...

34. All human communities, including nations, are characterized by a dominant culture that reflects the viewpoint and the interests of those with the power to ensure adherence to prescribed norms. The dominant culture is almost inevitably patriarchal in nature. ...

37. To enjoy equal cultural rights, women must become equal participants and decision makers in all the cultural affairs of their own specific communities, and in the wider "general" society. ...

65. The principle of universality of human rights can be a vehicle for building consensus, pluralism and democracy to enable women's attainment of full personhood through, inter alia, their cultural rights. The challenge, however, is that the complexities of gender inequality and the many layers and arenas it operates in cannot be addressed through a simple "one size fits all" theoretical model. Merely asserting the principle of "equality" is insufficient. Far greater and more rigorous attention needs to be devoted to formulating and implementing culturally relevant measures that catalyse transformative equality processes in each particular area of discrimination. It is suggested therefore that there is a need to understand universality as a transformative dialogue in which disparities in power are acknowledged, the diversity of the world is recognized and positively asserted, and the material necessities for ensuring human dignity are also addressed.

## B    Reflections and Questions

1. How can women own both their culture and human rights? In many ways this is really connected to the ability of women to have more influence and decision-making in the development and modification of cultural norms that work to their disadvantage with stereotypes and forms of discrimination. The increasing participation of women in the education, employment, public, and political lives of their countries is a precondition in many ways for women to transform patriarchal culture. As indicated *supra* in paragraph 37 of the U.N. Special Rapporteur's Report, the full protection of the rights of women to freedom of movement; opinion and expression, religion or belief; association; and to participate in social, economic, and political life are all important preconditions for women to become equal participants and decisionmakers in cultural affairs.

2. The Vienna Declaration and Programme of Action proclaimed human rights as universal, indivisible, interdependent, and interrelated.[30] Human rights – as recognized in the Universal Declaration of Human Rights, and other universal and regional human rights treaties – are supposed to apply equally to all cultures, religions, and historical circumstances. This notion has been challenged by the concept of *cultural relativism*, which represents the premise that individual beliefs, values, and practices should be conceived taking into consideration culture, and not just criteria imposed by external actors.[31] As we saw in Chapter 11, different regions have adopted their own treaties reflecting the experience and cultural history of Europe, the Americas, and Africa to the language of human rights. These regional human rights treaties, however, have also kept the essence of the civil, political, economic, social, and cultural rights protected by the international covenants. The regions of Asia and the Middle East have been more resistant to the notion of universalism embodied in the universal human rights treaties, as discussed in Chapter 11. Do you consider the principle of universalism useful or restrictive in the protection of the rights of women? Is universalism realistic? Should all cultures adhere to the principles of equality, non-discrimination, and freedom from gender-based violence according to universal standards?

## V    CONCLUSIONS: CULTURE AND RELIGION AS KEY TO THE HUMAN RIGHTS OF WOMEN

We are at a historical stage in which it is paramount that women can actively shape culture and religion. Their role should be transformative of patriarchal notions, norms, and stereotypes that work to their disadvantage. Women's autonomy and agency are key in this process. Only in this way will women be able to fully exercise their human rights in harmony with their rights to culture, freedom of religion, and to manifest religion and belief.

Culture and religion are also fundamental to the identity, history, and existence of many women. Human rights and the values of equality, non-discrimination, and non-violence should be part of every culture and religion. These are not just universal values. These are human values which are paramount to the advancement of women's autonomy, privacy, personal liberty, and dignity. Culture and religion should never be used to limit women's rights. To the contrary, they should be facilitators and enablers of women's rights. Women and LGBTI groups should be able to express their culture and religion without fearing that their human rights will be hindered or inhibited by fundamentalist views and religious tenets contrary to their human rights.

Even though the regulation of culture and religion reaches beyond the government and is relevant to individuals, society, and whole communities, states do have a mandate to reject practices which are harmful and not conducive to the full protection of the human rights of women in this arena. States also have a duty to prevent, supervise, and regulate the activities

---

[30]    *See* Vienna Declaration, World Conference on Human Rights, Vienna, 14–25 June 1993, U.N. Doc. A/CONF.157/24 (Part I) at 20 (1993), ¶ 5, https://www.un.org/en/development/desa/population/migration/generalassembly/docs/globalcompact/A_CONF.157_24.pdf.

[31]    For a discussion of the interplay of cultural relativism and women's rights in sub-Saharan Africa, *see* Norah Hashim Msuya, *Concept of Culture Relativism and Women's Rights in Sub-Saharan Africa*, 54(8) JOURNAL OF ASIAN AND AFRICAN STUDIES 1145–1158 (2019).

of state actors, private institutions, communities, and families invoking religion and culture which serve as barriers for women to fully enjoy their economic, social, civil, political, and cultural rights. This entails the reform of legislation, policies, and practices which are harmful to the exercise of the rights of women, girls, and LGBTI groups.

States can also be key entities in the transformations needed in culture and religion, thereby facilitating and opening spaces for women's leadership, influence, voices, and organizational work. The state's duties to act with due diligence; to respect and ensure non-discrimination and non-violence; to guarantee access to justice; and to ensure the right of women to effectively participate in public and private life acquire a special meaning and urgency in the case of culture and religion.

# 13. The human rights of women in the digital world

## I INTRODUCTION: THE GENDER DIGITAL DIVIDE

Every day the world is more digitalized and women are a part of this process. Women and girls increasingly use more computers, cell phones, the internet, virtual communication platforms, and social media. Technology is allowing all to communicate more transnationally, frequently, and in a more visible way. Technology was also paramount during the 2020–2021 COVID-19 pandemic to continue work, education, health care, and many other services during extended periods of lockdowns and quarantines. Technology and the internet today are paramount settings for discussions, decisions, reflections, and the finding of solutions.

Women's relationship with technology is very intricate and multifaceted. Women are users, participants, influencers, and creators. They can also be victims of human rights violations including forms of violence, hate speech, bullying, and forms of discrimination while using the internet and when participating in social media platforms. Even though the digital space can be empowering for women and girls, technology also magnifies the gender-based discrimination and violence they have faced historically, and can facilitate the curtailment of their right to effective participation.

This is an area in which international human rights law standards are still in development. There will no doubt be much more progress in the next decade, propelled by the increased digitalization during and after the COVID-19 pandemic.[1] One important issue is the role of states and non-state actors in this regulation. As discussed throughout this casebook, states are the primary holders of human rights obligations, and must act with due diligence to prevent, investigate, sanction, and grant reparations for all forms of discrimination and violence that women and girls may face in the realm of technology. However, there are many non-state actors involved in the use of technology, including increasingly large and well-resourced social media networks with millions of users. Sometimes these networks – though private – are wealthier and larger than countries themselves. These networks and their members also operate transnationally. How can states regulate, supervise, and oversee their activities? What are the responsibilities of these private actors themselves in the safeguarding of the rights of

---

[1]  For an overview of the impact of the COVID-19 pandemic on the problem of online violence against women, *see* UN Women, *Online and ICT facilitated violence against women and girls during COVID-19*, pp. 2–4, www.unwomen.org/-/media/headquarters/attachments/sections/library/publications/2020/brief-online-and-ict-facilitated-violence-against-women-and-girls-during-covid-19-en.pdf?la=en&vs=2519.

women and girls? What is the scope of the right to privacy in this realm? These are some of the questions explored in this chapter.

Another key issue explored is the role of women as users of technology. There is a well-documented gender digital divide, including financial and geographic barriers for women and girls to accessing needed forms of technology without delay.[2] Women and girls have also not been encouraged historically to enter STEM fields – Science, Technology, Engineering, and Mathematics.[3] This impairs their right to education, employment, effective participation, and social contributions. How can technological progress be used to advance gender equality and respect for the rights of women and girls?

This chapter discusses the different components of the human rights of women in the digital world, including the problem of violence against women online, women as users of technology, and the right to privacy.

## II   VIOLENCE AGAINST WOMEN ONLINE

Information and communication technologies (hereinafter "ICTs") have changed the way we interact, study, work, plan, and live. The readings below explore the way digitalization has also served to reproduce the existing inequalities faced by women and their consistent exposure to violence.

Even though ICTs have promoted women having more influence and voice in affairs related to their communities, and societies, they also serve as important settings for forms of gender-based violence and discrimination. Scholars and international organizations are beginning to recognize this alarming problem, its features, and ways to respond from a human rights, gender, and intersectional perspective. The readings below offer some examples of recent analysis produced in this area.

### A   Louise Arimatsu, *Silencing Women in the Digital Age*

8(2) CAMBRIDGE INTERNATIONAL LAW JOURNAL 187–217 (2019)[4]

Silence operates in multiple ways. It can represent an act of resistance or be a sign of deference, of unity, of solidarity, of remembrance, of contemplation. Silence can operate to establish and consolidate different formations of power, often hierarchical. In very many societies it functions as a manifestation of power.

In totalitarian states, silence is deployed as a technique to acquire and to reproduce power, through censorship and, as violence, in response to dissent. Thus, the ending of silence is often heralded as a marker or a sign of freedom, of liberty and of democracy. The breaking of silence

---

[2]   For more discussion on the impact of the digital revolution on women's rights issues, *see* Judy Wajcman, Erin Young, and Anna Fitzmaurice, UN Women, Discussion Paper: *The Digital Revolution: Implications for Gender Equality and Women's Rights 25 Years after Beijing*, pp. 4–5, 22–23, www.unwomen.org/-/media/headquarters/attachments/sections/library/publications/2020/the-digital-revolution-implications-for-gender-equality-and-womens-rights-25-years-after-beijing-en.pdf?la=en&vs=1837.

[3]   *See id.*, pp. 9–10.

[4]   Reproduced with permission of the Licensor through PLSclear.

constitutes a moment when what was suppressed is finally exposed, when hidden stories are released into public spaces, to be spoken about, documented and retold. But even in liberal democracies silence continues to operate in subtle and unveiled ways, including through structural silences. After all, contemporary forms of both democracy and international law are founded on the silencing of certain voices and narratives: who is entitled to speak, who they may speak to, what is heard, what is registered. Thus, to pay attention to the ways in which silence is employed or how it is interwoven in the formation and shaping of social relations is to gain an insight into the interests that are being protected and by whom.

The silencing of women, through political, social, cultural or legal exclusion, marginalization, diktat or violence has been, and remains, a common feature of patriarchy that is deeply embedded in all societies irrespective of political ideology, time or location. As an ideology or system of ideas and relations, patriarchy is adept at creating and utilizing silence to normalize and maintain gendered inequalities that privilege particular forms of masculinity over others, and over all forms of femininity through structures, practices, culture and law. …

As with international law, the field of technology is also highly gendered terrain. Often grouped with science, engineering and maths, technology is "firmly coded male", at least in contemporary Western society. The historical exclusion of women from these fields – commonly referred to as STEM – is widely acknowledged, although feminist scholars working in the field of Science and Technology Studies (STS) and feminist technoscience studies (FTS) have revealed a far more complex and ambiguous history of women's involvement in STEM, tracing the ways in which the political economy and patriarchy have operated to genderise these fields and the consequences that have followed. Through historical, sociological and cultural analyses, this scholarship, which critically explores the relationship between gender, science and technology, is not only reinstalling women's presence into the histories of the techno-sciences but is seeking to reconstitute our understanding of these fields, founded on the insight that each has been made masculine. …

The global growth in internet uptake has occurred at a rate well beyond all expectations. … For those operating within the international institutional structures, this was regarded as an important milestone since the prevailing view had long been that ICTs would enhance political, economic and social empowerment. Digital technologies would create new spaces of political engagement, promote greater transparency and accountability, and facilitate government and public-sector efficiency. …

Although the potential of ICTs to empower women had been recognized by the global women's movement by at least the mid-1990s, the primary focus of States during this early period was on expanding access to ICTs among and between States rather than as a means to further the political and social empowerment of women within States as was being urged by feminist activists and scholars. …

By the late 1990s the original euphoria was somewhat dampened by the realization that the digital revolution was deepening the socio-economic divide between countries, with the least developed being left further behind. Rather than closing the poverty gap, poverty was functioning to exclude access to ICTs, which was further entrenching material and non-material poverty. Today, 3.5 billion people still have no ICT access, the vast majority of whom are located in the poorest countries in Africa and Asia. Within countries, ICTs were reproducing the same pattern. Not only were 'new technologies travel[ling] on old social relations' but pre-existing disparities were being accentuated by digital technologies, further excluding already marginalized communities, including women. By 2003, the digital gender divide was high on the agenda of the international community. ...

The growing body of empirical research being generated by scholars, particularly in the field of development studies, is providing a far more contextual understanding of the impediments to access and use that are confronted by differently situated women most notably, but not exclusively, in the Global South. While these research outputs are providing granularity, for many working in the field the findings come as no surprise. For example, in too many societies girls and women continue to be prevented from acquiring basic literacy and language skills, let alone computer skills, by patriarchal structures, institutions and cultures. Studies show that common barriers include the diversion of family savings to providing dowries for girls rather than investing in their education; the prevalence of early marriage for girls; the failure to cater for the specific needs of girls and women in educational establishments; and gender stereo-typing. Even when women have managed to acquire basic IT skills, the fact that on average they spend 2.6 times more time than men on unpaid care and domestic work means that they have less time to acquire new IT skills and knowledge. The knock-on effect of this reality is that they are often confined to lower-skilled jobs and, with less income, accessibility to and use of ICTs becomes that much more unaffordable. The lack of dependable ICT infrastructure coupled with restricted access to public access sites, including internet cafes – which are often inhospitable sites for women and girls – further discriminate against women's ability to access ICTs. Patriarchal socio-cultural norms often mean that in traditional communities the male members of the household retain control over women's and girls' access to the technology. ...

In a world that is becoming increasingly digitized, the implications of exclusion from access to and use of ICTs raise serious concerns, direct and indirect, immediate and long-term. Exclusion is already leaving many women less equipped than men to exercise their human rights and to benefit from the technology on an equal footing with men. ...

As the digital economy has grown, women from all walks of life are being assimilated into the pre-existing gendered structures as users of the technology rather than as shapers and influencers. As such, their voices are silenced. ...

**B       Report of the Special Rapporteur on violence against women, its causes and consequences, Dubravka Šimonović, *Online violence against women and girls from a human rights perspective***

A/HRC/38/47
June 18, 2018

12. Online and ICT-facilitated forms of violence against women have become increasingly common, particularly with the use, every day and everywhere, of social media platforms and other technical applications. In today's digital age, the Internet and ICT are rapidly creating new social digital spaces and transforming how individuals meet, communicate and interact, and by this more generally, reshape society as a whole. This development is especially critical for new generations of girls and boys, who are starting their lives extensively using new technologies to mediate in their relationships, affecting all aspects of their lives. In the section below, the Special Rapporteur considers the phenomenon of

violence against women facilitated by new technologies and digital spaces from a human rights perspective.

13. Even though the core international human rights instruments, including those on women's rights, were drafted before the advent of ICT, they provide a global and dynamic set of rights and obligations with transformative potential, and have a key role to play in the promotion and protection of fundamental human rights, including a woman's rights to live a life free from violence, to freedom of expression, to privacy, to have access to information shared through ICT, and other rights.

14. When women and girls do have access to and use the Internet, they face online forms and manifestations of violence that are part of the continuum [of] multiple, recurring and interrelated forms of gender-based violence against women. Despite the benefits and empowering potential of the Internet and ICT, women and girls across the world have increasingly voiced their concern at harmful, sexist, misogynistic and violent content and behavior online. It is therefore important to acknowledge that the Internet is being used in a broader environment of widespread and systemic structural discrimination and gender-based violence against women and girls, which frame their access to and use of the Internet and other ICT. Emerging forms of ICT have facilitated new types of gender-based violence and gender inequality in access to technologies, which hinder women's and girls' full enjoyment of their human rights and their ability to achieve gender equality.

15. Terminology in this area is still developing and not univocal. In several official United Nations documents, and in particular the 2030 Agenda for Sustainable Development, reference is made to the general and inclusive term "information and communications technology" (or ICT), while in other reports "online violence", "digital violence" or "cyber-violence" are used. In the present report, the Special Rapporteur refers to "ICT-facilitated violence against women" as the most inclusive term, but mainly uses "online violence against women" as a more user-friendly expression. Where appropriate, she uses both terms, as well as the terms "cyberviolence" and "technology-facilitated violence" as alternatives. Mindful that many forms of online violence covered in the report are perpetrated against both women and girls, she uses the term "women" in an inclusive manner, which includes girls whenever applicable, while recognizing that girls are a frequent target of this form of violence.

16. Despite being a relatively new phenomenon and, consequently, the lack of comprehensive data, it has been estimated that 23 per cent of women have reported having experienced online abuse or harassment at least once in their life, and that 1 in 10 women has experienced some form of online violence since the age of 15.

17. At the normative level, the interaction between technology and women's human rights standards is marked by the recognition of the principle that human rights protected offline should also be protected online. Since women's rights are human rights and the prohibition of gender-based violence has been recognized as a principle of international human rights law, women's human rights as developed through comprehensive regional and international conventions, jurisprudence and norms should be protected online, including through the prohibition of gender-based violence in its ICT-facilitated and online forms. Furthermore, States have established positive obligations to ensure that fundamental human rights are protected, respected and fulfilled.

18. Protecting women's human rights and eliminating violence against women and girls in public and private life in the "real world" remains a global challenge that has now spread to the digital space of social media, such as Instagram, Twitter, Facebook, Reddit, YouTube and Tumblr, and in other mobile telephone communications technology, micro-blogging sites and messaging applications (such as WhatsApp, Snapchat, Messenger, Weibo and Line), which are now a part of everyday life for many people around the world.

19. This new global digital space has great potential for ensuring the faster and fuller promotion and enjoyment of all human rights, including women's rights. The power to use this potential for protecting women's human rights and achieving gender equality does not, however, reside only in the technologies themselves; much also depends on the ways that people access and use those new technologies. There is a significant risk that the use of ICT without a human rights-based approach and the prohibition of online gender-based violence could broaden sexual and gender-based discrimination and violence against women and girls in society even further. …

25. The consequences of and harm caused by different manifestations of online violence are specifically gendered, given that women and girls suffer from particular stigma in the context of structural inequality, discrimination and patriarchy. Women subjected to online violence are often further victimized through harmful and negative gender stereotypes, which are prohibited by international human rights law. The Internet has become a site of diverse forms of violence against women and girls, in the form of pornography, sexist games and breaches of privacy. For women who engage in public debate through the Internet, the risk of harassment is experienced online; for example, an anonymous negative campaign calling for the gang rape of a woman human rights defender, with racist abuse posted in her Wikipedia profile. Female ICT users have publicly protested about sexist attacks.

26. Acts of online violence may force women to retreat from the Internet. Research indicates that 28 per cent of women who had suffered ICT-based violence intentionally reduced their presence online. …

29. Women human rights defenders, journalists and politicians are directly targeted, threatened, harassed or even killed for their work. They receive online threats, generally of a misogynistic nature, often sexualized and specifically gendered. The violent nature of these threats often leads to self-censorship. Some resort to the use of pseudonyms, while others maintain low online profiles, an approach that can have a detrimental impact on their professional lives and reputations. Others decide to suspend, deactivate or permanently delete their online accounts, or to leave the profession entirely. …

31. ICT may be used directly as a tool for making digital threats and inciting gender-based violence, including threats of physical and/or sexual violence, rape, killing, unwanted and harassing online communications, or even the encouragement of others to harm women physically. It may also involve the dissemination of reputation-harming lies, electronic sabotage in the form of spam and malignant viruses, impersonation of the victim online and the sending of abusive emails or spam, blog posts, tweets or other online communications in the victim's name. ICT-facilitated violence against women may also be committed in the work place or in the form of so-called "honor-based" violence or of domestic violence by intimate partners. Women who speak out about their abuse online are frequently and increasingly threatened with legal proceedings, such as for defamation, which aims to

prevent them from reporting their situation. Such behavior may form part of a pattern of domestic violence and abuse. …

33. There are many new emerging forms of violence against women with ICT-related names, such as "doxing", "sextortion" and "trolling". Some forms of violence against women carry the prefix "online", such as online mobbing, online stalking and online harassment. New forms of violence have also developed, such as the non-consensual distribution of intimate contents ("revenge porn").

34. Online violence against women may be manifested in different forms and through different means, such as non-consensual accessing, using, manipulating, disseminating or sharing of private data, information and/or content, photographs and/or videos, including sexualized images, audio clips and/or video clips or Photoshopped images.

35. "Sextortion" refers to the use of ICT to blackmail a victim. In such cases, the perpetrator threatens to release intimate pictures of the victim in order to extort additional explicit photos, videos, sexual acts or sex from the victim.

36. "Doxing" refers to the publication of private information, such as contact details, on the Internet with malicious intent, usually with the insinuation that the victim is soliciting sex (researching and broadcasting personally identifiable information about an individual without consent, sometimes with the intention of exposing the woman to the "real" world for harassment and/or other purposes). It includes situations where personal information and data retrieved by a perpetrator is made public with malicious intent, clearly violating the right to privacy.

37. "Trolling" consists in the posting of messages, the uploading of images or videos and the creation of hashtags for the purpose of annoying, provoking or inciting violence against women and girls. Many "trolls" are anonymous and use false accounts to generate hate speech.

38. Online mobbing and harassment refer to the online equivalents of mobbing or harassment on social platforms, the Internet, in chat rooms, instant messaging and mobile communications.

39. Online stalking is the repeated harassment of individuals, perpetrated by means of mobile phones or messaging applications, in the form of crank calls or private conversations on online applications (such as WhatsApp) or in online chat groups.

40. Online sexual harassment refers to any form of online unwanted verbal or nonverbal conduct of a sexual nature with the purpose or effect of violating the dignity of a person, in particular by creating an intimidating, hostile, degrading, humiliating or offensive environment.

41. "Revenge porn" consists in the non-consensual online dissemination of intimate images, obtained with or without consent, with the purpose of shaming, stigmatizing or harming the victim.

42. All the above-mentioned forms of online violence create a permanent digital record that can be distributed worldwide and cannot be easily deleted, which may result in further victimization of the victim. Relevant data and surveys have shown that, in the majority of cases, online violence is not a gender-neutral crime. Surveys of the gender dimension of online violence indeed indicate that 90 per cent of those victimized by non-consensual digital distribution of intimate images are women. …

**C    Reflections and Questions**

1. Dr. Louise Arimatsu discusses in her article the ways that technology and the digital revolution are silencing women and furthering their exclusion and marginalization. Technology can serve to reproduce existing inequalities and gender-based violence against women and girls, as exemplified by the current problem of online violence and its forms, as well as the barriers women still face to access, use, and control technology. Technology can also be a very important facilitator of the rights of women. It can amplify the voices and perspectives of women and girls, offering an additional setting in which to present ideas, agendas, and plans, as well to influence and shape discourse. This was exemplified by the *MeToo* movement and the numerous women and girls voicing their views and expressing their creativity in social media platforms today. Social media platforms have become also paramount to the work and visibility of women human rights defenders, politicians, and journalists. Can you think of other ways in which technology has been beneficial for the participation of women and girls in society?

2. As discussed in Chapter 1, Article 2 of CEDAW and General Recommendation 28 of the CEDAW Committee have outlined three sets of obligations states have to meet to fully comply with CEDAW obligations. States have an obligation to respect and refrain from adopting laws, policies, and regulations that directly or indirectly impact the equal enjoyment by women of their civil, political, economic, social, and cultural rights. States also have an obligation to protect women from discrimination by private actors, and take steps to directly eliminate negative stereotypical practices. Thirdly, the obligation to fulfill requires state parties to take steps to ensure that women and men enjoy equal rights in the law, and in practice, which may entail temporary special measures. Which steps can states adopt to meet these three obligations towards women in the area of technology and digitalization?

3. Dr. Arimatsu also discusses the problem of non-state actors and online violence. This is probably one of the most challenging areas to regulate from a human rights perspective. A great deal of online violence against women is committed by individual users of social medial platforms and the internet.[5] These social media platforms are private companies which are very wealthy, having very limited government regulation. Many of the platforms are used frequently to commit acts of online violence against women. Some of the main social platforms have announced initiatives to prevent and address human rights violations. For example, Facebook has launched a corporate human rights policy, which includes international human rights standards that will govern its work, in harmony with the U.N. Ruggie Principles.[6] Facebook has also established an Independent Oversight Board, which

---

[5]    *See for example*, Melissa Davey, *Online violence against women "flourishing", and most common on Facebook, survey finds*, THE GUARDIAN, Oct. 4, 2020, www.theguardian.com/society/2020/oct/05/online-violence-against-women-flourishing-and-most-common-on-facebook-survey-finds; Amnesty International, *Toxic Twitter: A Toxic Place for Women* (March 15, 2018), www.amnesty.org/en/latest/research/2018/03/online-violence-against-women-chapter-1/#topanchor.

[6]    Miranda Sissons, Director of Human Rights, *Our Commitment to Human Rights*, Facebook (March 16, 2021), https://about.fb.com/news/2021/03/our-commitment-to-human-rights/.

reviews content decisions, considering safety and freedom of expression concerns.[7] Twitter has also issued its own policy against hateful conduct, prohibiting violence, direct attacks, and threats on the basis of gender and gender identity, including imagery and symbols.[8]

Article 2(e) of CEDAW mandates all states to take all appropriate measures to eliminate discrimination against women by any person, organization, or enterprise. The U.N. Ruggie Principles also mandate states to supervise the work of businesses and to prevent human rights violations. Under the U.N. Ruggie Principles, businesses themselves have an obligation to do no harm, and to guarantee access to remedies when human rights violations do occur. How can states regulate better the activity of social media platforms? What kind of policies, programs, and initiatives can social media platforms adopt to prevent and address gender-based violence and discrimination? How can social media platforms incorporate international human rights law standards in their daily work and operations?

4.  The U.N. Special Rapporteur on violence against women in her report discusses many forms of online violence against women. Her examples include harmful, sexist, and misogynistic behavior; the sharing of violent content and images; bullying; advocacy of sexual violence; and pornography. This behavior can have a very specific impact on girls, who are heavy users of the internet and social media platforms, and are growing up in societies in which these constitute an essential part of the way we communicate, receive education, work, and obtain information. The U.N. Special Rapporteur also gives very grim statistics of the magnitude of the problem of online violence. According to the U.N. Special Rapporteur, 23 percent of women have experienced online harassment and one in ten women have experienced online harassment since the age of 15.[9]

5.  The U.N. Special Rapporteur on violence against women also acknowledges in her report that the terminology is still evolving when it comes to online violence against women. She refers to emerging forms, including sextortion, doxing, and trolling.[10] She also discusses the problem of revenge porn which has garnered increased attention in the United States.[11] As the U.N. Special Rapporteur indicates, revenge porn typically refers to the online dissemination of intimate images – obtained with or without consent – with the objective of perpetrating harm on a victim. The online dissemination occurs without consent and with the intent to stigmatize or humiliate the woman or girl involved. There has been reporting indicating that the COVID-19 pandemic and the increased usage of the internet and digitalization have worsened the problem of revenge porn in the United States.[12] Can you think of

---

[7]   Nick Clegg, *Charting a Course for an Oversight Board for Content Decisions*, Facebook (Jan. 28, 2019), https://about.fb.com/news/2019/01/oversight-board/.

[8]   Twitter, *Hateful Conduct Policy*, https://help.twitter.com/en/rules-and-policies/hateful-conduct-policy (last visited on May 19, 2021).

[9]   *See* Report of the Special Rapporteur on violence against women, its causes and consequences, Dubravka Šimonović, *Online violence against women and girls from a human rights perspective*, A/HRC/38/47, ¶ 16 (June 18, 2018), discussed *supra*.

[10]   *Id.*, ¶¶ 35–37.

[11]   *Id.*, ¶ 41.

[12]   For more reading, *see* Jessica M. Goldstein, *Revenge porn was already commonplace. The pandemic has made things even worse*, THE WASHINGTON POST, Oct. 29, 2020, www.washingtonpost.com/lifestyle/style/revenge-porn-nonconsensual-porn/2020/10/28/603b88f4-dbf1-11ea-b205-ff838e15a9a6_story.html.

other forms of online violence against women and girls that could be eventually recognized as human rights violations?

6. The regional human rights protection systems have begun pronouncing over online violence. For example, the European Court of Human Rights ruled on the case of *Buturugă v. Romania* on February 11, 2020, in which the Court recognized cyberbullying as connected to domestic violence against women, and referred to its different forms, including the unauthorized intrusion into the victim's computer and Facebook account, the manipulation of data and images, and the breach of privacy.[13] The applicant reported acts of domestic violence before the authorities, including a breach of confidentiality of correspondence claim, and requested the search of her family computer, alleging that the perpetrator made copies of their private communications, documents, and photos.[14] The police rejected this request from the applicant considering this unrelated to the domestic violence acts alleged.[15] The Court found that the state had not complied with its positive obligations under Articles 3 and 8 of the European Convention on Human Rights to adequately address and sanction domestic violence by failing to consider the cyberviolence allegations.[16] Consider the different case applications that could be received by the European Court of Human Rights in the future, raising cyberbullying and cyberviolence claims affecting women and girls.

## III     ACCESS TO AND USE OF TECHNOLOGY

The existing inequalities women face socially are reproduced in their use of and access to technology. These differences are called frequently the gender digital divide. The United Nations High Commissioner for Human Rights has defined the gender digital divide as the gap between women and men in their access to, use of, ability to contribute to and influence information and communication technologies.[17]

Women and girls face important financial, geographic, educational, literacy, and information barriers to use, access, and control computers, the internet, social media, smartphones, and other key advances. Gender-based violence can also be a formidable impediment for the greater voice and presence of women in the digital space, as discussed in the previous section. All these variables can be detrimental to the education, employment, and effective participation of women and girls in their communities and society as a whole.

The readings below discuss some of these obstacles and their human rights implications.

**A       Organisation for Economic Co-operation and Development,** *Bridging the Digital Divide: Include, Upskill, and Innovate* **(2018), pp. 22–24**

www.oecd.org/digital/bridging-the-digital-gender-divide.pdf

---

[13]   *See* Buturugă v. Romania, App. No. 56867/15, Eur. Ct. H.R, ¶¶ 5–21, 74–79 (Feb. 11, 2020).

[14]   *See id.*, ¶¶ 5–21.

[15]   *See id.*

[16]   *See id.*, ¶¶ 74–79.

[17]   *See* United Nations High Commissioner for Human Rights, *Promotion, protection and enjoyment of human rights on the Internet: ways to bridge the gender digital divide from a human rights perspective*, A/HRC/35/9, ¶ 3 (May 5, 2017).

### The Gender Digital Divide and Its Root Causes

The digital transformation offers immense opportunities for economies and societies. However, the benefits of the digital transformation are currently not equally balanced between societal groups and genders and access, use and ownership of digital tools are not gender-neutral. The term "digital gender divide" is frequently used to refer to these types of gender differences in resources and capabilities to access and effectively utilize ICTs within and between countries, regions, sectors and socio-economic groups.

There are a number of root causes of the digital gender divide, including hurdles to access, affordability, education (or lack thereof) and lack of technological literacy, as well as inherent biases and socio-cultural norms that lead to gender-based digital exclusion. Women were found to do 2.6 times the amount of unpaid care and domestic work that men do, which leaves them less times to grow their careers. There is a recognition that action is needed across diverse areas to ensure all women and girls can fully participate in the online world.

Affordability is a challenge for all but affects disproportionally more women and girls, and remains one of the key hurdles in accessing ICTs. Also, the digital gender divide is found to increase as technological sophistication and functionality grows and with the cost of ownership. ...

Another reason why fewer women than men use digital tools is the lack of awareness of the potential benefits that the Internet may bring. Women are significantly more likely than men to not use the Internet because they think they "do not need it" or they "do not want it ..." Evidently, lack of trust in digital devices or the Internet may also play a role, despite women mainly reporting lack of interest or having low expectations about its usefulness and relevance to their local context.

Illiteracy further hinders women's and girls' ability to access online services. About 83% of women worldwide are literate, compared to 90% of men, and illiterate women only appear to be using online platform services, such as Skype and YouTube, that are more familiar to them or are easier to access and use. To try and address this hurdle, some search engines, such as Google, have installed voice navigation systems in local languages to make Internet search queries more accessible and inclusive.

The digital gender divide is also fueled by digital illiteracy, which often translates in lack of comfort in using technology and accessing the Internet. Such "technophobia" is often a result of concurrent factors including education, employment status and income level. ...

Additionally, socio-cultural reasons play an important role in explaining the digital gender divide. In India and Egypt, around one-fifth of women were found to believe that the Internet was not appropriate for them, for a number of cultural reasons. In India, around 12% of women report not to use the Internet because of the negative social perception associated to its use, and 8% due to the lack of acceptance by family members. In the case of women, in fact, family support emerges as a key enabler when it comes to using the Internet. Active female Internet users are three times more likely to have families who are "very supportive" of their Internet use, whereas female non-users are six times more likely to be exposed to family opposition. Such family hurdles can range from lack of support to outright discouragement or even prohibition.

Safety-related issues are often a key reason for families' opposition to the use of the Internet or the ownership of a mobile phone for both women and girls in developing and emerging economies. For example, for women in the People's Republic of China and Mexico, harassment is among the top barriers in owning and using a mobile phone. Women and girls using the Internet can be exposed to additional risks, including cyberstalking, online harassment or even sexual trafficking, and it thus becomes crucial to develop measures to protect and prevent gender-based violence online. …

OECD work finds that students spend a considerable amount of time online, making it crucial to understand whether and how Internet use influences students' well-being. On the one hand, Internet tools, including online networks, social media and interactive technologies, are giving rise to new learning styles where young people see themselves as agents of their own learning, where they can produce multimedia content, update and redefine their interests, and learn more about the world, others and themselves. On the other hand though, online activities pose several risks to well-being, ranging from peer pressure (cyber bullying) and stigmatization to sexting to being groomed by strangers. OECD finds that social networks can have an impact on girls' health as they are the object of more personal attacks and cyber bullying. When it happens to 15-year-old teenage girls, this can create risky situations and may impact their health and well-being. …

Finally, the ability of women to access and use digital technologies is directly and indirectly affected by market-related factors including investment dynamics, regulations, and competition, especially in rural areas. In rural areas, which are often scarcely populated, the investment and installation of infrastructures, such as broadband infrastructures and cell phone towers, is less economically profitable. This can affect disproportionally more women in developing countries as they seem to be more often located in rural areas, whereas working age men tend to be mainly in urban areas. Women and girls in rural areas of developing countries further face persistent structural constraints, including their higher probability to be out of school than boys – their likelihood is twice as high as girls in urban areas. …

**B**　　**Laura J. Dixon, Teresa Correa, Joseph Straubhaar, Laura Covarrubias, Dean Graber, Jeremiah Spence, Viviana Rojas,** *Gendered Space: The Digital Divide between Male and Female Users in Internet Public Access Sites*

19 JOURNAL OF COMPUTER-MEDIATED COMMUNICATION 991–1009, 993–996 (2014)
© 2014 International Communication Association
Reproduced with permission from Oxford University Press
Citations and footnotes omitted

### Gender and Technology
From the structuration framework of understanding the individual's relationship to their social structure, we have looked to more specific scholarship on women and technology. Despite having different approaches, many scholars have suggested that relationships with technology are gendered. Some even argue that the phenomenon of technology itself cannot be fully understood without reference to gender. …

Technology enables changes in society, so technology plays a role in the construction of gender by creating new possibilities of how gender roles might be performed in a new area. However, in the social shaping view, gender also shapes the construction and meanings of technology. For example, domestic technologies are strongly associated with women and femininity. Computer use was initially associated with males, such as in the stereotype of the computer geek, but that gendering began to change as more women in diverse roles began to use computers and go online. ...

## Socialization and gender gap

Perceiving technology as a gendered space illuminates the ways women and men are socialized to develop different relationships with technology from childhood, at home and school. When the computer was in its early stages of adoption, boys were three times more likely to use a computer and participate in computer-related activities. Although those gaps have diminished, there are strong differences in the way women relate to technology, particularly computers and the Internet. Statistics suggest that since 2000, women are equally likely to have access to the Internet; however, men are more frequent and intense users of the Internet than women. Men have also taken more technology classes and are more likely to have had a computer in their own room, which provides more opportunities to experiment and acquire confidence and skills associated with digital technologies. Males use the Internet more than women for a wide range of activities, particularly those that require greater technological skills such as job searching, e-banking, and posting or uploading materials. Regarding attitudes toward technology, there are no major gender differences in the actual abilities to locate online content in an effective and efficient way. However, women perceive that their abilities are significantly lower than men's, which eventually may affect their motivation and online behavior. Similarly, while women's interest in computers and technology has increased, they still feel more uncomfortable with technology than men.

What are the roots of these differences? Research on the gender divide points to the social development of boys and girls and the social expectations and stereotypes about what is appropriate for both genders. Generally, children are socialized to computers through video games. Video games are not only experienced through peer-learning, but educators also use them to make the learning experience in schools more enjoyable. The competitive nature of video games makes them more attractive to boys than girls. In addition, computer software is usually developed for and marketed toward males. As a result, boys feel more attracted to and develop more confidence with computers, while many girls develop negative attitudes, lowered interest, and anxiety. ...

Another reason behind the digital gender gap is the effect of household chores and childrearing. The second shift faced by women as workers in both their workplace and household leads to a gendering of leisure time. Often, women have less time than men to pass time, pursue hobbies, and experiment on the Internet.

## Internet public access and women

Because of awareness of the persistent digital divide in low-income communities, local and national policy initiatives have attempted to address the problem of the digital divide by providing access to Internet technologies through several venues, including community technology centers (CTCs), and public libraries.

As demonstrated by the research in The Persistence of Inequity, most Austin libraries, similarly to most libraries across the nation, have continued to change in the past decade to adapt to the evolving needs of patrons. In so doing, the space of libraries has become more dominated by technology. Card catalogs are almost exclusively accessible through the Internet; DVD,

CD, and laptop rentals are available; and of course, Internet access is provided. The modern library provides much of its information mediated through technology. The automated systems such as online catalogs and online databases provide access to more information sources but reduce access to information for the people who are not tech-savvy. ...

A survey drawn from Internet users of CTCs found that community technology centers were particularly important for connectivity for women and ethnic minorities. Many of these centers were forced to stop as federal funding decreased in the early 2000s. Previous research has indicated that men use public access at modestly higher rates than women. A survey conducted in the Colorado Public Libraries in 2002 revealed that men were somewhat more likely than women to use public libraries for Internet access (55% vs. 45%). Males also used library computers somewhat more frequently than women; 54% of males used them more than once a week compared to 43% of females. Moe has argued that this moderate difference may indicate that public access is contributing to the reduction of the gender gap. Nonetheless, it is also noteworthy that as public libraries become more technology-oriented, the places tradition-ally occupied and determined by women and children—as both employees and patrons—may become more masculine spaces. Another survey conducted only among women library patrons of Chester County Library in Exton, PA, found that females used the library mostly to borrow books and for children's activities. They also mentioned using public computers but it was not a first priority. Although 74% of female respondents felt comfortable using computers, 34% used them in the library.

Regarding attitudes toward libraries, the literature has found a strong association between computer anxiety and library anxiety, particularly among women. This finding suggests that the introduction of computer technology to the library has triggered negative emotional responses among women, especially because they feel lack of support. ...

## C    Reflections and Questions

1. The Organisation for Economic Co-operation and Development (hereinafter "OECD") in its *Gender Digital Divide* report discusses some of the most important causes of this problem affecting women and girls. Among some of the important challenges are affordability of technology, the lack of infrastructure in rural areas, and digital illiteracy. Other issues are social and parental biases; the burden of unpaid and domestic work on women and girls; and the safety and cyber violence issues discussed earlier. The OECD also discusses the lack of trust on the internet and digital devices that women and girls can have. Can you think of effective ways to disseminate information about the uses and advantages of technology among women, girls, and their families? Can you identify steps that can be adopted by states to increase the accessibility and affordability of technology for women and girls? How do you promote women's and girls' trust in technology?[18] Is promoting trust in technology a human rights obligation for states?

---

[18]    For more reading on ways to increase women's access to information and communications technologies, *see generally* Transcript of Hearing before Committee of Foreign Affairs, U.S. House of Representatives, *Women and Technology: Increasing Opportunity and Driving International Development* (Nov. 17, 2015), https://docs.house.gov/meetings/FA/FA00/20151117/104198/HHRG-114-FA00-Transcript-20151117.pdf.

2. The article on the *Gendered Space* discusses the relationship between technology and gender issues. It analyzes how the relationship with technology really stems in many ways from the different social development and raising of girls and boys. Other scholars have discussed how technology is frequently designed with male users in mind and marketed to men in general.[19] The COVID-19 pandemic, which affected the world between 2020 and 2021, propelled girls to conduct most of their education for close to two years virtually, remotely, and through technology. This means that the current generation of girls has had more exposure in general to technology and the virtual world. Can you think of ways in which this digital progression can change prevailing gender stereotypes of women's and girls' use of technology? Can technology become an important tool to promote the respect, protection, and fulfillment of the civil, political, economic, social, and cultural rights of women? How can women better exercise their rights to education, employment, and effective participation through technology?

3. The United Nations High Commissioner for Human Rights (hereinafter "OHCHR") has also expressed concern over the gender digital divide.[20] The OHCHR has documented how globally 250 million fewer women than men are online, and that women are less likely than men to use mobile telephones, social media applications, and SMS services.[21] It has identified important drivers of the gender digital divide, including challenges in access to equipment, solutions, connectivity and data, as well as the digital skills, knowledge, and opportunities to access ICTs.[22] The OHCHR recommended to states to apply a human rights-based approach to ensure that policies and programs geared to enhance access to technology are guided by the principles of accountability, equality and non-discrimination, participation, transparency, empowerment, and sustainability.[23] This also entails that individuals can challenge violations of their human rights and have adequate and effective access to remedies. Can you think of ways in which a gender and intersectional perspective can guide the implementation of this human rights framework by states in addressing the gender digital divide?

4. Every day women are undertaking more important roles using technology. They are engineers, scientists, researchers, network designers, innovators, and influencers. One interesting case has been women scientists and researchers who had a key role as the designers of vaccines and other forms of treatments during the 2020–2021 COVID-19 pandemic.[24] The 2020 Nobel Prize in Chemistry was also awarded to two women doctors for developing a method for genome editing.[25] However, the United Nations has reported that less than 30 percent of all researchers worldwide are women, and only 30 percent of female students

---

[19]    For more reading *see* Lori Andrews, *The Technology Enterprise: Systemic Bias Against Women*, 9 U.C. IRVINE L. REV. 1035, 1037–1045, 1050–1055 (2019).

[20]    *See generally* United Nations High Commissioner for Human Rights, *Promotion, protection and enjoyment of human rights on the Internet: ways to bridge the gender digital divide from a human rights perspective*, A/HRC/35/9 (May 5, 2017).

[21]    *See id.*, ¶¶ 5 and 7.

[22]    *Id.*, ¶ 9.

[23]    *Id.*, ¶ 14.

[24]    *See* Norah O'Donnell, *Meet the women at forefront of COVID-19 vaccine development*, CBS News, April 1, 2021, www.cbsnews.com/news/covid-vaccine-nita-patel-kizzmekia-corbett/.

[25]    *See* The Nobel Prize Press Release, *The Nobel Prize in Chemistry 2020*: *Emmanuelle Charpentier and Jennifer A. Doudna*, www.nobelprize.org/prizes/chemistry/2020/press-release/.

select STEM-related fields.[26] Can you think of ways to incentivize women and girls to enter STEM-related fields? What is the role of states and private actors in creating these incentives? Is this an international human rights law obligation?

# IV  THE RIGHT TO PRIVACY

The right to privacy is intimately connected with the use and access of technology by women. Concerns related to breaches of privacy in the use of computers, smartphones, the internet, social media, interactive virtual spaces, and other information and communication technologies can be a reality. These breaches of privacy can be propelled by both government and private actors.

The right to privacy is an important part of international human rights law. It is connected to the principles of autonomy, personal liberty, dignity, and equality. There is a presumption of intimate zones which should be free from arbitrary and unjustified intrusions without justification. The right to privacy applies to all spheres of human interaction, including the family, the community, employment, education, public and political life, and the digital setting. As discussed earlier, the digital space offers the opportunity to individuals and groups to amplify the experiences of the non-digital world. Therefore, it also increases the possibility of and exposure to breaches of privacy. These breaches are often combined with prevailing forms of gender-based violence, discrimination, and stereotypes, to place obstacles on women's and girls' ability to express their voices, views, influence, and participation in the virtual space.

The readings below present examples of breaches of privacy in connection with the digital setting and the contours of the human rights involved.

## A      Right to Privacy

Report of the Special Rapporteur on the right to privacy, A/HRC/40/63
October 16, 2019

50. While not an absolute right, the right to privacy is essential to the free development of an individual's personality and identity. It is a right that both derives from and conditions the innate dignity of the person and facilitates the exercise and enjoyment of other human rights. It is a right not restricted to the public sphere.
51. The right to privacy, as a necessary precondition for the protection of fundamental values, including liberty, dignity, equality and freedom from government intrusion, is an essential ingredient for democratic societies, and requires strong protection. The Human Rights Council has adopted resolutions highlighting the interdependent and mutually reinforcing relationship between democracy and human rights. …
55. It was reported that individuals' experience of digital technologies and privacy is affected by their gender, together with factors such as ethnicity, culture, race, age, social origin, wealth, economic self-sufficiency, education and legal and political frameworks. The right

---

[26]   United Nations, International Day of Women and Girls in Science, *Women Scientists at the Forefront of the Fight against COVID-19* (Feb. 11, 2021), www.un.org/en/observances/women-and-girls-in-science-day.

to privacy was said to be particularly important for those who face inequality, discrimination or marginalization on the basis of their gender, sexual orientation, gender identity, sex characteristics or expression. The Internet, with its reach and relative anonymity, has opened new ways for the interaction and mutual support of lesbian, gay, bisexual, transgender, queer and intersex (LGBTQI) people.

56. In submissions, it was recognized that digital technologies have a considerable effect upon privacy by amplifying the experiences of the non-digital world. The benefits of digital technologies were reported as unequally available, owing to structural inequity and discriminatory gender norms that fall heavily upon women, non-binary gender and cisnormative individuals, the poor and minority religious or cultural communities. Cybermisogyny and general cyberabuse of individuals of non-binary gender are enabled by new technologies with infinitely greater reach, durability and impact than previously.

57. The view was strongly expressed in submissions that that does not need to be the case, and digital technology can provide equality in the enjoyment of the right to privacy.

58. In submissions the benefits of smart devices, apps, search engines and social media platforms were recognized, but also their capacity to breach users' privacy according to gender. LGBTQI youth for example, use the Internet more frequently to engage in social media and networking than non-LGBTQI peers and are more likely than non-LGBTQI youth to be bullied or harassed online (42 per cent compared with 15 per cent).

59. Despite the benefits of digital technologies, those most at risk were seen as women, girls, children and LGBTQI individuals and communities, in particular transgender individuals, activists, gay teachers, human rights defenders, sex workers and women journalists. ...

61. It has been found in Canada that social media, while enabling social connections for women and girls, amplifies societal norms by intensifying commercial surveillance; reinforcing existing societal norms and increasing surveillance by family members and peers.

62. Fake accounts on LGBTQI dating apps and other social media platforms were reported as being used by State and non-State actors to entrap gay men and arrest or subject them to cruel and degrading treatment, or for blackmail.

63. It was reported that the media, including new media, publish the personal information of LGBTQI people and of human rights defenders, putting their safety at risk.

64. The Internet not only creates contemporary stories but can carry forward in perpetuity those of the pre-digital era, and associated violations of privacy.

65. Some submissions addressed the recognition of gender identity, autonomy and bodily integrity and the expression thereof and expressed their concern for inadequate privacy management in the context of name and gender changes in identity documents. Ordinary, everyday activities requiring identity documents, such as travel, banking, medical appointments, frequently impose deeply embarrassing and distressing privacy incursions for transgender individuals not experienced by individuals of binary genders.

66. The European Court of Human Rights has found States in violation of article 8 of the European Convention on Human Rights for the gender recognition procedures that violate the right to privacy of transgender people.

67. The online availability of public records, judicial notices and decisions concerning gender identity were a privacy concern, in particular in combination with big data and search engine capacity. ...

70. Digital technology and smart devices provide almost limitless ways to harass and control others. Technologically facilitated violence combines issues of gender inequality, sexualized violence, Internet regulation, Internet anonymity and privacy. ...

72. Domestic violence increasingly involves using smart home devices directed at women and dependents which enable new ways to infringe privacy, reduce autonomy and self-determination at home, or in communications. Sometimes legal protections are inadequate or there is a lack of police enforcement of breaches.

73. Cybermisogyny has been manifested on digital platforms. Twitter was reported as the main platform for promoting hate campaigns against women and dissemination of sexual content, while Facebook sees the most attacks on women who defend their rights.

74. Invasions of privacy and online violence are higher for men who do not conform to conventional masculine stereotypes and for lesbian, gay, or bisexual people.

75. The gendered experiences of privacy also affect the enjoyment of other rights, with, for example, women also suffering online censorship and profiling in campaigns targeting female activists and journalists.

76. Surveillance, unless undertaken lawfully, proportionately and necessarily, represents infringements of the human right to privacy. Gender, race, class, social origin, religion, opinions and their expression can become factors in determining who is watched in society and make certain individuals more likely to suffer violations of their right to privacy.

77. In a number of countries, gender bias is evident in the higher degree of surveillance of those who identify as members of LGBTQI groups. State surveillance of the LGBTQI community has been facilitated in some countries through legislation. An example given was the Anti-Cybercrime Law enacted in Egypt in 2018.

78. While State surveillance is generally presented as targeting males, counterterrorism measures have been said to disproportionately affect women and transgender asylum seekers, refugees and immigrants.

79. Women can expect that nearly every detail of their intimate lives will be subject to multiple forms of surveillance by State as well as private actors, from domestic violence to sexual objectification and reproduction.

80. Major platform providers now provide identity management via online identity authentication. Websites, apps and services now require login details and accept identity credentials as authentic following logon via Facebook or Google accounts. Facebook has 60 per cent of this "social log on" market, which provides access to vast amounts of information for the compilation of profiles, enabling insights, in which gender is a variable, into the behaviors of individuals, families, groups and communities.

81. The growth in the collection, storage and manipulation of data has increased the possibilities of privacy breaches, which can have different consequences according to gender.

82. Data processing can embed biases relating to gender roles and identities, in particular since data modelling for social intervention increasingly transcends the individual to focus on groups or communities.

83. Data analytics resulting in inferences being made about individuals or groups according to gender, and which lead to discrimination, are contrary to human rights law.

**B**     *Copland v. United Kingdom*

European Court of Human Rights
Application No. 62617/00
April 3, 2007
© Council of Europe, reproduced with permission
Citations and footnotes omitted

*This case is related to the unauthorized monitoring of the female applicant's telephone, email, and internet usage while working at the Carmarthenshire College, a state administered institution. The applicant alleged before the European Court of Human Rights that this monitoring amounted to a violation of her right to private life under Article 8 of the European Convention on Human Rights. In the excerpts below, the European Court examines whether the alleged monitoring was undertaken in contravention of the European Convention on Human Rights.*

43. The Court observes that the use of information relating to the date and length of telephone conversations and in particular the numbers dialled can give rise to an issue under Article 8 as such information constitutes an "integral element of the communications made by telephone". The mere fact that these data may have been legitimately obtained by the College, in the form of telephone bills, is no bar to finding an interference with rights guaranteed under Article 8. Moreover, storing of personal data relating to the private life of an individual also falls within the application of Article 8 § 1. Thus, it is irrelevant that the data held by the College were not disclosed or used against the applicant in disciplinary or other proceedings.

44. Accordingly, the Court considers that the collection and storage of personal information relating to the applicant's telephone, as well as to her e-mail and Internet usage, without her knowledge, amounted to an interference with her right to respect for her private life and correspondence within the meaning of Article 8. ...

45. The Court observes that it is well established in the case-law that the term "in accordance with the law" implies – and this follows from the object and purpose of Article 8 – that there must be a measure of legal protection in domestic law against arbitrary interferences by public authorities with the rights safeguarded by Article 8 § 1. This is all the more so in areas such as the monitoring in question, in view of the lack of public scrutiny and the risk of misuse of power.

46. This expression not only requires compliance with domestic law, but also relates to the quality of that law, requiring it to be compatible with the rule of law ... In order to fulfil the requirement of foreseeability, the law must be sufficiently clear in its terms to give individuals an adequate indication as to the circumstances in which and the conditions on which the authorities are empowered to resort to any such measures. ...

47. The Court is not convinced by the Government's submission that the College was authorised under its statutory powers to do "anything necessary or expedient" for the purposes of providing higher and further education, and finds the argument unpersuasive. Moreover, the Government do not seek to argue that any provisions existed at the relevant time, either in general domestic law or in the governing instruments of the College, regulating the circumstances in which employers could monitor the use of telephone, e-mail and the Internet

by employees. Furthermore, it is clear that the Telecommunications (Lawful Business Practice) Regulations 2000 (adopted under the Regulation of Investigatory Powers Act 2000) which make such provision were not in force at the relevant time.

48. Accordingly, as there was no domestic law regulating monitoring at the relevant time, the interference in this case was not "in accordance with the law" as required by Article 8 § 2 of the Convention. The Court would not exclude that the monitoring of an employee's telephone, e-mail or Internet usage at the place of work may be considered "necessary in a democratic society" in certain situations in pursuit of a legitimate aim. However, having regard to its above conclusion, it is not necessary to pronounce on that matter in the instant case.

49. There has therefore been a violation of Article 8 of the Convention in this regard.


## C      Reflections and Questions

1. The report of the U.N. Special Rapporteur discusses the non-absolute nature of the right to privacy and how it can be restricted under certain circumstances. Can you think of circumstances in which the right to privacy should be restricted in the digital space? Consider necessary restrictions to privacy in the use of computers, smartphones, social media, and internet activity platforms. When crafting your answers, contemplate the history of gender-based and intersectional discrimination and violence against women and girls. Does this history affect your determination of necessary restrictions to the right to privacy?

2. The report of the U.N. Special Rapporteur on the right to privacy presents a number of examples of breaches of the right to privacy which gravely affect women, girls, and LGBTQI individuals in the digital space. These include online harassment, bullying, criminal activities, and unjustified intrusions and surveillance by both government and non-government actors. The permanence of the information on the internet and language driven by hate and discrimination can also be aggravating factors. Women and girls can be subjected to attacks in their efforts to influence, voice their concerns, and advance human rights defenses on social media platforms. Can you think of other breaches of the right to privacy that affect women, girls, and LGBTQI groups in the digital world?

3. The European Court of Human Rights case of *Copland v. United Kingdom* exemplifies the problem of unjustified employee surveillance in the workplace. In this particular case, the applicant was working for a state college and its Deputy Principal insisted on monitoring her telephone, email, and internet usage. The applicant had received no warning that her activities would be monitored, and therefore had a reasonable expectation of privacy under Article 8(1) of the European Convention on Human Rights. The Court also noted the absence of domestic laws regulating this kind of monitoring at the time. The Court lastly observed that there may be times at which monitoring of employee telephone, email, and internet usage in the workplace may be "necessary in a democratic society," *see supra* para. 48. Please identify five instances in which this kind of workplace employee monitoring may be justified. Consider ways in which this interference could be regulated to comply with the human right to privacy.

4. The Rapporteurs on freedom of expression of the United Nations and the Inter-American Commission on Human Rights have actively expressed their concern over excessive surveillance of individuals by both government and non-government actors. In a joint dec-

laration, both Rapporteurs indicated their alarm over government programs and policies intercepting communications from private actors and other outside parties for national security and intelligence purposes.[27] In their declaration, the Rapporteurs expressed their concern over the rapid increase of the technology available to states for monitoring private communications and the large amount of data available on persons on the internet, which can be highly revealing.[28] According to the Rapporteurs, this rapid increase has not been met with appropriate regulation in states.[29] Therefore, the Rapporteurs make an explicit call to states to place limits on surveillance programs, to regulate these by law, and to establish legal limits regarding their nature, scope, and duration; the justification for ordering them; identifying the authorities with power to authorize and execute them; and the legal mechanisms to challenge them.[30] This is all key to ensuring a human rights perspective to these programs.

5. Surveillance has been historically particularly focused on marginalized populations based on race, class, gender, and sex. This problem has been referred to in scholarship as *intersectional surveillance*, recognizing these variables as determinants of who is watched and targeted by different government authorities.[31] Racial discrimination laws; police control, violence, and racial profiling; mass incarceration against African-Americans and other racial groups; the criminalization of the homeless; the revictimization of domestic violence victims when they report incidents to law enforcement authorities; revenge porn and online sexual harassment; and restrictive abortion laws have all been identified as contributing to discriminatory surveillance and breaches of privacy against women.[32] Even though most of the attention to surveillance practices has been afforded to government entities, surveillance can also come from private actors and their use of technology to monitor, collect personal data, control, and regulate the activity of women and other marginalized groups. Consider all the human rights that can be violated by unjustified surveillance against women and other marginalized groups.

## V    CONCLUSIONS: TECHNOLOGY AS A FACILITATOR TO THE EXERCISE OF WOMEN'S RIGHTS

As discussed in this chapter, technology and the digital world have grown at a very rapid pace, posing new opportunities and challenges for women and girls. The digital space can be a new setting which magnifies and worsens many of the human rights violations already faced by women and girls in terms of discrimination, violence, and harassment. One in ten

---

[27] *See* United Nations Special Rapporteur on the Promotion and Protection of the Right of Opinion and Expression and Special Rapporteur for Freedom of Expression of Inter-American Commission on Human Rights, *Joint Declaration on Surveillance Programs and their Impact on Freedom of Expression* (June 21, 2013), www.oas.org/en/iachr/expression/showarticle.asp?artID=926&lID=1.

[28] *See id.*, ¶ 4.

[29] *See id.*, ¶ 5.

[30] *See id.*, ¶ 8.

[31] For a discussion of intersectional surveillance and the ways marginalized groups are affected by surveillance practices, including women victims of domestic violence and revenge porn, *see* Mary Anne Franks, *Democratic Surveillance*, 30 HARV. J. L. & TECH. 425, 441–450, 464–473 (2017).

[32] *See id.*, 464–473.

women are already reporting suffering online violence since the age of 15. However, information and communications technology has also opened the door for many women and girls to increase their participation in public and political life, in education, work, and in society as a whole. Technology can be both empowering and disempowering for women, constituting a double-edged sword for their leadership and effective participation.

Technology is a fixture and one of the most important elements of our time. Most areas of human interaction and relations are currently driven or shaped in some way or other by technology. It is key that international human rights law evolves with the times and expands its standards to mandate states to act with the due diligence necessary to prevent, investigate, sanction, and grant reparations for forms of violence and discrimination against women and girls that are magnified in the digital space. The lens of international human rights law should also be focused on the extensive range of private actors in the internet and social media, and how to prevent, supervise, and regulate activities which may be harmful to women and girls. States need to adopt legislation, policies, and programs to prevent online violence and eliminate the discrimination and stereotypes which fuel these acts. At the core is the imperative need to work at the community, local, and national levels to eliminate all forms of intersectional discrimination against women and harmful gender-based discrimination and stereotypes.

It is also key for states to promote women's and girls' use of, access to, and participation in technological advancements. Girls are now growing up in a world very driven by technology, in which they are active participants. This all means at one level that states should continue promoting the use of technology by girls and women. At a second level, states should also incentivize, support, and create opportunities for girls and women to pursue STEM-related careers, and become creators, innovators, and shapers in the area of technology. Technology should be developed in the future considering a gender and intersectional perspective, and its use should be guided by the principles of non-discrimination, freedom from violence, personal liberty, autonomy, dignity, privacy, and human rights. The active participation and leadership of women and girls in the design and use of technology is a salient ingredient for achieving these goals.

# Index